STUDENT-DRIVEN, FACULTY-APPROVED!

THE HDEV SOLUTION

Visually Engaging Textbook

Online Study Tools

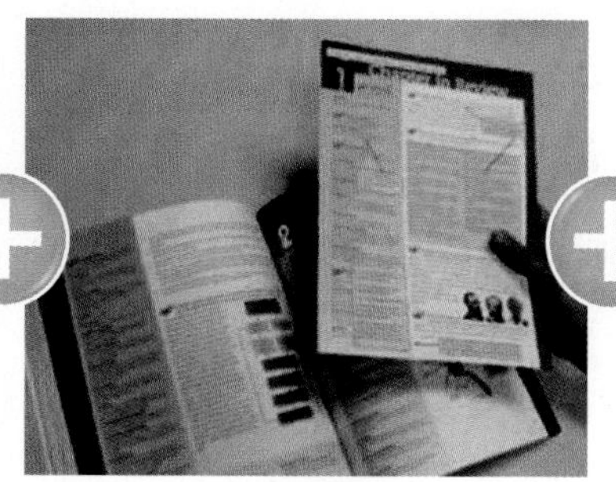

Tear-out Review Cards

Special Note To Students

It is important to begin reading this text with one thing in mind: *This business course does not have to be difficult*. We have done everything possible to eliminate the problems that students encounter in a typical class. All the features in each chapter have been evaluated and recommended by instructors with years of teaching experience. In addition, business students were asked to critique each chapter component. Based on this feedback, the text includes the following features:

- *Learning objectives* appear at the beginning of each chapter.
- *Inside Business* is a chapter-opening case that highlights how successful companies do business on a day-to-day basis.
- *Margin notes* are used throughout the text to reinforce both learning objectives and key terms.
- *Boxed features* highlight how both employees and entrepreneurs can be successful.
- *Spotlight* features highlight interesting facts about business and society and often provide a real-world example of an important concept within a chapter.

Interactive eBook

STUDENT RESOURCES:

- Chapter in Review Cards
- Build a Summary activities
- Observing Development Videos
- Games (Crossword and Beat the Clock)
- Flashcards
- Power Visuals
- Quizzes
- Weblinks

INSTRUCTOR RESOURCES:

- Enriched Instructor's Manual
- PowerPoint Slides
- Test Bank
- Image Library
- Lecture Prep Cards
- First-day-of-class Instructions

Students sign in at **www.nelsonbrain.com**

Instructors sign in at **www.nelson.com/login**

"The online learning is great and the review cards in the back make test review easy!"

– Kyle McConnell, Fanshawe College

NELSON EDUCATION

HDEV, Second Canadian Edition

by Spencer A. Rathus and Shauna Longmuir

Vice President, Editorial Higher Education:
Anne Williams

Executive Editor:
Lenore Taylor-Atkins

Marketing Manager:
Ann Byford

Developmental Editor:
Liisa Kelly

Photo Researcher and Permissions Coordinator:
Karen Hunter

Content Production Manager:
Jennifer Hare

Production Service:
Preeti Longia Sinha

Copy Editor:
Mariko Obokata

Proofreader:
MPS Limited

Indexer:
Maria Sosnowski

Design Director:
Ken Phipps

Managing Designer:
Franca Amore

Interior Design:
Carianne Sherriff

Cover Design:
Peter Papayanakis

Cover Image:
Zephyr Picture/Getty Images

Compositor:
MPS Limited

Printed and bound in the United States
1 2 3 4 17 16 15 14

For more information contact Nelson Education Ltd., 1120 Birchmount Road, Toronto, Ontario, M1K 5G4. Or you can visit our Internet site at http://www.nelson.com

Library and Archives Canada Cataloguing in Publication Data

Rathus, Spencer A., author
HDEV / Rathus, Longmuir. — Second Canadian edition.

Revision of: HDEV / Rathus, Longmuir. — Canadian ed. — Toronto : Nelson Education, c2012. Title from cover.
Includes bibliographical references and index.
ISBN 978-0-17-667311-6 (pbk.)

1. Developmental psychology—Textbooks. 2. Child development—Textbooks. 3. Aging—Psychological aspects—Textbooks. I. Longmuir, Shauna, author II. Title. III. Title: Human development.

BF713.R377 2014
155 C2013-907213-6

ISBN-13: 978-0-17-667311-6
ISBN-10: 0-17-667311-3

HDEV Brief Contents

Kiselev Andrey Valerevich/Shutterstock.com

Used by permission of Kaitlyn Howden

Jupiterimages/Getty Images

PART ONE Introduction

1 History, Theories, and Methods **2**

2 Heredity and Prenatal Development **22**

PART TWO Birth and Infancy

3 Birth and the Newborn Baby: In the New World **46**

4 Infancy: Physical Development **64**

5 Infancy: Cognitive Development **80**

6 Infancy: Social and Emotional Development **98**

PART THREE Early and Middle Childhood

7 Early Childhood: Physical and Cognitive Development **116**

8 Early Childhood: Social and Emotional Development **136**

9 Middle Childhood: Physical and Cognitive Development **152**

10 Middle Childhood: Social and Emotional Development **176**

PART FOUR Adolescence and Early Adulthood

11 Adolescence: Physical and Cognitive Development **192**

12 Adolescence: Social and Emotional Development **208**

13 Early Adulthood: Physical and Cognitive Development **224**

14 Early Adulthood: Social and Emotional Development **240**

PART FIVE Middle and Late Adulthood

15 Middle Adulthood: Physical and Cognitive Development **258**

16 Middle Adulthood: Social and Emotional Development **274**

17 Late Adulthood: Physical and Cognitive Development **286**

18 Late Adulthood: Social and Emotional Development **304**

19 Life's Final Chapter **320**

References **335**

Name Index **388**

Subject Index **395**

HDEV Contents

PART ONE Introduction

1 HISTORY, THEORIES, AND METHODS 2

The Development of the Study of Development **3**
The Study of Child and Adolescent Development 3
The Study of Adult Development 4
Theories of Development **4**
The Psychoanalytic Perspective 5
The Learning Perspective: Behavioural and Social Cognitive Theories 8
The Cognitive Perspective 10
The Biological Perspective 12
The Ecological Perspective 12
The Sociocultural Perspective 14
Debates in Development **15**
Nature and Nurture 16
Continuity and Discontinuity 16
Active and Passive Roles 16
How Do We Study Development? **17**
Gathering Information 17
Surveys 17
Correlation: Putting Things Together 18
The Experiment: Trying Things Out 18
Longitudinal Research: Studying Development over Time 19
Ethical Considerations 20

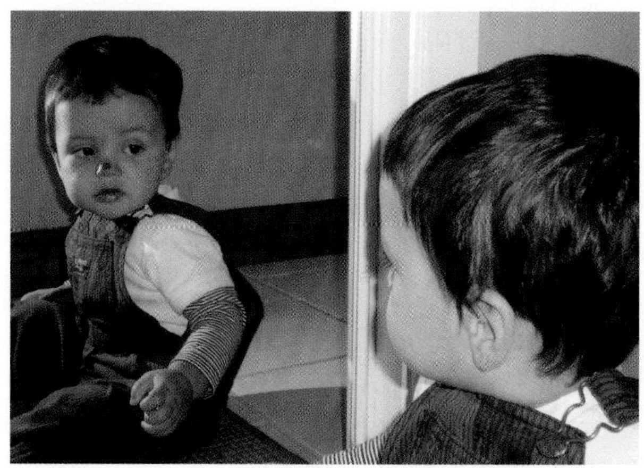

© Ashvin Mohindra

2 HEREDITY AND PRENATAL DEVELOPMENT 22

The Influence of Heredity on Development 23
Chromosomes and Genes 23
Mitosis and Meiosis 23
Identical and Fraternal Twins 24
Dominant and Recessive Traits 25
Chromosomal Abnormalities 26
Genetic Abnormalities 27
Genetic Counselling and Prenatal Testing 29
Heredity and the Environment **30**
Kinship Studies 30
Twin Studies: Looking in the Genetic Mirror 31
Adoption Studies 31
Conception: Against All Odds **31**
Ova 32
Sperm Cells 32
Infertility and Other Ways of Becoming Parents 33
Prenatal Development **35**
The Germinal (Zygotic) Stage: Wanderings 35
The Embryonic Stage 36
The Fetal Stage 37
Fetal Movements 38
Environmental Influences on Prenatal Development 38
Drugs Taken by the Parents 41
Environmental Hazards 43
Parents' Ages 44

© Louis B. Wallach Inc./Getty Images

PART TWO Birth and Infancy

3 BIRTH AND THE NEWBORN BABY: IN THE NEW WORLD 46

Countdown ... **47**

The Stages of Childbirth **47**

Methods of Childbirth **49**

Anesthesia 50

Prepared Childbirth 50

Midwives 50

Cesarean Section 50

Birth Problems **50**

Oxygen Deprivation 51

Preterm and Low-Birth-Weight Infants 51

The Postpartum Period 53

Maternal Depression 54

Bonding 55

Characteristics of Newborns **55**

Assessing the Health of Newborns 56

Reflexes 56

Sensory Capabilities 57

Learning: Really Early Childhood "Education" 59

Sleeping and Waking 60

Sudden Infant Death Syndrome (SIDS) 62

Shaken Baby Syndrome (SBS) 63

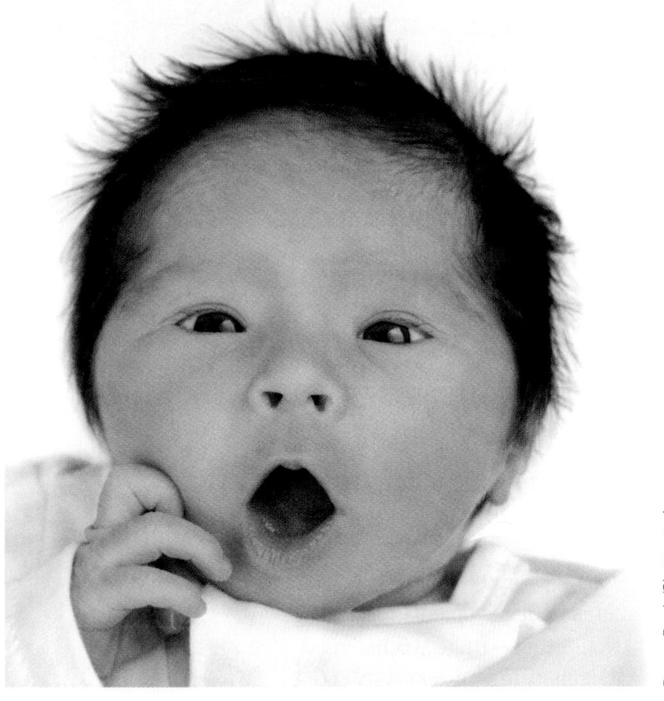

Darren Brode/Shutterstock.com

4 INFANCY: PHYSICAL DEVELOPMENT 64

Physical Growth and Development **65**

Sequences of Physical Development 65

Growth Patterns in Height and Weight 66

Nutrition: Fuelling Development 67

Breast Feeding versus Bottle Feeding 68

Development of the Brain and Nervous System **69**

Development of Neurons 69

Development of the Brain 69

Nature and Nurture in Brain Development 71

Motor Development **72**

Lifting and Holding the Torso and Head 72

Control of the Hands: Getting a Grip 72

Locomotion 73

Sensory and Perceptual Development **74**

Development of Vision 75

Development of Hearing 77

Development of Coordination of the Senses 78

The Active–Passive Controversy in Perceptual Development 78

Nature and Nurture in Perceptual Development 79

© Todd Taulman/Shutterstock.com

5 INFANCY: COGNITIVE DEVELOPMENT 80

Cognitive Development: Jean Piaget **81**

The Sensorimotor Stage 81

Development of Object Permanence 84

Evaluation of Piaget's Theory 85

Information Processing **85**

Infants' Memory 85

Imitation: Infant See, Infant Do? 86

Individual Differences in Intelligence among Infants **86**

Testing Infants: Why and with What? 88

Instability of Intelligence Scores Attained in Infancy 88

Use of Visual Recognition Memory 88

Language Development **89**

Early Vocalizations 89

Development of Vocabulary 89

Development of Sentences 91

Theories of Language Development 92

Views That Emphasize Nurture 92

© Lenore Taylor-Atkins, photo by Christopher Ellison

6 INFANCY: SOCIAL AND EMOTIONAL DEVELOPMENT 98

Attachment: Bonds That Endure **99**

Patterns of Attachment 100

Establishing Attachment 100

Stability of Attachment 101

Stages of Attachment 101

Theories of Attachment 101

When Attachment Fails **104**

Social Deprivation 104

Child Abuse and Neglect 105

Autism Spectrum Disorders 106

Day Care **108**

Emotional Development **109**

Fear of Strangers 110

Social Referencing: What Should I Do Now? 110

Emotional Regulation 111

Personality Development **111**

The Self-Concept 111

Temperament: Easy, Difficult, or Slow to Warm Up? 112

Sex Differences 113

© Radius Images/Jupiterimages

PART THREE Early and Middle Childhood

7 EARLY CHILDHOOD: PHYSICAL AND COGNITIVE DEVELOPMENT 116

Growth Patterns **117**
- *Height and Weight* 117
- *Development of the Brain* 117

Motor Development **118**
- *Gross Motor Skills* 118
- *Physical Activity* 119
- *Fine Motor Skills* 120
- *Children's Drawings* 120
- *Handedness* 120

Nutrition **121**

Health and Illness **123**
- *Minor Illnesses* 123
- *Major Illnesses* 123
- *Accidents* 123

Sleep **124**
- *Sleep Disorders* 124

Elimination Disorders **125**
- *Enuresis* 125
- *Encopresis* 125

Jean Piaget's Preoperational Stage **125**
- *Symbolic Thought* 125
- *Symbolic or Pretend Play* 126
- *Egocentrism: It's All About Me* 126
- *Causality: Why? Because.* 127
- *Focus on One Dimension at a Time* 128

Factors in Cognitive Development **129**
- *Scaffolding and the Zone of Proximal Development* 129
- *Effects of Early Childhood Education* 129
- *Television* 130

Theory of Mind **130**
- *False Beliefs: Where Are Those Crayons?* 130
- *Origins of Knowledge* 130
- *The Appearance–Reality Distinction* 131

Development of Memory **131**
- *Factors Influencing Memory* 131
- *Memory Strategies: Remembering to Remember* 132

Language Development: Why "Daddy Goed Away" **132**
- *Development of Vocabulary* 132
- *Development of Grammar* 132
- *Overregularization* 133
- *Pragmatics* 133
- *Language and Cognition* 134

8 EARLY CHILDHOOD: SOCIAL AND EMOTIONAL DEVELOPMENT 136

Dimensions of Child Rearing **137**
- *How Parents Enforce Restrictions* 138
- *Parenting Styles: How Parents Transmit Values and Standards* 139
- *Effects of the Situation and the Child on Parenting Styles* 140

Social Behaviours **141**
- *Influence of Siblings* 141
- *Birth Order* 141
- *Peer Relationships* 142
- *Play—Child's Play, That Is* 142
- *Prosocial Behaviour* 143
- *Development of Aggression* 144
- *Theories of Aggression* 144

Personality and Emotional Development **146**
- *The Self* 147
- *Fears: The Horrors of Early Childhood* 147

Development of Gender Roles and Sex Differences **148**
- *Sex Differences* 148
- *Theories of the Development of Sex Differences* 148
- *Psychological Androgyny* 150

9 MIDDLE CHILDHOOD: PHYSICAL AND COGNITIVE DEVELOPMENT 152

Growth Patterns **153**
- *Nutrition and Growth* 153
- *Overweight Children* 153

Motor Development **154**
- *Gross Motor Skills* 154
- *Fine Motor Skills* 155
- *Sex Differences* 155
- *Exercise and Fitness* 155

Children with Disabilities **155**
- *Attention-Deficit/Hyperactivity Disorder (ADHD)* 155
- *Learning Disabilities* 156
- *Educating Children Who Have Disabilities* 157

Cognitive Development **158**
- *Piaget: The Concrete-Operational Stage* 158

Moral Development: The Child as Judge **159**
- *Kohlberg's Theory of Moral Development* 159
- *Roots of Empathy: Character Education* 161

Information Processing: Learning, Remembering, Problem Solving **162**
- *Development of Selective Attention* 162
- *Developments in the Storage and Retrieval of Information* 162
- *Development of Recall Memory* 163
- *Development of Metacognition and Metamemory* 164

Intellectual Development, Creativity, and Achievement **164**
- *Theories of Intelligence* 164
- *Measurement of Intellectual Development* 165
- *Patterns of Intellectual Development* 169
- *Differences in Intellectual Development* 170
- *Creativity and Intellectual Development* 171
- *Determinants of Intellectual Development* 171

Language Development and Literacy **172**
- *Vocabulary and Grammar* 172
- *Reading Skills and Literacy* 172
- *Methods of Teaching Reading* 173
- *Bilingualism: Linguistic Perspectives on the World* 173

© JLP/Jose L. Pelaez/Corbis

10 MIDDLE CHILDHOOD: SOCIAL AND EMOTIONAL DEVELOPMENT 176

Theories of Social and Emotional Development in Middle Childhood **177**
- *Social Cognitive Theory* 177
- *Cognitive-Developmental Theory and Social Cognition* 177
- *Development of the Self-Concept in Middle Childhood* 178

The Family **180**
- *Parent–Child Relationships* 180
- *Same-Sex Parents* 180
- *What Happens to Children Whose Parents Divorce?* 181
- *When Mom Works* 182

Peer Relationships **182**
- *Peers as Socialization Influences* 182
- *Peer Acceptance and Rejection* 182
- *Development of Friendships* 183

The School **183**
- *Entry into School* 184
- *The School Environment: Setting the Stage for Success or …* 184
- *Teachers* 185

Social and Emotional Problems **186**
- *Conduct Disorders* 186
- *Childhood Depression* 187
- *Childhood Anxiety* 188

miskolin/Shutterstock.com

PART FOUR Adolescence and Early Adulthood

11 ADOLESCENCE: PHYSICAL AND COGNITIVE DEVELOPMENT 192

Puberty: The Biological Eruption **193**
- *The Adolescent Growth Spurt* 194
- *Changes in Boys* 195
- *Changes in Girls* 195
- *Early versus Late Maturers* 197

Health in Adolescence **198**
- *Death and Injuries* 198
- *Nutrition* 198
- *Teens and Alcohol and Illicit Drugs* 199
- *Eating Disorders* 199

Cognitive Development: Piaget's Stage of Formal Operations **201**
- *Hypothetical Thinking* 201
- *Sophisticated Use of Symbols* 201
- *Adolescent Egocentrism* 202

Sex Differences in Cognitive Abilities **202**
- *Verbal Ability* 202
- *Visual–Spatial Ability* 203
- *Mathematical Ability* 203

Moral Development and Kohlberg **204**
- *The Postconventional Level* 204
- *Moral Behaviour and Moral Reasoning* 204
- *Evaluation of Kohlberg's Theory* 204

The Adolescent in School **204**
- *Dropping Out* 205

Career Development and Work Experience **206**
- *Career Development* 206
- *Adolescents in the Workforce* 207

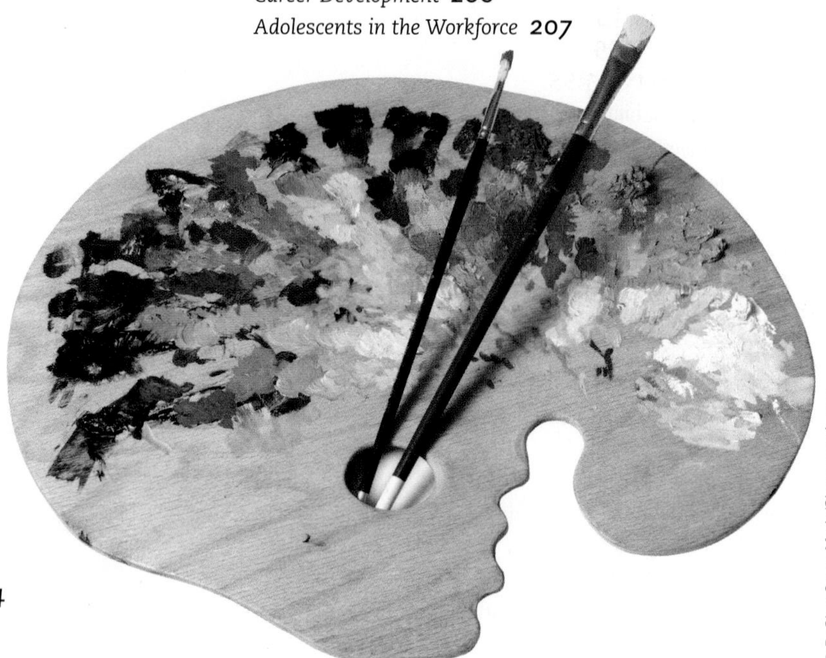

© R. Gino Santa Maria/Shutterstock.com

12 ADOLESCENCE: SOCIAL AND EMOTIONAL DEVELOPMENT 208

Development of Identity: "Who Am I?" **209**
- *Erikson and Identity Development* 209
- *Identity Statuses* 209
- *Ethnicity and Development of Identity* 211
- *Development of the Self-Concept* 212
- *Self-Esteem* 212

Relationships with Parents and Peers **213**
- *Relationships with Parents* 213
- *Relationships with Peers* 214

Sexuality **216**
- *Sexual Identity* 216
- *Masturbation* 217
- *Male–Female Sexual Behaviour* 217
- *Teenage Pregnancy* 218

Youth in Conflict with the Law **220**
- *Youth Crime in Canada* 220
- *Factors Associated with Youth Crime in Canada* 220
- *Reducing Youth Crime* 220
- *Aboriginal Culture and Community Justice* 221

Suicide: When the Adolescent Has Nothing—Except Everything—to Lose **221**
- *Risk Factors in Suicide* 221

Shauna Longmuir

13 EARLY ADULTHOOD: PHYSICAL AND COGNITIVE DEVELOPMENT 224

Emerging Adulthood **225**

Physical Development **226**

Health and Fitness **226**

Diet and Weight 227

Exercise 229

Substance Abuse and Dependence 229

Stress and Health 230

Sexuality **232**

The Origins of Sexual Orientation 232

Sexually Transmitted Infections (STIs) 233

Menstrual Problems 233

Sexual Assault: The Most Intimate Crime of Violence 235

Dating Violence 235

Sexual Harassment 236

Cognitive Development **236**

A New Way of Thinking 237

Labouvie-Vief's Theory of Pragmatic Thought 237

Postformal Thinking 237

Education 237

Career Development **238**

Choosing a Career and Stages of Career Development 238

Developmental Tasks in Beginning a Career 239

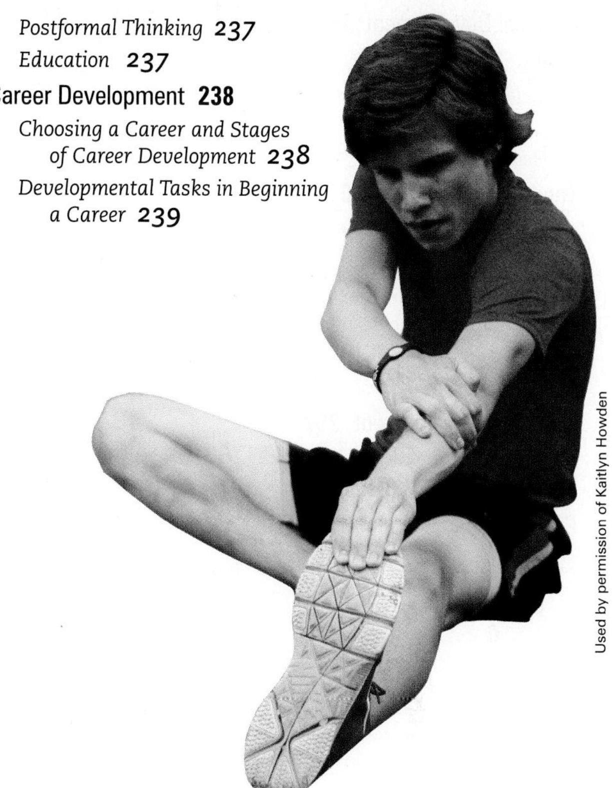

Used by permission of Kaitlyn Howden

14 EARLY ADULTHOOD: SOCIAL AND EMOTIONAL DEVELOPMENT 240

Separation **242**

Separation–Individuation 242

Intimacy versus Isolation **243**

Seasons of Life **243**

Attraction and Love: Forces That Bind? **244**

Attraction 244

Love 246

Loneliness **249**

The Single Life **249**

Living Together **251**

Marriage: Tying the Knot **251**

Why Do People Get Married? 251

Types of Marriage 252

Whom Do We Marry: Are Marriages Made in Heaven or in the Neighbourhood? 253

Marital Satisfaction 253

Parenthood **255**

Parenthood and Role Overload 255

Parenthood in Dual-Earner Families 256

Divorce: Breaking Bonds **256**

The Cost of Divorce 256

© Breanna Webster and Chad Glover, photo by Shauna Longmuir

PART FIVE Middle and Late Adulthood

15 MIDDLE ADULTHOOD: PHYSICAL AND COGNITIVE DEVELOPMENT 258

Physical Development **259**

Health **261**

Leading Causes of Death 261

Cancer 262

Heart Disease 264

The Immune System **264**

Stress and the Immune System 264

Sexuality **264**

Menopause, Perimenopause, and the Climacteric 265

Do Men Undergo an "Andropause"? 266

Sexual Dysfunctions 266

Cognitive Development **267**

Changes in Intellectual Abilities 268

Information Processing 269

Creativity and Learning **271**

Creativity 271

Mature Learners 271

ColorBlind Images/Blend Images/Jupiter Images

16 MIDDLE ADULTHOOD: SOCIAL AND EMOTIONAL DEVELOPMENT 274

Theories of Development in Middle Adulthood **276**

Erik Erikson's Theory of Psychosocial Development 276

Daniel Levinson's Seasons 277

Entering Midlife: Crisis, Turning Point, or Prime of Life? 277

The Life-Events Approach 278

Stability and Change in Middle Adulthood **279**

Are There Sudden Shifts in Personality? 280

Work in Middle Adulthood **280**

Job Satisfaction 281

Career Change in Middle Adulthood 281

Unemployment 281

Relationships in Middle Adulthood **282**

Evolving Parent–Child Relationships 282

Grandparenting 283

Middle-Aged Children and Aging Parents 284

Siblings 285

Friends 285

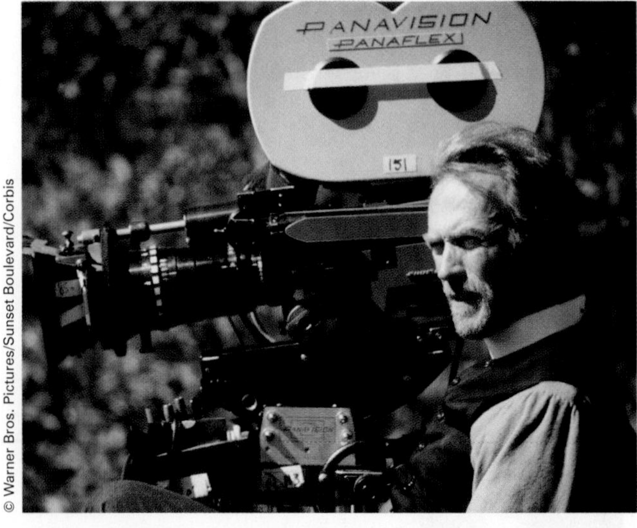

© Warner Bros. Pictures/Sunset Boulevard/Corbis

17 LATE ADULTHOOD: PHYSICAL AND COGNITIVE DEVELOPMENT 286

Physical Development 287

Longevity and Life Expectancy 287

Physical and Social Changes 288

Sleep 290

Sexuality 290

Theories of Aging **292**

Programmed Theories of Aging 292

Cellular Damage Theories of Aging 293

Health Concerns and Aging **293**

Cancer, Heart Disease, and Respiratory Disease 294

Arthritis 295

Substance Abuse 296

Accidents 297

Dementia and Alzheimer's Disease 297

Cognitive Development **298**

Memory: Remembrance of Things Past—and Future 298

Language Development 301

Problem Solving 301

Wisdom 302

Shauna Longmuir

18 LATE ADULTHOOD: SOCIAL AND EMOTIONAL DEVELOPMENT 304

Theories of Social and Emotional Development in Late Adulthood **305**

Life Review 305

Activity Theory 307

Socioemotional Selectivity Theory 307

Psychological Development **308**

Self-Esteem 308

Independence versus Dependence 309

Psychological Problems 309

Social Contexts of Aging **311**

Communities and Housing for Older People 311

Religion 311

Family and Social Relationships 312

Retirement **315**

Retirement Planning 315

Adjustment to Retirement 315

Leisure Activities and Retirement 316

Successful Aging **317**

Selective Optimization with Compensation 317

© Brand X Pictures/Jupiterimages

19 LIFE'S FINAL CHAPTER 320

Understanding Death and Dying **321**

Charting the Boundaries between Life and Death 321

Are There Stages of Dying? 322

Where People Die **323**

In the Hospital 323

Hospice Care 323

Supporting a Dying Person 324

Euthanasia: Is There a Right to Die? **325**

End-of-Life Definitions 325

The Living Will 326

Lifespan Perspectives on Death **327**

Children 327

Adolescents 329

Adults 330

Coping with Death **330**

What to Do When Someone Dies 330

Grief and Bereavement 331

Are There Stages of Grieving? 332

Advice for Coping 332

Look to Find the Lesson 334

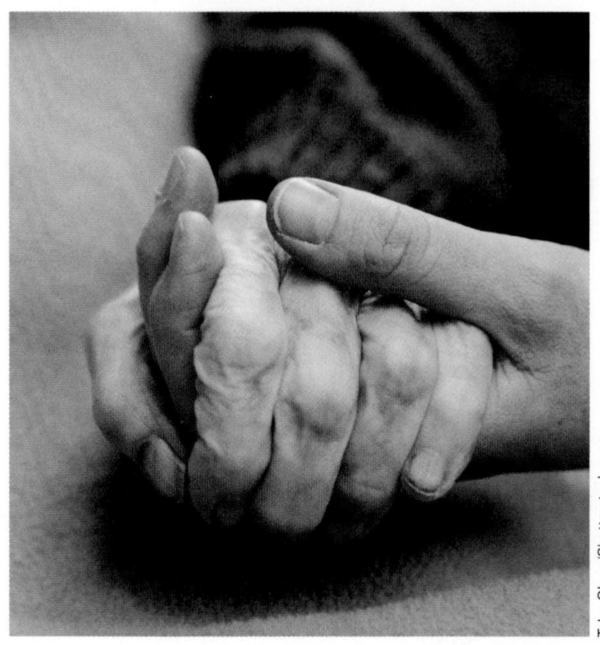

Tyler Olson/Shutterstock.com

References ***335***

Name Index ***388***

Subject Index ***395***

What's New in the Second Canadian Edition

© Duncan Walker/iStockphoto

© Michelle D. Milliman/Shutterstock.com

djedzura/Shutterstock.com

Overall

- A strong Canadian voice is retained throughout this edition
- Biopsychosocial framework of lifespan psychology has been emphasized
- New "Erikson Today" boxes introduce each Social and Emotional Development chapter, providing a framework for the content and contemporizing Erikson's theories for today's students
- New Emerging Canada boxes examine timely Canadian trends in the field and serve to integrate the latest information from Statistics Canada
- A refined focus on diversity matches the priorities of most Canadian colleges today: topics include aging, family structures, and cyberbullying in LGBT communities and preventative health education, youth empowerment, and heritage language recovery in Canada's Aboriginal communities.
- Updated figures, tables, and photos that highlight the most recent research and developments in the field of human development

Chapter 1

- Introduction to the biopsychosocial framework, "Erikson Today", and "Emerging Canada" boxes
- Coverage of female education, cardiovascular disease, and mental illness in Canada

Chapter 2

- Coverage of World Down Syndrome Day, colour blindness and sex-linked abnormalities, issues surrounding IVF, and the average age of mothers in Canada

Chapter 3

- Updated statistics on birthing choices among Canadian mothers
- Revised coverage of risks associated with high maternal age, changes in parental leave trends, stem cells, and postpartum depression

Chapter 4

- New discussions on infant growth spurts, breastfeeding trends, and "Superbaby" syndrome
- Special focus on Inuit parenting practices and results of deprivation in Romanian orphanages
- Updated discussion of the "visual cliff" phenomenon for pre- versus full-term babies

Chapter 5

- Further explanation of the role of habituation and dishabituation
- Discussion of bilingualism and educational videos such as "Baby Einstein" and their benefits for children
- Coverage of the growth of home languages, including Aboriginal languages

Chapter 6

- Revised coverage of child abuse and neglect in Canada, including two graphs on the Canadian

What's New in the Second Canadian Edition

Incidence Studies and the "duty to report"
- Updated discussion of autism, including the use of animal therapy treatment
- Revised discussion of attachment issues and daycare and coverage of infant-father interactions and effects on later behavior

Chapter 7

- New discussion of "Generation XL" and childhood obesity, the effects of second-hand smoke and screen time in children
- Coverage of handedness in infancy and scribbling and emerging childhood literacy
- Coverage of day care quality control and shortages

Chapter 8

- New conversations on helping Canadian children through divorce and gender stereotypes and play
- Focused coverage of Albert Bandura and Bem's inventory and psychological androgyny
- New coverage of "Baby Storm", a child being raised without gender roles

Chapter 9

- New discussion of individual education plans, universal classroom design, and character education in Canadian classrooms
- Tips for working with children with ADHD
- Coverage of heritage and Aboriginal languages

Chapter 10

- New discussion of issues surrounding all-day kindergarten, signs of childhood depression, and the Infinity Project in Canadian schools
- Revised coverage of same-sex parenting, divorce, and trends in Canadian families through the past 50 years

Chapter 11

- Discussion of average growth changes in Canada and internationally for boys and girls, including precocious puberty
- Coverage of teen alcohol and drug use, including prescription drugs
- Discussion of trends in eating disorders
- Exploration of Canadian dropout rates and career Holland Inventory samples

Chapter 12

- New coverage of teens and self-esteem, online friendships, cyberbullying, and suicide
- Discussion of teenage immigrant values and attitudes
- Exploration of parent-teen relationships and changes in the influence of parents on teens
- Revised coverage of coming-out issues for LGBT youth, including the International Day of Silence
- Updated statistics on youth sexual activity, including changes teenage girls' attitudes towards sexuality

Stockbyte/Thinkstock.com

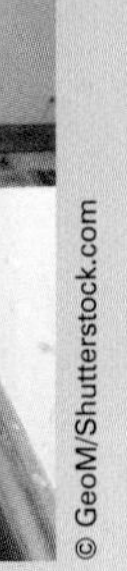
© GeoM/Shutterstock.com

© Jordan Chesbrough/iStockphoto

What's New in the Second Canadian Edition

Andresr/Shutterstock.com

Fuse/Thinkstock.com

Scape/Shutterstock.com

Chapter 13

- Revised coverage of health issues in Canadian young adults, including emerging perceptions of health, drug use, weight issues, and anxiety disorders
- Comparison of Canadian sexuality and international findings
- Coverage of groups most at risk for STIs and HIV/AIDs and dating violence
- Discussion of trends in post-secondary education, employment, and independence in youth

Chapter 14

- New coverage of the "boomerang generation"
- Discussion of the roles that science and culture play in attractiveness
- Coverage of online dating and of marriage statistics in the 2011 Canadian census

Chapter 15

- Revised discussion of health issues affecting "baby boomers", including lowering risks of cancer, increased rates of STIs, and risks associated with hormone replacement therapy
- Updated discussion of health self-assessment in middle age

Chapter 16

- New discussion of financial issues for baby boomers, including whether adult children or personal financial concerns should take precedence
- Revised discussions on the roots ageism in middle age, Elliott Jacques and the midlife crisis, second careers, and "coming out" to grandchildren

Chapter 17

- New division of the life span into young-old, old-old and oldest-old
- New discussions of online dating, STI rates, and the aging population
- Coverage of the baby boomers and the "silver tsunami"
- Examination of financial costs of Canadians on the health care system across the life span

Chapter 18

- New boxes on internet use among the "silver tsunami", LGBT retirement communities, and successful aging
- Discussion of suicide, seniors and ageism
- Exploration of the effects of widowhood

Chapter 19

- Revised coverage of the Robert Latimer case
- Canadianization of all material on euthanasia including definitions from the Canadian Medical Association, physician-targeted statistics, and targeted Canadian opinion polls
- New box on Canadian funeral costs
- Exploration of early experiences of grief and their impact on later grief responses
- Discussion on barriers to post-loss bereavement services for those who have utilized hospice care

PART ONE

CHAPTER 1

History, Theories, and Methods

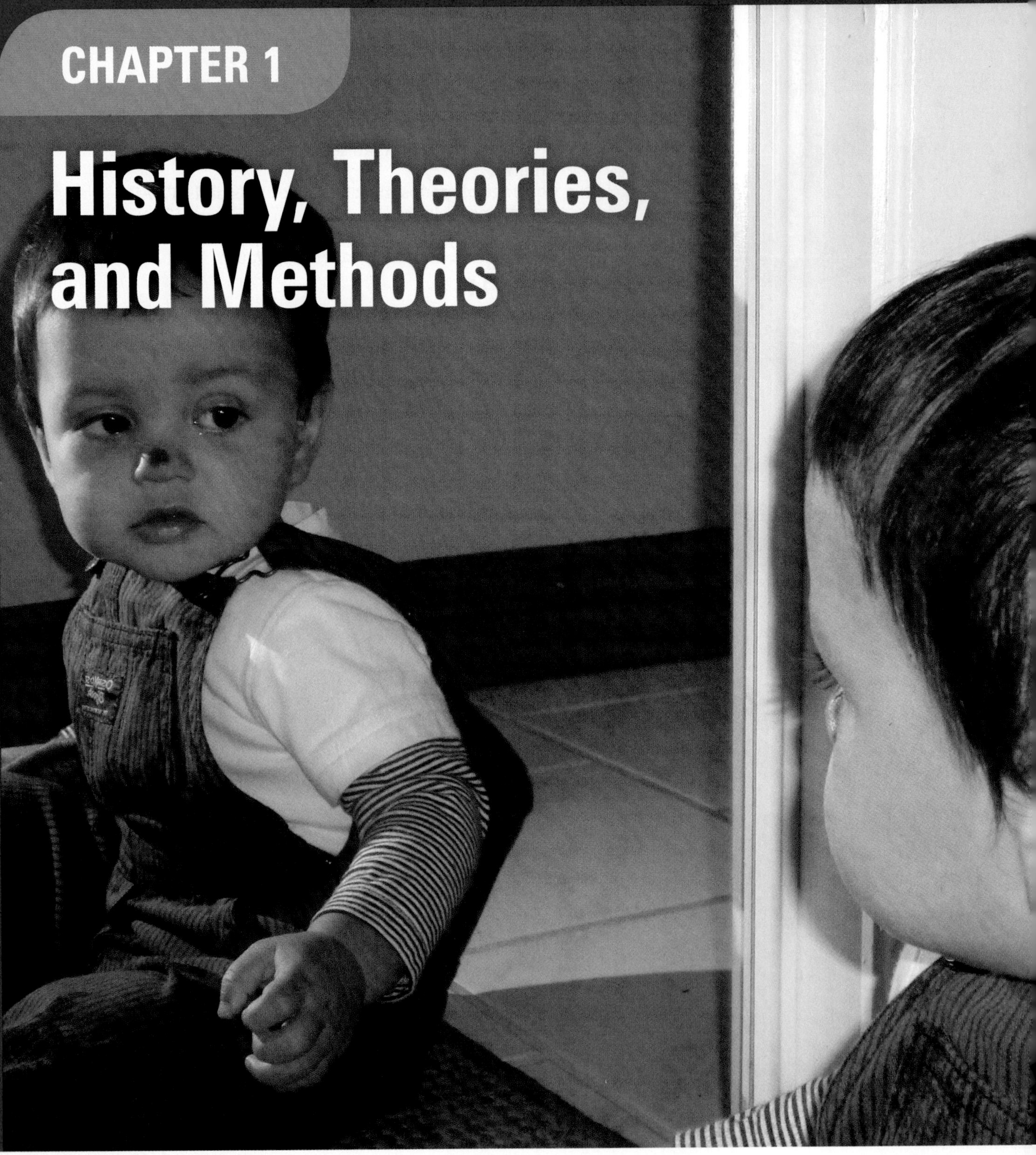

LEARNING OUTCOMES

LO1 Relate the history of the study of human development

LO2 Compare and contrast theories of human development

LO3 Enumerate key controversies in human development

LO4 Describe ways in which researchers study human development

© Ashvin Mohindra

> "You are unique, and things will happen to you, and because of you, that have never happened before."

This book has a story to tell. It is an important story—it is your story. It is about the remarkable journey you have already taken through childhood. It is about the unfolding of your adult life.

LO1 The Development of the Study of Development

Scientific inquiry into human development has existed for little more than a century. In ancient times and in the Middle Ages, children often were viewed as innately evil, and discipline was harsh. Children were nurtured until they were 7 years old, which was considered the "age of reason." After that age, they were expected to work alongside adults in the home and in the field.

> **DID YOU KNOW?**
>
> **During the Middle Ages, children were often treated as miniature adults.**
>
> Though more was expected of them, they weren't given additional privileges.

The Study of Child and Adolescent Development

The transition to modern thinking about children is marked by the writings of philosophers such as John Locke and Jean-Jacques Rousseau. Englishman John Locke (1632–1704) believed that the child came into the world as a *tabula rasa*—a "blank tablet" or clean slate—that was written on by experience. Locke did not believe that inborn predispositions toward good or evil played an important role in the conduct of the child. Instead, he focused on the role of the environment or of experience. Locke believed that social approval and disapproval are powerful shapers of behaviour. But Jean-Jacques Rousseau (1712–1778), a Swiss–French philosopher, argued that children are inherently good and that, if allowed to express their natural impulses, they will develop into generous and moral individuals.

Locke viewed children as a blank slate, or *tabula rasa*. What life experiences have been, and will be, written on your blank slate?

marekuliasz/iStockphoto

During the Industrial Revolution, family life came to be defined in terms of the nuclear unit of mother, father, and children rather than the extended family. Children became

developmental psychology the biological, psychological, and sociocultural study of human change across the lifespan.

behaviourism Watson's view that science must study observable behaviour only and investigate relationships between stimuli and responses.

more visible, fostering awareness of childhood as a special time of life. Still, children often laboured in factories from dawn to dusk through the early years of the 20th century.

In the 20th century, laws were passed to protect children from strenuous labour, to require that they attend school until a certain age, and to prevent them from getting married or being sexually exploited. Whereas children were once considered the property of parents to do with as they wished, laws now protect children from abuse by parents and other adults. Today, youth criminal justice courts ensure that children who break the law receive appropriate treatment in the criminal justice system. Childhood is now seen as a distinct psychological stage that needs protection.

Pioneers in the Study of Child Development

Various thoughts about child development emerged into a field of scientific study in the 19th and early 20th centuries. G. Stanley Hall (1844–1924) is credited with having founded child development as an academic discipline. The French psychologist Alfred Binet (1857–1911) worked with Theodore Simon to develop the first standardized intelligence test near the beginning of the 20th century. Binet's purpose was to identify elementary school children who were at risk of falling behind their peers in academic achievement. By the start of the 20th century, child development had emerged as a scientific field of study.

The Study of Adult Development

The traditional focus has been on childhood and adolescence because of the dramatic physical and cognitive changes that occur during those years. Many theorists today focus on the marked decline of late adulthood and on changes that occur during young and middle adulthood.

It has been said that play is the work of children. Children will often try on adult roles by playing make-believe.

© Banana Stock/Jupiterimages

TABLE 1.1

The Biopsychosocial Framework of Development

The study of human growth and development is built on the disciplines of biology, psychology, and sociology. This focus explains the formatting of your textbook. Each stage of development is addressed in a chapter focusing on biological and cognitive studies, followed by a chapter examining the psychological and sociological issues that shape lifespan development. These issues are then examined within the context of life-cycle forces.

Biological Force	How do genetics, health, and cognition shape our experiences?
Psychological Force	How do our perceptions and interpretations shape our inner world?
Sociological Force	How do the communities and cultures that we come in contact with influence our life experiences?
Life-Cycle Force	How is the same life event experienced by people in different stages of the lifespan?

Developmental psychology is the biological, psychological, and sociocultural study of development across the lifespan (see Table 1.1). Developmental psychology examines the progressive challenges and changes that an individual encounters from cradle to grave, which are prompted by maturation and the learning process.

LO2 Theories of Development

> Give me a dozen healthy infants, well-formed, and my own specified world to bring them up in, and I'll guarantee to train them to become any type of specialist I might suggest—doctor, lawyer, merchant, chief, and, yes, even beggar and thief, regardless of their talents, penchants, tendencies, abilities, vocations, and the race of their ancestors.
>
> —Watson, 1924, p. 82

John B. Watson, the founder of North American **behaviourism,** viewed development in terms of learning theory. He generally agreed with Locke that children's ideas, preferences, and skills are shaped by experience. The study of children has been subject to a longstanding nature–nurture debate. In Watson's theoretical approach to understanding children, he came down on the side of nurture—the importance of the physical and social environments—as found, for example, in parental training and approval.

Arnold Gesell expressed the opposing idea that biological **maturation** was the main principle of development: "All things considered, the inevitability and surety of maturation are the most impressive characteristics of early development. It is the hereditary ballast which conserves and stabilizes growth of each individual infant" (Gesell, 1928, p. 378). Whereas Gesell focused mainly on physical aspects of growth and development, Watson discussed the behaviour patterns that children develop.

Theories such as behavioural theory and maturational theory help developmentalists explain, predict, and influence the events they study. Let us consider theories that are popular among developmentalists today. They fall within broad perspectives on development.

The Psychoanalytic Perspective

Many theories fall within the psychoanalytic perspective. Each of these theories owes its origin to Sigmund Freud, and each views children—and adults—as caught in conflict. Early in development, the conflict is between the child and the world outside. The expressions of basic drives, such as sex and aggression, are in conflict with parental expectations, social rules, moral codes, even laws. But the external limits—parental demands and social rules—are brought inside or *internalized*. Once internalization occurs, the conflict takes place between opposing *inner* forces. The child's observable behaviour, thoughts, and feelings reflect the outcomes of these hidden battles.

Let us consider Freud's theory of **psychosexual development** and Erik Erikson's theory of psychosocial development. Each is a **stage theory** that sees children as developing through distinct periods of life. Each suggests that the child's experiences during early stages affect the child's emotional and social life at the time and later on.

Sigmund Freud's Theory of Psychosexual Development

Sigmund Freud's (1856–1939) theory of psychosexual development focused on emotional and social development and on the origins of psychological traits such as dependence, obsessive neatness, and vanity. Freud theorized three parts of the personality: *id, ego,* and *superego*. The id is present at birth and is *unconscious*. It represents biological drives and demands instant gratification, as suggested by a baby's wailing. The ego, or the conscious sense of self, begins to develop when children learn to obtain gratification consciously, without screaming or crying. The ego curbs the appetites of the id and makes plans that are in keeping with social conventions so that a person can find gratification but avoid social disapproval. The superego develops throughout infancy and early childhood. It brings inward the wishes and morals of the child's caregivers and other members of the community. This theory has become the basis of a favourite cartoon technique. Often a popular character is conflicted by what is desired (id) and what is the "right" thing to do (superego). The character (ego) is left to make the decision and deal with the consequences.

maturation
the unfolding of genetically determined traits, structures, and functions.

psychosexual development
the process by which libidinal energy is expressed through different erogenous zones during different stages of development.

stage theory
a theory of development characterized by distinct periods of life.

According to Freud, psychosexual development has five stages: *oral, anal, phallic, latency,* and *genital.* If a child receives too little or too much gratification during a stage, the child can become *fixated* in that stage. For example, during the first year of life, which Freud termed the *oral stage,* "oral" activities such as sucking and biting bring pleasure and gratification. A child who is weaned too early or breast-fed too long

The pull between "right" and "wrong" can be said to be the inner battle of the superego and the id, leaving the ego to make decisions.

psychosocial development Erikson's theory, which emphasizes the importance of social relationships and conscious choice throughout eight stages of development.

may become fixated on oral activities such as nail-biting or smoking, or may even show a "biting wit."

In the second, or *anal*, stage, gratification is obtained through control and elimination of waste products. Excessively strict or permissive toilet training can lead to the development of anal-retentive traits, such as perfectionism and neatness, or anal-expulsive traits, such as sloppiness and carelessness. In the third stage, the *phallic stage*, parent–child conflict may develop over masturbation, which many parents treat with punishment and threats. According to Freud's psychoanalytical perspective, it is normal for children in the phallic stage to develop strong sexual attachments to the parent of the opposite sex and to begin to view the parent of the same sex as a rival.

Freud believed that by the age of 5 or 6, children enter a *latency stage*, during which sexual feelings remain unconscious, children turn to schoolwork, and they typically prefer playmates of their own sex. The final stage of psychosexual development, the *genital stage*, begins with the biological changes that usher in adolescence. Adolescents generally desire sexual gratification through intercourse with a partner. Freud believed that oral or anal stimulation, masturbation, and male–male or female–female sexual activity are immature forms of sexual conduct that reflect fixations at early stages of development.

Evaluation Freud's views about the anal stage have influenced child-care workers to recommend that toilet training not be started too early or handled punitively. His emphasis on the emotional needs of children has influenced educators to be more sensitive to the possible emotional reasons behind a child's misbehaviour. Freud's work has also been criticized. For example, Freud developed his theory on the basis of contacts with adult patients (mostly women) (Schultz & Schultz, 2008), not by observing children directly. Freud may also have inadvertently guided patients into expressing ideas that confirmed his views. Although Freud's theory forms the basis of many psychological theories, many suggest that his ideas need to be placed within a more modern context that recognizes the role of relationships and the desire to achieve.

Erik Erikson's Theory of Psychosocial Development

Erik Erikson (1902–1994) modified Freud's theory and extended it through the adult years. Erikson's theory, like Freud's, focuses on the development of emotional life and psychological traits, but differs in its focus on social relationships rather than unconscious motivations, such as sexuality or aggressive instincts. Erikson emphasized the desire to achieve and to help others. Therefore, Erikson speaks of **psychosocial development** rather than of *psychosexual development*. Furthermore, Erikson

Freud: Imagno/Hulton Archive/Getty Images; Spiral notebook: © Image Source/Jupiterimages

Time & Life Pictures/Getty Images

Erik Erikson was married to his Canadian wife, Joan, for 64 years.

Hurricane Hank/Shutterstock.com

Erikson believed that who you are is primarily shaped by the influences of sociocultural forces.

places greater emphasis on the ego, or the sense of self. Erikson (1963) extended Freud's five stages to eight to include the concerns of adulthood. Rather than label his stages after parts of the body, Erikson labelled them after the **life crisis** that people might encounter during that stage (see Table 1.2). These life stages form the structure of lifespan development (and the structure of your textbook). Together we will explore these life challenges in the context of the changing world around us.

life crisis
an internal conflict that attends each stage of psychosocial development.

TABLE 1.2

Erik Erikson's Psychosocial Stages of Lifespan Development

Psychosocial Stage	Personality Crisis (Challenge)	Important Life Event	Outcome
Infancy (birth to 18 months)	Trust vs. Mistrust	Feeding	Trust is developed when caregivers are reliable and affectionate. Mistrust is developed when care is unpredictable and/or lacking in affection.
Early Childhood (19 months to 3 years)	Autonomy vs. Shame and Doubt	Toilet Training	Children develop a sense of personal control, skill, and independence. Success leads to feelings of self-rule and independence, whereas failure results in feelings of shame and self-doubt.
Preschool (4 to 5 years)	Initiative vs. Guilt	Exploration	Children need to take control over their own environment, which leads to a sense of purpose. If children exert too much power, they will encounter disapproval, which will result in guilt. Failure to control their environment will lead to a sense of inadequacy.
School Age (6 to 11 years)	Industry vs. Inferiority	School	Children learn to cope with new social and academic demands. Success leads to a sense of ability and accomplishment. In contrast, failure leads to a sense of nagging inferiority.
Adolescence (12 to 18 years)	Identity vs. Role Confusion	Social Relationships	Teens develop a sense of their personal identity. Success leads to their being able to clearly define themselves and to stay true to who they believe they are. Failure leads to unclear standards and a weak sense of self.
Young Adulthood (19 to 39 years)	Intimacy vs. Isolation	Relationships	Young adults need to form intimate and loving relationships. Success leads to patterns of strong relationship building. Failure to enter into loving relationships results in loneliness and isolation.
Middle Adulthood (40 to 64 years)	Generativity vs. Stagnation	Work and Parenthood	Adults thrive when they create and nurture things that will outlast them. Raising children or creating a positive change leads to feelings of usefulness and accomplishment. Failure results in shallow involvement and a realization that they will leave nothing lasting behind.
Later Life (65 to death)	Ego Integrity vs. Despair	Reflection on Life (Life Review)	Older adults need to actively look back on life and feel a sense that their life mattered. Success at this stage leads to feelings of wisdom and of contribution. Death is the logical next step and is received with grace. Failure to navigate this stage results in regret, bitterness, and despair. Death is feared.

identity crisis according to Erikson, a period of inner conflict during which individuals examine their values and make decisions about their life roles.

classical conditioning a simple form of learning in which one stimulus comes to bring forth the response usually brought forth by a second stimulus as a result of being paired repeatedly with the second stimulus.

operant conditioning a simple form of learning in which an organism learns to engage in behaviour that is reinforced.

reinforcement the process of providing stimuli following responses in an effort to increase the frequency of the responses.

Erikson proposed that social relationships and physical maturation give each stage its character. For example, the parent–child relationship and the infant's dependence and helplessness are responsible for the nature of the earliest stages of development. Early experiences affect future developments.

Erikson's views, like Freud's, have influenced child rearing, early childhood education, and child therapy. For example, Erikson's views about an adolescent **identity crisis** have entered the popular culture and have affected the way many parents and teachers deal with teenagers. Some schools help students master the crisis by means of life-adjustment courses and study units on self-understanding in social studies and literature classes.

Evaluation Erikson's views are appealing because they emphasize the importance of human consciousness and choice, and they portray us as social beings that are prosocial and helpful, whereas Freud portrayed us as social creatures that are selfish and need to be compelled to comply with social rules. Empirical findings support the Eriksonian view that positive outcomes of early life crises help put us on the path to positive development (Hoegh & Bourgeois, 2002).

The Learning Perspective: Behavioural and Social Cognitive Theories

Behaviourism

John B. Watson argued that a scientific approach to development must focus on observable behaviour only and not on unobservable activities, such as thoughts, fantasies, and other mental images.

Classical conditioning is a simple form of learning in which an originally neutral stimulus comes to bring forth, or elicit, the response usually brought forth by a second stimulus as a result of being paired repeatedly with the second stimulus.

For example, the opening of a can does not initially elicit a response from a dog. But once the dog learns to associate the opening of a can with being fed,

Used with permission of Kaitlyn Howden

The sound of a can opening will bring a dog running whether it is a can of dog food or a can of chicken noodle soup.

then anytime the dog hears the opening of a can, it will run toward that familiar sound from anywhere in the house. The can might contain dog food or a can of beans but, either way, the dog will associate the sound of it being opened with the act of being fed.

Behaviourists argue that much emotional learning is acquired through classical conditioning. In a different kind of conditioning, **operant conditioning**, children learn to do something because of its effects. B. F. Skinner introduced the key concept of **reinforcement**. Reinforcers are stimuli that are intended to increase the frequency of the behaviour they follow. Most children learn to adjust their

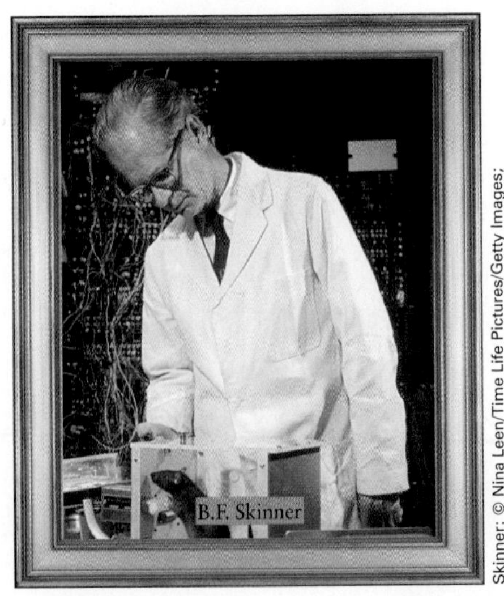

Skinner: © Nina Leen/Time Life Pictures/Getty Images; framer: © catnap72/iStockphoto

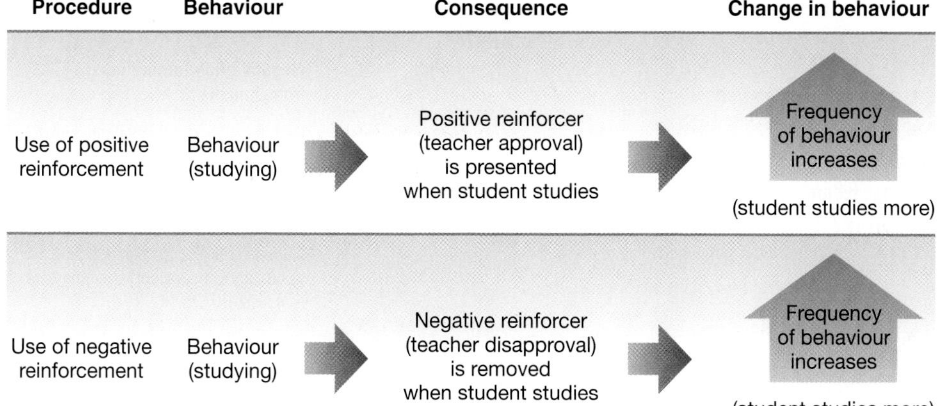

FIGURE 1.1

Positive versus Negative Reinforcers

All reinforcers *increase* the frequency of behaviour. In these examples, teacher approval is a positive reinforcer when students study harder to gain that approval. Teacher *disapproval* is a negative reinforcer when its *removal* increases the frequency of studying.

Go to www.nelson.com/4ltrpress/icanhdev2ce to access an interactive version of this figure.

behaviour to conform to social codes and rules so they can earn reinforcers, such as the attention and approval of their parents and teachers. Other children, ironically, learn to misbehave because misbehaviour also draws attention. Any stimulus that increases the frequency of the responses preceding it serves as a reinforcer. Skinner distinguished between positive and negative reinforcers. **Positive reinforcers** increase the frequency of behaviours when they are *applied*. Food and approval are common positive reinforcers. **Negative reinforcers** increase the frequency of behaviours when they are *removed*. Fear is a negative reinforcer because its removal increases the frequency of the behaviours preceding it. Figure 1.1 compares positive and negative reinforcers.

Extinction results from repeated performance of operant behaviour without reinforcement. After a number of trials, the operant behaviour is no longer shown. Children's temper tantrums and crying at bedtime can often be extinguished by parents' remaining out of the bedroom after the children have been put to bed. **Punishments** are aversive events that suppress or *decrease* the frequency of the behaviour they follow. (Figure 1.2 on page 10 compares negative reinforcers with punishments.) Many learning theorists agree that punishment should be used sparingly in child rearing and is most appropriate when mild and prompt, such as the case with time outs. Punishment on its own does not suggest an alternative, preferred behaviour and can lead to anger and resentment. Inappropriate behaviour will not be consistently suppressed unless punishment is guaranteed.

Research suggests that when teachers praise and attend to appropriate behaviour and ignore misbehaviour, studying and classroom behaviour improve while disruptive and aggressive behaviours decrease (McIlvane & Dube, 2003; Takahashi & Sugiyama, 2003). By ignoring misbehaviour or by using *time out* from positive reinforcement, caregivers can avoid reinforcing children's misbehaviour. When using time out, children who behave disruptively are placed in drab, restrictive environments for a specified time period, such as 10 minutes.

positive reinforcer
a reinforcer that, when applied, increases the frequency of a response.

negative reinforcer
a reinforcer that, when removed, increases the frequency of a response.

extinction
the cessation of a response that is performed in the absence of reinforcement.

punishments
aversive events that suppress or decrease the frequency of the behaviour they follow.

social cognitive theory
a cognitively oriented learning theory that emphasizes observational learning.

Bandura: © John Brenneis/Time Life Pictures/Getty Images; frame: © catnap72/iStockphoto

Social Cognitive Theory

Behaviourists tend to limit their view of learning to conditioning. Proponents of **social cognitive theorists**, such as Canadian-born Albert Bandura (1986, 2006a, 2006b), have shown that much learning also

Procedure	Behaviour	Consequence	Change in behaviour
Use of negative reinforcement	Behaviour (studying)	Negative reinforcer (teacher disapproval) is ***removed*** when student studies	Frequency of behaviour ***increases*** (student studies more)
Use of punishment	Behaviour (talking in class)	Punishment (detention) is ***presented*** when student talks in class	Frequency of behaviour ***decreases*** (student talks less in class)

FIGURE 1.2

Negative Reinforcers versus Punishments

Both negative reinforcers and punishments tend to be aversive stimuli. Reinforcers, however, *increase* the frequency of behaviour. Punishments *decrease* the frequency of behaviour. Negative reinforcers increase the frequency of behaviour when they are *removed.*

Go to www.nelson.com/4ltrpress/icanhdev2ce to access an interactive version of this figure.

cognitive-developmental theory
the stage theory that suggests children's abilities to mentally represent the world and solve problems are a result of the interaction of experience and the maturation of neurological structures.

occurs by observing other people, by reading, and by viewing individuals in the media. People may need practice to refine their skills, but they can acquire the basic know-how through observation and modelling.

Observational learning occurs when children notice how parents cook, clean, or interact with one another. It takes place when adults watch supervisors interact in the workplace or make important decisions. In social cognitive theory, the people after whom we pattern our own behaviour are termed *models*.

Evaluation of Learning Theories

Learning theories allow us to explain, predict, and influence many aspects of behaviour. Parenting magazines and websites are filled with tips for parents who want to learn how to control, observe, and make positive changes using the basics of learning theory. Many of the teaching approaches used in children's educational television are also based on these learning principles.

The Cognitive Perspective

Cognitive theorists focus on people's mental processes. They investigate how children perceive and mentally represent the world and how they develop thinking, logic, and problem-solving ability. One cognitive perspective is **cognitive-developmental theory**, advanced by Swiss biologist Jean Piaget (1896–1980) and further developed by many theorists such as Lev Semenovich Vygotsky, whose theories are discussed later in this chapter. Another perspective is information-processing theory.

Cognitive-Developmental Theory

During adolescence, Jean Piaget studied philosophy, logic, and mathematics, but years later he took his Ph.D. in biology. In 1920, he obtained a job at the Binet Institute in Paris, where research on intelligence tests was being conducted. Through his studies, Piaget realized that when children answered questions incorrectly, their wrong answers still often reflected consistent—although illogical—mental processes. Piaget regarded children as natural physicists who actively intend to learn about and take intellectual charge of their worlds. In the Piagetian view, children who squish their food and laugh enthusiastically are

© Farrell Grehan/Corbis

Piaget's early training as a biologist led to his view that children mentally assimilate and accommodate aspects of their environment.

often acting as budding scientists. They are studying both the texture and consistency of their food, as well as their parents' response.

Piaget used concepts such as *schemes, adaptation, assimilation, accommodation,* and *equilibration* to describe and explain cognitive development. Piaget defines the **scheme** as a pattern of action or mental structure involved when acquiring or organizing knowledge. For example, newborn babies might be said to have a sucking scheme (others call it a *reflex*) because they respond to objects put in their mouths as "things I can suck" versus "things I can't suck."

Adaptation refers to the interaction between the organism and the environment. According to Piaget, all organisms adapt to their environment. Adaptation consists of assimilation and accommodation, which occur throughout life. Cognitive **assimilation** refers to the process by which we respond to new objects or events according to existing schemes or ways of organizing knowledge. A 2-year-old who refers to horses as "doggies" is assimilating horses into the dog scheme. But sometimes a novel object or event cannot be made to fit into an existing scheme. In that case, the scheme may be changed or a new scheme may be created to incorporate the new event. This process is called **accommodation**. Consider the sucking reflex. Infants accommodate by rejecting objects that are too large, that taste bad, or that are of the wrong texture or temperature.

"Information processing in people is the process people use to encode (input) information, store it (in long-term memory), retrieve it (place it in short-term memory), and manipulate it to solve problems."

Piaget theorized that when children can assimilate new events to existing schemes, they are in a state of cognitive harmony, or equilibrium. When they encounter something that does not fit, their state of equilibrium is disturbed and they may try to accommodate. The process of restoring equilibrium is termed **equilibration**. Piaget believed that the attempt to restore equilibrium lies at the heart of a child's natural curiosity.

Piaget's Stages of Cognitive Development

Piaget (1963) hypothesized that children's cognitive processes develop in an orderly sequence, or series, consisting of four stages: *sensorimotor, preoperational, concrete operational,* and *formal operational*. These stages are discussed in greater detail in subsequent chapters.

Because Piaget's theory focuses on cognitive development, its applications are primarily in educational settings and provide the foundation for curriculum decisions made throughout the public school system in Canada. Teachers following Piaget's views actively engage children in solving problems. They gear instruction to children's developmental level and offer activities that challenge children to advance to the next level.

Evaluation Many researchers, using a variety of methods, find that Piaget may have underestimated the ages when children are capable of certain activities. Also, many cognitive skills seem to develop gradually and not in distinct stages. Nevertheless, Piaget has provided a strong theoretical foundation for researchers concerned with sequences in cognitive development.

scheme
an action pattern or mental structure involved in the acquisition and organization of knowledge.

adaptation
the interaction between the organism and the environment, consisting of assimilation and accommodation.

assimilation
the incorporation of new events or knowledge into existing schemes.

accommodation
the modification of existing schemes to permit the incorporation of new events or knowledge.

equilibration
the creation of an equilibrium, or balance, between assimilation and accommodation.

Information-Processing Theory

Another face of the cognitive perspective is information processing (Flavell et al., 2002; Siegler & Alabali, 2005). Many psychologists speak of people's working, or short-term, memory and a more permanent long-term memory (storage). If information has been placed in long-term memory, it must be retrieved before we can work on it. Retrieving

silver-john/Shutterstock.com

The human brain is very similar to a computer.

ethology
the study of behaviours that are specific to a species.

fixed action pattern (FAP)
a stereotyped pattern of behaviour that is evoked by a "releasing stimulus"; an instinct.

ecology
the branch of biology that studies the relationships between living organisms and their environment.

ecological systems theory
the view that explains child development in terms of the reciprocal influences between children and their environmental settings.

information from our own long-term memories requires certain cues; otherwise, the information may be lost.

Thus, many cognitive psychologists focus on people's information processing—the processes people use to encode (input) information, store it (in long-term memory), retrieve it (place it in short-term memory), and manipulate it to solve problems. Our strategies for solving problems are sometimes referred to as our "mental programs" or "software." In this computer metaphor, our brains are the "hardware" that runs our mental programs. Our brains—containing billions of brain cells called *neurons*—become our most "personal" computers. When psychologists who study information processing contemplate cognitive development, they are likely to talk in terms of the *size* of the person's short-term memory and the *number of programs* she or he can run simultaneously.

The Biological Perspective

The biological perspective directly relates to physical development: to gains in height and weight; development of the brain; and developments related to hormones, reproduction, and heredity. Here we consider one biologically oriented theory of development, *ethology*.

Ethology: "Doing What Comes Naturally"

Ethology was heavily influenced by the 19th-century work of Charles Darwin and by the work of 20th-century ethologists Konrad Lorenz and Niko Tinbergen (Washburn, 2007). Ethology is concerned with instinctive, or inborn, behaviour patterns.

The nervous systems of most, and perhaps all, animals are "prewired" to respond to some situations in specific ways. For example, birds raised in isolation from other birds will build nests during the mating season even if they have never seen a nest or have never seen another bird building a nest. Nest-building could not have been learned. Birds raised in isolation also sing the songs typical of their species. These behaviours are "built in," or instinctive. They are also referred to as inborn **fixed action patterns (FAPs)**.

Research seeks to answer two questions: Do human behaviour and human development involve instincts? If so, how powerful are human instincts?

Evaluation Research into the ethological perspective suggests that instinct may play a role in human behaviour. Research seeks to answer two questions: Do human behaviour and human development involve instincts? If so, how powerful are human instincts?

The Ecological Perspective

Ecology is the branch of biology that studies the relationships between living organisms and their environment. The **ecological systems theory** of development addresses aspects of psychological, social, and emotional development as well as aspects of biological development. Development is explained in terms of the interaction between people and the settings in which they live (Bronfenbrenner & Morris, 2006).

According to Urie Bronfenbrenner (1917–2005), for example, we need to focus on the two-way interactions between the child and the parents, not just maturational forces (nature) or child-rearing practices (nurture). Bronfenbrenner (Bronfenbrenner & Morris, 2006) suggested that we can view the setting or contexts of human development as consisting of multiple systems, each embedded within the next larger context. From narrowest to widest, these systems are the microsystem, the mesosystem, the exosystem, the macrosystem, and the chronosystem (see Figure 1.3).

Nesting is an instinctive behaviour, not a learned behaviour.

Vishnevskiy Vasily/Shutterstock.com

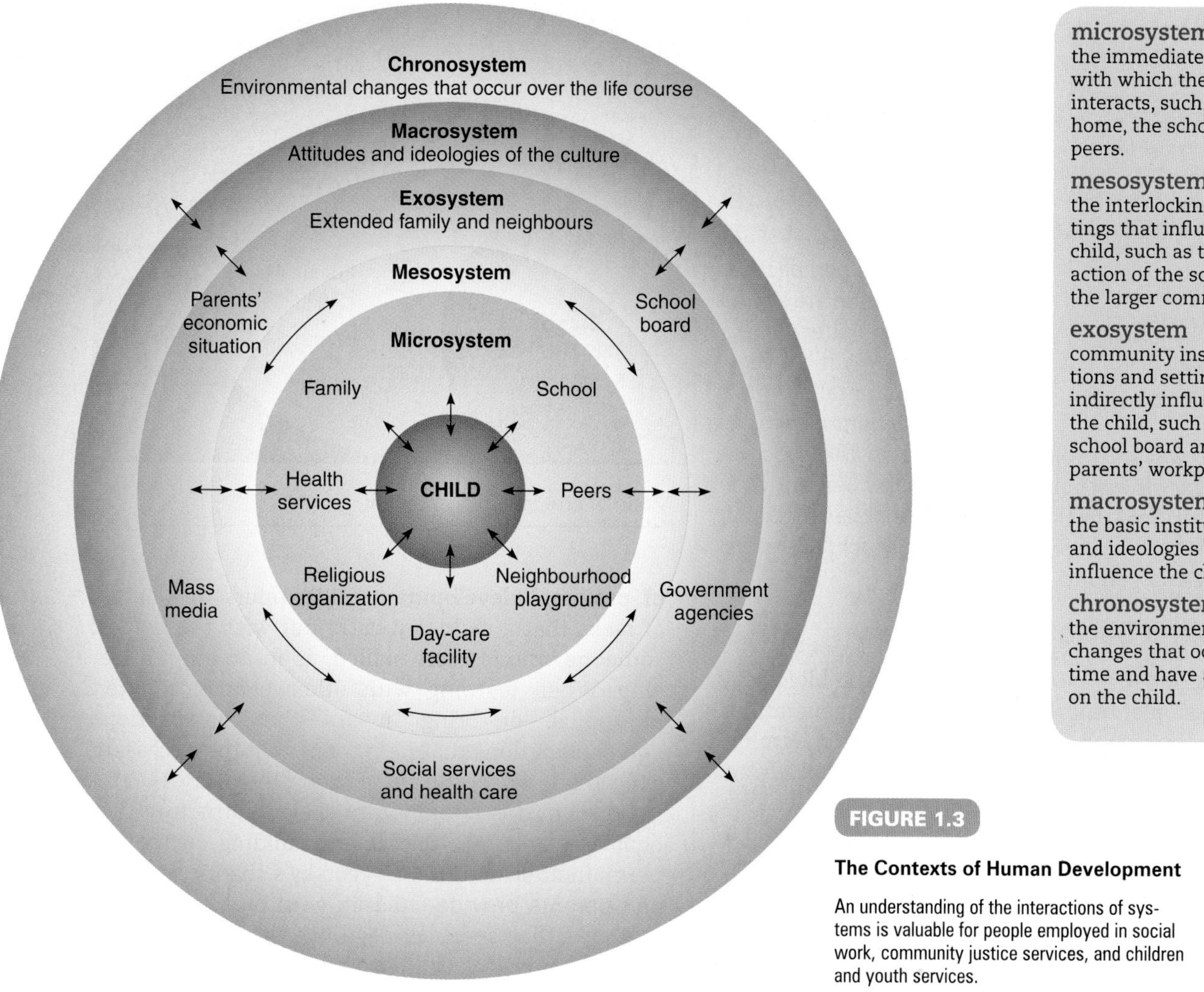

microsystem
the immediate settings with which the child interacts, such as the home, the school, and peers.

mesosystem
the interlocking settings that influence the child, such as the interaction of the school and the larger community.

exosystem
community institutions and settings that indirectly influence the child, such as the school board and the parents' workplaces.

macrosystem
the basic institutions and ideologies that influence the child.

chronosystem
the environmental changes that occur over time and have an effect on the child.

FIGURE 1.3

The Contexts of Human Development

An understanding of the interactions of systems is valuable for people employed in social work, community justice services, and children and youth services.

The **microsystem** involves the interactions of the child with other people in the immediate setting, such as the home, the school, or the peer group. Initially, the microsystem is small, involving caregiving interactions with the parents or others, usually at home. As children get older, they do more, with more people, in more places.

The **mesosystem** involves the interactions of the various settings within the microsystem. For instance, the home and the school interact during parent–teacher conferences. The school and the larger community interact when children go on field trips. The ecological systems approach addresses the joint effect of two or more settings on the child.

The **exosystem** refers to the institutions in which the child does not directly participate but which exert an indirect influence on the child. For example, the school board is part of the child's exosystem because board members design programs for the child's education, determine the textbooks to be used, and so forth. In similar fashion, parents' workplaces and their economic situations determine the hours when they are available to the child, and so on (Kaminski & Stormshak, 2007). As a result, children may misbehave at home and in school.

The **macrosystem** refers to the interaction of children with the beliefs, values, expectations, and lifestyles of their cultural settings. Cross-cultural studies examine children's interactions with their macrosystem. Macrosystems exist within a particular culture. In Canada, three different macrosystems are the dual-earner family; the low-income, single-parent household; and the family with father as sole breadwinner. Each has its lifestyle, set of values, and expectations (Bronfenbrenner & Morris, 2006; Silbereisen, 2006).

The **chronosystem** considers the changes that occur over time. For example, the effects of divorce peak about a year after the event, and then children begin to recover. The breakup has more of an effect on boys than on girls. The ecological approach broadens the strategies for intervention in issues

zone of proximal development (ZPD) Vygotsky's term for the range of tasks a child can carry out with the help of someone who is more skilled.

scaffolding Vygotsky's term for temporary cognitive structures or methods of solving problems that help children as they learn to function independently.

such as prevention of teenage pregnancy, child abuse, youth in conflict with the law, and substance abuse (Kaminski & Stormshak, 2007).

The Sociocultural Perspective

The sociocultural perspective teaches that people are social beings who are affected by the cultures in which they live. Developmentalists use the term *sociocultural* in two different ways: to refer specifically to the *sociocultural theory* of Russian psychologist Lev Semenovich Vygotsky (1896–1934) and to address the effect on people by human diversity, including such factors as ethnicity and gender.

Vygotsky's Sociocultural Theory

Whereas genetics is concerned with the biological transmission of traits from generation to generation, Vygotsky's (1978) theory is concerned with the transmission of information and cognitive skills from generation to generation. The transmission of skills involves teaching and learning, but Vygotsky did not view learning in terms of conditioning. Rather, he focused on how the child's social interaction with adults, mostly in the home, organizes a child's learning experiences in such a way that the child can obtain cognitive skills—such as computation or reading skills—which it uses to acquire information. Like Piaget, Vygotsky sees the child's functioning as adaptive (Kanevsky & Geake, 2004), and the child adapts to his or her social and cultural interactions.

Key concepts in Vygotsky's theory include the *zone of proximal development* and *scaffolding*. The **zone of proximal development (ZPD)** refers to a range of tasks that a child can carry out with the help of someone who is more skilled, as in an apprenticeship. When learning with other people, children internalize—or bring inward—the conversations and explanations that help them gain the necessary skills (Ash, 2004; Umek et al., 2005; Vygotsky, 1962).

A *scaffold* is a temporary skeletal structure that enables workers to fabricate a building or another permanent structure. In Vygotsky's theory, teachers and parents provide children with problem-solving methods that serve as cognitive **scaffolding** while the child gains the ability to function independently. For example, children may be offered scaffolding that enables them to use their fingers or their toes to do simple calculations. Eventually, the scaffolding is removed and the cognitive structures stand alone.

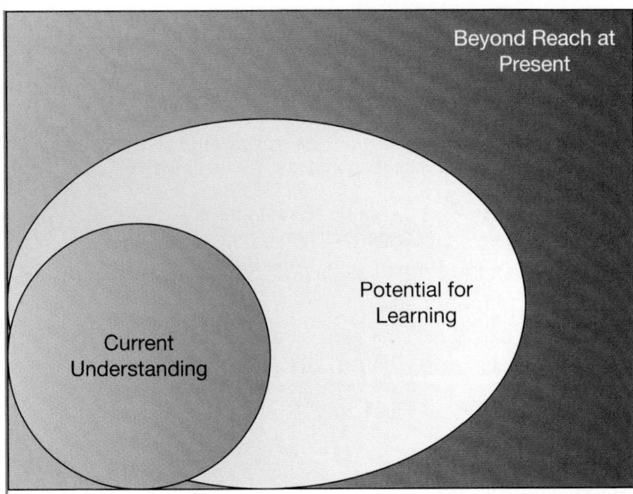

Zone of proximal development

Lev Semenovich Vygotsky

Vygotsky: UIG via Getty Images; frame: © catnap72/iStockphoto

According to Vygotsky's theory, teachers and parents provide children with problem-solving methods that serve as cognitive scaffolding.

jh Fotografie/Shutterstock.com/© Brand X Pictures/Jupiterimages

The Sociocultural Perspective and Human Diversity

The sociocultural perspective asserts that we cannot understand individuals without awareness of the richness of their diversity (Fouad & Arredondo, 2007). For example, people differ in their ethnicity, gender, and socioeconomic status.

People's ethnic groups involve their cultural heritage, their race, their language, and their common history. Figure 1.4, from the website of Citizenship and Immigration Canada, highlights more than 200 multicultural groupings that populate our country. Canadian society is built on the acceptance and promotion of multiculturalism. Diversity within the Canadian population must not be taken for granted but should be fostered and developed.

© Duncan Walker/iStockphoto

FIGURE 1.4

Diversity in Canada 1996–2006, and 2017 Projections

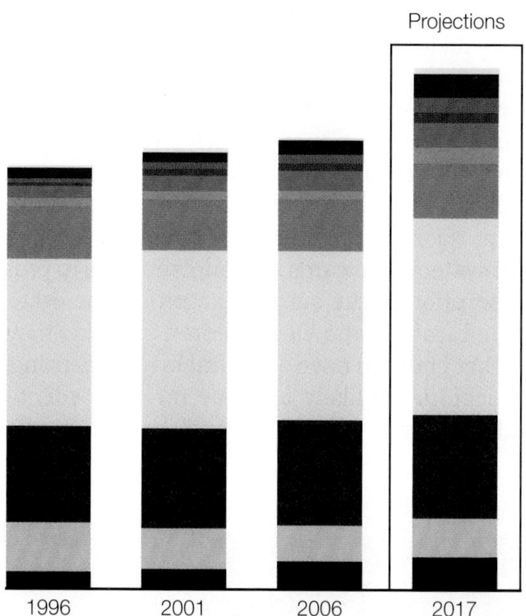

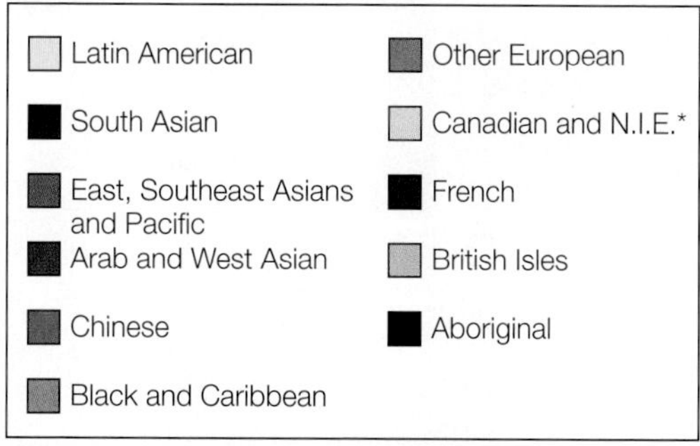

* not included elsewhere, Statistics Canada 2006

Source: *Annual Report on the Operation of the Canadian Multiculturalism Act 2007-2008*, Citizenship and Immigration Canada, 2009

Reproduced with the permission of the Minister of Public Works and Government Services Canada, 2013

Gender is another aspect of human diversity. Gender refers to the psychological state of being male or being female, as influenced by cultural concepts of gender-appropriate behaviour. Expectations of females and males are often polarized by cultural rules. That is, gender differences may be exaggerated, as in the case of intellectual abilities. For example, although males differ from females in some respects, history has created more burdens for women than for men. Historically, females have been discouraged from careers in the sciences, politics, and business. However, women today are making inroads into academic and vocational spheres that were traditionally male preserves—such as medicine, law, engineering, and the military. It is worth noting that, until relatively recently, females were not considered qualified for education. But even today, in many parts of the world, women still prevented from obtaining an education.

EMERGING CANADA

Canadians are better educated than they were a decade ago and have some of the highest graduation rates in the free world. More Canadian women graduate from high school and postsecondary institutions than men but women continue to earn far less in the workplace (Morrow, 2010).

LO3 Debates in Development

The discussion of theories of development reveals that developmentalists can see things in very different ways. Let us consider how they react to three of the most important debates in the field.

nature
the processes within an organism that guide it to develop according to its genetic code.

nurture
environmental factors that influence development.

Nature and Nurture

Researchers are continually trying to sort out the extent to which human behaviour is the result of **nature** (heredity) and of **nurture** (environmental influences). What aspects of human behaviour originate in our genes and are biologically programmed to unfold as time goes on, as long as we receive minimal nutrition and social experience? What aspects of human behaviour can be traced mostly to such environmental influences as nutrition and learning?

Most researchers agree that both nature and nurture play important roles in nearly every area of development. Consider the significant health threat that cardiovascular disease presents to Canadians. A person may be genetically predisposed to this disease (nature), but lifestyle choices (nurture) will also strongly affect this person's health outcome. Modern theorists rarely view nature and nurture as mutually exclusive.

Tomas 111/Shutterstock.com

Those viewing development as discontinuous recognize distinct changes comparable to the caterpillar and the butterfly.

Continuity and Discontinuity

Some developmentalists view human development as a continuous process, in which the effects of learning increase gradually, with no sudden major qualitative changes. In contrast, other theorists believe that numerous rapid qualitative changes usher in new stages of development. Maturational theorists point out that the environment, even when enriched, provides us with little benefit until we are ready, or mature enough, to develop in a certain way. For example, newborn babies will not imitate their parents' speech, even when parents speak clearly and deliberately because developmentally, they are not yet ready to speak. Stage theorists such as Sigmund Freud and Jean Piaget saw development as discontinuous. They saw biological changes as providing the potential for psychological changes.

Sari O'Neal/Shutterstock.com

EMERGING CANADA

In Canada, tens of thousands of people die every year from heart disease or stroke. Over the past 40 years, the rate has significantly declined as a result of education and changes in lifestyle. The rate has declined 25 percent over the past 10 years, 50 percent over the past 20 years, and 70 percent between 1956 and today (Heart and Stroke Foundation, 2013).

Active and Passive Roles

Historical views of children as willful and unruly suggest that people have generally viewed children as being active, even if mischievous (at best) or evil (at worst). John Locke introduced a view of children as passive beings (blank tablets); he believed that experience "wrote" features of personality and moral virtue on children.

At one extreme, educators who view children as passive may assume that instructors must motivate children to learn. Such educators are likely to provide a rigorous traditional curriculum with a powerful system of rewards and punishments to promote absorption of the subject matter. At the other extreme, educators who view children as active may assume that children have a natural love of learning. Such educators are likely to argue for open education and encourage children to explore and pursue

© Shauna Longmuir

Girls usually spurt in growth before boys do, which these graduating grade eights are very much aware of.

their unique likes and talents, focusing on a love of learning for learning's sake.

These debates are theoretical. Scientists value theory for its ability to tie together observations and suggest new areas of investigation, but they also follow an **empirical** approach. That is, to find evidence for or against various theoretical positions, they engage in research methods, such as those described in the next section.

LO4 How Do We Study Development?

Gathering Information

Researchers use various methods to gather information. For example, they may ask teachers or parents to report on the behaviour of children, use interviews or questionnaires with adults, or study statistics compiled by the government or the United Nations. They also directly observe children in the laboratory, the playground, or the classroom. Let us discuss two ways of gathering information: the naturalistic-observation method and the case-study method.

Naturalistic Observation

Naturalistic-observation studies are conducted in "the field," that is, in the natural, or real-life, settings in which the activities being studied occur. For example, in field studies, investigators observe the natural behaviour of children in settings such as homes, playgrounds, and classrooms. Because researchers do not want their presence to interfere with children's normal behaviour, they may try to "blend into the woodwork" by sitting quietly in the back of a classroom or by observing the class through a one-way mirror.

The Case Study

The **case study** is a carefully written account of the behaviour of an individual. Parents who keep diaries of their children's activities are writing informal case studies. Case studies themselves often use different kinds of information. In addition to direct observation, case studies may include questionnaires, **standardized tests**, and interviews. Information gleaned from public records may also be included. Scientists who use the case-study method try to record all relevant factors in a person's behaviour, and they are cautious in drawing conclusions about the source of any behaviour.

CHARLES FOX/MCT/Landov

The researcher is able to observe children in this two-way mirror without disrupting their play. The children are unaware they are being observed.

Surveys

empirical based on observation and experimentation.

case study a carefully written account of the behaviour of an individual.

standardized test a test that compares an individual's score with the scores of a group of similar individuals.

Researchers also collect information by posing well-designed questions to gather statistics on a wide variety of topics. For example, Statistics Canada collects data to ensure that the government can make appropriate planning decisions while collecting the most recent and accurate information on Canadian trends. The Canadian Census of Population is gathered every five years and is mandatory for every citizen to complete.

The Canadian Psychological Association also routinely conducts surveys. This initiative aids in the collecting of information concerning the characteristics of the clients they assess and treat. The survey results are used to attempt to address the data gap that exists in the area of mental health needs in Canada. For example, a recent 2011 survey conducted by the Canadian Psychological Association found that Canadians face "significant barriers" to accessing psychological care (Canadian Psychological Association, 2011).

Remember that survey results are sterile and are subject to interpretation. The individual is responsible to give the information collected significant meaning. Throughout this textbook, you will read Emerging Canada features that describe the information being collected on emerging Canadian trends. Your challenge is to apply this information in a meaningful way, by going beyond the statistics presented.

correlation coefficient a number ranging from +1.00 to −1.00 that expresses the direction (positive or negative) and strength of the relationship between two variables.

positive correlation a relationship between two variables in which one variable increases as the other increases.

negative correlation a relationship between two variables in which one variable increases as the other decreases.

Correlation: Putting Things Together

Researchers use the correlational method to determine whether one behaviour or trait being studied relates to, or correlates with, another. Consider intelligence and achievement. These variables are assigned numbers such as intelligence test scores and grade point averages. The numbers or scores are then mathematically related and expressed as a **correlation coefficient**—a number that varies between +1.00 and −1.00.

EMERGING CANADA

Mental illness indirectly affects all Canadians at some time through a family member, friend, or colleague. Consider that 20 percent of Canadians will personally experience a mental illness in their lifetime, and suicide accounts for 24 percent of all deaths among 15- to 24-year-olds and 16 percent of all deaths among 25- to 44-year-olds. In other words, 1 in 5 Canadians will experience mental illness, and suicide is one of the leading causes of death for young Canadians (Canadian Mental Health Association, 2013c). What questions arise from this finding? Why are Canadians so secretive about mental illness when it is clearly a significant Canadian issue?

In general, the higher people score on intelligence tests, the more likely they are to have better academic performance (and income). The scores attained on intelligence tests are **positively correlated** (about +0.60 to +0.70) with overall academic achievement (and income). A **negative correlation** exists between adolescents' grades and delinquent acts. That is, the higher an adolescent's grades, the less likely he or she is to engage in criminal behaviour. Figure 1.5 illustrates positive and negative correlations.

Limitations of Correlational Information

Correlational information can reveal relationships between variables, but does not show cause and effect. Assuming that exposure to violent media makes people more aggressive may seem logical, but it may also be that more aggressive people *choose* violent media. This research bias is termed a *selection factor*.

Similarly, studies report that children (especially boys) in divorced families tend to show more behavioural problems than children in intact families (Greene et al., 2006; Lansford et al., 2006). These studies, however, do not show that divorce causes these adjustment problems. It could be that the factors that led to divorce—such as parental conflict—also led to adjustment problems among the children (Hetherington, 2006). To investigate cause and effect, researchers turn to the experimental method.

The Experiment: Trying Things Out

The experiment is the preferred method for investigating questions of cause and effect. In the **experiment**, one group of subjects receives a treatment and another group does not. The subjects are then observed to determine whether the treatment changes their behaviour. Experiments are usually

Positive correlation

As one variable increases, the other variable increases.

A

Time spent studying

Grades in school

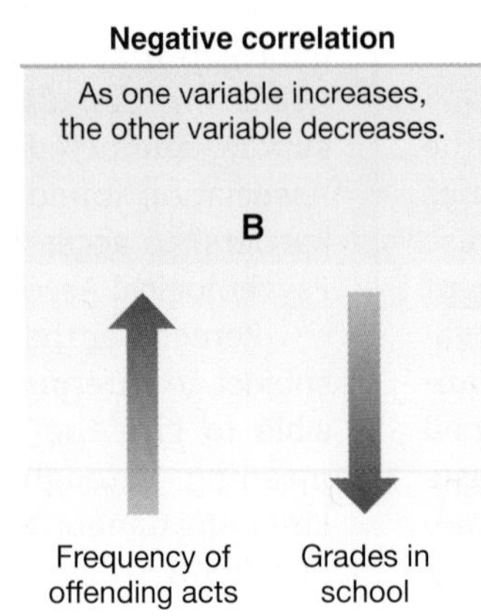

FIGURE 1.5

Examples of Positive and Negative Correlations

When two variables are correlated positively, one increases as the other increases. For example, as shown in Part A, a positive correlation exists between the amount of time spent studying and grades. When two variables are correlated negatively, one increases as the other decreases. For example, as shown in Part B, a negative correlation exists between the frequency of a child's offending acts and his or her grades. As offending behaviour increases, grades tend to decline.

undertaken to test a **hypothesis**. For example, a researcher might hypothesize that TV violence will cause aggressive behaviour in children.

Independent and Dependent Variables

© Lilyana Vynogradova/iStockphoto

In an experiment to determine whether TV violence causes aggressive behaviour, subjects in the experimental group would be shown a TV program containing violence, and then its effects on behaviour would be measured. TV violence would be considered an **inde- pendent variable**, a variable whose presence is manipulated by the experimenters so that its effects can be determined. The measured result—in this case, the child's behaviour—is called a **dependent variable**. Its presence or level presumably depends on the independent variable.

Experimental and Control Groups

Experiments use experimental and control groups. Subjects in the **experimental group** receive the treatment, whereas subjects in the **control group** do not. All other conditions are held constant for both groups. Thus, we can have confidence that experimental outcomes reflect the treatments and not chance factors.

Random Assignment

Subjects should be assigned to experimental or control groups on a chance or random basis. We could not conclude much from an experiment on the effects of TV violence if the children were allowed to choose whether they would be in a group that watched TV violence or in a group that did not. In such an experiment, a *selection factor*, not the treatment itself might be responsible for the results of the experiment.

Ethical and practical considerations also prevent researchers from doing experiments on the effects of many life circumstances, such as divorce or different patterns of child rearing. We cannot randomly assign some families to divorce or conflict and assign other families to "bliss." We can also not randomly assign parents to rearing their children in an authoritarian or permissive manner. In some areas of investigation, we must settle for correlational evidence.

When experiments cannot ethically be performed on humans, researchers sometimes carry them out with animals and try to generalize the findings to humans. No researcher would separate human infants from their parents to study the effects of isolation on development, yet experimenters have deprived monkeys of early social experience. Such research has helped psychologists investigate the formation of parent–child bonds of attachment.

Longitudinal Research: Studying Development over Time

The processes of development occur over time, and researchers have devised different strategies for comparing children of one age with children or adults of other ages. In **longitudinal research**, the same people are observed repeatedly over time, and researchers record their changes in development, such as gains in height or changes in mental abilities.

experiment
a method of scientific investigation that seeks to discover cause-and-effect relationships by introducing independent variables and observing their effects on dependent variables.

hypothesis
a proposition to be tested.

independent variable
a condition in a scientific study that is manipulated so that its effects can be observed.

dependent variable
a measure of an assumed effect of an independent variable.

experimental group
a group of subjects who receive a treatment in an experiment.

control group
a group of subjects in an experiment who do not receive the treatment but for whom all other conditions are comparable with those of the experimental group.

longitudinal research
the study of developmental processes by taking repeated measures of the same group of participants at various stages of development.

DID YOU KNOW?

Research with monkeys has helped psychologists understand the formation of attachment in humans.

Scientists cannot ethically research the formation of attachments on humans, so they conduct tests on animals that are genetically similar to people and then extrapolate their findings.

cross-sectional research the study of developmental processes by taking measures of participants of different age groups at the same time.

cohort effect similarities in behaviour among a group of peers as a result of being of approximately the same age.

In **cross-sectional research**, children of different ages are observed and compared.

Longitudinal Studies

The National Longitudinal Survey of Children and Youth (NLSCY) began in Canada in 1994. The NLSCY collects information on the factors that influence children's social, emotional, and behavioural development and studies the impact of these factors on children's development over time. Also gathered are data concerning Canadian children's social environment (family, friends, schools, and communities) (Statistics Canada, 2008c).

> **DID YOU KNOW?**
>
> **To learn how a person develops over a lifetime, researchers have tracked some individuals for more than 50 years.**
>
> Lewis Terman's Genetic Studies of Genius, which began in the 1920s, tracked the professional achievements of male subjects with high IQs.

These studies allow long-term vision; however, they are also costly and require an extensive time commitment.

Longitudinal studies have drawbacks. For example, researchers find it difficult to enlist volunteers to participate in a study that will last a lifetime. Many subjects fall out of touch as the years pass; others die. The researchers must be patient or arrange to enlist future generations of researchers.

Cross-Sectional Studies

Because of the drawbacks of longitudinal studies, most research that compares children of different ages is cross-sectional. In other words, most investigators gather data on what the "typical" 6-month-old is doing by finding children who are 6 months old today. When they expand their research to the behaviour of typical 12-month-olds, they seek another group of children, and so on.

© Polina Lobanova/Shutterstock.com

© Martin Rogers/Stock, Boston

A major challenge to cross-sectional research is the **cohort effect**. A cohort is a group of people born at about the same time. As a result, they experience cultural and other events unique to their age group. In other words, children and adults of different ages are not likely to have shared similar cultural backgrounds. For example, people who are 80 years old today grew up without TV. Today's children grow up taking iPods and the Internet for granted.

Children of past generations also grew up with different expectations about gender roles and appropriate social behaviour.

In longitudinal studies, we know that we have the same individuals as they have developed over 5, 25, even 50 years or more. In cross-sectional research, we can only hope that the individuals being studied will be comparable.

Ethical Considerations

The Canadian Psychological Association (2000) has designed an extensive 32-page Code of Ethics for psychologists conducting research in Canada. Although this document often makes the completion of research more difficult, it ultimately safeguards the welfare of Canadians.

Some of the governing principles of the document include the following:

1. Respect for the Individual, including standards such as informed consent, confidentiality, and protection for vulnerable persons (including children, seniors, and those with intellectual disabilities);
2. Responsible Care, such as risk/benefit analysis and minimizing harm;
3. Integrity in Relationships, including honesty, lack of bias, and complete disclosure;
4. Responsibility to Society, including the pursuit of beneficial research for the development of society.

This strict and detailed code of ethics reflects the responsibility and integrity that must govern all psychological research conducted in Canada. The code promotes the dignity of the individual, fosters human welfare, and maintains scientific integrity.

CHAPTER 2

Heredity and Prenatal Development

LEARNING OUTCOMES

LO1 Describe the influences of heredity on development

LO2 Describe the influences of the environment on development

LO3 Explain what happens in the process of conception

LO4 Recount the major events of prenatal development

> “The structures we inherit make our behaviour possible and place limits on it.”

LO1 The Influence of Heredity on Development

Heredity makes possible all things human. The structures we inherit make our behaviour possible and place limits on it. The field of biology that studies heredity is called **genetics**.

Genetic influences are fundamental in the transmission of physical traits, such as height, hair texture, and eye colour. Genetics also appears to play a role in psychological traits such as intelligence, activity level, sociability, shyness, anxiety, empathy, effectiveness as a parent, happiness, and even interest in arts and crafts (Johnson & Krueger, 2006; Knafo & Plomin, 2006a, 2006b; Leonardo & Hen, 2006). Genetic factors are also involved in psychological problems such as schizophrenia; depression; and dependence on nicotine, alcohol, and other substances (Farmer et al., 2007; Hill et al., 2007; Metzger et al., 2007).

genetics
the branch of biology that studies heredity.

chromosomes
rod-shaped structures that are composed of genes and are found within the nuclei of cells.

genes
the basic units of heredity. Genes are composed of deoxyribonucleic acid (DNA).

polygenic
resulting from many (poly) genes.

deoxyribonucleic acid (DNA)
genetic material that takes the form of a double helix and is composed of phosphates, sugars, and bases.

mitosis
the form of cell division in which each chromosome splits lengthwise to double in number. Half of each chromosome combines with chemicals to retake its original form and then moves to the new cell.

Chromosomes and Genes

Traits are transmitted by chromosomes and genes. **Chromosomes** are rod-shaped structures found in cells. Typical human cells contain 46 chromosomes organized into 23 pairs. Each chromosome contains thousands of segments called genes. **Genes** are the biochemical materials that regulate the development of traits. Some traits, such as blood type, appear to be transmitted by a single pair of genes, one derived from each parent. Other traits are **polygenic**; that is, they are determined by many (poly) pairs of genes.

Our heredity is governed by 20,000 to 25,000 genes (International Human Genome Sequencing Consortium, 2006). Genes are segments of strands of **deoxyribonucleic acid (DNA)**. DNA takes the form of a double spiral, or helix, similar to a twisting ladder (see Figure 2.1).

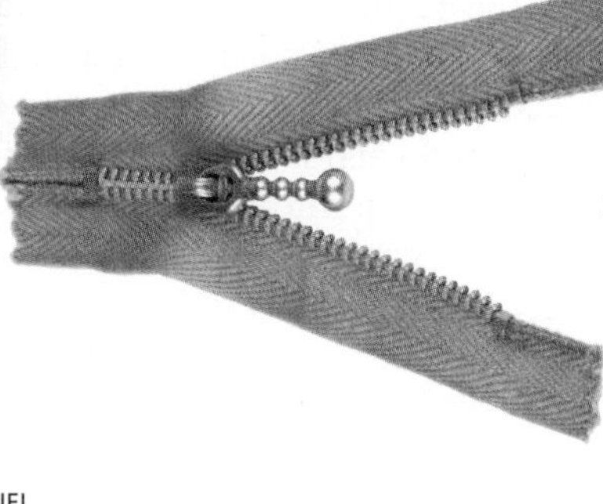

Mitosis and Meiosis

We begin life as a single cell, or zygote, that divides repeatedly. There are two types of cell division: *mitosis* and *meiosis*. In **mitosis**, strands of DNA break apart, or “unzip.” The double helix then duplicates. The DNA forms two camps on either side of the cell, and then the cell divides. Each incomplete rung combines with the appropriate “partner” to form a new complete ladder. The two resulting identical copies of the DNA strand will separate when the cell divides so that

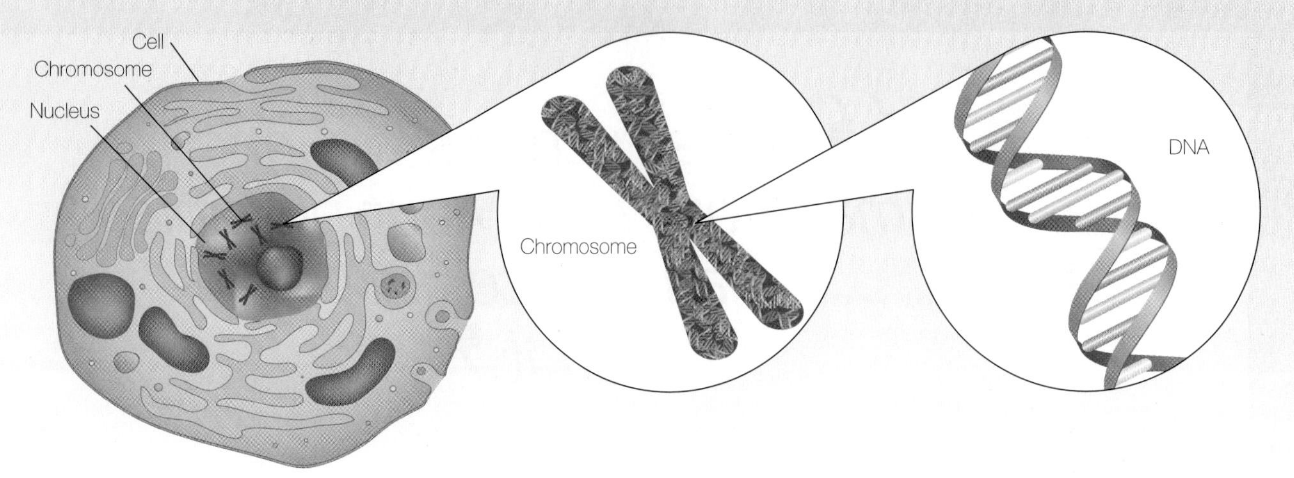

FIGURE 2.1

The Double Helix of DNA

DNA takes the form of a double spiral, or helix.

WWW Go to www.nelson.com/4ltrpress/icanhdev2ce to access an interactive version of this figure.

mutation
a sudden, or accidental, variation in a heritable characteristic that affects the composition of genes.

meiosis
the form of cell division in which each pair of chromosomes splits so that one member of each pair moves to the new cell. As a result, each new cell has 23 chromosomes.

autosome
a pair of chromosomes (with the exception of sex chromosomes).

sex chromosome
a chromosome in the shape of a Y (male) or X (female) that determines the sex of the child.

monozygotic (MZ) twins
twins that derive from a single zygote that has split into two; identical twins. Each MZ twin carries the same genetic code.

dizygotic (DZ) twins
twins that derive from two separate zygotes; fraternal twins with different genetic codes.

each becomes a member of a newly formed cell. As a result, the genetic code is identical in new cells unless **mutations** occur through radiation or other environmental influences. Mutations also occur by chance, but not often.

Sperm and ova (egg cells) are produced through **meiosis**, or *reduction division*. In meiosis, the 46 chromosomes within the cell nucleus first line up into 23 pairs. The DNA ladders then unzip, leaving unpaired halves of chromosomes. When the cell divides, one member of each pair goes to each newly formed cell. Each new cell nucleus contains only 23 chromosomes, not 46.

When a sperm cell fertilizes an ovum (an egg cell), we receive 23 chromosomes from our father's sperm cell and 23 from our mother's ovum, and the combined chromosomes form 23 pairs (see Figure 2.2). Twenty-two of the pairs are **autosomes**—pairs that look alike and possess genetic information concerning the same set of traits. The 23rd pair, the **sex chromosomes**, looks different from the autosome pairs and determines our sex. We all receive an X sex chromosome (so called because of its X shape) from our mother. Our father supplies either a Y or an X sex chromosome. If we receive an X sex chromosome from our father, we develop into a female, and if we receive a Y chromosome (named after its Y shape), we develop into a male.

DID YOU KNOW?

Your father determined whether you are female or male.

Males supply either an X or a Y chromosome, which determines the sex of the baby. Imagine how shocked King Henry VIII would be if he were a student in this class. Many women were isolated in medieval times for "their" inability to produce a male heir.

Identical and Fraternal Twins

Now and then, a zygote divides into two cells that separate so that each develops into an individual with the same genetic makeup. These individuals are identical twins, or **monozygotic (MZ) twins**. In very rare cases, the eggs do not completely separate on the 13th day after conception, and the result is conjoined twins, as was the case for Tatiana and Krista, born in British Columbia in March 2007. If a woman produces two ova in the same month, and each is fertilized by different sperm cells, they develop into fraternal twins, or **dizygotic (DZ) twins**. DZ twins run in families. If a woman is a twin, if her mother was a twin, or if she has previously borne twins, the chances rise that she will bear twins (Office of National Statistics, 2006).

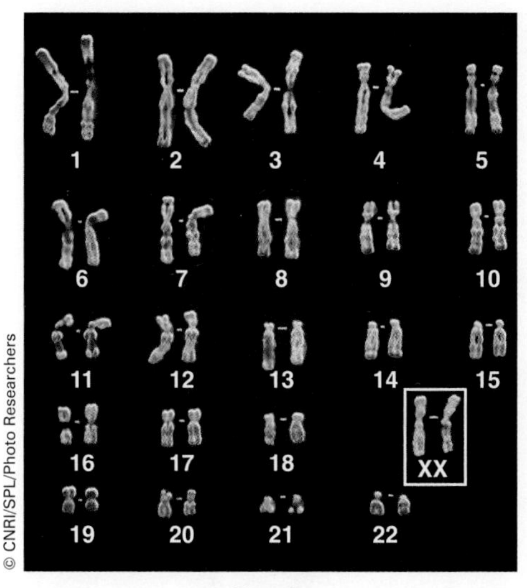

Female

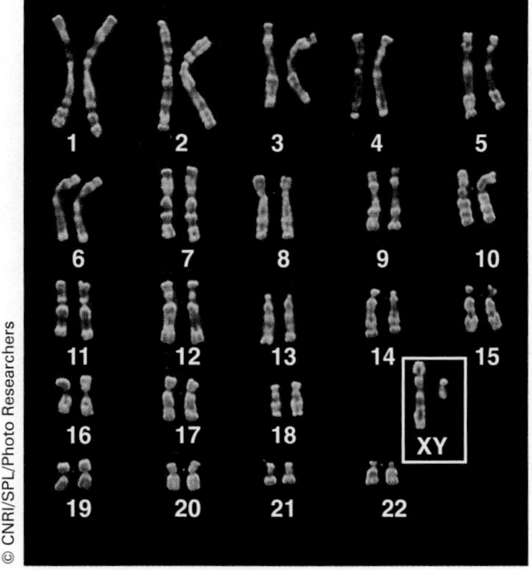

Male

FIGURE 2.2

The 23 Pairs of Human Chromosomes

People normally have 23 pairs of chromosomes. Females have two X chromosomes, whereas males have an X and a Y sex chromosome.

As women reach the end of their childbearing years, **ovulation** becomes less regular, resulting in months when more than one ovum is released. Thus, the chances of twins increase with parental age (National Guideline Clearinghouse, 2007). Adding to this likelihood is the social reality in Canada that women are postponing parenting later than their mothers and grandmothers. Of the mothers who gave birth in 2005, 48.9 percent were 30 years of age or older, more than double the percentage in 1974 (Human Resources and Skills Development Canada, 2010a). Fertility drugs also enhance the chances of multiple births by causing more than one ovum to ripen and be released during a woman's cycle (National Guideline Clearinghouse, 2007).

Dominant and Recessive Traits

Traits are determined by pairs of genes. Each member of a pair of genes is termed an **allele**. When both of the alleles for a trait, such as hair colour, are the same, the person is said to be **homozygous** for that trait. When the alleles for a trait differ, the person is **heterozygous** for that trait. Some traits result from an "averaging" of the genetic instructions carried by the parents. When the effects of both alleles are shown, the trait is said to have incomplete dominance, or codominance. When a *dominant* allele is paired with a *recessive* allele, the trait determined by the dominant allele appears in the offspring. For example, the offspring from the crossing of brown eyes with blue eyes have brown eyes, suggesting that brown eyes are a **dominant trait** and blue eyes are a **recessive trait**.

If one parent carried genes for only brown eyes and if the other parent carried genes for only blue eyes, the children would invariably have brown eyes. But brown-eyed parents can also carry recessive genes for blue eyes, as shown in Figure 2.3. If the recessive gene from one parent combines with the recessive gene from the other parent, the recessive trait will be shown. As suggested by Figure 2.3, approximately 25 percent of the children of brown-eyed parents who carry recessive blue eye colour will have blue eyes. Table 2.1 shows some dominant and recessive traits in humans.

People who bear one dominant gene and one recessive gene for a trait are said to be **carriers** of the recessive gene. In the cases of recessive genes that cause illness, carriers of those genes are fortunate to have dominant genes that cancel the effects of the recessive genes.

Chromosomal or genetic abnormalities can cause health problems. Some chromosomal disorders reflect abnormalities in the 22 pairs of autosomes (e.g., Down syndrome); others reflect abnormalities in the sex chromosomes (e.g., XYY syndrome). Some genetic abnormalities, such as cystic fibrosis, are caused by a single pair of genes; others are caused by combinations of genes. Diabetes mellitus, epilepsy, and peptic ulcers are **multifactorial problems**; they reflect both a genetic predisposition and environmental contributors.

ovulation
the releasing of an ovum from an ovary.

allele
a member of a pair of genes.

homozygous
having two identical alleles.

heterozygous
having two different alleles.

dominant trait
a trait that is expressed.

recessive trait
a trait that is not expressed when the gene or genes involved have been paired with dominant genes.

carrier
a person who carries and transmits characteristics but does not exhibit them.

multifactorial problems
problems that stem from the interaction of heredity and environmental factors.

FIGURE 2.3

Transmission of Dominant and Recessive Traits

These two brown-eyed parents each carry a gene for blue eyes. Their children have an equal opportunity of receiving genes for brown eyes and blue eyes.

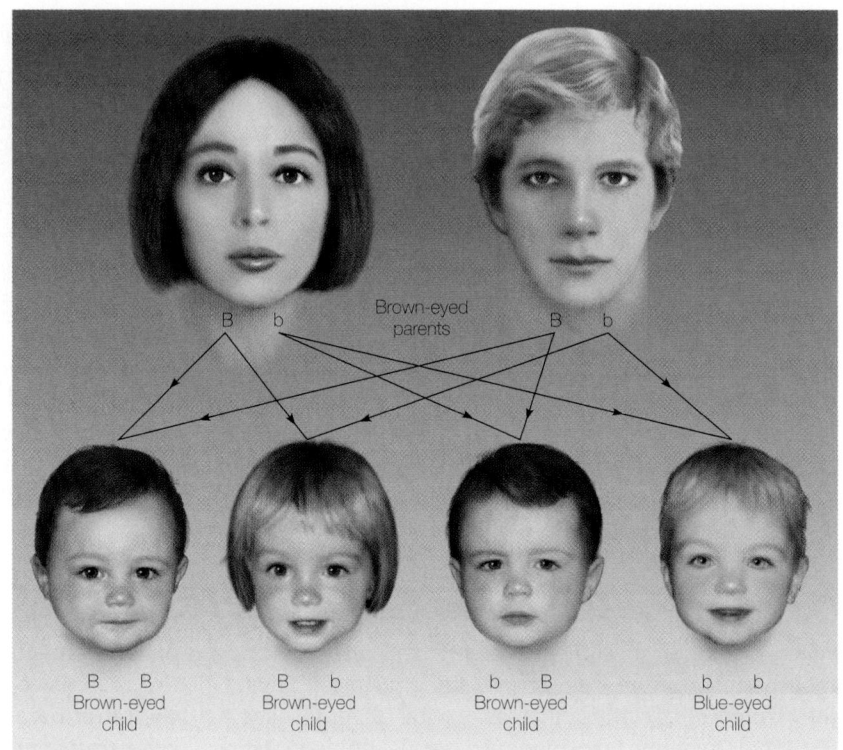

Down syndrome a chromosomal abnormality characterized by intellectual challenges and caused by an extra chromosome in the 21st pair.

sex-linked chromosomal abnormalities abnormalities that are transmitted from generation to generation and are carried by a sex chromosome.

Chromosomal Abnormalities

People normally have 46 chromosomes. Children with more or fewer chromosomes usually experience health problems or behavioural abnormalities. The risk of chromosomal abnormalities rises with the age of the parents (American Fertility Association, 2007).

TABLE 2.1

Examples of Dominant and Recessive Traits in Humans

Dominant Trait	Recessive Trait
Dark hair	Blond hair
Dark hair	Red hair
Curly hair	Straight hair
Normal colour vision	Red-green colour blindness
Normal vision	Myopia (nearsightedness)
Farsightedness	Normal vision
Normal pigmentation	Deficiency of pigmentation in skin, hair, and retina (albinism)
Normal sensitivity to touch	Extremely fragile skin
Normal hearing	Some forms of deafness
Dimples	Lack of dimpling
Type A blood	Type O blood
Type B blood	Type O blood

Down Syndrome

Down syndrome is usually caused by an extra chromosome on the 21st pair, resulting in 47 chromosomes. The probability of having a child with Down syndrome increases with the age of the parents. People with Down syndrome have characteristic features that include a rounded face; a protruding tongue; a broad, flat nose; and a sloping fold of skin over the inner corners of the eyes (see Figure 2.4). They show deficits in cognitive development (Rondal & Ling, 2006) and motor development (Virji-Babul et al., 2006) and usually die from cardiovascular problems by middle age, although modern medicine has extended their life expectancy.

EMERGING CANADA

The Canadian Down Syndrome Society (CDSS) is proud to celebrate World Down Syndrome Day, March 21. This day of recognition celebrates the lives of people with Down syndrome and was ratified by the United Nations in 2012.

Sex-Linked Chromosomal Abnormalities

Numerous disorders stem from an abnormal number of sex chromosomes and are therefore called **sex-linked chromosomal abnormalities**. Most

FIGURE 2.4

Down Syndrome

Development and adjustment of individuals with Down syndrome are greatly enhanced through family and community encouragement.

individuals with an abnormal number of sex chromosomes are infertile. Beyond that common finding, these individuals experience many differences, some of them associated with "maleness" or "femaleness" (Wodrich, 2006).

Genetic Abnormalities

Numerous disorders have been attributed to genes.

Phenylketonuria

The enzyme disorder **phenylketonuria (PKU)** is transmitted by a recessive gene. The Canadian PKU and Allied Disorders (2008) estimates that 1 in 12,000 newborns in North America have PKU, approximately 300 newborns per year. Children with PKU cannot metabolize an amino acid called phenylalanine, which builds up in their bodies and impairs the functioning of the central nervous system, resulting in intellectual challenges, psychological disorders, and physical problems. PKU has no cure, but in Canada, newborns are screened for PKU at birth. Those testing positive can be placed on diets low in phenylalanine within three to six weeks of birth and will develop normally (Brazier & Rowlands, 2006).

Huntington Disease

Huntington disease (HD) is a fatal, progressive degenerative disorder and a dominant trait. According to the Huntington Society of Canada (n.d.), one in every 10,000 Canadians has HD, but one in every 1,000 is touched by HD, whether by being at risk or by being a caregiver, family member, or friend. Physical symptoms include uncontrollable muscle movements (Jacobs et al., 2006). Psychological symptoms include loss of intellectual functioning and personality change (Robins Wahlin et al., 2007). Because the onset of HD is delayed until middle adulthood, many individuals with the defect have borne children only to discover years later that they and possibly half their offspring will inevitably develop it. Medicines can help deal with some symptoms.

phenylketonuria (PKU)
a genetic abnormality in which phenylalanine builds up and causes intellectual challenges.

Huntington disease (HD)
a fatal genetic neurologic disorder whose onset takes place in middle age. It is a dominant trait, which is rare for a fatal genetic disorder.

sickle-cell anemia
a genetic disorder that decreases the blood's capacity to carry oxygen.

Sickle-Cell Anemia

Sickle-cell anemia is caused by a recessive gene. Sickle-cell anemia is most common among black North Americans. In Canada, many refer to sickle-cell anemia as the "neglected disease" because Health Canada does not keep statistics on the disease (CBC News, 2003). Nearly 1 black North American in 10 is a carrier. In sickle-cell anemia, red blood cells take

Genetic Abnormalities

Phenylketonuria
Huntington Disease
Sickle-Cell Anemia
Tay-Sachs Disease
Cystic Fibrosis
Hemophilia
Muscular Dystrophy

Tay-Sachs disease a fatal genetic neurological disorder that causes degeneration and premature death.

cystic fibrosis a fatal genetic disorder in which mucus obstructs the lungs and pancreas.

hemophilia a genetic disorder in which blood does not clot properly.

sex-linked genetic abnormalities abnormalities resulting from genes that are found on the X sex chromosome. They are more likely to be shown by male offspring (who do not have an opposing gene from a second X chromosome) than by female offspring.

muscular dystrophy a chronic disease characterized by a progressive wasting away of the muscles.

on the shape of a sickle and clump together, obstructing small blood vessels and decreasing the oxygen supply. The reduced oxygen supply can impair cognitive skills and academic performance (Hogan et al., 2005; Ogunfowora et al., 2005). Episodes of acute pain are also common, as are complications such as blindness and failure of the heart, kidney, and liver, which can be fatal.

Tay-Sachs Disease

Tay-Sachs disease is also caused by a recessive gene. It causes the central nervous system to degenerate, resulting in death. The disorder is commonly found among children in Jewish families of Eastern European background, where 1 person in 30 carries the recessive gene. A disproportionate rate of Tay-Sachs disease has also been found in French Canadian communities. Such genetic concerns have led doctors to recommend Tay-Sachs testing for Canadians who either have a family history of the disease or live in a population with a high incidence of the disease (WebMD, 2010). Children with the disorder progressively lose control over their muscles, experience sensory losses, develop intellectual challenges, become paralyzed, and usually die by about the age of 5.

Cystic Fibrosis

Cystic fibrosis, also caused by a recessive gene, is the most common fatal hereditary disease among Canadian children and young adults, according to the Canadian Cystic Fibrosis Foundation (2010). Approximately 1 in every 3,500 children in Canada is born with this disease. Children with the disease suffer from excessive production of thick mucus that clogs the pancreas and lungs. Mucus and protein build up in the digestive tract, resulting in extreme difficulty digesting food and absorbing adequate nutrients. Most victims die of respiratory infections in their 20s. Lung transplantation can enable individuals with end-stage lung disease to regain their health, but Canada has a limited number of organ donors. The Canadian Cystic Fibrosis Foundation supports organ donor awareness and encourages Canadians to discuss organ donation with their loved ones.

Sex-Linked Genetic Abnormalities

Some genetic defects, such as **hemophilia** and colour blindness, are carried on only the X sex chromosome. For this reason, they are referred to as **sex-linked genetic abnormalities**. These defects also involve recessive genes. Females, who have two X sex chromosomes, are less likely than males to show sex-linked disorders because the genes that cause the disorder need to be present on both of a female's sex chromosomes for the disorder to be expressed. Sex-linked diseases are more likely to afflict sons of female carriers because males have only one X sex chromosome, which they inherit from their mothers.

One form of **muscular dystrophy**, Duchenne muscular dystrophy, is sex-linked. Muscular dystrophy is characterized by a weakening of the muscles, which can lead to wasting away, inability to walk, and sometimes death. Other sex-linked abnormalities include diabetes, colour blindness, and some types of night blindness.

Queen Victoria was a carrier of hemophilia and transmitted the sex-linked blood disorder to many of her children, who in turn carried it into many of the ruling houses of Europe. For this reason, hemophilia has been dubbed the "royal disease."

Genetic Counselling and Prenatal Testing

Genetic counsellors can detect the genetic abnormalities that are responsible for many diseases. They compile information about a couple's genetic heritage to explore whether their children might develop genetic abnormalities. Couples who face a high risk of passing genetic defects to their children sometimes choose to adopt or to not have children rather than conceive their own. In addition, **prenatal** testing can indicate whether the embryo or fetus carries genetic abnormalities.

EMERGING CANADA

Most people have mild forms of colour blindness that doesn't interfere with daily life. Of Caucasians, 8 percent of males and 1 percent of female have either red or green colour blindness. The condition is rare among people of Asian, First Nations, and African decent (Body and Health Canada, 2010).

Amniocentesis

prenatal before birth.

amniocentesis a procedure for drawing and examining fetal cells sloughed off into amniotic fluid to determine the presence of various disorders.

Amniocentesis is usually performed on the mother at 14–16 weeks after conception, although many physicians now perform the procedure earlier ("early amniocentesis"). During this procedure, the health professional uses a syringe (needle) to withdraw fluid from the amniotic sac (see Figure 2.5). The fluid contains cells that have been sloughed off by the fetus. The cells are separated from the amniotic fluid, grown in a culture, and then examined microscopically for genetic and chromosomal abnormalities.

Amniocentesis has become routine among Canadian women who become pregnant past the age of 35 because the chances of Down syndrome and other chromosomal abnormalities increase dramatically as women approach or pass the age of 40. In Canada, the

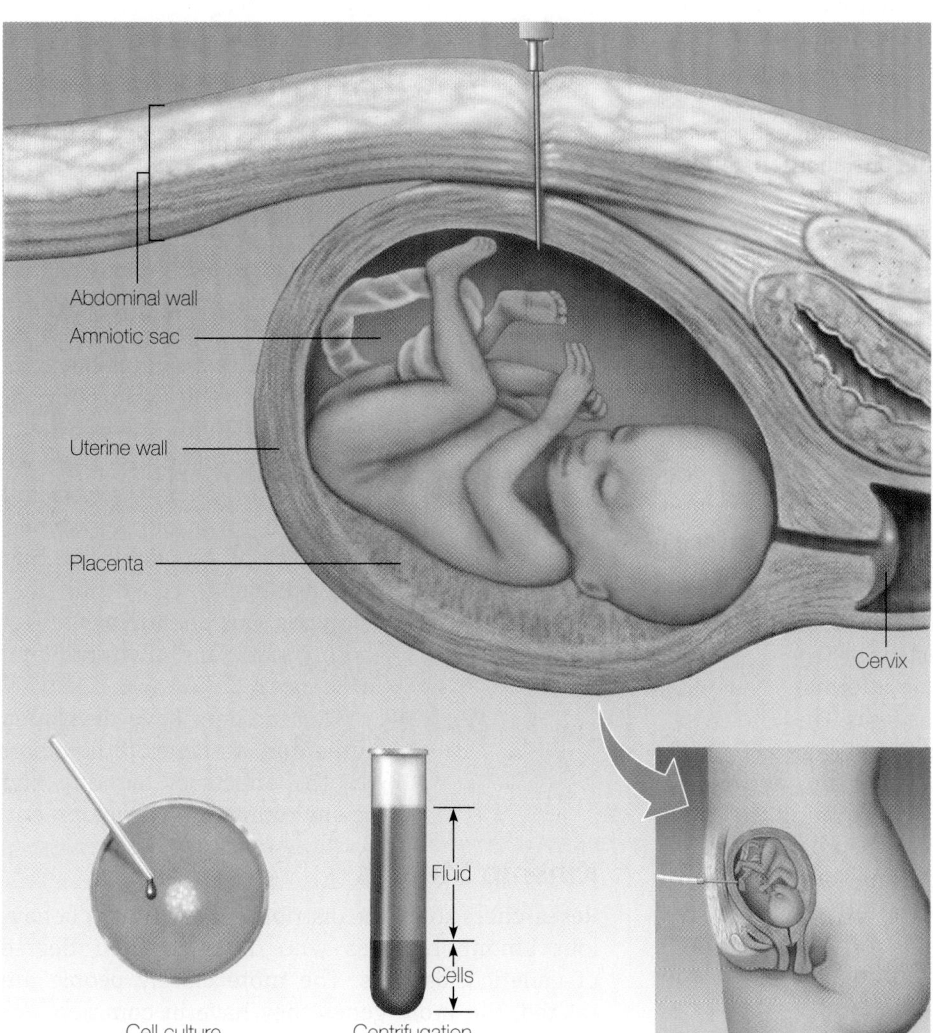

FIGURE 2.5

Amniocentesis

Amniocentesis allows prenatal identification of certain genetic and chromosomal disorders by examining genetic material sloughed off by the fetus into amniotic fluid.

chorionic villus sampling (CVS) a method for the prenatal detection of genetic abnormalities that samples the membrane enveloping the amniotic sac and fetus.

uterus the hollow organ within females in which the embryo and fetus develop.

ultrasound sound waves too high in pitch to be sensed by the human ear.

alpha-fetoprotein (AFP) assay a blood test that assesses the mother's blood level of alpha-fetoprotein, a substance that is linked to fetal neural tube defects.

reaction range the interaction between nature (genetic potential) and nurture (the set of circumstances that we encounter in life).

genotype the genetic form or constitution of a person as determined by heredity.

phenotype the actual form or constitution of a person as determined by heredity and environmental factors.

risk of fetal loss because of an amniocentesis procedure is one half of one percentage of all pregnancies (Wilson et al., 2007). Amniocentesis is not conducted simply to learn the sex of the child, which can be determined earlier through an ultrasound.

Chorionic Villus Sampling

Chorionic villus sampling (CVS) is similar to amniocentesis but is carried out earlier, between the 9th and 12th week of pregnancy. A small syringe is inserted through the vagina into the **uterus** and sucks out some threadlike projections (villi) from the outer membrane that envelops the amniotic sac and fetus. Results are available within days. CVS has not been used as frequently as amniocentesis because CVS carries a slightly greater risk of spontaneous abortion. Studies suggest that both amniocentesis and CVS increase the risk of miscarriage and that the risks might not be equal (Alfirevic et al., 2003; Philip et al., 2004).

Ultrasound

Health professionals also use sound waves that are too high in frequency to be heard by the human ear—**ultrasound**—to obtain information about the fetus. Ultrasound waves are reflected by the fetus, and a computer uses the information to generate a picture of the fetus. The picture is termed an ultrasound (see Figure 2.6).

Ultrasound is used to guide the syringe in amniocentesis and CVS by determining the position of the fetus. Ultrasound is also used to locate fetal structures when intrauterine transfusions are necessary for the survival of a fetus with Rh disease. Ultrasound also is used to track the growth of the fetus, to determine fetal age and sex, and to detect multiple pregnancies and structural abnormalities.

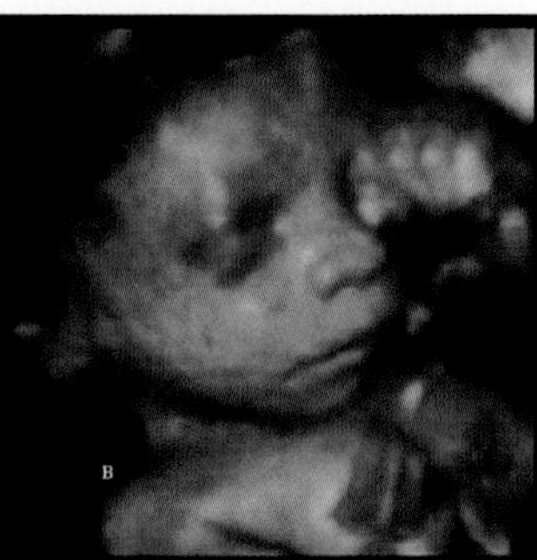

FIGURE 2.6

3-D Ultrasound Image

In the ultrasound technique, sound waves are bounced off the fetus to provide an image that enables medical professionals to detect various abnormalities. 3-D ultrasounds now give a much more complete view of the fetus. Parents often refer to 3-D ultrasounds as simply an ultrasound.

Denver Post via Getty Images

Blood Tests

Parental blood tests can reveal the presence of genetic disorders such as sickle-cell anemia, Tay-Sachs disease, and cystic fibrosis. The **alpha-fetoprotein (AFP) assay** is used to detect neural tube defects such as spina bifida and certain chromosomal abnormalities. Neural tube defects cause an elevation in the AFP level in the mother's blood. Elevated AFP levels also are associated with increased risk of fetal death. Because the mother's blood is tested, the fetus is not at risk.

LO2 Heredity and the Environment

The development of our traits is influenced by inheritance and by nutrition, learning, exercise, and—unfortunately—accident and illness. **Reaction range** refers to the interaction between nature (genetic potential) and nurture (the set of circumstances that we encounter in life). A potential Shakespeare who is reared in poverty and never taught to read or write will not create a *Hamlet*. Our traits and behaviours represent the interaction of heredity and environment. The sets of traits that we inherit from our parents are referred to as our **genotypes**. The actual sets of traits that we exhibit are called our **phenotypes**. Our phenotypes reflect both genetic and environmental influences.

The Reaction Range (the interaction between nature and nurture) sets a genetic potential for developmental outcomes.

Researchers have developed numerous strategies to help sort out the effects of heredity and the environment on development.

Kinship Studies

Researchers study the distribution of a trait or behaviour among relatives who differ in their degree of genetic closeness. The more closely people are related, the more genes they have in common. For example, parents and children have a 50 percent overlap in their genetic endowments, as do siblings (brothers and sisters). Aunts and uncles have a 25 percent overlap with nieces and nephews, as do grandparents with grandchildren. First cousins share 12.5 percent of their genetic endowment. If genes are implicated in a trait, people who are more closely related are more likely to share it.

Twin Studies: Looking in the Genetic Mirror

Monozygotic (MZ) twins share 100 percent of their genes, whereas dizygotic (DZ) twins have a 50 percent overlap, similar to other siblings. When MZ twins show greater similarity on some trait or behaviour than DZ twins do, a genetic basis for the trait or behaviour is indicated.

A potential Shakespeare who is reared in poverty and never taught to read or write will not create a *Hamlet*.

But do MZ twins resemble each other so closely in part because they are often treated so similarly? One way to answer this question is to compare MZ twins who were reared apart. Except for the uterine environment, similarities between MZ twins reared apart would appear to be a result of heredity. In the Minnesota Study of Twins Reared Apart (Bouchard et al., 1990; DiLalla et al., 1999; Lykken, 2006b), researchers have been measuring the physiological and psychological characteristics of 56 sets of MZ adult twins who were separated in infancy and reared in different homes. The MZ twins reared apart are about as similar as MZ twins reared together on measures of intelligence, personality, temperament, occupational and leisure-time interests, and social attitudes. These traits would thus appear to have a genetic underpinning.

EMERGING CANADA

In Canada, more than 11,000 multiple-birth babies are born every year. Between 1997 and 2006, the multiple-birth rate increased about 35 percent (Launslager, 2009).

Adoption Studies

Adoption studies in which children were separated from their natural parents at an early age and reared by adoptive parents provide special opportunities for looking at the effects of nature and nurture. When children reared by adoptive parents exhibit a trait more similar to their natural parents, a powerful argument is made for a genetic role in the appearance of that trait.

Traits are determined by pairs of genes. One member of each pair comes from each parent in the process called conception.

LO3 Conception: Against All Odds

Conception is the union of an ovum and a sperm cell. Conception, from one perspective, is the beginning of a new human life. From another perspective, though, conception is also the end of a fantastic voyage in which one of several hundred thousand ova produced by the woman unites with one of hundreds of million sperm produced by the man in the average ejaculate.

conception
the union of a sperm cell and an ovum that occurs when the chromosomes of each of these cells combine to form 23 new pairs.

© Joan Coll/iStockphoto.com / © Blend Images/Jupiterimages

The developing organism is a random genetic combination that will develop into a unique individual.

waters. Among Canada's First Nations, a growing body of research and concerns are focused on the health effects posed to children and unborn fetuses as a result of exposures to toxic chemicals and other environmental hazards. Recent research has linked environmental contaminants to adverse child health outcomes, including learning and developmental disabilities, birth defects, low birth weight, Fetal Alcohol Spectrum Disorder (FASD), some cancers, and asthma (Assembly of First Nations, 2008).

Experiments with mice show that fetal exposure to radiation in high doses can damage the eyes, central nervous system, and skeleton (e.g., Hossain et al., 2005). Pregnant women are advised to avoid unnecessary exposure to X-rays. (Ultrasound, which is not an X-ray, has not been shown to harm the fetus.) Even a house cat can pose a life-threatening risk to a fetus if the mother is exposed (through litter boxes or gardening) to cat feces infected with the tiny parasite that causes toxoplasmosis. Exposure to this parasite can result in severe birth defects or even death for the fetus (Kidshealth, 2010).

Parents' Ages

What about the parents' ages? During a parental "age window," the health of the baby is better ensured. For example, sperm production slows in old age but remains throughout men's lifespan, though older fathers are more likely to produce abnormal sperm. The mother's age also matters. From a biological vantage point, the 20s may be the ideal age for women to bear children in terms of reducing the risk of genetic abnormalities. The offspring of teenage mothers have a higher incidence of infant mortality and are more likely to have a low birth weight (Phipps et al., 2002; Save the Children, 2004). Girls who become pregnant in their early teens may place a burden on their bodies that may not have adequately matured to facilitate pregnancy and childbirth (Berg et al., 2003).

© Louis B. Wallach Inc./Getty Images

Women's fertility declines gradually until the mid-30s, after which it declines more rapidly. Women who wait until their 30s or 40s to have children also increase the likelihood of having stillborn or preterm babies (Berg et al., 2003). With adequate prenatal care, however, the risk of bearing a premature or unhealthy baby still is relatively small, even for older first-time mothers (Berg et al., 2003).

Whatever the age of the mother, the events of childbirth provide some of the most memorable moments in the lives of parents. In Chapter 3, we continue our voyage with the process of birth and the characteristics of the newborn child.

EMERGING CANADA

In 2009, the average age of mothers at the birth of their children was 29.4 years. This age has been increasing over the past three decades. Half of all mothers who gave birth were age 30 or older. Births to teenage mothers have been decreasing constantly from 30 births per 1,000 in 1974 to 12 in 2009 (Human Resources and Skills Development Canada, 2013a).

Medical Discovery versus Bioethics

In 1996, the cloning of Dolly the Sheep (or the Dolly Lamba, as she is often called) prompted Canada and the world to examine how far they were willing to stretch the boundaries of medical discovery and ethics. The Canadian government enacted legislation in March of 2004 banning human and stem cell cloning, rent-a-womb contracts, the sale of human eggs and sperm, and the creation of people with animal DNA. This legislation was designed to keep children safe and to ensure research into new reproductive technology is ethically sound (CBC News, 2009a).

Canadians needed to decide where to draw the line

Scenario One: In April 2007, a Quebec woman froze some of her eggs for the future use of her 7-year-old daughter, who has a genetic disorder that causes infertility.

Scenario Two: In April 2007, England approved the right of a couple to have doctors select embryos free from a gene that carries a greater risk of breast cancer. The presence of this gene does not necessarily mean the cancer will develop. The embryos free of the gene would be implanted, and the embryos with the gene would be aborted.

Scenario Three: In February 2009, 60-year-old Ranjit Hayer gave birth to twin boys in Calgary after undergoing in vitro fertilization procedures in India, after decades of trying the old-fashioned way.

Scenario Four: Stem cells are cells with the potential to develop into many different cells within the body. They hold much promise for curing diseases such as diabetes and muscular dystrophy. In 2010, the Canadian Institute of Health Research revised the set of guidelines for use of stem cells (CBC News, 2010). Most stem cell research is conducted on embryonic stem cells.

Canada has limited research to the use of embryos that have been created for reproductive purposes but are now no longer required. Permission to use the embryos must be obtained from the parents for whom the embryos were created. In the case of experimental stem cell research, are Canadian parents currently able to create an embryo so that they can harvest the stem cells? Do you believe they should have this right?

Where do you, as an individual, draw the line?

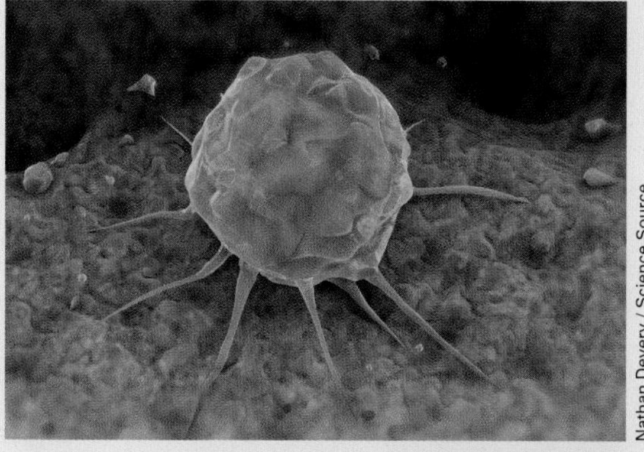

Nathan Devery / Science Source

AP Photo/Paul Clements/CP Images

Jim Barber/Shutterstock.com

Go online at
www.nelson.com/4ltrpress/icanhdev2ce
And access the essential Study Tools online for this chapter:

- **Practice Quizzes**, which will help you to prepare for tests
- **Games**, to help test your knowledge
- **Flashcards**, to test your understanding of key terms
- **Observing Development Videos**
- **Internet Activities**

PART TWO

CHAPTER 3

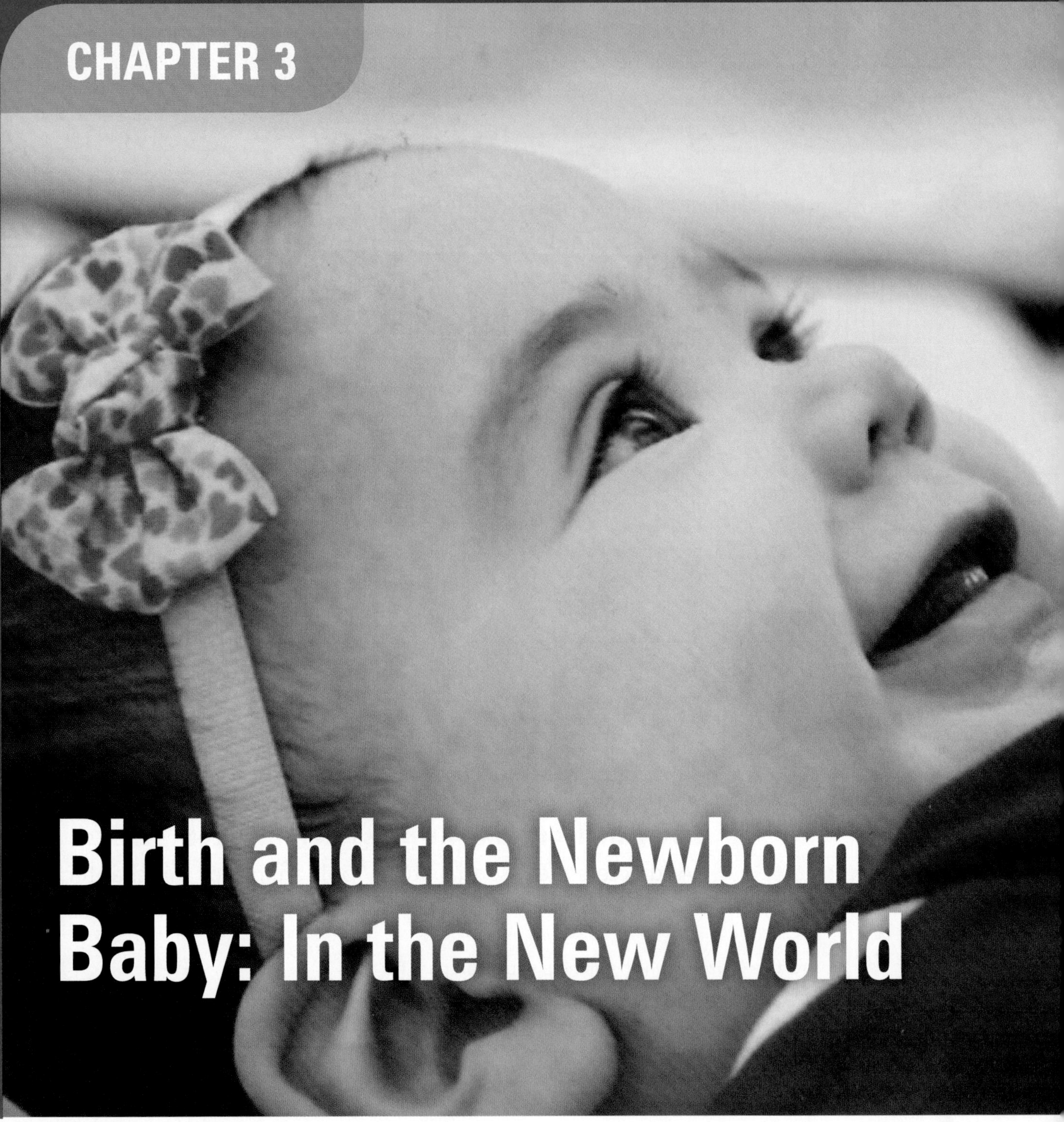

Birth and the Newborn Baby: In the New World

LEARNING OUTCOMES

LO1 Identify the stages of childbirth

LO2 Describe the different methods of childbirth

LO3 Discuss potential problems with childbirth

LO4 Describe the key events of the postpartum period

LO5 Describe the characteristics of the newborn

> “Nearly all mothers struggle through the last weeks of pregnancy and worry about the mechanics of delivery.”

Countdown ...

Early in the last month of pregnancy, the head of the fetus settles in the mother's pelvis. This process is called dropping or lightening. Because lightening decreases pressure on the diaphragm, the mother may, in fact, feel lighter.

The first uterine contractions are called **Braxton-Hicks contractions**, or false labour contractions. They are relatively painless and may be experienced as early as the sixth month of pregnancy. These contractions increase in frequency as the pregnancy progresses and may serve to tone the muscles that will be used in delivery. True labour contractions are more painful and regular, and are usually intensified by walking.

A day or so before labour begins, increased pelvic pressure from the fetus may rupture blood vessels in the birth canal so that blood appears in vaginal secretions. Mucous that had plugged the cervix and protected the uterus from infection becomes dislodged. About 1 woman in 10 has a rush of warm liquid from the vagina at this time. This liquid is amniotic fluid, and its discharge means that the amniotic sac has burst. The sac usually does not burst until the end of the first stage of childbirth, as described later. Other signs that labour is beginning include indigestion, diarrhea, an ache in the small of the back, and cramps.

The fetus may actually signal the mother when it is ready to be born by secreting hormones that stimulate the placenta and uterus to secrete **prostaglandins** (Snegovskikh et al., 2006). Prostaglandins not only cause the cramping women may feel before or during menstruation, they also excite the muscles of the uterus to engage in labour contractions. As labour progresses, the pituitary gland releases the hormone **oxytocin**, which stimulates contractions powerful enough to expel the baby.

Braxton-Hicks contractions
the first, usually painless, contractions of childbirth.

prostaglandins
hormones that stimulate uterine contractions.

oxytocin
a hormone that stimulates labour contractions.

efface
to become thin.

dilate
to widen.

LO1 The Stages of Childbirth

Regular uterine contractions signal the beginning of childbirth. Childbirth occurs in three stages. In the first stage, uterine contractions **efface** and **dilate** the cervix, which needs to widen to about 10 cm (4 in.) to allow the baby to pass. Dilation of the cervix causes most of the pain of childbirth.

The first stage of childbirth is the longest. For first-time mothers, this stage may last from a few hours to more than a

transition
movement of the head of the fetus into the birth canal.

day. Subsequent pregnancies take less time. The first contractions are not usually painful. They are spaced 10 to 20 minutes apart and may last from 20 to 40 seconds each. As the process continues, the contractions become more powerful, frequent, and regular. Women are usually advised to go to the hospital or birthing centre when the contractions are 4 to 5 minutes apart. Until the end of the first stage of labour, the mother is usually in a labour room.

During the first stage of childbirth, fetal monitoring may be used. One kind of monitor is an electronic device strapped around the woman's abdomen that measures both the fetal heart rate and the mother's contractions. When the cervix is nearly fully dilated, the head of the fetus begins to move into the vagina. This process is called **transition**. During transition, which lasts 30 minutes or less, contractions are frequent and strong.

The second stage of childbirth begins when the baby appears at the opening of the vagina (now called the birth canal; see Figure 3.1). The second stage is briefer than the first, possibly lasting minutes or a few hours and ending with the birth of the baby. For this stage, the woman may be taken to a delivery room.

The contractions of the second stage stretch the skin surrounding the birth canal farther and propel the baby forward. The baby's head is said to have crowned when it begins to emerge from the birth canal. Once crowning has occurred, the baby normally emerges completely within minutes.

The physician, nurse, or midwife may perform an episiotomy once crowning takes place. The purpose of the episiotomy is to prevent random tearing when the area between the birth canal and the anus becomes severely stretched. The incision may cause

FIGURE 3.1

Stages of Childbirth

In the first stage, uterine contractions efface and dilate the cervix. The second stage begins with movement of the baby into the birth canal and ends with birth of the baby. During the third stage, the placenta separates from the uterine wall and is expelled through the birth canal.

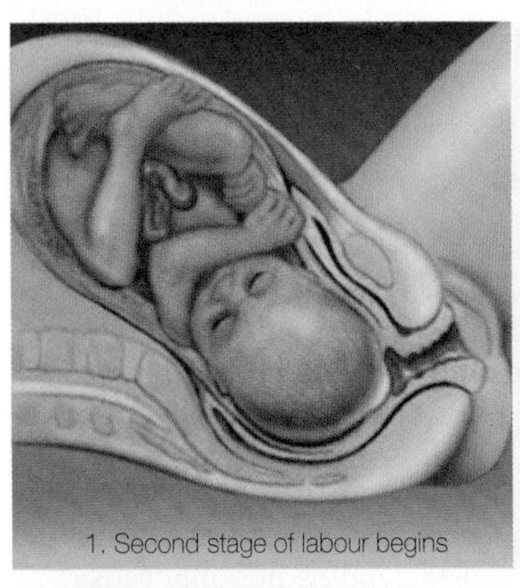

1. Second stage of labour begins

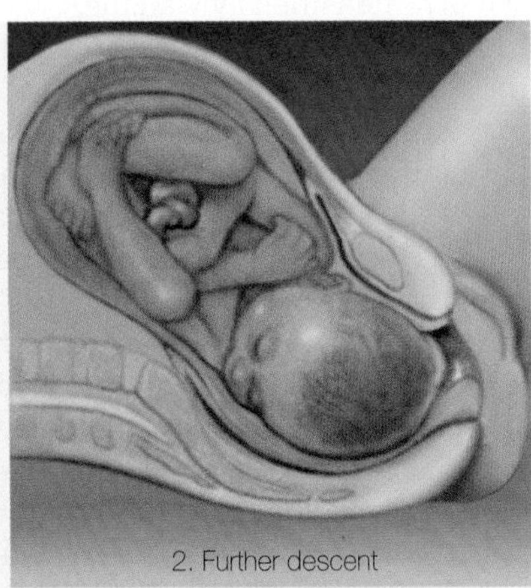

2. Further descent

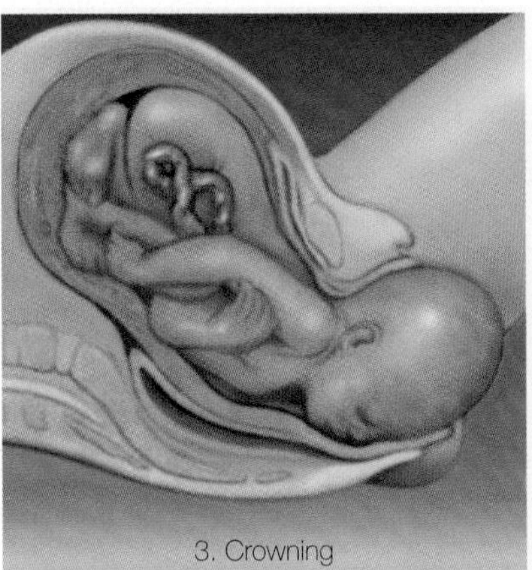

3. Crowning

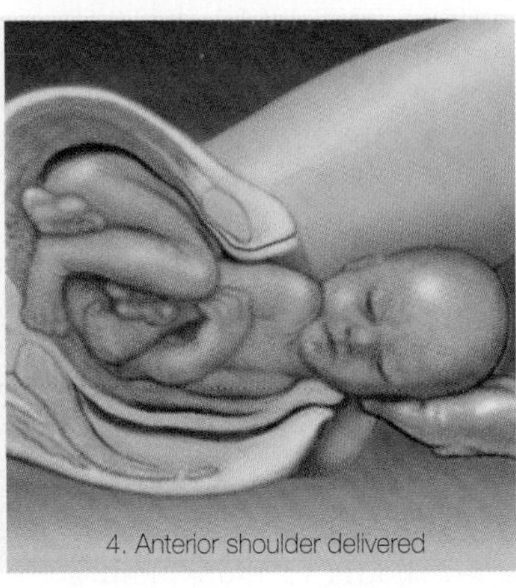

4. Anterior shoulder delivered

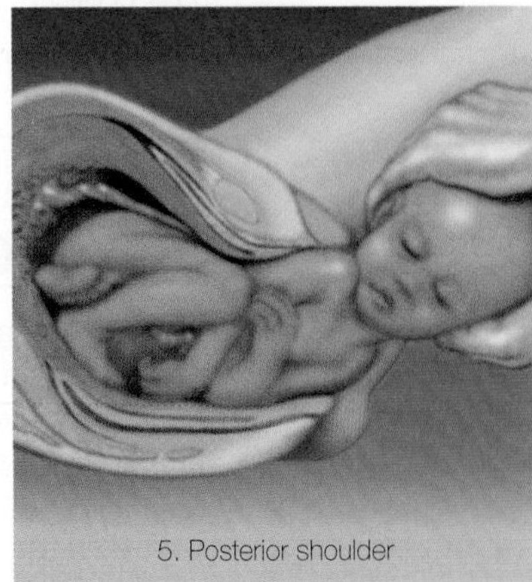

5. Posterior shoulder

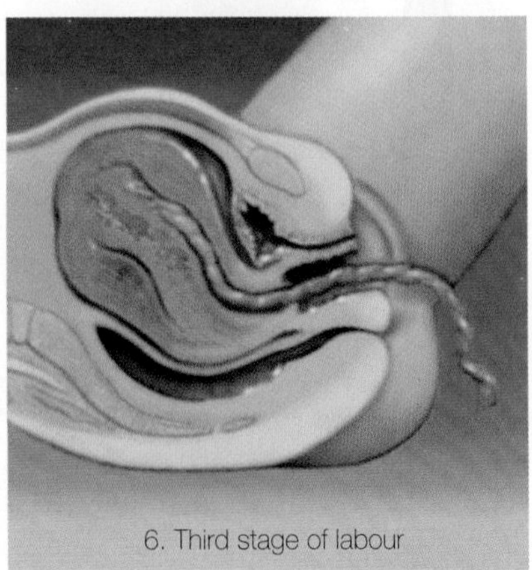

6. Third stage of labour

itching and discomfort as it heals. In 1992, half of all women who had vaginal deliveries in Canada had an episiotomy. This rate fell to 14.1 percent in 2012 (Chalmers et al., 2012). According to research conducted at the Ottawa Hospital Research Institute, an episiotomy provides no advantage other than speeding up the delivery.

To clear any obstructions from the passageway for breathing, mucous is suctioned from the baby's mouth when the head emerges from the birth canal. When the baby is breathing adequately on its own, the umbilical cord is clamped and severed (Figure 3.2). Mother and infant are now separate beings. The stump of the umbilical cord will dry and fall off on its own in about 7 to 10 days.

> **DID YOU KNOW?**
>
> **Slapping babies on the bottom to stimulate breathing is an outdated Hollywood image.**
>
> Though this image is often seen in old movies, it does not happen in today's hospitals. To allow for independent breathing, mucous is suctioned from the baby's nose and mouth when the head emerges from the birth canal.

The baby is now often whisked away by a nurse, who will perform various procedures, including footprinting the baby, supplying an ID bracelet, administering antibiotic ointment or drops of silver nitrate into the baby's eyes to prevent bacterial infections, and injecting the baby with vitamin K to help its blood clot properly if it bleeds (newborn babies do not manufacture vitamin K). In Canada, one drop of blood is taken from newborns to screen for more than 50 obscure disorders and anomalies (such as PKU) that may be treatable if detected early (CBC News, 2007b). During these procedures, the mother is in the third stage of labour, which can last from minutes to hours.

During the third stage of labour, the placenta separates from the uterine wall and is expelled through the birth canal. Some bleeding is normal. The obstetrician then sews the episiotomy, if one has been performed.

© Brand X Pictures/Jupiterimages

FIGURE 3.2

A Clamped and Severed Umbilical Cord

The stump of the umbilical cord dries and falls off in about 10 days.

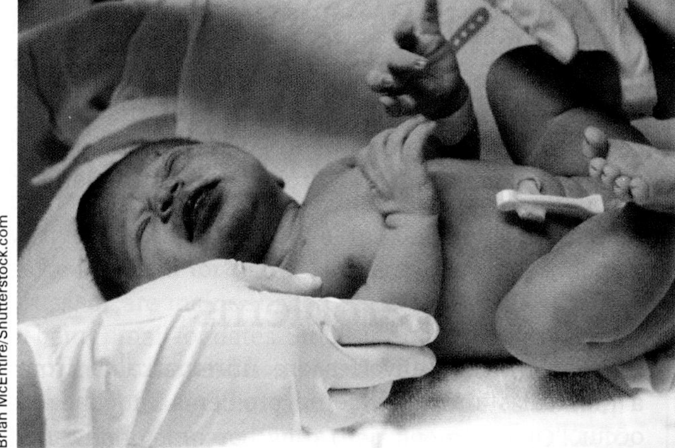

Brian McEntire/Shutterstock.com

LO2 Methods of Childbirth

Childbirth was once a more intimate procedure that usually took place in the woman's home and involved the mother, perhaps a **midwife**, and family members. This pattern is followed in many less developed nations today but fewer than 5 percent of babies born in Canada are delivered under the care of a midwife (Picard, 2013). Despite of these low numbers, using a midwife is a growing trend in Canada, particularly within the Aboriginal population. Modern medicine has undeniably saved countless lives of both newborn babies and their mothers, but childbearing has also become more impersonal. Some argue that modern methods take control from women over their own bodies.

> **midwife**
> an individual who helps women in childbirth.

> **EMERGING CANADA**
>
> Chalmers et al. (2012) surveyed mothers' experiences of the birthing process in Canada. Birthing in Canada varies greatly in response to the situation encountered. The following experiences were reported:
>
> - 30.9% were induced
> - 53.7% received an epidural
> - 37.9% received continuous electronic fetal monitoring
> - 14.1% received an episiotomy (a surgical incision between the birth canal and the anus to widen the vaginal opening)
> - 48.3% did not receive an episiotomy but did need to be "stitched"
> - 42.2% lay flat during the delivery
> - 35.7% delivered in stirrups

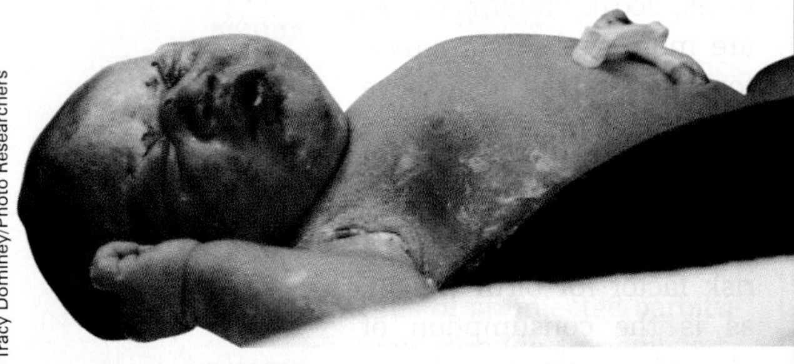

© Tracy Dominey/Photo Researchers

This newborn shows lanugo and vernix, both characteristics of prematurity.

Preterm babies have immature muscles, so their sucking and breathing reflexes are weak. In addition, the walls of the tiny air sacs in their lungs may tend to stick together because the babies do not yet secrete substances that lubricate the walls of the sacs. As a result, babies born more than a month before full term may breathe irregularly or may suddenly stop breathing, evidence of **respiratory distress syndrome**. Compared with full-term infants, preterm infants with respiratory stress syndrome show poorer development in cognitive, language, and motor skills over the first 2 years of development. Injecting pregnant women at risk for delivering preterm babies with corticosteroids increases the babies' chances of survival (Crowther et al., 2006).

respiratory distress syndrome weak and irregular breathing, typical of preterm babies.

incubators heated, protective containers for premature infants.

Strides have been made in helping low-birth-weight children survive, but those children often have below-average verbal ability and academic achievement and various motor and perceptual impairments (Saigal et al., 2006).

Treatment of Preterm Babies

Because of their physical frailty, preterm infants usually remain in the hospital and are placed in **incubators**, which maintain a temperature-controlled environment and afford some protection from disease. The babies may be given oxygen, although excessive oxygen can cause permanent eye injury.

Parents and Preterm Newborns

Parents often do not treat preterm newborns as well as they treat full-term newborns. For one thing, preterm infants usually do not have the robust, appealing appearance of many full-term babies. Their cries are more high-pitched and grating, and they are more irritable (Bugental & Happaney, 2004; Eckerman et al., 1999). The demands of caring for preterm babies can lead to depression in mothers (Davis et al., 2003; Drewett et al., 2004). Mothers of preterm babies frequently report that they feel alienated from their babies and harbour feelings of failure, guilt, and low self-esteem (Bugental & Happaney, 2004). Fear of hurting preterm babies can further discourage parents from handling them, but encouraging mothers to massage their preterm infants can help them cope with this fear (Feijó et al., 2006). Once preterm infants are taken home from the hospital, they remain more passive and less sociable than full-term infants (Larroque et al., 2005; McGrath et al., 2005). Preterm infants fare better when they have responsive and caring parents.

Intervention Programs

Preterm infants benefit from early stimulation just as full-term babies do—by being cuddled, rocked, talked to, and sung to; by being exposed to recordings of their mothers' voices; by having mobiles in view; and by hearing live and recorded music in their environment (Arnon et al., 2006; Lai et al., 2006). Other forms of stimulation include massage (Field et al., 2006) and "kangaroo care" (Lai et al., 2006), in which the baby spends time each day lying skin to skin and chest to chest with a parent. In general, stimulated preterm infants tend to gain weight more rapidly, show fewer respiratory problems, and make greater advances in motor, intellectual, and neurological development than control infants (Caulfield, 2000; Dombrowski et al., 2000)

Maternal and Infant Mortality around the World

Modern medicine has made vast strides in decreasing the rates of maternal and infant mortality, but the advances are not equally spread throughout the world. Save the Children, a nonprofit relief and development organization, tracks the likelihood that a woman will die in childbirth and that an infant will die during its first year. The likelihood of maternal and infant mortality relates to such factors as the percentage of births that are attended by trained people, the literacy rate of adult women (one measure of women's level of education), and the participation of women in national government (one measure of the extent to which a society empowers women). In Canada, the infant mortality rate in 2007 was 5.1 per 1,000 babies born (Statistics Canada, 2010b). Factors contributing to this lower number are our system of universal health care, our high literacy rate (99 percent), and strong female leadership within the country. In contrast, in Afghanistan, one woman in six will die as a result of pregnancy, and 165 children of 1,000 will die during their first year. In Afghan society, the literacy rate for women is only 21 percent, only 12 percent of women receive any professional assistance during childbirth, and women have virtually no role in government.

UNICEF Report: Leaving No Child Behind

In the past 20 years, the world has reduced the infant mortality rate by 30 percent. If we can achieve this change in some of the poorest nations in the world, why are infant mortality rates for some Aboriginal children much higher than they are for other Canadian children (see Figure 3.4)? In 2009, UNICEF asked, why are Aboriginal children generally not as healthy as other Canadian children (UNICEF Canada, 2009)?

In the past, Canadians attributed their health to biological and medical causes. Then we began to also factor in the effects of lifestyle choices. Now we know that our health is much more complicated. Health depends on a web of economic, social, political, and environmental factors. Some of the factors affecting the health of Aboriginal children include the following:

- poverty
- lack of education
- substandard housing
- poor nutrition
- lack of access to health care and social services
- a legacy of family, community, and cultural breakdown left by residential school policies

Prenatal care and infant mortality rates are the starting point of a child's health. We have the knowledge, technology, and information to make changes. The UNICEF document states the priority of leaving no child behind. We are, however, leaving some Canadian children behind, which must change.

Source: Adapted from The State of The World's Children 2009: Aboriginal Children's Health; Leaving No Child Behind, Canadian Supplement, UNICEF, 2009.

FIGURE 3.3

Stimulating a Preterm Infant

Preterm infants usually benefit from stimulation.

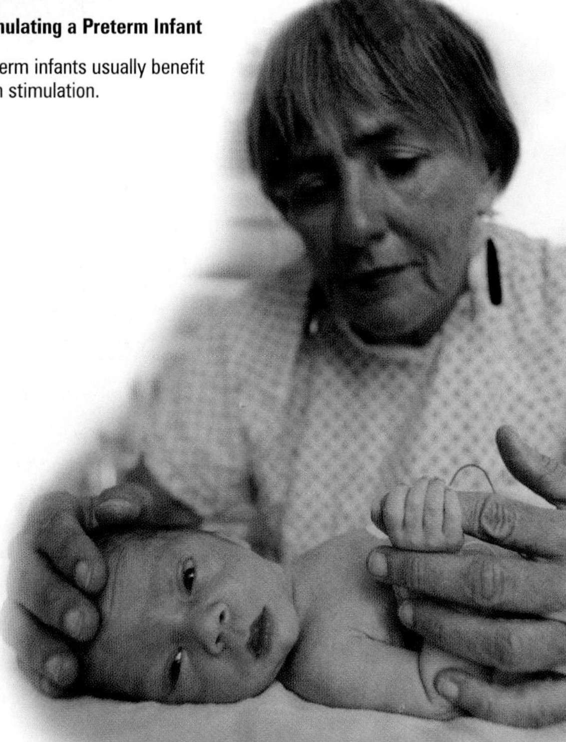

(see Figure 3.3). Studies on a "cuddling program" reported by the Harvard Medical Teaching Hospital show that tactile stimulation—cuddling, massage, and human touch in general—helps improve weight gain in newborns, especially premature babies still developing.

postpartum period the period immediately following childbirth.

LO4 The Postpartum Period

The **postpartum period** refers to the weeks following delivery, but has no specific limit. The family's long wait is over. Concerns about pregnancy and labour are over, fingers and toes have been counted, and despite some local discomfort, the mother finds her "load" to be lightened—literally. According to the Canadian Paediatric Society (Province of British Columbia, 2010), about 80 percent of new mothers can expect to experience periods of tearfulness, sadness, and irritability that the association refers to as the "baby blues."

postpartum depression (PPD) serious maternal depression following delivery; characterized by sadness, apathy, and feelings of worthlessness.

Maternal Depression

Problems related to maternal depression include the "baby blues" and more serious mood disorders, such as postpartum depression, which is is a treatable medical illness characterized by feelings of sadness, indifference, exhaustion, and anxiety following the birth of a baby (Depression and Bipolar Support Alliance, n.d.). Postpartum mood problems are so common that they are statistically normal (Gavin et al., 2005). Researchers believe that they are often due to hormonal changes that follow delivery (Kohl, 2004). They last about 10 days and are generally not severe enough to impair the mother's functioning.

FIGURE 3.4

United Nations Statistics on the Health of Canadian Children

1 in 9 On average, the number of Canadian children living in poverty	1 in 4 The number of children in First Nations communities living in poverty
5 Infant deaths per 1,000 infants born in Canada	16 Infant deaths per 1,000 infants born in Nunavut (where 85% of the population is Inuit)
3 out of 177 Canada's ranking in the Human Development Index (HDI), a United Nations standard that measures a country's achievements in three basic aspects of human development: health, knowledge, and decent standard of living	68 out of 177 The HDI ranking of Canada's First Nations communities
85 The percentage of all children in Canada who accessed a doctor in 2000–01	63 The percentage of First Nations children on selected reserves who accessed a doctor in 2000–01
21 The percentage of non-Aboriginal children in census metropolitan areas living in low-income families	45 The percentage of Inuit children in census metropolitan areas living in low-income families
2 to 3× The multiple by which First Nations, Inuit, and Métis children are worse off than other Canadian children. They are less likely to see a doctor. As teens, they are more likely to become parents, and they are more likely to commit suicide.	

Source: Adapted from Canadian Supplement to The State of the World's Children 2009: Aboriginal Children's Health: Leaving No Child Behind, UNICEF.

Perhaps as many as 13 percent of Canadian mothers will encounter the more serious mood disorder frequently referred to as **postpartum depression (PPD)**, which begins about a month after delivery and may linger for weeks or months. PPD is characterized by serious sadness; feelings of hopelessness, helplessness, and worthlessness; difficulty concentrating; mood swings; and major changes in appetite (usually loss of appetite) and sleep patterns (frequently insomnia). Some women show obsessive concern for the well-being of their babies.

Many researchers suggest that PPD is caused by a sudden drop in estrogen (Kohl, 2004). The focus is on physiological factors because of the major changes in body chemistry during and after pregnancy and because women around the world seem to experience similar disturbances in mood, even when their life experiences and support systems are radically different from those found here in Canada (Cohen et al., 2006).

The Canadian Press Images/Mario Beauregard

Margaret Trudeau, controversial former wife of late Prime Minister Pierre Trudeau, has waged a lonely battle against depression and bipolar disorder, which first became an issue after the birth of her son Sacha. She now shares her personal story with Canadians and the world, in the hope of helping others.

In extreme cases, mothers who experience psychotic features may experience a break with reality that leads to delusional thoughts about their infant that place the infant at risk of injury or death. This illness was brought to the forefront of Canadian news when 37-year-old Suzanne Killinger-Johnson leapt in front of a moving subway with her sleeping child. Killinger-Johnson had a psychotherapy practice. Her mother was a psychotherapist who had written books on stress, depression, and anxiety, and her father was a medical doctor. The tragic irony was that even those trained in the field can fall victim to the despair of depression that, when left untreated, can lead to violent outcomes (CBC News, 2000). Even loved ones can miss the signs.

Women who experience PPD usually benefit from social support and counselling, even if it does little more than explain that many women encounter PPD and that it usually eases and ends as time goes on. Some women find help in drugs that increase estrogen levels or act as antidepressants.

DID YOU KNOW?

It is normal to feel depressed following childbirth.

Postpartum mood problems are so common that they are statistically normal (Gavin et al., 2005).

Bonding

Bonding—that is, the formation of bonds of attachment between parents and their children—is essential to the survival and well-being of children.

Parent–child bonding has been shown to be a complex process involving desire to have the child; parent–child familiarity with one another's sounds, odours, and tastes; and caring. On the other hand, serious maternal depression can delay bonding with newborns (Klier, 2006), and a history of rejection by parents can interfere with women's bonding with their own children (Leerkes & Crockenberg, 2006).

Parents do not, however, require early contact with their newborn children for adequate bonding to occur. Many parents, for instance, adopt children at advanced ages and bond closely with them.

DID YOU KNOW?

Parents do not require early contact with their newborn child for adequate bonding to occur.

For instance, many parents adopt children at advanced ages and bond closely with them.

© Comstock Images/Jupiterimages

© Edyta Pawlowska/Shutterstock.com

bonding
formation of parent–infant attachment.

EMERGING CANADA

In December 2000, Canada made family a social priority by making important changes to maternity and parental leave. As part of the new benefits package, after a baby is born or adopted, either the mother or father can take 35 weeks of parental leave, or the parents can share the leave to better accommodate the needs of their family and the new family member. For eligible parents, the benefits equal 55 percent of the average weekly insurable wage (up to 80 percent for low-income families), up to a maximum of $485 per week (Service Canada, 2013).

LO5 Characteristics of Newborns

Many newborns come into the world seeing things a bit fuzzy, but even though they are utterly dependent on others, they are probably more aware of their surroundings than you can imagine. Newborns also make rapid adaptations to the world around them.

Apgar scale
a measure of a newborn's health that assesses appearance, pulse, grimace, activity level, and respiratory effort.

Brazelton Neonatal Behavioural Assessment Scale
a measure of a newborn's motor behaviour, response to stress, adaptive behaviour, and control over physiological state.

reflexes
unlearned responses to a stimulus.

rooting reflex
the response of turning the mouth and head toward the stroking of the cheek or the corner of the mouth.

Moro reflex
the response of arching the back, flinging out the arms and legs, and drawing them back to the chest in response to a sudden change in position.

Assessing the Health of Newborns

The newborn's overall level of health is usually evaluated at birth according to the **Apgar scale** (Table 3.1). Apgar scores are based on five signs of health: appearance, pulse, grimace, activity level, and respiratory effort. For each sign, the newborn is assigned a score of 0, 1, or 2. The total Apgar score can therefore vary from 0 to 10. A score of 7 or more usually indicates that the baby is not in danger. Parents should not be concerned if a baby does not receive a perfect score as its breathing may not be functioning perfectly but quickly rebounds. A score of less than 4 suggests that the baby is in critical condition and requires medical attention. By 1 minute after birth, most normal babies attain scores of 8 to 10 (Clayton & Crosby, 2006).

The **Brazelton Neonatal Behavioural Assessment Scale** measures newborns' reflexes and other behaviour patterns. This test screens for behavioural and neurological problems by assessing four areas of behaviour: motor behaviour, response to stress, adaptive behaviour, and control over physiological state.

Reflexes

Reflexes are unlearned, automatic responses that occur without thinking and are elicited by certain types of stimulation. Of these reflexes, most are exhibited by newborns shortly after birth, disappear within a few months, and—if the behaviours still serve a purpose—are replaced by corresponding voluntary actions.

Pediatricians learn about a newborn's neural functioning by testing its reflexes. The absence or weakness of a reflex may indicate immaturity (as in prematurity), slowed responsiveness (which can result from anesthetics used during childbirth), brain injury, or retardation.

The rooting and sucking reflexes are basic to survival. In the **rooting reflex**, the baby turns its head and mouth toward a stimulus that strokes its cheek, chin, or corner of the mouth. The rooting reflex facilitates finding the mother's nipple in preparation for sucking. Babies will suck almost any object that touches their lips. The sucking reflex grows stronger during the first days after birth and can be lost if not stimulated, which can lead to difficulty feeding and may result in malnourishment. As the months go on, reflexive sucking becomes replaced by voluntary sucking.

In the startle reflex, or **Moro reflex** (the startle response), the back arches and the legs and arms are flung out and then brought back toward the chest, with the arms in a hugging motion. The Moro reflex occurs when a baby's position is suddenly changed or when support for the head and neck is suddenly

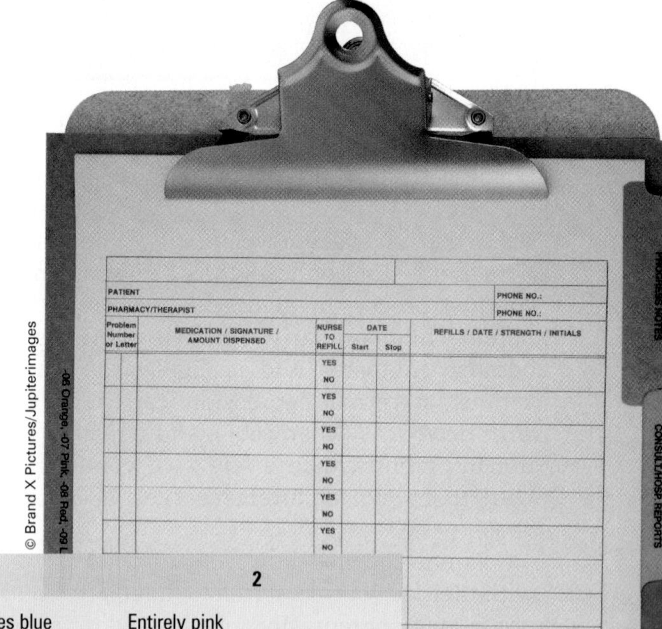
© Brand X Pictures/Jupiterimages

TABLE 3.1

The Apgar Scale

POINTS	0	1	2
Appearance: Colour	Blue, pale	Body pink, extremities blue	Entirely pink
Pulse: Heart Rate	Absent (not detectable)	Slow—below 100 beats/minute	Rapid—100–140 beats/minute
Grimace: Reflex Irritability	No response	Grimace	Crying, coughing, sneezing
Activity level: Muscle tone	Completely flaccid, limp	Weak, inactive	Flexed arms and legs; resists extension
Respiratory effort: Breathing	Absent (infant is apneic)	Shallow, irregular, slow	Regular breathing; lusty crying

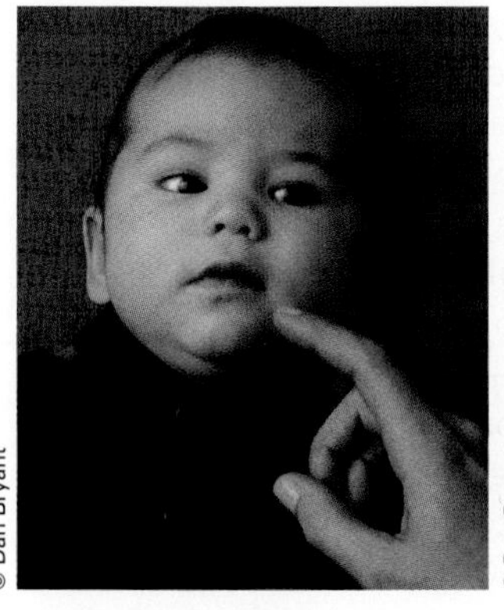
© Dan Bryant

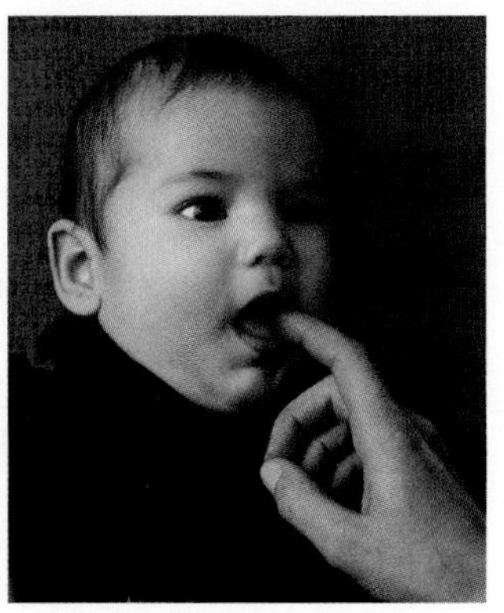
© Dan Bryant

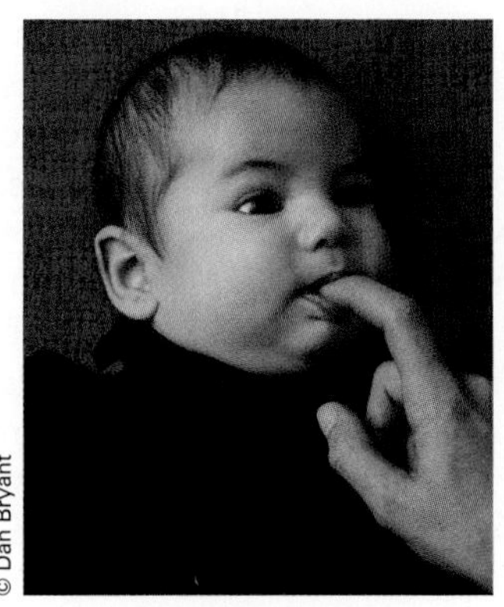
© Dan Bryant

The Rooting Reflex

grasping reflex the response of grasping objects that touch the palms.

stepping reflex the response of taking steps when held under the arms and leaned forward so the feet press the ground.

Babinski reflex the response of fanning the toes when the soles of the feet are stroked.

tonic-neck reflex the response of turning the head to one side, extending the arm and leg on that side, and flexing the limbs on the opposite side.

lost. It can also be elicited by loud noises or sudden movements. The Moro reflex is usually lost within 6 to 7 months after birth. Absence of the Moro reflex can indicate immaturity or brain damage.

During the first few weeks following birth, babies show an increasing tendency to reflexively grasp fingers or other objects pressed against the palms of their hands. In this **grasping reflex**, or palmar reflex, they use four fingers only (the thumbs are not included). Absence of the grasping reflex may indicate depressed activity of the nervous system, which can stem from use of anesthetics during childbirth. The grasping reflex is usually lost within 3 to 4 months of age, and babies generally show voluntary grasping within 5 to 6 months.

Within 1 or 2 days after birth, babies show a reflex that mimics walking. When held under the arms and tilted forward so that the feet press against a solid surface, a baby will show a **stepping reflex** in which the feet advance one after the other. A full-term baby "walks" heel to toe, whereas a preterm infant is more likely to remain on tiptoe. The stepping reflex usually disappears by about 3 or 4 months of age.

In the **Babinski reflex**, the newborn fans or spreads its toes in response to stroking of the underside of the foot from heel to toes. The Babinski reflex normally disappears toward the end of the first year, to be replaced by the toes curling downward.

The **tonic-neck reflex** is observed when the baby is lying on its back and turns its head to one side. The arm and leg on that side extend, while the limbs on the opposite side flex. This reflex is believed to aid the baby in the rolling process later on when greater mobility is apparent.

Some reflexes, such as breathing regularly and blinking the eye in response to a puff of air, remain with us for life. Others, such as the sucking and grasping reflexes, are gradually replaced after several months by voluntary sucking and grasping. Still others, such as the Moro and Babinski reflexes, disappear, indicating that the nervous system is maturing on schedule.

Sensory Capabilities

In 1890, William James, a founder of modern psychology, wrote that the newborn must sense the world "as one great blooming, buzzing confusion." We now study the sensory capabilities of newborns, and we see that James, for all his eloquence, exaggerated their disorganization.

Vision

Newborns can see, but they are nearsighted. They can best see objects that are about 18 to 23 cm (7 to 9 in.) from their eyes (Kellman & Arterberry, 2006), which is roughly the distance of a caregiver's face when a baby is being held. Newborns also do not have the peripheral vision of older children (Candy et al., 1998). They can visually detect movement, and many infants can visually follow, or track, movement the first day after birth. In fact, they appear to prefer (i.e., they spend more time looking at) moving objects to stationary objects (Kellman & Arterberry, 2006).

The Moro Reflex

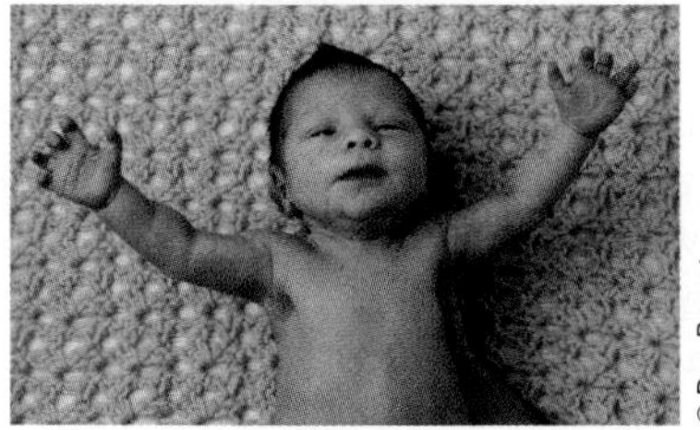
© Dan Bryant

The Grasping Reflex

© Praefice/G&J/Stockphoto/Black Star

The Stepping Reflex

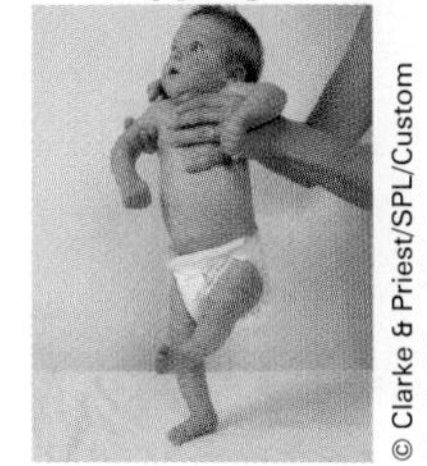
© Clarke & Priest/SPL/Custom Medical Stock Photo

The Tonic-Neck Reflex

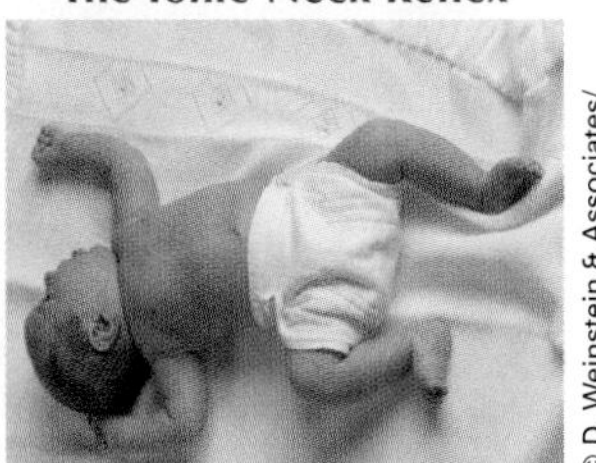
© D. Weinstein & Associates/Custom Medical Stock Photo

visual accommodation automatic adjustments of the lenses to focus on objects.

convergence inward movement of the eyes to focus on an object that is drawing nearer.

amplitude loudness (of sound waves).

pitch highness or lowness (of a sound), as determined by the frequency of sound waves.

Visual accommodation refers to the self-adjustments made by the eye's lens to bring objects into focus. Newborns show little or no visual accommodation; rather, they see as through a fixed-focus camera. Objects placed about 18 to 23 cm (7 to 9 in.) away are in clearest focus for most newborns, but visual accommodation improves dramatically during their first 2 months (Kellman & Arterberry, 2006).

Newborns do not have the muscle control to converge their eyes on an object that is close to them. For this reason, babies may appear cross-eyed but parents should not be concerned. **Convergence** with nearby objects does not occur until 7 or 8 weeks of age (Kellman & Arterberry, 2006).

The degree to which newborns perceive colour remains an open question. By 4 months, however, infants can see most, if not all, colours of the visible spectrum (Franklin et al., 2005). To stimulate infants, distinct black and white patterns should be used (Boston Children's Hospital, 2011).

Even at birth, babies do not simply passively respond to visual stimuli. Babies placed in absolute darkness will open their eyes wide and search around (Kellman & Arterberry, 2006).

Hearing

Fetuses respond to sound for months before they are born, and expecting parents might discover that a baby may kick or jump in response to loud noises and may even be quieted with soft, soothing music (Boston Children's Hospital, 2011). Although myelination of the auditory pathways is not complete before birth, a fetus's middle and inner ears normally reach their mature shapes and sizes before birth. A newborn typically hears well unless its middle ears are clogged with amniotic fluid (Priner et al., 2003). Usually, a newborn will turn its head toward unusual sounds, such as the shaking of a rattle.

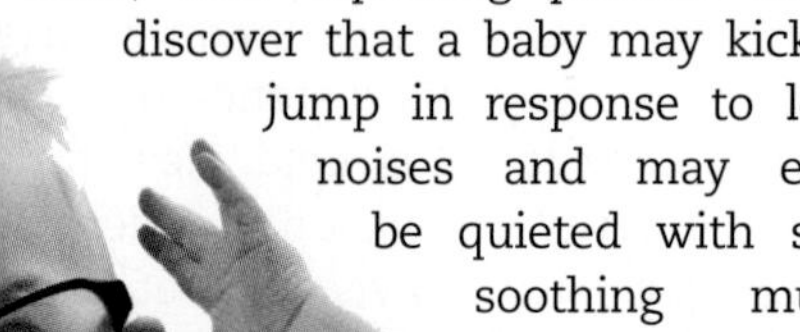

Newborns have the capacity to respond to sounds of different **amplitude** and **pitch**. They are more likely to respond to high-pitched sounds than to low-pitched sounds—especially voices (Trehub & Hannon, 2006). By contrast, softly speaking or singing to infants, in a relatively low-pitched voice, can have a soothing effect (Volkova et al., 2006). The sense of hearing may play a role in the formation of affectional bonds between newborns and mothers that goes well beyond the soothing potential of the mothers' voices.

Smell: The Nose Knows—Early

Newborns can discriminate distinct odours, such as those of onions and licorice. They show more rapid breathing patterns and increased bodily movement in response to powerful odours. They also turn away from unpleasant odours, such as ammonia and vinegar, as early as the first day after birth (Werner & Bernstein, 2001). The nasal preferences of newborns are similar to those of older children and adults (Werner & Bernstein, 2001).

Within the first few days of life, infants show a preference for the smell of their own mother, especially her breast milk (Boston Children's Hospital, 2011). Like hearing, the sense of smell may provide a vehicle for mother–infant recognition and attachment. Newborns may be sensitive to the smell of milk because, when held by the mother, they tend to turn toward her nipple before they have had a chance to see or touch it. In one classic experiment, Macfarlane (1975, 1977) placed nursing pads above and to the sides of newborns' heads. One pad had absorbed milk from the mother, the other was clean. Newborns less than 1 week old spent more time turning to look at their mothers' pads than at the new pads. Smell may contribute to the early development of recognition and attachment.

Taste

Taste buds begin to form early in fetal development. Thus, newborns are sensitive to different tastes, and their preferences, as suggested by their facial expressions in response to various fluids, are like those of adults (Werner & Bernstein, 2001). When distilled water is placed on the tongue, newborns swallow without showing any facial expression suggestive of a positive or negative response. Sweet solutions, however, are met with smiles, licking, and eager sucking, as in Figure 3.5a (Rosenstein & Oster, 1988). Newborns discriminate among solutions with salty, sour, and bitter tastes, as suggested by reactions in the lower part of the face (Rosenstein & Oster, 1988). Sour fluids (Figure 3.5b) elicit pursing of the lips, nose wrinkling, and eye blinking. Bitter solutions (Figure 3.5c) stimulate spitting, gagging, and sticking out the tongue.

Sweet solutions have a calming effect on newborns (Blass & Camp, 2003). Babies also show a strong preference for breast milk (Boston Children's Hospital, 2011).

Touch

Throughout the last months of pregnancy, a baby is snuggly cocooned in the uterus with its arms and legs tucked inward. At birth, babies are suddenly thrust into a bright, cold world where their arms and legs can suddenly move about freely. The newborn might feel insecure, so cuddling the baby closely can make it feel more protected. Swaddling (wrapping snugly in a blanket) is another technique for soothing an infant. Feedings will also ensure that the baby spends several hours in the caregiver's arms (Boston Children's Hospital, 2011).

The sense of touch is also an extremely important avenue of babies' learning and communication. Not only do the skin senses provide information about the external world but the sensations of skin against skin also appear to provide feelings of comfort and security that may be major factors in the formation of bonds of attachment between infants and their caregivers. Baby massage has become an increasingly popular method of promoting a relationship between baby and caregiver.

© Blend Images/Jupiterimages

Learning: Really Early Childhood "Education"

The limited sensory capabilities of newborns suggest that they may not learn as rapidly as older children do. After all, we must sense clearly those things we are to learn about. Newborns do, however, seem capable of conditioning.

Classical Conditioning of Newborns

In classical conditioning of newborns, involuntary responses are conditioned to new stimuli. In a typical study (Lipsitt, 2002), newborns were taught to blink in response to a tone, much like the dog in Chapter 1

FIGURE 3.5

Facial Expressions Elicited by Sweet, Sour, and Bitter Solutions

Newborns are sensitive to different tastes, as shown by their facial expressions when tasting (a) sweet, (b) sour, and (c) bitter solutions.

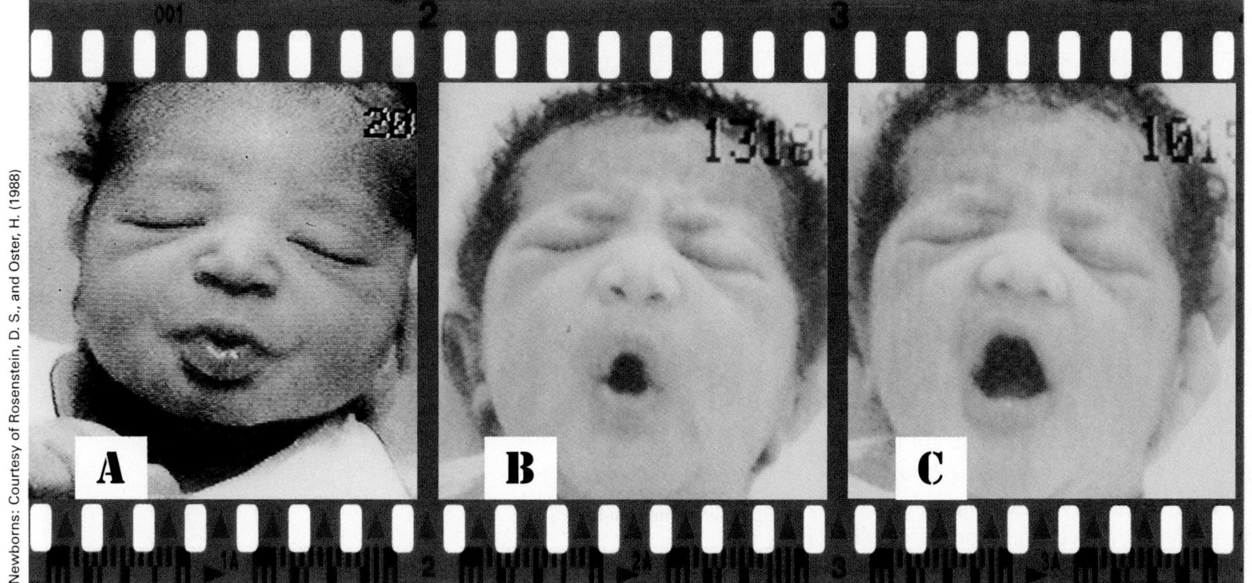

Newborns: Courtesy of Rosenstein, D. S., and Oster, H. (1988)

Filmstrip: © Nicholas Belton/iStockphoto.com

rapid-eye-movement (REM) sleep
a sleep period when dreams are likely, as suggested by rapid eye movements.

non-rapid-eye-movement (non-REM) sleep
a sleep period when dreams are unlikely.

learns to respond to the opening of a can of dog food. Blinking (the unconditioned response) was elicited by a puff of air directed toward the infant's eye (the unconditioned stimulus). A tone was sounded (the conditioned stimulus) as the puff of air was delivered. After repeated pairings, sounding the tone caused the newborn to blink (the conditioned response). This response indicates that newborns are equipped to learn that events peculiar to their own environments (touches or other conditioned stimuli) may mean that a meal is at hand. The conditioned stimuli are culture specific; the capacity to learn is universal.

Operant Conditioning of Newborns

Operant conditioning, like classical conditioning, can take place in newborns. A prime example of operant conditioning is the experiment from Chapter 2 in which newborns learned to suck on a pacifier in such a way as to activate a recording of their mothers reading *The Cat in the Hat* (DeCasper & Fifer, 1980; DeCasper & Spence, 1991).

Sleeping and Waking

As adults, we spend about one-third of our time sleeping. Newborns greatly outsleep us, spending two-thirds of their time, or about 16 hours per day, in sleep. And, in one of life's basic challenges to parents, newborns do not sleep their 16 hours consecutively.

Several different states of sleep and wakefulness have been identified in newborns and infants, as shown in Table 3.2 (Cornwell & Feigenbaum, 2006; Salzarulo & Ficca, 2002; Wulff & Siegmund, 2001). Although individual babies differ in the amount of time they spend in each of these states, sleep clearly predominates over wakefulness in the early days and weeks of life.

Different infants require different amounts of sleep and follow different patterns of sleep, but virtually all infants distribute their sleeping throughout the day and night through a series of naps. The typical infant has about six cycles of waking and sleeping in a 24-hour period. The longest nap typically approaches 41/2 hours, and the newborn is usually awake for a little more than 1 hour during each cycle.

TABLE 3.2

States of Sleep and Wakefulness in Infancy

STATE	COMMENTS
Quiet sleep (non-REM)	Regular breathing, eyes closed, no movement
Active sleep (REM)	Irregular breathing, eyes closed, rapid eye movement, muscle twitches
Drowsiness	Regular or irregular breathing, eyes open or closed, little movement
Alert inactivity	Regular breathing, eyes open, looking around, little body movement
Alert activity	Irregular breathing, eyes open, active body movement
Crying	Irregular breathing, eyes open or closed, thrashing of arms and legs, crying

After a month or so, the infant has fewer but longer sleep periods and will usually take longer naps during the night. By the ages of about 6 months to 1 year, many infants begin to sleep through the night. Some infants start sleeping through the night even earlier (Salzarulo & Ficca, 2002). Some infants begin to sleep through the night for a week or so and then revert to their wakeful ways again for a while.

REM and Non-REM Sleep

Sleep can be divided into **rapid-eye-movement (REM) sleep** and **non-rapid-eye-movement (non-REM) sleep** (see Figure 3.6). REM sleep is characterized by rapid

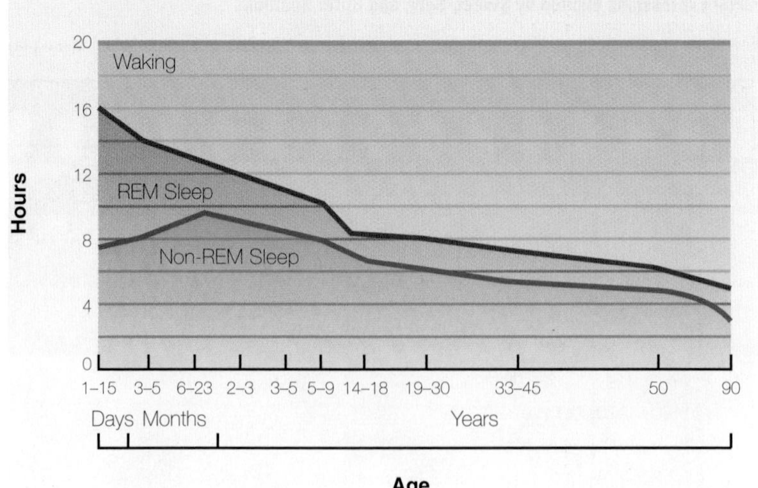

FIGURE 3.6

REM Sleep and Non-REM Sleep

The percentage of time spent in REM sleep declines as people age.

Source: Roffwarg et al. (1966).

eye movements that can be observed beneath closed lids. About 80 percent of adults who are roused during REM sleep report that they have been dreaming. Is the same true of newborns?

Note from Figure 3.6 that newborns spend about half their time sleeping in REM sleep. As they develop, the percentage of sleeping time spent in REM sleep declines. By 6 months or so, REM sleep accounts for only about 30 percent of the baby's sleep. By 2 to 3 years, REM sleep drops off to about 20–25 percent (Salzarulo & Ficca, 2002). As we develop, we experience a dramatic falling-off in the total number of hours spent in sleep (Salzarulo & Ficca, 2002).

What is the function of REM sleep in newborns? Research with humans and other animals, including kittens and rat pups, suggests that the brain requires a certain amount of stimulation for the creation of proteins that are involved in the development of neurons and synapses (Dang-Vu et al., 2006). Perhaps newborns create this stimulation by means of REM sleep, which most closely parallels the waking state in terms of brain waves. Preterm babies spend an even greater proportion of their time in REM sleep, perhaps because they need relatively more stimulation of the brain.

Crying

No discussion of the sleeping and waking states of the newborn would be complete without mentioning crying, a comment that parents will view as an understatement. The main reason babies cry seems to be simple enough. Studies suggest a one-word answer: pain (Gormally et al., 2001; Zeifman, 2004). Whether crying is healthful remains an open question, but some crying among babies seems to be universal.

Before parenthood, many people wonder whether they will be able to recognize the meaning of their babies' cries, but it usually does not take them long. Parents typically learn to distinguish cries that signify hunger, anger, and pain. The pitch of an infant's cries appears to provide information (Zeifman, 2004). Adults perceive high-pitched crying to be more urgent, distressing, and sick sounding than low-pitched crying (Zeifman, 2004). A sudden, loud, insistent cry associated with flexing and kicking of the legs may indicate colic, that is, pain resulting from gas or other sources of distress in the digestive tract. Crying from colic can be severe and persistent; it may last for hours (Barr et al., 2005). Much to the relief of parents, colic tends to disappear by the third to sixth month, as a baby's digestive system matures.

Certain high-pitched cries, when prolonged, may signify health problems. The cries of chronically distressed infants differ from those of nondistressed infants in both rhythm and pitch. Patterns of crying may be indicative of chromosomal abnormalities, infections, fetal malnutrition, and exposure to narcotics (Zeifman, 2004).

Infant crying increases after birth, peaking at around 5–6 weeks and goes away by about 3 months. This early period of crying can be a source of great concern for parents. During early infancy, the pattern of crying has some significant differences. For example, depending on the child, the age at which crying peaks can range from 3 to 12 weeks. The amount of crying also varies, ranging from a daily total crying duration of less than 20 minutes in mild cases, to more than 3 hours in severe cases. Many infants continue to have symptoms after 3 months (Shinohara & Kodama, 2012). At first, crying communicates pain and hunger that is correctable. Because persistent crying can strain the mother–infant relationship, it is important to provide support for new caregivers (Reijneveld et al., 2004).

In extreme cases of crying, parents can become very frustrated. Extended crying can be confusing and concerning and is often labelled as colic. Because crying sounds like an illness, it can seem abnormal, but crying is a very normal developmental phase. Dr. Ronald Barr, a developmental pediatrician who studies infant crying,

pacifier a device such as an artificial nipple or teething ring that soothes babies when sucked.

sudden infant death syndrome (SIDS) the death, while sleeping, of apparently healthy babies who stop breathing.

came up with the phrase "the period of purple crying." Purple does not refer to the colour a baby turns. It is an acronym that stands for P(peak of) U(unexpected) R(resists) P(pain-like) L(long) E(evening). PURPLE crying begins at about 2 weeks of age and continues until about 3–4 months of age. The baby seems to resist soothing and nothing helps. Parents often say their baby looks like he or she is in pain yet the baby is healthy and happy at other times during the day. This crying is a very normal part of development and, although frustrating, is only temporary—this period will come to an end. The best thing a caregiver can do is stay calm, which may sound simple but is very difficult when you are tired, frazzled, and worried about your baby (Barr, 2013).

Soothing

Sucking seems to be a built-in tranquilizer. Sucking on a **pacifier** decreases crying and agitated movement in hungry newborns (Field, 1999). Therefore, the soothing function of sucking need not be learned through experience.

Parents soothe infants by picking them up, patting them, caressing and rocking them, swaddling them, and speaking to them in a low voice. Parents then usually try to find the specific cause of the distress by offering a bottle or pacifier or checking the diaper. Parents learn by trial and error the types of embraces and movements that are likely to soothe infants, and infants learn quickly that crying is followed by being picked up or other interventions. Whether it is possible to spoil a crying baby remains a hotly debated question.

More Canadian children die from sudden infant death syndrome (SIDS) than die from cancer, heart disease, pneumonia, child abuse, AIDS, cystic fibrosis, and muscular dystrophy combined.

Sudden Infant Death Syndrome (SIDS)

More children die from **sudden infant death syndrome (SIDS)** than die from cancer, heart disease, pneumonia, child abuse, AIDS, cystic fibrosis, and muscular dystrophy combined (Lipsitt, 2003). SIDS—also known as crib death—is a disorder of infancy that apparently strikes while a baby is sleeping. In the typical case, a baby goes to sleep, apparently in perfect health, and is later found dead. There is typically no sign that the baby struggled or was in pain. The awareness campaign "Back to Sleep" was initiated in 1994; however, despite a 50 percent decrease in incidence, each week in Canada, three babies succumb to SIDS (Canadian Foundation for the Study of Infant Deaths, 2005).

The incidence of SIDS has been declining, but each year many infants in Canada still die of SIDS. It is the most common cause of death during the first year, and most of these deaths occur between 2 and 5 months of age (Paterson et al., 2006). New parents frequently live in dread of SIDS and check a sleeping baby regularly to whether it is still breathing. Babies occasionally suspend their breathing for a moment, which heightens caregiver anxiety.

What should *you* do about SIDS? Place your baby to sleep on its back. Keep current with research data on SIDS by checking with your pediatrician and by exploring websites such as those of the Centers for

SIDS is more common among the following (Hunt & Hauck, 2006; Paterson et al., 2006):

- Babies aged 2–4 months
- Babies who are put to sleep on their stomachs or their sides
- Premature and low-birth-weight infants
- Male babies
- Babies whose mothers smoked during or after pregnancy or whose mothers used narcotics during pregnancy

*Note that these characteristics are risk factors for, not causes of, SIDS

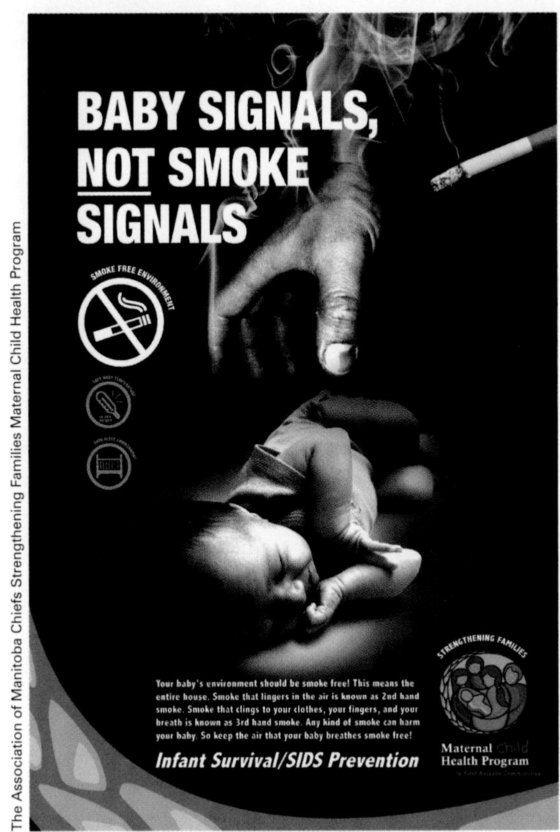

The Association of Manitoba Chiefs Strengthening Families Maternal Child Health Program

EMERGING CANADA

The health of First Nations children was the focus of a discussion paper published by the Assembly of First Nations in Canada. The aim of this paper was to provide a basic overview of the issues and concerns that affect the health of First Nations children's. A major point of concern is that First Nations infant mortality rate is 1.5 times higher than the mainstream Canadian population. Several studies also show that SIDS rates range from 3 to 10 times higher among First Nations than across Canada (Assembly of First Nations, 2008). The Assembly of Manitoba Chiefs created an education campaign to help protect First Nations families in a culturally relevant way. Education is a key strategy in protecting all parents and families against the risk factors associated with Sudden Infant Death Syndrome (Assembly of First Nations, 2008).

Disease Control and Prevention and the SIDS Network.

Shaken Baby Syndrome (SBS)

Shaken Baby Syndrome (SBS) and Abusive Head Trauma (AHT) are terms used to describe the injuries sustained by an infant or young child who is roughly shaken. In a Canadian study of 364 victims of SBS and AHT who were admitted to hospital (King et al., 2003), 81 percent of the children survived but suffered neurological deficit, visual impairment, and ongoing care issues; the other 19 percent died. The authors concluded that any estimate of the number of SBS cases was likely just the "tip of the iceberg," as the incidence of SBS and AHT is likely significantly underestimated due to misdiagnoses and underreporting.

We all need to realize that shaking a baby *can happen to anyone*. SBS is an impulsive act of an often exhausted or frustrated caregiver. SBS happens in all cultural and socioeconomic groups. If you know someone who has a baby, and you are able to help out, offer your assistance. If you have a baby and you need support, ask (Alberta SBS Prevention Campaign, 2010). Shaken Baby Syndrome: Take a Break—Don't Shake.

Shaken Baby Syndrome is the result of an impulsive act of an often exhausted or frustrated caregiver. SBS cases happen in all cultural and socioeconomic groups.

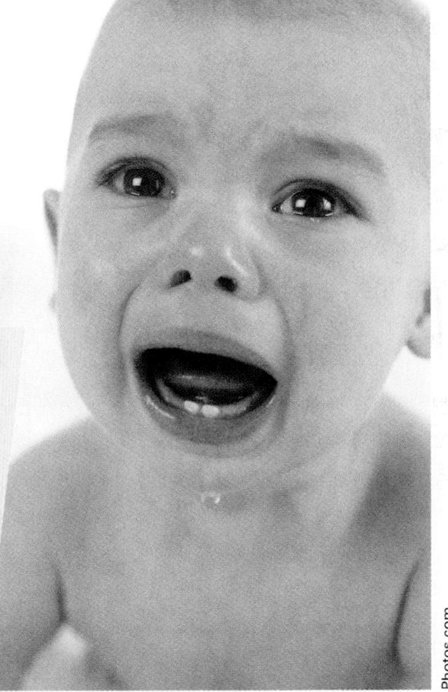

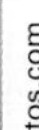

Photos.com

Monkey Business Images/Shutterstock.com

CHAPTER 4

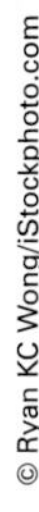

Infancy: Physical Development

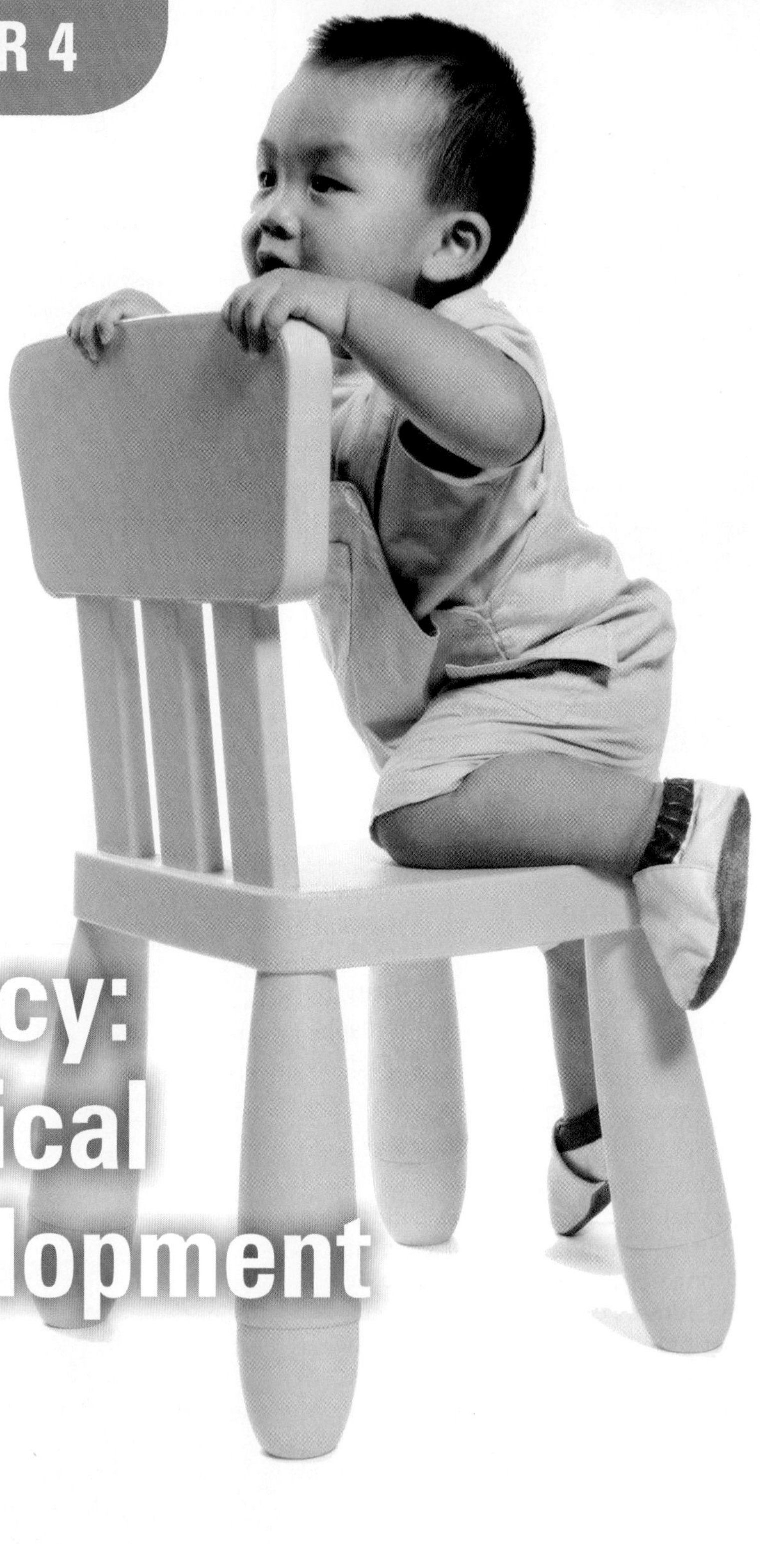

© Ryan KC Wong/iStockphoto.com

LEARNING OUTCOMES

LO1 Describe trends in the physical development of the infant

LO2 Describe the physical development of the brain and the nervous system

LO3 Describe the key events in the motor development of the infant

LO4 Describe patterns of sensory and perceptual development in infancy

> "Three key sequences of physical development are cephalocaudal development, proximodistal development, and differentiation."

What a fascinating creature the newborn is: tiny, delicate, apparently oblivious to its surroundings, yet perfectly formed and fully capable of letting its caregivers know when it is hungry, thirsty, or uncomfortable. And what a fascinating creature is this same child 2 years later: running, playing, talking, hugging, and kissing.

It is hard to believe that only 2 short years—the years of infancy—bring about so many changes. It seems that nearly every day brings a new accomplishment. But as we will see, not all infants share equally in the explosion of positive developments. Therefore, we will also enumerate some developmental problems and what can be done about them.

LO1 Physical Growth and Development

During the first 2 years, children make enormous strides in physical growth and development. In this section, we explore sequences of physical development, changes in height and weight, and nutrition. As we will see next, development is "head first."

Sequences of Physical Development

Three key sequences of physical development are cephalocaudal development, proximodistal development, and differentiation.

Cephalocaudal Development

Development proceeds from the upper part of the head to the lower parts of the body (tip to toe). When we consider the central role of the brain, which is contained within the skull, the cephalocaudal sequence appears quite logical. The brain regulates essential functions, such as heartbeat. Through the secretion of hormones, the brain also regulates the growth and development of the body and influences basic drives, such as hunger and thirst.

The head develops more rapidly than the rest of the body during the embryonic stage. By 8 weeks after conception, the head constitutes half the entire length of the embryo. The brain develops more rapidly than the spinal cord. Arm buds form before leg buds. Most newborn babies have a strong, well-defined sucking reflex, although their legs are spindly and their limbs move back and forth only in diffuse excitement or agitation. Infants can hold up their heads before they gain control over their arms, their torsos, and, finally, their legs. They can sit up before they can crawl and walk.

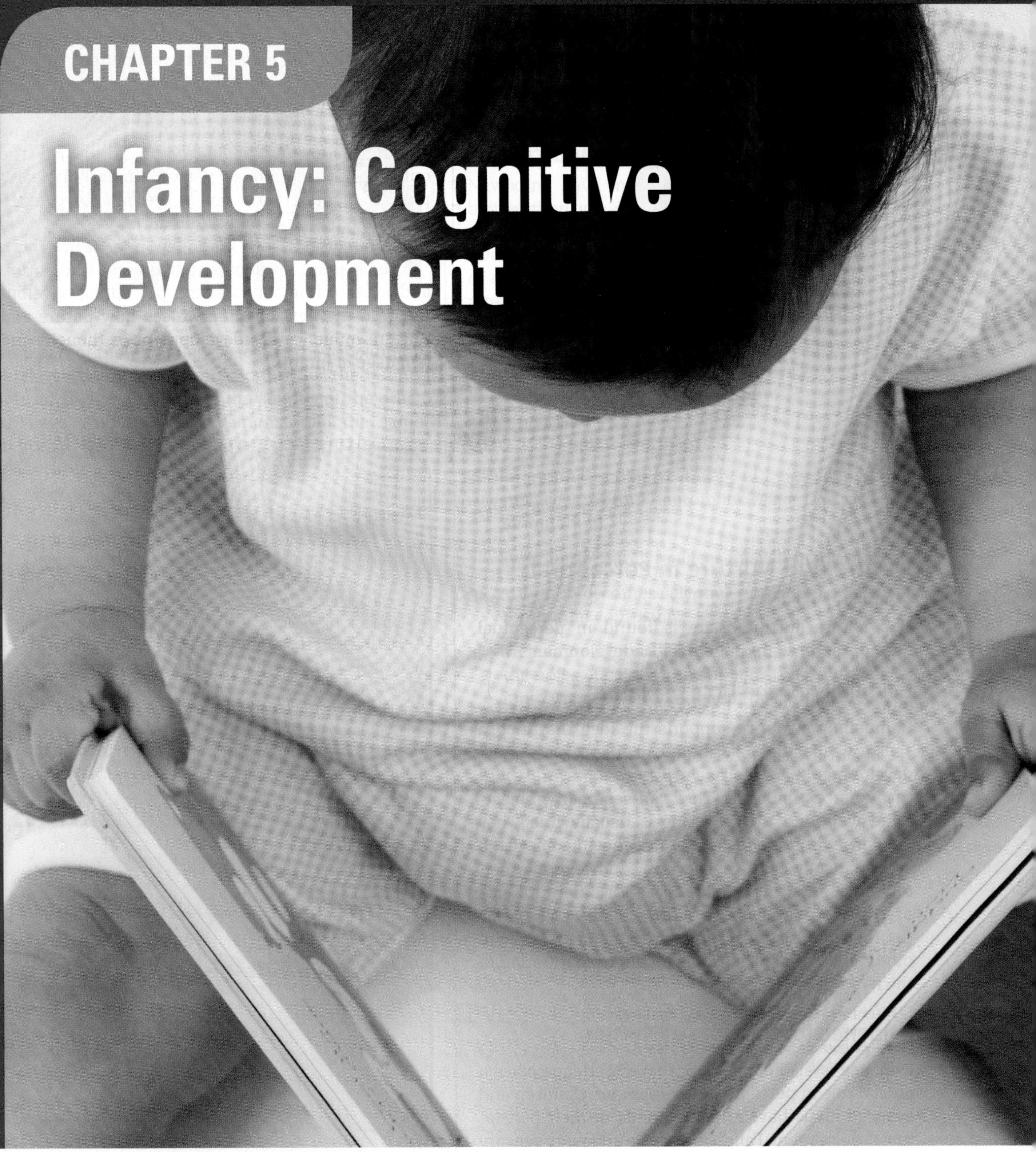

CHAPTER 5

Infancy: Cognitive Development

LEARNING OUTCOMES

LO1 Examine Jean Piaget's studies of cognitive development

LO2 Discuss the information-processing approach

LO3 Identify individual differences in intelligence among infants

LO4 Examine language development in children

"Cognitive development focuses on the development of children's ways of perceiving and mentally representing the world."

Alana plays in the bathtub slapping the water making sounds and bubbles. She does the same movements over and over . . . just like she did the day before. She pours water from one cup to the other and back again.

Is this description one of a scientist at work? In a way, it is. Swiss psychologist Jean Piaget (1963 [1936]) felt children of this age frequently act like scientists, performing what he called "experiments in order to see."

LO1 Cognitive Development: Jean Piaget

Cognitive development focuses on the development of children's ways of perceiving and mentally representing the world. Piaget labelled children's concepts of the world *schemes*. He hypothesized that children try to use *assimilation* to absorb new events into existing schemes. When assimilation does not allow the child to make sense of novel events, children try to modify existing schemes through *accommodation*.

Piaget (1963 [1936]) hypothesized that cognitive processes develop in an orderly sequence of stages. Some children may advance more quickly than others, but the sequence remains constant (Flavell et al., 2002; Siegler & Alibali, 2005). Piaget identified four stages of cognitive development: sensorimotor, preoperational, concrete operational, and formal operational. In this chapter, we discuss the sensorimotor stage.

The Sensorimotor Stage

Piaget's sensorimotor stage refers to the first 2 years of cognitive development, a time during which infants progress from responding to events with reflexes, or ready-made schemes, to goal-oriented behaviour. Piaget divided the sensorimotor stage into six substages. In each substage, earlier forms of behaviour are repeated, varied, and coordinated.

Simple Reflexes

The first substage covers the first month after birth. It is dominated by the assimilation of sources of stimulation into inborn reflexes such as grasping or visual tracking. At birth, reflexes seem like automatic responses but even within the first few hours, neonates begin to modify reflexes as a result of experience. For example, infants will adapt their patterns of sucking to the shape of the nipple and the rate of flow of fluid. During the first month or so, however, infants apparently make no connection between stimulation perceived through different sensory modalities. They make no effort to grasp objects that they visually track.

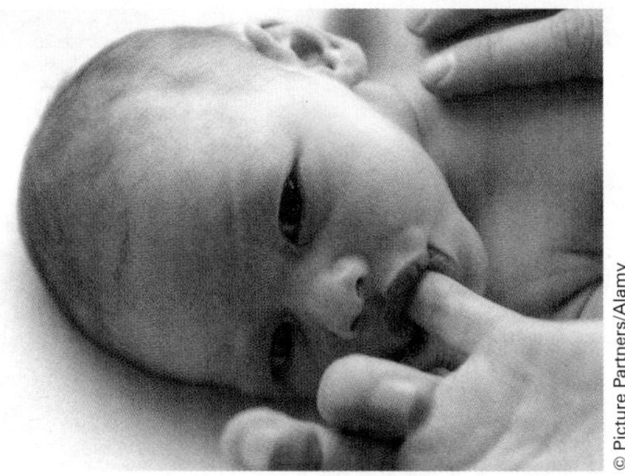

At birth, neonates assimilate objects into reflexive responses.

Infants repeat actions that involve their bodies (primary circular reactions).

Patterns of activity are repeated because of their effect on the environment (secondary circular reactions).

primary circular reactions the repetition of actions that first occurred by chance and that focus on the infant's own body.

secondary circular reactions the repetition of actions that produce an effect on the environment.

Primary Circular Reactions

The second substage, primary circular reactions, lasts from about 1 to 4 months of age and is characterized by the beginnings of the ability to coordinate various sensorimotor schemes. Infants tend to repeat stimulating actions that first occurred by chance. For example, an infant may lift its arm repeatedly to bring it into view. **Primary circular reactions** focus on the infant's own body rather than on the external environment. Piaget noticed the following primary circular reaction in his son Laurent:

> At 2 months 4 days, Laurent by chance discovers his right index finger and looks at it briefly. At 2 months 11 days, he inspects for a moment his open right hand, perceived by chance. At 2 months 17 days, he follows its spontaneous movement for a moment, then examines it several times while it searches for his nose or rubs his eye.
>
> —Piaget (1963 [1936], pp. 96–97)

Thus, Laurent, early in the third month, visually tracks the behaviour of his hands, but his visual observations do not affect their movement. In terms of assimilation and accommodation, the child is attempting to assimilate the motor scheme (moving the hand) into the sensory scheme (looking at it). But the schemes do not automatically fit. Several days of apparent trial and error pass, during which the infant seems to be trying to make accommodations so that they will fit. By the third month, infants may examine objects repeatedly and intensely. It seems that the infant is no longer simply looking and seeing but is now "looking in order to see."

Because Laurent (and other infants) will repeat actions that allow them to see, cognitive-developmental psychologists consider sensorimotor coordination to be self-reinforcing. Laurent is acting on his hands to keep them in his field of vision. Piaget considers the desire to prolong stimulation to be as "basic" as the drives of hunger or thirst.

Secondary Circular Reactions

The third substage lasts from about 4 to 8 months and is characterized by **secondary circular reactions**, in which patterns of activity are repeated because of their effect on the environment. In the second substage (primary circular reactions), infants are focused on their own bodies, as in the example given with Laurent. In the third substage (secondary circular reactions), the focus shifts to objects and environmental events. Infants may now learn to pull strings in order to make a plastic face appear or to shake an object in order to hear it rattle.

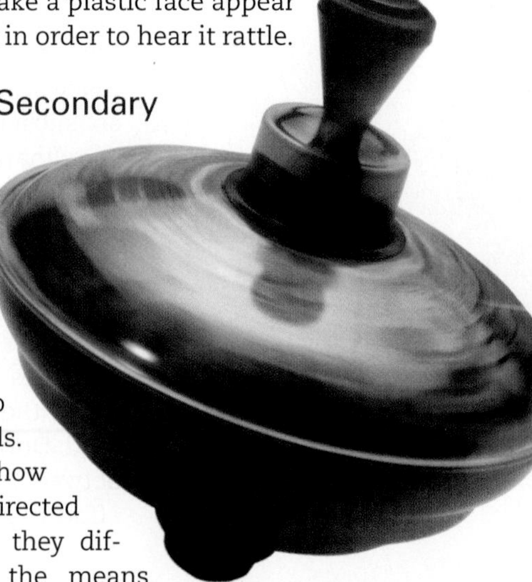

Coordination of Secondary Schemes

In the fourth substage, infants no longer act simply to prolong interesting occurrences. Now they can coordinate schemes to attain specific goals. Infants begin to show intentional, goal-directed behaviour in which they differentiate between the means of achieving a goal and the goal or end itself. For example, they may lift a piece of cloth to reach a toy that they had seen a parent place there earlier. In this example, the scheme of picking up the cloth (the means) is coordinated with the scheme of reaching for the toy (the goal or end). This example indicates that the infant has mentally represented the toy placed under the cloth.

During the fourth substage, infants also gain the capacity to imitate gestures and sounds that they had previously ignored. The imitation of a facial gesture implies an infant has mentally represented his or her own face and, through feedback from facial muscles, can tell what parts of the face he or she is moving.

DID YOU KNOW?

For 2-month-old infants, "out of sight" is "out of mind."

Infants delight at playing peek-a-boo because once you disappear from view they don't realize you still exist!

Tertiary Circular Reactions

In the fifth substage, which lasts from about 12 to 18 months of age, Piaget looked on the behaviour of infants as characteristic of budding scientists. Infants now engage in **tertiary circular reactions**, or purposeful adaptations of established schemes to specific situations. Behaviour takes on a new experimental quality, and infants may vary their actions dozens of times in a deliberate trial-and-error fashion to learn how things work.

Piaget reported an example of tertiary circular reactions by his daughter Jacqueline. The episode was an experiment in which Piaget placed a stick outside Jacqueline's playpen, which had wooden bars (Piaget, 1963 [1936]). At first, Jacqueline grasped the stick and tried to pull it sideways into the playpen. The stick was too long and could not fit through the bars. After days of overt trial and error, however, Jacqueline discovered that she could bring the stick between the bars by turning it upright. In the sixth substage, described next, infants apparently engage in mental trial and error before displaying the correct overt response.

tertiary circular reactions
the purposeful adaptation of established schemes to new situations.

Invention of New Means through Mental Combinations

The sixth substage lasts from about 18 to 24 months of age. It serves as a transition between sensorimotor development and the development of symbolic thought. External exploration is replaced by mental exploration. At about 18 months, children may also use imitation to symbolize or stand for a plan of action.

Piaget presented his other children, Lucienne and Laurent, with the playpen and stick problem when each was 18 months old. Rather than engage in overt trial and error, at age 18 months, each child sat and studied the situation for a few moments. Then each grasped the stick, turned it upright, and brought it into the playpen with little overt effort. Lucienne and Laurent apparently mentally represented the stick and the bars of the playpen and then perceived that the stick would not fit through as it was. They then needed to rotate the mental image of the stick until they perceived a position that would allow the stick to pass between the bars.

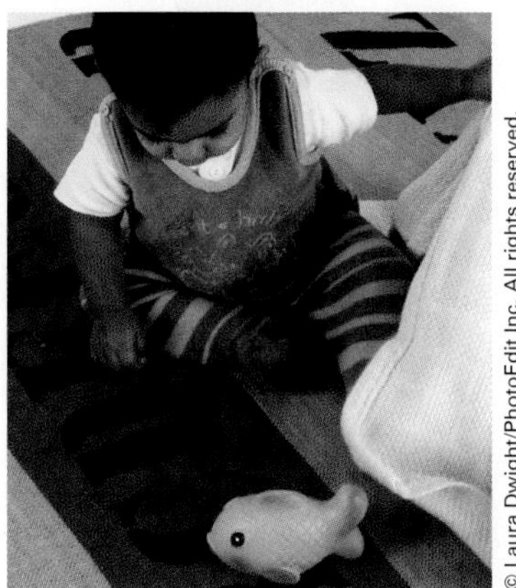

Infants coordinate their behaviour to attain specific goals (coordinating secondary schemes).

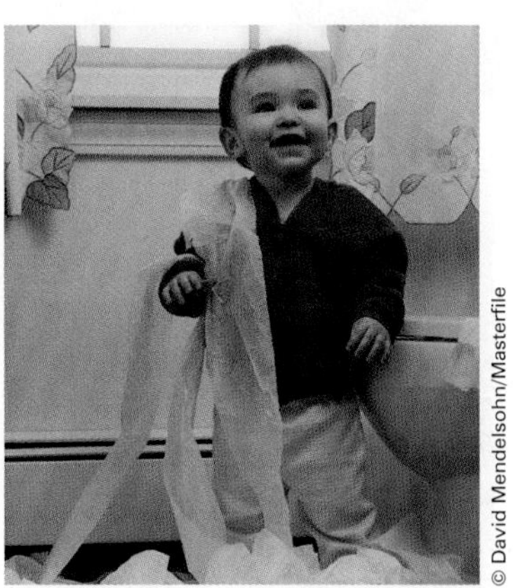

Infants use trial and error to learn how things work (tertiary circular reactions).

The Bayley scales measure an infant's mental and motor development. (More on pp. 87–88.)

object permanence recognition that objects continue to exist when they are not in view.

Development of Object Permanence

The appearance of **object permanence** is an important aspect of sensorimotor development. Object permanence is the recognition that an object or person continues to exist when out of sight. For example, your textbook continues to exist when you leave it in the library after studying for the big test, and an infant's mother continues to exist even when she is in another room. The development of object permanence is tied into the development of infants' working memory and reasoning ability (Aguiar & Baillargeon, 2002; Saiki & Miyatsuji, 2007).

Newborns show no tendency to respond to objects that are not within their immediate sensory grasp. By the age of 2 months, infants may show some surprise if an object (such as a toy duck) is placed behind a screen and then taken away so that when the screen is lifted, it is absent. However, they make no effort to search for the missing object (see Figure 5.1). Through the first 6 months or so, when the screen is placed between the object and the infant, the infant behaves as though the object is no longer there. Apparently, they do not yet reliably mentally represent objects they see. For 2-month-old infants, "out of sight" is truly "out of mind."

By about the sixth month, some interesting advances occur in the development of the object concept (Piaget's substage 3). For example, an infant at this age will tend to look for an object that has been dropped, behaviour that suggests some form of object permanence. We have reason to believe that a 6-month-old perceives a mental representation (image) of an object, such as a favourite toy, in response to sensory impressions of part of the object. This perception is shown by the infant's reaching for an object that is partly hidden.

FIGURE 5.1

Development of Object Permanence

To the infant who is in the early part of the sensorimotor stage, out of sight is truly out of mind. After a sheet of paper is placed between the infant and the toy monkey (top two photos), the infant loses all interest in the toy. Using similar evidence, Piaget concluded that the infant does not have a mental representation of the toy. The bottom series of photos shows a child in a later part of the sensorimotor stage. This child does mentally represent objects, indicated by his pushing through a towel to reach an object that has been screened from sight.

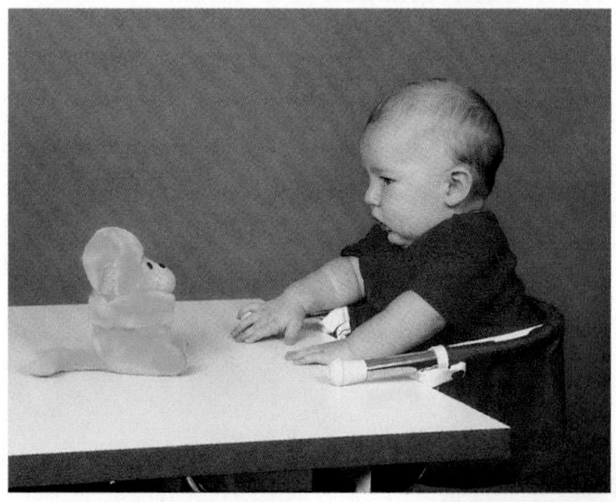

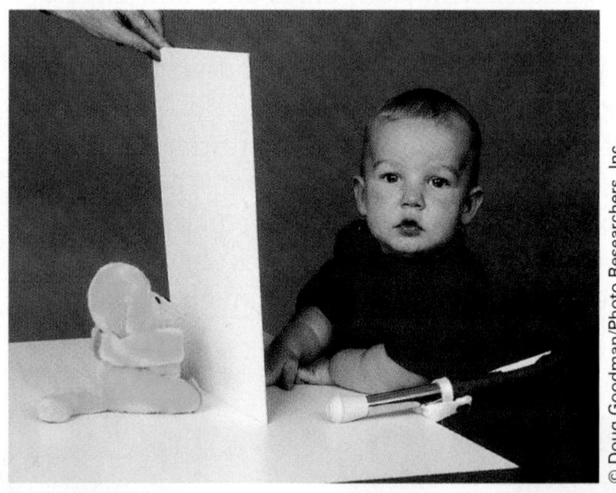

© Todd Taulman/Shutterstock

By 8 to 12 months of age (Piaget's substage 4), infants will seek to retrieve objects that have been completely hidden. But in observing his own children, Piaget (1963 [1936]) noted an interesting error known as the A-not-B error. Piaget repeatedly hid a toy behind a screen (A), and each time, his infant removed the screen and retrieved the toy. Then, as the infant watched, Piaget hid the toy behind another screen (B) in a different place. Still, the infant tried to recover the toy by pushing aside the first screen (A). It was as though the child had learned that a certain motor activity would reinstate the missing toy. The child's concept of the object did not, at this age, extend to recognition that objects usually remain in the place where they have been most recently mentally represented.

Under certain conditions, 9- to 10-month-old infants do not show the A-not-B error (Bremner & Bryant, 2001; Marcovitch & Zelazo, 2006). If infants are allowed to search for the object immediately after seeing it hidden, the error often does not occur. But if they are forced to wait 5 or more seconds before looking, they are likely to commit the A-not-B error (Wellman et al., 1986).

Evaluation of Piaget's Theory

Piaget's theory remains a comprehensive model of infant cognition. Many of his observations of his own infants have been confirmed by others. The pattern and sequence of events he described have been observed among infants in North America, Europe, Africa, and Asia (Werner, 1988). Still, research has raised questions about the validity of many of Piaget's claims (Siegler & Alibali, 2005).

First, most researchers now agree that cognitive development is not as tied to discrete stages as Piaget suggested (Krojgaard, 2005; Siegler & Alibali, 2005). Although later developments seem to build on earlier ones, the process appears to be more gradual than discontinuous.

Second, Piaget emphasized the role of maturation, almost to the point of excluding adult and peer influences on cognitive development. However, these interpersonal influences have been shown to play important roles in cognitive development (Kuhn, 2007; Maratsos, 2007).

deferred imitation the imitation of previously encountered people and events.

Third, Piaget appears to have underestimated infants' competence (Siegler & Alibali, 2005). For example, infants display object permanence earlier than he believed (Wang et al., 2005). Also, consider studies on the presence of **deferred imitation** (imitation of an action that may have occurred hours, days, or even weeks earlier), which suggest that children have mentally represented behaviour patterns. Piaget believed that deferred imitation appears at about 18 months, but others such as (Barr, et. al., 2005; Campanella & Rovee-Collier, 2005) found that infants as young as 6 months of age could imitate an action after a time delay. For example, a child can observe and adult push a button to produce a beep and after a time delay, they can re-produce the same action. One day later, when the infants were given a chance to play with the same objects, many of them imitated the actions they had witnessed.

LO2 Information Processing

The information-processing approach to cognitive development focuses on how children manipulate or process information that is coming in from the environment or is already stored in the mind. Infants' tools for processing information include their memory and imitation.

Infants' Memory

Many of the cognitive capabilities of infants—recognizing the faces of familiar people, developing object permanence, and, in fact, learning in any form—depend on one critical aspect of cognitive development: their memory (Daman-Wasserman et al., 2006; Hayne & Fagen, 2003). Even newborns demonstrate their memory for stimuli they have previously been exposed to. For example, neonates adjust their rate of sucking to hear a recording of their mother reading a story she had read aloud during the last weeks of pregnancy, as discussed in Chapter 2 (DeCasper & Fifer, 1980; DeCasper & Spence, 1991). Much of our current understanding of infant perceptions and cognitive abilities comes from the study of the visual habituation–dishabituation model. Habituation takes place when the infant encodes information and begins to predict outcomes. Dishabituation takes place when memory performance becomes apparent. In other words, infants disengage from the source of interest and shift their attention to something new (Kavšek, 2012).

Memory improves dramatically between 2 and 6 months of age and then again by 12 months (Pelphrey et al., 2004; Rose et al., 2001). The improvement may indicate that older infants are more capable than younger ones at encoding (i.e., storing) information, retrieving information already stored, or both (Hayne & Fagen, 2003).

Imitation: Infant See, Infant Do?

Imitation is the basis for much of human learning. To assist infants remembering imitated acts, a practise period enhances success of deferred imitation. But in one study, 12-month-old infants were prevented from practising the behaviour they imitated. Yet, they were able to demonstrate it 4 weeks later, suggesting that they had mentally represented the act (Klein & Meltzoff, 1999).

DID YOU KNOW?

A 1-hour-old infant may imitate an adult who sticks out his or her tongue.

True, but that imitation may be reflexive rather than an action of choice.

FIGURE 5.2

Imitation in Infants

These 2- to 3-week-old infants are imitating the facial gestures of an adult experimenter. How are we to interpret these findings? Can we say that the infants "knew" what the experimenter was doing and "chose" to imitate the behaviour, or is there another explanation?

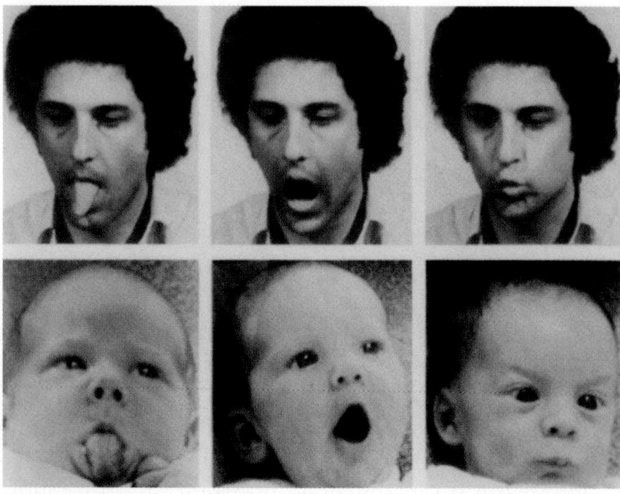

Source: A. N. Meltzoff and M. K. Moore, "Imitation of facial and manual gestures by human neonates." *Science*, 1977, 198, 75–78.

But infants can imitate certain actions at a much earlier age. Neonates only 0.7 to 71 hours old have been found to imitate adults who open their mouths or stick out their tongues (Meltzoff & Prinz, 2002; Rizzolatti et al., 2002; see Figure 5.2).

Before you become too impressed with this early imitative ability of neonates, you should know that some studies have not found imitation in early infancy (Abravanel & DeYong, 1991). One key factor may be the infants' age. Most of the studies that find imitation were done with very young infants—up to 2 weeks old—whereas the studies that do not find imitation tended to use older infants. Therefore, the imitation of neonates is likely to be reflexive. Thus, imitation might disappear when reflexes are "dropping out" and then re-emerge when it has a firmer cognitive footing.

Why might newborns possess some sort of imitation reflex? Answers lie in the realm of speculation. One possibility is that such a built-in response would contribute to the formation of caregiver–infant bonding and the survival of the newborn (Meltzoff & Prinz, 2002). Some theorists speculate that the imitation reflex is made possible by *mirror neurons* that are found in human brains. Such neurons are maintained by evolutionary forces because they enhance the probability of survival as a result of caregiving (Oztop et al., 2006; Rizzolatti et al., 2002).

LO3 Individual Differences in Intelligence among Infants

Cognitive development does not proceed in the same way or at the same pace for all infants (Newman et al., 2006; Rose et al., 2001, 2005). Efforts to understand the development of infant differences in cognitive development have relied on so-called scales of infant development or infant intelligence.

Measuring cognition, or intelligence, in infants is quite different from measuring it in adults. Infants cannot, of course, be assessed by asking them to explain the meanings of words, the similarity between concepts, or the rationales for social rules. Very different kinds of items are used in one of the most important tests of intellectual development among infants—the Bayley Scales of Infant Development, first constructed in 1933 by psychologist Nancy Bayley, and later revised.

The Bayley test currently consists of 178 mental-scale items and 111 motor-scale items. The mental scale assesses verbal communication, perceptual skills, learning and memory, and problem-solving skills. The motor scale assesses gross motor skills, such as standing, walking, and climbing, and fine motor skills, as shown by the ability to manipulate the hands and fingers. Also used is a behaviour rating scale that is based on an examiner's observation of the child during the test. The behaviour rating scale assesses attention span, goal directedness, persistence, and aspects of social and emotional development. Table 5.1 contains sample items from the mental and motor scales and shows the ages at which 50 percent of the infants taking the test passed the items.

DID YOU KNOW?

Psychologists can begin to measure intelligence in infancy.

This is true, but they use different test items from those used with older children and adults. We can't ask infants to explain themselves, so we need to observe their behaviours and draw conclusions instead.

EMERGING CANADA

Baby Einstein and other popular baby DVDs are designed and marketed to promote infant learning. Dr. Hoecker (2011), of the Mayo Clinic, argues that these videos might grab the child's attention but they aren't likely to promote development. A 2007 study of children aged 8 to 16 months concluded that infants exposed to baby DVDs scored lower on language development than children with no screen time. Another study in 2009 of 2-month-olds to 4-year-olds indicated that turning on the television actually reduces interaction time between caregivers and children. Reading does boost language ability for babies and toddlers. If you enjoy baby DVDs, then it might be a productive way to spend time with a child but be cautious about their value and use.

djedzura/Shutterstock.com

TABLE 5.1

Items from the Bayley Scales of Infant Development (BSID–II)

Age	Mental-Scale Items	Motor-Scale Items
1 month	The infant quiets when picked up.	The infant makes a postural adjustment when placed on the examiner's shoulder.
2 months	When examiner presents two objects (bell and rattle) above the infant in a crib, the infant glances back and forth from one to the other.	The infant holds his or her head steady when being carried about in a vertical position.
5 months	The infant is observed to transfer an object from one hand to the other during play.	When seated at a feeding-type table and presented with a sugar pill that is out of reach, the infant attempts to pick it up.
8 months	When an object (toy) in plain view of the infant (i.e., on a table) is covered by a cup, the infant removes the cup to retrieve the object.	The infant raises herself or himself into a sitting position.
12 months	The infant imitates words that are spoken by the examiner.	An infant lying on his or her back will stand up when requested to do so by the examiner.
14–16 months	The infant builds a tower with two cubes (blocks) after the examiner demonstrates the behaviour.	The infant walks alone with good coordination.

visual recognition memory the kind of memory shown in an infant's ability to discriminate previously seen objects from novel objects.

Even though psychologists can begin to measure intelligence in infancy, they use different test items from those used with older children and adults. It remains unclear how well results obtained in infancy predict intellectual functioning at later ages.

Testing Infants: Why and with What?

As you can imagine, testing an infant is no easy matter. The test items must be administered on a one-to-one basis by a patient tester, and it can be difficult to judge whether the infant is showing the targeted response. Why, then, do we test infants?

One reason is to screen infants for handicaps. A tester may be able to detect early signs of sensory or neurological problems, as suggested by development of visual–motor coordination. In addition to the Bayley scales, several other tests have been developed to screen infants for such difficulties, including the Brazelton Neonatal Behavioural Assessment Scale (see Chapter 3) and the Denver Developmental Screening Test.

Instability of Intelligence Scores Attained in Infancy

Researchers have also tried to use infant scales to predict development, but this effort has been less than successful. One study found that scores obtained during the first year of life correlated moderately at best with scores obtained a year later (Harris et al., 2005). Certain items on the Bayley scales appear to predict related intellectual skills later in childhood. For example, Bayley items measuring infant motor skills predict subsequent fine motor and visual–spatial skills at 6 to 8 years of age (Siegel, 1992). Bayley language items also predict language skills at the same age (Siegel, 1992).

One study found that the Bayley scales and socioeconomic status were able to predict cognitive development among low-birth-weight children from 18 months to 4 years of age (Dezoete et al., 2003). But overall scores on the Bayley and other infant scales apparently do not reliably predict school grades or IQ scores among schoolchildren (Colombo, 1993). Perhaps the sensorimotor test items used during infancy are not strongly related to the verbal and symbolic items used to assess intelligence at later ages.

The overall conclusion seems to be that the Bayley scales can identify gross lags in development and relative strengths and weaknesses. However, they are only moderate predictors of intelligence scores even one year later, and are still poorer predictors of scores taken beyond longer stretches of time.

Infant intelligence scores are unstable; that is, a score in infancy cannot be considered to have accurate predictive power for scores obtained later in life.

Use of Visual Recognition Memory

In a continuing effort to find aspects of intelligence and cognition that might remain consistent from infancy through later childhood, researchers have recently focused on visual recognition memory (Courage et al., 2004). **Visual recognition memory** is the ability to discriminate previously seen objects from novel objects. This procedure is based on *habituation*.

Let us consider longitudinal studies of this type. Susan Rose and her colleagues (Rose et al., 1992) showed 7-month-old infants pictures of two identical faces. After 20 seconds, the pictures were replaced with one picture of a new face and a second picture of the familiar face. The amount of time the infants spent looking at each face in the second set of pictures was recorded. Some infants spent more time looking at the new face than at the familiar face, suggesting that they had better memory for visual stimulation. The children were given standard IQ tests yearly from ages 1 through 6. It was found that the children with greater visual recognition memory later attained higher IQ scores.

Rose and her colleagues (2001) also showed that, from age to age, individual differences in the capacity for visual recognition memory remain stable. This finding is important because intelligence—the quality that many researchers seek to predict from visual recognition memory—is also theorized to be a reasonably stable trait.

In sum, scales of infant development may provide useful data as screening devices, as research instruments, or simply as a way to describe the activities that infants do and do not do.

LO4 Language Development

As children develop language skills, they often begin speaking about the things more closely related to their environments and their needs. Children enjoy playing with language. In physical development, the most dramatic developments come early—fast and furious—long before the child is born. Language does not come quite as early, and its development may not seem quite so fast and furious. Nevertheless, during the years of infancy, most children develop from creatures without language to little people who understand nearly all the things that are said to them and who relentlessly sputter words and simple sentences for everyone to hear.

Early Vocalizations

Children develop language according to an invariant sequence of steps, or stages, as outlined in Table 5.2. Infants typically begin with **prelinguistic** vocalizations. True words are symbols of objects and events. Prelinguistic vocalizations, such as cooing and babbling, do not represent objects or events, so infant crying is not a primitive form of language.

Newborns, as parents are well aware, have an unlearned but highly effective form of verbal expression: crying and more crying. Crying is about the only sound that infants make during the first month. During the second month, infants begin **cooing**. Infants use their tongues when they COO. For this reason, coos are more articulated than cries. Coos are often vowel-like and may resemble extended "oohs" and "ahs." Cooing appears to be linked to feelings of pleasure or positive excitement. Infants tend not to coo when they are hungry, tired, or in pain.

Most children develop from creatures without language to little people who understand nearly all the things that are said to them.

Cries and coos are innate but can be modified by experience (Volterra et al., 2004). When parents respond positively to cooing, such as by talking to their infants, smiling at them, and imitating them, cooing increases. Early parent–child "conversations," in which parents respond to coos and then pause as the infant coos, may foster infant awareness of taking turns as a way of verbally relating to other people.

DID YOU KNOW?

Infant crying is not a primitive form of language.

Cries do not represent objects or events, so they are not considered language.

By about 8 months of age, cooing decreases markedly. Somewhere between 6 and 9 months, children begin to babble. **Babbling** is the first vocalizing that sounds like human speech. When babbling, infants frequently combine consonants and vowels, as in *ba*, *ga*, and, sometimes, the much valued *dada* (Stoel-Gammon, 2002). At first, *dada* is purely coincidental (sorry, you dads), despite the family's jubilation over hearing it.

In verbal interactions between infants and adults, the adults frequently repeat the syllables produced by their infants. They are likely to say "dadada" or "bababa" instead of simply "da" or "ba." Such redundancy apparently helps infants discriminate these sounds from others and further encourages them to imitate their parents (Elkind, 2007; Tamis-LeMonda et al., 2006).

prelinguistic vocalizations made by the infant before the use of language.

cooing prelinguistic vowel-like sounds that reflect feelings of positive excitement.

babbling the child's first vocalizations that have the sounds of speech.

echolalia the automatic repetition of sounds or words.

intonation the use of pitches of varying levels to help communicate meaning.

receptive vocabulary the number of words one understands.

expressive vocabulary the number of words one can use in the production of language.

After infants have been babbling for a few months, parents often believe that their children are having conversations with themselves. At 10 to 12 months, infants tend to repeat syllables, showing what linguists refer to as **echolalia**. Parents overhear them going on and on, repeating consonant–vowel combinations ("ah-bah-bah-bah-bah"), pausing, and then switching to other combinations.

Toward the end of the first year, infants use patterns of rising and falling **intonation** that resemble the sounds of adult speech. It may sound as though the infant is trying to speak the parents' language.

Development of Vocabulary

Vocabulary development refers to the child's learning the meanings of words. In general, children's **receptive vocabulary** development outpaces their **expressive vocabulary** development (Lickliter, 2001; Ouellette, 2006). In other words, at any given time, they can understand more words

TABLE 5.2

Milestones in Language Development in Infancy

Approximate Age	Vocalization and Language
Birth	• Cries
12 weeks	• Cries less • Smiles when talked to and nodded at • Engages in squealing and gurgling sounds (cooing) • Sustains cooing for 15–20 seconds
16 weeks	• Responds to human sounds more definitely • Turns head, searching for the speaker • Chuckles occasionally
20 weeks	• Cooing becomes interspersed with consonant-like sounds • Vocalizations differ from the sounds of mature language
6 months	• Cooing changes to single-syllable babbling • Neither vowels nor consonants have fixed pattern of recurrence • Common utterances sound like *ma*, *mu*, *da*, or *di*
8 months	• Continuous repetition (reduplication) enters into babbling • Patterns of intonation become distinct • Utterances can signal emphasis and emotion
10 months	• Vocalizations mixed with sound play, such as gurgling and bubble blowing • Effort made to imitate sounds made by others, with mixed success
12 months	• Identical sound sequences replicated more often • Words (e.g., *mama* or *dada*) emerge • Many words and requests understood (e.g., "Show me your eyes")
18 months	• Repertoire of 3–50 words • Explosive vocabulary growth • Babbling consists of several syllables with intricate intonation • Little effort to communicate information • Little joining of words into spontaneous two-word utterances • Understanding of nearly everything spoken
24 months	• Vocabulary more than 50 words, naming everything in the environment • Spontaneous creation of two-word sentences • Clear efforts to communicate

Note: Ages are approximations. Slower development does not necessarily indicate language problems. Albert Einstein did not talk until the age of 3.

Source: Table items adapted from Lenneberg (1967, pp. 128–130).

than they can use. One study, for example, found that 12-month-olds could speak an average of 13 words but could comprehend the meaning of 84 (Tamis-LeMonda et al., 2006). Infants usually understand much of what others are saying well before they themselves utter any words. Their ability to segment speech sounds into meaningful units—or words—before 12 months is a good predictor of their vocabulary at 24 months (Newman et al., 2006).

The Child's First Words

Ah, that long-awaited first word! What a milestone! Sad to say, many parents miss it. They are not quite sure when their infants utter their first word, often because the first word is not pronounced clearly or because pronunciation varies from usage to usage.

A child's first word typically is spoken between the ages of 11 and 13 months, but a range of 8 to 18 months is considered normal (Hoff, 2006; Tamis-LeMonda et al., 2006). First words tend to be brief, consisting of one or two syllables. Each syllable is likely to consist of a consonant followed by a vowel. Vocabulary acquisition is slow at first. It may take children 3 or 4 months to achieve a vocabulary of 10 to 30 words after the first word is spoken (de Villiers & de Villiers, 1999).

By about 18 months of age, children may be producing up to 50 words. Many of them are quite familiar, such as *no*, *cookie*, *mama*, *hi*, and *eat*. Others, such as *all gone* and *bye-bye*, may not be found in the dictionary, but they function as words. That is, they are used consistently to symbolize the same meaning.

More than half (65 percent) of children's first words make up "general nominals" and "specific nominals" (Hoff, 2006; Nelson, 1973). General nominals are similar to nouns in that they include the names of classes of objects (*car*, *ball*), animals (*doggy*, *cat*), and people (*boy*, *girl*), but they also include both personal and relative pronouns (*she*, *that*). Specific nominals are proper nouns, such as *Daddy* and *Rover*. Words expressing movement are frequently found in early speech.

At about 18 to 22 months of age, children have a rapid burst in vocabulary (Tamis-LeMonda et al., 2006). The child's vocabulary may increase from 50 to more than 300 words in only a few months. This vocabulary spurt could also be called a naming explosion because almost 75 percent of the words added during this time are nouns. The rapid pace of vocabulary growth continues through the preschool years, with children acquiring an average of nine new words per day (Hoff, 2006).

Referential and Expressive Styles in Language Development

Some children prefer a referential approach in their language development, whereas others take a more expressive approach (Hoff, 2006; Nelson, 1981).

© Stephen Orsillo/Shutterstock

Infants have a rapidly expanding vocabulary that helps them identify objects in their environment.

Children who show the **referential language style** use language primarily to label objects in their environment. Children who use an **expressive language style** use language primarily as a means for engaging in social interactions. (Tamis-LeMonda et al., 2006).

Overextension

Young children try to talk about more objects than they have words for. To accomplish their linguistic feats, children often extend the meaning of one word to refer to things and actions for which they do not have words (McDonough, 2002). This process is called **overextension**. Eve Clark (1973, 1975) studied diaries of infants' language development and found that overextensions are generally based on perceived similarities in function or form between the original object or action and the new one. She provides the example of the word *mooi*, which one child originally used to designate the moon. The child then overextended *mooi* to designate all round objects, including the letter o and cookies and cakes. Overextensions gradually pull back to their proper references as the child's vocabulary and ability to classify objects develop (McDonough, 2002).

Development of Sentences

The infant's first sentences are typically one-word utterances, but they express complete ideas and therefore can be thought of as sentences. Roger Brown (1973) referred to brief expressions that have the meanings of sentences as **telegraphic speech**. Because the cost of telegrams was determined by the number of words used, the principles of syntax were used to cut out all the unnecessary words. In a telegram, the message "Home Tuesday" might have stood for "I expect to be home on Tuesday." Similarly, only the essential words are used in children's telegraphic speech—in particular, nouns, verbs, and some modifiers.

referential language style
use of language primarily as a means for labelling objects.

expressive language style
use of language primarily as a means for engaging in social interaction.

overextension
use of words in situations in which their meanings become extended.

telegraphic speech
type of speech in which only the essential words are used.

holophrase
a single word that is used to express complex meanings.

Holophrases

Holophrases are single words that are used to express complex meanings. For example, *Mama* may be used by the child to signify meanings as varied as "There goes Mama," "Come here, Mama," and "You are Mama." Most children readily teach their parents what they intend by augmenting their holophrases with gestures, intonations, and reinforcers. That is, they act delighted

© Thomas Perkins/iStockphoto.com / © catnap72/iStockphoto

Language development in young children is enhanced when caregivers engage the infant "in conversation."

sensitive period the period from about 18 months to puberty when the brain is especially capable of learning language.

previous studies. Bilingual toddlers outperform their unilingual peers on doing tasks while being distracted. The bilingual advantage provides an enhancement in attention control (Science Daily, 2011).

The Sensitive Period

Language learning is most efficient during the **sensitive period**, which begins at about 18 to 24 months and lasts until puberty (Clancy & Finlay, 2001; Uylings, 2006).

Evidence for a sensitive period is found in some people's recovery from brain injuries. Injuries to the hemisphere that controls language (usually the left hemisphere) can impair or destroy the ability to speak (Werker & Tees, 2005). But before puberty, children who have left-hemisphere injuries frequently recover a good deal of their speaking ability due to brain plasticity. In young children, left-hemisphere damage may encourage the development of language functions in the right hemisphere. But adaptation ability wanes in adolescence, when brain tissue has reached adult levels of differentiation (Snow, 2006).

EMERGING CANADA

The following home languages showing the highest growth in Canada:

Tagalog (Philippine-based language)	64% growth
Mandarin	50% growth
Arabic	50% growth
Hindi	44% growth
Creole languages	42% growth
Bengali	40% growth
Persian	33% growth
Spanish	32% growth

Across Canada, there are more than 50 individual languages that belong to 11 Aboriginal language families. Currently, only a minority of the Aboriginal population in Canada is able to speak or understand an Aboriginal language; however, 60 percent of parents in non-reserve areas believe it is very important or somewhat important for their children to speak and understand the language (Statistics Canada, 2012c).

The Genie Project

The best way to determine whether people are capable of acquiring language once they have passed puberty would be to run an experiment in which one or more children were reared in such severe isolation that they were not exposed to language until puberty. Of course, because of ethical reasons, such an experiment could not be conducted. However, human circumstance sometimes presents such an opportunity, such as the disturbing case history of Genie, which offers insights into whether children have a sensitive period for language development (Fromkin et al., 2004; LaPointe, 2005).

The PBS *Nova* documentary "Secret of the Wild Child" (Garmon, 1997) explores Genie's tragic life. Genie's father locked her in a small room at the age of 20 months and kept her confined until she was 13 years old. Her social contacts during this period were limited to her mother, who entered the room only to feed Genie, and to her father, who beat her. When Genie was rescued, she weighed only about 27 kg (60 lb.), did not speak, had not been toilet trained, and could barely stand. She was observed scientifically in the *Genie Project* and thereafter her language development followed the normal sequence of much younger children in several ways.

Five years after her liberation, however, Genie's language remained largely telegraphic. She still showed significant problems with syntax, such as failing to reverse subjects and verbs to phrase questions. Genie's language development provides support for *the sensitive-period hypothesis*, although her language problems might also be partly attributed to her years of malnutrition and abuse. Her efforts to acquire English after puberty were laborious, and the results were substandard, comparable with the language of many 2- and 3-year-olds. She never acquired the linguistic or social skills of an adult, perhaps as a result of synaptic pruning. The synapses that could have facilitated this learning may simply have disappeared through lack of use.

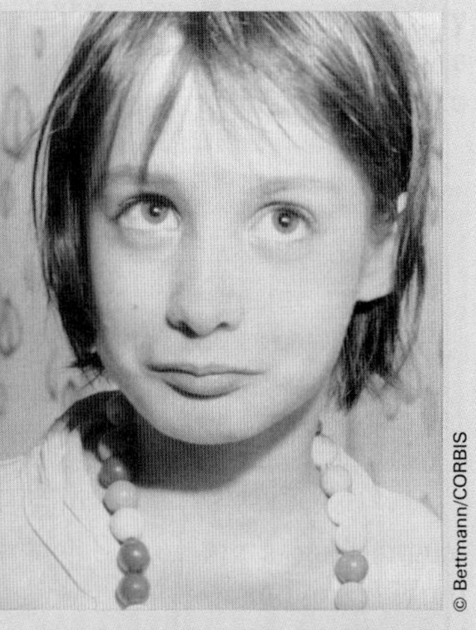
© Bettmann/CORBIS

In sum, the development of language in infancy represents the interaction of environmental and biological factors. Children bring a built-in readiness to the task of language acquisition, whereas houseplants and other organisms do not. Children must also have the opportunity to hear spoken language and to interact verbally with others. In the next chapter, we see how interaction with others affects social development.

CHAPTER 6

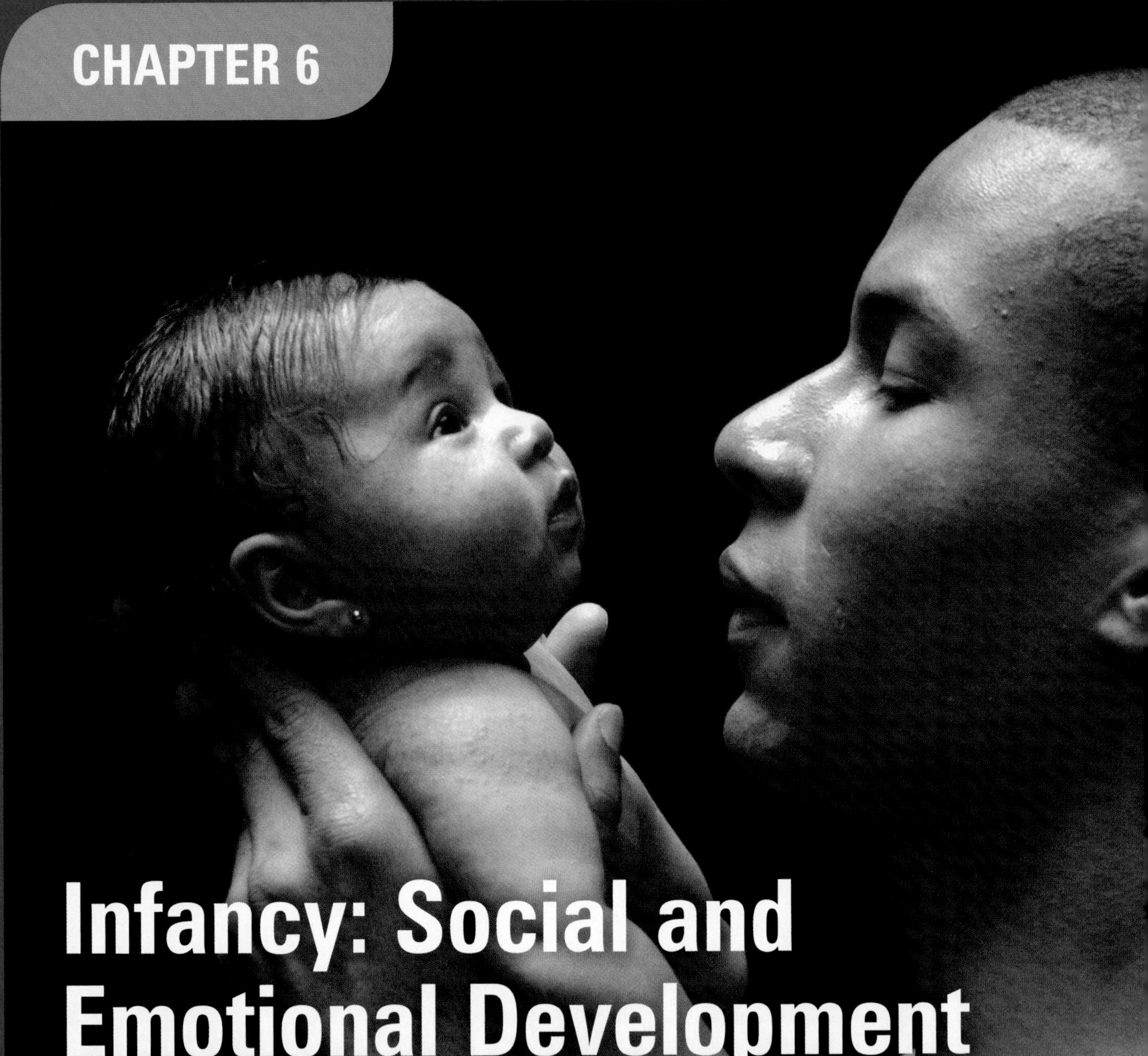

Infancy: Social and Emotional Development

LEARNING OUTCOMES

LO1 Describe the development of attachment in infancy and theoretical views of how it occurs

LO2 Discuss the effects of social deprivation, abuse and neglect, and autism spectrum disorders on attachment

LO3 Discuss the effects of day care

LO4 Describe the emotional development of the infant

LO5 Describe the personality development of the infant, focusing on the self-concept, temperament, and sex differences

> "Babies are born with behaviours—crying, smiling, clinging—that stimulate caregiving from adults."

As discussed in Chapter 1, Erikson's theory of psychosocial development focuses on age-based stages of development. Each stage has a specific developmental "crisis," or challenge. When the challenge is handled successfully, it leads to a sense of mastery that sets the groundwork for the next developmental challenge. When a stage is not successfully navigated, it may lead to a sense of inadequacy. As a result, the next life stages may not fit together as neatly as puzzle pieces. During each developmental period, the potential for personal growth is high—but so is the potential for failure. We explore Erikson's first stage of psychosocial development:

Erikson Today

Stage 1: Basic Trust versus Mistrust (birth to 18 months)

The initial task of the ego is the development of trust. The infant is not able to care for itself and is therefore completely dependent on primary caregivers for all of its needs. The development of trust is an ongoing challenge that will be faced throughout the lifespan but it has particular importance during the first stage of development. The child must develop a sense that the primary caregivers will be both reliable and predictable. The quality of care received will set the stage for all other social interactions that follow. If the caregiver is unreliable or inconsistent, a sense of mistrust is established, which may become the template for future relationships.

LO1 Attachment: Bonds That Endure

Attachment is what most people refer to as affection or love. Canadian-born Mary Ainsworth (1989) defines attachment as an enduring emotional bond between one animal or person and another. John Bowlby adds that attachment is essential to the survival of the infant (Bowlby, 1988). He notes that babies are born with behaviours—crying, smiling, clinging—that encourage care-giving from adults.

Consider THIS

Can You Spoil Your Baby?
Please see page 104 for a discussion on this topic.

attachment an affectional bond characterized by seeking closeness with another and distress upon separation.

separation anxiety fear of separation from a target of attachment.

Infants try to maintain contact with caregivers to whom they are attached. They engage in eye contact, pull and tug at them, and ask to be picked up. When they cannot maintain contact, they show **separation anxiety**—thrash about, fuss, cry, screech, or whine.

secure attachment a type of attachment characterized by mild distress at leave-takings and being readily soothed by reunion.

avoidant attachment a type of insecure attachment characterized by apparent indifference to leave-takings by and reunions with an attachment figure.

ambivalent/resistant attachment a type of insecure attachment characterized by severe distress at leave-takings by and ambivalent behaviour at reunions.

disorganized–disoriented attachment a type of insecure attachment characterized by dazed and contradictory behaviours toward an attachment figure.

Patterns of Attachment

Ainsworth and her colleagues (1978) identified various patterns of attachment. Broadly, infants show **secure attachment** or insecure attachment. Most North American children are securely attached (Belsky, 2006a; McCartney et al., 2004).

Ainsworth developed the *strange-situation method* as a way of measuring the development of attachment (see Figure 6.1). In this method, an infant is exposed to a series of separations and reunions with a caregiver (usually the mother) and a stranger who is working with the researchers. In the test, secure infants mildly protest their mother's departure, seek interaction upon reunion, and are readily comforted by her.

Insecurity, or "insecure attachment," can be divided into two types: **avoidant attachment** and **ambivalent/resistant attachment**. Infants who show avoidant attachment are the least distressed by their mothers' departure. They play without fuss when alone and ignore their mothers upon reunion. Ambivalent/resistant babies are the most emotional. They show severe signs of distress when their mothers leave and, upon reunion, show ambivalence by alternately clinging to their mothers and pushing them away. Additional categories of insecure attachment have been proposed, including **disorganized–disoriented attachment**, exhibited by babies who seem dazed, confused, or disoriented. They may show contradictory behaviours, such as moving toward the mother while looking away from her.

Not surprisingly, secure infants and toddlers are happier, more sociable, and more cooperative with caregivers. At ages 5 and 6, they get along better with peers and are better adjusted in school than insecure children (Belsky, 2006a; McCartney et al., 2004; Spieker et al., 2003). Insecure attachment at 1 year of age predicts psychological disorders by age 17 (Sroufe, 1998; Steele, 2005a).

Establishing Attachment

Attachment is related to the quality of infant care (Belsky, 2006a; Coleman, 2003). Compared with parents of insecure infants, the parents of secure infants tend to be more affectionate, cooperative, and predictable. These parents also respond more sensitively to their infants' smiles and cries (Harel & Scher, 2003).

Security is also related to the infant's temperament (Belsky, 2006a; Kerns et al., 2007). The mothers of so-called "difficult" children tend to be less responsive to them and report feeling more

FIGURE 6.1

The Strange Situation

These historic photos show a 12-month-old child in the Strange Situation. In (a), the child plays with toys, glancing occasionally at mother. In (b), the stranger approaches with a toy. While the child is distracted, mother leaves the room. In (c), mother returns after a brief absence. The child crawls to her quickly and clings to her when picked up. In (d), the child cries when mother again leaves the room.

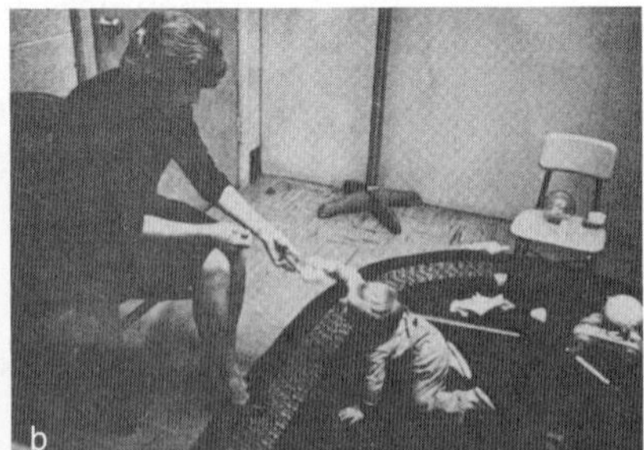

distant from them (Morrell & Steele, 2003; Stams et al., 2002).

Involvement of Fathers

How involved is the average father with his children? The brief answer, in developed nations, is more so than in the past (Grossmann et al., 2002). But mothers typically engage in more interactions with their infants. Most fathers are more likely to play with their children than to feed or clean them (Laflamme et al., 2002). Fathers, more often than mothers, engage in rough-and-tumble play, whereas mothers are more likely to play games involving toys, patty-cake, and peek-a-boo (Laflamme et al., 2002).

How strongly, then, do infants become attached to their fathers? The more affectionate the interaction between father and infant is, the stronger the attachment (R. A. Thompson et al., 2003).

Stability of Attachment

Patterns of attachment tend to persist when caregiving conditions remain constant (Ammaniti et al., 2005; Karavasilis et al., 2003). But children can also become less securely attached to caregivers when home life deteriorates (Belsky, 2006a). Children adopted at various ages can become securely attached to adoptive parents (Verissimo & Salvaterra, 2006). Early attachment patterns tend to endure into middle childhood, adolescence, and even adulthood (Ammaniti et al., 2005; Karavasilis et al., 2003).

Stages of Attachment

From studies, Ainsworth and her colleagues (1978) identified the following three phases of attachment:

1. The **initial-preattachment phase** lasts from birth to about 3 months and is characterized by indiscriminate attachment.

Ainsworth: © Robert S. Marvin; frame: © catnap72/iStockphoto

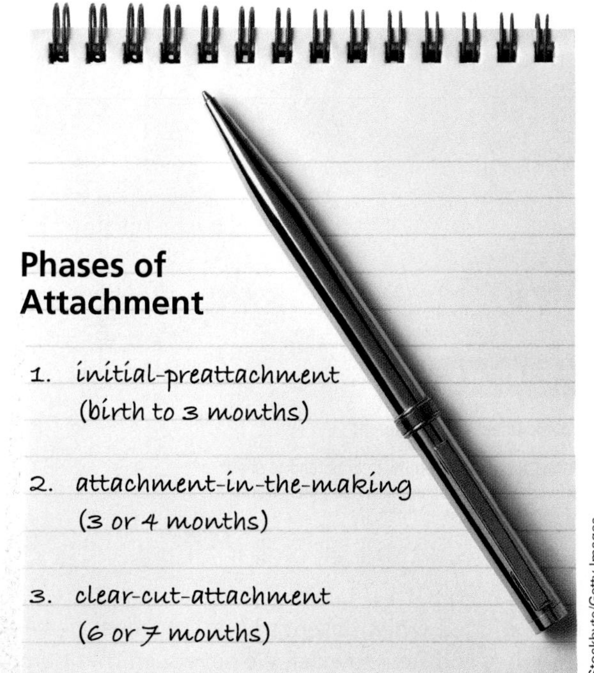

© Stockbyte/Getty Images

2. The **attachment-in-the-making phase** occurs at about 3 or 4 months and is characterized by preference for familiar figures.
3. The **clear-cut-attachment phase** occurs at about 6 or 7 months and is characterized by intensified dependence on the primary caregiver, usually the mother.

But most infants have more than one adult caregiver and are likely to form multiple attachments: to the father, day-care providers, grandparents, and other caregivers, as well as the mother. The development of attachment is shown graphically in Figure 6.2.

initial-preattachment phase the first phase in development of attachment, characterized by indiscriminate attachment.

attachment-in-the-making phase the second phase in development of attachment, characterized by preference for familiar figures.

clear-cut-attachment phase the third phase in development of attachment, characterized by intensified dependence on the primary caregiver.

Theories of Attachment

There are several theories of the development of attachment.

Cognitive View of Attachment

The cognitive view suggests that an infant must develop the concept of object permanence before specific attachment becomes possible. If caregivers are

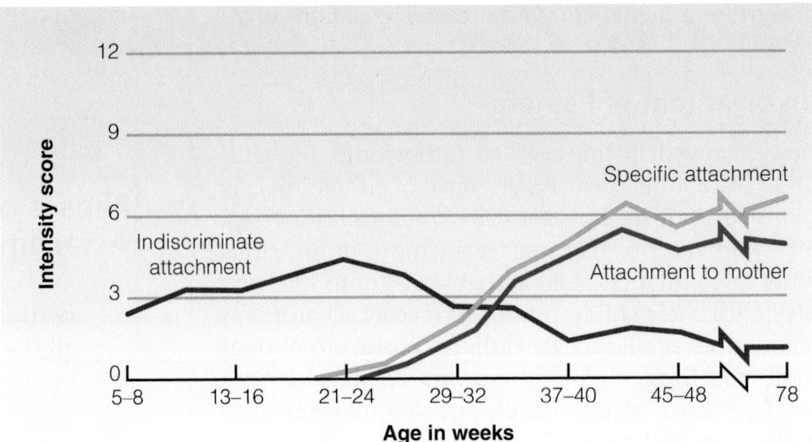

FIGURE 6.2

Development of Attachment

During the first 6 months, infants tend to show indiscriminate attachment, which then wanes as specific attachments intensify.

to be missed when absent, the infant must perceive that they continue to exist. We have seen that infants tend to develop specific attachments at about the age of 6 to 7 months. Basic object permanence concerning objects usually develops earlier (see Chapter 5).

Behavioural View of Attachment

Early in the 20th century, behaviourists argued that attachment behaviours were conditioned. Caregivers feed their infants and tend to their other physiological needs. Thus, infants associate their caregivers with gratification and learn to approach them to meet their needs. From this perspective, a caregiver becomes a conditioned reinforcer.

Psychoanalytic Views of Attachment

According to psychoanalytic theorists, the caregiver, usually the mother, becomes not just a "reinforcer" but also a love object who forms the basis for all later attachments. Sigmund Freud emphasized the importance of oral activities, such as eating, in the first year. Freud believed that the infant becomes emotionally attached to the mother during this time because she is the primary satisfier of the infant's needs for food and sucking.

Erik Erikson believed that the first year is critical for developing a sense of trust in the mother, which fosters attachment.

Caregiver as a Source of Contact Comfort

Harry and Margaret Harlow conducted classic experiments to demonstrate that feeding is not critical to the attachment process, as Freud suggested (Harlow & Harlow, 1966). In one infamous study, the Harlows placed rhesus monkey infants in cages with two surrogate mothers (see Figure 6.3). One "mother" was made from wire mesh, from which a baby bottle was extended. The other surrogate mother was made of soft, cuddly terry cloth. Infant monkeys spent most of their time clinging to the cloth mother, even

FIGURE 6.3

Contact Comfort

Although this rhesus monkey infant is fed by the "wire-mesh mother," it spends most of its time clinging to a soft, cuddly "terry-cloth mother."

© Martin Rogers/Stock, Boston

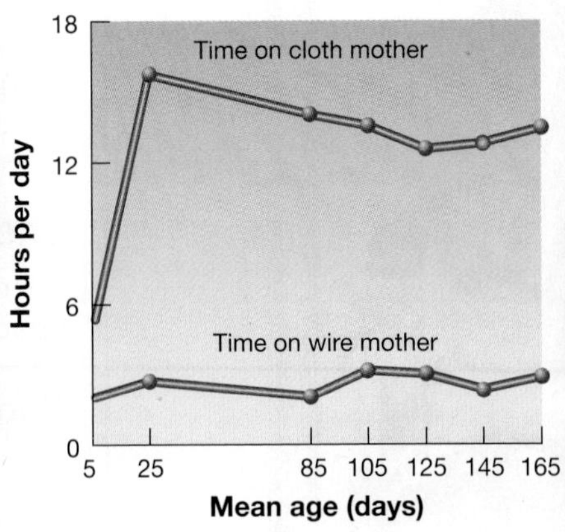

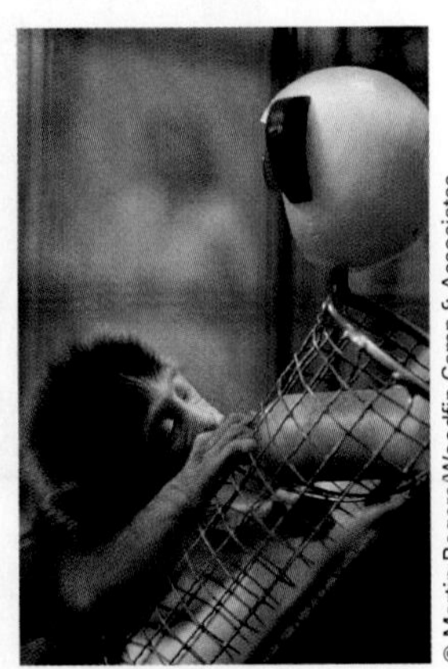
© Martin Rogers/Woodfin Camp & Associates

though she did not offer food. The Harlows concluded that monkeys—and perhaps humans—have a need for **contact comfort** that is as basic as the need for food.

Ethological View of Attachment

Ethologists note that for many animals, attachment is an inborn, or instinctive, response to a specific stimulus. Some researchers theorize that a baby's cry stimulates caregiving in women. By 2 to 3 months of age, the human face begins to elicit a **social smile** in infants, helping to ensure survival by eliciting affection (Ainsworth & Bowlby, 1991; Bowlby, 1988). In circular fashion, the mother's social response to her infant's face can reliably produce infant smiling by 8 months of age (Jones & Hong, 2005). The pattern contributes to a mutual attachment, or the *social dance*.

In many nonhumans, attachment occurs during a **critical period** of life. Waterfowl become attached during this period to the first moving object they encounter. Because the image of the moving object seems to become "imprinted" on the young animal, the process is termed **imprinting**.

Ethologist Konrad Lorenz (1962, 1981) became well known when pictures of his "family" of goslings (baby geese) were made public. Lorenz acquired his "following" by being present when the goslings hatched and allowing them to follow him. The critical period for geese and ducks begins when they first engage in locomotion and ends when they develop fear of strangers. The goslings followed Lorenz persistently, ran to him when frightened, honked with distress at his departure, and tried to overcome barriers placed between them. If you substitute crying for honking, it sounds quite human.

© Time Life Pictures/Getty Images/ © catnap72/iStockphoto

Konrad Lorenz with his "family" of goslings. This type of attachment is known as imprinting.

Ethology, Ainsworth, and Bowlby

Let us return to Ainsworth and Bowlby (1991), who wrote that "the distinguishing characteristic of the theory of attachment that we have jointly developed is that it is an ethological approach" (p. 333). They address several distinctions for humans, noting that caregiving in humans is largely learned and not inborn. Ainsworth and Bowlby also note that the critical period for attachment in humans—if one exists—extends to months or years (Ainsworth & Bowlby, 1991; Verissimo & Salvaterra, 2006). Caregiving itself promotes attachment, as does infant responsiveness, such as smiling.

contact comfort the pleasure derived from physical contact with another.

ethologists scientists who study the behaviour patterns characteristic of various species.

social smile a smile that occurs in response to a human voice or face.

critical period a period during which imprinting can occur.

imprinting the process by which waterfowl become attached to the first moving object they follow.

EMERGING CANADA

Mary (Salter) Ainsworth (1913–1999) was born in Ohio and moved to Canada when she was 5 years old. She attended the University of Toronto, where she earned her Ph.D. She was offered a teaching position at Queen's University in 1939; however, 2 weeks later, her offer of employment was withdrawn, as the Senate refused to appoint a woman. This refusal is not surprising, given the time period. Ainsworth then spent 4 years in the army. She then returned to the University of Toronto, where she met her future husband. After marriage, they moved to England. There, she was offered a position with John Bowlby, studying the effects of early separation from mothers and personality development. She used this learning to support her naturalistic observation of attachment between caregivers and children. Ainsworth proudly considered herself a feminist, though some claimed her groundbreaking work on attachment and early caregiving was used to argue that mothers should stay at home with their children in the early years. Ainsworth commented, saying that attachment in early childhood is vital; however, if she had been blessed with the children that she had wanted, she believed she could have balanced the responsibilities of motherhood with the demands of a career (Held, 2010).

Consider **THIS** *Can you spoil your baby?*

All new parents fear that they will make a mistake that will last a lifetime. Complicating the matter is that we were all raised in different families and may have grown up with varying expectations. Our early family experiences often become our parenting templates. Babies do not have language, and they use crying to communicate that they are hungry, are soggy, or simply want attention and affection.

According to Erikson, at this first stage of ego development, newborns are establishing whether their parents are reliable and predictable. But parents may be aware of looks of disapproval from expert parent observers and whispers of "You're spoiling them. They are going to rule your household." It's no wonder many new parents worry their decisions may have long-reaching developmental effects. According to attachment theory and research, early child–parent relationships lay the foundation for children's later social, emotional, and school functioning (Appleyard & Berlin, 2007).

In the 1960s, a generation of babies were raised on the advice of Dr. Spock, who stated that yes, you could spoil your baby. Current research disagrees, as babies are unable to understand cause and effect until at least 8 or 10 months of age (Faris & McCarroll, 2010). Dr. Spock was replaced by Dr. Sears (Pickert, 2012), known as the man who remade motherhood. His book, *The Attachment Parenting Book* (Sears & Sears, 2001), defined a modern relationship between mother and baby in terms of breast feeding (into toddlerhood of desired), immediately responding to a baby's cries, and co-sleeping and baby-carrying ideas. This book was criticized and contradicted by the 2011 blockbuster *Battle Hymn of the Tiger Mother* (Chua, 2011), a book about why parents should demand more of their children and not the other way around (Pickert, 2012).

Parents need to not only do their research but also be aware of cultural beliefs (those unasked-for words of parenting advice) that will influence how quickly parents respond to the demands and needs of their babies. Ultimately, parents must decide what approach work best with their understanding of the theory, their past family experiences, and their individual styles of parenting. So consider this: is it possible to spoil your baby?

Julian Schattner/Shutterstock.com

LO2 When Attachment Fails

What happens when children are reared with little or no contact with caregivers, when they are abused, or when they have disorders that prevent forms of attachment?

Social Deprivation

Studies of children reared in institutions where they receive little social stimulation from caregivers are limited because they are correlational. In other words, family factors that led to the children's placement in those institutions may also have contributed to their developmental problems. Tragic real-life examples, such as the Romanian orphans studied earlier, are thankfully few and far between. Ethical considerations prevent us from conducting experiments in which children are randomly assigned to social deprivation. Such experiments have been undertaken with rhesus monkeys, and the results are consistent with correlational studies of children.

Experiments with Monkeys

The Harlows and their colleagues conducted studies of rhesus monkeys that were "reared by" wire-mesh and terry-cloth surrogate mothers. In later studies, rhesus monkeys were reared without even this questionable "social" support—without seeing any other animal, monkey, or human (Harlow et al., 1971).

The Harlows found that rhesus infants reared in this most solitary confinement later avoided other monkeys. Instead, they cowered in the presence of others and made little attempt to fend off attacks by other monkeys. Rather, they sat in the corner, clutching themselves and rocking back and forth. The isolated females who later bore children ignored or abused them.

Can the damage from social deprivation be overcome? When monkeys deprived for 6 months or more are placed with younger, 3- to 4-month-old females for a couple of hours a day, the younger monkeys attempt to interact with their deprived elders. After a few weeks, many of the deprived monkeys begin to play with the youngsters, and many eventually expand their social contacts to older monkeys (Suomi et al., 1972). Similarly, socially withdrawn 4- and 5-year-old children make gains in their social and emotional development when provided with younger playmates (Furman et al., 1979). Although we need to be cautious when drawing connections between animal studies and the human population, the correlations are undeniable.

Child Abuse and Neglect

Child abuse and neglect provide an unfortunate view into the effects of child maltreatment. The Canadian Incidence Study (CIS) of Reported Child Abuse and Neglect is a national attempt to profile levels of child abuse in Canada. The 2008 report is the third attempt at such Canadian data collection (Public Health Agency of Canada, 2010a). However, because of the secrecy that often surrounds cases of child abuse, gathering reliable data is very difficult, if not impossible (Statistics Canada, 2013f).

Graphs provide a visual understanding of issues associated with child abuse. Statistical data is sometimes dated by the time it is collected, analyzed, and reported. Figure 6.4 reports the number of child maltreatment investigations in Canada and future maltreatment investigations. Figure 6.5 represents the types of abuse cases reported and their level of substantiation. Figure 6.6 depicts the category of the abuse collected in the data. Together these charts give us a more complete picture of the issues associated with child abuse in Canada.

Changes in rates from 1998 to 2008 may be due to changes in public awareness, changes in legislation and definitions, and/or changes in the rates of maltreatment.

Costs of Child Abuse

Consequences of child abuse and neglect vary widely, depending on the circumstances of the abuse and the resilience of the child. Several studies have shown a physical consequence of abuse reflected in the relationship between abuse and poor health. The immediate emotional effects of abuse and neglect—isolation, fear, and an inability to trust—can translate into lifelong consequences of depression, relationship difficulties, and low self-esteem. Not all survivors of abuse experience these behaviour consequences; however, those who experienced abuse are more likely to encounter delinquency, risky sexual behaviour, and substance abuse. They are also more likely to display abusive behaviour

FIGURE 6.4

Number of Child Maltreatment Investigations and Risk of Future Maltreatment Investigations in Canada in 1998, 2003, and 2008*

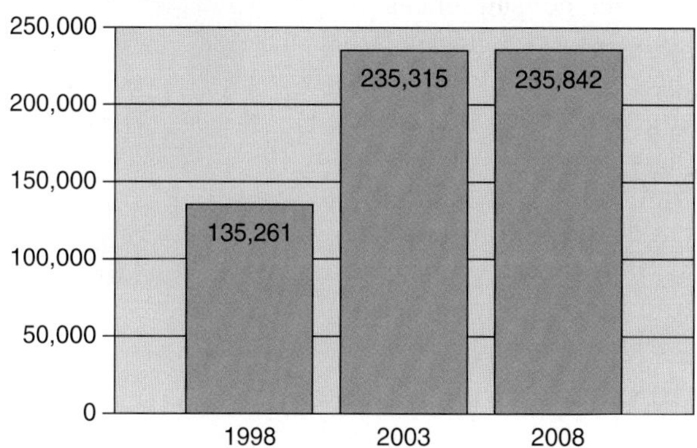

* Based on a sample of 7,633 investigations in 1998, 14,200 in 2003, and 15,980 in 2008.

Source: Canadian Incidence Study of Reported Child Abuse and Neglect: Major Findings. Public Health Agency of Canada, 2008. © Reproduced with permission from the Minister of Health, 2013.

FIGURE 6.5

Type of Child Maltreatment Investigations and Level of Substantiation in Canada in 2008*

* Total estimated number of investigations is 235,842, based on a sample of 15,980 investigations.

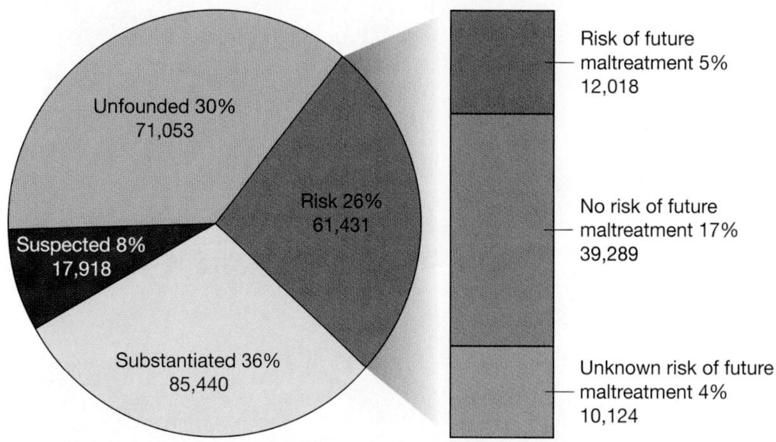

Source: Canadian Incidence Study of Reported Child Abuse and Neglect: Major Findings. Public Health Agency of Canada, 2008. © Reproduced with permission from the Minister of Health, 2013.

FIGURE 6.6

Primary Category of Substantiated Child Maltreatment in Canada in 2008*

*Total estimated number of substantiated investigations is 85,440, based on a sample of 6,163 substantiated investigations.

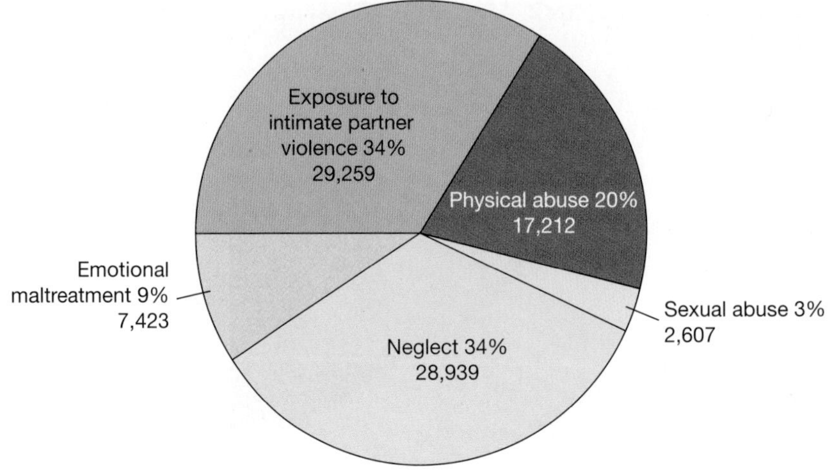

Source: Canadian Incidence Study of Reported Child Abuse and Neglect: Major Findings. Public Health Agency of Canada, 2008. ©Reproduced with permission from the Minister of Health, 2013.

autism spectrum disorders (ASDs) developmental disorders characterized by impairment in communication and social skills, and by repetitive, stereotyped behaviour.

themselves. Society pays the cost of maintaining costly welfare systems to support individuals who experience these indirect consequences of abuse and neglect. Early intervention and proactive support reduces the impact of abuse but the widespread costs of abuse are felt by the child, the family, and society as a whole (Child Welfare Information Gateway, 2013).

Scyther5/Shutterstock.com

Causes of Child Abuse

Various risk factors contribute to child abuse, including alcohol and drug abuse, health issues, inadequate social supports for the caregiver, and a history of domestic violence (Public Health Agency, 2010a).

Abused children are at a greater risk for delinquency, risky sexual behaviour, and substance abuse.

Neale Cousland/Shutterstock.com

What to Do

Numerous techniques have been developed to help prevent child abuse. One approach focuses on strengthening parenting skills among the general population, while providing information about abuse and providing support for families. Another approach focuses on groups at high risk for abuse, such as people living in poverty and single teenage mothers. In some programs, home visitors help new parents develop their care-giving and home-management skills (Duggan et al., 2004).

Autism Spectrum Disorders

Autism spectrum disorders (ASDs) are characterized by impairment in communication skills and social interaction and by repetitive, stereotyped behaviour (see Table 6.1). ASDs tend to become evident by the age of 3 and sometimes before the end of the first year. The term *spectrum* refers to a continuum of severity. Diagnoses of ASDs share common characteristics, but the conditions of ASDs cover a wide range, with many individual differences. Autism is the major type of ASD but, according to the Autism Society of Canada (2009), other forms include the following:

- *Asperger disorder* (20 in 10,000 Canadians). Characterized by social deficits and stereotyped behaviour but without the significant cognitive or language delays associated with autism.
- *Rett disorder* (1 in 10,000 female births). Characterized by a range of physical, behavioural, motor, and cognitive abnormalities that begin after a few months of normal development; found almost exclusively in females.

EMERGING CANADA

Because child welfare is a provincial and territorial responsibility, each province and territory and each Aboriginal child welfare organization has a different mandate regarding the duty to report. Our laws require that anyone who has reasonable grounds to suspect child abuse must report that situation. Reasonable grounds refer to any suspicions of abuse that an average person would identify, given that person's training, background, and experience, when exercising normal and honest judgment. This duty to report is ongoing, which means that even if a previous report has been made, additional reasonable grounds must also be reported. The reporting person must communicate directly with the appropriate provincial or territorial protection agency and cannot rely on anyone else to report on their behalf. The reporter has no responsibility to collect any information, a task that is best left to the authorities. Parents who experience difficulty in controlling their aggressive impulses toward their children are also encouraged to call for support (Ontario Association of Children's Aid Societies, 2010).

- *Childhood disintegrative disorder* (0.2 in 10,000 Canadians). Abnormal functioning and loss of previously acquired skills that begins after approximately 2 years of apparently normal development.

Autism

Autism is four to five times more common among boys than girls (Autism Society of Canada, 2009). Children with autism show limited interest in social interaction and may avoid eye contact. Attachment to others is weak or absent.

TABLE 6.1

Characteristics of Autism Spectrum Disorders (ASDs)

Key Indicators
Does not babble, point, or make meaningful gestures by 1 year of age
Does not speak one word by 16 months
Does not combine two words by 2 years
Does not respond to name
Loses language or social skills
Other Indicators
Poor eye contact
Doesn't seem to know how to play with toys
Excessively lines up toys or other objects
Is attached to one particular toy or object
Doesn't smile
At times seems to be hearing impaired

Source: Adapted from Strock (2004).

Other features of autism include communication problems, difficulty adapting to change, and ritualistic or stereotypical behaviour (Georgiades et al., 2007) (see Table 6.1). Some individuals with autism demonstrate self-harming behaviours, such as slapping their faces or biting their hands. Parents of children with autism often say they were "good babies," which usually means they made few demands. But as children with autism develop, they tend to shun traditional forms of affectionate contacts such as hugging, cuddling, and kissing.

autism a disorder characterized by extreme aloneness, communication problems, preservation of sameness, and ritualistic behaviour.

mutism refusal to speak.

echolalia automatic repetition of sounds or words.

Speech development is often delayed, with little babbling and few communicative gestures during the first year. Children with autism may show **mutism**, **echolalia**, and pronoun reversal, referring to themselves as "you" or "he." By middle childhood, approximately half of all children with autism use language, but their speech is often unusual.

The Autism Society of Canada warns that we need to distinguish between clinical descriptions and our knowledge of people who live with ASDs. Many terms are seen as labels that have limiting effects, often "medicalizing" people to the point that, despite their unique skills, abilities, and values, they become forgotten by communities or eclipsed by their "disorder." When referring to children with autism, take care to use person-first language. That is, use "children with autism" in place of the dated reference to "the autistic child," where the word *autism* defines the child.

Causes of Autism

Research evidence shows no correlation between the development of autism and deficiencies in child rearing (Mackic-Magyar & McCracken, 2004). Various lines of evidence suggest biological factors play a key role in autism. For example, very low birth weight and advanced maternal age may heighten the risk of autism (Maimburg & Vaeth, 2006). A role for genetic mechanisms is suggested by kinship studies (Constantino et al., 2006; Gutknecht, 2001). The concordance (agreement) rates for autism are about 60 percent among pairs of identical (MZ) twins, who fully share the same genes, compared with about 10 percent for pairs of fraternal (DZ) twins, whose genetic codes overlap by half (Plomin et al., 1994).

Biological factors focus on neurological involvement. Many children with autism have abnormal brain wave patterns or seizures (Canitano, 2007; Roulet-Perez & Deonna, 2006). Other researchers

© Robin Nelson/Photo Edit

Autism is a spectrum disorder. Many individuals with autism are able to thrive in a supportive environment.

have found that the brains of children with autism have abnormal sensitivities to neurotransmitters such as serotonin, dopamine, acetylcholine, and norepinephrine (Bauman et al., 2006). Other researchers note unusual activity in the motor region of the cerebral cortex (Mueller et al., 2001) and less activity in some other areas of the brain (Lam et al., 2006; Penn, 2006).

Individuals with autism should be valued for their differences and not viewed as persons who should be changed.

Treatment of Autism

Treatment for autism is mainly based on principles of learning, although investigation of biological approaches is also under way (Strock, 2004).

Because children with autism show behavioural deficits, behaviour modification is used to help them develop new behaviours. Although children with autism often experience difficulty relating to people, many can be taught to accept people or animals as reinforcers, rather than objects, by pairing praise with food treats (Drasgow et al., 2001). Praise can then be used to encourage speech and social play.

The most effective treatment programs focus on individualized instruction (Rapin, 1997). In a classic study conducted by Lovaas and colleagues (1989), children with autism received more than 40 hours of one-to-one behaviour modification a week for at least 2 years. Significant intellectual and educational gains were reported for 9 of the 19 children (47 percent) in the program. Less intensive educational programs have yielded some positive results with toddlers who have autism (Stahmer et al., 2004).

Researchers are studying biological approaches for the treatment of autism. For example, drugs that enhance serotonin activity (selective serotonin reuptake inhibitors, or SSRIs) can help prevent self-injury, aggressive outbursts, depression, anxiety, and repetitive behaviour (Kwok, 2003). Drugs that are usually used to treat schizophrenia—so-called "major tranquilizers"—are helpful with stereotyped behaviour, hyperactivity, and self-injury, but not with cognitive and language problems (Kwok, 2003; McClellan & Werry, 2003).

Autistic behaviour generally continues into adulthood to one degree or another. Many individuals with autism go on to be productive, happy, and successful individuals.

Recent research on autism has introduced animal intervention as a treatment technique for working with children with autism spectrum disorder. Marguerite E. O'Haire and colleagues compared the social interactions of 5- to 13-year-old children with ASD after they had played with two guinea pigs as opposed to toys. They found that in the presence of animals, the children presented more social behaviours, such as talking, face gazing, and making physical contact. They were also more open to social advances from peers in the presence of animals than when they were playing with toys. The presence of the animals increased the frequency of smiling and laughing and reduced negative social behaviours such as frowning, whining, and crying (Science Daily, 2013).

DID YOU KNOW?

Children with autism spectrum disorder often grow up to be independent, productive, happy, and successful professionals.

We must resist the stereotypes and consider the individual.

LO3 Day Care

Have you seen the bumper sticker that suggests we should choose our children's day care wisely because our children will one day choose our retirement home? Most parents, including mothers with infants, are in the workforce (Carey, 2007a). About 54 percent of Canadian children aged 6 months to 5 years attend some type of nonparental child care (Bushnik, 2006).

Many parents wonder whether day care will affect their children's attachment to them. The issue is not whether their children should attend day care, but the quality of their children's day care (Johnson, 2008). Day cares should do more than provide routine care; they should be warm and nurturing environments. Whenever possible, the child's diaper should be changed by the same person. Meals should be eaten together, and the care provider should be emotionally available for activities with the children. Attachment with a care provider does not replace the love of a parent. The parent and the caregiver should work together. The child's development benefits from having numerous opportunities to form a secure attachment. Despite parents' concerns, research finds that, for the most part, infants who attend full-time day care are as securely attached as infants raised at home (Timmerman, 2006).

Some studies report that infants with day-care experience are more peer-oriented and play at higher developmental levels than do home-reared infants. Children in high-quality day care are more likely to share their toys. They also tend to be more independent, self-confident, outgoing, affectionate, and more helpful and cooperative with peers and adults (Lamb & Ahnert, 2006; Pierce & Vandell, 2006). Participation in day care is also linked to better academic performance in elementary school (Belsky, 2006b).

A study funded by the National Institute on Child Health and Human Development (NICHD) agrees that high-quality day care can result in scores on tests of cognitive skills that rival or exceed those of the children reared in the home by their mothers (Belsky et al., 2007). The quality of the day care was defined in terms of the richness of the learning environment (availability of toys, books, and other materials), the ratio of caregivers to children (high-quality meant more caregivers), the amount of individual attention received by the child, and the extent to which caregivers talked to the children and asked them questions.

About 54 percent of Canadian children aged 6 months to 5 years attend some type of nonparental child care.

© PhotoObjects.net/Jupiterimages

However, the researchers also found that children placed in day care may be less cooperative and more aggressive toward peers and adults than children who are reared in the home.

DID YOU KNOW?

Children placed in day care are more aggressive than children who are cared for in the home.

True, but children in day care are not abnormally aggressive; compared with home-raised children, they are reportedly more peer-oriented and more likely to play at higher developmental levels.

Teacher ratings found that children who had attended day care were significantly more likely than children cared for in the home to interrupt in class and to tease or bully other children (Belsky et al., 2007). The degree of disturbance generally remained "within normal limits." *The quality of the day-care centre made no difference.* Children from high-quality day-care centres were also more likely to be disruptive than children cared for in the home. Moreover, the behavioural difference persisted through Grade 6.

EMERGING CANADA

Canada is experiencing a repeat baby boom, referred to as an echo boom (an echo of the earlier baby boom that followed World War II). The population of children 4 years of age and younger increased 11.0 percent between 2005 and 2011, the highest birthrate since the baby boom of 1956–61 (Statistics Canada, 2012b). Statistics Canada informs us that in 2002–03, 54 percent of Canadian children aged 6 months to 5 years attended some type of nonparental child care, up 42 percent in just eight years (CBC News, 2009b). In addition, half of all Canadian mothers that gave birth were older than age 30. Women are waiting longer to start their families, as they establish themselves in their careers (Human Resources and Skills Development Canada, 2013a). The need to be proactive in demanding high-quality day care is more important than ever.

LO4 Emotional Development

An emotion is a state of feeling that has physiological, situational, and cognitive components. Physiologically, when emotions are strong, our hearts may beat more rapidly and our muscles may tense. Situationally, we may feel anger when frustrated, or pleasure or relief when we being held by a loved one.

social referencing using another person's reaction to a situation to form one's own response.

Cognitively, anger may be triggered by the idea that someone is purposefully withholding something we need.

It is unclear how many emotions babies have, and they cannot tell us what they are feeling. We can only observe how they behave, including changes in their facial expressions (Oster, 2005). Facial expressions appear to be universal in that they are recognized in different cultures around the world, so they are considered a reliable index of emotion.

© Ryan Gerber

Researchers have long debated whether newborns are born with specific emotions (Soussignan & Schaal, 2005). They have asked whether the newborn baby's crying is nothing more than a reflex in response to discomfort. It seems clear enough that as infants develop through the first year, their cognitive appraisal of events, including their interaction with their caregivers, becomes a key part of their emotional life and their emotional expression (Camras et al., 2007; Soussignan & Schaal, 2005).

Infants' initial emotional expressions appear to comprise two basic states of emotional arousal: a positive attraction to pleasant stimulation and withdrawal from aversive stimulation.

Infants' initial emotional expressions appear to comprise two basic states of emotional arousal: a positive attraction to pleasant stimulation, such as the caregiver's voice or being held, and withdrawal from aversive stimulation, such as a sudden loud noise. By the age of 2 to 3 months, social smiling has replaced reflexive smiling. Social smiling is usually highly endearing to caregivers. At 3 to 5 months, infants laugh at active stimuli, such as repetitively touching their bellies or playing "Ah, boop!"

In sum, researchers agree that infants show only a few emotions during the first few months. They agree that emotional development is linked to cognitive development and social experience. They do not necessarily agree, however, on exactly when specific emotions are first shown or whether discrete emotions are present at birth (Camras et al., 2007).

Fear of Strangers

We live in an increasingly transient world where many adult children find themselves living across the country, or at least in a different province, from their parents. It is a proud moment to introduce your child to your parents for the first time. The new grandparents expectantly shower their grandchild with joy and affection, only to be met by screams that rival any carefully scripted horror movie. What have they done wrong? They simply existed within sight of their grandchild, who is going through the cognitive stage of stranger anxiety.

Fear of strangers—also called *stranger anxiety*—is normal. Most infants develop it. Stranger anxiety appears at about 6 to 9 months of age. By 4 or 5 months of age, infants may compare the face of a stranger with their mother's face, looking back and forth. Older infants show distress by crying, whimpering, gazing fearfully, and crawling away. Fear of strangers often peaks at 9–12 months, just in time for that first picture with Santa Claus, and declines in the second year.

DID YOU KNOW?

Fear of strangers is normal among infants.

Most infants develop some form of stranger anxiety around 6 to 9 months of age. This behaviour is not an indicator of an insecure attachment.

Children who have a fear of strangers show less anxiety when their mothers are present (Thompson & Limber, 1990). Children also are less fearful when they are in familiar surroundings, such as their homes, rather than in new and unfamiliar environments (Sroufe et al., 1974).

© Olga Sweet/Shutterstock.com

Social Referencing: What Should I Do Now?

Social referencing is the seeking out of another person's perception of a situation to help us form our own view of it (Hertenstein & Campos, 2004). Leslie Carver and Brenda Vaccaro (2007)

Eric Isselee/Shutterstock.com

A parent may need to suppress a personal fear of spiders and play with one to keep a child free from the same fear.

suggest that social referencing requires three components: (1) looking at another, usually older individual in a novel, ambiguous situation; (2) associating that individual's emotional response with the unfamiliar situation; and (3) regulating one's own emotional response in accord with the response of the older individual.

Infants also display social referencing, as early as 6 months of age. They use caregivers' facial expressions or tone of voice as clues on how to respond (Hertenstein & Campos, 2004). In one study, 8-month-old infants were friendlier to a stranger when their mothers exhibited a friendly facial expression in the stranger's presence than when she looked worried (Boccia & Campos, 1989). Parents quickly learn that smiling when their child has a gentle fall will help to diffuse the situation. A parent may need to suppress a personal fear of spiders and play with one to keep a child free from that same fear.

Emotional Regulation

Emotional regulation refers to the ways in which young children control their own emotions. Even infants display certain behaviours to control unpleasant emotional states. For example, an infant may look away from a disturbing event or suck its thumb (Rothbart & Sheese, 2007). Caregivers help infants learn to regulate their emotions. A two-way communication system develops, in which the infant signals the caregiver that help is needed and the caregiver responds. Claire Kopp (1989, p. 347) provides an example of such a system:

> A 13-month-old, playing with a large plastic bottle, attempted to unscrew the cover, but could not. Fretting for a short time, she initiated eye contact with her mother and held out the jar. As her mother took it to unscrew the cover, the infant ceased fretting.

Research evidence suggests that the children of secure mothers are not only likely to be securely attached themselves but also are likely to regulate their own emotions in a positive manner (Grolnick et al., 2006; Thompson & Meyer, 2007). A German longitudinal study (Zimmermann et al., 2001) related emotional regulation in adolescence with patterns of attachment during infancy, as assessed using the strange-situation method. Forty-one adolescents, aged 16 and 17, were placed in complex problem-solving situations with friends. Those adolescents who were secure as infants were more capable of regulating their emotions to interact cooperatively with their friends.

emotional regulation techniques for controlling one's emotional states.

LO5 Personality Development

In this section, we look at the emergence of the self-concept. We then turn to a discussion of temperament. Finally, we consider sex differences in behaviour.

The Self-Concept

At birth, we may find the world to be a confusing blur of sights, sounds, and inner sensations—yet the "we" may be missing, at least for a while. When we first see our hands, we do not yet realize that the hands belong to us and that we are separate and distinct from the world outside.

The self-concept appears to emerge gradually during infancy. At some point, infants understand that the hands they are moving in and out of sight are their hands. At some point, they understand that their own bodies extend only so far and then external objects and the bodies of others begin.

Development of the Self-Concept

Psychologists have devised ingenious methods to assess the development of the self-concept among infants. One of these methods uses the mirror technique, which involves a mirror and a dot of lipstick. Before the experiment begins, the researcher observes the infant for baseline data on how frequently the infant touches his or her nose. The mother then applies a red lipstick dot on the infant's nose and places the infant in front of a mirror. While looking in the mirror, infants do not touch their own nose until about the age of 18 months (Campbell et al., 2000; Keller et al., 2005).

Nose touching suggests that children recognize themselves and that they perceive the red dot to be an abnormality. Most 2-year-olds can point to pictures of themselves, and they begin to use "I" or their

separation–individuation the process of becoming separate from and independent of the mother.

temperament individual difference in style of reaction that is present early in life.

own name spontaneously (Smiley & Johnson, 2006).

Self-awareness affects the infant's social and emotional development (Foley, 2006). Knowledge of the self permits the infant and child to develop notions of sharing and cooperation. In one study, 2-year-olds with a better developed sense of self were more likely to cooperate with other children (Brownell & Carriger, 1990).

Self-awareness also facilitates the development of self-conscious emotions such as embarrassment, envy, empathy, pride, guilt, and shame (Foley, 2006). In one study, Deborah Stipek and her colleagues (1992) found that children older than 21 months often seek their mother's attention and approval when they have successfully completed a task, whereas younger toddlers do not.

Psychoanalytic Views of the Self-Concept

Margaret Mahler, a psychoanalyst, has proposed that development of self-concept comes about through a process of **separation–individuation**, which lasts from about 5 months until 3 years of age (Mahler et al., 1975). Separation involves the child's growing perception that her mother is a separate person. Individuation refers to the child's increasing sense of independence and autonomy.

One of the ways toddlers demonstrate growing autonomy, much to the dismay of caregivers, is by refusing to comply with caregivers' requests. "No!" becomes a universal reply to many parental interactions. Studies of toddlers and preschoolers between the ages of 11/2 and 5 years have found that as children grow older, they adopt more skillful ways of expressing resistance to caregivers' requests (Smith et al., 2004; Stifter & Wiggins, 2004). For example, young toddlers are more likely to ignore a caregiver's request or defy it. Older toddlers and preschoolers are more likely to make excuses or negotiate.

Temperament: Easy, Difficult, or Slow to Warm Up?

Each child has a characteristic **temperament**, a stable way of reacting and adapting to the world that is present early in life (Wachs, 2006). Many researchers believe that temperament involves a strong genetic component (Goldsmith et al., 2003; Wachs, 2006). The child's temperament includes many aspects of behaviour, including activity level, smiling and laughter, regularity in eating and sleep habits, approach or withdrawal, adaptability to new situations, intensity of responsiveness, general cheerfulness or unpleasantness, distractibility or persistence, and soothability (Gartstein et al., 2003; Thomas & Chess, 1989).

Myron Pronyshyn/Shutterstock.com

At about 18 months, children recognize themselves in the mirror and see the red dot as an abnormality.

Types of Temperament

Thomas and Chess (1989) found that from the first days of life, many of the children in their study (65 percent) could be classified into one of three types of temperament: "easy" (40 percent of their sample), "difficult" (10 percent), and "slow to warm up" (15 percent). Some of the differences among these three types of children are shown in Table 6.2. The easy child is generally cheerful, has regular sleep and feeding schedules, approaches new situations (such as a new food or a new school) enthusiastically, and adapts easily to change. Some children, though, are more inconsistent and show a mixture of temperament traits.

The difficult child, for example, has irregular sleep and feeding schedules, is slow to accept new people and situations, takes a long time to adjust to new routines, and responds to frustrations with tantrums and crying. The slow-to-warm-up child falls between the other two.

Stability of Temperament

Although not all children are born with the same temperament, as Thomas and Chess found, at least moderate consistency is shown in the development of temperament from infancy onward (Wachs, 2006). The infant who is highly active and cries in novel situations often becomes a fearful toddler. Difficult children are, in general, at greater risk for developing psychological disorders and adjustment problems later in life (Pauli-Pott et al., 2003; Rothbart

TABLE 6.2

Types of Temperament

Temperament Category	Easy	Difficult	Slow to warm up
Regularity of biological functioning	Regular	Irregular	Somewhat irregular
Response to new stimuli	Positive approach	Negative withdrawal	Negative withdrawal
Adaptability to new situations	Adapts readily	Adapts slowly or not at all	Adapts slowly
Intensity of reaction	Mild or moderate	Intense	Mild
Quality of mood	Positive	Negative	Initially negative; gradually more positive

Sources: Chess & Thomas (1991) and Thomas & Chess (1989).

goodness of fit agreement between the parents' expectations of a child and the child's temperament.

et al., 2004). A longitudinal study tracked the progress of infants with a difficult temperament from 11/2 through 12 years of age (Guerin et al., 1997). A difficult temperament correlated both with parental reports of behavioural problems from ages 3 to 12 and with teachers' reports of problems with attention span and aggression.

DID YOU KNOW?

Children are born with varying temperaments that are believed to have a significant genetic component.

Though not all children are born with the same temperament, at least moderate consistency is shown in the development of temperament from infancy onward.

Goodness of Fit: The Role of the Environment

Our daughter was a difficult infant, but we weathered the storm. Then, at the age of 15, she climbed out the second-storey bedroom window at 2 a.m. to be with friends. When we caught her, she sarcastically asked if we disapproved. "Yes," we said. "Use the front door; you're less likely to get hurt." She graduated college with honours. She has occasional outbursts, but that's her boyfriend's problem. And they love her on the job. She's a hard worker and the most creative thing they've ever seen.

The environment also affects the development of temperament. An initial biological predisposition to a certain temperament may be strengthened or weakened by the parents' reaction to the child. Parents may react to a difficult child by imposing rigid care-giving schedules, which in turn can cause the child to become even more difficult (Schoppe-Sullivan et al., 2007). This example illustrates a poor fit between the child's behaviour style and the parents' response.

On the other hand, parents may modify a child's initial temperament in a more positive direction to achieve a **goodness of fit** between child and parent. Realization that their youngster's behaviour does not mean that the child is weak or deliberately disobedient, or that they are bad parents, helps parents modify their attitudes and behaviour toward the child, whose behaviour may then improve (Bird et al., 2006; Schoppe-Sullivan et al., 2007).

Sex Differences

All cultures distinguish between females and males and have expectations about how they ought to behave. For this reason, a child's sex is a key factor in society's efforts to shape its personality and behaviour.

Behaviour of Infant Girls and Boys

In infancy, girls tend to advance more rapidly than boys in their motor development: They sit, crawl, and walk earlier than boys (Matlin, 2008). Although a few studies have found that infant boys are more active and irritable than girls, others have not (Matlin, 2008).

© Radius Images/Jupiterimages

iStockphoto/Thinkstock.com

Girls and boys are similar in their social behaviours. They are equally likely to smile at people's faces, for example, and they do not differ in their dependency on adults (Maccoby & Jacklin, 1974). Girls and boys do begin to differ early in their preference for certain toys and play activities. By 12 to 18 months of age, girls tend to play with dolls, doll furniture, dishes, and toy animals; boys more commonly play with transportation toys (trucks, cars, airplanes, and the like), tools, and sports equipment as early as 9 to 18 month of age (Campbell et al., 2000; Serbin et al., 2001). Sex differences that show up later, such as differences in spatial relations skills, are not necessarily evident in infancy (Örnkloo & von Hofsten, 2007). By 24 months, both girls and boys appear to be aware of which behaviours are considered appropriate or inappropriate for their sex, according to cultural stereotypes (Hill & Flom, 2007). Thus, girls and boys appear to play more often with gender stereotypical toys before they have been socialized and possibly before they understand their own sex.

Parents tend to provide baby girls and boys with different bedroom decorations and toys, sometimes before they are even born.

Adults' Behaviour toward Infants

Adults interact differently with girls and boys. Researchers have presented adults with an unfamiliar infant who is dressed in boy's clothes and has a boy's name or an infant who is dressed in girl's clothing and has a girl's name. (In reality, it is the same baby who simply is given different names and clothing.) When adults believe they are playing with a girl, they are more likely to offer "her" a doll; when they think the child is a boy, they are more likely to offer a football or a hammer. "Boys" also are encouraged to engage in more physical activity than "girls" (Worell & Goodheart, 2006).

Parents, especially fathers, are more likely to encourage rough-and-tumble play in sons than daughters (Eccles et al., 2000; Fagot et al., 2000). On the other hand, parents talk more to infant daughters than to infant sons. They smile more at daughters and are more emotionally expressive toward them (Powlishta et al., 2001).

Infant girls are likely to be decked out in a pink or yellow dress and embellished with ruffles and lace, whereas infant boys wear blue or red (Eccles et al., 2000; Powlishta et al., 2001). Parents tend to provide baby girls and boys with different bedroom decorations and toys, sometimes even before they are born. Examination of the contents of rooms of children from 5 months to 6 years of age found that boys' rooms were often decorated with animal themes and with blue bedding and curtains. Girls' rooms featured flowers, lace, ruffles, and pastels. Girls owned more dolls; boys had more vehicles, military toys, and sports equipment.

pearleye/iStockphoto

Parents react favourably when their infant daughters play with "girls' toys" and their sons play with "boys' toys." In spite of best efforts not to stereotype their children, adults, especially fathers, show more negative reactions when girls play with boys' toys and boys play with girls' toys (Martin et al., 2002; Worell & Goodheart, 2006). Parents thus try to shape their children's behaviour during infancy and lay the foundation for development in early childhood.

Infant–Father Interaction as a Predictor of Later Infant Behaviour

Recently, research has increasingly focused on the earliest years of life. Relatively few studies have focused on father–infant interactions despite the

Dragon Images/Shutterstock.com

importance of this relationship on child behavioural development. A recent study conducted by Ramchandani et al. (2013) studied whether father–infant interactions at age 3 months independently predicted child behavioural problems at 1 year of age. Fathers and their children were observed in their own homes in two different play scenarios. Fathers were asked to play with their child in each setting without toys or other object for 3 minutes. When fathers were disengaged and remote (lost in their thoughts or simply "going through the motions"), their negative interaction reliably predicted early behavioural problems. Interestingly, boys seemed more sensitive to this pattern of association. This study reinforces the importance of the father–infant relationship and promotes an opportunity for preventative intervention (Ramchandani et al., 2013).

Go online at
www.nelson.com/4ltrpress/icanhdev2ce
And access the essential Study Tools online for this chapter:

- **Practice Quizzes**, which will help you to prepare for tests
- **Games**, to help test your knowledge
- **Flashcards**, to test your understanding of key terms
- **Observing Development Videos**
- **Internet Activities**

PART THREE

CHAPTER 7

Early Childhood: Physical and Cognitive Development

LEARNING OUTCOMES

LO1 Describe trends in physical development in early childhood

LO2 Describe motor development in early childhood

LO3 Describe nutritional needs in early childhood

LO4 Describe trends in health and illness in early childhood

LO5 Describe sleep patterns in early childhood

LO6 Discuss elimination disorders

LO7 Describe Piaget's preoperational stage

LO8 Discuss influences on cognitive development in early childhood

LO9 Explain how "theory of mind" affects cognitive development

LO10 Describe memory development in early childhood

LO11 Describe language development in early childhood

Rebekah Littlejohn Photography www.littlejohnphotography.com

> "During the preschool years, physical and motor development proceeds, literally, by leaps and bounds."

The years from 2 to 6 are referred to as early childhood, or the preschool years, even though many Canadian children can begin junior kindergarten as early as 3 years 8 months of age. During early childhood, physical growth is slower than in infancy. Children become taller and leaner, and, by the end of early childhood, they look more like adults than infants. As their motor skills develop, children become stronger, faster, and better coordinated.

Language improves enormously, and children begin to carry on conversations with others. As cognitive skills develop, a new world emerges of make-believe, or "pretend" play. Most preschoolers are curious and eager to learn. Increased physical and cognitive capabilities enable children to emerge from total dependence on caregivers to become part of the broader world outside the family.

LO1 Growth Patterns

During the preschool years, physical and motor development proceeds, literally, by leaps and bounds.

Height and Weight

After the dramatic gains in height in a child's first 2 years, the growth rate slows during the preschool years (Kuczmarski et al., 2002). Girls and boys tend to gain about 5 to 8 cm (2 to 3 in.) in height per year, and weight gains remain fairly even at about 2 to 3 kg (4 to 6 lb.) per year. Children become increasingly slender as they gain in height and shed some "baby fat." Boys as a group become slightly taller and heavier than girls. Noticeable variations in growth occur from child to child.

Development of the Brain

The brain develops more quickly than any other organ in early childhood and needs to be supported by proper nutrition. At 2 years of age, the brain already has attained 75 percent of its adult weight. By the age of 5, the brain has reached 90 percent of its adult weight, even though the body weight of the 5-year-old is barely one-third of what it will be as an adult (Tanner, 1989).

The increase in brain size is due in part to the continuing myelination of nerve fibres. Completion of myelination of the neural pathways that link the cerebellum to the cerebral cortex facilitates development of fine motor skills, balance, and coordination (Nelson & Luciana, 2001; Paus et al., 1999).

Brain Development and Visual Skills

Brain development also improves the processing of visual information (Yamada et al., 2000), which facilitates learning to read. The parts of the brain that enable the child to sustain attention and screen out distractions (reticular formation) become

corpus callosum the thick bundle of nerve fibres that connects the left and right hemispheres of the brain.

plasticity the tendency of new parts of the brain to take up the functions of injured parts.

gross motor skills skills employing the large muscles used in locomotion.

increasingly myelinated between the ages of about 4 and 7 (Nelson & Luciana, 2001), enabling most children to focus on schoolwork. The speed of processing visual information improves throughout childhood, reaching adult levels at the onset of adolescence (Chou et al., 2006; Paus et al., 1999).

Right Brain, Left Brain?

We often hear people described as being "right-brained" or "left-brained." The notion is that the hemispheres of the brain are involved in different kinds of intellectual and emotional activities. Research does suggest that in right-handed individuals, the left hemisphere is relatively more involved in intellectual undertakings that require logical analysis, problem-solving language, and computation (Grindrod & Baum, 2005; O'Shea & Corballis, 2005). In contrast, the right hemisphere is usually superior in visual–spatial functions (such as piecing puzzles together), aesthetic and emotional responses, and understanding metaphors.

But it is not true that some children are left-brained and others are right-brained. The functions of the left and right hemispheres overlap, and the hemispheres respond simultaneously when we focus on one thing or another. They are aided in "cooperation" by the myelination of the **corpus callosum**, a thick bundle of nerve fibres that connects the hemispheres (Kinsbourne, 2003). This process is largely complete by the age of 8, enabling the integration of logical and emotional functioning.

Plasticity of the Brain

Many parts of the brain have specialized functions, allowing our behaviour to be more complex. But it also means that injuries to certain parts of the brain can result in loss of these functions. However, the brain also shows **plasticity**, or the ability to compensate for injuries to particular areas. Plasticity is greatest at about 1 to 2 years of age and then gradually declines (Kolb & Gibb, 2007; Nelson et al., 2006). When we, as adults, experience damage to the areas of the brain that control language, we may lose the ability to speak or understand language. However, when the same damage occurs in a preschooler, other areas of the brain may assume these functions. As a result, preschoolers with brain damage may regain the ability to speak or comprehend language (Nelson et al., 2006). Neurological factors that enable plasticity include the growth of new dendrites ("sprouting") and the redundancy of neural connections (Nelson et al., 2006; Szaflarski et al., 2006).

LO2 Motor Development

The preschool years witness an explosion of motor skills, as children's nervous systems mature and their movements become more precise and coordinated.

Gross Motor Skills

Gross motor skills involve the large muscles used in locomotion (see Table 7.1). At about the age of 3, children can balance on one foot. By age 3 or 4, they can walk up stairs as adults do, by placing one foot on each step. By age 4 or 5, they can skip and pedal a tricycle (McDevitt & Ormrod, 2002). Older preschoolers are better able to coordinate two tasks at the same time, such as singing and running. In general, preschoolers appear to acquire motor skills by teaching themselves and observing other children. At this age, imitating other children seems more important than adult instruction.

Throughout early childhood, girls and boys are similar in motor skills. Girls are generally better at balance and precision. Boys show some advantage in throwing and kicking (McDevitt & Ormrod, 2002).

Throughout early and middle childhood, individual differences are larger than sex differences. Some children are genetically predisposed to developing better coordination or more strength. Motivation and practice also are important.

TABLE 7.1

Development of Gross Motor Skills in Early Childhood

2 Years (24–35 Months)	3 Years (36–47 Months)	4 Years (48–59 Months)	5 Years (60–71 Months)
• Runs well straight ahead • Walks up stairs, two feet to a step • Kicks a large ball • Jumps a distance of 10 to 35 cm (4 to 14 in.) • Throws a small ball without falling • Pushes and pulls large toys • Hops on one foot, for two or more hops • Tries to stand on one foot • Climbs on furniture to look out of window	• Goes around obstacles while running • Walks up stairs, one foot to a step • Kicks a large ball easily • Jumps from the bottom step • Catches a bounced ball, using torso and arms to form a basket • Goes around obstacles while pushing and pulling toys • Hops on one foot, for up to three hops • Stands on one foot • Climbs on playground equipment	• Turns sharp corners while running • Walks down stairs, one foot to a step • Jumps from a height of 30 cm (12 in.) • Throws a ball overhand • Turns sharp corners while pushing and pulling toys • Hops on one foot, for four to six hops • Stands on one foot for 3 to 8 seconds • Climbs ladders • Skips on one foot • Rides a tricycle well	• Runs lightly on toes • Jumps a distance of 1 metre (3 ft.) • Catches a small ball, using hands only • Hops on one foot for 2 to 3 m (2 to 3 yd.) • Stands on one foot for 8 to 10 seconds • Climbs actively and skillfully • Skips on alternate feet • Rides a bicycle with training wheels

Note: The ages are averages; there are individual variations.

Physical Activity

Preschoolers spend an average of more than 25 hours a week in large-muscle activity (D. W. Campbell et al., 2002). Younger preschoolers are more likely than older preschoolers to engage in physically oriented play, such as grasping, banging, and mouthing objects (D. W. Campbell et al., 2002).

Rough-and-tumble play, which is not the same as aggressive behaviour, helps develop physical and social skills.

Motor activity level begins to decline after 2 or 3 years of age. Children become less restless and are able to sit still longer. Between the ages of 2 and 4, children show an increase in sustained, focused attention.

Rough-and-Tumble Play

Rough-and-tumble play consists of running, chasing, fleeing, wrestling, hitting with an open hand, laughing, and making faces. Rough-and-tumble play is not the same as aggressive behaviour, which involves hitting with a fist, pushing, taking, grabbing, and angry looks. Rough-and-tumble play helps develop physical and social skills (Fry, 2005; Smith, 2005).

Active Parents Have Active Children

A recent study suggests that active parents raise active children. Regular parental activity seems to protect children from the risk of obesity (Khamsi, 2007).

Several reasons may explain this relationship. First, active parents may serve as role models for activity. Second, sharing of activities by family members may have an influence. Active parents may be more likely to encourage their child's participation in physical activity. In other words, children seem to learn physical activity habits through example.

TABLE 7.2

Development of Fine Motor Skills in Early Childhood

2 Years (24–35 Months)	3 Years (36–47 Months)	4 Years (48–59 Months)	5 Years (60–71 Months)
• Builds tower of 6 cubes • Copies vertical and horizontal lines • Imitates folding of paper • Prints on easel with a brush • Places simple shapes in correct holes	• Builds tower of 9 cubes • Copies circle and cross • Copies letters • Holds crayons with fingers, not fist • Strings 4 beads using a large needle	• Builds tower of 10 or more cubes • Copies square • Prints simple words • Imitates folding paper three times • Uses correct hand grip to hold a pencil • Strings 10 beads	• Builds 3 steps from 6 blocks, using a model • Copies triangle and star • Prints first name and numbers • Imitates folding a piece of square paper into a triangle • Traces around a diamond drawn on paper • Laces shoes

Note: The ages are averages; there are individual variations.

fine motor skills skills employing the small muscles used in manipulation, such as those in the fingers.

Fine Motor Skills

Fine motor skills develop gradually and later than gross motor skills. Fine motor skills involve the small muscles used in manipulation and coordination. Control over the wrists and fingers enables children to hold a pencil properly, dress themselves, and stack blocks (see Table 7.2). Preschoolers can labour endlessly, while trying to tie their shoelaces and get their jackets zipped.

Children's Drawings

The development of drawing is linked to the development of motor and cognitive skills. Children first begin to scribble during the second year of life. Initially, they seem to make marks for the sheer joy of it (Eisner, 1990). Rhoda Kellogg (1959, 1970) found a meaningful pattern in the scribbles. She identified 20 basic scribbles that she considered the building blocks of art (see Figure 7.1).

Two-year-olds scribble in various locations on the page (e.g., in the middle of the page or near one of the borders). By age 3, children are starting to draw basic shapes: circles, squares, triangles, crosses, Xs, and odd shapes. As soon as they can draw shapes, children begin to combine them in the design stage. Between ages 4 and 5, children reach the pictorial stage, when their designs begin to resemble recognizable objects.

A more recent study by Yang and Noel (2006) confirmed earlier findings by Kellogg that four- and five-year-olds prefer single line drawings with centred placement patterns. This preference is possibly because their eye–hand coordination is still developing, so centred drawings dominate over drawings on other areas of the paper. The concept of symmetry is also still developing, which may explain why a child often considers a drawing in the centre of the page to be complete. Another finding of this study is that drawings help to encourage emerging literacy. Children seem to prefer the letters in their own name over other letters and readily add their names to their drawings. Yang and Noel concluded that children should be encouraged to freely explore scribbles and placement patterns in their drawing and that drawing are an excellent starting point for the practice of name writing.

Handedness

Handedness emerges during infancy. By the age of 2 to 3 months, a rattle placed in an infant's hand is held longer with the dominant hand (Fitzgerald et al., 1991). By 4 months of age, most infants show a clear-cut

© Ryan McVay/Photodisc/Getty Images

FIGURE 7.1

The 20 Basic Scribbles

By the age of 2, children can scribble. Rhoda Kellogg has identified these 20 basic scribbles as the building blocks of young children's drawings.

Source: Kellogg (1970).

right-hand preference when exploring objects (Streri, 2002). Preference for grasping with one hand or the other increases markedly between 7 and 11 months (Hinojosa et al., 2003). Handedness becomes more strongly established during early childhood (McManus et al., 1988). Most people are right-handed, although studies vary as to how many are left-handed.

A study conducted by Rat-Fischer et al. (2012) had 16- to 22-month-olds reach for a toy rake. Most of the younger infants used their hand of preference, while most older infants used the hand that would provide the easiest retrieval. Older children were better able to anticipate the most successful strategy and could use either hand.

The origins of handedness apparently have a genetic component (Geschwind, 2000; McManus, 2003). If both of your parents are right-handed, your chances of being right-handed are about 92 percent. If both of your parents are left-handed, your chances of being left-handed are about 50 percent (Annett, 1999; Clode, 2006). An environmental component also comes into play if children are discouraged from using their left hand.

Left-Handedness

Being a "lefty" was once seen as a deficiency, but, today, the 14 percent of the population that are left-handed are usually quite proud of their uniqueness. Being left-handed may matter because it appears to be related to language problems, such as dyslexia and stuttering, and with health problems, such as high blood pressure and epilepsy (Andreou et al., 2002; Bryden et al., 2005). Left-handedness is also related to psychological disorders, including schizophrenia and depression (Annett & Moran, 2006; Dollfus et al., 2005).

Even so, being left-handed has its advantages. A disproportionately high percentage of math whizzes are left-handed, as found on the math portion of the SAT among 12- and 13-year-olds (O'Boyle & Benbow, 1990). Twenty percent of the highest-scoring group was left-handed, while only 10 percent of the general population is left-handed.

Left-handedness (and ambidexterity, the use of both hands with similar or equal dexterity) also has been associated with success in athletic activities such as handball, fencing, boxing, basketball, and baseball (Coren, 1992; Dane & Erzurumluoglu, 2003). Higher frequencies of left-handedness are found among musicians, architects, and artists (Natsopoulos et al., 1992).

DID YOU KNOW

A disproportionately high percentage of math whizzes are left-handed.

Twenty percent of the highest-scoring group on the math SATs was left-handed, while only 10 percent of the general population is left-handed.

LO3 Nutrition

Today's generation of children has been referred to as Generation XL, which is a comment on the most overweight generation of children our country has known. Statistics Canada reports that 31 percent of Canadian children between the ages of 5 and 17 are either overweight or obese (Roberts et al., 2012).

When it comes to our food, we have bought into the notion that bigger is better. Today's children are part of

That Was Then ... This Is Now

20 Years Ago	Today
Two pieces of pizza: 500 calories	Two pieces of pizza: 850 calories
Cheeseburger: 333 calories	Cheeseburger: 590 calories
Movie popcorn tub: 270 calories	Movie popcorn tub: 630 calories
Can of coke (351 ml): 145 calories	Bottle of coke (500 ml): 242 calories
Kids who walk or bike to school: 58%	Kids who walk or bike to school: 28%

Source: Boyle, T. (2013, May 21). Canadian children don't walk to school, study says. *Toronto Star*, retrieved from http://www.thestar.com/life/health_wellness/2013/05/21/canadian_children_dont_walk_to_school_study_says.html; Gottesman, N. (2012). Generation XL. *Parenting School Years, 26*(7), p. 76; Monte, L. (2013). Portion size, then and now. Retrieved from http://www.divinecaroline.com/self/wellness/portion-size-then-vs-now

The following are some tips given by Nancy Gottesman (2012):

- Use smaller dishware (Cornell University scientists have proven we eat and drink less when using smaller dishes).
- Use the palm of your hand to gauge portions. Consider that many portions purchased in restaurants are usually 2 to 3 times the daily recommended serving size.
- When grabbing snacks, one serving size is what you can grab in one hand, not what comes in a prepackaged serving size.

the supersizing phenomenon. For example, many cookies today are 700 percent bigger than they were in the 1970s (Gottesman, 2012). Look at the following comparisons of common food servings compared with the 1970s.

Health Canada recommends that a healthy diet for children should focus on the number of food guide servings, not on calorie intake (Health Canada, 2007b) (see Figure 7.2). During the second and third years, a child's appetite typically varies, but because the child is growing more slowly than in infancy, he or she needs fewer calories. Children who eat little at one meal may compensate by eating more at another (Cooke et al., 2003).

Many children eat too much sugar and salt, which can be harmful to their health. Preferences for these types of food increase with repeated exposure. Parents serve as role models in the development of food preferences (Hannon et al., 2003).

EMERGING CANADA

The Hospital for Sick Children and Toronto Public Health have launched Canada's first obesity program targeting 3- to 5-year-olds. Currently, 14 percent of Canadian children in this age group are overweight, and 6 percent are obese. Without strong intervention, these numbers will increase as these children age. Cardiologists are now focusing on early childhood to prevent weight-related diabetes, heart disease, and stroke. The focus of the program is less on obesity and more on the healthy-active living of young children and their families. Experts believe that tackling the Canadian obesity epidemic will require tackling the early childhood age group. This cutting-edge program focuses on physical games, meal planning, and family activities to create healthy habits that can last a lifetime (Alphonso, 2012).

FIGURE 7.2

Canada's Food Guide for a Toddler

Your health and safety... our priority. *Votre santé et votre sécurité... notre priorité.*

My Food Guide

Name: ______________________

My Recommended *Food Guide Servings* per day

My **Numbers** (Boy aged 2 to 3)	My **Examples** (Each example represents 1 Food Guide Serving)
Milk and Alternatives 4 Drink skim, 1% or 2% milk each day. Select lower fat milk alternatives.	Milk, 1%, 2%, skim, 250 mL, 1 cup; Milk, chocolate, 250 mL, 1 cup; Cheese, 50 g, 1 ½ oz; Pudding/custard 125 mL, ½ cup; Yogurt, 175 g, ¾ cup; Yogurt drink, 200 mL
Grain Products 3 Make at least half of your grain products whole grain each day. Choose grain products that are lower in fat, sugar or salt.	Cereal, cold, 30 g; Whole wheat crackers, 30 g; Whole wheat tortilla, ½ piece, 35 g; Pancake, 1 small, 35 g; Pasta/noodles, 125 mL, ½ cup cooked; Rice, white, 125 mL, ½ cup cooked
Vegetables and Fruit 2 Eat at least one dark green and one orange vegetable each day. Choose vegetables and fruit prepared with little or no added fat, sugar or salt. Have vegetables and fruit more often than juice.	Broccoli, 125 mL, ½ cup; Carrots, 125 mL, ½ cup, 1 large; Snow peas, 125 mL, ½ cup; Apple, 1 medium; Banana, 1 medium; Grapes, 20 fruits
Meat and Alternatives 1 Have meat alternatives such as beans, lentils and tofu often. Eat at least two Food Guide Servings of fish each week. Select lean meat and alternatives prepared with little or no added fat or salt.	Eggs, 2; Peanut/nut butter, 30 mL, 2 Tbsp; Beef, 75 g (2 ½ oz) / 125 mL (½ cup); Chicken, 75 g (2 ½ oz) / 125 mL (½ cup); Fish and shellfish, canned, 75 g (2 ½ oz) / 125 mL (½ cup); Ham, 75 g (2 ½ oz) / 125 mL (½ cup)

Build at least 90 minutes of physical activity into your day everyday

Here are the examples you chose:

- Gymnastics
- Running
- Skipping

Use with Canada's Food Guide

www.healthcanada.gc.ca/foodguide

Source: *My Food Guide.* Health Canada, 2008. Reproduced with permission from the Minister of Health, 2013.

LO4 Health and Illness

Minor Illnesses

Minor illnesses refer to respiratory infections, such as colds, and to stomach upsets, such as nausea, vomiting, and diarrhea. These conditions are normal in that most children experience them. Minor illnesses typically last a few days or less and are not life threatening. Although diarrheal illness in Canada is usually mild, it is a leading killer of children in developing countries (UNICEF, 2006).

Canadian children will have lots of colds, some as many as 8 to 10 each year before they are 2 years old (Canadian Paediatric Society, 2010). Childhood illnesses can lead to the creation of antibodies that may prevent children from coming down with the same illnesses in adulthood, when illnesses can do more harm.

Joe Belanger/iStockphoto

DID YOU KNOW

Some diseases are normal.

Minor illnesses are generally normal, insofar as most children get them and may actually be healthier in adulthood as a result of the immunities they acquire.

EMERGING CANADA

The Canadian Lung Association educates Canadians about the health risks associated with second-hand smoke. Children are especially vulnerable because they have less developed immune systems and they have a faster breathing rate, which means their bodies absorb more smoke. Children also have less control about whether their environment will be smoke-free or not. The nonprofit group Physicians for a Smoke-free Canada estimates that in Canada, second-hand smoke is responsible for the following:

- 13% of ear infections
- 13% of asthma cases
- 16% of physician visits for cough
- 20% of lung infections in children younger than age 5
- 15 deaths per year due to deaths from fires
- 80–270 deaths per year from Sudden Infant Death Syndrome.

Data collected by Health Canada in 2007 reported that 7 percent of children younger than age 12 are exposed to second-hand smoke at home (Canadian Lung Association, 2012).

Major Illnesses

Advances in immunization and the development of antibiotics and other medications have dramatically reduced the incidence and effects of serious childhood diseases in Canada. Because most preschoolers and schoolchildren have been inoculated against major childhood illnesses such as rubella (German measles), measles, tetanus, mumps, whooping cough, diphtheria, and polio, these diseases no longer pose the threat they once did.

More than 80 percent of kids aged 11 to 17 surveyed by the University of Alberta had one or more risk factors for chronic diseases (Sinnema, 2009). These illnesses include such major disorders as arthritis, diabetes, heart disease, and lung disease.

Although many major childhood diseases have been largely eliminated in Canada and other industrialized nations, they remain fearsome killers of children in developing countries. Around the world, 8 million to 9 million children die each year from only six diseases: pneumonia, diarrhea, measles, tetanus, whooping cough, and tuberculosis (UNICEF, 2006). Air pollution from the combustion of fossil fuels used for heating and cooking causes many respiratory infections, which are responsible for nearly one death in five among children who are younger than 5 years of age (UNICEF, 2006). Diarrhea kills nearly 2 million children under the age of 5 each year. Diarrheal diseases are mostly related to unsafe drinking water, inadequate sanitation, and poor hygiene (UNICEF, 2006).

Infants fed formulas made with tap water are at risk of lead poisoning, because water pipes sometimes contain lead. Lead causes neurological damage and may result in lowered cognitive functioning and other delays.

Accidents

Accidents cause more deaths in early childhood than the next six most frequent causes combined (National Center for Injury Prevention and Control, 2007a). The single most common cause of death in early childhood is motor vehicle accidents. Boys are more likely than girls to incur accidental injuries at all ages and in all socioeconomic groups. Children living in poverty are five times as likely as other children to die from fires and more than twice as likely to die in motor vehicle accidents (National Center for Injury Prevention and Control, 2007a).

sleep terrors frightening dreamlike experiences that occur during the deepest stage of non-REM sleep, shortly after the child has gone to sleep.

somnambulism sleepwalking.

LO5 Sleep

According to the National Sleep Foundation, toddlers need 12 to 14 hours of sleep in a 24-hour period. In other words, children should be spending half of their time sleeping. Getting this amount of sleep is incredibly difficult in a world that has become increasingly busier and more scheduled. If the toddler has siblings or parents that need to be in other places, the toddler's sleep schedules may need to be juggled to fit into a busy family routine. At about 18 months of age, naps decrease to once a day, usually early in the afternoon. If naps are too close to bedtime, sleep issues may surface. Toddlers will sleep better when they have a daily sleep schedule and a consistent bedtime. The bedroom environment should be the same every night. Limits around bedtime behaviour need to be well communicated, consistent, and enforced. Security objects should be encouraged (National Sleep Foundation, 2011). If children do not receive sufficient sleep, they may experience changes in their behaviour. Whereas adults who lack sleep are sleepy, children who lack sleep are often hyperactive; they may act aggressively, cry, and act inappropriately (Peters, 2013).

Security objects allow children to become masters of their bedtime routines.

Sleep Disorders

In this section, we focus on the sleep disorders of sleep terrors, nightmares, and sleepwalking.

Sleep Terrors and Nightmares

Sleep terrors are more severe than the anxiety dreams we refer to as nightmares. Sleep terrors usually occur during deep sleep. Nightmares take place during lighter, rapid-eye-movement (REM) sleep, when about 80 percent of normal dreams occur.

Sleep terrors usually begin in childhood or early adolescence and are outgrown by late adolescence. They are sometimes associated with stress, as caused by moving to a new neighbourhood, beginning school, adjusting to parental divorce, or being in a war zone. Children with sleep terrors may wake suddenly with a surge in heart and respiration rates, talk incoherently, and thrash about. Children may then fall back into more restful sleep. The incidence of sleep terrors wanes as children develop.

Children who have frequent nightmares or sleep terrors may come to fear going to sleep. They may show distress at bedtime, refuse to get into their pajamas, and insist that the lights be kept on. As a result, they can develop insomnia. Children with frequent nightmares or sleep terrors need caregivers' understanding and affection. They also benefit from a regular routine in which they are expected to get to sleep at the same time each night (Christophersen & Mortweet, 2003).

Sleepwalking

Sleepwalking, or **somnambulism**, is more common among children than adults. As with sleep terrors, sleepwalking tends to occur during deep sleep (Stores & Wiggs, 2001). Onset is usually between the ages of 3 and 8.

When children sleepwalk, they may rearrange toys, go to the bathroom, or walk to the refrigerator to get a glass of milk. Then they return to their room and go back to bed. Many myths surround sleepwalking, such as the suggestion that sleepwalkers' eyes are closed, that they will avoid harm, and that they will become violently agitated if awakened during an episode. All these notions are false.

Sleepwalking in children is assumed to reflect immaturity of the nervous system. As with sleep terrors, the incidence of sleepwalking drops as children develop. If a child has persistent sleep terrors or sleepwalking, it may be helpful to talk with a health professional.

LO6 Elimination Disorders

During toilet training, a child's maturation plays a crucial role. During the first year, only an exceptional child can be toilet trained. Most Canadian children are toilet trained between the ages of 2 and 3 (Bracht, 2007). Expectations around toilet training are culturally influenced, and in our busy Western culture, the initiation of toilet training is sometimes postponed. In a study conducted by Horn et al. (2006), both race and socioeconomic status seemed to play a role in the age when toilet training was initiated. In this study, Caucasian parents initiated toilet training at 25.4 months, African American parents started at 18.2 months, and other racial groups began at 19.4 months. In addition, higher-income groups also initiated attempts later. The researchers suggest the reasons for the different ages might include the cost of diapers and an expanded option of day care day-trained children. Although children may be toilet trained during the day, they may continue to have night-time "accidents" for another year or so. Children who do not become toilet trained within reasonable time frames may be diagnosed with enuresis, encopresis, or both.

DID YOU KNOW

For most Canadian children, toilet training takes place between the ages of 2 and 3.

It is important to allow the child to set the pace for toilet training. The average age can vary significantly, and night-time accidents can be expected to occur for an additional year after daytime training has been achieved.

Enuresis

Enuresis is failure to control the bladder (urination) once the "normal" age for achieving bladder control has been reached.

A night-time "accident" is termed **bed-wetting**. Night-time control is more difficult to achieve than daytime control. At night, children must first wake up when their bladders are full. At 5 years of age, 15 percent of Canadian children wet the bed. By 8 years, only 6–8 percent wet the bed (Canadian Paediatric Society, 2007). Bed-wetting is about twice as common among boys and tends to occur during the deepest stage of sleep, the stage when sleep terrors and sleepwalking may also occur.

Just as children outgrow sleep terrors and sleepwalking, they tend to outgrow bed-wetting (Mellon & Houts, 2006). Scientists have discovered a gene for bed-wetting. If one parent wet the bed as a child, the child has a 25 percent risk of bed-wetting. If both parents wet the bed as children, this likelihood increases to about 65 percent (Canadian Paediatric Society, 2007)

enuresis
failure to control the bladder (urination) once the normal age for control has been reached.

bed-wetting
failure to control the bladder during the night.

encopresis
failure to control the bowels once the normal age for bowel control has been reached. Also called soiling.

preoperational stage
the second stage in Piaget's scheme, characterized by inflexible and irreversible mental manipulation of symbols.

Encopresis

Soiling, or **encopresis**, is lack of control over the bowels. Soiling, like enuresis, is more common among boys. About 1–2 percent of children at the ages of 7 and 8 have continuing problems controlling their bowels (Mellon, 2006; von Gontard, 2007). Soiling, in contrast to enuresis, is more likely to occur during the day. Thus, encopresis can be embarrassing to the child, especially when it occurs at school.

Encopresis stems from both physical causes, such as chronic constipation, and psychological factors (Mellon, 2006; von Gontard, 2007). Soiling may follow harsh punishment of toileting accidents, especially in children who are already anxious or experiencing stress. Punishment may cause the child to tense up on the toilet, whereas moving one's bowels requires relaxation. Soiling, punishment, and anxiety can become a vicious cycle.

LO7 Jean Piaget's Preoperational Stage

According to Piaget, the **preoperational stage** of cognitive development lasts from about age 2 to age 7. At this stage, young children's logic is at best "under construction."

Symbolic Thought

Preoperational thought is characterized by the use of symbols to represent objects and relationships among them. According to Piaget, preschoolers' drawings are symbols of objects, people, and events in children's lives. Symbolism is part of pretend play.

© Thinkstock Images/Jupiterimages

symbolic play play in which children make-believe that objects and toys are other than what they are. Also called pretend play.

egocentrism putting oneself at the centre of things such that one is unable to perceive the world from another person's point of view.

Symbolic or Pretend Play

Children's **symbolic play**—the "let's pretend" type of play—may seem immature to busy adults meeting the realistic demands of the business world, but this type of play requires cognitive sophistication (Feldman & Masalha, 2007; Keen et al., 2007).

Piaget (1962 [1946]) wrote that pretend play usually begins in the second year, when the child begins to symbolize objects. The ability to engage in pretend play is based on children's mental representations of their experiences or things they have heard about.

Children first engage in pretend play at about 12 or 13 months. They make-believe they are performing familiar activities, such as sleeping or feeding themselves. By 15 to 20 months, they can shift their focus from themselves to others. A child may pretend to feed her doll. By 30 months, she or he can make-believe that the other object takes an active role. The child may pretend that the doll is feeding itself (Paavola et al., 2006).

© C Squared Studios/Getty Images

The quality of pretend play influences preschoolers' later academic performance, their creativity, and their social skills (Russ, 2006; Stagnitti et al., 2000).

Imaginary friends are an example of pretend play. As many as 65 percent of preschoolers have imaginary friends; they are most common among first-born and only children (Gleason et al., 2003). Having an imaginary playmate does not mean that the child has problems with real relationships (Gleason, 2004; Hoff, 2005). In fact, children with imaginary friends are usually less aggressive, more cooperative, and more creative than children without them (Gleason, 2002). They have more real friends, show greater ability to concentrate, and are more advanced in language development (Taylor, 1999).

DID YOU KNOW

Children pursuing a relationship with an invisible friend show many developmental advantages.

Children with imaginary friends are usually less aggressive, more cooperative, and show greater language development and concentration.

Egocentrism: It's All About Me

Sometimes the attitude "It's all about me" is a sign of early childhood, not of selfishness. One consequence of one-dimensional thinking is **egocentrism**. Egocentrism, in Piaget's use of the term, means that preoperational children do not understand that other people may have different perspectives on the world. When children want to hide from you, they will cover their eyes, thinking that if they can't see anything, neither can you.

Piaget used the "three-mountains test" (see Figure 7.3) to learn whether egocentrism prevents young children from taking the viewpoints of others. In this demonstration, the child sits at a table before a model of three mountains. One has a house on it, and another has a cross at the summit.

Piaget then placed a doll elsewhere on the table and asked the child what the

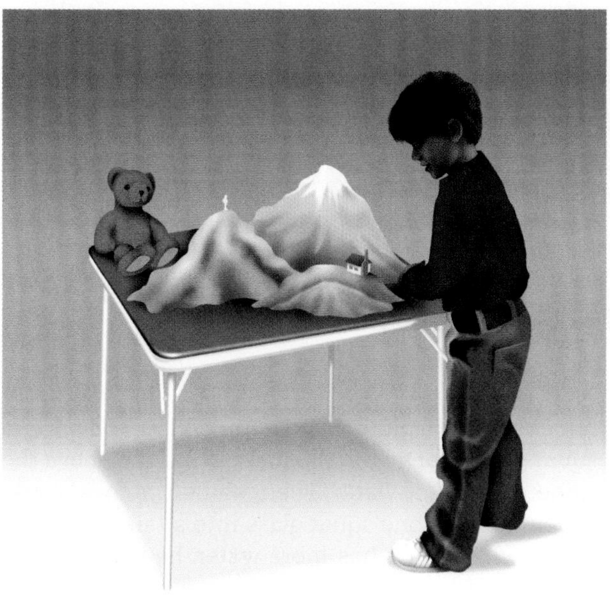

FIGURE 7.3

The Three-Mountains Test

Piaget used the three-mountains test to learn whether children at certain ages are egocentric or can take the viewpoints of others.

doll sees. The language abilities of very young children do not permit them to provide verbal descriptions of what can be seen from where the doll is situated, so they can answer in one of two ways. They can either select a photograph taken from the proper vantage point, or they can construct another model of the mountains as they would be seen by the doll. The results of a classic experiment with the three-mountains test suggest that 5- and 6-year-olds usually select photos or build models that correspond to their own viewpoints (Laurendeau & Pinard, 1970).

DID YOU KNOW

Two-year-olds tend to assume that their parents are aware of everything that is happening to them, even when their parents are not present.

This attitude is a product of early childhood one-dimensional thinking and egocentrism.

Causality: Why? Because.

Preoperational children's responses to questions such as "Why does the sun shine?" show other sides of egocentrism. At the age of 2 or so, they may answer that they do not know, or they may change the subject. Three-year-olds may report themselves as doing things because they want to do them or "Because Mommy wants me to." In egocentric fashion, this explanation of behaviour is extended to inanimate objects. The sun may be thought of as shining because it wants to shine or someone wants it to shine.

precausal
a type of thought in which natural cause-and-effect relationships are attributed to will and other preoperational concepts.

transductive reasoning
faulty reasoning that links one specific isolated event to another specific isolated event.

animism
the attribution of life and intentionality to inanimate objects.

artificialism
the belief that environmental features were made by people.

Piaget labels this structuring of cause and effect **precausal**. Unless preoperational children know the natural causes of an event, their reasons are likely to have an egocentric flavour and not be based on science. Consider the question, "Why does it get dark outside?" The preoperational child usually does not have knowledge of Earth's rotation and is likely to answer something like, "So I can go to sleep."

DID YOU KNOW

"Because Mommy wants me to" may be a perfectly good explanation for a 3-year-old.

This line of reasoning is also a reflection of early childhood egocentrism. Unfortunately, this response is not frequently heard in the teenage years.

In **transductive reasoning**, children reason by going from one specific isolated event to another. For example, a 3-year-old may argue that she should go to sleep *because* it is dark outside. That is, separate events, darkness and going to sleep, are thought to have cause-and-effect relationships.

Preoperational children also show **animism** and **artificialism** in their attributions of causality. In animistic thinking, they attribute life and intentions to inanimate objects, such as the sun and the moon. ("Why is the moon gone during the day?" "It is afraid of the sun.") Artificialism assumes that environmental features such as rain and thunder have been designed and made by people.

© Jitloac/Shutterstock

a

b

c

FIGURE 7.4

Conservation

(a) The boy in this illustration agreed that the amount of water in two identical containers is equal. (b) He then watched as water from one container was poured into a tall, thin container. (c) When asked whether the amounts of water in the two containers are now the same, he says no.

conservation
in cognitive psychology, the principle that properties of substances such as weight and mass remain the same (are conserved) when superficial characteristics such as their shapes or arrangement are changed.

Focus on One Dimension at a Time

To gain further insight into preoperational thinking, consider two problems. First, imagine that you pour water from a low, wide glass into a tall, thin glass, as in Figure 7.4(b). Does the tall, thin glass contain more than, less than, or the same amount of water as in the low, wide glass? We won't keep you in suspense. If you said the same amount, you were correct.

Next, if you flatten a ball of clay into a pancake, do you wind up with more, less, or the same amount of clay? If you said the same amount, you are correct once more.

To arrive at the correct answers to these questions, you must understand the law of **conservation**. The law of conservation holds that properties of substances such as volume, mass, and number remain the same—or are conserved—even if you change their shape or arrangement.

Preoperational children tend to focus on only one aspect of a problem at a time, a characteristic of thought that Piaget called *centration*. Conservation requires the ability to focus on two aspects of a situation at once, such as height and width. A preoperational child focuses, or centres, on only one dimension at a time. First, the child is shown two squat glasses of water and agrees that they have the same amount of water. Then, as he watches, water is poured from one squat glass into a tall, thin glass. Asked which glass has more water, he points to the tall glass. Why? When he looks at the glasses, he is swayed by the fact that the thinner glass is taller.

The preoperational child's failure to show conservation also comes about because of *irreversibility*. In the case of the water, the child does not realize that pouring water from the wide glass to the tall glass can be reversed, restoring things to their original condition.

After you have tried the experiment with the water, try this experiment on conservation of number. Make two rows with four pennies in each. As the 3-year-old child watches, move the pennies in the second row to about 2.5 cm (1 in.) apart, as in Figure 7.5. Ask the child which row has more pennies. What do you think the child will say? Why?

Class Inclusion

Class inclusion, as we are using it here, refers to the inclusion of new objects or categories in broader mental classes or categories. Class inclusion requires children to focus on two aspects of a situation at once. In one of Piaget's class-inclusion tasks, the child is shown several pictures from two

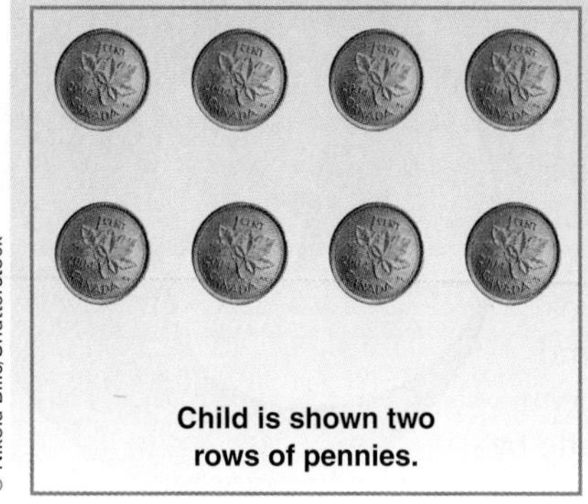

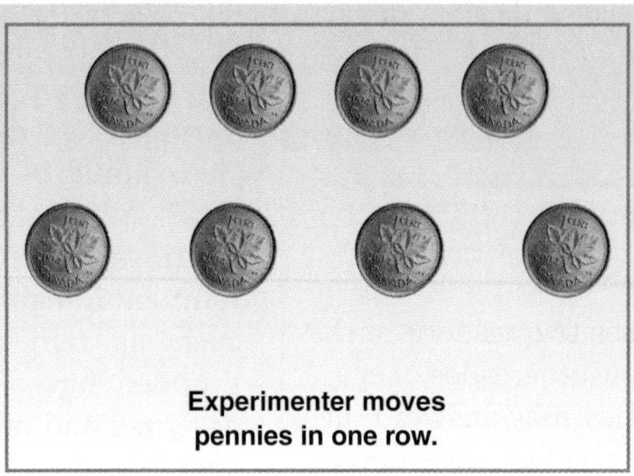

FIGURE 7.5

Conservation of Number

In this demonstration, we begin with two rows of pennies that are spread out equally, as shown in the left-hand drawing. One row of pennies is then spread out, as shown in the drawing on the right-hand side. We then ask the child, "Do the two rows still have the same number of pennies?" In arriving at an answer, do you think a preoperational child will conserve the number of pennies or focus on the length of the longer row?

subclasses of a larger class, for example, four cats and six dogs. She is asked whether there are more dogs or more animals. What do you think she will say? Preoperational children typically answer that there are more dogs than animals (Piaget, 1963 [1936]).

Why do preoperational children make this error? According to Piaget, they cannot think about the two subclasses and the larger class at the same time. Therefore, they cannot easily compare them. Children view dogs as dogs, or as animals, but find it difficult to see them as both dogs and animals at once (Branco & Lourenço, 2004).

LO8 Factors in Cognitive Development

Scaffolding and the Zone of Proximal Development

Parental responsiveness and interaction with children are key ingredients in children's cognitive development. One component of this interaction is **scaffolding**. Cognitive scaffolding refers to temporary support provided by a parent or teacher to learning children. The guidance provided by adults decreases as children become capable of carrying out the task on their own (Lengua et al., 2007; Sylva et al., 2007).

A related concept is Vygotsky's **zone of proximal development (ZPD)**. The zone refers to the gap between what children are capable of doing now and what they could do with help from others. Adults or older children can best guide children through this zone by gearing their assistance to children's capabilities (Lantolf & Thorne, 2007; Wennergren & Rönnerman, 2006). These researchers argue that the key forms of children's cognitive activities develop through interaction with older, more experienced individuals who teach and guide them. Consider working on a jigsaw puzzle with children. They will model your strategies of locating the corners and the edges first. With practice they will be able to build the puzzle on their own.

Effects of Early Childhood Education

Research suggests that preschool education enables children to get an early start on achievement in school. Children reared in poverty generally perform less well on standardized intelligence tests than children of higher socioeconomic status, and they are at greater risk for school failure (Stipek & Hakuta, 2007; Whitehouse, 2006). As a result, preschool programs were begun in the 1960s to enhance children's cognitive development and readiness for elementary school. Canada has one of the earliest educational starts in the world, with children able to enter the school system as early as 3 years 8 months. Children in these programs typically are exposed to letters and words, numbers, books, exercises in drawing, pegs and pegboards, puzzles, and toy animals and dolls—materials and activities that middle-class children usually take for granted.

scaffolding Vygotsky's term for temporary cognitive structures or methods of solving problems that help the child as he or she learns to function independently.

zone of proximal development (ZPD) Vygotsky's term for the situation in which a child carries out tasks with the help of someone who is more skilled, frequently an adult who represents the culture in which the child develops.

The Aboriginal Head Start on Reserve program encourages the development of locally controlled projects in First Nation communities that strive to instill in children a sense of pride and a desire to learn, enhance parenting skills that contribute to the healthy development of children, improve family relationships, foster emotional and social development, and increase confidence (Health Canada, 2009). Studies of Head Start and other intervention programs show that environmental enrichment can enhance the cognitive development of economically disadvantaged children (Stipek & Hakuta, 2007; P. Wilson, 2004).

EMERGING CANADA

The ability to access quality day care is becoming a national concern in Canada. Since the late 1990s, demand for day-care spaces has been rapidly rising in both urban and rural centres. In 2005, the Organisation for Economic Co-operation and Development (2005) released a report that described Canada's child-care system as a chronically underfunded patchwork of programs with no overarching goals. The report ranked Canada last among developed countries in terms of access to child-care spaces and public investment in child care. The report also found a shortage of available regulated child-care spaces—enough for fewer than 20 percent of children aged 6 and younger whose parents work. In the United Kingdom, 60 percent of children find regulated child care; in Belgium, 63 percent; in France, 69 percent; and in Denmark, 78 percent. According to the Child Care Advocacy Association of Canada, given that the 2009 federal budget allocated no new money to day cares, the government must be content with this last-place standing. In addition, day-care costs are increasing. Statistics Canada reported in 2008 that the consumer price index rose by 2.3 percent but the average cost of day care across the country was up by 6.1 percent (CBC News, 2009b).

John Lamparski/WireImage/Getty Images

theory of mind
a commonsense understanding of how the mind works.

Television

The National Longitudinal Survey of Children and Youth (NLSCY) reported from data collected in 2004–05 that 27 percent of children aged 2 to 3 years, and 22 percent of children aged 4 to 6, are watching more than 2 hours of TV per day (Active Healthy Kids Canada, 2010). The good news is that some programs, such as *Sesame Street,* have mild to positive effects on preschoolers' cognitive development (Calvert & Kotler, 2003). The goal of *Sesame Street* is to promote the intellectual growth of preschoolers, particularly those of lower socioeconomic status. Large-scale evaluations of the effects of *Sesame Street* have concluded that regular viewing increases children's learning of numbers, letters, and cognitive skills such as sorting and classification (Fisch, 2004). Caregivers are reminded to limit the number of hours that children spend watching television. TV watching should be a conscious decision that is periodically reviewed. Caregivers should be wary of the trap of television—that it easily becomes a mindless distraction for children.

EMERGING CANADA

The Canadian Paediatric Society recommends that children have no more than 2 hours of screen time daily (from television, DVDs, computers, social media, and video games) but research shows that just 15 percent of youth meet this guideline. Studies show that the more time kids spend in front of a screen, the less likely they are to be physically active, which leads to weight issues. Research has also shown excessive screen time to be a risk factor for anxiety, depression, and a low sense of belonging. Caregivers need to set limits in early childhood to avoid the pattern of too much screen time that seems to be developing for older children. Canadians aged 10 to 16 spend an average of six hours watching TV, playing video games, and/or using the computer (Fernandes, 2011).

LO9 Theory of Mind

Adults appear to have a commonsense understanding of how the mind works—that is, a **theory of mind**. We know the distinction between actual and mental events and between how things appear and how they really are. We can infer the perceptions, thoughts, and feelings of others. We understand that mental states affect behaviour.

Piaget might have predicted that preoperational children are too egocentric and too focused on misleading external appearances to have a theory of mind, but research has shown that even preschoolers can accurately predict and explain human action and emotion in terms of mental states (Wellman et al., 2006).

False Beliefs: Where Are Those Crayons?

False belief is a concept that involves children's ability to separate their beliefs from the beliefs of another person who has false knowledge. It is illustrated in a study of 3-year-olds by Louis Moses and John Flavell (1990). The children were shown a videotape in which a girl named Cathy found some crayons in a bag. When Cathy left the room briefly, a clown entered the room. The clown removed the crayons from the bag, hid them in a drawer, and put rocks in the bag instead. When Cathy returned, the children were asked whether Cathy thought the bag contained rocks or crayons. Most of the 3-year-olds incorrectly answered "rocks," demonstrating their difficulty in understanding that the other person's belief would be different from their own. But by the age of 4 to 5 years, children do not have trouble with this concept and correctly answer "crayons" (Flavell, 1993).

Origins of Knowledge

Another aspect of theory of mind is how we acquire knowledge. By age 3, most children begin to realize that people gain knowledge about something by looking at it (Pratt & Bryant, 1990). By age 4, children understand that particular senses provide information about only certain qualities of an object; for example, we come to know an object's colour through our eyes, but we learn about its weight by feeling it (O'Neill & Chong, 2001). In a study by Daniela O'Neill and Alison Gopnik (1991), 3-, 4-, and 5-year-olds learned about the contents of a toy tunnel in three different ways: They saw the contents, were told about them, or felt them. The children were then asked to state what was in the tunnel and how they knew. Although 4- and 5-year-olds had no trouble identifying the sources of their knowledge, the 3-year-olds had difficulty. For example, after feeling

Older children realize that appearances can be different from reality.

but not seeing a ball in the tunnel, some 3-year-olds told the experimenter that they could tell it was a blue ball. The children did not realize they could not learn the ball's colour by feeling it.

The Appearance–Reality Distinction

Children must acquire an understanding of the difference between, on the one hand, real events, and on the other hand, mental events, fantasies, and misleading appearances (Bialystok & Senman, 2004; Flavell et al., 2002). This understanding is known as the **appearance–reality distinction**.

Piaget's view was that children do not differentiate reality from appearances or mental events until the age of 7 or 8. In a study by Marjorie Taylor and Barbara Hort (1990), children age 3 to 5 were shown objects that had misleading appearances, such as an eraser that looked like a cookie. The children initially reported that the eraser looked like a cookie. However, once they learned that it was actually an eraser, they tended to report that it looked like an eraser. Apparently, these children could not mentally represent the eraser as both being an eraser and looking like a cookie.

Three-year-olds also apparently cannot understand changes in their mental states. In one study (Gopnik & Slaughter, 1991), 3-year-olds were shown a crayon box with candles inside. Before it was opened, they consistently said they thought crayons were inside. When asked what they had thought was in the box before it was opened, the children now said "candles."

appearance–reality distinction
the difference between real events on the one hand and mental events, fantasies, and misleading appearances on the other hand.

scripts
abstract, generalized accounts of familiar repeated events.

autobiographical memory
the memory of specific episodes or events.

LO10 Development of Memory

Children, like adults, often remember what they want to remember (Ghetti & Alexander, 2004; Sales et al., 2003). By the age of 4, children can remember events that occurred at least 11/2 years earlier (Fivush & Hammond, 1990). Furthermore, young children seem to form **scripts**, which are abstract, generalized accounts of these repeated events. For example, in describing what happens during a birthday party, a child might say, "You play games, open presents, and eat cake" (Fivush, 2002). However, an unusual experience, such as a hurricane, may be remembered in detail for years (Fivush et al., 2004).

Young children can remember a great deal, but compared with older children, they depend more on cues from adults to help them retrieve their memories.

Even though children as young as 1 and 2 years of age can remember events, these memories seldom last into adulthood. This memory of specific events—known as **autobiographical memory**—is facilitated by children talking about the events with others (Nelson & Fivush, 2004).

Factors Influencing Memory

Factors that affect memory include what the child is asked to remember, the interest level of the child, the availability of retrieval cues or reminders, and the memory measure being used. First, children

rehearsal
a strategy that uses repetition to remember information.

fast mapping
a process of quickly determining a word's meaning, which facilitates children's vocabulary development.

find it easier to remember events that follow a fixed and logical order than events that do not follow a fixed order. Research consistently shows that most preschool boys are more interested in playing with toys such as cars and weapons, whereas most preschool girls are more interested in playing with dolls, dishes, and teddy bears. Later, the children typically show better recognition and recall for the toys that interest them the most (Martin & Ruble, 2004).

Young children can remember a great deal, but compared with older children, they depend more on cues from adults to help them retrieve their memories. By elaborating on the child's experiences and by asking questions that encourage the child to contribute information to the narrative, adults can generally help children remember an episode (Nelson & Fivush, 2004).

Memory Strategies: Remembering to Remember

Adults and older children use strategies to help them remember things. One strategy is mental repetition, or **rehearsal**. If you are trying to remember a new friend's phone number, for example, you might repeat it several times. Another strategy for remembering is to organize things into categories. Most preschoolers do not engage in rehearsal until about 5 years of age (Labrell & Ubersfeld, 2004). They also rarely group objects into related categories to help them remember. By about age 5, many children have learned to verbalize information silently to themselves by counting mentally, for example, rather than aloud.

© Walter Lockwood/CORBIS

LO11 Language Development: Why "Daddy Goed Away"

Children's language skills mushroom during the preschool years. By the fourth year, children are asking adults and each other questions, taking turns talking, and engaging in lengthy conversations.

Development of Vocabulary

The development of vocabulary proceeds at an extraordinary pace. Preschoolers learn an average of nine new words per day (Tamis-LaMonda et al., 2006). But how can that be possible when each new word has so many potential meanings? Consider the following example. A toddler observes a small, black dog running through the park. His older sister points to the animal and says, "Doggy." The word *doggy* could mean this particular dog, or all dogs, or all animals. It could refer to one part of the dog (e.g., its tail), or to its behaviour (running, barking), or to its characteristics (small, black) (Waxman & Lidz, 2006). Does the child consider all these possibilities before determining what doggy actually means?

Word learning, in fact, does not occur gradually but is better characterized as a **fast-mapping** process in which the child quickly attaches a new word to its appropriate concept (Homer & Nelson, 2005; Waxman & Lidz, 2006). Children apparently have early cognitive biases or constraints that lead them to prefer certain meanings over others (Waxman & Lidz, 2006).

Development of Grammar

A "grammar explosion" occurs during children's third year (Tamis-LeMonda et al., 2006). Children's sentence structure expands to include the words missing in telegraphic speech. Children usually add to their vocabulary an impressive array of articles (*a, an, the*), conjunctions (*and, but, or*), possessive adjectives (*your, her*), pronouns (*she, him, one*), and prepositions (*in, on, over, around, under, through*). Between the ages

© Andy Sands/naturepl.com

of 3 and 4, children usually show knowledge of rules for combining phrases and clauses into complex sentences, as in "You goed and Mommy goed, too."

Overregularization

The apparent basis of one of the more intriguing language developments—**overregularization**—is that children acquire grammatical rules as they learn language. At young ages, they tend to apply these rules rather strictly, even in cases that call for exceptions (Jacobson & Schwartz, 2005; Stemberger, 2004). Consider the formation of the past tense and plurals in English. We add *d* or *ed* to regular verbs and *s* to regular nouns. Thus, *walk* becomes *walked* and *dog* becomes *dogs*. But then there are irregular verbs and irregular nouns. For example, *sit* becomes *sat* and *go* becomes *went*. *Sheep* remains *sheep* (plural) and *child* becomes *children*.

As children become aware of the syntactic rules for forming the past tense and plurals in English, they often misapply them to irregular words. As a result, they tend to make charming errors (Stemberger, 2004). Some 3- to 5-year-olds are more likely to say "Mommy sitted down" than "Mommy sat down" or talk about the "sheeps" they "seed" on the farm and about all the "childs" they ran into at the playground.

overregularization the application of regular grammatical rules for forming inflections to irregular verbs and nouns.

pragmatics the practical aspects of communication, such as adaptation of language to fit the social situation.

Some parents recognize that their children were forming the past tense of irregular verbs correctly but then began to make errors. Some of these parents become concerned that their children are "slipping" in their language development and attempt to correct them. However, overregularization reflects accurate knowledge of grammar, not faulty language development. In another year or two, *mouses* will be boringly transformed into *mice*, and Mommy will no longer have *sitted* down. Parents might as well enjoy overregularization while they can.

Asking Questions

Children's first questions are telegraphic and characterized by a rising pitch at the end, which, in English, signifies a question. Depending on the context, "More milky?" can be translated into "May I have more milk?", "Would you like more milk?", or "Is there more milk?" Usually toward the latter part of the third year, the *wh* questions start. Consistent with the child's general cognitive development, certain *wh* questions (*what, who,* and *where*) appear earlier than others (*why, when, which,* and *how*) (Tamis- LeMonda et al., 2006). *Why* is usually too philosophical for a 2-year-old, and *how* is too involved. Two-year-olds are also likely to be now-oriented, so *when* is of less than immediate concern. By the fourth year, most children are spontaneously producing *why, when,* and *how* questions. These *wh* words are initially tacked on to the beginnings of sentences. "Where Mommy go?" can stand for "Where is Mommy going?", "Where did Mommy go?", or "Where will Mommy go?", and its meaning must be derived from context. Later on, the child will add the auxiliary verbs *is, did,* and *will* to indicate whether the question concerns the present, past, or future.

Pragmatics

Pragmatics refers to the practical aspects of communication. Children show pragmatism when they adjust their speech to fit the social situation (Nelson, 2006). For example, children show greater formality in their choice of words and syntax when their make-believe games include role-playing high-status figures, such as teachers or physicians. They say "please" more often when making requests of high-status people or when they use Motherese in talking to an infant.

Preschoolers tend to be egocentric; therefore, a 2-year-old who tells another child "Gimme my book," without specifying which book, may assume that the other child knows what she herself knows. Once children can perceive the world through the eyes of others, they advance in their abilities to make themselves understood. The child can then recognize that the other child needs a description of the book or of its location to carry out the request.

Language and Cognition

Language and cognitive development are interwoven (Homer & Nelson, 2005; Waxman & Lidz, 2006). For example, the child gradually gains the capacity to discriminate between animals on the basis of distinct features, such as size, patterns of movement, and the sounds they make. At the same time, the child also is acquiring words that represent broader categories, such as *mammal* and *animal*.

But which comes first? Does the child first develop concepts and then acquire the language to describe them, or does the child's increasing language ability lead to the development of new concepts?

KITTY

Does Cognitive Development Precede Language Development?

Piaget (1976) believed that cognitive development precedes language development. He argued that children must understand concepts before they use words to describe them. From Piaget's perspective, children learn words to describe classes or categories that they have already created (Nelson, 2005). Children can learn the word *kitty* because they have perceived the characteristics that distinguish cats from other things.

Some studies support the notion that cognitive concepts may precede language. For example, the vocabulary explosion that occurs at about 18 months of age is related to the child's ability to group a set of objects into two categories, such as "dolls" and "cars" (Gopnik & Meltzoff, 1992). Other research suggests that young children need to experience an action themselves or by observation to learn the meaning of a verb (Pulverman et al., 2006).

Does Language Development Precede Cognitive Development?

Although many theorists argue that cognitive development precedes language development, others reverse the causal relationship and claim that children create cognitive classes to understand things that are labelled by words (Clark, 1983). When children hear the word *dog*, they try to understand it by searching for characteristics that separate dogs from other things.

The Interactionist View: Outer Speech and Inner Speech

Today, most developmentalists find something of value in each of these cognitive views (Waxman & Lidz, 2006). In the early stages of language development, concepts often precede words, and many of the infant's words describe classes that have already developed. But later, language influences thought.

Vygotsky believed that during most of the first year, vocalizations and thought are separate. But during the second year, thought and speech combine forces. Children discover that objects have labels. Their learning of the labels becomes more self-directed. Children ask what new words mean. Learning new words fosters the creation of new

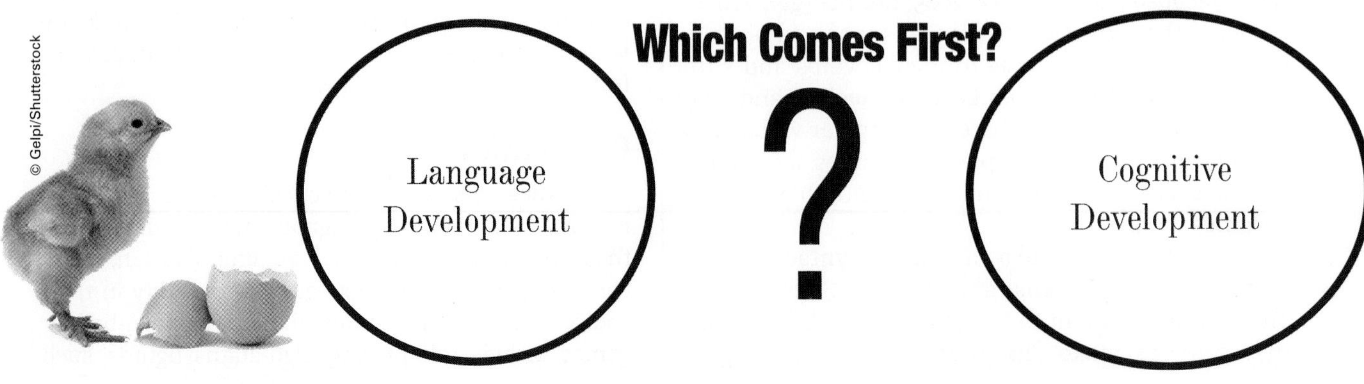

categories, and new categories become filled with labels for new things.

Vygotsky's concept of **inner speech** is a key feature of his position. At first, children's thoughts are spoken aloud. You can hear the 3-year-old instructing herself as she plays with toys. At this age, her vocalizations serve to regulate her behaviour, but they gradually become internalized. What was spoken aloud at ages 4 and 5 becomes an internal dialogue by age 6 or 7. Inner speech is the ultimate binding of language and thought. It facilitates learning and is involved in the development of planning and self-regulation.

inner speech
Vygotsky's concept of the ultimate binding of language and thought. Inner speech originates in vocalizations that may regulate the child's behaviour and become internalized by age 6 or 7.

Go online at
www.nelson.com/4ltrpress/icanhdev2ce
And access the essential Study Tools online for this chapter:

- **Practice Quizzes,** which will help you to prepare for tests
- **Games,** to help test your knowledge
- **Flashcards,** to test your understanding of key terms
- **Observing Development Videos**
- **Internet Activities**

CHAPTER 8

© David H. Lewis/iStockphoto.com

Early Childhood: Social and Emotional Development

LEARNING OUTCOMES

LO1 Describe the dimensions of child rearing and styles of parenting

LO2 Explain how siblings, birth order, peers, and other factors affect social development during early childhood

LO3 Discuss personality and emotional development during early childhood, focusing on the self, Erikson's views, and fears

LO4 Discuss the development of gender roles and sex differences

> **"Most parents want preschoolers to develop a sense of responsibility and develop into well-adjusted individuals."**

LO1 Dimensions of Child Rearing

Parents have different approaches to rearing their children. Investigators of parental patterns of child rearing have found it useful to classify parents' approaches according to two broad dimensions: warmth–coldness and restrictiveness–permissiveness (Baumrind, 1989, 2005).

Warm parents are affectionate toward their children. They tend to hug and kiss them and smile at them frequently. Warm parents are caring and supportive. They communicate their enjoyment of being with their children. Warm parents are less likely than cold parents to use physical discipline (Bender et al., 2007).

Cold parents may not enjoy their children and may have few feelings of affection for them. They are likely to complain about their children's behaviour, saying they are naughty or have "minds of their own."

Clearly, it is better to be warm than cold toward children. The children of parents who are warm and accepting are more likely to develop internal standards of conduct, a moral sense or conscience (Bender et al., 2007; Lau et al., 2006). Parental warmth also is related to the child's social

Time & Life Pictures/Getty Images

Erikson Today

Stage 2: Autonomy versus Shame, Doubt (19 months to 3 years)

The next step along the road of personality development involves the challenge of autonomy vs. shame and doubt. As children become older and are able to explore their own environment, they need to develop a sense of autonomy or control. Between the ages of 18 months and 3 years, children have the opportunity to build self-esteem as they learn new skills and the difference between right and wrong. Well-cared-for children will carry themselves with pride rather than shame. This stage focuses on the ability (or inability) to master certain skills as children become the controller of their universe by mastering social rules and such important cultural rules as toilet training and sleeping.

Time & Life Pictures/Getty Images

Erikson Today

Stage 3: Initiative versus Guilt (4 to 5 years)

The third piece of the puzzle focuses on the life stage when children begin to copy the important people in their lives by taking initiative in creating play situations. They make up stories and play out character roles in their pretend universe. They experiment with their ideas of who people are, both within the context of their family and in the world around them.

Consider **THIS**

How can you determine whether a child is securely attached and building the foundation for autonomy and independence?

Please see page 140 for a discussion on this topic.

inductive
based on an attempt to foster understanding of the principles behind parental demands; characteristic of disciplinary methods, such as reasoning.

and emotional well-being (Lau et al., 2006; Leung et al., 2004).

Where does parental warmth come from? Some of it reflects parental beliefs about how to best rear children, and some reflects parents' tendencies to imitate the behaviour of their own parents.

It is not true that parents who are strict and demand mature behaviour end up raising rebellious children. Consistent control and firm enforcement of rules can have positive consequences for the child, particularly when combined with strong support and affection (Grusec, 2006). This parenting style is termed the *authoritative style*. On the other hand, if "restrictiveness" means physical punishment, interference, or intrusiveness, it can give rise to disobedience, rebelliousness, and lower levels of cognitive development (Paulussen-Hoogeboom et al., 2007; Rudy & Grusec, 2006).

Permissive parents supervise their children less closely than restrictive parents do. Permissive parents allow their children to do what is "natural," such as make noise, treat toys carelessly, and experiment with their bodies. They may also allow their children to show some aggression, intervening only when its continuation presents a danger.

How Parents Enforce Restrictions

Inductive methods aim to teach knowledge that will enable children to generate desirable behaviour on their own. The main inductive technique is "reasoning," or explaining why one kind of behaviour is good and another is not. Reasoning with a 1- or 2-year-old can be basic. "Don't do that—it hurts!" qualifies as reasoning with toddlers. "It hurts!" is an explanation, though brief. The inductive approach helps the child understand moral behaviour and fosters prosocial behaviours such as helping and sharing (Paulussen-Hoogeboom et al., 2007).

Power-assertive methods include physical punishment and denial of privileges. Parents often justify physical punishment with sayings such as "Spare the rod, spoil the child." Parents may insist that power assertion is necessary because their children are noncompliant. However, use of power assertion is related to both parental authoritarianism and children's behaviour (Roopnarine et al., 2006; Rudy & Grusec, 2006). Parental power assertion is associated with children's lower acceptance by peers, poorer grades, and more antisocial behaviour. The more parents use power-assertive techniques, the less children appear to develop internal standards of conduct. Parental punishment and rejection are often linked to children's aggression and delinquency.

Consistent control and firm enforcement of rules can have positive consequences for the child, particularly when combined with strong support and affection.

Some parents control children by threatening the withdrawal of love. They isolate or ignore misbehaving children. Because most children need parental approval and contact, loss of love can be more threatening than physical punishment. Although withdrawal of love may foster compliance, it may also instill guilt and anxiety (Grusec, 2002).

Preschoolers more readily comply when asked to do something than when asked to *stop* doing something (Kochanska et al., 2001). One way to manage children who are doing something wrong or bad is to involve them in something else.

Parenting Styles: How Parents Transmit Values and Standards

Diana Baumrind (1989, 1991b) focused on the relationship between parenting styles and the development of competent behaviour in young children. She used the dimensions of warmth–coldness and restrictiveness–permissiveness to develop a grid of four parenting styles based on whether parents are high or low in each dimension (see Table 8.1).

The parents of the most capable children are rated high in both dimensions (see Table 8.1). They are highly restrictive and make strong demands for maturity. However, they also reason with their children and show strong support and feelings of love. Baumrind applies the label **authoritative** to these parents; they know what they want their children to do but also respect their children and are warm toward them.

Compared with other children, the children of authoritative parents tend to show self-reliance and independence, high self-esteem, high levels of activity and exploratory behaviour, and social competence. They are highly motivated to achieve and do well in school (Baumrind, 1989, 1991b; Grusec, 2006).

"Because I say so" could be the motto of parents who Baumrind labels **authoritarian**. Authoritarians value obedience for its own sake. They have strict guidelines for right and wrong and demand that their children accept those guidelines without question. Like authoritative parents, they are controlling. But unlike authoritative parents, their enforcement methods rely on force. Moreover, authoritarian parents do not communicate well with their children or respect their children's viewpoints. Most researchers find them to be generally cold and rejecting (Grusec, 2002).

authoritative
a child-rearing style in which parents are restrictive and demanding yet communicative and warm.

authoritarian
a child-rearing style in which parents demand submission and obedience.

permissive–indulgent
a child-rearing style in which parents are warm and not restrictive.

rejecting–neglecting
a child-rearing style in which parents are neither restrictive and controlling nor supportive and responsive.

Baumrind found the sons of authoritarian parents to be relatively hostile and defiant and the daughters to be low in independence and dominance (Baumrind, 1989). Other researchers have found that the children of authoritarian parents are less competent socially and academically than children of authoritative parents. Children of authoritarian parents tend to be anxious, irritable, and restrained in their social interactions (Grusec, 2002). As adolescents, they may be conforming and obedient but have low self-reliance and self-esteem.

Baumrind found two types of parents who are permissive as opposed to restrictive. One is permissive–indulgent and the other rejecting–neglecting. **Permissive–indulgent** parents are low in their attempts to control their children and in their demands for mature behaviour. They are easygoing and unconventional. Their brand of permissiveness is accompanied by high nurturance (warmth and support).

Rejecting–neglecting parents are also low in their demands for mature behaviour and in their attempts to control their children. Unlike indulgent parents, however, they are low in support and responsiveness. The children of neglectful parents are the least competent, least responsible, and least mature. The children of permissive–indulgent parents, like those of neglectful parents, are less competent in school and show more misconduct and substance abuse than children of more restrictive,

TABLE 8.1

Baumrind's Patterns of Parenting

	Parental Behaviour Patterns	
Parental Style	***Restrictiveness and Control***	***Warmth and Responsiveness***
Authoritative	↑	↑
Authoritarian	↑	↓
Permissive–Indulgent	↓	↑
Rejecting–Neglecting	↓	↓

secure attachment a type of attachment characterized by mild distress when caregivers physically leave a space, and being readily soothed upon their return.

controlling parents. But children from permissive–indulgent homes, unlike those from neglectful homes, are fairly high in social competence and self-confidence (Baumrind, 1991a).

Effects of the Situation and the Child on Parenting Styles

Parenting styles are not merely a one-way street, from parent to child. Parenting styles also depend partly on the situation and partly on the characteristics of the child (Grusec, 2006). For example, parents are most likely to use power-assertive techniques when dealing with aggressive behaviour (Casas et al., 2006; Lipman et al., 2006). Parents prefer power assertion to induction when they believe that children understand the rules they have violated and are capable of acting appropriately. Stress also contributes to the parents' use of power.

Baumrind's research suggests that we can make an effort to avoid some of the pitfalls of being authoritarian or overly permissive. Some recommended techniques that parents can use to help control and guide their children's behaviour are listed in Table 8.2.

EMERGING CANADA

The Canadian government (Health Canada, 2000) has compiled a publication to help children (at every age) through the difficulties of divorce. In this document, parents are reminded that young children see and experience divorce much differently from adults. Young children have a limited ability to understand the complex emotions they are experiencing yet they often create their own "big picture." Often they view themselves as the cause of their parents' separation, and they ultimately believe or wish their parents will get back together. Because early childhood is a time when children learn and build their sense of self by watching and interacting with their parents, those children who witness arguing often experience it as though they were personally involved.

The publication *Because Life Goes On* provides tips on the following:

- Talking to your children about your separation and divorce
- Communicating effectively with children at different stages of development
- Maintaining your child's community of support
- Learning when to get help for yourself and your child
- Dealing with violence in the home
- Helping a child who experiences abandonment
- Helping a child in distress

Consider THIS

How can you determine whether a child is securely attached and building the foundation for autonomy and independence?

We study the individual stages of development separately but it is important to recognize that each stage sets the foundation for the next stage. The stages interact with one another in a complex puzzle of personality development. Life experiences shape personality development but some life events are timely, having more significance within the psychosocial stage where they are encountered. Trust or mistrust lays the foundation for attachment in early childhood. The next step is the development of autonomy, which requires an examination of attachment quality (secure or insecure), one of the strongest predictors of later development. A **secure attachment** is characterized by children's ability to use their parent(s) for comfort, treating them as a home base for exploration. Secure attachment will lead to independence. Confident in the primary caregivers' availability, children with secure attachment are free to fully explore and play on their own.

- **Parental behaviours:** sensitive, consistent supervision; responsive interaction; the ability to recognize the uniqueness of children and their individual needs; and the ability to vary their responses to the context of the situation.
- **Early childhood behaviours:** infants use their parents as a home base; they seek out the parent for help or comfort; they exhibit a willingness to comply with requests; infants do not show patterns of directing the caregivers' behaviour for their own purposes.
- **Insecure attachment:** characterized by children's inability or unwillingness to access their parent for comfort; obviously dependent children have difficulty with separation or independent play; other children are under-dependent, barely noticing when the parents leave; some children may seem frightened or very confused in the presence of their parents.
- **Parental behaviours:** interfering with child exploration; inconsistent supervision and expectations; ignoring the child's cues; exhibiting hostile behaviour; placing their own needs above those of the child.
- **Early childhood behaviours:** excessive dependence; marked shyness and withdrawal; failure to seek contact or comfort; aggressive or bossy behaviours; confusion in the presence of their parents.

Given the psychosocial importance of developing a sense of autonomy in this stage of personality development, intervention is necessary if behaviours seem to indicate an insecure attachment. Failure to disrupt the pattern of insecure attachment will lead to the child developing a sense of shame or doubt. Drawing from the lessons of attachment theory and research, professionals can support parents to raise secure, well-adjusted children (Appleyard & Berlin, 2007).

TABLE 8.2

Advice for Parents in Guiding Young Children's Behaviour

DO ...	DON'T ...
• Reward good behaviour with praises, smiles, and hugs. • Give clear, simple, realistic rules appropriate to the child's age. • Enforce rules with reasonable consequences. • Ignore annoying behaviour such as whining and tantrums. • Childproof the house, putting dangerous and breakable items out of reach. Then establish limits. • Be consistent.	• Pay attention only to a child's misbehaviour. • Issue too many rules or enforce them haphazardly. • Try to control behaviour solely in the child's domain, such as thumb sucking, which can lead to frustrating power struggles. • Nag, lecture, shame, or induce guilt. • Yell or spank. • Be overly permissive.

regression
a return to behaviour characteristic of earlier stages of development

LO2 Social Behaviours

During early childhood, children make tremendous advances in social skills and behaviour. Their play increasingly involves other children. They learn how to share, cooperate, and comfort others. But young children, like adults, can be aggressive as well as loving and helpful.

Influence of Siblings

Siblings serve many functions, including giving physical care, providing emotional support and nurturance, offering advice, serving as role models, providing social interaction that helps develop social skills, making demands, and imposing restrictions (McHale et al., 2006; Parke & Buriel, 2006).

In early childhood, siblings' interactions have positive aspects (cooperation, teaching, nurturance) and negative aspects (conflict, control, competition) (Parke & Buriel, 2006). Older siblings tend to be more caring but also more dominating than younger siblings. Younger siblings are more likely to imitate older siblings and accept their direction.

In many cultures, older girls care for their younger siblings (Clark, 2005). Parents often urge their children to stop fighting among themselves, and at times, these conflicts look deadly. But garden-variety sibling conflict can enhance children's social competence, their development of self-identity (who they are and what they stand for), and their ability to rear their own children (Ross et al., 2006).

More conflicts occur between siblings when the parents play favourites (Scharf et al., 2005). Conflict between siblings is also greater when the relationships between the parents or between the parents and children are troubled (Kim et al., 2006).

Adjusting to the Birth of a Sibling

The birth of a sister or brother leads to changes in family relationships, which are often a source of stress for preschoolers (Volling, 2003). When a new baby comes into the home, the mother pays relatively more attention to that child and spends less time with the older child. As a result, the older child may feel displaced and resentful.

Children show a mixture of negative and positive reactions to the birth of a sibling. Negative responses include **regression** to baby-like behaviours, such as increases in clinging, crying, and toilet accidents. Anger and naughtiness may also increase. But the same children may also show more independence and maturity, insisting on feeding or dressing themselves and helping to care for the baby (Volling, 2003). Parents can help a young child cope with the arrival of a baby by explaining in advance what is to come (Kavcic & Zupancic, 2005).

Birth Order

Differences in personality and achievement have been linked to birth order. First-born children, as a group, are more highly motivated to achieve than later-born children (Latham & Budworth, 2007). First-born and only children perform better academically and are more cooperative (Healy & Ellis, 2007). They are more adult-oriented and less aggressive than later-born children (Beck et al., 2006; Zajonc, 2001). They obtain higher standardized test scores, including IQ and SAT scores (Kristensen & Bjerkedal, 2007; Sulloway, 2007). On the

dramatic play
play in which children enact social roles

negative side, first-born and only children show greater anxiety and are less self-reliant than later-born children.

Later-born children may learn to act aggressively to compete for the attention of their parents and older siblings (Carey, 2007b). Their self-concepts tend to be lower than those of first-born or only children, but the social skills later-born children acquire from dealing with their family position seem to translate into greater popularity with peers (Carey, 2007b). They also tend to be more rebellious and liberal than first-born children (Beck et al., 2006; Zweigenhaft & Von Ammon, 2000).

By and large, parents are more relaxed and flexible with later-born children. Many parents see that the first-born child is turning out well and perhaps they assume that later-born children will also turn out well.

> **DID YOU KNOW?**
>
> **First-born children are more highly motivated to achieve than later-born children.**
>
> As a group, this is true, but individual variances always occur.

Peer Relationships

Peer interactions foster social skills—sharing, helping, taking turns, and dealing with conflict. Groups teach children how to lead and how to follow. Physical and cognitive skills develop through peer interactions. Peers also provide emotional support (Dishion & Stormshak, 2007; Grusec, 2006).

By about 2 years of age, children imitate one another's play and engage in social games such as follow-the-leader (Fontaine, 2005; Kavanaugh, 2006). By the age of 2, children show preferences for particular playmates—an early sign of friendship (Sherwin-White, 2006). Friendship is characterized by shared positive experiences and feelings of attachment (Grusec, 2002). Even early friendships can be fairly stable (Rubin et al., 2006).

© Shauna Longmuir

First-born children tend to be more cooperative, and later-born children tend to be more social.

When preschoolers are asked what they like about their friends, they typically mention the toys and activities they share (Gleason & Hohmann, 2006). Primary-school children usually report that their friends are the children with whom they do things and have fun (Gleason & Hohmann, 2006). The importance of friends' traits and notions of trust, communication, and intimacy do not emerge until late childhood and adolescence.

Play—Child's Play, That Is

Play is more than fun; it is also meaningful, voluntary, and internally motivated (Elkind, 2007). Play helps children develop motor skills and coordination. It contributes to social development, as children learn to share their play materials, take turns, and, through **dramatic play**, try on new roles (Elkind, 2007). Play also supports the development of such cognitive qualities as curiosity, exploration, symbolic thinking, and problem solving. Play may even help children learn to control impulses (Elkind, 2007).

Play and Cognitive Development

Play contributes to and expresses milestones in cognitive development. Jean Piaget (1962 [1946]) identified kinds of play, each characterized by increasing cognitive complexity:

- *Functional play.* Beginning in the sensorimotor stage, the first kind of play involves repetitive motor activity, such as rolling a ball or running and laughing.
- *Symbolic play.* Also called pretend play, imaginative play, or dramatic play, symbolic play emerges toward the end of the sensorimotor stage and increases during early childhood. In symbolic play, children create settings, characters, and scripts (Kavanaugh, 2006).
- *Constructive play.* Children use objects or materials to draw something or make something, such as a tower of blocks.
- *Formal games.* Games with rules include board games, which are sometimes enhanced or invented by children, and games involving motor skills, such as marbles and hopscotch, ball games involving sides or teams, and video games. Such games may involve social interaction as well as physical activity and rules. People play such games for a lifetime.

Sex Differences in Play

Girls and boys differ both in their toy preferences and in their choice of play environments and activities. During the preschool and early elementary school years, boys prefer vigorous physical outdoor activities, such as climbing, playing with large vehicles, and rough-and-tumble play (Else-Quest et al., 2006).

In middle childhood, boys spend more time than girls in play groups of five or more children and in competitive play (Crombie & Desjardins, 1993; Else-Quest et al., 2006). Girls are more likely than boys to engage in arts and crafts and domestic play. Girls' activities are more closely directed and structured by adults (A. Campbell et al., 2002).

Why do children show these early preferences for gender-stereotyped toys and activities? Biological factors may play a role: boys tend to have slightly greater strength and higher activity levels than girls, whereas girls tend to have slightly greater physical maturity and coordination than boys. But adults treat girls and boys differently. They provide gender-stereotyped toys and room furnishings and encourage gender typing in play and household chores (Leaper, 2002). Children, moreover, tend to seek out information on which kinds of toys and play are "masculine" or "feminine" and then to conform to the label (Martin & Ruble, 2004).

This socialization process of parents and peers encouraging play with gender specific toys has always been believed to be the primary force shaping sex differences in toy preference. Hasset et al. (2008) conducted a study to consider the role of biology in determining preferences for specific types of toys. They noted that sex differences in child play, such as rough and tumble play, were shared by monkeys. If activity preference was similar, perhaps toy preference was also similar. They found that, like boys, male monkeys showed a strong and consistent preference for wheeled toys, whereas female monkeys preferred more variety, much like their human counterparts. This finding raises an interesting question about the role of nature and nurture in play.

Another well-documented finding is that by age 2, many children begin to prefer playmates of the same sex. Girls tend to develop this preference earlier than boys (Fagot, 1990; Hay et al., 2004). This tendency strengthens during middle childhood.

EMERGING CANADA

This is the "hot toy list" published by The Canadian Toy Association for the 2012 holiday season. What influences are at play when it comes to the toys we choose for our children?

- Furby, Elmo, Tigger, and The Teenage Mutant Ninja Turtles are making a comeback.
- Construction toys have targeted girls, with toys ranging from castles to stables to playgrounds.
- Preschool toys have become electronic with an emphasis throughout the age groups on touch screens, built-in cameras, and downloadable apps for iPads.
- Arts and crafts remain on the top toy list.
- Also making the list was an environmentally friendly recycling truck and a popular new series of interactive sound books called *Meet the Farties* (Abraham, 2012).

Prosocial Behaviour

Prosocial behaviour, also known as *altruism*, is intended to benefit another without expectation of reward. Prosocial behaviour includes sharing, cooperating, and helping and comforting others in distress (Strayer & Roberts, 2004). This behaviour is exhibited by children in their preschool and early school years (Knafo & Plomin, 2006a, 2006b) and is linked to the development of empathy and perspective taking.

Empathy

Empathy refers to sensitivity to the feelings of others and shown by such activities as sharing and cooperation. Infants frequently begin to cry when they hear other children crying, although this early agitated response may be largely reflexive (Strayer & Roberts, 2004). Empathy promotes prosocial behaviour and decreases aggressive behaviour, and these links are evident by the second year (Hastings et al., 2000). During the second year, many children approach other children and adults who are in distress and try to help them. They may hug a crying child or tell the child not to cry. Toddlers who are rated as emotionally unresponsive to the feelings of others are more likely to behave aggressively throughout their school years (Olson et al., 2000).

Girls show more empathy than boys (Strayer & Roberts, 2004). It is unclear whether this sex difference reflects genetic factors or the socialization of girls to be attuned to the emotions of others.

Perspective Taking

According to Piaget, preoperational children tend to be egocentric. They tend not to be able to see things from the vantage points of others. Various cognitive abilities, such as being able to take another person's perspective, are related to knowing when someone is in need or distress. Perspective-taking skills improve with age, as do prosocial skills. Among children of the same age, those with better developed perspective-taking ability also show more prosocial behaviour and less aggressive behaviour (Hastings et al., 2000).

Influences on Prosocial Behaviour

Although altruistic behaviour is defined as prosocial behaviour that occurs in the absence of rewards or the expectations of rewards, it is, in reality, influenced by rewards and punishments. The peers of nursery-school children who are cooperative, friendly, and generous respond more positively to them than they do to children whose behaviour is self-centred (Hartup, 1983). Children who are rewarded for acting prosocially are likely to continue these behaviours (Knafo & Plomin, 2006a, 2006b).

Parents foster prosocial behaviour when they use inductive techniques such as explaining how behaviour affects others ("You made Josh cry. It's not nice to hit."). Parents of prosocial children are more likely to expect mature behaviour from their children. They are less likely to use power-assertive techniques of discipline (Strayer & Roberts, 2004).

Development of Aggression

Children, like adults, can also be aggressive. Aggression refers to behaviour intended to hurt or injure another person.

Aggressive behaviour, similar to other social behaviour, seems to follow developmental patterns.

Stockbyte/Thinkstock.com

The aggression of preschoolers is frequently instrumental or possession oriented (Persson, 2005). For example, younger preschoolers tend to use aggression to obtain the toys and situations they want, such as a favoured seat at the table or in the car. Older preschoolers are more likely to resolve conflicts over toys by sharing rather than fighting (Caplan et al., 1991). Anger and aggression in preschoolers usually cause other preschoolers to reject them (Henry et al., 2000; Walter & LaFreniere, 2000).

By age 6 or 7, aggression becomes hostile and person oriented. Children taunt and criticize one another and call one another names; they also attack one another physically.

Aggressive behaviour appears to be generally stable and predictive of social and emotional problems later on, especially among boys (Nagin & Tremblay, 2001; Tapper & Boulton, 2004). Toddlers who are perceived as difficult and defiant are more likely to behave aggressively throughout their school years (Olson et al., 2000).

Theories of Aggression

Evidence suggests that genetic factors may be involved in aggressive behaviour, including criminal and antisocial behaviour (Hicks et al., 2007; Lykken, 2006a; E. O. Wilson, 2004). If genetics is involved in aggression, genes may do their work at least in part through the male sex hormone testosterone. Testosterone is apparently related to feelings of self-confidence, high activity levels, and—the negative side—aggressiveness (Archer, 2006; Cunningham & McGinnis, 2007; Popma et al., 2007). Cognitive research with primary-school children has found that children who believe that aggression is an acceptable way to settle matters are more likely to behave aggressively when provoked (Tapper & Boulton, 2004).

Social cognitive explanations of aggression focus on environmental factors such as reinforcement and observational learning. When children repeatedly push, shove, and hit to grab toys or break into line, other children usually let them have their way (Kempes et al., 2005). Children who are thus rewarded for acting aggressively are likely to continue to use aggressive means, especially if they have no other means to achieve their ends. Aggressive children may also associate with peers who value and encourage aggression (Stauffacher & DeHart, 2006).

Children who are physically punished are more likely to be aggressive themselves than children who are not physically punished (Patterson, 2005). Physically aggressive parents serve as models for aggression and also stoke their children's anger.

DID YOU KNOW?

Children who are physically punished are more likely to be aggressive than children who are not physically punished.

This is true, and it raises important discipline issues.

Media Influences

Real people are not the only models of aggressive behaviour in children's lives. A classic study by Albert Bandura and his colleagues (1963) suggested that televised models had a powerful influence on children's aggressive behaviour. One group of preschoolers observed a film of an adult model hitting and kicking an inflated Bobo doll, whereas a control group saw an aggression-free film. The experimental and control children were then left alone in a room with the same doll as hidden observers recorded their behaviour. The children who had observed the aggressive model showed significantly more aggressive behaviour toward the doll themselves (see Figure 8.1). Many children imitated the bizarre attack behaviours they had observed in the film, behaviours they would not have thought up themselves.

greenland/Shutterstock.com

DID YOU KNOW?

Children who watch 2 to 4 hours of TV a day will see 8,000 murders and another 100,000 acts of violence by the time they have finished elementary school.

What are our children watching?

FIGURE 8.1

Photos from Albert Bandura's Classic Experiment in the Imitation of Aggressive Models

In the top row, an adult model strikes a clown doll. The second and third rows show a boy and a girl imitating the aggressive behaviour.

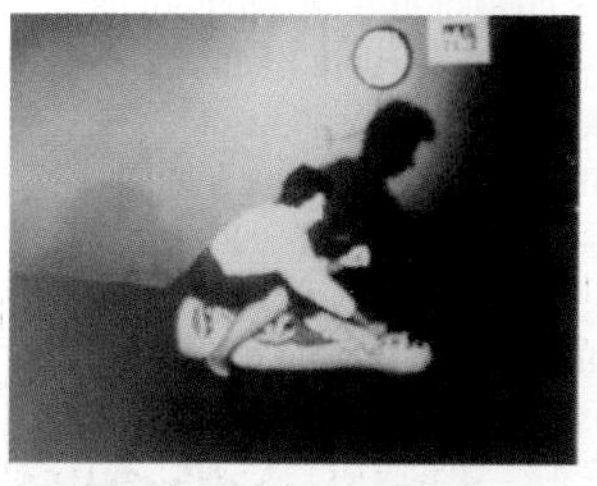

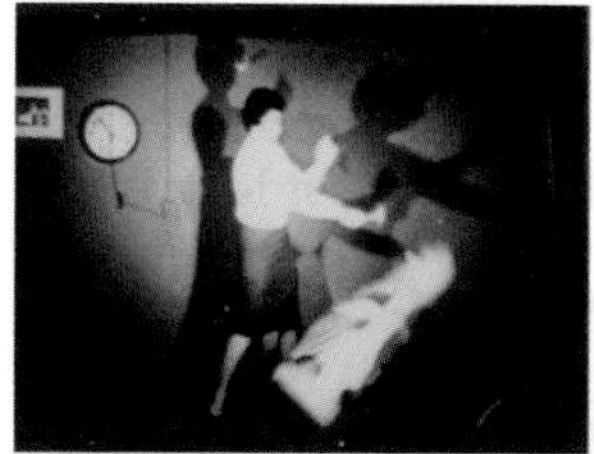
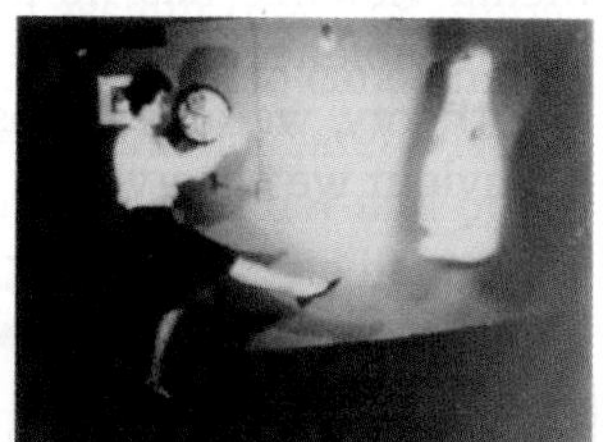

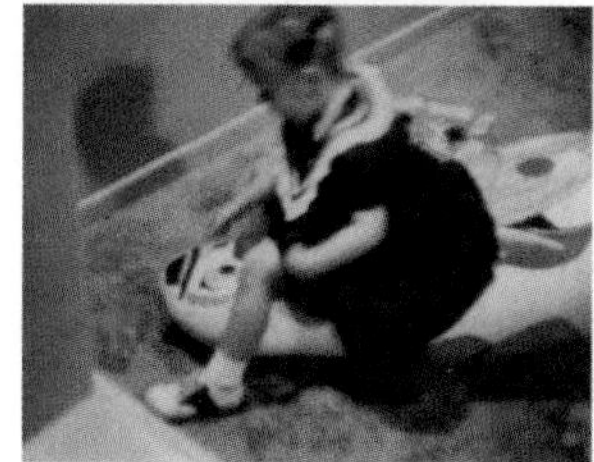

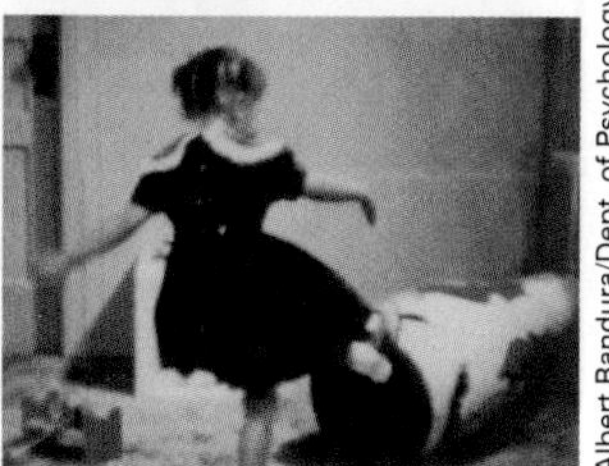

Albert Bandura/Dept. of Psychology, Stanford University

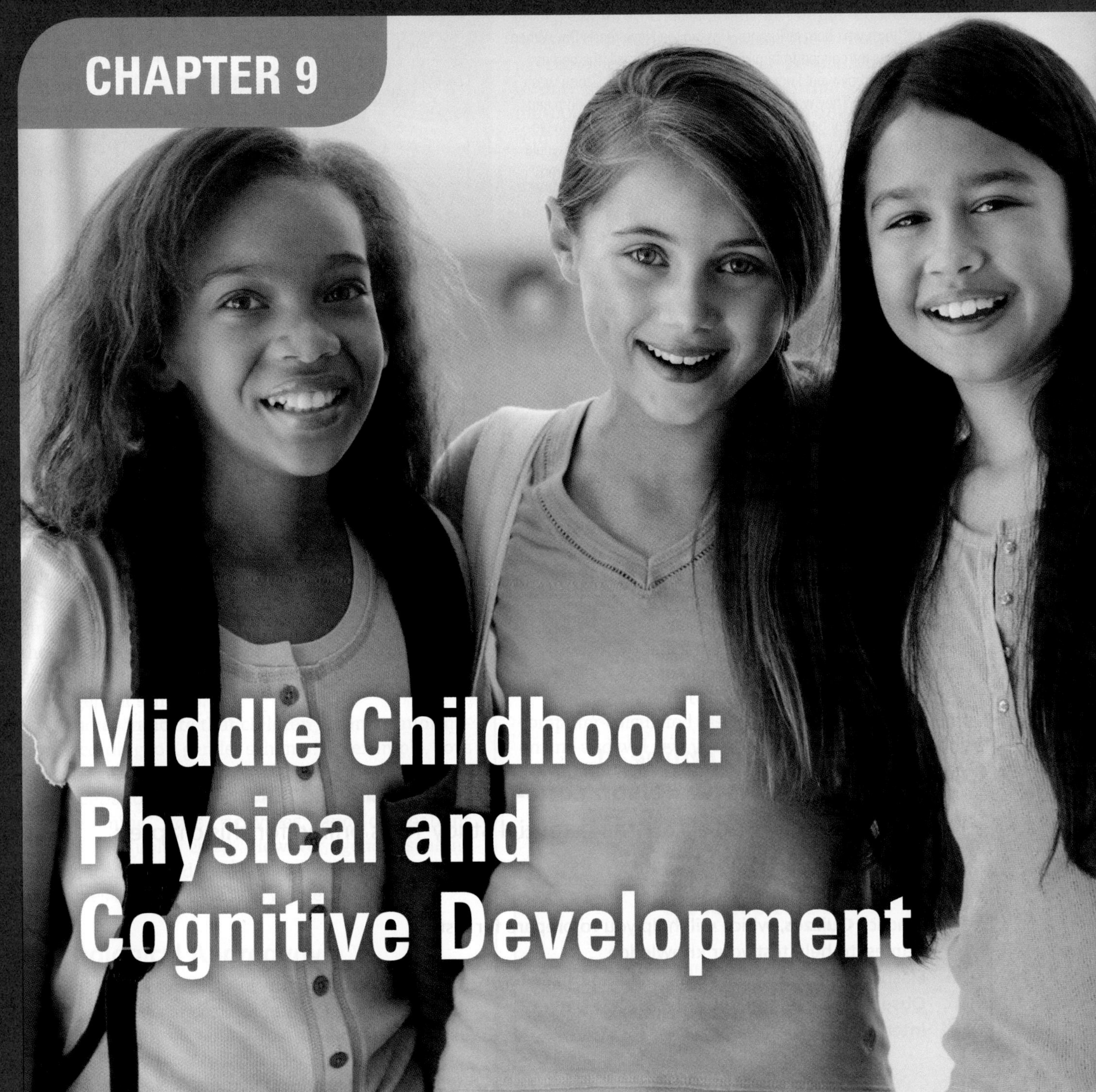

CHAPTER 9

Middle Childhood: Physical and Cognitive Development

LEARNING OUTCOMES

LO1 Describe trends in physical development in middle childhood

LO2 Describe changes in motor development in middle childhood

LO3 Discuss ADHD and learning disabilities

LO4 Describe Piaget's concrete-operational stage

LO5 Discuss Kohlberg's theories of moral development

LO6 Describe developments in information processing in middle childhood

LO7 Describe intellectual development in middle childhood, focusing on theories of intelligence

LO8 Describe language development in middle childhood, including reading and bilingualism

Monkey Business Images/Shutterstock.com

> "Boys are slightly heavier and taller than girls through to the age of 9 or 10. Girls then begin their adolescent growth spurt."

LO1 Growth Patterns

Following the growth trends of early childhood, boys and girls continue to gain a little more than 5 cm (2 in.) in height per year until the adolescent **growth spurt**. The average gain in weight between the ages of 6 and 12 is 2.25 to 3 kg (5 to 7 lb.) a year, but children grow less stocky and more slender (Kuczmarski et al., 2002).

growth spurt a period during which growth advances at a dramatically rapid rate compared with other periods.

Nutrition and Growth

In middle childhood, the average child's body weight doubles. Children also spend a good deal of energy in physical activity and play. To fuel this growth and activity, schoolchildren eat more than preschoolers. The average 4- to 6-year-old needs 1,400 calories per day, but the average 7- to 10-year-old requires 2,000 calories, though healthy choices from Canada's Food Guide should be the highest priority when considering nutritional needs in middle childhood.

Nutrition involves more than calories. Good nutrition requires making healthful choices from Canada's Food Guide, including fruits and vegetables, fish, poultry (without skin), and whole grains. Limit the intake of fats, sugar, and starches. However, most foods in school cafeterias and elsewhere are heavy in sugar, animal fats, and salt (Bauer et al., 2004). Portions have also grown over the decades, especially at fast-food restaurants (Nielsen & Popkin, 2003).

Sex Similarities and Differences in Physical Growth

Boys are slightly heavier and taller than girls through to the age of 9 or 10. Girls then begin their adolescent growth spurt and surpass boys in height and weight until about age 13 or 14, when boys spurt and grow taller and heavier than girls. The steady gains in height and weight in middle childhood are paralleled by increased muscle strength in both sexes. Beginning at about age 11, boys develop relatively more muscle, and girls develop relatively more fat.

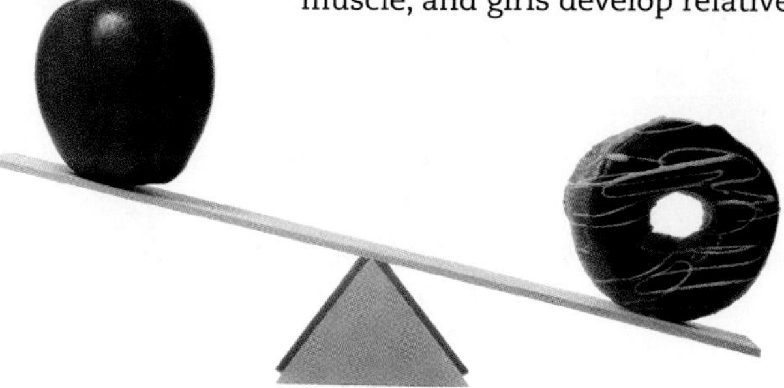
Encouraging healthy food choices is important.

© Mike Kemp/Rubberball/Getty Images

Overweight Children

The Canadian Heart and Stroke Foundation (2008) reports that, in 2004, 8 percent of Canadian children and youth (ages 6 to 11) were obese, and 18 percent were overweight, representing 1 child in 4, or 26 percent. Although parents often assume that heavy children will "outgrow" their "baby

DID YOU KNOW?

"Baby fat" in early childhood can remain a lifelong struggle.

Statistically, most overweight children become overweight adults.

fat," most overweight children become overweight adults (Daniels, 2006).

Overweight children are often rejected by peers or become a focus of ridicule (Storch et al., 2007). They are usually poor at sports and less likely to be considered attractive in adolescence (Storch et al., 2007). Overweight children are at greater risk of health problems throughout life (American Heart Association, 2007).

Strategies for Weight Loss

Parents need to support their children in healthy living without encouraging "dieting." Here are a few basic strategies:

- Eliminate sugary drinks from your house. Choose water instead.
- Eliminate unhealthy snacks from your house. Focus on variety and nutrition.
- Control portions and follow the "handful" method for serving sizes.
- Provide fun activities. Be a good role model and spend time with your children.
- Most importantly, adopt the same strategies to help children adjust to a lifetime of healthy choices. When parents are involved, children are more likely to be successful (Sessoms, 2010).

Causes of Being Overweight

Heredity plays a role in being overweight. Some people inherit a tendency to burn up extra calories, whereas others inherit a tendency to turn extra calories into fat (Kolata, 2007).

Family, peers, and environmental factors can influence children's eating habits (Moens et al., 2007). Overweight parents may serve as examples of poor exercise habits, encourage overeating, and keep unhealthful foods in the home. Dining out frequently can become an unhealthy family habit. Children who watch TV extensively burn fewer calories and are more likely to become overweight adolescents than children who exercise frequently (Schumacher & Queen, 2007). Figure 9.1 shows how common it has become for Canadians aged 5 to 17 to be overweight or obese.

LO2 Motor Development

The school years are marked by increases in the child's speed, strength, agility, and balance. These developments lead to more skillful motor activities.

Gross Motor Skills

Throughout middle childhood, children show steady improvement in their ability to perform gross motor

FIGURE 9.1

Body Mass Index of Canadian Children and Youth, 2009 to 2011

Distribution of Household Population Aged 5–17, by Body Mass Index Norms† and age group, Canada, 2009 to 2011

Overweight and obesity is becoming common for Canadians aged 5 to 17.

E Use with caution (data with a coefficient of variation (CV) from 16.6% to 33.3%)

F Too unreliable to be published (data with a coefficient of variation (CV) greater than 33.3%; suppressed due to extreme sampling variability)

†BMI classification based on de Onis M et al.

Source: Statistics Canada. Overweight and obesity rates, by age group, household population aged 2 to 17, Canada excluding territories, 1978/79 and 2004. 2004 Canadian Community Health Survey: Nutrition; Canada Health Survey 1978/79. http://www.statcan.gc.ca/pub/82-620-m/2005001/c-g/child-enfant/4053584-eng.htm .

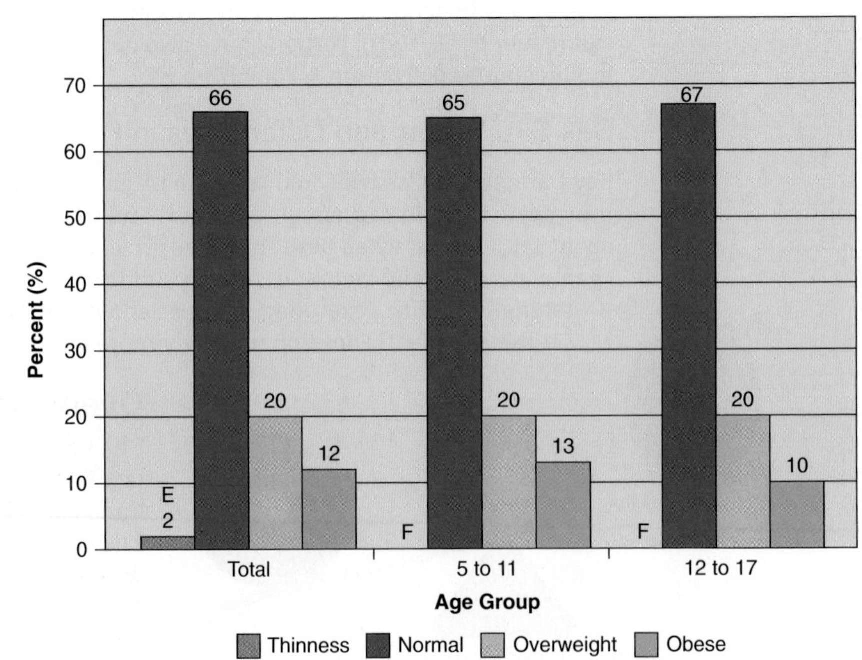

EMERGING CANADA

In 2005, Statistics Canada conducted a survey to gather information on Canadian youth in sports. Many factors influence children's participation in sport activities, including gender, age, household income, parental education, parental involvement in sports, geography, and immigrant status of parents.

Boys are more likely than girls to participate in sports but the gender gap is not as large as it once was. Early teens are more likely to be involved in sports than younger children. Children in higher-income households and those with parents with more than a high-school education are much more likely to be sports participants. The five most popular organized sports in Canada are soccer, swimming, hockey, basketball, and baseball.

Parents who are involved in sports (either as players or spectators) are more likely to enroll their children in sports. Children living in smaller towns and cities are more likely participate in sports than children in Canada's three largest cities. Children of recent immigrants are least likely to participate (Clark, 2009).

skills. Children are hopping, jumping, and climbing by age 6 or so; by age 6 or 7, they are usually capable of balancing and pedalling on a bicycle. By the ages of 8 to 10, children are showing the balance, coordination, and strength that allow them to engage in gymnastics and team sports.

During these years, children's muscles grow stronger, and their neural pathways that connect the cerebellum to the cortex become more myelinated. Experience refines their sensorimotor abilities, but some differences are inborn. For example, some people are born with better visual acuity, depth perception, or coordination than others.

Reaction time is basic to the child's estimate of when to swing a bat or hit a tennis ball. Children's reaction time gradually improves (decreases) from early childhood to about age 18, but individual differences are common (Karatekin et al., 2007). Reaction time increases again in adulthood.

Fine Motor Skills

By the age of 6 to 7, children can usually tie their shoelaces, in spite of Velcro, and hold pencils as adults do. Their abilities to fasten buttons, zip zippers, brush teeth, wash themselves, coordinate a knife and fork, and use chopsticks all develop during the early school years and improve during childhood (Beilei et al., 2002).

Sex Differences

Throughout middle childhood, boys and girls perform similarly in most motor activities. Boys show slightly greater strength, especially in their forearms, which aids them in sports (Butterfield & Loovis, 1993). Girls show slightly greater limb coordination and overall flexibility, which are valuable in dancing, balancing, and gymnastics (Abdelaziz et al., 2001; Cumming et al., 2005).

reaction time the amount of time required to respond to a stimulus.

Prior to puberty, boys are more likely than girls to receive social encouragement and opportunities in sports (A. M. Thompson et al., 2003). Between middle childhood and adolescence, children increasingly stereotype physical activities as being masculine (e.g., football) or feminine (e.g., dance) (Meaney et al., 2002).

Exercise and Fitness

Exercise reduces the risk of heart disease, stroke, diabetes, and certain forms of cancer (Atkinson & Davenne, 2007). Physically active adolescents also have a better self-image and coping skills than those who are inactive (Kirkcaldy et al., 2002). More than half of Canadians aged 5 to 17 are not active enough for optimal growth and development (Heart and Stroke Foundation of Canada, 1993).

Cardiac and muscular fitness are developed through aerobic exercises, such as running, walking quickly, swimming laps, bicycling, or jumping rope for several minutes at a time. However, Canadian schools have seen physical education programming declining over several decades (Physical and Health Education Canada, 2009).

LO3 Children with Disabilities

The school setting requires that a child sit still, pay attention, and master certain academic skills. But some children have difficulty with these demands.

Attention-Deficit/Hyperactivity Disorder (ADHD)

Nine-year-old Sebastian is a problem in class. His teacher complains that he distracts the the other students. He constantly creates reasons to be up from his desk or talking to his neighbours, and he rarely completes his work. And when he does complete his work, he often forgets to hand it in.

Psychological testing shows Eddie to be average in academic ability but to have no attention span.

attention-deficit/hyperactivity disorder (ADHD) a disorder characterized by excessive inattention, impulsiveness, and hyperactivity.

hyperactivity excessive restlessness and overactivity; a characteristic of ADHD.

stimulants drugs that increase the activity of the nervous system.

learning disabilities disorders characterized by inadequate development of specific academic, language, and speech skills.

A child who has attention-deficit/hyperactivity disorder (ADHD) shows excessive inattention, impulsivity, and hyperactivity. The degree of hyperactive behaviour is crucial because many normal children are overactive and fidgety from time to time.

ADHD typically occurs by age 7. The hyperactivity and restlessness impair children's ability to function in school. They cannot sit still and have difficulty getting along with others. ADHD is diagnosed in about 1–5 percent of school-age children and is many times more common in boys than girls.

ADHD is sometimes "overdiagnosed" (Weisler & Sussman, 2007). Some children who misbehave in school are diagnosed with ADHD and medicated to encourage more acceptable behaviour (Reddy & De Thomas, 2007).

Causes of ADHD

ADHD may have a genetic component, involving the brain chemical dopamine (Thapar et al., 2007; Walitza et al., 2006). Studies in brain imaging have found differences in the brain chemistry of children with ADHD.

In the 1970s, according to a widely held view, ADHD was related to food additives. Researchers now generally agree that food colouring and preservatives do not cause ADHD (Cruz & Bahna, 2006). Joel Nigg and his colleagues (2006) note that ADHD is due to a lack of executive control of the brain over motor and more primitive functions.

DID YOU KNOW?

Chemical food additives are not a cause of hyperactivity.

In the 1970s, according to a widely held view, ADHD was related to food additives. Researchers now generally agree that food colouring and preservatives do not cause ADHD.

Treatment and Outcome

Stimulants such as Ritalin are the most common treatment for ADHD. These stimulants promote the activity of the brain chemicals dopamine and noradrenaline, which stimulate the "executive centre" of the brain to control more primitive areas of the brain. Stimulants increase children's attention span and improve their academic performance (Posey et al., 2007). Most children with ADHD continue to have problems in attention, conduct, or learning in adolescence and adulthood (Nigg et al., 2004).

Tips for Working with Children with ADHD

1. Make directions clear and short (repeat if necessary).
2. Avoid giving multiple directions at once.
3. Give reminders often.
4. Start one task and don't stop until it is completed.
5. Organization is key for feeling in control.
6. Talk less.
7. Break more.
8. Allow for movement

Source: U.S. Department of Education, (2006). Teaching children with attention deficit hyperactivity disorder: Instructional strategies and practices. Washington, DC.

DID YOU KNOW?

Stimulants are often used to treat children who are already hyperactive.

Stimulants such as Ritalin are the most common treatment for ADHD.

Learning Disabilities

Some children, despite being intelligent and living in enriched home environments, encounter difficulties when learning how to read or when attempting to solve simple math problems. Many such children have learning disabilities. Children with learning disabilities may have difficulties in math, writing, or reading, in spite of scoring in the average range for intelligence on IQ tests. Some have difficulties in articulating the sounds of speech or in understanding spoken language. Others have problems in motor coordination. Children are usually diagnosed with a learning disability when they are performing below the level expected for their age and intelligence, and when the child shows no evidence of other handicaps such as vision or hearing problems, retardation, or socioeconomic disadvantage (Joshi, 2003; Lyon et al., 2003). Learning disabilities may persist through life, but early recognition and remediation can help many children learn how to compensate for their disability (Vellutino et al., 2004). Strategies for adapting are key to success for children with learning disabilities.

Origins of Dyslexia

Theories of **dyslexia** focus on how sensory and neurological problems may contribute to the reading problems we find in individuals with dyslexia. Genetic factors appear to be involved; 25–65 percent of children who have one dyslexic parent are dyslexic themselves (Plomin & Walker, 2003). About 40 percent of the siblings of children with dyslexia are dyslexic.

Genetic factors may give rise to neurological problems or circulation problems in the left hemisphere of the brain (Grigorenko, 2007). The circulation problems would result in oxygen deficiency. The part of the brain called the angular gyrus "translates" visual information, such as written words, into auditory information (sounds). Problems in the angular gyrus may give rise to reading problems by making it difficult for the reader to associate letters with sounds (Grigorenko, 2007; Shaywitz et al., 2006b).

Most researchers also focus on *phonological processing*. That is, dyslexic children may not discriminate sounds as accurately as other children do (Halliday & Bishop, 2006). As a result, *b*'s and *d*'s and *p*'s may be hard to tell apart, creating confusion that impairs reading ability (Shaywitz et al., 2006a). Figure 9.2 shows a writing sample from a child with dyslexia.

FIGURE 9.2

Writing Sample from a Child with Dyslexia

Children with dyslexia may perceive letters as upside down (confusing *w* with *m*) or reversed (confusing *b* with *d*). Their misperception leads to rotations or reversals in writing, as shown here.

dyslexia
a reading disorder characterized by letter reversals, mirror reading, slow reading and reduced comprehension.

classroom inclusion
placing children with disabilities in classrooms with children without disabilities.

Educating Children Who Have Disabilities

In childhood, treatment of dyslexia focuses on remediation (Bakker, 2006). Children are given highly structured exercises to help them become aware of how to blend sounds to form words, such as by identifying word pairs that rhyme and do not rhyme. Later in life, the focus tends to be on accommodation rather than on remediation. For example, postsecondary students who have dyslexia may be allowed extra time for the reading portion of tests.

A philosophy of **classroom inclusion** is adopted in Canada where, whenever possible, children with disabilities are placed in regular classrooms that have been adapted to their needs. Most students who have mild learning disabilities spend most of their school day in regular classrooms (Fergusson, 2007).

EMERGING CANADA

Education is a provincial and territorial responsibility so each province and territory will have different procedures for dealing with students with special educational needs. The Canadian Human Rights Code states that equal treatment for all students is required by law, requiring all schools to make accommodations for students identified as having a special educational need. In Ontario, for example, students with learning disabilities are given an Individual Education Plan (IEP) that ensures they have equal access to education. This written plan describes the services required by students who have been thoroughly assessed and identified as having a learning disability by an education psychologist.

The IEP is a record of the specific accommodations required to help students achieve learning expectations given their identified learning strengths and needs. These accommodations may include access to such computer programs as Dragon NaturallySpeaking, which is set up so that a student's spoken works are transcribed onscreen as written text. The IEP might also require access to a calculator when other students would not normally be allowed access to one. Or it might require that the student be provided a quiet room to write tests with an extra amount of time assigned to the task. The IEP is an accountability tool for the students, students' parents, and everyone who has responsibilities to help the children progress toward their learning goals (Ontario Ministry of Education, 2004).

FIGURE 9.7

Performance Items on an Intelligence Test

This figure shows items that resemble those found on the Wechsler Intelligence Scale for Children.

© Comstock Images/Jupiterimages

different intellectual tasks. For this reason, subtests compare a person's performance on one type of task (such as defining words) with another (such as using blocks to construct geometric designs). The Wechsler scales thus suggest children's strengths and weaknesses and provide overall measures of intellectual functioning.

Wechsler described some subtests as measuring verbal tasks and others as assessing performance tasks. In general, verbal subtests require knowledge of verbal concepts, whereas performance subtests (see Figure 9.7) require familiarity with spatial–relations concepts. Wechsler's scales permit the computation of verbal and performance IQs.

Figure 9.8 on page 169 indicates the labels that Wechsler assigned to various IQ scores and the approximate percentages of the population who attain IQ scores at those levels. Most children's IQ scores cluster around the average. Only about 5 percent of the population have IQ scores above 130 or below 70.

The Testing Controversy

Most psychologists and educational specialists consider intelligence tests to be biased, at least to some degree, against minority groups and members of lower social classes (Snyderman & Rothman, 1990). If scoring well on intelligence tests requires a certain type of cultural experience, the tests are said to have a **cultural bias**. For this reason, psychologists have tried to construct **culture-free** or culture-fair intelligence tests. Such culture-free tests are of particular importance for Canada because of our large multicultural population.

Some tests do not rely on expressive language at all. For example, Raymond Cattell's (1949) Culture-Fair Intelligence Test evaluates reasoning ability through the child's comprehension of the rules that govern a progression of geometric designs, as shown in Figure 9.9 on page 169.

But culture-free tests have not lived up to their promise. First, middle-class children still outperform lower-class children on these tests (Rushton et al., 2003). Middle-class children, for example, are more likely to have basic familiarity with materials such as blocks and pencils and paper. They are also more likely to have played with blocks (a practice relevant to the Cattell test). Second, culture-free tests do not predict academic success as accurately

cultural bias
a factor in intelligence tests that provides an advantage for test takers from certain cultural backgrounds.

culture-free
descriptive of a test in which cultural biases have been removed.

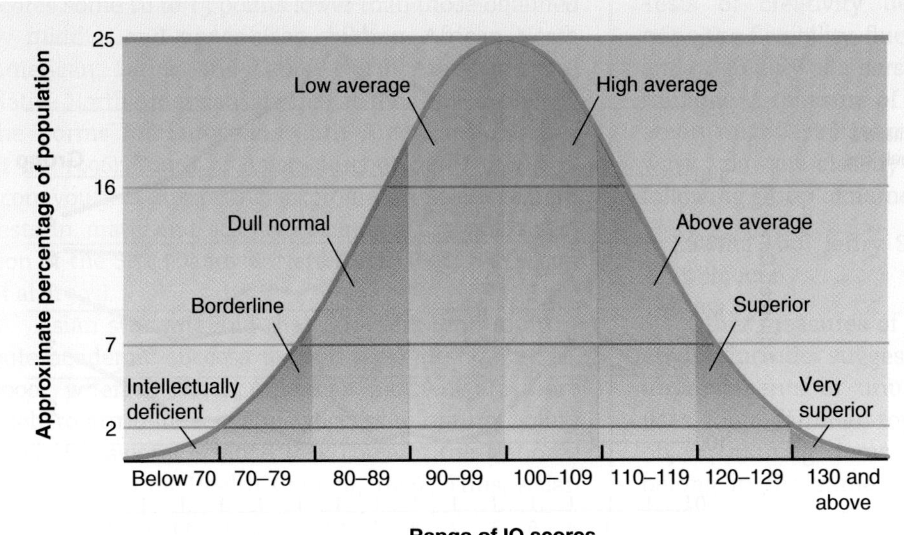

FIGURE 9.8

Variations in IQ Scores

IQ scores generally vary according to a bell-shaped, or "normal," curve.

as other intelligence tests do, and scholastic aptitude remains the central concern of educators (Keogh & Whyte, 2006).

Patterns of Intellectual Development

Intellectual growth seems to occur in at least two major spurts. The first occurs at about the age of 6. It coincides with entry into school and also with the shift from preoperational to concrete-operational thought. School may help crystallize children's intellectual functioning. The second spurt occurs at about age 10 or 11.

An individual should never be referred to as "retarded" or "a retard."

Once children reach middle childhood, their gains in intellectual functioning appear to follow more stable patterns, although some spurts still occur (Deary et al., 2004). As a result, by middle childhood, intelligence tests gain greater predictive power. In a classic study by Marjorie Honzik and her colleagues (1948), intelligence test scores taken at the age of 9 correlated strongly (+0.90) with scores at age 10 and more moderately (+0.76) with scores at age 18. Testing at age 11 even shows a moderate to high relationship with scores at age 77 (Deary et al., 2004).

Despite the increased predictive power of intelligence tests during middle childhood, individual differences exist. In the classic Fels Longitudinal Study (see Figure 9.10 on page 170), two groups of children (Groups 1 and 3) made reasonably consistent gains in intelligence test scores between the ages of 10 and 17, whereas three groups showed declines. Group 4, children who had shown the most intellectual promise at age 10, went on to show the most precipitous decline, although they still wound up in the highest 2–3 percent of the population (McCall et al., 1973). Many factors influence changes in IQ scores, including changes in the home, socioeconomic circumstances, and education (Deary et al., 2004).

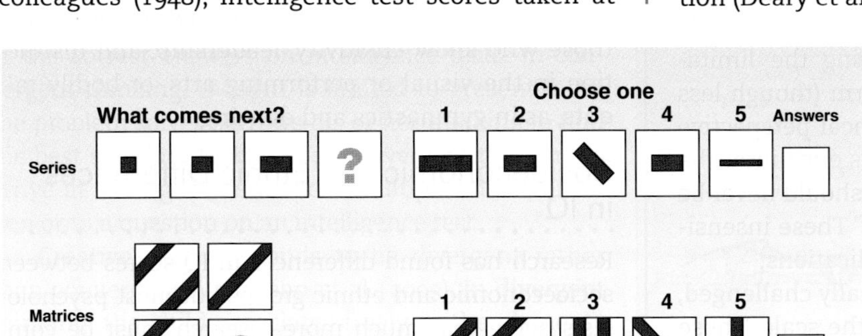

FIGURE 9.9

Sample Items from Cattell's Culture-Fair Intelligence Test

Culture-fair tests attempt to exclude items that discriminate on the basis of cultural background rather than intelligence.

© Image Source

Monolingual children are more likely to think erroneously that the word dog is somehow intertwined with the nature of the beast. Bilingual children therefore tend to have more cognitive flexibility.

EMERGING CANADA

Language development is central to how children gain knowledge and learn to participate and grow within their cultures. Children who learn their cultural languages experience all the benefits of other bilingual children, and they remain connected with their culture of origin. Canada's numerous heritage language programs support children in maintaining skills in speaking the cultural language of their families. Heritage language program offerings range from Italian, to Gaelic, to Mohawk and typically take place outside of regularly scheduled class time, such as weekends, after school, or evenings.

Low literacy development in Aboriginal languages is a significant issue in Canada. It is largely the result of the policies and practices carried out in residential schools, which instilled a belief among many Aboriginal adults that their language was inferior and their cultural ways were primitive. Assisting Aboriginal children to learn their Indigenous language is an excellent way to effectively communicate important thoughts of cultural identity, cultural knowledge and connectedness with their cultural community (Ball, 2008).

Roxana Gonzalez/Shutterstock.com

Go online at
www.nelson.com/4ltrpress/icanhdev2ce
And access the essential Study Tools online for this chapter:

- **Practice Quizzes,** which will help you to prepare for tests
- **Games,** to help test your knowledge
- **Flashcards,** to test your understanding of key terms
- **Observing Development Videos**
- **Internet Activities**

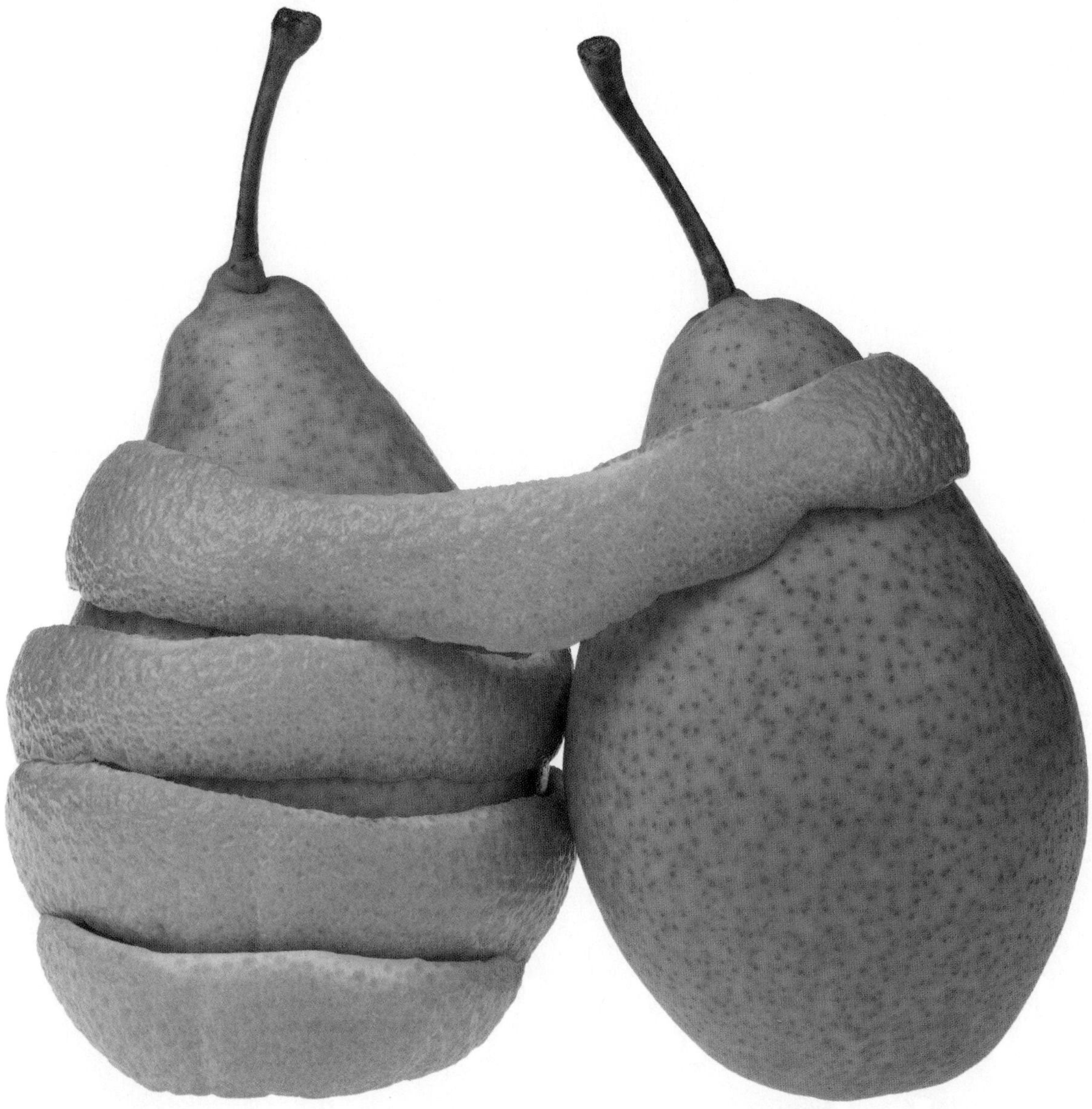

CHAPTER 10

Middle Childhood: Social and Emotional Development

LEARNING OUTCOMES

LO1 Explain theories of social and emotional development in middle childhood

LO2 Discuss the influences of the family on social development in middle childhood

LO3 Discuss the influences of peers on social development in middle childhood

LO4 Discuss the influence of the school on development in middle childhood

LO5 Discuss social and emotional problems that tend to develop in middle childhood

MANDY GODBEHEAR/Shutterstock.com

> "In the years between 6 and 12, peers take on greater importance and friendships deepen."

In the years between 6 and 12, the child's social world expands. Peers take on greater importance and friendships deepen. Entry into school exposes the child to the influence of teachers. Relationships with parents change as children develop greater independence.

LO1 Theories of Social and Emotional Development in Middle Childhood

Social Cognitive Theory

Social cognitive theory, advanced by Albert Bandura, focuses on the importance of rewards and modelling in middle childhood. During these years, children depend less on external rewards and punishments and increasingly regulate their own behaviour. Children are exposed to an increasing variety of models. Their influential models include parents, teachers, other adults, peers, and symbolic models (such as TV characters or the heroine in a story) (Anderson et al., 2007; Oates & Messer, 2007).

Cognitive-Developmental Theory and Social Cognition

According to Piaget, middle childhood coincides with the stage of concrete operations and is partly characterized by a decline in egocentrism and an expansion of the capacity to view the world and oneself from the perspective of others. This cognitive advance affects the child's social relationships (Mischo, 2004; Zan & Hildebrandt, 2003).

Time & Life Pictures/Getty Images

Erikson Today

Stage 4: Industry versus Inferiority (6–11 years)

As children become more capable, they master additional layers of personality and face new developmental challenges. Children's lives become more focused on learning, creating, and accomplishing a variety of new skills and knowledge, which results in a sense of industry. Children begin to look outward to compare themselves with their peers. This constant social comparison can result in unresolved feelings of inadequacy and even inferiority. Ability and self-esteem are at the forefront of this psychosocial challenge to be a productive and important member of the group. Parents are no longer the only authority in the life of their child, whose world grows in size with the introduction of the classroom, peers, and more unsupervised play experiences.

Consider THIS

Should we be keeping score and standings for young children in organized sport?

Please see page 179 for a discussion on this topic.

social cognition our understanding of the relationship between ourself and others.

Social cognition refers to perception of the social world, and our concern is the development of children's perspective-taking skills. Robert Selman and his colleagues (Selman, 1980; Selman & Dray, 2006) studied the development of these skills by presenting children with a social dilemma such as the following:

Holly is an 8-year-old girl who likes to climb trees. She is the best tree climber in the neighbourhood. One day while climbing down from a tall tree, she falls off the bottom branch but does not hurt herself. Her father sees her fall. He is upset and asks her to promise not to climb trees any more. Holly promises. Later that day, Holly and her friends meet Sean. Sean's kitten is caught up in a tree and can't get down. Something has to be done right away, or the kitten may fall. Holly is the only one who climbs trees well enough to reach the kitten and get it down, but she remembers her promise to her father (Selman, 1980, p. 36).

The children then were asked questions such as "How will Holly's father feel if he finds out she climbed the tree?" Using the children's responses, Selman (1976) described five levels of perspective-taking skills in childhood (see Table 10.1). Children

Sergey Petrov/Shutterstock.com

with better perspective-taking skills tend to have better peer relationships (Selman & Dray, 2006).

Development of the Self-Concept in Middle Childhood

In early childhood, children's self-concepts focus on concrete external traits, such as appearance,

TABLE 10.1

Levels of Perspective Taking

Level	Approximate Age (Years)	What Happens
0	3–6	Children are egocentric and do not realize that other people have perspectives different from their own. A child of this age will typically say that Holly will save the kitten because she likes kittens and that her father will be happy because he likes kittens, too. The child assumes that everyone feels as she does.
1	5–9[a]	Children understand that people in different situations may have different perspectives. The child still assumes that only one perspective is "right." A child might say that Holly's father would be angry if he did not know why she climbed the tree. But if she told him why, he would understand. The child recognizes that the father's perspective may differ from Holly's because of lack of information. But once he has the information, he will assume the "right" perspective (i.e., Holly's).
2	7–12[a]	The child understands that people may think or feel differently because they have different values or ideas. The child also recognizes that others are capable of understanding the child's own perspective. Therefore, the child is better able to anticipate reactions of others. The typical child of this age might say that Holly knows that her father will understand why she climbed the tree and that he therefore will not punish her.
3	10–15[a]	The child finally realizes that both she and another person can consider each other's point of view at the same time. The child may say something similar to this reasoning: Holly's father will think that Holly shouldn't have climbed the tree. But now that he has heard her side of the story, he would feel that she was doing what she thought was right. Holly realizes that her father will consider how she felt.
4	12 and above[a]	The child realizes that mutual perspective taking does not always lead to agreement. The perspectives of the larger social group also must be considered. A child of this age might say that society expects children to obey their parents and therefore that Holly should realize why her father might punish her.

[a]Ages may overlap.

Source: Selman (1976).

activities, and living situations. But as children undergo the cognitive developments of middle childhood, more abstract internal traits, or personality traits, begin to play a role. Social relationships and group memberships take on significance (Harter, 2006; Thompson, 2006).

Self-Esteem

As children enter middle childhood, they evaluate their self-worth in many different areas (Tassi et al., 2001). Preschoolers tend to see themselves as either generally "good at doing things" or not. But by 5 to 7 years of age, children are able to judge their performance in seven different areas: physical ability, physical appearance, peer relationships, parent relationships, reading, math, and general school performance. They also report a general self-concept (Harter, 2006).

Children's self-esteem declines throughout middle childhood, reaching a low ebb at age 12 or 13. Self-esteem then increases during adolescence (Harter, 2006). What accounts for the decline? Because preschoolers are egocentric, their self-concepts may be unrealistic. By middle childhood, children can compare themselves with other children and arrive at a more honest and critical self-appraisal. Whereas girls tend to have more positive self-concepts regarding reading, general academics, and helping others, boys tend to have more positive self-concepts in terms of math, physical ability, and physical appearance (Jacobs et al., 2005; Wang, 2005).

Authoritative parenting apparently contributes to children's self-esteem (Baumrind, 1991a, 1991b; Supple & Small, 2006). Children with a favourable self-image tend to have parents who are restrictive, involved, and loving. Children with low self-esteem are more likely to have authoritarian or rejecting–neglecting parents.

Social acceptance by peers is related to self-perceived competence in academic, social, and athletic domains (Nesdale & Lambert, 2007). Parents and classmates have an equally strong effect on children's self-esteem in middle childhood. Friends and teachers have relatively less influence but also matter (Harter, 2006).

DID YOU KNOW?

Children's self-esteem tends to decline in middle childhood.

Children's self-esteem declines throughout middle childhood, reaching a low ebb at age 12 or 13 and rising again in adolescence.

Consider THIS

Should we be keeping score and standings for young children in organized sport?

In 2013, the Ontario Soccer Association made a controversial decision to discontinue scoring and the maintenance of standings for players under the age of 12 in non-competitive soccer leagues (Kennedy, 2013). This decision is currently being considered throughout minor leagues in Canada. Part of the reasoning behind this decision is the belief that keeping score and handing out trophies can be damaging to the self-esteem of young children. The Ontario Soccer Association acknowledges that adults are often the source of issues in youth sport, but the fallout is experienced by the youths playing the sports.

Until recent years, children tended to get the bulk of their athletic exposure in "sandlot" games, where kids handled all the organizing, team selection, rule enforcement, and conflict resolutions during their games (McCormick, 2010). Yes, scores were kept, and every game led to winners and losers, but another game was always just about to begin. This scenario is no longer the case. Now, from a very young age, kids inhabit and compete in an adult-organized world that can restrict the fun and damage the self-esteem of young players. A scoreless game puts a renewed focus on skills development, a sense of fun, and more equal playing time, which benefits young players who may still be developing or are slower in mastering the skills of the game.

Some argue that taking away the scoring takes away important life lessons. Competition leads to learning experiences. When competition has a score attached to it, children learn ethics and experience positive interactions with other children. Exposing young children to competition early on prepares them for competition and adversity later in life. Losing a game teaches young children how to regroup and do better, and scores can encourage youth to push themselves to achieve more. These games become the training places for the real world.

Two very different viewpoints are at play. You can compete to win and to be victorious over others in a bid to be the best, or you can compete for the sake of learning and for the pursuit of excellence without the fear of measurement. Is the removal of scoring and standings just one more example of an overly protective world that "bubble-wraps" its children? Or, should we use sport, instead, to guide children into the realities of life? Or does a scoreless game allow children to have fun and to focus on process without damaging the self-esteem of young players who just want to enjoy the game. In terms of this particular stage of psychosocial development, should we be keeping score and standings for young children in organized sport?

Design Pics Inc./Alamy

Should we be keeping score?

learned helplessness an acquired (hence, learned) belief that one is unable to control one's environment.

co-regulation a gradual transferring of control from parent to child, beginning in middle childhood.

transsexuals persons who prefer to be of the other sex and who may undergo hormone treatments, cosmetic surgery, or both to achieve the appearance of being of the other sex.

Learned Helplessness

One outcome of low self-esteem in academics is known as **learned helplessness**. Learned helplessness is the acquired belief that one is unable to obtain the rewards that one seeks. "Helpless" children tend to quit following failure, whereas children who believe in their own ability tend to persist or change their strategies (Zimmerman, 2000). One reason for this difference is that children with learned helplessness believe both that success is due more to ability than effort and that they have little ability in a particular area. Consequently, persistence seems futile (Bandura et al., 2001). Helpless children typically obtain lower grades and lower scores on IQ and achievement tests (Goldstein & Brooks, 2005).

LO2 The Family

In middle childhood, the family continues to play a key role in socializing the child, although peers, teachers, and other outsiders begin to play a greater role (Harter, 2006).

Parent–Child Relationships

Parent–child interactions focus on some new concerns during middle childhood. They include school-related matters, assignment of chores, and peer activities (Collins et al., 2003). Parents do less monitoring of children's activities and provide less direct feedback than they did in the preschool years. Control is gradually transferred from parent to child in a process known as **co-regulation** (Maccoby, 2002; Wahler et al., 2001). Children begin to internalize the standards of their parents.

Children in middle childhood spend less time with their parents than they did in their preschool years. Children typically still spend more time with their mother than with their father. Mothers' interactions with school-age children continue to revolve around caregiving; fathers are relatively more involved in recreational activities (Wolfenden & Holt, 2005).

Because of their developing cognitive ability, 10- to 12-year-olds evaluate their parents more harshly than they did in early childhood (Selman & Dray, 2006). But throughout middle childhood, children rate their parents as their best source of emotional support (Cowan & Cowan, 2005; Katz et al., 2005).

Same-Sex Parents

Research on same-sex parenting is divided into two general categories: the general adjustment of the children of same-sex parents and whether the children of same-sex parents are more likely than other children to be lesbian or gay. Research by Charlotte Patterson (2006) has generally found that the psychological adjustment of children of same-sex parents is comparable with that of children of heterosexual parents. Similar to their heterosexual counterparts, lesbians and gay men often sustain positive family relationships (Wainright et al., 2004). With the legalization of gay marriage in Canada in 2005, social stigmas regarding homosexuality have lessened.

What have researchers learned about the sexual orientation of the children of same-sex parents? Green (1978) observed 37 children and young adults, ages 3 to 20, who were being reared—or had been reared—by lesbians or **transsexuals**. All but one of the children reported or recalled preferences for toys, clothing, and friends (male or female) that were typical for their sex and age. All the 13 older children who reported sexual fantasies or sexual behaviour were heterosexually oriented. It seems that the concerns of those opposed to families with same-sex parents are not supported through research.

© GeoM/Shutterstock.com

EMERGING CANADA

Fifty years of families in Canada: 1961 to 2011

The traditional family of a mother and a father and three children is no longer the reality in Canadian society. Over the past 50 years, the Canadian family has evolved to the point that there no longer is a "typical" family. Many Canadians live alone, have remarried, are empty nesters, or live with multiple generations in one household. In 1961, the average Canadian family had 3.9 people. In 2011, the average Canadian family had 2.9 people. Anne Milan, a Statistics Canadian demographer observed that the Canadian family is more complex and is definitely more diverse than ever before (Scoffield, 2012).

The following are some of the significant changes to the Canadian family that were observed in the Statistics Canada document titled *Fifty Years of Families in Canada: 1961 to 2011* (Statistics Canada, 2013b):

- Married couples accounted for 91.6 percent of census families in 1961. By 2011, this number had declined to 76 percent. This decrease is likely due to the growth of common-law couples.
- The number of married couples rose 19.7 percent, while the number of common-law couples more than quadrupled, with an increase of 345.2 percent.
- The percentage of lone-parent families almost doubled, from 8.4 percent in 1961 to 16.3 percent in 2011. In 2011, lone-parent families were head by a parent who was divorced or separated (50.8 percent), never married (31.5 percent), or widowed (17.7%).
- Same-sex couples made up only 0.8 percent of all recorded couples in 2011.
- In 1961, 9.3 percent of households consisted of one person. In 2011, 27.6% of all Canadian households consisted of one person.

What Happens to Children Whose Parents Divorce?

Much of our popular culture information about divorce comes from the United States but Canadians do not divorce at the same rates as our neighbours. The Canadian divorce rate has remained fairly stable, at 37.6 divorces per 100 marriages by the 30th wedding anniversary in 2002 and 38.3 in 2003. Divorce rates for remarried individuals are higher (Statistics Canada, 2005).

Divorce may be tough on parents; it can be even tougher on children (Amato, 2006). No longer do children participate with both parents in daily activities such as eating. No longer do children go with both parents to ball games, movies, or Disneyland. The parents are now often supporting two households, resulting in a lowering of the family's financial status and, thus, fewer resources for the children (Tashiro et al., 2006).

Most children live with their mothers after a divorce (Amato, 2006). Many fathers remain devoted to their children despite the split, but others tend to spend less time with their children as time goes on. Time must be spent discussing children's emotions and reassuring them that although things will be different, they will always be loved.

The children of divorce do not fare well in the statistics, and they are more likely to experience conduct disorders, drug abuse, and poor grades in school (Amato, 2006). Their physical health may also decline (Troxel & Matthews, 2004). In general, the fallout for children is worst during the first year after the breakup. After a couple of years or so, children tend to rebound (Malone et al., 2004). Focused parenting is key to successfully making this significant social adjustment. Parents who are devoted to their children and are aware of the statistics can protect their children from the harms associated with divorce.

Should We Remain Married "for the Sake of the Children"?

Many readers believe—for moral or personal reasons—that marriage and family life must be permanent, no matter what. Readers will need to consider their personal beliefs about divorce in the light of their own value systems. But—from a purely psychological perspective—what should bickering parents do? The answer seems to relate to how they behave in front of the children. Research shows that severe parental bickering is linked to the same kinds of problems that children experience when their parents separate or divorce (Troxel & Matthews, 2004). When children are exposed to adult or marital conflict, they display

PART FOUR

CHAPTER 11

Adolescence: Physical and Cognitive Development

LEARNING OUTCOMES

LO1 Describe the key events of puberty and their relationship to social development

LO2 Discuss health in adolescence, focusing on causes of death and eating disorders

LO3 Discuss adolescent cognitive development and the key events of Piaget's stage of formal operations

LO4 Discuss sex differences in cognitive abilities

LO5 Discuss Kohlberg's theory of moral development in adolescence

LO6 Discuss the roles of the school in adolescence, focusing on dropping out

LO7 Discuss career development and work experience during adolescence

Used by permission of Kaitlyn Howden

> "Many teens are taller and stronger than their parents, and they have the responsibilities associated with reproduction. But to their frustration, they face social restrictions in terms of driving, voting, and consuming alcohol."

Perhaps no other period of life is as exciting—and bewildering—as adolescence. Except for infancy, more changes occur during adolescence than any other time of life. Adolescence is a time of being in between. Adolescents are physically able to become parents yet they cannot attend R-rated films. Given the restrictions placed on adolescents, their growing yearning for independence, and a sex drive heightened by high levels of sex hormones, it is not surprising that adolescents are occasionally in conflict with their parents.

puberty
the biological stage of development characterized by changes that lead to reproductive capacity.

feedback loop
a system in which glands regulate each other's functioning through a series of hormonal messages.

The idea that adolescence is an important and separate developmental stage was proposed by G. Stanley Hall (1904). Hall believed that adolescence is marked by turmoil and used the German term *Sturm und Drang* ("storm and stress") to refer to the conflicts of adolescence. Contemporary theorists no longer see adolescent storm and stress as inevitable (Smetana, 2005). Instead, they see adolescence as a period when biological, cognitive, social, and emotional functioning are reorganized. Nevertheless, adolescents need to adapt to numerous changes.

Krivosheev Vitaly/Shutterstock.com

LO1 Puberty: The Biological Eruption

Puberty is a stage of development characterized by reaching sexual maturity and the ability to reproduce. The onset of adolescence coincides with the advent of puberty. Puberty is controlled by a **feedback loop** involving the hypothalamus, pituitary gland, hormones, and the gonads—the ovaries in females and the testes in males. The hypothalamus signals the pituitary gland, which, in turn, releases hormones that control physical growth and the gonads. The gonads respond to pituitary hormones by increasing their production of sex hormones (androgens and estrogens). The sex hormones further stimulate the hypothalamus, perpetuating the feedback loop.

primary sex characteristics the structures that make reproduction possible.

secondary sex characteristics physical indicators of sexual maturation—such as changes to the voice and growth of bodily hair—that do not directly involve reproductive structures.

asynchronous growth imbalanced growth, such as the growth that occurs during the early part of adolescence and causes many adolescents to appear gawky.

The sex hormones also trigger the development of primary and secondary sex characteristics. The **primary sex characteristics** are the structures that make reproduction possible. In girls, these are the ovaries, vagina, uterus, and fallopian tubes. In boys, they are the penis, testes, prostate gland, and seminal vesicles. The **secondary sex characteristics** are physical indicators of sexual maturation that are not directly involved in reproduction. They include breast development, deepening of the voice, and the appearance of facial, pubic, and underarm hair.

The Adolescent Growth Spurt

The stable growth patterns in height and weight that characterize early and middle childhood end abruptly with the adolescent growth spurt. Girls start to spurt in height sooner than boys, at an average age of a little older than 10. Boys start to spurt about 2 years later. Girls and boys reach their peak growth in height about 2 years after the growth spurt begins (see Figure 11.1). The spurt in height for both girls and boys continues for about another 2 years at a gradually declining pace. The Canadian Paediatric Society (2013a) reports the growth spurt for boys and girls can be quite dramatic. They may grow 2 to 8 inches (5 to 20 cm) in one year, but puberty is a long process that will take place over several years.

Adolescents begin to spurt in weight about half a year after they begin to spurt in height. The period of peak growth in weight occurs about a year and a half after the onset of the spurt. As with height, the growth spurt in weight then continues for a little more than 2 years. Because the spurt in weight lags the spurt in height, many adolescents are relatively slender compared with their preadolescent stature. However, adolescents tend to eat enormous quantities of food to fuel their growth spurts. Active 14- and 15-year-old boys may consume 3,000 to 4,000 calories a day without becoming obese.

Girls' and boys' body shapes begin to differ during adolescence. Girls develop relatively broader hips compared with their shoulders (Canadian Paediatric Society, 2013b), whereas the opposite is true for boys. A girl's body shape is more rounded than a boy's because girls gain almost twice as much fatty tissue as boys. Boys gain twice as much muscle tissue as girls.

Asynchronous Growth

Adolescents may be awkward and gawky due to **asynchronous growth**; different parts of the body grow at different rates. The hands and feet mature before the

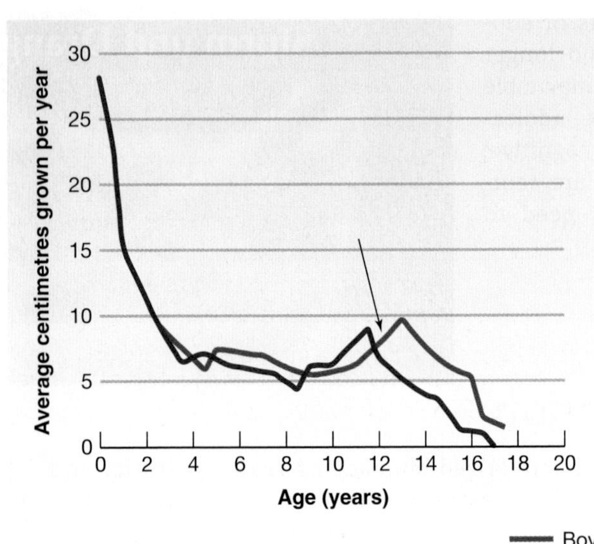

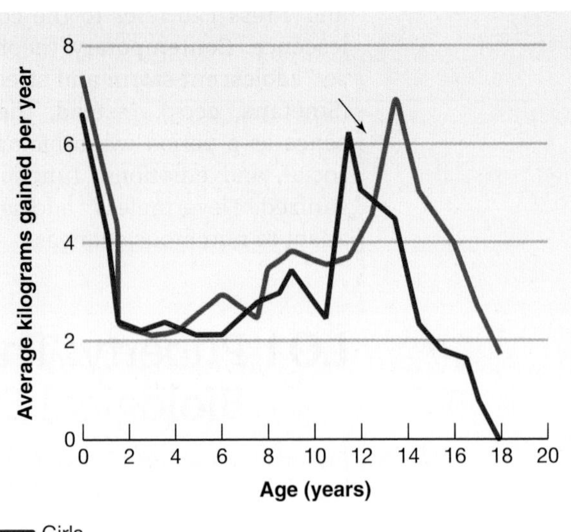

FIGURE 11.1

Spurts in Growth

The adolescent growth spurt begins at about age 10½ for girls and age 13 for boys.

Source: From Kail/Cavanaugh. *Human Development*, 2e. © 2009 Nelson Education Ltd. Reproduced by permission. www.cengage.com/permissions

arms and legs do. As a consequence, adolescent girls and boys may complain of big hands or feet. Legs reach their peak growth before the shoulders and chest. Boys stop growing out of their pants about a year before they stop growing out of their jackets.

The Secular Trend

During the 20th century, children in the Western world grew dramatically more rapidly and ended up taller than children from earlier times (Sun et al., 2005). This historical trend toward increasing adult height was also accompanied by an earlier onset of puberty, and is known as the **secular trend.** This trend that has been observed worldwide is likely due to improved health care and improved nutrition.

Growth and height are recognized as a measure of the health and wellness of individuals. Adult height among different ethnic groups differs significantly with males normally being taller than females within each group. In the 18th and 19th century, European North Americans were the tallest people in the world. Today, the heights of people from many nations (particularly those in Europe) have surpassed the typical heights in the United States. Americans, on average, are taller than Canadians. What human growth and development factors are at play to create such shifts? Table 11.1 shows the average male and female heights reported by selected countries (Disabled World, 2008).

© James Worrell/Getty Images

Changes in Boys

At puberty, the pituitary gland stimulates the testes to increase their output of testosterone, leading to further development of the male genitals. The first visible sign of puberty is accelerated growth of the testes, which begins at an average age of about 11½, plus or minus 2 years. Testicular growth further accelerates testosterone production and other pubertal changes. The penis spurts about a year later, and still later, pubic hair begins to spurt.

Underarm and facial hair appears at about age 15. Only half of Canadian boys shave (of necessity) by age 17. At age 14 or 15, the voice deepens because of growth of the "voice box," or larynx, and the lengthening of the vocal cords. The process is gradual, and adolescent boys sometimes encounter an embarrassing cracking of the voice (see Figure 11.2 on page 196).

TABLE 11.1

Average Male and Female Heights in Selected Countries

Country	Average Male Height	Average Female Height
Canada	174 cm (5′ 8.5″)	161.0 cm (5′ 3.4″)
India	165.3 cm (5′ 5″)	165.3 cm (5′ 5″)
Netherlands	184.8 cm (6′ 0.8″)	168.7 cm (5′ 6.4″)
Philippines	163.5 cm (5′ 4.4″)	151.8 cm (4′ 11.8″)
United States	178.2 cm (5′ 10.2″)	164.1 cm (5′ 4.6″)

Used with permission of Disabled World

Testosterone also triggers the development of acne, which afflicts 75–90 percent of adolescents (Goldstein, 2004). Severe acne is manifested by pimples and blackheads on the face, chest, and back. Although boys are more prone to acne, we cannot say that girls suffer less from it. A smooth complexion has a higher value for girls.

Males can have erections in early infancy, but erections are infrequent until age 13 or 14. Adolescent males may experience unwanted erections. The organs that produce **semen** grow rapidly, and boys typically ejaculate seminal fluid by age 13 or 14. About a year later, they begin to have **nocturnal emissions,** also called wet dreams because of the myth that emissions necessarily accompany erotic dreams. Mature sperm are found in ejaculatory emissions by about the age of 15.

Nearly half of all boys experience enlargement of the breasts, or **gynecomastia**, which usually declines in a year or two. Gynecomastia stems from the small amount of female sex hormones (estrogen) secreted by the testes.

At age 20 or 21, men stop growing taller because testosterone causes **epiphyseal closure**, which prevents the long bones from making further gains in length. Puberty for males draws to a close.

secular trend a historical trend toward increasing adult height and earlier puberty.

semen the fluid that contains sperm and substances that nourish and help transport sperm.

nocturnal emission emission of seminal fluid while asleep.

gynecomastia enlargement of breast tissue in males.

epiphyseal closure the process by which the cartilage that separates the long end of a bone from the main part of the bone turns to bone.

Changes in Girls

In girls, the pituitary gland signals the ovaries to boost estrogen production at puberty. Estrogen

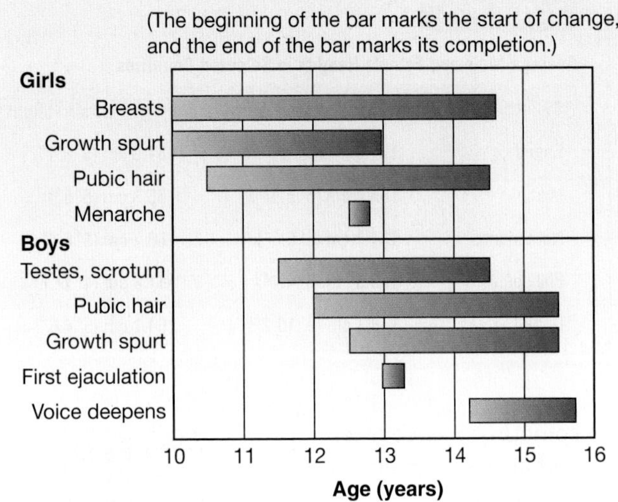

FIGURE 11.2

Average Timing of Pubertal Changes in North American Youth

Because girls' growth spurt occurs earlier, girls are taller and heavier than boys from about age 9 or 10 until about age 13. Once boys begin their spurt, they catch up with girls and eventually become taller and heavier.

Source: From Kail/Cavanaugh. *Human Development*, 2e. © 2009 Nelson Education Ltd. Reproduced by permission. www.cengage.com/permissions

EMERGING CANADA

Canadian society is kinder to boys than it is to girls in terms of issues of physical change. Most parents are proud to see their boys growing stronger and taller and becoming young men. If you are a female helping a male understand his body changes, you may have knowledge but you have no first-hand experience. The following are some concerns young men may have but they may not be prepared to voice:

- Some boys may gain weight before a spurt in height. Reassure that this change is normal and will likely be temporary if he is eating properly and exercising.
- Another source of concern is breast development. As many as one in three boys can expect swelling under the nipples. This growth is also temporary, though boys may be concerned that they are growing breasts or they have cancer.
- Let the young man know that the penis first grows long and then wide. The process takes several years, and some may be concerned that their penis will never grow.
- Sometimes one testicle grows faster than the other and this difference is normal.
- Erotic dreams accompanied by ejaculation (a wet dream) are also normal but can be alarming if the boy is unprepared.
- Spontaneous erections, though potentially embarrassing, are also normal, as are erections every morning.

Starting a conversation around body changes might be embarrassing at first but establishing that the adolescent can ask you any questions without judgment is important. If you don't know the answers, let them know that together you can find them (Langlois, 2013).

menarche the onset of menstruation.

may stimulate the growth of breast tissue ("breast buds") as early as age 8 or 9, but the breasts usually begin to enlarge during the 10th year. The development of fatty tissue and ducts elevates the areas of the breasts surrounding the nipples and causes the nipples to protrude. The breasts typically reach full size in about 4 years, but the *mammary glands* do not mature fully until a woman has a baby. Estrogen also promotes the growth of the fatty and supporting tissue in the hips and buttocks, which, along with the widening of the pelvis, causes the hips to round. Beginning at about the age of 10½ or 11, girls develop pubic and underarm hair (see Figure 11.2).

Ron Sumners/Dreamstime

Estrogen causes the labia, vagina, and uterus to develop during puberty, and androgens cause the clitoris to develop. The vaginal lining varies in thickness according to the amount of estrogen in the bloodstream. Estrogen typically brakes the female growth spurt some years before testosterone brakes the growth spurt of males.

Menarche

Menarche (first menstruation) commonly occurs between the ages of 11 and 14, plus or minus 2 years (Capron et al., 2007; Mendle et al., 2006). The average age of menarche for a Canadian girl is 12½.

What accounts for the earlier age of puberty? One hypothesis is that girls must reach a certain body weight to trigger pubertal changes such

EMERGING CANADA

Canadian girls can experience changes to their bodies as early as age 8 or 9, so cognitively they are not as prepared to deal with changes to their body. Girls changing into young women bring concerns of sexuality that are prevalent in Canadian society. Speak openly with female adolescents and make sure they know they can ask you any questions they have. The following are some changes that may cause concerns.

- A girl's hips and thighs begin to widen before growth, and she may develop a rounded belly that will be an energy store for puberty. With a healthy diet and active lifestyle, this change will be temporary.
- Budding begins breast growth. These buds may be tender to the touch and may be irritated by clothing and normal play. It is normal for breasts to grow unevenly. One might grow earlier or faster. Reassure that this uneven growth is not a sign of cancer.
- Sweat glands will produce odour, which, if not properly looked after, can lead to ridicule from classmates.
- She will begin to discharge a clear white fluid from her vagina that she will see on her underwear. This too is normal but should be discussed openly.
- This age is a good time for a discussion about her period. If a young girl receives her first period without being prepared, she may think she is hurt or even dying.
- Dysmenorrhea is the medical term for painful menstruation that affects every woman at some point in her life. This pain can be particularly difficult when at school. Symptoms may include severe abdominal cramping, headaches, nausea, and vomiting. Effects can last two to three days. Serious medical conditions should always be ruled out by visiting a doctor. Sleep and exercise might reduce the effects.
- Skin and hair can become oily and may become a point of frustration in a society that is so driven by appearances.

Working with adolescent girls and establishing a sense of trust allows you to help them to understand and properly care for their bodies. Let them know that if you don't have the answers, you will find them together (Langlois, 2013).

as menarche. Body fat could trigger the changes because fat cells secrete a protein that signals the brain to secrete hormones that raise estrogen levels. Menarche comes later to girls who have a lower percentage of body fat, such as athletes and girls with eating disorders (Bosi & de Oliveira, 2006; Frisch, 1997). The average body weight for triggering menarche depends on the girl's height (Frisch, 1994). Today's girls are larger than those of the early 20th century because of improved nutrition and health care. As a result, menarche now occurs earlier than it did for previous generations.

Early versus Late Maturers

Early maturing boys tend to be both more popular than their late-maturing peers and more likely to be leaders in school (Graber et al., 2004). They are more poised, more relaxed, and good-natured. Their edge in sports and the admiration of their peers heighten their sense of worth. On the negative side, early maturation is associated with greater risks of aggression and delinquency (Lynne et al., 2007) and abuse of alcohol and other drugs (Costello et al., 2007). Coaches may expect too much of early maturing boys in sports, and peers may want them to fight their battles. Sexual opportunities may create demands before they know how to respond (Lam et al., 2002).

Late maturers have the advantage of not being rushed into maturity. On the other hand, late-maturing boys often feel dominated by early maturing boys. They have also been found to be more dependent and more insecure and may be more easily influenced by peer pressure (Ge et al., 2003).

Although boys who mature early usually have higher self-esteem than those who mature late, early maturing girls may feel awkward because they are among the first of their peers to begin the physical changes of puberty. They become conspicuous with their height and their developing breasts. Early maturing girls are at greater risk for psychological problems and substance abuse than girls who mature later on (Ge et al., 2003; Lynne et al., 2007). Many girls who mature early obtain lower grades in school and are involved in sexual

DID YOU KNOW?

Girls are not usually fertile immediately after their first menstrual period.

Girls should not assume they cannot become pregnant at this time because variations in the timing of ovulation are common.

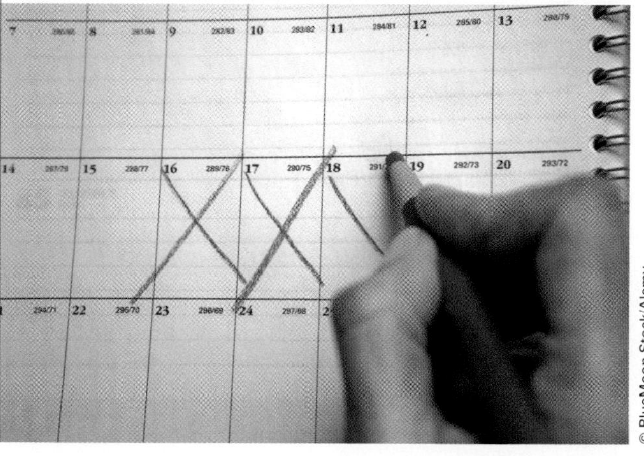

© BlueMoon Stock/Alamy

EMERGING CANADA

Precocious puberty (PP) is happening more often in Canada. PP is the onset of puberty before age 7 or 8 in girls, and before age 9 in boys. In general, girls are now developing earlier than ever before, and breast development is the most noticeable marker. Many jump to the conclusion that PP is caused by hormones in food or chemicals in water, but research attributes this change to better nutrition, greater consumption of animal protein, and higher levels of body fat. According to researchers, PP is merely a change in development being experienced across a new generation. Many children who develop early do not have PP, which is confirmed through blood and urine tests that indicate elevated levels of sex hormones and through an X-ray of hands that detects "bone age." Normal early onset of puberty does raise social and emotional concerns but does not appear to have significant lasting physical effects (Curtis, 2012).

activity earlier (Lam et al., 2002). For reasons such as these, the parents of early maturing girls may increase their vigilance and restrictiveness, leading to new child–parent conflicts.

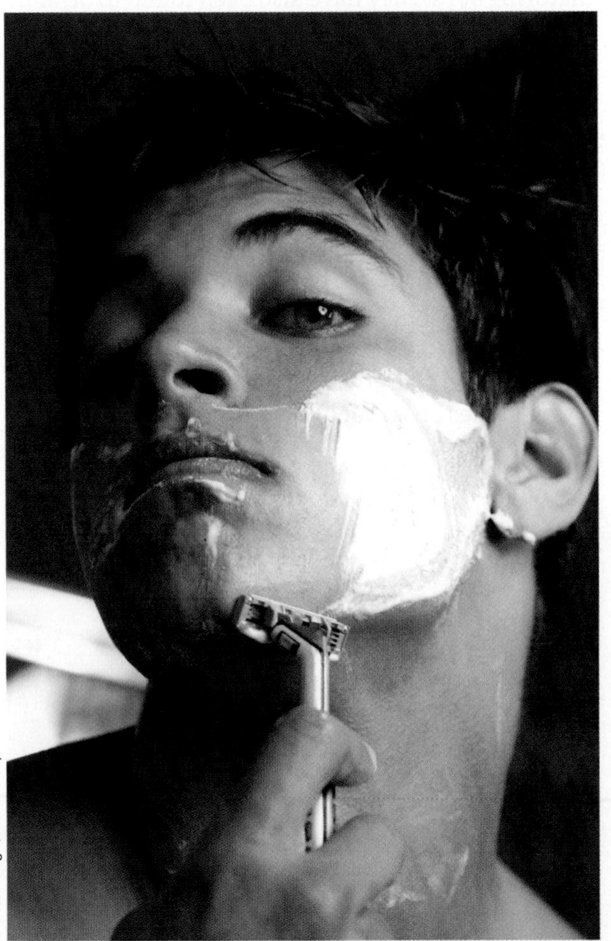

© Susan Vogel/Photolibrary

DID YOU KNOW?

Physical maturity influences boys' and girls' self-esteem differently.

Although boys who mature early often have higher self-esteem, early maturing girls can encounter negative social experiences.

Body Image

The Public Health Agency of Canada reports that dangerous and unrealistic cultural ideals of slimness (particularly in females) and muscularity (particularly in males) have filtered down to Canadian children and adolescents. Dissatisfaction with body weight and size is, in many situations, reported by young people with a healthy weight (Janssen, 2012). Adolescents tend to be concerned about their physical appearance, particularly in early adolescence, during the rapid physical changes of puberty (Jones & Crawford, 2006). By age 18, girls and boys are more satisfied with their bodies (Eisenberg et al., 2006). In our society, adolescent females tend to be more preoccupied with body weight and slimness than adolescent males (Paxton et al., 2006). Many adolescent males want to gain weight to build their muscle mass (Stanford & McCabe, 2005).

LO2 Health in Adolescence

Death and Injuries

Death rates are, in general, low in adolescence, but they are nearly twice as great for male adolescents as female adolescents. Unintentional injury is the number one cause of death (73 percent) with 1 youth dying every 5 hours in Canada. Motor vehicle accidents cause 60 percent of these deaths. According to MacDonald, Yanchar, and Hebert (2007), this overwhelming rate of teen deaths can be traced to teenagers' increased likelihood of taking chances, their tendency to act impulsively, their overestimation of their skills, and their feeling of invincibility.

Nutrition

Physical growth occurs more rapidly in the adolescent years than at any other time after birth, with

DID YOU KNOW?

Accidents are the number one cause of death for Canadian adolescents.

Each week, 32 Canadian youths die in motor vehicle accidents (MacDonald et al., 2007).

Raymond Forbes/First Light

the exception of the first year of infancy. Health Canada recommends that Canadian teens need to build a healthy diet based on Canada's Food Guide selections rather than following the dated method of counting calories. Recommendations for female teens include seven servings of fruits and vegetables, six servings of grains, three to four servings of milk and milk alternatives, and two servings of meat and meat alternatives; male teens have slightly higher requirements of eight servings of fruits and vegetables, seven servings of grains, three to four servings of milk and milk alternatives, and three servings of meat and meat alternatives (Health Canada, 2007c). The nutritional needs of adolescents vary according to their activity level and stage of pubertal development.

One reason for adolescents' nutritional deficits is their irregular eating patterns. Breakfast is often skipped, especially by dieters (Niemeier et al., 2006). Teenagers may rely on fast food and junk food, which are convenient but high in fat and calories. A diet heavy in junk food can lead to being overweight, and being overweight in adolescence can lead to chronic illness and premature death in adulthood (Niemeier et al., 2006).

Teens and Alcohol and Illicit Drugs

Although teens cannot legally use alcohol or illicit drugs, we know that these substances are a significant part of adolescent social life in Canada. The Canadian Medical Association released a 10-year study on alcohol and drug use in Canada. Of the teens surveyed, ⅔ had used alcohol, ⅓ had used marijuana, and 1 in 20 had tried LSD, ecstasy, or cocaine.

A closer look at adolescent drug and alcohol use patterns is more revealing. In Alberta, 79 percent of people over the age of 15 drink. Of Ontario Grade 12 students, 83 percent reported drinking regularly, and 49 percent responded that they binge drink. Among Grade 11 students who drink, age 13 was the average age of their first alcoholic drink and 14 was the average age of their first intoxication. The average age of drug use was 15.7 (Teen Challenge Canada, 2013). Teenagers in Canada may not be able to legally use illicit drugs and alcohol but clearly, it is an issue that must be discussed openly to protect our youth and to avoid exposure to potential lifelong addictions.

EMERGING CANADA

A disturbing trend dramatically on the rise is teen abuse of prescription drugs. A recent national survey finds that 1 in 4 teens has misused or abused a prescription drug at least once, representing a jump of 33 percent in five years.

- Of the teens reporting having used or abused prescription drugs, 20 percent did so before age 4.
- Of all teens surveyed, 27 percent mistakenly believe that misusing and abusing prescription drugs to get high is safer than using street drugs.
- Ritalin and Adderal (medication for attention deficit hyperactivity disorder, or ADHD) are among the most commonly abused medications. They are misused as a study aid and an aid to reducing hunger for teens wanting to lose weight.
- Painkillers were taken by 16 percent of the teens surveyed, and their use seems to be on the decrease.

Knowing that prescription drug abuse is on the rise presents a good opportunity for conversations with teens. Be sure to safely store prescription medications, given the high likelihood of abuse. A majority of teens (81 percent) said they have discussed the use of marijuana with their parents, (80 percent) have discussed alcohol use, but a shockingly low number of teens (16 percent) say that their parents have discussed the abuse of prescription medication. Talk with teens to discuss the dangers associated with this activity (Nauert, 2013).

ajt/Shutterstock.com

Eating Disorders

The Canadian ideal has slimmed down to the point that most Canadian females of normal weight are dissatisfied with the size and shape of their bodies (Paxton et al., 2005). In the section on cognitive

TABLE 11.3

Number of Dropouts and the Dropout Rate, by Province, 1990–1993 and 2007–2010

	1990–1993		2007–2010	
	thousands	*percent*	*thousands*	*percent*
Newfoundland and Labrador	10.0	19.9	2.2	7.4
Prince Edward Island	1.8	18.9	0.9	8.9
Nova Scotia	11.9	17.8	5.2	8.6
New Brunswick	8.6	15.4	3.8	8.1
Quebec	84.2	17.4	55.5	11.7
Ontario	114.3	14.8	68.6	7.8
Manitoba	12.4	16.0	9.1	11.4
Saskatchewan	10.4	16.2	6.7	9.4
Alberta	30.7	15.7	28.3	10.4
British Columbia	31.5	13.3	19.1	6.2

Dropouts are defined as 20- to 24-year-olds without a high-school diploma who do not attend school.
Note: due to small sample sizes in many provinces, all provincial data are based on a 3-year average (1990–1993 and 2007–2010).

Source: Statistics Canada, Labour Force Survey. http://www23.statcan.gc.ca/imdb/p2SV.pl?Function=getSurvey&SDDS=3701&lang=en&db=imdb&adm=8&dis=2

LO7 Career Development and Work Experience

Deciding what job or career we will pursue after completion of school is one of the most important choices we make.

Career Development

Children's first career aspirations may not be practical; however, they become increasingly realistic as children mature and gain experience. In adolescence, ideas about the kind of work one wants to do tend to become more firmly established, but a particular occupation may not be chosen until the postsecondary years or later (Rottinghaus et al., 2003).

Holland's Career Typology

John Holland's (1997) RIASEC method of predicting adjustment in a career matches six personality types (realistic, investigative, artistic, social, entrepreneurial, and conventional) to various kinds of careers. Within each "type" of career, some are more sophisticated than others and require more education and training.

- Realistic people are concrete in their thinking and are mechanically oriented. They tend to be best adjusted in occupations that involve motor activity, such as attending gas stations, farming, auto repairs, or construction work.
- Investigative people are abstract in their thinking, creative, and open to experience. They tend to do well in higher-level education and in research.
- Artistic people also tend to be creative and open to experience. They are emotional and intuitive. They tend to be content in the visual and performing arts.
- Socially oriented people tend to be outgoing (extraverted) and concerned for social welfare. They gravitate toward occupations in teaching (kindergarten through high school), counselling, and social work.
- Enterprising people tend to be adventurous, outgoing, and dominant. They gravitate toward leadership roles in industry and organizations.
- Conventional people thrive on routine and have needs for order, self-control, and social approval. They gravitate toward occupations in banking, accounting, clerical work, and the military.

Many people combine several vocational types (Nauta, 2007). For example, a copywriter in an advertising agency might be both artistic and enterprising. Holland's Vocational Preference Inventory assesses these personality types, as do various vocational tests used in high schools, colleges, and universities.

All in all, thousands of occupations are available, but most young people choose from a relatively small range of traditional occupations on the basis of their personalities, experiences, and opportunities (Nauta, 2007). Holland's Career Inventory is available online and is an interesting starting point for uncovering your interests. It asks simple questions such as: Are you a nature lover? Are you insightful? Do you like to be physically

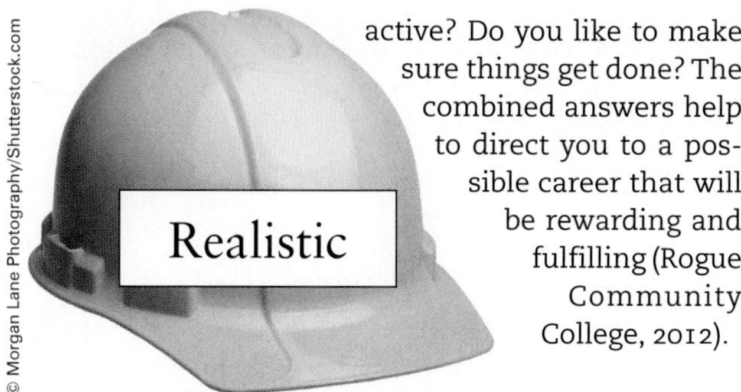

© Morgan Lane Photography/Shutterstock.com

active? Do you like to make sure things get done? The combined answers help to direct you to a possible career that will be rewarding and fulfilling (Rogue Community College, 2012).

Adolescents in the Workforce

Life experiences help shape vocational development. One life experience common among most North American teenagers is holding a job.

According to Statistics Canada (2008a), in 2004–05, 31 percent of high-school students between the ages of 15 and 17 held a job. Those not working reported preferring to focus on schoolwork or other activities.

Pros and Cons of Adolescent Employment

The potential benefits of adolescent employment include developing a sense of responsibility, self-reliance, and discipline; learning to appreciate the value of money and education; acquiring positive work habits and values; and enhancing occupational aspirations (Porfeli, 2007). Working a reasonable amount of time per week (less than 10 hours) prompts students to schedule their study time appropriately and lends structure to the week. On the other hand, most working adolescents are in jobs with low pay, high turnover, little authority, and little chance for advancement (Staff et al., 2004). Some question the benefits of such jobs. Students who work lengthy hours—more than 11 to 13 hours per week—report lower grades, higher rates of drug and alcohol use, more delinquent behaviour, lower self-esteem, and higher levels of psychological problems than students who do not work or who work only a few hours (Brandstätter & Farthofer, 2003). Students working 30 hours or more per week were the most likely to drop out of high school (Statistics Canada, 2008a). Perhaps the safest course is for parents and educators to limit the number of hours adolescents work, particularly during the school year.

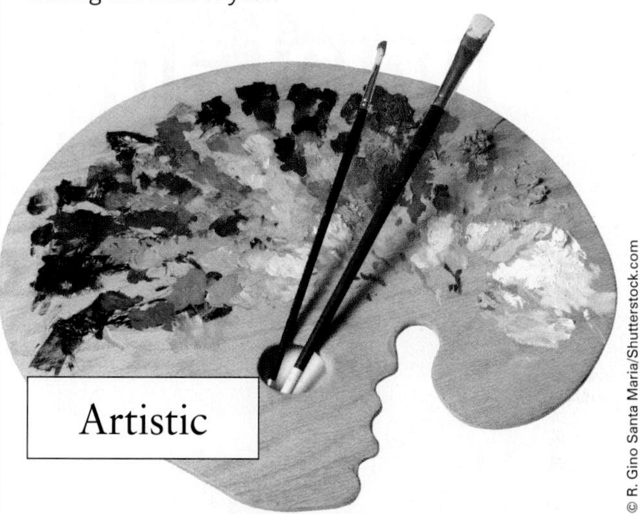

© R. Gino Santa Maria/Shutterstock.com

DID YOU KNOW?

The number of hours worked after school can affect school performance.

This is true. Working 30 hours per week or more places students at a high risk to drop out of school. Working less than 10 hours can prompt students to manage their time productively.

CHAPTER 12

Adolescence: Social and Emotional Development

LEARNING OUTCOMES

LO1 Discuss the formation of identity in adolescence

LO2 Discuss relationships with parents and peers during adolescence

LO3 Discuss sexuality during adolescence, focusing on sexual identity and teenage pregnancy

LO4 Discuss the statistics specific to youth in conflict with the law and measures that can reduce youth crime in Canada

LO5 Discuss risk factors in adolescent suicide

> "Adolescents are preoccupied not only with their present selves but also with what they want to become."

LO1 Development of Identity: "Who Am I?"

Canadian teens search for an answer to the question "Who am I?" They struggle to balance different selves and contradictory traits and behaviours to determine the "real me." Adolescents are preoccupied not only with their present selves but also with what they want to become.

ego identity according to Erikson, one's sense of who one is and what one stands for.

psychological moratorium a time-out period when adolescents experiment with different roles, values, beliefs, and relationships.

identity crisis a turning point in development during which one examines one's values and makes decisions about life roles.

Erikson and Identity Development

The primary developmental task is for adolescents to develop **ego identity**: a sense of who they are and what they stand for. They face choices about their future occupation, political and religious beliefs, and gender roles. Because of formal-operational thinking, adolescents can weigh options they have not directly experienced (Roeser et al., 2006).

One aspect of identity development is a **psychological moratorium** during which adolescents experiment with different roles, values, beliefs, and relationships (Erikson, 1968). During this time, adolescents undergo an **identity crisis** in which they examine their values and make decisions about their life roles. Should they attend college or university? What career should they pursue? Should they become sexually active? With whom? Adolescents in developed nations may feel overwhelmed by their options.

Erikson Today

Stage 5: Identity versus Role Confusion (12–18)

Psychosocial Theory: Up until now, development has been dependent on events that happen to the child. In adolescence, development shifts to focus on what the person does. Adolescents struggle to discover their own identity. While negotiating and struggling in a complex social world, they must find their own sense of self in terms of their morality. Those who do not embrace responsibility will be unsuccessful as they face the challenges of this life stage and, as a result, may experience emotional upheaval and role confusion. Adolescents must construct their own sense of beliefs, ideals, and friends.

Consider THIS

What issues are associated with social media and identity formation in the teenage years?

Please see page 215 for a discussion onthis topic.

Identity Statuses

Building on Erikson's approach, James Marcia (1991) theorized four identity statuses that represent the four possible combinations of the dimensions of exploration and commitment that Erikson believed

CHAPTER 13

Early Adulthood: Physical and Cognitive Development

LEARNING OUTCOMES

LO1 Discuss the (theoretical) stage of emerging adulthood

LO2 Describe trends in physical development in early adulthood

LO3 Discuss health in early adulthood, focusing on causes of death, diet, exercise, and substance abuse

LO4 Discuss sexuality in early adulthood, focusing on homosexuality, STIs, menstrual problems, and sexual coercion

LO5 Discuss cognitive development in early adulthood, focusing on "postformal" developments and effects of life after high school

LO6 Describe career choice and development during early adulthood

> "Adulthood is usually defined in terms of what people do, not how old they are."

Today in Canada, many young people have abundant opportunities to spend time in what some theorists consider a new period of development, roughly spanning the ages of 18 to 25: *emerging adulthood* (Arnett, 2007).

Adulthood is usually defined in terms of what people do, not how old they are. Over the years, developmentalists have considered marriage to be a key standard for adulthood (Carroll et al., 2007). Other criteria include holding a full-time job and living independently. Today, the transition to adulthood is mainly marked by adjustment issues, such as settling on one's values and beliefs, accepting self-responsibility, becoming financially independent, and establishing an equal relationship with one's parents (Gottlieb et al., 2007).

Adulthood itself has been divided into stages, and the first of these, early adulthood, has been largely seen as the period of life when people focus on establishing their careers or pathways in life. The transition to adulthood can be rapid or piecemeal. Many individuals in their late teens and early 20s remain dependent on their parents and are reluctant or unable to make enduring commitments in terms of identity formation or intimate relationships. The question is whether another stage of development bridges adolescence and early adulthood. Many developmental theorists believe in a bridging stage, including Jeffrey Arnett (2007), who terms this stage *emerging adulthood.*

LO1 Emerging Adulthood

Emerging adulthood is theorized to be a distinct period of development found in societies that allow young people an extended opportunity to explore their roles in life. Some parents are affluent enough to continue to support their children through their postsecondary education. Some students will receive assistance from the government by qualifying for student loans. These supports allow young people the luxury of sorting out their identity issues and creating meaningful life plans. But even in Canada, of course, many people cannot afford the luxury of exploring educational opportunities in emerging adulthood.

Overall, Canadian youth and young adults are leading healthy lives and are in a positive transition toward becoming healthy adults. Some young adults will experience significant health issues. Most mental illnesses, which are often an issue throughout life, begin to appear in early adulthood. Eating disorders and intentional self-harm are of particular concern. Accidents are the number one cause of death and injury in young adults. Sadly, many of such accidents are preventable. Substance abuse and risky sexual behaviour are also major health issues. Several factors have a positive outcome on the life of the young adult. Positive relationships with peers and parents are reported by most young adults. Academic engagement and involvement in extracurricular activities also protect the well-being of young Canadians (Public Health Agency of Canada, 2011).

emerging adulthood
a theoretical period of development, spanning the ages of 18 to 25, when young people in developed nations engage in extended role exploration.

CHAPTER 14

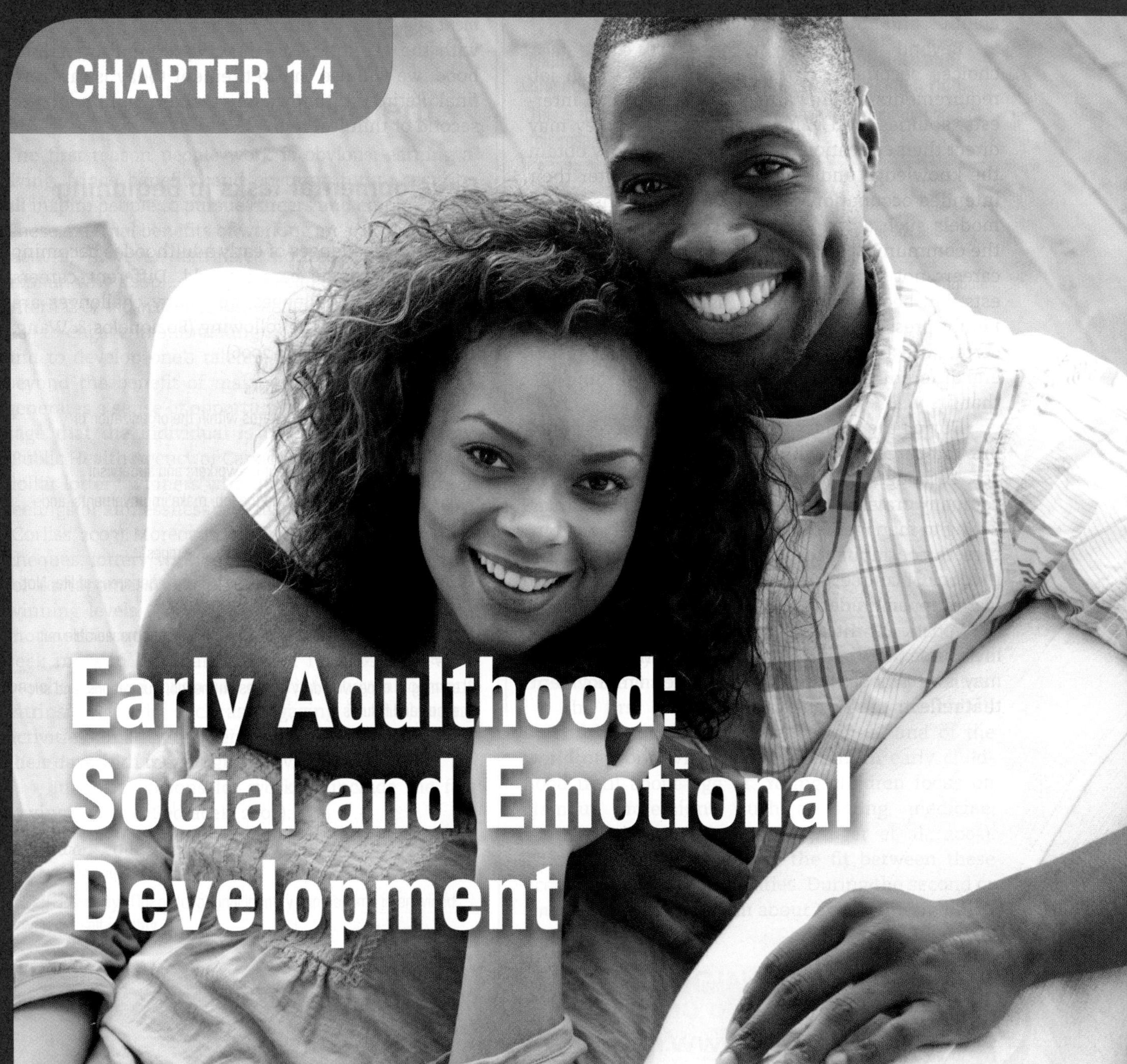

Early Adulthood: Social and Emotional Development

LEARNING OUTCOMES

LO1 Examine the issues involved in early adulthood separation

LO2 Describe the conflict between intimacy and isolation

LO3 Discuss the stage of life for entry into adulthood

LO4 Examine the emotional forces of attraction and love

LO5 Explain why people get lonely and what they do in response

LO6 Discuss the lifestyle of being single

LO7 Describe the practice of living together

LO8 Describe the practice of marriage

LO9 Discuss the state of parenthood

LO10 Discuss divorce and its repercussions

oliveromg/Shutterstock.com

> **"Erik Erikson saw the establishment of intimate relationships as the key "crisis," or challenge, of early adulthood."**

Early adulthood generally covers the two decades from ages 20 to 40, although some theorists suggest this stage begins at age 17 or 18, when the teen goes off to college or university, or enters the workforce. Others believe that since Canadians are living longer, middle age doesn't really start at 40 anymore. The traditional view of development in early adulthood was laid down by developmental psychologist Robert Havighurst (1972) more than 40 years ago. He believed that each stage of development involved accomplishing certain "tasks," and the tasks he describes for early adulthood include the following:

1. Getting started in an occupation
2. Selecting a life partner
3. Learning to live contentedly with one's partner
4. Starting a family and becoming a parent
5. Assuming the responsibilities of managing a home
6. Assuming social responsibilities

Many young adults will laugh at this list of tasks. Others will think that it doesn't sound too bad at all. Does this list remain valid, or does it need to be adjusted for the realities of today's life? For example, many young adults (and older adults) remain single. Some may choose stable and long-term relationships but not the traditional label of marriage to legitimize these relationships. Some couples choose not to have children, and others may discover they are infertile. For some, community contributions are not a priority. Havighurst did not list *separation* from one's family of origin, which seems to define today's Canadian reality.

Time & Life Pictures/Getty Images

Erikson Today

Stage 6: Intimacy vs. Isolation (19 to 39)

Psychosocial Theory: If a clear sense of self is established, the individual will begin to look outward to find companionship and love. The more solid the earlier foundations of personality development have been constructed, the easier this transition will be. Young adults seek deep intimacy and satisfying relationships. Individuals who are unsuccessful in this challenge will begin to isolate themselves from lasting unions.

Consider THIS

Are the "boomerang kids" creating a new stage in lifespan development?

Please see page 242 for a discussion on this topic.

PART FIVE

CHAPTER 15

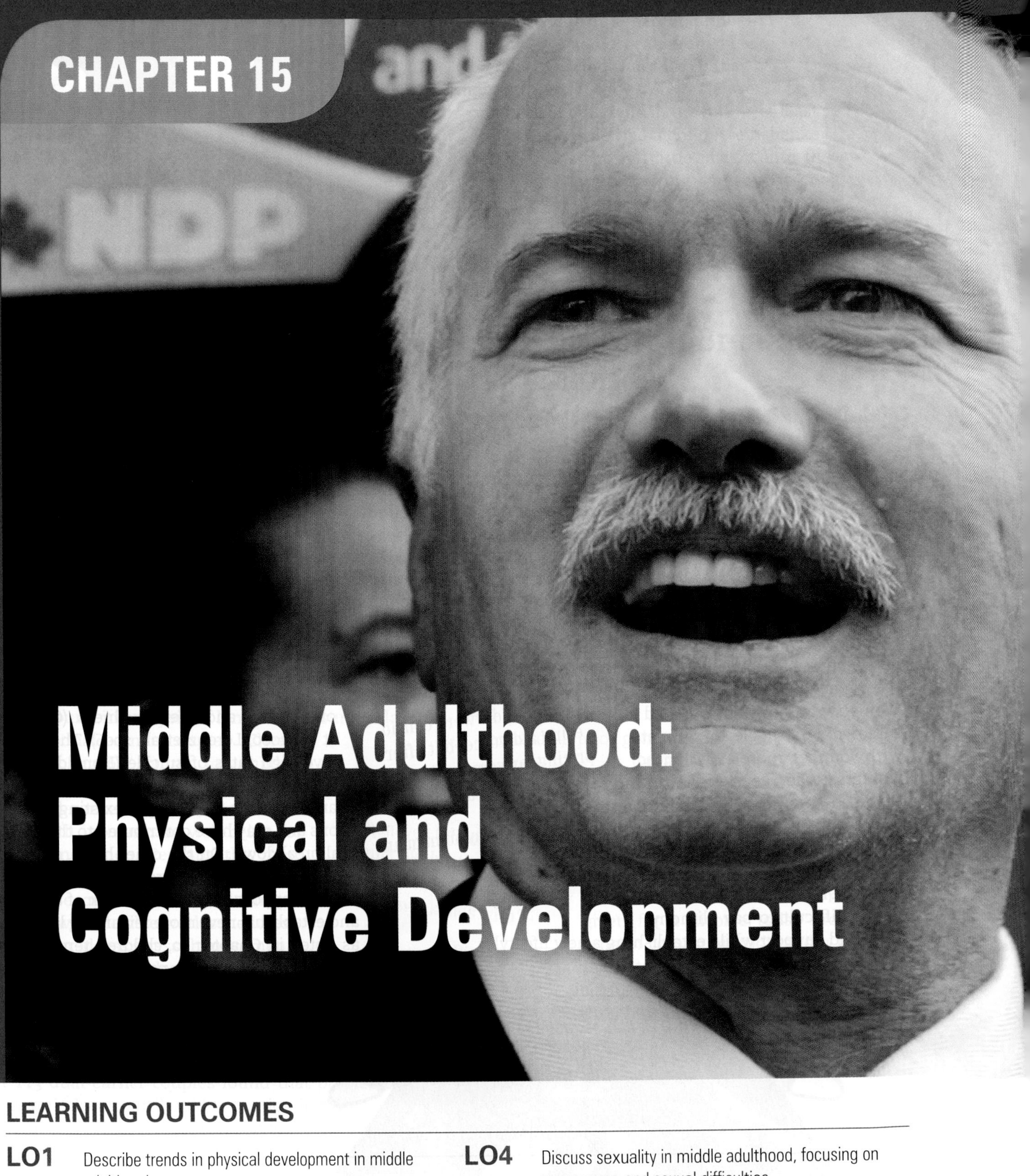

Middle Adulthood: Physical and Cognitive Development

LEARNING OUTCOMES

LO1 Describe trends in physical development in middle adulthood

LO2 Discuss the major health concerns of middle adulthood, including cancer and heart disease

LO3 Discuss the functioning of the immune system

LO4 Discuss sexuality in middle adulthood, focusing on menopause and sexual difficulties

LO5 Describe cognitive development in middle adulthood, distinguishing between crystallized and fluid intelligence

LO6 Discuss opportunities for exercising creativity and continuing education in middle adulthood

MIKE CASSESE/Reuters/Landov

> "Some theorists view middle age as a time of peak performance, whereas others portray it as a time of crisis or decline."

The **baby boomers** are those people who were born between 1946 and 1965. Canada saw a population increase of 11 percent, as the result of postwar babies. On average, 3.7 babies were born to each woman, compared with the average of 1.7 more recently (Statistics Canada, 2013c). The baby boomers are now middle-aged adults.

Some theorists view middle age as a time of peak performance, and others have portrayed it as a time of crisis or decline (Lachman, 2004). Physically speaking, we are at our peak in early adulthood, but in general, those who eat right and exercise will, in many ways, undergo only a gradual and relatively minor physical decline in middle adulthood. As we age, we become more vulnerable to a variety of illnesses, but we also become less prone to irresponsible behaviour that may result in injury or death. On the other hand, some sensory and sexual changes might well become major issues. Cognitively speaking, we are at our peak in many intellectual functions in middle adulthood, but may experience some loss of processing speed and some lapses in memory. Even so, these declines are often made up for in expertise.

LO1 Physical Development

No two people age in the same way or at the same rate. This phenomenon is called **interindividual variability**. But whatever individual differences may exist, physiological aging is defined by changes in the body's integumentary system (the body's system of skin, hair, and nails), senses, reaction time, and lung capacity. These changes may well be unavoidable. Changes in metabolism, muscle mass, strength, bone density, aerobic capacity, blood-sugar tolerance, and ability to regulate body temperature may be moderated and sometimes reversed through exercise and diet.

Skin and Hair

Hair usually begins to grey in middle adulthood as the production of *melanin*, the pigment responsible for hair colour, decreases. Hair loss also accelerates with aging, especially in men. Much of the wrinkling associated with aging is caused by exposure to ultraviolet (UV) rays.

Beginning gradually in early adulthood, the body produces fewer proteins that give the skin its elasticity. The body also produces fewer *keratinocytes*—the cells in the outer layer of the skin that are regularly shed and renewed, leaving the skin dryer and more brittle.

baby boomers
postwar babies whose births between 1946 and 1965 spiked the Canadian population 11 percent.

interindividual variability
the notion that people do not age in the same way or at the same rate.

presbyopia loss of elasticity in the lens that makes it harder to focus on nearby objects.

Sensory Functioning

Normal age-related changes in vision begin to appear by the mid-30s and assert themselves as significant problems in middle adulthood. **Presbyopia** (Latin for "old vision") refers to loss of elasticity in the lens that makes it harder to focus on, or accommodate to, nearby objects or fine print. Cataracts, glaucoma, and hearing loss are usually problems of late adulthood.

Reaction Time

Reaction time—the amount of time it takes to respond to a stimulus—increases with age, mainly because of changes in the nervous system. At age 25 or so, we begin to lose neurons, which are responsible for sensing signals such as sights and sounds and for coordinating our muscular responses.

Lung Capacity

Lung tissue stiffens with age, diminishing the lungs' capacity to expand, such that breathing capacity may decline by half between early and late adulthood. Regular exercise can offset much of this loss, and beginning to exercise regularly in middle adulthood can expand breathing capacity beyond what it was earlier in life.

Lean-Body Mass and Body Fat

Beginning at age 20, we lose nearly 3.2 kg (7 lb.) of lean-body mass with each decade. The rate of loss accelerates after age 45. Fat replaces lean-body mass, which includes muscles. Consequently, the average person's body mass index (BMI) rises.

Muscle Strength

Loss of muscles reduces strength. However, the change is gradual, and in middle adulthood, exercise can readily compensate, by increasing the size of the remaining muscle cells. Exercise will not re-achieve the prowess of the athlete in early adulthood, but will contribute to vigour, health, and a desirable body shape.

Metabolism

Metabolism is the rate at which the body processes or "burns" food to produce energy. The resting metabolic rate—also called the *basal metabolic rate (BMR)*—declines as we age. Fatty tissue burns fewer calories than muscle, and the decline in BMR is largely attributable to the loss of muscle tissue and the corresponding increase in fatty tissue. Since we require fewer calories to maintain our weight as we age, middle-aged people (and older adults) are likely to gain weight if they eat as much as they did as young adults.

Bone Density

Bone, which consists largely of calcium, begins to lose density and strength at around the age of 40. As bones lose density, they become more brittle and prone to fracture. Bones in the spine, hip, thigh (femur), and forearm lose the most density as we age. We discuss osteoporosis in Chapter 17.

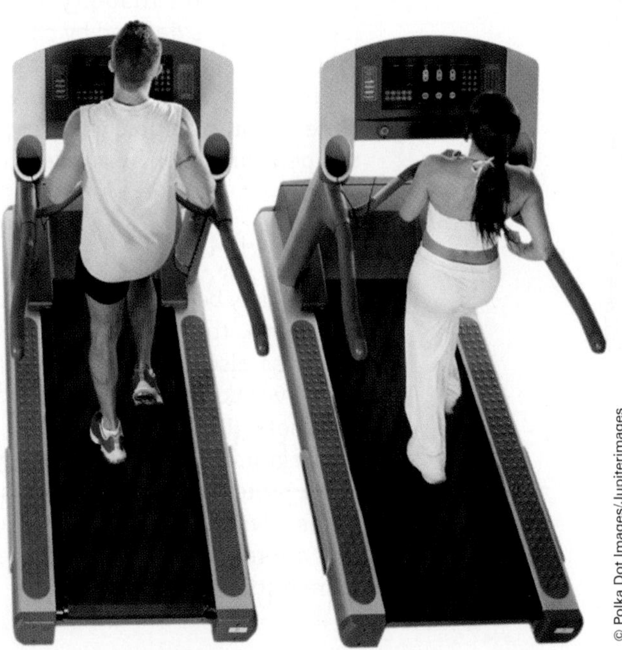

Aerobic Capacity

As we age, the cardiovascular system becomes less efficient. Heart and lung muscles shrink. Aerobic capacity declines as less oxygen is taken into the lungs and the heart pumps less blood. The maximum heart rate declines, but exercise expands aerobic capacity at *any* age.

Blood-Sugar Tolerance

Blood sugar, or glucose, is the basic fuel and energy source for cells. The energy from glucose supports cell activities and maintains body temperature. Glucose circulates in the bloodstream and enters cells with the help of insulin, a hormone secreted by the pancreas.

As we age, the tissues in our body become less capable of taking up glucose from the bloodstream. Body tissues lose their sensitivity to insulin; the pancreas must thus produce more insulin to achieve the same effect. Therefore, blood-sugar levels rise, increasing the risk of adult-onset diabetes.

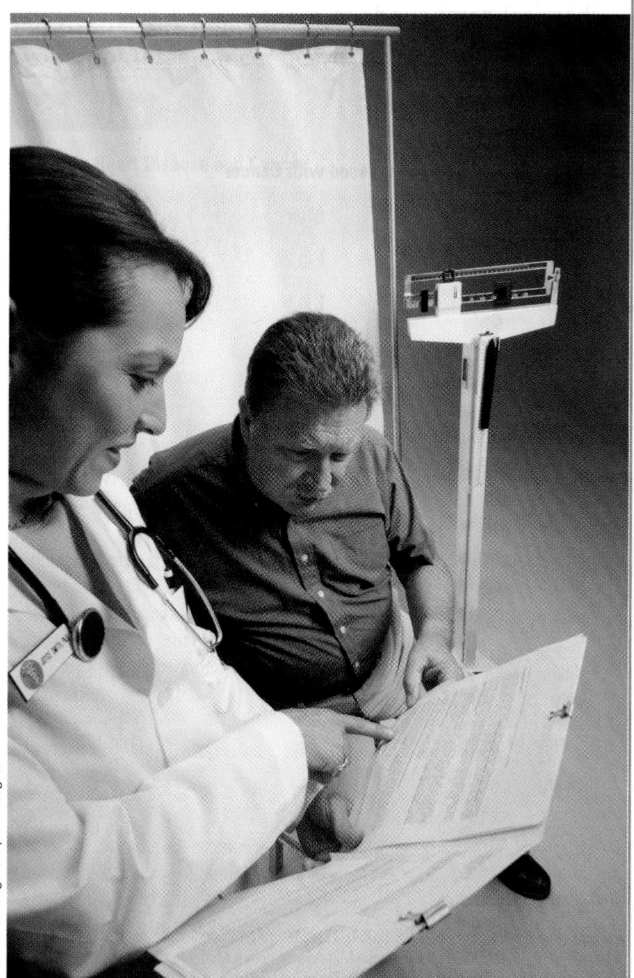

LO2 Health

The health of people aged 40–65 in developed nations such as Canada is better than ever. Nearly everyone has been vaccinated for preventable diseases. Many, perhaps the majority, practise preventive health care. Once people reach 40, they are advised to have annual physical checkups. Fortunately, more is known today about curing or treating illnesses than ever before.

Racial, ethnic, and sex differences affect the incidence and treatment of various diseases. People from certain groups appear to be more likely to develop certain chronic conditions, such as hypertension and specific types of cancer. Canadians are very proud of their health care system, but reduced access and lengthy wait times make it apparent that much work is needed to restore health care to the level of our pride.

As we consider the health of people in middle adulthood, we focus on many things that can go wrong. For most of us, things go quite well if we get regular medical checkups, pay attention to our diets, exercise, avoid smoking, drink in moderation if at all, regulate stress, and—ideally—enjoy supportive relationships.

DID YOU KNOW?

Canadians are proud of their health care system.

Reduced access and lengthy wait times make it clear that we need to focus on our health care system if we want to protect it.

Leading Causes of Death

In early adulthood, the leading causes of death—accidents and suicide—screamed out their preventability. In middle adulthood, diseases come to the fore (see Table 15.1). Cancer and heart disease are numbers one and two, and accidents are now in third place. Cancer and heart disease are also preventable to some degree, of course. Cancer Care Ontario (2013) recommends women have mammograms to screen for breast cancer beginning at age 50, and men and women be screened for cancer of the colon also beginning at age 50. Most men should have digital rectal exams (in which the doctor uses a gloved finger to feel the prostate gland) and blood tests for prostate-specific antigen (PSA) at age 40 (Prostate Cancer Canada, 2013). However, Canadian men of Black African or Black

EMERGING CANADA

Only 56 percent of Canadians between the ages of 45 to 65 consider themselves to be in very good or excellent health, and 14 percent say their health is fair or poor (Human Resources and Skills Development, 2013d).

Speed of Information Processing

The speed of information processing can be measured in several ways. One is simply physical: *reaction time*, which is the time it takes to respond to a stimulus. If you touch a hot stove, how long does it take to pull your hand away? In one assessment of reaction time, people push a button when a light is flashed. Compared with young adults, those in middle adulthood respond to the light more slowly—their reaction time is greater (Hartley, 2006). The difference in reaction time is only a fraction of a second, but it is enough to keep the typical middle-aged adult out of the firing line in the military and on the sidelines of professional sports (Salthouse & Berish, 2005). It can also make a difference when trying to avoid an accident on the highway.

Reaction time is only one aspect of processing speed. The broad cognitive aspect of perceptual speed is also intertwined with fluid intelligence. As with reaction time, the changes in middle adulthood are not that dramatic, but are measurable. Because of continuous experience with reading and writing, an educated person in middle adulthood may be better than ever at doing crossword puzzles (largely dependent on crystallized intelligence), but she might find it more difficult to navigate new cities than when she was younger (largely dependent on fluid intelligence) (Salthouse & Siedlecki, 2007).

Most researchers believe that the decline in processing speed reflects changes in the integrity of the nervous system. But the hypotheses run rampant, from the death of neurons in the brain to changes in specific parts of the brain and changes in the secretion of neurotransmitters (Hartley, 2006).

Memory

K. Warner Schaie's (1994) longitudinal research found that memory is one intellectual factor that showed improvement through most of the years of middle adulthood and then stability from age 53 to 60. Not all researchers agree. Researchers use several kinds of memory tasks, which do not necessarily lead to the same results (Salthouse et al., 2006). Despite Schaie's results, most researchers conclude that people in middle adulthood and late adulthood perform less well than young adults at memorizing lists of words, numbers, and passages of prose (Salthouse & Davis, 2006).

The main strategies for memorization are *rote rehearsal* and *elaborative rehearsal*. Once we are in the latter part of middle adulthood, we are less likely than when we were younger to be able to learn new information by rote repetition (Salthouse & Babcock, 1991). We are also less capable of screening out distractions (Radvansky et al., 2005). Elaborative rehearsal may also suffer because we are also apparently less capable of rapid classification or categorization (Hultsch et al., 1998).

We have been speaking of working, or short-term, memory. Let's look at storage, or long-term, memory. Not all types of memory functions decline in middle adulthood. We are typically more likely to retain or expand our general knowledge in middle adulthood (Prull et al., 2000; Zacks et al., 2000), such as by learning more about an area in which we have little knowledge or experience.

Procedural memory is a kind of motor memory of how to do things—how to ride a bicycle, how to use a keyboard, how to write with a pen, how to drive a car. One of my favourite photos is of the older Jean Piaget riding a bicycle. The "student of children" looks childlike, but the message for the student of psychology or education is that we can maintain procedural memories for a lifetime.

DID YOU KNOW?

Not all types of memory functioning decline in middle adulthood.

Long-term memory and general knowledge often improve with age.

Expertise and Practical Problem Solving

Any employer with some knowledge of human development would want to hire someone in middle adulthood. Middle-aged people have verbal abilities that match or exceed those of younger people, have lost very little in the way of fluid intelligence, and have a greater store of expertise and practical problem-solving skills (Leclerc & Hess, 2007). Despite interindividual variations, as a group, middle-aged adults show their skills every day in every way.

Over the years, they have acquired social skills that enable them to deal better with subordinates and with supervisors. They have a better feeling for other people's limitations and potentials, and they have a better understanding of how to motivate them. They may also have experience that will help them remain calm in stressful situations.

The parent who was so distraught when the first child cried may now be relaxed when the grandchildren cry. Part of the difference may be the "distance"—the generation of removal. But their patience is also the result of having learned that whether or not children cry, they will usually survive and develop into normal human beings—whatever that means.

In terms of vocations, the initial training or education of middle-aged people has now had the benefits of years of experience. People in middle adulthood have learned what works and what does not work for them. In terms of professions, for instance, "book learning" and perhaps internships have been supplemented by years of experience in the real world. Pianist Arthur Rubinstein became so accomplished as the years wore on that he often practised "mentally"—he needed the physical keyboard only intermittently. Although he lost some speed when playing rapid passages, he compensated by slowing before beginning those passages, and he created drama when he escalated his pacing.

LO6 Creativity and Learning

Middle adulthood offers numerous opportunities for exercising creativity, expanding knowledge, and enjoying the intellectual experience.

Creativity

People in middle adulthood can be creative, and many middle-aged adults are at the height of their creativity. At age 56, Pablo Picasso painted *Guernica*, one of the best known images in art and a protest against the Spanish Civil War. Author Toni Morrison wrote the Pulitzer Prize–winning novel *Beloved* at age 57. Inventor Thomas Edison built the kinetoscope, an early peephole method for watching films, at age 44. Yet researchers have found some differences in creativity among young adults and middle-aged people. Aspects of creativity that are relatively more likely to be found among young adults include creativity in music, mathematics, and physics (Norton et al., 2005; Simonton, 2006b). Wolfgang Amadeus Mozart, considered by many critics to be the greatest composer in history, died at the age of 35. Albert Einstein published his general theory of relativity at the age of 36.

Writers and visual artists often continue to improve into middle adulthood, although their most emotional and fervent works may be produced at younger ages. The most emotionally charged works of poets tend to be penned in early adulthood (Simonton, 2007).

DID YOU KNOW?

Creativity continues well into middle adulthood.

Pablo Picasso, Toni Morrison, and Thomas Edison all had great creative achievements during middle age.

Mature Learners

For most adults, learning is a perpetual process. We learn when a new store opens in the neighbourhood or when we watch or listen to the media. We learn when we hear what is happening with a family member or observe a pet. But when psychologists

and educators use the term "adult learning," they are usually speaking of learning as it occurs within a formal educational setting.

Even when we limit our discussion to educational settings, we find vast diversity and interindividual variation. But research on mature learners suggests that they are likely to have some things in common: They are apt to be highly motivated, and they are more likely than younger learners to find the subject matter interesting for its own sake (Bye et al., 2007).

In 2007, a higher percentage of women (69 percent) than men (62 percent) aged 25–44 had completed a college or university program. Canada has the second highest rate of postsecondary attainment in the world, bettered only by Korea. You might assume that women who have families and have returned to school would be the women with the least exacting combinations of family and work demands. Actually, it's the other way around (Hostetler et al., 2007). Women with the greatest demands on them from family and work are those most likely to return to school. But once they're back, their major source of stress is time constraints; those who receive the emotional support of their families and employers experience the least stress and do best (Kirby et al., 2004).

Research on mature learners suggests that they are apt to be highly motivated, and they are more likely than younger learners to find the subject matter interesting for its own sake.

Government assistance programs, such as Ontario's Second Careers, report an increasing number of laid-off adult workers are enrolling in postsecondary schools. Others in middle adulthood may choose to pursue educational goals they were not able to realize in their youth. When returning students come to campus, they often feel a bit on the periphery of things because rules, regulations, and activities are generally designed for younger students (Brady, 2007). The returning students are often unsure whether to share their thoughts or perspectives with the class; perhaps, they may think, their ideas are out of date. Then again, some returning students have achieved commanding positions at work or in social roles and may find it difficult to accept their subordinate status in the teacher–student relationship (Marron & Rayman, 2002). However, all in all, research suggests that both younger and returning students, and instructors, benefit from the mix of views that includes returning students (Brady, 2007).

© Shauna Longmuir

Student diversity in age enhances the learning process. Who is the student and who is the instructor?

CHAPTER 16

Middle Adulthood: Social and Emotional Development

LEARNING OUTCOMES

LO1 Discuss theories of development in middle adulthood

LO2 Discuss stability and change in social and emotional development in middle adulthood

LO3 Discuss career developments typical of middle adulthood

LO4 Discuss trends in relationships in middle adulthood, focusing on grandparenting and being in the "sand-wich generation"

“Many of us ‘launch’ our children into the outside world during middle adulthood and help them establish themselves.”

Social perceptions have changed greatly since the time of *Happy Days* and *Leave it to Beaver*. Robert Havighurst's vision of normalcy may have been based on these "typical" American families when he proposed his "developmental tasks" of middle adulthood in the 1970s. He didn't account for same-sex families, people who cannot or choose not to have children, people who choose the single life, or people who do not undertake "meaningful" social and civic responsibilities. But we must admit that Havighurst did arrive at a list of issues that affect many of us at midlife, and we will discuss many of these issues in this chapter.

Erikson Today

Stage 7: Generativity versus Stagnation (40–64 years)

Family life and career are the defining features of this stage of development. Middle adulthood is defined by greater responsibility and a more established sense of control. Middle-aged individuals are working toward establishing stability in their life. Erikson spoke of generativity, which is the attempt to produce something that will be long-lasting and worthwhile. Inactivity and meaninglessness are feared. Major life shifts also occur during this stage of development, as children leave home, careers come to an end, and aging parents die. The challenge is to find purpose. Those who are successful boldly step into the last challenge of the lifespan. Those who fail to capture a sense of accomplishment will be ill-equipped for the final stage of life.

Consider THIS

Should middle-aged parents be more focused on their own futures given that their children are now adults?

Please see page 276 for a discussion on this topic.

Many of us do "launch" our children into the outside world during our middle adulthood, and we do help them establish themselves—sometimes for much longer than we might have anticipated. We may find that our preferences in leisure activities have changed over the years, or we may continue activities we have long enjoyed—athletic, cultural, and social pursuits. Some of us are establishing deeper relationships with life partners, but some are living alone, having never partnered or perhaps having divorced, and some are living with stepfamilies and possibly struggling along. Some of us are involved in meaningful social or civic activities, but some of us are loners. As we will see, going it alone can have negative consequences for our mental and physical well-being.

Havighurst sounds pessimistic about work—when he mentions keeping our performance at a satisfactory level. Many of us reach our peak performance or first come into our own in middle adulthood. We have gained expertise, as noted in Chapter 15, and our abilities remain generally intact.

Yes, we may have issues in adjusting to physical aging. Our bodies will be changing. We may encounter illnesses we really weren't thinking all that much about

Robert Havighurst's Developmental Tasks of Middle Adulthood

- ✓ Helping our children establish themselves in the outside world
- ✓ Developing a range of enjoyable leisure activities
- ✓ Establishing a deeper relationship with our life partner
- ✓ Becoming involved in meaningful social and civic responsibilities
- ✓ Keeping our performance at work at a satisfactory level
- ✓ Adjusting to the physical changes that accompany aging through the midlife period
- ✓ Adjusting to the demands and responsibilities of caring for aging parents

during young adulthood. We may need to come to the aid of aging parents. On the other hand, we may also find new rewards in our relationships with our aging parents, now that all of us are "grown up."

generativity the ability to generate or produce, as in bearing children or contributing to society.

LO1 Theories of Development in Middle Adulthood

Theories of development in middle adulthood largely deal with the issue of whether we can consider middle adulthood to be a distinct stage or phase of life.

Erik Erikson's Theory of Psychosocial Development

Erikson believed that the major psychological challenge of the middle years is *generativity versus* stagnation. **Generativity** is the ability to generate or produce. We have an instinctive drive to leave something of

Consider THIS

Should middle-aged parents be more focused on their own futures, given that their children are now adults?

In earlier chapters, we looked at "the boomerang" generation, referring to the baby boomers' children who just keep coming back. The boomerang generation has created a unique set of problems for their parents, the baby boomers. Canada's baby boomers face the financial worries of reduced pensions, low returns on their savings, and high debt. One more additional burden is their boomerang kids. According to a survey, one in five Canadian baby boomers is prepared to risk their own financial security to help out their adult children. Free room and board is the largest financial strain, followed by major purchases (such cars and furniture), rent expenses, groceries, and credit lines for their children. But by taking on these expenses, the baby boomers run the risk of doing too much and placing their retirement plans in jeopardy (Beltrame, 2013).

As Canada's largest demographic group moves closer to retirement, 46 percent of Canadians aged 45–64 are still working to pay off their mortgage—including 33 percent of those between 55 and 64 years of age (Toneguzzi, 2011). According to Erikson, middle-aged adults are trying to establish stability in their life. They are torn between helping their adult children gain a financial footing and leaving behind a legacy that proves to themselves and others that their time has made a difference. Naturally, parents are inclined to help their children find a place in the world but at what cost to themselves? How do aging parents protect their own futures? Should they be helping their adult children, or should they be focusing on their own financial stability and security? What impact will these choices have on the last stage of psychosocial development?

meaning behind for future generations. Failure to achieve this goal leads to **stagnation.** For those that have raised their families and completed their careers, grandparenting offers an interesting opportunity for satisfying generativity in later adulthood.

© Jeffrey Coolidge/Getty Images

Daniel Levinson's Seasons

When we walk down the street and encounter others, we begin a sociological process of automatically categorizing each person into three dimensions: race, gender, and age. For decades, researchers have studied the influence of race- and gender-based categorization but what about ageism? Ageism includes all prejudices that are based on age. In our society, a billion-dollar industry is devoted toward making us look and feel younger. Birthday cards clearly deliver the notion that getting one year older is very undesirable. Canada has seen the first wave of baby boomers hit the retirement age. Demographers predict that by 2030 the population older than 65 will have doubled. The roots of ageism begin to become firmly established in middle age (Nelson, 2005). A **social clock** guides our judgment regarding the "appropriateness" of certain behaviours, life events, and trajectories (Paglia & Room, 1998). We judge what is appropriate fashion, appropriate behaviour, and even the appropriate roles that middle-aged persons should fulfill.

According to Daniel Levinson and his colleagues, the years from 40 to 45 comprise a **midlife transition**—a psychological shift into middle adulthood that is often accompanied by a crisis during which people fear they have more to look back on than to look forward to. In the 1960s, a Canadian psychoanalyst, Elliott Jaques, coined the term *midlife crisis* based on his studies of clinical patients who were dealing with depression and angst about getting older. The term became an instant popular culture sensation because, after all, everyone knew someone who fit the stereotype, so it must be true (Nixon, 2011). This crisis is termed a **midlife crisis** and is defined as a time of dramatic self-doubt and anxiety, during which people sense the passing of their youth and become preoccupied with concerns about the imminence of their own mortality. Levinson believed that marker events such as menopause, the death of a parent or a friend, a divorce, or a child's leaving "the nest" could trigger the crisis.

Once beset by the crisis, some people attempt to deny the realities of aging, such as by having an extramarital affair to prove to themselves they are still sexually attractive, buying a sports car (red, of course), or suddenly shifting careers. Many people, however, view the years from age 45 onward as a type of second adulthood, filled with opportunities for new direction and fulfillment.

stagnation
the state of no longer developing, growing, or advancing.

social clock
the social norms that guide our judgment regarding the age-related "appropriateness" of certain behaviours.

midlife transition
a psychological shift into middle adulthood that is theorized to occur between the ages of 40 and 45, as people begin to believe they have more to look back on than to look forward to.

midlife crisis
a time of dramatic self-doubt and anxiety, during which people sense the passing of their youth and become concerned with their own aging and mortality.

DID YOU KNOW?

The midlife crisis is more the creation of Hollywood than a reflection of real life.

A midlife crisis may be more the exception than the rule.

Entering Midlife: Crisis, Turning Point, or Prime of Life?

With people now often living into their late 70s, 80s, and beyond, age 40 has become accepted as a midlife turning point (Wethington et al., 2004). When people turn 40, they often realize they have as much to look back on as they have to look forward to.

Daniel Levinson and his colleagues (1978) considered the transition to midlife at about the age of 40 to be a crisis, a midlife crisis, characterized by taking stock and often recognizing that one has fallen short of one's dream or dreams. The promising lead vocalist in a local band never made it. The Queen's University business major never sat at the Fortune 500 merger that brought in $25 million. The police college graduate at the top of her class never made RCMP commissioner. Thus, argues Becker (2006), the value of psychotherapy at this time of life should not be minimized.

David Svetlik/Shutterstock.com

Who's Having a Crisis?

According to psychiatrist Richard A. Friedman (2008), one excuse for human messing up is "My dog ate my homework." Another is "I'm going through a midlife crisis." As mortality begins to loom on the horizon, some people experience the impulse to do things in denial of their age, such as buy a new, fast, expensive car; suddenly quit a job; or leave a loyal spouse for a younger version.

Friedman reports on the experiences of middle-aged men who cheated on their wives, claiming to have had midlife crises. They may say that they love their wives and don't know what got into them, but they're usually seeking novelty and risking too much for a few moments of fun. Being bored with routine is not what is meant by the term *midlife crisis*.

empty nest syndrome
a feeling of loneliness or loss of purpose that parents, and especially mothers, are theorized to experience when the youngest child leaves home.

These portraits are negative, to say the least. Other observers of adult development note that while some theorists present portraits of middle-aged people suddenly focusing on tragedy, loss, or doom, others find people to be in or entering the "prime of life" (Almeida & Horn, 2004; Lachman, 2004). People can develop certain illnesses at almost any time of life, but as described in Chapter 15, most people in middle adulthood encounter little decline in physical prowess. Intellectually, little fluid intelligence, if any, is lost, and crystallized intelligence is growing—especially among professionals who continue to develop skills in their chosen fields.

Middle-aged adults, especially professionals, are also often earning more money than young adults. They are more likely to be settled geographically and vocationally, although they may experience midlife career changes and movement from one organization or business to another. By now, many have built systems of social support and may be involved in enduring romantic and social relationships and have children. The flip side, as we will see, may be overwhelming responsibility, such as caring for adolescent children, a spouse, aging parents, and remaining in the workplace all at once—quite a juggling act! But many in middle adulthood are at the height of their productivity and resilience, despite these challenges.

The Life-Events Approach

The life-events approach to middle age focuses on the particular challenges and changes that people are likely to face at this time of life rather than on phases or stages of life. Numerous researchers have found that the most stressful life events of middle adulthood tend to include the death of a spouse or a child; the death of a parent or a sibling; marital divorce or separation, or separation from a cohabitant; hospitalization or change in the health status of oneself, one's child, one's parent, or one's sibling; the need to care for one's parents; a change in the relationship with one's children; financial difficulties; concern about one's appearance, weight, or aging; moving; change or loss of employment; a change in a relationship with an important friend; or a change in responsibilities at work (Etaugh & Bridges, 2006; Lorenz et al., 2006).

One common change in middle adulthood occurs when the last child leaves the home. Although we once assumed that mothers whose children have moved out would experience a painful "**empty nest syndrome**," this time can just as often be a positive stage (Etaugh & Bridges, 2006). Today, many middle-aged women in developed nations find they are "as young as they feel." Most are in the workforce and find life satisfaction in activities other than childrearing and homemaking.

DID YOU KNOW?

Modern mothers no longer experience an "empty-nest syndrome" when the last child leaves home.

Having the last child leave home is often a positive event for middle-aged women.

As sources of stress, negative life events, including physical illness and depression, have been shown to be harmful to people's health in middle adulthood (Lorenz et al., 2006; Ryff et al., 2002). Some stressed people resort to a host of medicines, both prescribed and over-the-counter (Outram et al., 2006). An accumulation of stressful

© Blend Images/Jupiterimages

© Image Source

life events even seems capable of accelerating age-related declines in memory functioning (VonDras et al., 2005).

Nevertheless, middle-aged people's situations—such as having understanding and helpful family members or friends—and attitudes can have moderating effects on stressors (Etaugh & Bridges, 2006). A sense of control has been shown to override the effects of stress and foster feelings of well-being among midlife adults (Windsor et al., 2008). Middle-aged adults are less likely to be depressed by negative life events when they perceive such events as capable of being changed and as specific rather than global problems (Adler et al., 2006).

EMERGING CANADA

When it comes to Freedom 55, Canadians aren't retiring, they are leaving their spouses. Despite an overall decline in the Canadian divorce rate, the over-50 crowd is the only age group experiencing more divorces. In 2007, the divorce rate for those over age 65 had doubled since 1980. As the lifespan unfolds, children leave the family, and couples have limited years left to be truly happy. This realization seems to be affecting people's decisions to remain married, leading to the new trend of the "27-year itch" (Kingston, 2007).

LO2 Stability and Change in Middle Adulthood

Many researchers use five basic factors of personality isolated by Robert McCrae and Paul Costa and their colleagues to study stability and change in the personality development of adults over several decades (McCrae & Costa, 2006; Terracciano et al., 2006). These factors include extraversion, agreeableness, conscientiousness, neuroticism (emotional instability), and openness to experience (see Table 16.1). Cross-cultural research has found that these five factors appear to define the personality structure of North American, German, Portuguese, Hebrew, Chinese, Korean, and Japanese people (McCrae & Costa, 1997). A study of more than 5,000 German, British, Spanish, Czech, and Turkish people suggests that the factors are related to people's basic temperaments, which are considered to be largely inborn (McCrae et al., 2000). The researchers interpret the results to suggest that our personalities tend to mature rather than be shaped by environmental conditions, although the expression of personality traits is certainly affected by culture. (For example, a person who is "basically" open to new experience is likely to behave less openly in a traditional, fundamentalist society than in an open society.)

© Stuart McClymont/Getty Images

TABLE 16.1

The "Big Five": The Five-Factor Model of Personality

Factor	Name	Traits
I	Extraversion	Contrasts talkativeness, assertiveness, and activity with silence, passivity, and reserve
II	Agreeableness	Contrasts kindness, trust, and warmth with hostility, selfishness, and distrust
III	Conscientiousness	Contrasts organization, thoroughness, and reliability with carelessness, negligence, and unreliability
IV	Neuroticism	Contrasts nervousness, moodiness, and sensitivity to negative stimuli with coping ability
V	Openness to experience	Contrasts imagination, curiosity, and creativity with shallowness and lack of perceptiveness

© Comstock Images/Jupiterimages

"big five" personality traits basic personality traits derived from contemporary statistical methods: extraversion, agreeableness, conscientiousness, neuroticism (emotional instability), and openness to experience.

Are There Sudden Shifts in Personality?

The notions of crises or turning points in emotional development also suggest that people undergo rather sudden changes or shifts in personality. As pointed out by Robert McCrae and Paul Costa, Jr. (2006), we have widely assumed that our personalities are deeply affected by adult life events such as getting married, working our way up in a vocation, and having and rearing children. However, according to two decades of longitudinal research, the **"big five" personality traits** tend to show a good deal of stability over time, at least after age 30 (Roberts & DelVecchio, 2000). McCrae and Costa suggest that this stability brings into question whether it makes sense for developmentalists, such as the Levinson group (1978), to suggest that phases or stages of adult development are predictable.

Longitudinal and cross-sectional research has shown some consistent trends in group personality change over the years, but by and large, those who are, say, most extraverted in young adulthood will remain most extraverted in middle adulthood (Roberts & DelVecchio, 2000; Roberts et al., 2006). However, for adults as a group, male and female, the traits of agreeableness and conscientiousness tend to increase from young adulthood to middle adulthood. Neuroticism declines throughout the same period, meaning that people become more emotionally stable. Extraversion and openness to new experience either remain the same or decline slightly in middle adulthood, suggesting again greater stability in personality, or "maturity." The trait of being open to new experience decreases once more in late adulthood.

DID YOU KNOW?

The events of middle adulthood do not tend to cause major shifts in personality.

According to two decades of longitudinal research, the "big five" personality traits tend to show a good deal of stability over time (Roberts & DelVecchio, 2000).

DID YOU KNOW?

Women who have a college or university education do not typically experience increased personal distress as they advance from middle adulthood to late adulthood.

Aside from increased concern with aging, this is generally true.

LO3 Work in Middle Adulthood

As suggested by Erikson and Levinson, many workers are at their peak in middle adulthood. They have had years to "learn the ropes," and many have advanced into the highest ranks of their trades or professions. One's work can continue to provide social benefits, a sense of identity, and self-esteem.

Job Satisfaction

Canadians are among the most satisfied workers in the world. In a global study of workers in 23 countries, only those in Denmark and Norway had a higher satisfaction level with their current employer (Fortier, 2010).

A study of more than 2,000 university employees found that job satisfaction increased steadily throughout middle adulthood (Hochwarter et al., 2001). The gains were greatest for men, and especially for men who were white-collar workers, for example, professors. Some workers—particularly blue-collar workers—reported feelings of alienation and dissatisfaction. Some complain that supervisors treated them with disrespect and failed to ask them how to improve working conditions and productivity (Judge & Klinger, 2008). These feelings are particularly painful for middle-aged workers when their supervisors are young adults. Middle-aged women are often balancing the demands of the workplace and a family, and they may still experience a "glass ceiling" on the job (Casini & Sanchez-Mazas, 2005). Although women may be sought out in the hiring process, they will not necessarily have an easy time advancing. Still, most women and blue-collar workers reported more satisfaction on the job throughout middle age—just not as much as white-collar men.

DID YOU KNOW?

Job satisfaction increases throughout middle adulthood.

A study of more than 2,000 university employees found that job satisfaction increased steadily throughout middle adulthood (Hochwarter et al., 2001).

The growing job satisfaction throughout middle age can be linked to factors such as increases in both expertise and income. Workers in middle adulthood may also have more realistic perceptions of their career goals. They may have come to terms with recognition that (most of them) will never be the CEO of Apple, Inc.; the lead singer in a famous rock band; or the first person to set foot on Mars.

Career Change in Middle Adulthood

People change careers for many reasons, such as more money, more job security, greater prestige, and more stimulation (Jepsen & Choudhuri, 2001; Sullivan et al., 2003). Most people who change their careers do so in young adulthood. By middle adulthood, people tend to have greater responsibilities and to have become more "entrenched" in their pursuits. They may also wonder whether they have the time and the ability to start over.

EMERGING CANADA

Second Careers is a government program designed to fund and retrain Ontarians who are unemployed, forcing a career change at a time when most didn't expect it. With the emergence of a knowledge economy, it is projected that by 2026, 77 percent of the Canadian labour force will need a postsecondary education to be employable. Currently, only 60 percent of the Canadian workforce aged 35 or older meets this requirement, so the government is sending them back to school. This opportunity is exciting for some middle-aged students and a terrifying prospect for others. By 2032, a projected 1.73 million workers will need to be retrained for a second career in Ontario alone (Miner, 2010).

For reasons such as these, most career changes in midlife involve shifts into related fields (Shultz & Adams, 2007). For example, in the entertainment world, an actor might become a director or a producer. In the field of education, a teacher might move into educational administration. More radical shifts can occur, and they can also be successful (Hall, 2004). A laboratory chemist who has spent 20 years working for a pharmaceuticals company might decide she wants to work with people and to have more time for herself, so she might choose to teach high-school chemistry and travel during the summers. We know of a social worker who decided to become a rabbi at the age of 43 and undertook several years of study. She said that she didn't feel she was really changing much at all, just getting better at Hebrew.

These are all "voluntary," planned changes. Some middle-aged people change careers following a personal crisis such as a divorce, conflict with coworkers, or being fired. In such cases, middle-aged people sometimes pick up whatever work they can to sustain themselves (Shultz & Adams, 2007).

Unemployment

Our friend lost her executive position in her late 40s, when her company was bought out and a new management team came in. She knew she was in a vulnerable position because the company taking over usually "chops off the head" of the acquired company; still, she thought she might have enough seniority to escape notice. Not so. New management cut in half the number of professionals at her level. At first she focused on her generous severance package. She thought she would take a month off to relax and then use the head-hunting firm hired by the company to

CHAPTER 17

Late Adulthood: Physical and Cognitive Development

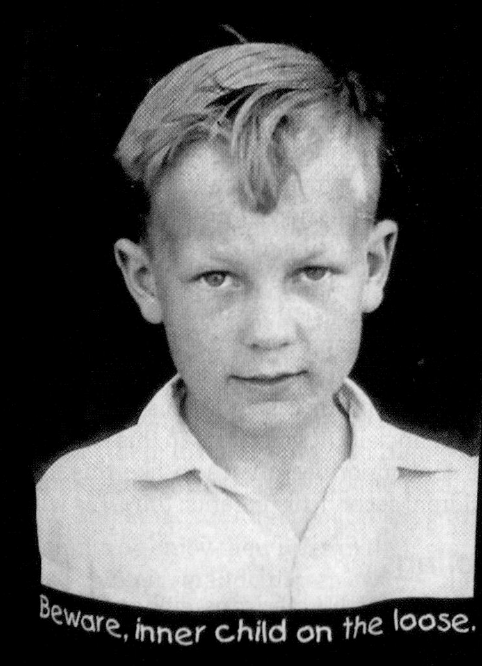

LEARNING OUTCOMES

LO1 Describe trends in physical development in late adulthood, focusing on life expectancy

LO2 Compare programmed and cellular damage theories of aging

LO3 Identify common health concerns associated with late adulthood

LO4 Discuss cognitive development in late adulthood

Shauna Longmuir

“People age 65 and older are the most rapidly growing segment of the Canadian population.”

An Agequake Is Coming. People age 65 and older are the most rapidly growing segment of the Canadian population. So many people are living longer that we are in the midst of a “greying of Canada,” an aging of the population that is having significant effects on many aspects of society.

LO1 Physical Development

In 1900, only 1 person in 25 was over the age of 65. Today, that figure has more than tripled, to 1 in 8 of us. By the year 2050, more than 1 in 5 North Americans will be 65 years of age or older, and the percentage of North Americans over the age of 75 will have doubled (Kawas & Brookmeyer, 2001). To put these numbers in historical context, consider that through virtually all of human history, until the beginning of the 19th century, only a small fraction of humans lived to the age of 50. The population over age 65 is usually divided into the young-old (65–74), the old-old (75–84), and the oldest-old (85 and over). The groups are assigned according to the likelihood that they will be dependent on family members or the medical community. Gender differences in death rates also shift significantly across the age groupings (Rowland, 2009).

DID YOU KNOW?

Canadians have a higher life expectancy than our neighbours in the United States.

This difference is likely due to our health care system.

Thomas Fricke/First Light/Getty Images

Being a centenarian means you have celebrated your 100th birthday.

Longevity and Life Expectancy

One’s **life span**, or **longevity**, is the length of time a person can live under the best of circumstances. The life span of a species, including humans, depends on its genetic programming. With the right genes and environment, and with the good fortune to avoid serious accidents or illnesses, people have a life span of about 115 years.

One’s **life expectancy** refers to the number of years a person in a given population group can actually expect to live. The average European American child born 100 years ago in the United States could expect to live 47 years. The average African American could expect a shorter life of 35.5 years (Andersen & Taylor, 2009). Great strides have been made in increasing life expectancy. A century ago, lower life expectancy rates were, in part, the result of high infant mortality rates due to diseases such as German measles, smallpox, polio, and diphtheria. These diseases have since been

life span (longevity) the maximum amount of time a person can live under optimal conditions.

life expectancy the amount of time a person can actually be expected to live in a given setting.

© Emma Wood/Alamy

After we reach our physical peak in our 20s, our biological functions begin a gradual decline.

brought under control or eliminated. Other major killers, including bacterial infections such as tuberculosis, are now largely controlled by antibiotics. Factors that contribute to longevity include public health measures such as safer water supplies, improved dietary habits, and more accessible health care. Life expectancy across the provinces has also changed significantly.

Life expectancy varies from province to province and between the provinces and the territories.

Sex Differences in Life Expectancy

Although the longevity gap between men and women is narrowing, life expectancy among men trails that among women by about 4.7 years (78 years for men versus 82.7 years for women) (CBC News, 2008).

Why the gap? For one thing, heart disease typically develops later in life in women than in men because estrogen provides women some protection against heart disease. Also, men are more likely to die from accidents, cirrhosis of the liver, strokes, suicide, homicide, HIV/AIDS, and some forms of cancer. Many of these causes of death reflect unhealthful habits that are more typical of men, such as drinking, reckless behaviour, and smoking.

ageism
prejudice against people because of their age.

cataract
a condition characterized by clouding of the lens of the eye.

glaucoma
a condition involving abnormally high fluid pressure in the eye.

Many men are also reluctant to have regular physical examinations or to talk about health concerns with their doctors. Many men avoid medical attention until problems that could have been easily prevented or treated become serious or life-threatening. For example, women are more likely to examine themselves for signs of breast cancer than men are to examine their testicles for unusual lumps.

Physical and Social Changes

After we reach our physical peak in our 20s, our biological functions begin a gradual decline. Aging also involves adapting to changing physical and social realities. People who were once "newbies" in the workplace become the "old guard." One-time newlyweds come to celebrate their silver and golden anniversaries. Yet aging can involve more than adjustment; it can also bring about personal growth and exciting changes. Even advanced age can bring greater harmony and integration to our personalities. However, we must learn to adapt to changes in our mental skills and abilities. Although older people's memories and fluid intelligence may not be as keen as they once were, older people often have the maturity and experience that make them sources of wisdom.

Aging also has social aspects. Our self-concepts and behaviour as "young," "middle-aged," or "old" stem in large measure from cultural beliefs and our social clock. In historical times, "mature" people had great prestige, leading men to routinely claim to be older than they were. Women, whose reproductive capacity was valued, did not want to be viewed as being older than they were. By contrast, the modern era has been marked by **ageism**—prejudice against people because of their age. Stereotypes that paint older people as crotchety, sluggish, forgetful, and fixed in their ways shape the way people respond to older people and can actually impair their performance (Horton, 2008).

DID YOU KNOW?

In historical times, aging was viewed so positively that men often claimed to be older than they actually were.

Maturity was considered a mark of prestige but asking job applicants their age is illegal in Canada.

Changes in Sensory Functioning

Beginning in one's middle age, the lenses of the eyes become brittle, leading to presbyopia, as discussed in Chapter 15. Chemical changes of aging can lead to vision disorders such as **cataracts** and **glaucoma**.

Ten Ways to Recognize Hearing Loss

The following questions from the NIDCD* will help you determine whether you need to have your hearing evaluated by a medical professional:

1. Do you have a problem hearing over the telephone?
2. Do you have trouble following the conversation when two or more people are talking at the same time?
3. Do people complain that you turn the TV volume up too high?
4. Do you strain to understand conversation?
5. Do you have trouble hearing in a noisy background?
6. Do you find yourself asking people to repeat themselves?
7. Do many people you talk to seem to mumble (or not speak clearly)?
8. Do you misunderstand what others are saying and respond inappropriately?
9. Do you have trouble understanding the speech of women and children?
10. Do people get annoyed because you misunderstand what they say?

If you answered "yes" to three or more of these questions, you may want to schedule a hearing evaluation with an ear, nose, and throat specialist or an audiologist.

*NIDCD (National Institute on Deafness and Other Communication Disorders). (2008, April 16). Ten Ways to Recognize Hearing Loss. http://www.nidcd.nih.gov/health/hearing/10ways.asp

Cataracts cloud the lenses of the eyes, reducing vision. Today, outpatient surgery for correcting cataracts is routine. If performed before the condition progresses too far, the outcome for regained sight is excellent. Glaucoma is a buildup of fluid pressure inside the eyeball. Glaucoma can lead to tunnel vision (lack of peripheral vision) or blindness. Glaucoma rarely occurs before age 40, but affects about 1 in 250 people over the age of 40, and 1 in 25 people over 80. Rates are higher among diabetics than nondiabetics. Glaucoma is treated with medication or surgery.

presbycusis
loss of acuteness of hearing due to age-related degenerative changes in the ear.

osteoporosis
a disorder in which bones become more porous, brittle, and subject to fracture, due to loss of calcium and other minerals.

The sense of hearing, especially the ability to hear higher frequencies, also declines with age. **Presbycusis** is age-related hearing loss that affects about 1 person in 3 over the age of 65 (Sommers, 2008). Hearing ability tends to decline more quickly in men than in women. Hearing aids magnify sound and can compensate for hearing loss. The Ten Ways to Recognize Hearing Loss questionnaire from the National Institute on Deafness and other Communication Disorders shows how to recognize hearing loss.

Taste and smell become less acute as we age. Our sense of smell decreases almost ninefold from youth to advanced late adulthood. We also lose taste buds in the tongue with aging. As a result, foods may need to be more strongly spiced to yield the same flavour.

Bone Density

Bones begin to lose density in middle adulthood, becoming more brittle and vulnerable to fracture. Bones in the spine, hip, thigh, and forearm lose the most density as we age. **Osteoporosis** is a disorder in

FIGURE 17.7

Answer to the Duncker Candle Problem

adults, abstract problem-solving ability, as in complex math problems, is not related to their quality of life. "Real-world" or everyday problem-solving skills are usually of greater concern (Gilhooly et al., 2007).

Moreover, when older adults encounter interpersonal conflicts, they tend to regulate their emotional responses differently from young and middle-aged adults. Whereas younger groups are relatively more likely to express feelings of anger or frustration, to seek support from other people, or to solve interpersonal problems, older adults are more likely to focus on remaining calm and unperturbed (Coats & Blanchard-Fields, 2008). The difference appears to be partially due to older adults' decreased tendency to express anger and increased priority on regulating emotion. Perhaps the older adults do not wish to be "jarred," but it also sounds a bit like wisdom.

Wisdom

We may seek athletes who are in their 20s, but we prefer coaches who are decades older. It may be desirable to hire high-school teachers and college and university professors who have recently graduated, but we usually seek high-school principals and department chairpersons who are older. It is helpful to have 18-year-olds who are bursting with energy knocking on doors to get out the vote, but we want our presidential candidates to be older. Why? Because we associate age with *wisdom*.

Among the numerous cognitive hazards of aging, older people tend to be more distractible than young adults. Developmental psychologist Lynn Hasher (2008) suggests that distractibility can enable older adults to take a broader view of various situations: "A broad attention span may enable older adults to ultimately know more about a situation and . . . what's going on than their younger peers. . . . [This] characteristic may play a significant role in why we think of older people as wiser."

Kunzmann and Baltes (2005) note that wise people approach life's problems in a way that addresses the meaning of life. They consider not only the present but also the past, the future, and the contexts in which the problems arise. They tend to be tolerant of other people's value systems and to acknowledge that life holds uncertainties and that one can only attempt to find workable solutions in an imperfect world. Ardelt (2008a, 2008b) adds emotional and philosophical dimensions to the definition of wisdom. She suggests that wise people tend to possess an unselfish love for others and tend to be less afraid of death. We will examine the role of the elder in Aboriginal culture in the next chapter in the context of Erikson's life review.

© Comstock Images/Jupiterimages

CHAPTER 18

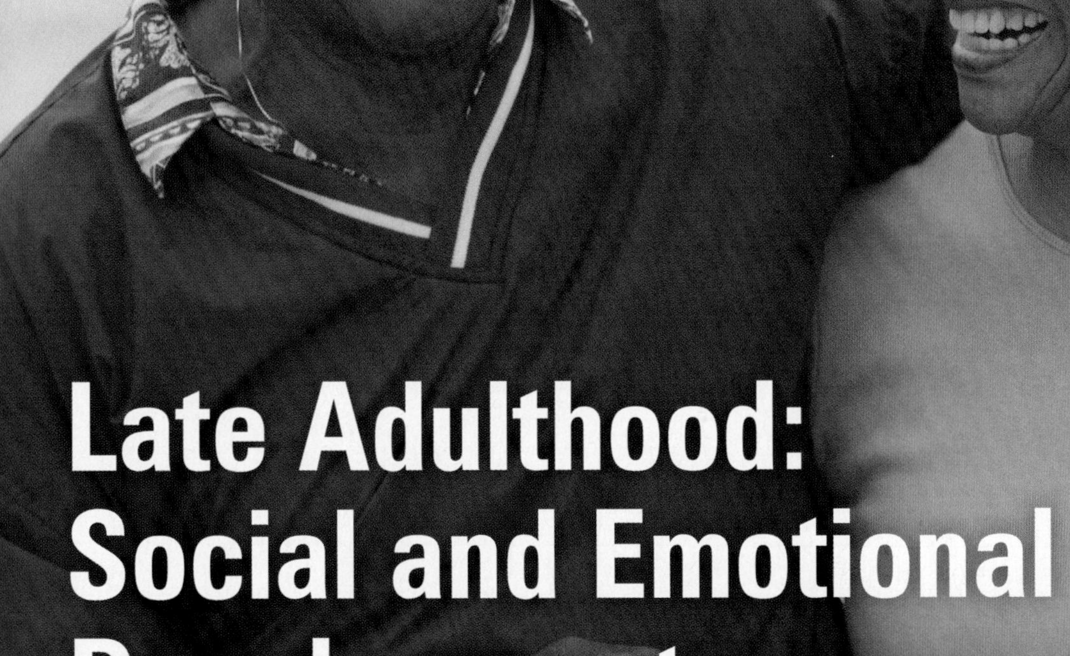

Late Adulthood: Social and Emotional Development

LEARNING OUTCOMES

LO1 Evaluate various theories of social and emotional development in late adulthood

LO2 Discuss psychological development in late adulthood, focusing on self-esteem and maintaining independence

LO3 Discuss the social contexts in which people age, focusing on housing, religion, and family

LO4 Discuss factors that contribute to adjustment to retirement

LO5 Discuss factors in "successful aging"

bikeriderlondon/Shutterstock.com

> "For many people, the later years are the best years—especially when they are filled with meaningful activity."

LO1 Theories of Social and Emotional Development in Late Adulthood

Life Review

Robert Peck's Developmental Tasks

Erikson labelled his eighth and final life stage as the crisis of **ego integrity or despair**. The crisis was defined by the battle between two competing beliefs. According to ego integrity, life is meaningful and worthwhile despite physical decline and impending death. The other belief, despair, views life and death as overwhelming, resulting in feelings of depression and hopelessness.

Robert Peck (1968) amplified Erikson's stage of ego integrity versus despair by outlining three developmental tasks that people face in late adulthood:

- *Ego differentiation versus work-role preoccupation.* After retirement, people need to find new ways of defining their self-worth outside of their achievements in the workplace, perhaps in terms of roles in the community, activities with friends and family, or in spiritual undertakings.
- *Body transcendence versus body preoccupation.* At some point in late adulthood, people face inevitable physical decline, and it is in their best interests to come to terms with it by shifting more value to cognitive activities and social relationships. Some people, of course, run into chronic illnesses or disabilities years earlier and must face the need to transcend body preoccupation prior to late adulthood.

Time & Life Pictures/Getty Images

Erikson Today

Stage 8: Ego Integrity vs. Despair (65 years to death)

Much of our early life is spent preparing for midlife but the last stage is characterized by reflection. As older adults look back to review their life's meaning, many do so with a feeling of integrity, which results from their sense of contentment and fulfillment. They realize that they have led a good life that had meaning and value and that they have been contributing members of society. They will be content in the knowledge that they have lived a good life. Those that have not been successful in their life journey will often feel a sense of despair with the realization that they have run out of time and that they have led a meaningless life.

Consider THIS

How do you want to be perceived, and treated, in your final years?

Please see pages 306 and 318 for discussions on this topic.

ego integrity or despair
Erikson's eighth life crisis, defined by maintenance of the belief that life is meaningful and worthwhile despite physical decline and the inevitability of death versus depression and hopelessness.

DID YOU KNOW?

The majority of people aged 65 and older consider themselves to be in good or excellent health, compared with other people of their age.

According to the National Health Survey, this is true.

- *Ego transcendence versus ego preoccupation.* Ego transcendence means preparing in some way to go beyond the physical limitations of one's own life expectancy. As death comes nearer, some prepare to transcend death by helping secure the futures of their children or grandchildren. Others work more broadly to benefit their church, synagogue, or mosque, or to leave planet Earth in "better shape" than they found it.

Based on extensive interviews with small samples, Monika Ardelt (2008b) writes that ego transcendence grows out of self-reflection and a willingness to learn from experience. She believes ego transcendence—which she also calls *the quieting of the ego*—is characterized by a concern for the well-being of humankind in general, not only for the self and close loved ones.

The Life Review

Daniel Levinson theorized that one aspect of the "midlife crisis" was that people realized they had more to look back on than to look forward to. Older adults often engage in reminiscence—that is, relating stories from the distant past. At times, some older people may seem to live in the past, possibly in denial of their current decline and the approach of death.

Reminiscence was once considered a symptom of dementia, but contemporary researchers now consider it to be a normal aspect of aging (Kunz, 2007). In working with healthy older volunteers as individuals and in groups, Robert Butler (2002) found that life reviews can be complex and nuanced; incoherent and self-contradictory; or even replete with irony, tragedy, and comedy. Butler believes that older people engage in life reviews to attempt to make life meaningful, to move on with new relationships as contemporaries pass on, and to help them find ego integrity and accept the end of life.

Butler (2002) also argues that health care professionals rely far too much on drugs to ease the discomforts of older adults. Pilot programs suggest that therapists may be able to relieve depression and other psychological problems in older adults by helping them reminisce about their lives (Bohlmeijer et al., 2005).

© SuperStock/Getty Images

Consider THIS

How do you want to be perceived, and treated, in your final years?

For many people, the later years are the best years—especially when they are filled with meaningful activity. The stresses involved in building and maintaining a career, selecting a mate, and rearing children are likely gone. Questions of identity may have become settled.

Troubling emotions such as depression and anxiety tend to decline as we age, whereas positive emotions remain fairly steady (Charles et al., 2001). On the whole, older Canadians are at least as happy as younger people. Yet, as we will see, aging has its challenges. Older people are more likely to be bereaved by the loss of their spouse and close friends. Older people may need to cope with declining health, retirement, and relocation.

Robert Peck's Three Developmental Tasks

1. Ego differentiation versus work-role preoccupation
2. Body transcendence versus body preoccupation
3. Ego transcendence versus ego preoccupation

© Image Source

Fuse/Thinkstock.com

Activity theory states that older adults are more content when they are active and social.

Activity Theory

It seems that well-being among older adults is generally predicted by pursuing goals, rather than the stereotype of the older adult who withdraws socially (Frazier et al., 2007). This stereotype is supported by **disengagement theory**, which is the view that older adults and society withdraw from one another as older adults approach death. A less stereotypical view is rooted in **activity theory**, which states that older adults are better adjusted when they are more active and involved in physical and social activities. Activity theory perceives many barriers to such activity in social attitudes, such as beliefs that older people should "take it easy," and in structural matters, such as forced retirement, rather than considering the desires of the individual.

© Andrea Pistolesi/Getty Images

Research shows that physical activity is associated with a lower mortality rate in late adulthood (Talbot et al., 2007). Leisure and informal social activities also contribute to life satisfaction among retired people (Joung & Miller, 2007). An Israeli study found particular benefits for life satisfaction in activities involving the next generation, the visual and performing arts, and spiritual and religious matters (Nimrod, 2007). However, value was also found in independent activities in the home.

Socioemotional Selectivity Theory

Socioemotional selectivity theory addresses the development of older adults' social networks. Charles and Carstensen (2007) hypothesize that as we age, increasing emphasis is placed on emotional experience, leading to a greater focus on emotionally fulfilling experiences.

To regulate their emotional lives as they grow older, people limit their social contacts to a few individuals who are of major importance. By the time older adults reach their 80s, they are likely to have whittled their social network down to a few family members and friends. This small social grouping does not mean that older adults are antisocial. It means that they see themselves as having less time to waste and they are more

disengagement theory the view that older adults and society withdraw from one another as older adults approach death.

activity theory the view that older adults fare better when they engage in physical and social activities.

socioemotional selectivity theory the view that we place increasing emphasis on emotional experience as we age but limit our social contacts to regulate our emotions.

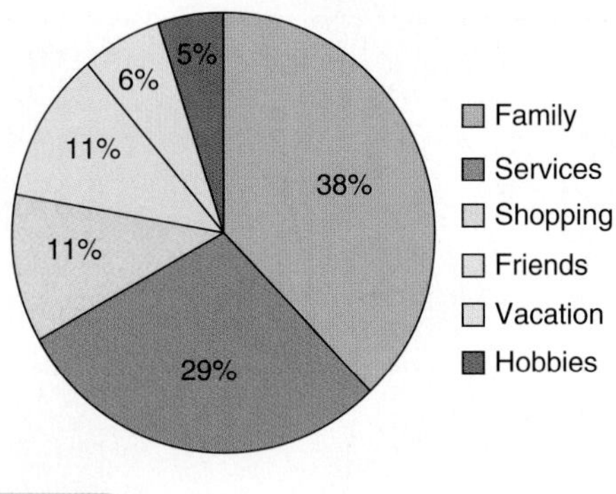

FIGURE 18.1

Reasons for Use of Social Media by Silver Surfers

Source: © Media Badger

EMERGING CANADA

Statistics Canada reports that 2/3 of seniors 65 years of age and older use the Internet daily, making them the fastest growing group of users (Statistics Canada, 2010c). Simon Fraser University is conducting the Silver Surfer Project to examine senior citizens and their use of the Internet. Most seniors use the Internet to communicate and maintain relationships. Figure 18.1 illustrates the reasons given for their engagement on the Internet. The Silver Surfer Project reports that using the Internet leads to seniors having feelings of empowerment, control, and optimism (Simon Fraser University, 2011).

LO2 Psychological Development

Self-esteem, as we will see, is tied to both independence and dependence. Also, the psychological problems of depression and anxiety can affect us at any age, but they warrant special focus in late adulthood.

Self-Esteem

To study the lifetime development of self-esteem, Richard Robins and his colleagues (2002) recruited more than 300,000 individuals to complete an extensive online questionnaire that provided demographic information (age, sex, ethnic background, and so forth) and measures of self-esteem. About 66 percent of the respondents were from the United States, and 57 percent were female. Results are shown in Figure 18.2. In general, the self-esteem of males was higher than that of females. Self-esteem was highest in childhood (likely an inflated estimate) and dipped precipitously in adolescence, a finding consistent with studies reported in Chapter 12. Self-esteem then rose gradually throughout middle adulthood and declined in late adulthood, with most of the decline occurring between the ages of 70 and 85. However, these results are all relative. Even for people in their 80s, self-esteem levels were above the mid-point of the questionnaire.

Robins and Trzesniewski (2005) suggest two possible reasons for the drop in self-esteem among people in their 80s. The first theory suggests that it results from life changes such as retirement, loss of a spouse or partner, reduced social support, declining health, and downward movement in socioeconomic status. The other hypothesis is more optimistic, namely that risk-averse; that is, they do not want to involve themselves in painful social interactions.

Other researchers (e.g., Ersner-Hershfield et al., 2008) also note that older people's perceived limitation on future time increases their appreciation for life, which brings about positive emotions. On the other hand, the same constraints on future time heighten awareness that such positive experiences will be drawing to a close, thus giving rise to mixed emotional states that have a poignant quality.

Volunteering and the Older Adult in Canada

Being able to care for oneself is important but caring for others is also a key factor in personal well-being. Volunteering helps charitable and nonprofit organizations deliver needed programs and services. It also provides a social outlet and structure that allow older generations to feel valuable and involved in the community where they live.

In 2004, Canadians volunteered about 2 billion hours. Although both men and women volunteer a similar amount of time, according to Human Resources and Skills Development Canada (2010b), the average number of hours volunteered increases with age. Those in the youngest age group (aged 15–24) volunteered, on average, 63 hours per year, whereas those 65 years and older volunteered an average of 111 hours per year.

People in later life contribute significantly to the communities in which they live.

© Jim West / Photo Edit

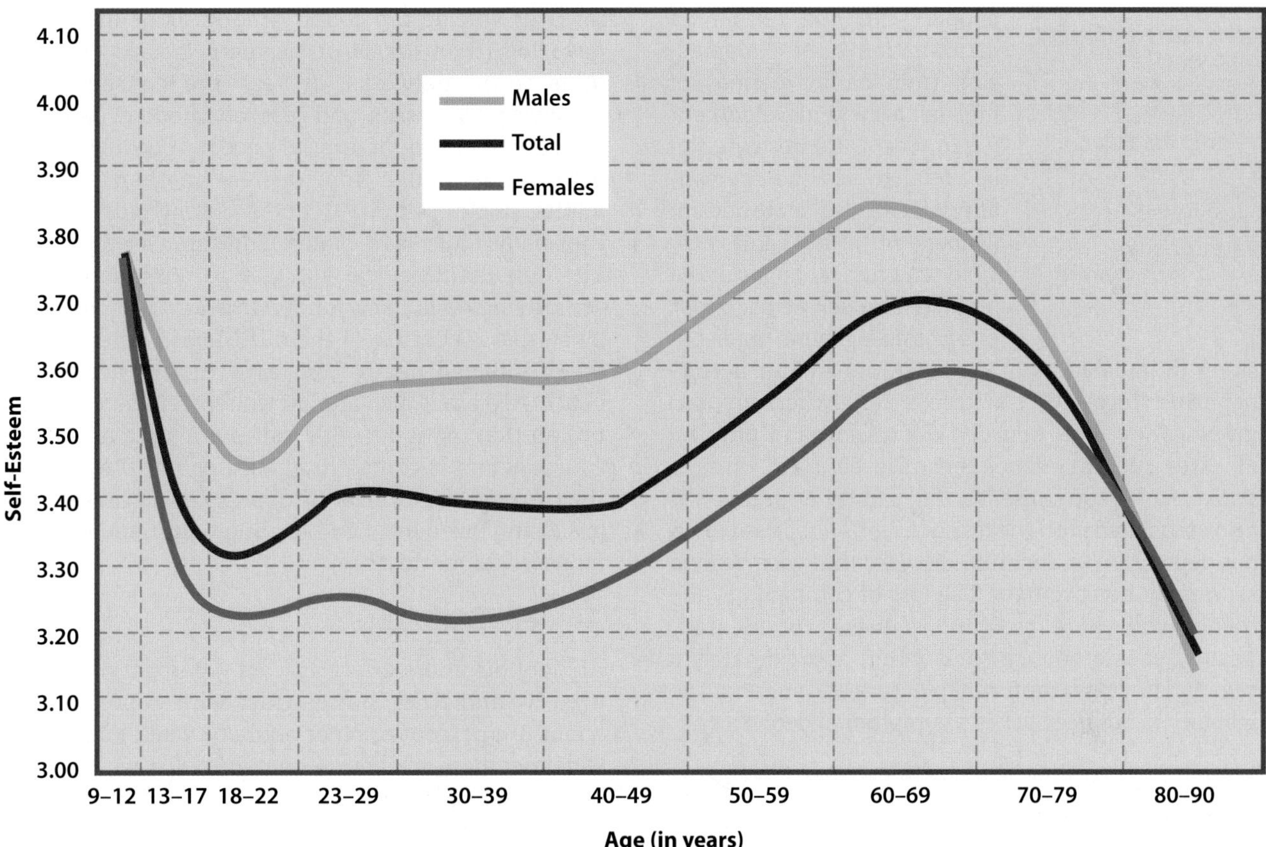

FIGURE 18.2

Mean Level of Self-Esteem as a Function of Age, for Total Sample, Males, and Females

Self-esteem is highest in childhood, dips in adolescence, rises gradually throughout middle adulthood, and declines in late adulthood (Robins & Trzesniewski, 2005).

Source: Richard W. Robins, Kali H. Trzesniewski, Jessica L. Tracy, Samuel D. Gosling, & Jeff Potter. (2002). Global self-esteem across the lifespan. *Psychology and Aging, 17*(3), 423–434.

older people are wiser and more content. Erikson (1968) and other theorists suggest that ego transcendence may occur in this stage of life, leading people to accept themselves as they are, "warts and all," making it no longer necessary to inflate their self-esteem.

As the years wear on in late adulthood, people express progressively less "body esteem"—that is, less pride in the appearance and functioning of their bodies. There is also a gender difference, with older men expressing less body esteem than older women do (Kaminski & Hayslip, 2006). Men are more likely to accumulate fat around the middle, whereas women accumulate fat in the hips. Sexual arousal problems are usually more distressing for men. Older adults with poor body esteem tend to withdraw from sexual activity, which often frustrates their partners (Mohan & Bhugra, 2005).

Independence versus Dependence

Being able to care for oneself appears to be a core condition of successful aging. Older people who are independent tend to think of themselves as leading a "normal life," whereas those who are dependent on others, even if they are only slightly dependent, tend to worry more about aging and encountering physical disabilities and stress (Sousa & Figueiredo, 2002). A study of 441 healthy people aged 65 to 95 found that dependence on others to carry out the activities of daily living increased with age (Perrig-Chiello et al., 2006). A particularly sensitive independence issue is toileting, as found in a study of stroke victims (Clark & Rugg, 2005). Interviewers found that independence in toileting is especially important in enabling older people to avoid a loss in their self-esteem.

Psychological Problems

Problems in coping with aging are associated with psychological problems, including depression and anxiety.

Depression

Depression affects some 10 percent of people aged 65 and older (Kvaal et al., 2008). Depression in older

generalized anxiety disorder general feelings of dread and foreboding.

phobic disorder irrational, exaggerated fear of an object or situation.

agoraphobia fear of open, crowded places.

people can be either a continuation of depression from earlier periods of life, or a new development (Fiske, 2006). Depression can be related to the personality factor of neuroticism (Duberstein et al., 2008), possible structural changes in the brain (Ballmaier et al., 2008), or a possible genetic predisposition to imbalances of the neurotransmitter norepinephrine (Togsverd et al., 2008). Researchers are also investigating links between depression and physical illnesses such as Alzheimer's disease, heart disease, stroke, Parkinson's disease, and cancer. Depression is also associated with the loss of friends and loved ones, but depression is a mental disorder that goes beyond sadness or bereavement. The loss of companions and friends will cause profound sadness, but mentally healthy people bounce back within approximately a year and find new sources of pleasure and support. The inability to bounce back is a symptom of depression.

DID YOU KNOW?

When friends and loved ones die, sadness is a normal reaction; depression is not.

It is normal to be sad when we suffer loss. Depression is a mental disorder.

Depression often goes undetected and untreated in older people (Cochran, 2005). Depression may be overlooked because its symptoms are masked by physical complaints such as low energy, loss of appetite, and insomnia. Health care providers also tend to focus more on older people's physical health than their mental health. Many older people are reluctant to admit to depression because when they were young, psychological problems carried a stigma. Depression is also associated with memory lapses and other cognitive impairment, such as difficulty concentrating (Ballmaier et al., 2008). Some cases of depression are wrongly attributed to the effects of aging or are misdiagnosed as dementia or Alzheimer's disease. Depression in older people can usually be treated successfully, using the same means that work in younger people, such as antidepressant drugs and cognitive-behavioural psychotherapy (Schuurmans et al., 2006).

Suicide

Untreated depression can lead to suicide, which is not uncommon among older people. The highest rates of suicide are found among older men who have lost their wives or partners, no longer have their social networks, or fear the consequences of physical illnesses and loss of freedom (Johnson et al., 2008; Schmidtke et al., 2008). Although fewer older adults suffer from depression than younger adults, suicide is more frequent among older adults, especially Caucasian males (Eddleston et al., 2006). The Canadian Medical Association reminds us that senior suicide is likely understated and uncaptured by statistics because of the difficulty in determining a self-inflicted death from a natural or accidental death. Ageism is also at play. Our society has a faulty notion that mental health issues are just par for the course when it comes to elderly people. We expect they experience a level of depression because they are losing loved ones and dealing with more chronic illnesses (Monette, 2012).

Anxiety Disorders

Anxiety disorders affect at least 3 percent of people aged 65 and older, but co-exist with depression in about 8–9 percent of older adults (Kvaal et al., 2008). Older women are approximately twice as likely to be affected as older men (Stanley & Beck, 2000). The most common anxiety disorders among older adults are **generalized anxiety disorder** and **phobic disorders**. Most cases of **agoraphobia** affecting older adults tend to be of recent origin and may involve the loss of social support systems due to the death

Zurijeta/Shutterstock.com

of a spouse or close friends. Then again, some older individuals who are frail may have realistic fears of falling on the street and may be misdiagnosed as being agoraphobic if they refuse to leave the house alone. Generalized anxiety disorder may arise from the perception that one lacks control over one's life.

Anxiety disorders can be harmful to older people's physical health. When older adults with anxiety disorders are subjected to stress, their levels of cortisol (a stress hormone) rise, then take some time to subside (Chaudieu et al., 2008). Cortisol suppresses the functioning of the immune system, making people more vulnerable to illness.

Mild tranquilizers (such as Valium) are commonly used to quell anxiety in older adults. Psychological interventions, such as cognitive-behaviour therapy, have proven beneficial and do not carry the risk of side effects or potential dependence (Caudle et al., 2007).

LO3 Social Contexts of Aging

Communities and Housing for Older People

According to surveys, older people consistently report that they prefer to remain in their homes as long as their physical and mental conditions allow them to do so (Sabia, 2008). The older people most likely to remain in their homes are those who have plentiful financial resources, large amounts of equity in their homes, and strong ties to their communities. Conversely, the older people most likely to need to consider residing elsewhere are those experiencing declining health conditions, changes in their family composition, and significant increases in property taxes and costs of utilities (Sabia, 2008). In many suburban communities, for example, property taxes have been skyrocketing to keep pace with the costs of public education. Older people no longer have children in the schools nor—more crucially—sufficient income to pay the increased taxes, and so they sell their homes.

Older adults may be reluctant to relocate to a nursing home, which signifies their loss of independence.

Older people who live in urban areas are highly concerned about exposure to crime, particularly crimes of violence. Ironically, people aged 80 and older are significantly less likely to be victimized than people in other age groups (Beaulieu et al., 2008). Social support helps older people cope with their concerns about victimization (Beaulieu et al., 2008). If they are victimized, social support helps them avoid some of the problems that characterize post-traumatic stress disorder, such as intrusive thoughts and nightmares (Sexton, 2008).

DID YOU KNOW?

Despite experiencing heightened anxiety about being exposed to crime, older people are less likely than younger people to be victims of crime.

It is still important to take steps so that older people feel safe in their homes.

When older people can no longer manage living on their own, they may consider utilizing the services of in-home care and visiting nurses to help them remain in the home. Others may move in with adult children. Still others may move into assisted-living residences, where they have their own apartment, community dining room, 24-hour nursing aid, and on-call physician care.

When older adults relocate to a seniors' residence, which may or may not have facilities for assisted living, their existing social networks tend to be disrupted. As a result, the new residents are challenged to find new friends and create new networks (Dupuis-Blanchard, 2008). Such residences often have communal dining facilities and organized activities, including transportation to nearby shopping and entertainment. Residents typically take time in engaging with other people socially and are selective in forming new relationships (Dupuis-Blanchard, 2008).

Older adults may be reluctant to relocate to a nursing home (often referred to as a long-term care facility), which signifies their loss of independence. Surveys indicate that older adults are relatively more willing to enter into long-term care when they perceive themselves to be in poor health and when one or more close family members live nearby (Jang et al., 2008).

Some frightening stories emerge of what happens in nursing homes, but we also hear heartening stories. Occasionally, cases of elder abuse occur, in which staff act harshly toward residents, sometimes in response to cognitively impaired residents acting aggressively toward the staff (Rosen et al., 2008). However, a well-selected and well-trained staff can deal well with impaired residents, many of whom are disoriented and frightened (Kazui et al., 2008).

Religion

Religion involves beliefs and practices centred on claims about the nature of reality and moral behaviour, usually codified as rituals, religious laws, and prayers. Religions also usually encompass cultural traditions and myths, faith, spiritual experience, and both communal and private worship.

We discuss religion as part of the social context in which older adults (and others) live because, in addition to offering the opportunity to worship, religion often involves participating in the congregation's social, educational, and charitable activities. Therefore, religion and religious activities provide older adults with a vast arena for social networking.

Religion also has a special allure as people approach the end of life. As people undergo physical decline, religion asks them to focus, instead, on moral conduct and spiritual "substance" such as the soul. People who experience physical suffering in this world are advised to look forward to relief in the next.

Therefore, it is not surprising that studies find that religious involvement in late adulthood is usually associated with less depression (Braam et al., 2008) and more life satisfaction (Korff, 2006). Frequent churchgoing has also been shown to be associated with fewer problems in older people's activities of daily living (Park et al., 2008). Here, of course, we can assume that older people reap benefits both from social networking and from church attendance per se.

Consider some of the benefits of frequent churchgoing found in studies of older African Americans. Older African Americans who attend services more than once a week were found to live 13.7 years longer, on average, than their counterparts who *never* attend church (Marks et al., 2005). In-depth interviews with the churchgoers found several reasons for their relative longevity, including having a sense of hopefulness, having social support, evading being victimized by violence, and avoidance of negative coping methods such as aggressive behaviour and drinking alcohol.

© Shauna Longmuir

DID YOU KNOW?

African Americans who attend church more than once a week live more than 13 years longer than African Americans who never attend.

This is true on average.

Family and Social Relationships

Family and social relationships provide some of the most obvious—and most important—elements in the social lives of older adults.

Marriage

Approximately 38 percent of Canadian marriages end in divorce, but for many people, marriage lasts, like the traditional words, "until death do us part." Married people face very different life tasks as young adults, middle-aged adults, and older adults. Also likely to vary from stage to stage are the qualities in relationships that help people fulfill these tasks. For example, the core issues in early adulthood are the selection of a partner, the development of a shared life, and emotional intimacy. Given these needs, two people's similarities in personality may foster their feelings of attachment and intimacy, providing them with a sense of equity in contributing to the relationship (Shiota & Levenson, 2007).

By middle adulthood, the partners' concerns appear to shift toward meeting their shared and individual responsibilities (Moen et al., 2001). The partnership needs to handle tasks such as finances, household chores, and parenting. Conflicts may easily arise over a division of labour unless the couple can divide the tasks readily (Hatch & Bulcroft, 2004; Shiota & Levenson, 2007). At this stage, similarity in personality may work against the couple, with each partner competing to handle—or avoid—the same task. For example, as Shiota and Levenson (2007) found in their study of marital satisfaction and the Big Five personality factors in middle-aged and older adults, *difference rather than similarity* in conscientiousness and extraversion predicts marital satisfaction when the couple are in their 40s, whereas similarity does just as well in their 60s.

Shiota and Levenson (2007) suggest that conscientious people want to get things done, but by middle adulthood they have their own way of doing things. When two people in close quarters each want a task completed in their own way, conflicts are likely. The relationship is likely smoother if one partner is detail-oriented while the other is more easygoing. It is also useful if one partner is the workaholic and the other is the "people person" or social butterfly.

They each then have their domains of expertise and are less likely to clash.

When couples reach their 60s, many midlife responsibilities such as childrearing and work have declined, allowing the partners to spend more time together. As a result, intimacy becomes a central issue once more. In this stage, couples report less disagreement over finances, household chores, and parenting (or grandparenting), but may have concerns about emotional expression and companionship (Hatch & Bulcroft, 2004). A similarity in personality is less of a contributor to conflict than it is in midlife, consistent with the finding that similarity in conscientiousness and extraversion is no longer strongly associated with marital dissatisfaction.

© Dole/Shutterstock.com

DID YOU KNOW?

Older married couples are focused on each other, and intimacy becomes a primary focus of their relationship.

Because work and child rearing are removed from the relationship, many couples can now focus primarily on each other and intimacy.

On the other hand, older couples may complain they spend too much time together, especially women whose husbands have just retired (Shiota & Levenson, 2007). If similarity in personality is a problem in this stage of life, perhaps it is because highly similar spouses become bored with one another (Amato & Previti, 2003).

In a study of 120 older Israeli couples, Kulik (2004) found that sharing power in the relationship and dividing household tasks contributed to satisfaction in the relationships. Past assistance from one's spouse in a time of need also positively affected the quality of the marriage and life satisfaction for both partners.

Divorce, Cohabitation, and Remarriage

Having worked out most of the problems in their relationships and having learned to live with those issues that remain, older adults are less likely than younger adults to seek divorce. The ideal of lifelong marriage retains its strength (Amato et al., 2007). Because of fear of loss of assets, family disruption, and relocation, older adults do not enter into divorce lightly. When they do, it is often because they belong to an unacceptable marriage that is particularly negative or because one of the partners has taken up a relationship with an outsider (Bengtson et al., 2005).

Older people are increasingly likely to cohabit today, making up about 4 percent of the unmarried population (Brown et al., 2006). Nearly 90 percent of cohabiting older adults have previously been married, and they are less likely than younger people to want to remarry (Mahay & Lewin, 2007). Although they are less likely than younger cohabiters to marry their partners, older cohabiters report being in more intimate, stable relationships (King & Scott, 2005). They cite reasons for avoiding remarriage, such as concern about ramifications for pensions and disapproval by adult children, who may be concerned about their inheritance (King & Scott, 2005).

Same-Sex Relationships

Most of the research on gay men and lesbians has focused on adolescents and young adults (Grossman et al., 2003). However, a growing body of information about older gay males and lesbians has shown that, similar to heterosexual couples, gay men and lesbians in long-term partnerships tend to enjoy higher self-esteem, less depression, fewer suicidal urges,

© Michael Krasowitz/Getty Images

and less alcohol and drug abuse (D'Augelli et al., 2001). Individuals in long-term partnerships are also less likely to incur sexually transmitted infections (Wierzalis et al., 2006).

An interesting pattern has emerged, in which gay men or lesbians sometimes form long-term intimate relationships with straight people of the other sex (Muraco, 2006). These relationships do not involve sexual activity, but the couples consider themselves to be "family" and are confidants.

EMERGING CANADA

LGBTQ (lesbian, gay, bisexual, trans [gendered, sexual, twin-spirited], and questioning) seniors often lack the traditional support network of spouses and children enjoyed by their heterosexual counterparts. Research conducted by SAGE (Services and Advocacy for Gay, Lesbian, Bisexual, and Transgendered Elders) found that, compared with heterosexual seniors, LGBTQ seniors are twice as likely to age alone, four-and-a-half times more likely to have no children to rely on, and five times less likely to access seniors' services. Many LGBTQ seniors report heightened fear and anxiety when they disclose their sexual orientation, and they have little faith they will not experience further victimization. Inclusive retirement homes, with specific diversity training for staff are becoming more popular, as many LGBTQ seniors report not feeling well-served within the mainstream health care system (Thomson et al., 2013).

Widowhood

By the age of 65, about 50 percent of all women and 10 percent of all men have experienced the loss of a spouse. By the age of 85, these figures rise to 80 percent and 40 percent. The loss of a life partner is one of the most traumatic experiences of one's life. Most older adults emerge from such a loss as resilient individuals; however, the loss of a loved one has a profoundly negative impact on life for 10–20 percent of individuals. A severe grief reaction places the individual at a higher risk for high blood pressure, heart problems, cancer, and suicide ideation (Holland et al., 2013).

Being widowed is much more likely than marital separation to lead to social isolation.

Men in their 70s seem to have the most difficulty coping, especially when they have retired and were expecting to spend more time with their wives during the coming years (Lund & Caserta, 2001).

Widowhood leads to a decline in physical and mental health, including increased mortality and deterioration in memory functioning (Aartsen et al., 2005). Loss of a spouse also heightens the risks of depression and suicide among older adults, and more so among men than women (Ajdacic-Gross et al., 2008).

Among people who are widowed, men are more likely than women to remarry, or at least to form new relationships with the opposite sex. One reason is simply that women tend to outlive men, so more older women are available. Also, women, more so than men, make use of the web of kinship relations and close friendships available to them. Men may also be less adept than women at various aspects of self and household care, and therefore seek that help from a new partner.

Singles and Older People without Children

Single, never-married, and non-cohabiting adults without children make up a small minority of the adult Canadian population. According to data from the United States, Japan, Europe, Australia, and Israel, single older adults without children are just as likely as people who have had children—married or not—to be socially active and involved in volunteer work (Wenger et al., 2007). They also tend to maintain close relationships with siblings and long-time friends. Very old (mean age = 93) mothers and women who have not had children report equally positive levels of well-being (Hoppmann & Smith, 2007).

On the other hand, married older men without children appear to be especially dependent on their spouses (Wenger et al., 2007). Parents also seem to be more likely than people without children to have a social network that permits them to avoid nursing homes or other residential care when their physical health declines (Wenger et al., 2007).

Siblings

In general, older sibling pairs tend to shore each other up with emotional support (Taylor et al., 2008). This support is especially seen among sisters (as women are more likely than men to talk about feelings) who are close in age and geographically near one another. After a spouse dies, the widowed person's siblings (and children) tend to ramp up their social contacts and emotional support (Guiaux et al., 2007). Often, the widowed person's sibling, especially a sister, will take the place of a spouse as a confidant (Wenger & Jerrome, 1999).

A longitudinal developmental study of twin relationships found that, compared with other sibling relationships, twin relationships were more intense in terms of frequency of contacts, intimacy, conflict, and emotional support (Neyer, 2002). Frequency of

© Purestock/Jupiterimages

contact and emotional closeness declined from early to middle adulthood, but increased again in late adulthood (mean age at time of study = 71.5 years).

Friendships

You can't pick your relatives—at least not your blood relatives—but you can choose your friends. Older people have often narrowed their friendships to friends who are most like them and enjoy the same kinds of activities. As a way of regulating their emotions, they tend to avoid people with whom they have had conflict over the years. Friends serve many functions in the lives of older adults, including providing social networks, acting as confidants, and offering emotional closeness and support, especially when a family member or another friend dies.

Grandchildren

Although grandparent–grandchild relationships have great variation, research suggests that both cohorts view each other in a positive light and see their ties as deep and meaningful (Kemp, 2005). They conceptualize their relationship as distinct family connection that involves unconditional love, emotional support, obligation, and respect. As they experience life events together, their relationship can seem precious and capable of being cut short at any time. Grandparents and their adult grandchildren often act as friends and confidants. The grandparent–grandchild relationship often differs from the relationship the grandparents had with their own children. A popular bumper sticker declares, "If I had known grandchildren would be this much fun, I would have had them first."

LO4 Retirement

Once upon a time, when it was assumed that work was, by definition, mind-numbing, it was also assumed that people retired as soon as they could afford to do so, usually at age 65. According to the Statistics Canada data surveyed earlier in this text, at age 65, the average person has two decades of life to look forward to. That number has been increasing and is likely to continue to increase. Moreover, because of medical advances, 65-year-olds are more and more likely to be robust. Therefore, many people, especially professionals, are working beyond the age of 65.

Retirement Planning

One of the keys of a successful retirement is retirement planning (Reitzes & Mutran, 2004). Retirement planning may include regularly putting money aside in plans such as a Registered Retirement Savings Plan (RRSP) and various pension plans in the workplace; investing in stocks, bonds, or a second home; and, perhaps, investigating recreational activities available in other geographic areas of interest. People who are thinking about moving or extended travelling will also be interested in learning about the weather (including effects on allergies) and crime statistics.

People who live alone may do their retirement planning as individuals. However, couples in relationships—including married heterosexuals, cohabiting heterosexuals, and gay and lesbian couples—usually make their retirement plans collaboratively (Mock et al., 2006; Moen et al., 2006). By and large, the greater the satisfaction in the relationship, the more likely the partners are to make their retirement plans together (Mock & Cornelius, 2007). Phyllis Moen and her colleagues (2006) found that in married couples, husbands more often than wives tended to be in control of the plans, although control was also related to the partner's workload and income level. Men in same-sex couples are more likely than women in same-sex couples to do retirement planning, but women who do such planning are more likely to do it collaboratively.

Hemera/Thinkstock.com

Adjustment to Retirement

Let's begin this section with two questions: Is the key to retirement doing as little as possible? Does adjustment to retirement begin with retirement? The answer to both questions is no.

Research has consistently shown that older adults who are best adjusted to retirement are highly involved in a variety of activities, such as community activities and organizations (Kloep & Hendry, 2007). In the case of community activities, the experience and devotion of retirees renders their participation an important asset for the community, and the activities promote the adjustment of older adults into retirement.

DID YOU KNOW?

The key to successful retirement is knowing how to relax.

This is true. However, "relaxing" does not necessarily mean doing as little as possible.

Pinquart and Schindler (2007) found in a retirement study that retirees could be divided into three groups, according to their satisfaction with retirement and various other factors. The group that was most satisfied with retirement maintained leisure and other non-work–related activities as sources of life satisfaction, or replaced work with more satisfying activities. They retired at a typical retirement age and had a wealth of resources to compensate for the loss of work: they were married, in good health, and of high socioeconomic status. The majority of a second group retired at a later age and tended to be female; the majority of the third group retired at a younger age and tended to be male. The second and third groups were not as satisfied with retirement. They were in poorer health, less likely to be married, and lower in socioeconomic status than the first group. The third group had a spotty employment record. Another way to look at this data is to suggest that retirement per se didn't change these people's lives in major ways.

A 2-year longitudinal study found that the adjustment of older retirees was affected by their pre-retirement work identities (Reitzes & Mutran, 2006). For example, upscale professional workers continued to be well-adjusted and had high self-esteem. They weren't simply "retirees"; they were retired professors or retired doctors or retired lawyers and the like. On the other hand, hourly wage earners and other blue-collar workers tended to have lower self-esteem and were more likely to think of themselves as simply "retirees."

Data from Dutch and American retirees found that the following factors impeded adjustment to retirement: a lengthy attachment to work, lack of control over the transition to retirement (e.g., forced retirement at age 65), worrying prior to retirement about what retirement would bring, and lack of self-confidence (Reitzes & Mutran, 2004; van Solinge & Henkens, 2005). Nevertheless, a wide range of feelings about giving up work tend to surface just before retirement. Some people are relieved; others are worried—about finances, about surrendering their work roles, or both. Even so, most retirees report that their well-being has increased a year after they have retired, and that much of the stress they felt before retiring has diminished (Nuttman-Shwartz, 2007).

Leisure Activities and Retirement

Once people retire, they have the opportunity to fill most of their days with activities they enjoy. Research has shown that engaging in recreational and leisure activities is essential for retirees' physical and psychological health (Hansen et al., 2008). A recent Japanese study found that older men's failure to engage in leisure activities with neighbours, social organizations, and friends was strongly associated with feelings of depression (Arai et al., 2007). Similarly, older women appeared to need to engage in leisure activities with social groups, children, and grandchildren in order to avoid depression.

Joint leisure activities also contribute to the satisfaction of marital and other intimate partners and to family well-being (Ton & Hansen, 2001). Such activities reduce stress (Melamed et al., 1995) and help retirees avert boredom (Sonnentag, 2003). Contributing to civic activities or volunteering at hospitals and the like also enhances retirees' self-esteem and fosters feelings of self-efficacy (Siegrist et al., 2004).

Kleiber and Kelly (1980) proposed a model of leisure development in which the final period includes retirement and aging. Leisure takes on special importance after retirement and may become central to the retiree's identity and self-acceptance. If the retiree's health remains robust, leisure activities tend to carry over from working days and may ease the transition to retirement. On the other hand, the physical aspects of aging and the death of companions can force changes in the choice of activities and diminish the level of satisfaction received from them.

A British study of adults with an average age of 72 reported that 73 percent engaged in leisure activities (Ball et al., 2007): 23 percent engaged in

TABLE 18.1

Factor Analysis of Leisure Activities of Retirees

Factor #	Name	Items
I	Athletic-Competitive-Outdoors	Adventure sports, team sports, hunting & fishing, individual sports, camping & outdoors, building & repair, cards & games, computer activities, collecting
II	Artistic-Cultural-Self Expressive	Shopping, arts & crafts, entertaining & culinary arts, cultural arts, dancing, literature & writing, socializing, gardening & nature, community involvement, travel
III	Social	Partying

Source: Jo-Ida C. Hansen, Bryan J. Dik, & Shuangmei Zhou. (2008). An examination of the structure of leisure interests of college students, working-age adults, and retirees. *Journal of Counseling Psychology, 55*(2), 133–145.

"active leisure" (sailing, walking); 18 percent, "passive leisure" (listening to music, watching television); 24 percent, social activities; 20 percent, hobbies; and 15 percent, other activities. The key motives for leisure activity were pleasure and relaxation.

Jo-Ida Hansen and her colleagues (Hansen et al., 2008) administered a questionnaire about leisure activities to 194 retirees, also with an average age of 72. They mathematically correlated the respondents' self-reported leisure activities and found that they fell into three clusters or factors, as shown in Table 18.1. Factor I included athletic, competitive, and outdoor activities. Factor II involved artistic, cultural, and self-expressive activities. Partying was the sole activity that defined Factor III. Partying isn't just for youngsters.

LO5 Successful Aging

Despite the stereotype of "grumpy old men and women," a recent study found that 44 percent of seniors perceive their health to be excellent or very good. In the same year, 37 percent of seniors reported that they had taken some action to improve their health: 71 percent said they had increased their physical activity, 21 percent said they had lost weight, and 13 percent had changed their eating habits (Public Health Agency of Canada, 2010b).

There are many definitions of successful aging. One journal article identified 28 studies with 29 definitions of the concept (Depp & Jeste, 2006). By and large, the definitions included physical activity, social contacts, self-rated good health, the absence of cognitive impairment and depression, nonsmoking, and the absence of disabilities and chronic diseases such as arthritis and diabetes.

selective optimization with compensation reshaping of one's life to concentrate on what one finds to be important and meaningful in the face of physical decline and possible cognitive impairment.

EMERGING CANADA

The Public Health Agency of Canada (2010b) released a report indicating a positive relationship between the number of social activities seniors participate in and their self-perceived health, loneliness, and life satisfaction. Social activities also decrease the odds of loneliness and life dissatisfaction. It is not the number of social interactions that seems to make the difference, but the quality of the activities. Seniors reported that barriers to participating in social activities included health issues, being too busy, and lack of income (CBC News, 2012b).

Selective Optimization with Compensation

A different view of successful aging is being advanced by researchers who focus on the processes by which individuals attempt to provide better person–environment fits to the changing physical, cognitive, and social circumstances of late adulthood (e.g., Baltes & Baltes, 1990). From this point of view, often referred to as **selective optimization with compensation**, older people manage to maximize their gains while minimizing their losses.

Margaret Baltes and Laura Carstensen (2003) note that a good deal of the research carried on by developmentalists focuses on decline and loss as major themes associated with late adulthood, and therefore tends to deflect attention from the many older people who experience late adulthood as a satisfying and productive stage of life. The concept of selective optimization with compensation is related to socioemotional selectivity theory and is a key theme in adaptive aging (now also known as successful aging). In keeping with socioemotional selectivity theory, successful agers tend to seek emotional fulfillment by reshaping their lives to concentrate on what they find to be important and meaningful. Baltes and Carstensen (2003) define the process of selection as a narrowing of the array of goals and arenas to which older people direct their resources. In fact, Baltes and Carstensen go so far as to consider selective optimization with compensation to be the "cardinal principle of lifespan development" (2003, p. 81).

Research on people aged 70 and older reveals that successful agers form emotional goals that bring them satisfaction (Löckenhoff & Carstensen, 2004). In applying the principle of selective optimization with compensation, successful agers may no longer compete in certain athletic or business activities (Bajor & Baltes, 2003; Freund & Baltes, 2002). Instead, they focus on matters that allow them to maintain a sense of control over their own lives.

Though late adulthood is often viewed as a time to sit back and rest, it is an excellent opportunity to engage in new challenges and activities, such as going back to school.

Successful agers also tend to be optimistic. Such an outlook may be derived from transcendence of the ego, from spirituality, or sometimes from one's genetic heritage. (Yes, there is a genetic component to happiness [Lykken & Csikszentmihalyi, 2001].) However, retaining social contacts and building new ones also contributes to a positive outlook, as does continuing with one's athletic activities, where possible, and one's artistic and cultural activities.

The stereotype is that retirees look forward to late adulthood as a time when they can rest from life's challenges. But sitting back and allowing the world to pass by is a prescription for depression, not for living life to its fullest. In one experiment, Sandman and Crinella (1995) randomly assigned people (average age = 72) either to a foster grandparent program with neurologically impaired children or to a control group. They followed both groups for 10 years. The foster grandparents carried out physical challenges, such as walking a few miles each day, and engaged in new kinds of social interactions. Those in the control group did not engage in these activities. After 10 years, the foster grandparents showed superior overall cognitive functioning, including memory functioning, and better sleep patterns, compared with those in the control group.

In the more normal course of events, many successful agers challenge themselves by taking up new pursuits such as painting, photography, or writing. Some travel to new destinations. Others return to school, taking special courses for older students, sitting in on regular college or university classes, or participating in seminars on special topics of interest. What will your retirement years look like?

© Journal-Courier/Clayton Stalter/The Image Works

Consider THIS

How do you want to be perceived, and treated, in your final years?

Elders are considered the "heart" of First Nations learning and are the gatekeepers of wisdom, knowledge, and history. Elders pass down tradition, culture, values, and lessons using oral storytelling and by role-modelling traditional practices. At the end of life, Aboriginal elders are seen as an important source of cultural power and voice within their communities (First Nations Pedagogy Online, 2009).

Erikson argues that life satisfaction is based on life review. In life review, the Aboriginal elder is the keeper of knowledge and is actively sought out for information and guidance. Elders are the centrepiece of families, communities, and nations, lending itself to a sense of fulfillment and the assessment of a life well spent (Statistics Canada, 2010a).

Seniors in Canada often encounter an opposite experience that was reflected in a 2012 survey of 1,500 seniors that questioned whether ageism had become the most tolerated form of social discrimination. Of the Canadians surveyed, 89 percent associated aging with negative outcomes, such as being alone and losing independence. According to the survey, the three most common forms of discrimination faced by Canadian seniors are being ignored or treated like they are invisible (41 percent), being treated like they have nothing to contribute (38 percent), and assuming that seniors are incompetent (27 percent). These findings pose a significant obstacle for life review and the completion of Erikson's stage of ego integrity vs. despair (CTV News, 2012). Consider this: what is your perception of aging in Canada? How do you want to be perceived and treated in your final years?

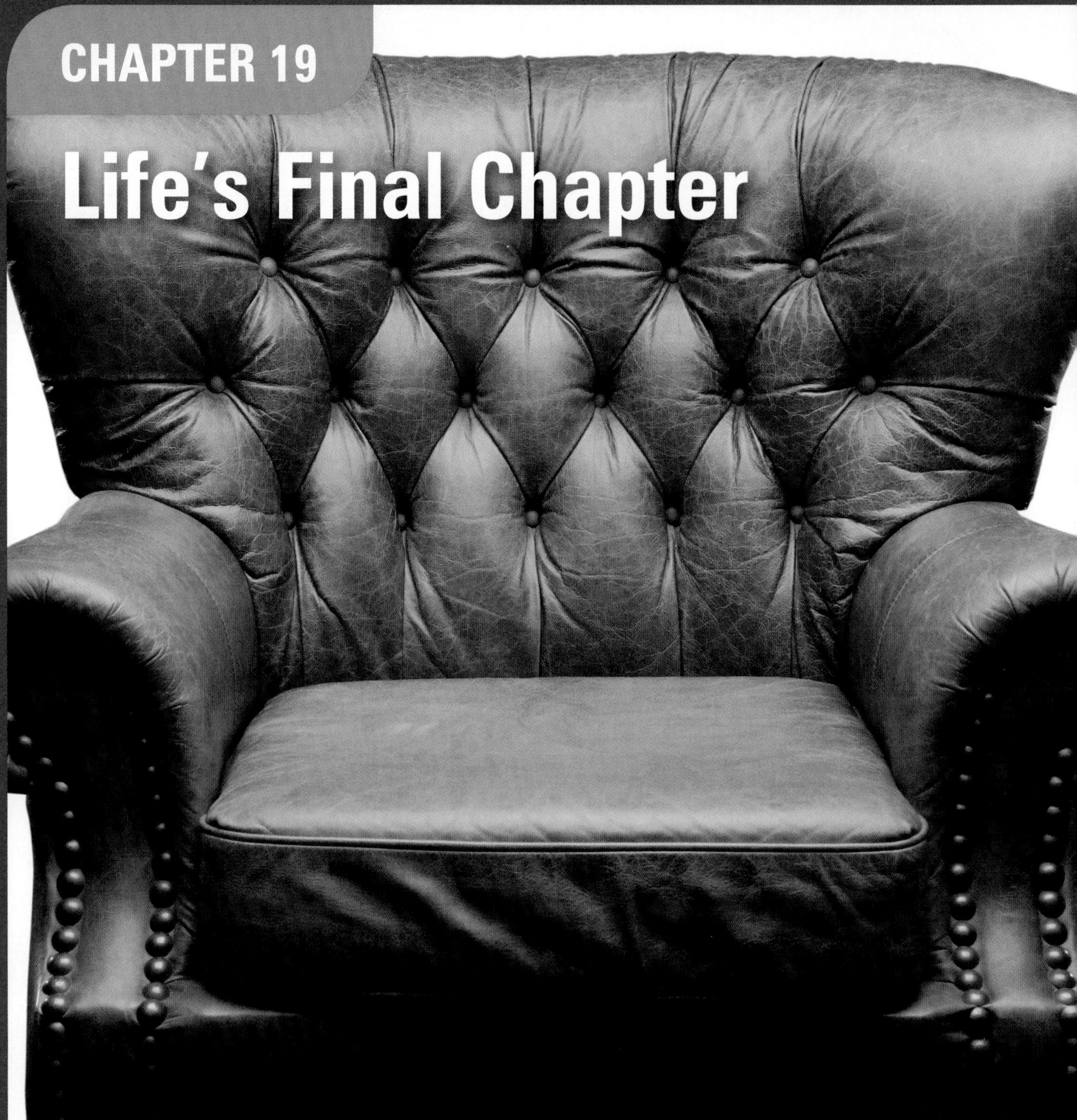

CHAPTER 19

Life's Final Chapter

LEARNING OUTCOMES

LO1 Define death and dying, and evaluate views on stages of dying

LO2 Identify settings in which people die, distinguishing between hospitals and hospices

LO3 Discuss the various types of euthanasia and their controversies

LO4 Discuss people's perspectives on death at various stages of development

LO5 Discuss coping with death, focusing on the funeral, and possible stages of grieving

© Roy McMahon/Corbis

> **"Today, only a small minority of Canadians die in their own homes—typically those who are in advanced old age or those who are gravely or terminally ill."**

When we are young and our bodies are supple and strong, it may seem that we will live forever. All we have to do is eat right, exercise, and avoid smoking and driving recklessly. We may have but a dim awareness of our own mortality. We parcel thoughts about death and dying into a mental file cabinet to be opened later in life, along with items like retirement, Old Age Security, and varicose veins. But death can occur at any age—by accident, violence, or illness. We can also be affected deeply at any stage of life through the deaths of others.

The denial of death is deeply embedded in our culture. Many people prefer not to think about their death or plan ahead for their eventual demise, as though thinking about it or planning for it might bring it about sooner. Elisabeth Kübler-Ross (1969, p. 21) wrote that "We use euphemisms, we make the dead look as if they were asleep, we ship the children off to protect them from the anxiety and turmoil around the house if the [person] is fortunate enough to die at home, [and] we don't allow children to visit their dying parents in the hospitals." When we think about death and dying, many questions arise:

- How do we know when a person has died?
- Are there stages of dying?
- What is meant by the "right to die"? Do people have a right to die?
- What is a living will?
- Is there a proper way to mourn? Are there stages of grieving?

This chapter addresses these questions and many more.

LO1 Understanding Death and Dying

Death is commonly defined as the cessation of life. Many people think of death as a part of life, but death is the termination of life and not a part of life. **Dying**, though, is a part of life. It is the universal end-stage of life in which bodily processes decline, leading to death. Yet life holds significance and meaning even in the face of impending death.

death the irreversible cessation of vital life functions.

dying the end-stage of life in which bodily processes decline, leading to death.

brain death cessation of activity of the cerebral cortex.

Charting the Boundaries between Life and Death

How do we know when a person has died? Is it the stoppage of their hearts? Of their breathing? Of their brain activity?

Medical authorities generally use **brain death** as the basis for determining that a person has died (Appel, 2005). The most

whole-brain death cessation of activity of the cerebral cortex and brain stem.

widely used criterion for establishing brain death is the absence of activity of the cerebral cortex, as shown by a flat EEG (electroencephalography) recording. When the cerebral cortex no longer shows signs of activity, consciousness—the sense of self and all psychological functioning—has ceased. The broader concept of **whole-brain death** includes death of the brain stem, which is responsible for certain automatic functions, such as the reflex of breathing. Thus, a person who is "brain dead" can continue to breathe. On the other hand, some people who are "whole-brain dead" can be been kept "alive" by life-support equipment that takes over their breathing and circulation.

Death is also a legal matter. In Canada, a person is considered legally dead when there is an irreversible cessation of breathing and circulation or when an irreversible cessation of brain activity occurs, including activity in the brain stem, which controls breathing (Appel, 2005).

TABLE 19.1

Stages of Dying

1. Denial	In this stage, people think, "It can't be me. The diagnosis must be wrong." Denial can be flat and absolute, or it can fluctuate so that one minute the patient accepts the medical verdict, and the next, the patient chats animatedly about future plans.
2. Anger	Denial usually gives way to anger and resentment toward the young and healthy, and, sometimes, toward the medical establishment: "It's unfair. Why me?" or "They didn't catch it in time."
3. Bargaining	People may bargain with God to postpone death, promising, for example, to do good deeds if they are given another six months, or another year.
4. Depression	With depression come feelings of grief, loss, and hopelessness—at the prospect of leaving loved ones and life itself.
5. Final Acceptance	Ultimately, inner peace may come as a quiet acceptance of the inevitable. This "peace" is not contentment; it is nearly devoid of feeling. The patient may still fear death, but comes to accept it with a sense of peace and dignity.

DID YOU KNOW?

A person may stop breathing and have no heartbeat but still be alive.

People whose hearts and lungs have ceased functioning can often be revived using cardiopulmonary resuscitation (CPR).

Are There Stages of Dying?

Our overview of the process of dying has been influenced by the work of Elisabeth Kübler-Ross (1969). From her observations of terminally ill patients, Kübler-Ross found some common responses to news of impending death. She hypothesized that dying patients pass through five stages of dying (see Table 19.1). She suggested that older people who suspect that death is near may undergo similar responses.

Much current "death education" suggests that hospital staff and family members can help support dying people by understanding the stages they are going through, by not imposing their own expectations, and by helping patients achieve final acceptance when they are ready to do so. But critics note that staff may be imposing Kübler-Ross's expectations.

Another critic, Joan Retsinas (1988), notes that Kübler-Ross's stages are limited to cases in which people receive a diagnosis of a terminal illness. As Retsinas points out, most people die because of their advanced years, not because of a specific terminal diagnosis. Thus, Kübler-Ross's approach may not be much use in helping us understand reactions under circumstances other than terminal illness.

Edwin Shneidman (1977) acknowledges that dying people may have feelings such as those described by Kübler-Ross, but his research shows that individuals behave in dying more or less as they behaved during their earlier life when they experienced stress, failure, and threat. A gamut of emotional responses and psychological defences emerge, especially denial, and can be observed in every death. However, the process of dying does not necessarily follow any progression of stages, as suggested by Kübler-Ross. The key factors that appear to affect the adjustment of the dying individual include the type and extent of organic cerebral impairment, pain and weakness, the time or phase of the person's life, the person's philosophy of life (and death), and prior experiences with crises.

DID YOU KNOW?

The five stages of dying provide insight into the dying process but should not be used as a template.

Although Kübler-Ross identified five stages that dying individuals commonly experience, other factors also appear to affect the adjustment of the dying individual.

Life and Death Issues: A Blurring Line

Because of medical advances, people are now able to live longer and delay death. But the ability to live longer does not necessarily walk hand in hand with quality of life. Such is the case for those who are living with degenerative or incurable diseases. Examine the following Canadian cases and ask yourself where you would draw your lines.

- In 1992, Sue Rodriquez, a woman with amyotrophic lateral sclerosis (ALS, or Lou Gehrig's disease), sought the right to secure physician-assisted suicide in Canada. She argued that her right to "life, liberty, and security of the person" included individual control over the circumstances and the timing of her inevitable death. The Supreme Court denied her argument, stating that to allow this act would erode the belief of the Canadian people in the sanctity of life. The state would not condone suicide and would protect the rights of the vulnerable.
- Nancy B. was a young woman who was living with an incurable disease (Guillain-Barré syndrome) and bedridden for life. She requested that doctors disconnect the respirator that was keeping her alive, arguing that no one can be made to undergo treatment without consent. The courts allowed this request in 1992, stating that the doctors would not be aiding the patient to commit suicide because Nancy B.'s death would result from the underlying disease.
- Robert Latimer is the father who, in 1993, took the life of his daughter, who had been living with severe disabilities. As a result, he received a minimum 10-year sentence. He stated that the personal consequences were not a consideration and that her daily pain and suffering were the only things on his mind (Johnson, 2011).

The line becomes even blurrier when we consider legal advanced directives known as "living wills."

An *instruction directive* sets out the types of treatment a person does not want to receive in the event that he or she cannot personally voice these decisions at the appropriate time. A *proxy directive* allows an individual to select, in advance, someone who can make health care decisions on his or her behalf.

So the lines blur, and questions surround the laws of Canada. The lines are drawn between active and passive assistance and the timing of clearly thought-out decisions that are documented in advance of a medical crisis.

Stockstudio X/iStockphoto

These issues are not new philosophical discussions and are likely to continue to be challenged in Canadian public and legal arenas (Butler et al., 2013).

LO2 Where People Die

A hundred years ago, most people died in their homes, surrounded by family members. Today, only a small minority of Canadians die in their own homes—typically those who are in advanced old age or who are gravely or terminally ill. When asked, most people respond that they would prefer to die at home with loved ones, yet 70 percent of Canadians die in a hospital (Canadian Hospice Palliative Care Association, 2010). Many people, of course, die suddenly wherever they happen to be at the time, either because of accidents, heart attacks, or other unanticipated events.

In the Hospital

Dying in a hospital can seem impersonal. Hospitals function to treat diseases, not to help prepare patients and their families for death. Instead of dying in familiar surroundings, comforted by family and friends, patients in hospitals often face death alone, cut off from their usual supports. On the other hand, patients and their families may assume that going to the hospital gives them the best chance of averting death.

Hospice Care

hospice an organization that treats dying patients by focusing on palliative care rather than curative treatment.

Depending on where they live, only 16–30 percent of Canadians who die will have access to or will receive hospice services (Canadian Hospice Palliative Care Association, 2010). Because of our rapidly aging population, demand for these services will continue to rise. Increasing numbers of dying people and their families are turning to **hospices** to help make their final days as meaningful and pain-free as possible. The word *hospice* derives from the Latin *hospitium*, meaning "hospitality," the same root of the words *hospital* and *hospitable*. The derivation is fitting, as hospices provide a homelike atmosphere to help terminally ill patients approach death with a maximum of dignity and a minimum of pain and discomfort. When necessary, hospices can provide care in inpatient settings, such as a hospitals, nursing facilities, or hospice centres, but most hospice care is provided in the patient's home.

Hospice workers typically work in teams that include physicians, nurses, social workers, mental health or pastoral counsellors, and home care aides

palliative care treatment focused on the relief of pain and suffering, not on a cure.

who provide physical, medical, spiritual, and emotional support to the entire family, not just the patient. Bereavement specialists assist the family to prepare for the loss and help them through grieving after the death. In contrast to hospitals, hospices provide the patient and family with as much control over decision making as possible. Hospice workers honour the patient's wishes not to be resuscitated or not to be kept alive on life-support equipment. Patients are given ample amounts of pain-killing narcotics to alleviate their discomfort.

Compared with hospital care, hospice care provides a more supportive environment for both the patient and the family; it is also less costly, especially when provided in the patient's home.

Hospice care has the following characteristics:

- Hospices offer **palliative care**, not a curative treatment. They control pain and symptoms to enable the patient to live as fully and comfortably as possible.
- Hospices treat the person, not the disease. The hospice team addresses the medical, emotional, psychological, and spiritual needs of patients, family, and friends.
- Hospices emphasize the quality of life, not the length of life, neither hastening nor postponing death.
- The hospice considers the unit of care to be the entire family, not just the patient. Bereavement counselling is provided after the death.
- Hospices provide 24-hour help and support to the patient and family.

The hospice considers the unit of care to be the entire family, not just the patient.

Supporting a Dying Person

First of all, you must be there for the person who is dying. Put yourself at the same eye level and don't withhold touching. Be available to listen, to talk, and to share experiences. Give the person the opportunity to talk about death and to grieve, but don't be afraid to also talk about the ongoing lives of mutual acquaintances. People who are dying often need to focus on topics other than their impending death, and some enjoy humorous stories. They may be comforted to hear about your life experiences—your concerns and worries as well as your joys, hopes, and dreams. But be aware of the person's emotional state on any given day. Some days are better than others. Don't attempt to minimize the person's emotional pain or his or her need to grieve by refusing to acknowledge it or changing the subject. Be sensitive to the person's feelings, and offer consolation and support. People with cognitive impairment may repeat certain thoughts many times; you can go with it or gently guide the conversation in another

Tyler Olson/Shutterstock.com

Characteristics of Hospice Care

- offers palliative care, not curative care
- treats the person, not the disease
- emphasizes the quality of life, not the length of life
- considers the entire family, not just the patient
- provides 24-hour help and support

© Ryan McVay/Photodisc/Getty Images

EMERGING CANADA

Once again in this textbook, we see the evolution of social media in the lives of Canadians. Blogging is very popular option for family and friends facing health events. Daily journal entries can keep loved ones updated. Blogs often include guest books that allow for messages of support and written words of encouragement without burdening the patient with having to respond to multiple well-meaning messages. CaringBridge is a nonprofit organization providing social-media support for anyone coping with illness (CaringBridge, 2013).

Courtesy of The Caring Bridge

direction now and then. He or she may repeatedly ask whether certain tasks have been taken care of, and a simple yes may do each time.

LO3 Euthanasia: Is There a Right to Die?

The word **euthanasia**, literally meaning "good death," is derived from the Greek roots *eu* ("good") and *thanatos* ("death"). Also called "mercy killing," it refers to the purposeful taking of a person's life through gentle or painless means to relieve pain or suffering. There are several types of euthanasia.

DID YOU KNOW?

Even the medical community is divided on the hot-button issue of physician-assisted suicide.

Even if physician-assisted suicide were legal, 42 percent of Canadian doctors say they would refuse to grant the patient's request.

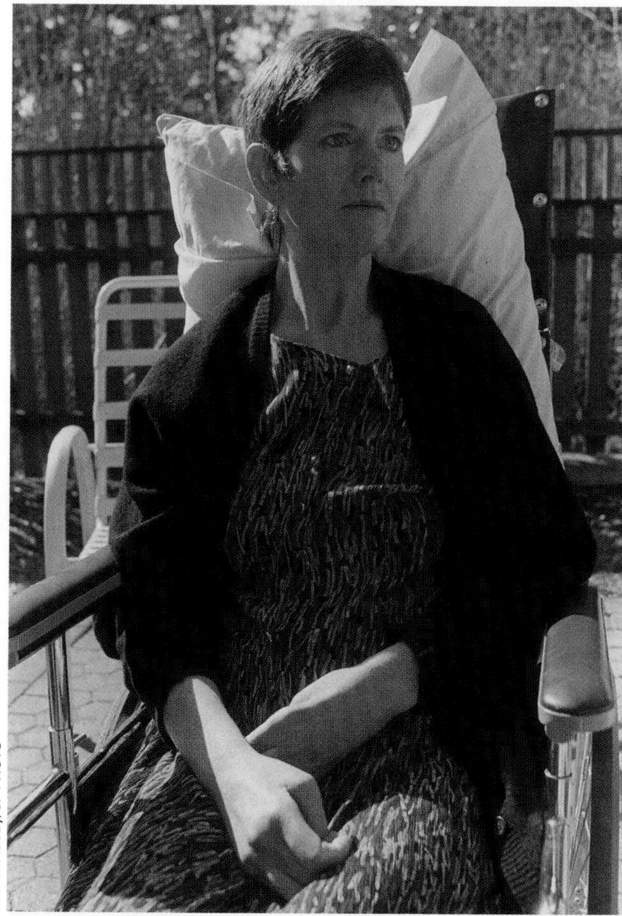

Chuck Stoody/CP PHOTO

For many Canadians who followed Sue Rodriguez's brave fight against ALS, she will be remembered as the face of "the right to die" issue in Canada.

End-of-Life Definitions

The Canadian Medical Association (CMA) has developed several definitions to be used when discussing end-of-life medical decisions. Euthanasia means knowingly and intentionally performing an act intended to end another person's life. In euthanasia, the subject (patient) has an incurable illness, the agent (who assists) is aware of the life-threatening condition, the primary intent of the agent's act is to end life, and the act is undertaken with empathy and compassion and without personal gain.

The CMA identifies three types of euthanasia. **Voluntary euthanasia** refers to an assisted death where the subject is competent, informed, and voluntarily asks to have his or her life ended. **Non-voluntary euthanasia** refers to an assisted death where the person has not expressed his or her preference in terms of an assisted death. **In-voluntary euthanasia** refers to an assisted death where the person made an informed choice and expressed his or her refusal to accept assistance in dying (Canadian Medical Association, 2007).

Assisted suicide refers to a self-inflicted death as a result of someone intentionally providing the knowledge or means to die by suicide. An alternative to euthanasia is **terminal sedation**, the practice of relieving distress in a terminally ill patient in the last hours or days of his or her life, usually by means of a continuous intravenous infusion of a sedative drug, such as a tranquilizer. Terminal sedation is not intended to hasten death, although whether it has that effect is often debated (Cellarius, 2008).

euthanasia the purposeful taking of life to relieve suffering.

voluntary euthanasia the intentional ending of life as a result of a competent, informed person having made a personal decision to have an assisted death.

non-voluntary euthanasia the intentional ending of the life of a person who has not expressed his or her preference in terms of an assisted death.

in-voluntary euthanasia the intentional ending of the life of a person who made an informed choice and expressed his or her refusal to have an assisted death.

assisted suicide a self-inflicted death as a result of someone intentionally providing the knowledge or means to die by suicide.

terminal sedation the practice of relieving distress in the last hours or days of life with the use of sedatives.

The Canadian Medical Association's Perspective

Both euthanasia and assisted suicide are illegal in Canada, and the CMA voices concerns about the "slippery slope." For example, if changes occur to

living will
a document prepared when a person is well, directing medical care providers to terminate life-sustaining treatment in the event of incapacitation or inability to speak; also known as a health care directive.

Canadian law and social policy regarding euthanasia, enabling competent people to legally pursue this option, can it be long before the legal system considers proxies for decision making for neurologically impaired patients and incurably ill babies? The CMA supports providing palliative care services to all Canadians as an alternative to euthanasia. The CMA further suggests that rational people requesting assisted suicide should petition the courts for physician-assisted suicide rather than take matters into their own hands and potentially legally jeopardizing their loved ones who help (Canadian Medical Association, 2007).

The Canadian Physician's Point of View

The section above states the official stand of the CMA, but how do individual doctors feel? The CMA polled more than 2,000 doctors. Only 20 percent said they would be willing to perform euthanasia. More than double that number, 42 percent said they would refuse to do so. Some 23 percent were not sure how they would respond, and 15 percent chose not to answer (see Figure 19.1).

Recent Court Decisions and Public Opinion

Gloria Taylor, a British Columbia woman with ALS (the same disease that afflicted Sue Rodriguez, mentioned earlier in the chapter), won her legal fight to obtain doctor-assisted suicide in Canada. The BC court ruled that it was unconstitutional to deny her this right if she could find a physician prepared to help her. Gloria died before pursuing this option (CBC News, 2012a).

In 2011, 67 percent of Canadians said they were in favour of legalizing medically assisted suicide in spite of Canadian doctors' reluctance to be part of the process. Withholding a life-saving medical procedure is legal in Canada. Of the physicians surveyed, 59 percent said they had withheld such a procedure at a patient's request. Every competent Canadian has the right to refuse any treatment. One in six doctors, or 16 percent, reported that they had been asked to perform euthanasia within the past five years (Kirkey, 2013).

Studio Smart/Shutterstock.com

The Living Will

Pierre was in a tragic accident that left him in an irreversible coma and dependent on artificial life support—a respirator to maintain his breathing and feeding tubes to supply his body with nutrients. Would Pierre want his life to be maintained by whatever means were at the disposal of modern medicine, or would he prefer doctors to withdraw life support, allowing him to die naturally?

Keisha has been in pain day after day. She has a terminal disease, and her heart suddenly stops due to cardiac arrest. Would she want the doctors to resuscitate her by whatever means necessary in an effort to prolong her life for another few days or weeks? Who decides when it is time for her to die—Keisha or the doctors managing her care?

A **living will**, also known as a health care directive, is a legal document that people draft when they are well. It directs health care workers to not use aggressive medical procedures or life-support equipment to prolong vegetative functioning in the event they became permanently incapacitated and unable to communicate their wishes. Terminally ill patients can insist, for example, that "Do Not Resuscitate"

FIGURE 19.1

How Do Doctors Feel about Euthanasia?

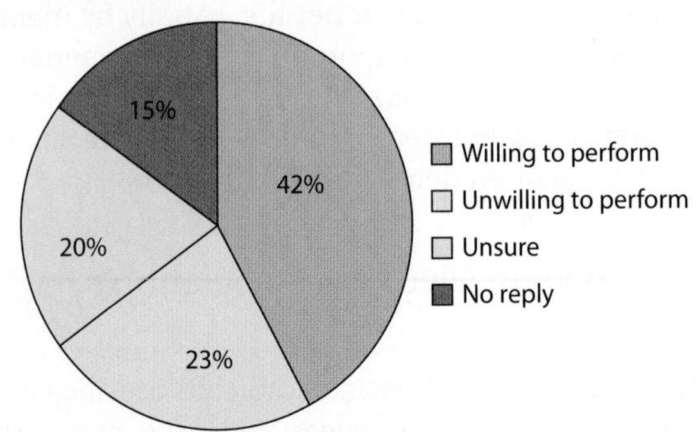

Source: Canadian Medical Association

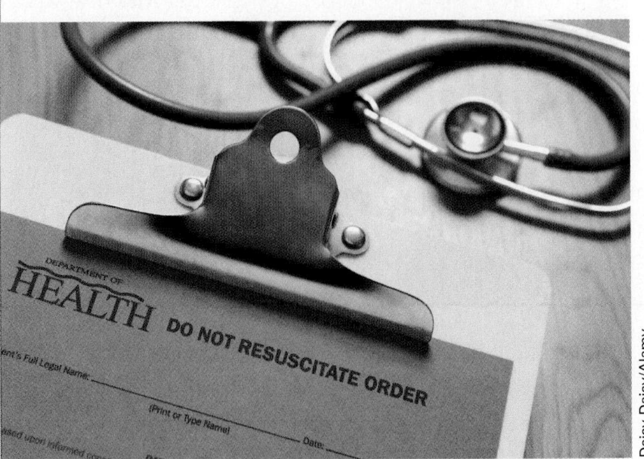

Daisy-Daisy/Alamy

orders be included in their charts, directing doctors not to use CPR in the event they have a cardiac arrest.

The withdrawal of life-sustaining treatment is a form of passive euthanasia. Unlike active euthanasia, death is not induced by administering a drug or assisting in the patient's suicide.

Living wills must be drafted in accordance with provincial or territorial laws (see Figure 19.2 on page 328). The terms of the document take effect only when patients are unable to speak for themselves. For this reason, living wills usually identify a proxy, such as the next of kin, who can make decisions in the event that the signer cannot communicate.

Still, many living wills are ignored. Some are disregarded by their proxies, often because the proxies don't judge the patient's wishes accurately or because they can't bear the emotional burden of asking health care workers to remove life support. Physicians, too, may not comply with health care directives, perhaps because the directives weren't available when needed or weren't clear. Physicians are more likely to follow specific health care directives (e.g., "Do not resuscitate") than general guidelines.

DID YOU KNOW?

People who have living wills can hope their wishes will be carried out if they become unable to speak for themselves.

A living will may not be carried out for many reasons. Specific health care directives have a better chance of being carried out than general guidelines.

Organ Donation: The Gift of Life

One winter day, I lost a dear student and friend to a sudden brain aneurism. Greg died as he had lived, with dignity and with charity. Upon his death, seven people received a gift of life because Greg had previously agreed to donate his organs. One donor can save up to eight lives, and the gift of tissue donation can enhance the lives of another 75.

Donating your organs for transplant after your death gives the gift of hope and a second chance at life to someone else in need. Living donors—often family members—can sometimes donate a kidney or a portion of their liver for transplant. In deceased donation, all organs and tissues must be taken from the donor shortly after death. Organs and tissues that can be donated include heart, kidneys, liver, lungs, pancreas, skin, small bowel, stomach, bone, connective tissue, corneas, heart valves, and islet cells of the pancreas. Only organs that are healthy at the time of death are suitable for transplantation.

In Canada, in 2011:

- 4,543 people were on the waiting list for an organ transplant
- 2,124 transplants took place
- Those transplants were made possible because of 1,033 organ donors (living and deceased) (Canadian Institute for Health Information, 2013).

Organ donations save lives but, regardless of your decision, make your wishes known to your family to relieve them of the burden of this decision in the time of their grief.

Gift of Life

Courtesy of Trillium Gift of Life Network

LO4 Lifespan Perspectives on Death

Psychologists have found interesting developments in people's understanding of death and their reactions to death. Children, for example, seem to follow something of a Piagetian route in their cognitive development although their sense of reversibility is reversed. In other words, they begin by thinking of death as reversible, but, by about the time they enter school, they see it as irreversible (Poltorak & Glazer, 2006). People who truly understand the finality of death appear to take some reasonable steps to avert it, even "risk-taking" adolescents (Mills et al., 2008).

Without taking sides in what some might think of as a religious debate, we note that many people at most ages assume, or are encouraged to assume, a form of spiritual reversibility in their thinking about death (Balk et al., 2007; Lattanzi-Licht, 2007). Religious traditions inform people that the soul of the person who has passed on will dwell in heaven or in Paradise forever, or that it will be reincarnated on Earth.

Children

Younger children lack the cognitive ability to understand the permanent nature of death (Slaughter & Griffiths, 2007). Preschoolers may think that death is reversible or temporary, a belief reinforced by cartoon characters that die and come back to life (Poltorak & Glazer, 2006). Nevertheless, their thinking becomes increasingly realistic as they progress through the ages of 4, 5, and 6 (Li-qi & Fu-xi, 2006). Children's understanding of death appears to increase as they learn about the biology of the human body and how various organs contribute to the processes of life (Slaughter & Griffiths, 2007).

children to attend funerals, including funerals with open caskets. These experiences challenge the adolescent's sense of immortality that is associated with the personal fable (see Chapter 11; Noppe & Noppe, 2004). Even though adolescents come to recognize that the concept of death applies to them, they continue to engage in riskier behaviour than adults do. On the other hand, those adolescents who perceive certain behaviours to be highly risky are less likely to engage in them (Mills et al., 2008).

Adults

Most young adults in developed nations need not spend much time thinking about the possibility of their death. The leading causes of death in early adulthood are accidents and suicide. In middle adulthood, heart disease and cancer have become the leading causes of death. People are advised to become proactive in their screenings for cardiovascular problems and for several kinds of cancer. Some cancers have sex differences, but educated women and men are aware that age is a risk factor in both heart disease and cancer, and they are likely aware of middle-aged people who died "untimely" deaths from one or the other.

Heart disease and cancer remain the leading causes of death in late adulthood. As people move into advanced old age, many should no longer be driving due to loss of sensory acuity and slowed reaction time. Older adults are also more prone to falls, Alzheimer's disease, and other dementias. Some older people come to fear disability and discomfort nearly as much as they fear death.

Theorists of social and emotional development in late adulthood suggest that ego transcendence, or concern for the well-being of humankind in general, enables some people to begin to face death with an inner calm (see Chapter 18; Ardelt, 2008b). On the other hand, continuing with physical, leisure, and informal social activities are all associated with greater life satisfaction among older, retired people (Joung & Miller, 2007; Talbot et al., 2007). There is no single formula for coping with physical decline and the approach of death.

LO5 Coping with Death

For most of us, coping with death is at best complicated, and at worst painful and disorienting. Losing a loved one is generally considered to be the most stressful life change we can endure.

What to Do When Someone Dies

If you are present at someone's death, call the family doctor, the police, or 911. A doctor is needed to complete the death certificate and to indicate the cause of death. If the cause of death cannot be readily determined, a coroner or medical examiner may become involved to determine the cause of death. Once the body has been examined by the doctor and the death certificate has been completed, a funeral director may be contacted to remove the body from the home or the hospital and to make arrangements for burial, cremation, or placement in a mausoleum. If death occurs unexpectedly or foul play is involved or suspected, an autopsy may be performed to determine the cause and circumstances of death. Sometimes an autopsy is performed, with the family's consent, if the knowledge gained from the procedure could benefit medical science.

Funeral Arrangements

Funerals respond to death in an organized way that is tied to religious custom and cultural tradition. Funerals offer family and community a ritual for grieving publicly and saying farewell to the person who died. Funerals grant a closure that can help observers begin to move on with their lives.

Family members of the deceased decide how simple or elaborate they prefer the funeral to be, whether they want embalming, and whether the deceased's body should be buried or cremated. Sometimes these matters are spelled out by religious or family custom. Sometimes these decisions lead to family conflicts.

After their homes, automobiles, and children's educations, funerals may be a Canadian family's next largest expense. Consider these guidelines to arrange a funeral that meets your needs and remains in your budget. Have a good friend, who will be able to make decisions, go with you to arrange the funeral. Funerals can be expensive. Make decisions based on reason and good sense, not on emotions or guilt. If a funeral home has not yet been selected, shop around; you can and should ask about their services and costs. Be aware that some cemeteries offer

© Robert Pears/iStockphoto

Different cultures often have very different approaches to funerary traditions. For example, compare these musicians, who are part of a cremation ceremony in Bali, Indonesia, with the mourners in black on page 332.

the plot for free but then make their profit from charging exorbitant maintenance fees, opening and closing fees, costs for monuments, and other fees. Caskets are often the major burial expense and can range from $500 to $50,000 or more! Recognize that the type of casket you choose makes no difference to the deceased person, and tell the funeral director to show you models that fall within the price range that you are comfortable paying.

Funerals can be expensive. Make decisions based on reason and good sense, not on emotions or guilt.

Legal and Financial Matters

Many legal and financial matters require attention following a death. Family members will need to deal with issues concerning estates, inheritance, outstanding debts, insurance, and amounts owed for funeral expenses. Focusing on these matters can be difficult during a time of grief. Family members should seek legal counsel to protect their own financial interests and for guidance on handling the deceased person's affairs. An attorney is usually needed to settle the estate, especially when it is sizeable or when complex matters arise in sorting through the deceased person's affairs.

bereavement
the state of deprivation brought about by the death of a family member or close friend.

grief
emotional suffering resulting from a death.

mourning
customary methods of expressing grief.

Grief and Bereavement

The death of a close friend or family member can be a traumatic experience. It typically leads to a state of **bereavement**, an emotional state of longing and deprivation characterized by feelings of **grief** and a deep sense of loss. **Mourning** is synonymous with grief over the death of a person, but also describes culturally prescribed ways of displaying grief. Different cultures prescribe different periods of mourning and different rituals for expressing grief. The tradition of wearing unadorned black clothing for mourning dates at least to the Roman Empire. In rural parts of Mexico, Italy, and Greece, widows are often still expected to wear black for the remainder of their lives. In England and North America, the wearing of black is on the decline, replaced by wearing joyous colours as the life of the deceased person is celebrated.

Coping with loss requires time and the ability to come to terms with the loss and move ahead with one's life. Having a supportive social network is important in navigating this major transition.

EMERGING CANADA

It is highly recommended that family members compare the costs associated with burials and cremations. Helping the family through these decisions is one way that a supporter can provide assistance to a family that has just lost a loved one and may not be thinking clearly. The costs differ among providers and across services. On average, cremations cost 25 percent of the cost of a burial. This lower cost might be one reason why 60 percent of deceased people are now cremated. The average burial in Canada costs $10,000 (Demont, 2012).

© Russell Underwood/CORBIS

Grieving

There is no one right way to grieve and no fixed period of time for which grief should last. Sometimes, especially for parents who have lost a child, grief never ends, though people do learn over time to live with the loss. People grieve in different ways. Some grieve more publicly, while others reveal their feelings only in private. You may not always know when someone is grieving. Early experiences of the non-acceptance of loss are the best predictors of later grief experiences. Early non-acceptance indicates a much higher likelihood for a prolonged grief response (Holland et al., 2013)

Grief usually involves a combination of emotions, especially depression, loneliness, feelings of emptiness, disbelief and numbness, apprehension about the future ("What will I do now?"), guilt ("I could have done something."), even anger ("They could have handled this better."). Grief may also be punctuated by relief that the deceased person is no longer suffering intense pain and by a heightened awareness of one's own mortality. Grief may also compromise the immune system, leaving the person more vulnerable to disease. Researchers also find that the death of a loved puts one at greater risk of death by suicide, especially during the first weeks following the loss (Ajdacic-Gross et al., 2008).

The Widow Who Wasn't a Bride

What do you call a widow who isn't a widow? Part of the problem, according to Shatz (2006), is that we have no word for a woman who has cohabited with a man who has died, even if she has been with him for decades. In her doctoral dissertation, Shatz describes the experiences of nine women who experienced "disenfranchised grief" following the loss of their partners. The bereaved women felt marginalized by society and cut off from their partners' biological children. Not only had these men taken care of their children in their wills, to the exclusion of their cohabiting partners, but they had arranged to be buried next to their late spouses at some time in the past but had never changed that arrangement. Apparently these men did not want to be thought of badly by their biological children.

Are There Stages of Grieving?

John Bowlby (1961), the attachment theorist, was the first to propose a stage theory of grief for coping with bereavement. It included four stages: shock-numbness, yearning-searching, disorganization-despair, and reorganization. Elisabeth Kübler-Ross (1969) adapted Bowlby's stage theory to describe her five-stage reaction of terminally ill patients to knowledge of their own impending death: denial-isolation, anger, bargaining, depression, and acceptance. The stage theory of grief has become generally accepted when applied to various kinds of losses, including children's responses to parental separation, adults' responses to marital separation (Gray et al., 1991), and hospital staff's responses to the death of a patient. Medical education currently relies heavily on the Kübler-Ross model of grief (Kübler-Ross & Kessler, 2005; Maciejewski et al., 2007).

Jacobs (1993) modified the stage theory of grief to include the following stages: numbness-disbelief, separation distress (yearning-anger-anxiety), depression-mourning, and recovery. Jacobs' stage theory, like the theories that preceded it, is largely based on anecdotes and case studies.

To test Jacobs' theory, Paul Maciejewski and his colleagues (2007) administered five items measuring disbelief, yearning, anger, depression, and acceptance of death to 233 bereaved individuals from 1 to 24 months following their losses. Several findings are clear. Disbelief was highest just after the loss and gradually waned over the course of two years. Acceptance of the loss shows the opposite course, being nonexistent at the outset, growing gradually, and peaking two years later. Yearning, anger, and depression rise suddenly in the predicted order and then each wanes gradually.

Maciejewski and his colleagues (2007) believe they found support for the theory, and to some degree they did. The predicted feelings were present and arose in the predicted order. However, others reviewing the same data noted that the investigators tested for only these five emotions; the emotions they neglected could have been more powerful (Bonanno & Boerner, 2007; Silver & Wortman, 2007). Also, given their overlap, one wonders just how stage-like these emotions are. But no observer can deny that, in this sample, all five emotions are present and occur in a predictable order.

Advice for Coping

What can you do if someone you know is faced with the death of a close family member or friend?

Consider some combination of the following: First, tell them to take care of themselves. When people are grieving, they can become so absorbed with their loss that they fail to attend to their own personal needs. Some people do not eat or bathe. They may feel guilty doing things for themselves and avoid any pleasurable experiences. Remember to reassure them that they can grieve without withdrawing from life.

Encourage them to feel their loss. Some people prefer to bottle up their feelings, but covering up feelings or trying to erase them with tranquilizers may prolong the grieving process. When they feel the time is right, they will turn to a trusted support. Make yourself available and invite the person to lean on you for support.

Bereaved persons can find comfort knowing that they are not alone in their suffering; sharing experiences can help bereaved persons cope and process what they are feeling.

Remember that 70 percent of family members enrolled in hospice do not access post-loss bereavement services; and even of those who have major depressive disorders, less than 50 percent draw on outside resources. These findings suggest that many of the people who could benefit from those services do not seek them out (Holland et al., 2013). Be an advocate and offer to go with the bereaved individual so he or she can get the help that is needed.

Reassure the individual that it takes time to come to terms with loss. There is no fixed timetable for grief to run its course. Remind them not to let other people push them into moving on "to the next stage" unless they are prepared to do so.

Encourage the individual to join a bereavement support group. They will find that they are not alone in their suffering. Sharing experiences can help people cope better and work through their grief in a supportive environment where others can share similar experiences. Bereavement groups provide hope that, with time, life will continue.

© David Harry Stewart/Getty Images

Advice for Helping a Bereaved Friend or Relative Cope

When someone you know has lost a loved one, you will naturally want to reach out to them. Yet you may not know how to help, or you may fear that you'll say the wrong thing. *Don't worry about what to say*. Just spending time with the bereaved person can help. Don't expect to have all the answers; sometimes there are no answers. Sometimes what matters is simply being a good listener. Don't be afraid to talk about the deceased person. Take your cue from the bereaved person. Not talking about the departed person brings down a curtain of silence that can make it more difficult for the bereaved person to work through feelings of grief. By the same token, don't force bereaved persons to talk about their feelings. Keep in touch regularly, but don't assume that because you don't get a call, the person doesn't want to talk. The bereaved person may be too depressed or lack the energy to reach out. Offer to help with chores such as shopping, running errands, and babysitting.

Don't minimize the loss, and avoid clichés like "You're young, you can have more children" or "It was for the best."

DID YOU KNOW?

When helping someone cope with a death, don't expect to have all the answers.

Sometimes there are no answers. Simply listening and being supportive is a wise course of action.

Look to Find the Lesson

Scape/Shutterstock.com

Death is a universal developmental event that we all encounter. Some of us fear the shadow that it casts, while others embrace the lessons that come from the loss of our loved ones. Fittingly, those that have taken us by the hand in life also often serve as our most insightful teachers—through their death.

Randy Pausch is an excellent example of this. A famous lecture series asks the question, "If you knew you were going to die, and you had one last lecture, what would you say to your students?" Randy brought an interesting perspective to this question as he was dying of pancreatic cancer and he delivered his famous last lecture at Carnegie Mellon University on September 18, 2007. He chose not to speak about death, but about the lessons to be learned in life.

Randy spoke about moments that change our lives forever. He explored the notion that lessons are learned through disappointment and that we need to realize that brick walls aren't designed to keep us out but to show us how much we want to achieve something. Experience is what we get when we don't get what we want. Randy talked about embracing the negative feedback that you receive in life because when people stop saying anything to you anymore, they have given up on you. Finally, Randy challenged us to determine whether we are "Tiggers" or "Eeyores." Do we search for the fun in every situation, or do we choose to wallow in self-misery (Pausch & Zaslow, 2008)?

Death holds the gift of wisdom.

As our loved ones pass—and as we ultimately take our final journey into death—we must look to find the lesson. Death holds the gift of wisdom. Death teaches us that, through memories, loved ones live on forever.

Go online at
www.nelson.com/4ltrpress/icanhdev2ce
And access the essential Study Tools online for this chapter:

- **Practice Quizzes**, which will help you to prepare for tests
- **Games**, to help test your knowledge
- **Flashcards**, to test your understanding of key terms
- **Observing Development Videos**
- **Internet Activities**

References

A

AAIDD. (2007). American Association on Intellectual and Developmental Disabilities. Retrieved from www.aamr.org. Accessed May 24, 2007.

Aalsma, M. C., Lapsley, D. K., & Flannery, D. J. (2006). Personal fables, narcissism, and adolescent adjustment. *Psychology in the Schools, 43*(4), 481–491.

Aartsen, M. J., et al. (2005). Does widowhood affect memory performance of older persons? *Psychological Medicine, 35*(2), 217–226.

Abdelaziz, Y. E., Harb, A. H., & Hisham, N. (2001). *Textbook of clinical pediatrics.* Philadelphia: Lippincott Williams & Wilkins.

Aber, J. L., Bishop-Josef, S. J., Jones, S. M., McLearn, K. T., & Phillips, D. A. (Eds.). (2007). *Child development and social policy: Knowledge for action. APA Decade of Behavior volumes*. Washington, DC: American Psychological Association.

Abraham, L. (2012). Holiday toys: Canadian Toy Association lists hottest toys for 2012. Retrieved from http://www.huffingtonpost.ca/2012/11/01/holiday-toys-_n_2060340.html

Abravanel, E., & DeYong, N. G. (1991). Does object modeling elicit imitative-like gestures from young infants? *Journal of Experimental Child Psychology, 52,* 22–40.

Acevedo, A., & Loewenstein, D. A. (2007). Nonpharmacological cognitive interventions in aging and dementia. *Journal of Geriatric Psychiatry and Neurology, 20*(4), 239–249.

Active Healthy Kids Canada. (2010). Healthy habits start earlier than you think: The Active Healthy Kids Canada report card on physical activity for children and youth. Toronto: Author. Retrieved from http://www.activehealthykids.ca/ecms.ashx/2010 ActiveHealthyKids CanadaReportCard-longform.pdf

A.D.A.M. Medical Encyclopedia. (2012). Premenstrual dysphoric disorder. Retrieved from http://www.ncbi.nlm.nih.gov/pubmedhealth/PMH0004461/

Adams, G. R., Berzonsky, M. D., & Keating, L. (2006). Psychosocial resources in first-year university students: The role of identity processes and social relationships. *Journal of Youth and Adolescence, 35*(1), 81–91.

Adams, R. G., & Ueno, K. (2006). Middle-aged and older adult men's friendships. In V. H. Bedford & B. Formaniak Turner (Eds.), *Men in relationships: A new look from a life course perspective* (pp. 103–124). New York: Springer Publishing Co.

Adler, J. M., Kissel, E. C., & McAdams, D. P. (2006). Emerging from the CAVE: Attributional style and the narrative study of identity in midlife adults. *Cognitive Therapy and Research, 30*(1), 39–51.

Adolph, K. E., & Berger, S. E. (2005). Physical and motor development. In M. H. Bornstein & M. E. Lamb (Eds.), *Developmental science: An advanced textbook* (5th ed.) (pp. 223–281). Hillsdale, NJ: Erlbaum.

Aguiar, A., & Baillargeon, R. (2002). Developments in young infants' reasoning about occluded objects. *Cognitive Psychology, 45*(2), 267–336.

Ainsworth, M. D. S. (1989). Attachments beyond infancy. *American Psychologist, 44,* 709–716.

Ainsworth, M. D. S., Blehar, M. C., Waters, E., & Wall, S. (1978). *Patterns of attachment: A psychological study of the strange situation.* Hillsdale, NJ: Erlbaum.

Ainsworth, M. D. S., & Bowlby, J. (1991). An ethological approach to personality development. *American Psychologist, 46*(4), 333–341.

Ajdacic-Gross, V., et al. (2008). Suicide after bereavement. *Psychological Medicine, 38*(5), 673–676.

Akman, Y. (2007). Identity status of Turkish university students in relation to their evaluation of family problems. *Social Behavior and Personality, 35*(1), 79–88.

Alberta SBS Prevention Campaign. (2010). Parents and caregivers of young children. Retrieved from http://www.shakenbaby.ca

Alfirevic, Z., Sundberg, K., & Brigham, S. (2003). Amniocentesis and chorionic villus sampling for prenatal diagnosis. *Cochrane Database of Systematic Reviews*, DOI: 10.1002/14651858.CD003252.

Allain, P., Kauffmann, M., Dubas, F., Berrut, G., & Le Gall, D. (2007). Executive functioning and normal aging: A study of arithmetic word-problem-solving. *Psychologie & NeuroPsychiatrie Du Vieillissement, 5*(4), 315–325.

Alloway, T. P., Gathercole, S. E., Willis, C., & Adams, A. (2004). A structural analysis of working memory and related cognitive skills in young children. *Journal of Experimental Child Psychology, 87*(2), 85–106.

Almeida, D. M., & Horn, M. C. (2004). Is daily life more stressful during middle adulthood? In O. G. Brim, C. D. Ryff, & R. C. Kessler (Eds.), *How healthy are we? A national study of well-being at midlife* (pp. 425–451). *The John D. and Catherine T. MacArthur Foundation series on mental health and development. Studies on successful midlife development.* Chicago: University of Chicago Press.

Alphonso, C. (2012, November 26). Canada's first childhood obesity program targets unhealthy lifestyles. Retrieved from http://www.theglobeandmail.com/news/national/canadas-first-childhood-obesity-program-targets-unhealthy-lifestyles/article5711928/

Alzheimer Society. (2010). *Rising tide: The impact of dementia on Canadian society.* Retrieved from http://www.alzheimer.ca/~/media/Files/national/Advocacy/ASC_Rising%20Tide_Full%20Report_Eng.ashx

Amato, P. R. (2006). Marital discord, divorce, and children's well-being: Results from a 20-year longitudinal study of two generations. In A. Clarke-Stewart & J. Dunn (Eds.), *Families count: Effects on child and adolescent development. The Jacobs Foundation series on adolescence* (pp. 179–202). New York: Cambridge University Press.

Amato, P. R., Booth, A., Johnson, D. R., & Rogers, S. J. (2007). *Alone together: How marriage in America is changing.* Cambridge, MA: Harvard University Press.

Amato, P. R., & Previti, D. (2003). People's reasons for divorcing. *Journal of Family Issues, 24,* 602–626.

Ambert, A.-M. (2005). *Cohabitation and marriage: How are they related.* Contemporary Family Trends series. Ottawa: The Vanier Institute of the Family. Retrieved from http://www.vifamily.ca/sites/default/files/cohabitation_and_marriage.pdf

Ambert, A.-M. (2009). *Divorce: Facts, causes & consequences* (3rd. ed.). Ottawa: Vanier Institute of the Family. Retrieved from http://www.vifamily.ca/node/80

American Cancer Society. (2007). www.cancer.org.

American Fertility Association. (2007). Retrieved from http://www.theafa.org/fertility/malefactor/index.html. Accessed February 6, 2007.

American Heart Association. (2007). Overweight in children. Retrieved from http://www.americanheart.org/presenter.jhtml?identifier=4670. Accessed May 18, 2007.

American Psychiatric Association. (1998). *Diagnostic and statistical manual of mental disorders: DSM-IV-TR,* (4th ed.). Washington, DC: Author.

Ammaniti, M., Speranza, A. M., & Fedele, S. (2005). Attachment in infancy and in early and late childhood: A longitudinal study. In K. A Kerns & R. A. Richardson (Eds.), *Attachment in middle childhood* (pp. 115–136). New York: Guilford.

Amodio, D. M., & Showers, C. J. (2005). "Similarity breeds liking" revisited: The moderating role of commitment. *Journal of Social and Personal Relationships, 22*(6), 817–836.

Andersen, M. L., & Taylor, H. H. (2009). *Sociology: The essentials* (5th ed.). Belmont, CA: Wadsworth.

Anderson, C. A., Gentile, D. A., & Buckley, K. E. (2007). *Violent video game effects on children and adolescents: Theory, research, and public policy*. New York: Oxford University Press.

Andreou, G., Krommydas, G., Gourgoulianis, K. I., Karapetsas, A., & Molyvdas, P. A. (2002). Handedness, asthma, and allergic disorders: Is there an association? *Psychology, Health, and Medicine, 7*(1), 53–60.

Andrews, G., Clark, M., & Luszcz, M. (2002). Successful aging in the Australian longitudinal study of aging: Applying the MacArthur Model cross-nationally. *Journal of Social Issues, 58,* 749–765.

Angier, N. (2007, June 12). Sleek, fast, and focused: The cells that make dad dad. *New York Times,* pp. F1, F6.

Annett, M. (1999). Left-handedness as a function of sex, maternal versus paternal inheritance, and report bias. *Behavior Genetics, 29*(2), 103–114.

Annett, M., & Moran, P. (2006). Schizotypy is increased in mixed-handers, especially right-handed writers who use the left hand for primary actions. *Schizophrenia Research, 81*(2–3), 239–246.

Antonucci, T. C., & Birditt, K. S. (2004). Lack of close relationships and well-being across the life span. Paper presented to the American Psychological Association.

Anxiety BC. (2010). Separation anxiety. Retrieved from http://www.anxietybc.com/parent/separation.php

Appel, J. M. (2005). Defining death. *Journal of Medical Ethics, 31*(11), 641–642.

Appleyard, K., & Berlin, L. J. (2007). Supporting healthy relationships between young children and their parents. Policy brief. Center for Child and Family Policy, Duke University. Retrieved from https://childandfamilypolicy.duke.edu/pdfs/pubpres/SupportingHealthyRelationships.pdf

Aquilino, W. S. (2005). Impact of family structure on parental attitudes toward the economic support of adult children over the transition to adulthood. *Journal of Family Issues, 26*(2), 143–167.

Arai, A., et al. (2007). Association between lifestyle activity and depressed mood among home-dwelling older people. *Aging & Mental Health, 11*(5), 547–555.

Archer, J. (2006). Testosterone and human aggression: An evaluation of the challenge hypothesis. *Neuroscience & Biobehavioral Reviews, 30*(3), 319–345.

Archibald, L. M. D., & Gathercole, S. E. (2006). Short-term memory and working memory in specific language impairment. In T. P. Alloway & S. E. Gathercole (Eds.), *Working memory and neurodevelopmental disorders* (pp. 139–160). New York: Psychology Press.

Ardelt, M. (2008a). Wisdom, religiosity, purpose in life, and death attitudes of aging adults. In A. Tomer, G. T. Eliason, T. Grafton, & P. T. P. Wong (Eds.), *Existential and spiritual issues in death attitudes* (pp. 139–158). Mahwah, NJ: Erlbaum.

Ardelt, M. (2008b). Self-development through selflessness: The paradoxical process of growing wiser. In H. A. Wayment, & J. J. Bauer (Eds.), *Transcending self-interest: Psychological explorations of the quiet ego. Decade of behavior* (pp. 221–233). Washington, DC: American Psychological Association.

Arija, V., et al. (2006). Nutritional status and performance in test of verbal and non-verbal intelligence in 6-year-old children. *Intelligence, 34*(2), 141–149.

Arnett, J. J. (2007). Socialization in emerging adulthood: From the family to the wider world, from socialization to self-socialization. In J. E. Grusec & P. D. Hastings (Eds.), *Handbook of socialization: Theory and research* (pp. 208–231). New York: Guilford.

Arnon, S., et al. (2006). Live music is beneficial to preterm infants in the neonatal intensive care unit environment. *Birth: Issues in Perinatal Care, 33*(2), 131–136.

Aronson, E., Wilson, T. D., & Akert, R. M. (2010). *Social psychology* (7th ed.). Upper Saddle River, NJ: Prentice Hall.

Arranz, L., Guayerbas, N., & De la Fuente, M. (2007). Impairment of several immune functions in anxious women. *Journal of Psychosomatic Research, 62*(1), 1–8.

Aschermann, E., Gülzow, I., & Wendt, D. (2004). Differences in the comprehension of passive voice in German- and English-speaking children. *Swiss Journal of Psychology, 63*(4), 235–245.

Ash, D. (2004). Reflective scientific sense-making dialogue in two languages: The science in the dialogue and the dialogue in the science. *Science Education, 88*(6), 855–884.

Aslin, R. N., & Schlaggar, B. L. (2006). Is myelination the precipitating neural event for language development in infants and toddlers? *Neurology, 66*(3), 304–305.

Aspy, C. B., et al. (2007). Parental communication and youth sexual behaviour. *Journal of Adolescence, 30*(3), 449–466.

Assembly of First Nations. (2008). *Health of First Nations Children and the Environment*. Retrieved from http://www.afn.ca/uploads/files/rp-discussion_paper_re_childrens_health_and_the_environment.pdf_

Association of American Colleges & Universities. (2007). Case Study Facilitation Guidelines: February Fifth Forum: Cultivating Community. Retrieved from http://www.diversityweb.org/diversity_innovations/institutional_leadership/institutional_statements_plans/knox.cfm. Accessed November 1, 2007.

Atkinson, G., & Davenne, D. (2007). Relationships between sleep, physical activity and human health. *Physiology & Behavior, 90*(2–3), 229–235.

Auger, R. W., Blackhurst, A. E., & Wahl, K. H. (2005). The development of elementary-aged children's career aspirations and expectations. *Professional School Counseling, 8*(4), 322–329.

August, D., Carlo, M., Dressler, C., & Snow, C. (2005). The critical role of vocabulary development for English language learners. *Learning Disabilities Research & Practice, 20*(1), 50–57.

Autism Society of Canada. (2009). What are autism spectrum disorders? Retrieved from http://www.autismsocietycanada.ca/understanding_autism/what_are_asds/index_e.htm

Axford, J., Heron, C., Ross, F., & Victor, C. R. (2008). Management of knee osteoarthritis in primary care: Pain and depression are the major obstacles. *Journal of Psychosomatic Research, 64*(5), 461–467.

B

Bäckström T., et al. (2003). The role of hormones and hormonal treatments in premenstrual syndrome. *CNS Drugs, 17*(5), 325–342.

Bahrick, H. P., Bahrick, P. O., & Wittlinger, R. P. (1975). Fifty years of memory for names and faces: A cross-sectional approach. *Journal of Experimental Psychology: General, 104*(1), 54–75.

Bahrick, H. P., Hall, L. K., & Da Costa, L.A. (2008). Fifty years of memory of college grades: Accuracy and distortions. *Emotion, 8*(1), 13–22.

Bailey, J. M., & Pillard, R. C. (1991). A genetic study of male sexual orientation. *Archives of General Psychiatry, 48,* 1089–1096.

Bajor, J. K., & Baltes, P. B. (2003). The relationship between selection optimization with compensation, conscientiousness, motivation, and performance. *Journal of Vocational Behavior, 63*(3), 347–367.

Bakker, D. J. (2006). Treatment of developmental dyslexia: A review. *Pediatric Rehabilitation, 9*(1), 3–13.

Balk, D., Wogrin, C., Thornton, G., & Meagher, D. (2007). *Handbook of thanatology.* New York: Routledge/Taylor & Francis Group.

Ball, J. (2008). Aboriginal early language promotion and early intervention. In *Encyclopedia of language and literacy development* (pp. 1–8). London, ON: Canadian Language and Literacy Research Network. Retrieved from http://www.literacyencyclopedia.ca/pdfs/topic.php?topId=257

Ball, V., Corr, S., Knight, J., & Lowis, M. J. (2007). An investigation into the leisure occupations of older adults. *British Journal of Occupational Therapy, 70*(9), 393–400.

Ballmaier, M., et al. (2008). Hippocampal morphology and distinguishing late-onset from early-onset elderly depression. *American Journal of Psychiatry, 165*(2), 229–237.

Baltes, P. B., & Baltes, M. M. (1990). Psychological perspectives on successful aging: The model of selective optimization with compensation. In P. B. Baltes & M. M. Baltes (Eds.), *Successful aging: Perspectives from the behavioral sciences* (pp. 1–34). New York: Cambridge University Press.

Baltes, M., & Carstensen, L. L. (2003). The process of successful aging: Selection, optimization and compensation. In U. M. Staudinger, & U. Lindenberger (Eds.), *Understanding human development: Dialogues with lifespan psychology* (pp. 81–104). Dordrecht, Netherlands: Kluwer Academic Publishers.

Bancroft, J., Carnes, L., & Janssen, E. (2005a). Unprotected anal intercourse in HIV-positive and HIV-negative gay men: The relevance of sexual arousability, mood, sensation seeking, and erectile problems. *Archives of Sexual Behavior, 34,* 299–305.

Bancroft, J, Carnes, L. & Janssen, E., Goodrich, D., & Long, J. S. (2005b). Erectile and ejaculatory problems in gay and heterosexual men. *Archives of Sexual Behavior, 34,* 285–297.

Bandura, A. (1986). *Social foundations of thought and action: A social-cognitive theory.* Englewood Cliffs, NJ: Prentice Hall.

Bandura, A. (2006a). Going global with social cognitive theory: From prospect to paydirt. In S. I. Donaldson, D. E. Berger, & K. Pezdek (Eds.), *Applied psychology: New frontiers and rewarding careers* (pp. 53–79). Hillsdale, NJ: Lawrence Erlbaum Associates Publishers.

Bandura, A. (2006b). Toward a psychology of human agency. *Perspectives on Psychological Science, 1*(2), 164–180.

Bandura, A., Barbaranelli, C., Vittorio Caprara, G., & Pastorelli, C. (2001). Self-efficacy beliefs as shapers of children's aspirations and career trajectories. *Child Development, 72*(1), 187–206.

Barnard, C. J., Collins, S. A., Daisley, J. N., & Behnke, J. M. (2005). Maze performance and immunity costs in mice. *Behaviour, 142*(2), 241–263.

Barnett, J. E., & Dunning, C. (2003). Clinical perspectives on elderly sexuality. *Archives of Sexual Behavior, 32*(3), 295–296.

Barr, M. What is the period of PURPLE crying? Retrieved from http://www.purplecrying.info/what-is-the-period-of-purple-crying.php

Barr, R. G., Paterson, J. A., MacMartin, L. M., Lehtonen, L., & Young, S. N. (2005). Prolonged and unsoothable crying bouts in infants with and without colic. *Journal of Developmental & Behavioral Pediatrics, 26*(1), 14–23.

Barr, R., Rovee-Collier, C., & Campanella, J. (2005). Retrieval protracts deferred imitation by 6-month-olds. *Infancy, 7*(3), 263–283.

Barry, C. M., & Wentzel, K. R. (2006). Friend influence on prosocial behavior: The role of motivational factors and friendship characteristics. *Developmental Psychology, 42*(1), 153–163.

Barua, B., & Rovere, M. (2012). Canada's aging Medicare burden. *Fraser Forum*, May/June. Retrieved from http://www.fraserinstitute.org/uploadedFiles/fraser-ca/Content/research-news/research/articles/canadas-aging-medicare-burden.pdf

Basic Behavioral Science Task Force of the National Advisory Mental Health Council. (1996). Basic behavioral science research for mental health: Sociocultural and environmental practices. *American Psychologist, 51,* 722–731.

Batsche, G. M., & Porter, L. J. (2006). Bullying. In G. G. Bear & K. M. Minke (Eds.), *Children's needs III: Development, prevention, and intervention* (pp. 135–148). Washington, DC: National Association of School Psychologists.

Bauer, K. W., Yang, Y. W., & Austin, S. B. (2004). "How can we stay healthy when you're throwing all of this in front of us?" Findings from focus groups and interviews in middle schools on environmental influences on nutrition and physical activity. *Health Education and Behavior, 31*(1), 33–46.

Bauman, M. L., Anderson, G., Perry, E., & Ray, M. (2006). Neuroanatomical and neurochemical studies of the autistic brain: Current thought and future directions. In S. O. Moldin & J. L. R. Rubenstein (Eds.), *Understanding autism: From basic neuroscience to treatment* (pp. 303–322). Boca Raton, FL: CRC Press.

Baumrind, D. (1989). Rearing competent children. In W. Damon (Ed.), *Child development today and tomorrow.* San Francisco: Jossey-Bass.

Baumrind, D. (1991a). The influence of parenting style on adolescent competence and substance use. *Journal of Early Adolescence, 11,* 56–95.

Baumrind, D. (1991b). Parenting styles and adolescent development. In J. Brooks-Gunn, R. Lerner, & A. C. Petersen (Eds.), *Encyclopedia of adolescence.* New York: Garland.

Baumrind, D. (2005). Taking a stand in a morally pluralistic society: Constructive obedience and responsible dissent in moral/character education. In L. Nucci (Ed.), *Conflict, contradiction, and contrarian elements in moral development and education* (pp. 21–50). Mahwah, NJ: Erlbaum.

BC Partners for Mental Health and Addictions Information. (2004). *Wellness module 2: Stress and well-being.* Retrieved from http://www.heretohelp.bc.ca/skills/module2

Beaulieu, M-D., et al. (2008). When is knowledge ripe for primary care? *Evaluation & the Health Professions, 31*(1), 22–42.

Beck, E., Burnet, K. L., & Vosper, J. (2006). Birth-order effects on facets of extraversion. *Personality and Individual Differences, 40*(5), 953–959.

Becker, D. (2006). Therapy for the middle-aged: The relevance of existential issues. *American Journal of Psychotherapy, 60*(1), 87–99.

Bedford, V. H., & Avioli, P. S. (2006). "Shooting the bull": Cohort comparisons of fraternal intimacy in midlife and old age. In V. H. Bedford & B. Formaniak Turner (Eds.), *Men in relationships: A new look from a life course perspective* (pp. 81–101). New York: Springer Publishing Co.

Beidel, D. C., & Turner, S. M. (2007). Clinical presentation of social anxiety disorder in children and adolescents. In D. C. Beidel & S. M. Turner (Eds.), *Shy children, phobic adults: Nature and treatment of social anxiety disorders* (2nd ed.) (pp. 47–80). Washington, DC: American Psychological Association.

Beilei, L., Lei, L., Qi, D., & von Hofsten, C. (2002). The development of fine motor skills and their relations to children's academic achievement. *Acta Psychologica Sinica, 34*(5), 494–499.

Bell, J. H., & Bromnick, R. D. (2003). The social reality of the imaginary audience: A grounded theory approach. *Adolescence,* 38: 205–219.

Belsky, J. (2006a). Determinants and consequences of infant–parent attachment. In L. Balter & C. S. Tamis-LeMonda (Eds.), *Child psychology: A handbook of contemporary issues* (2nd ed.) (pp. 53–77). New York: Psychology Press.

Belsky, J., et al. (2007). Are there long-term effects of early child care? *Child Development, 78*(2), 681–701.

Beltrame, J. (2013, May 7). Unemployed kids a burden for boomer parents: Report. *Huffington Post*. Retrieved from http://www.huffingtonpost.ca/2013/05/07/baby-boomers-children-money_n_3230204.html

Bem, S. L. (1974). The measurement of psychological androgyny. *Journal of Consulting and Clinical Psychology, 42*, 155–162.

Bem, S. L. (1993). *The lenses of gender: Transforming the debate on sexual inequality.* New Haven, CT: Yale University Press.

Bender, H. L., et al. (2007). Use of harsh physical discipline and developmental outcomes in adolescence. *Development and Psychopathology, 19*(1) 227–242.

Bengtson, V. L., et al. (Eds.). (2005). *Sourcebook of family theory and research.* Thousand Oaks, CA: Sage Publications, Inc.

Berg, C. J., Chang, J., Callaghan, W. M., & Whitehead, S. J. (2003). Pregnancy-related mortality in the United States, 1991–1997. *Obstetrics and Gynecology, 101*, 289–296.

Berndt, T. J. (2004). Friendship and three A's (aggression, adjustment, and attachment). *Journal of Experimental Child Psychology, 88*(1), 1–4.

Berndt, T. J., Miller, K. E., & Park, K. E. (1989). Adolescents' perceptions of friends and parents' influence on aspects of their school adjustment. *Journal of Early Adolescence, 9,* 419–435.

Bernstein, I. M., et al. (2005). Maternal smoking and its association with birth weight. *Obstetrics & Gynecology, 106,* 986–991.

Berscheid, E. (2003). On stepping on land mines. In Sternberg, R. J. (Ed.). *Psychologists defying the crowd: Stories of those who battled the establishment and won*. (pp. 33–44). Washington, DC: American Psychological Association.

Berscheid, E. (2006). Searching for the meaning of "love." In R. J. Sternberg & K. Weis (Eds.), *The new psychology of love* (pp. 171–183). New Haven, CT: Yale University Press.

Bertoni, A., et al. (2007). Stress communication, dyadic coping and couple satisfaction: A cross-sectional and cross-cultural study. *Età Evolutiva, 86,* 58–66.

Bertrand, L. D., MacRae-Krisa, L. D., Costello, M., & Winterdyk, J. (2013). Ethnic diversity and youth offending: An examination of risk and protective factors. *International Journal of Child, Youth and Family Studies, 1*, 166–188.

Berzonsky, M. D. (2005). Ego identity: A personal standpoint in a postmodern world. *Identity, 5*(2), 125–136.

Berzonsky, M. D., & Kuk, L. S. (2005). Identity style, psychosocial maturity, and academic performance. *Personality and Individual Differences, 39*(1), 235–247.

Beth Israel Deaconess Medical Center. (2001). NICU programs benefit premature babies and their parents. Retrieved from http://www.bidmc.org/YourHealth/HealthNotes/WomensHealth/Pregnancy/NICUProgramsBenefitPrematureBabiesandTheirParents.aspx

Bialystok, E., & Senman, L. (2004). Executive processes in appearance–reality tasks: The role of inhibition of attention and symbolic representation. *Child Development, 75*(2), 562–579.

Bialystok, E. K., & Craik, F. I. M. (2007). Bilingualism and naming: Implications for cognitive assessment. *Journal of the International Neuropsychological Society, 13*(2), 209–211.

Bibby, R. (2004). *The Future Families Project: A survey of Canadian hopes and dreams.* Ottawa: Vanier Institute of the Family. Retrieved from http://www.vifamily.ca/node/177

Bielski, Z. (2012, June 8). Dating violence on the rise, Statistics Canada finds. *Globe and Mail*. Retrieved from http://www.theglobeandmail.com/life/relationships/dating-violence-on-the-rise-statistics-canada-finds/article4240601

Bird, A., Reese, E., & Tripp, G. (2006). Parent–child talk about past emotional events: Associations with child temperament and goodness-of-fit. *Journal of Cognition and Development, 7*(2), 189–210.

Bissell, M., & McKay, A. (2005). Taking action on chlamydia literature review. Retrieved from http://www.toronto.ca/health/sexualhealth/checkuponchlamydia/pdf/chlamydia_research_3.pdf

Black, D. W. (2007). Antisocial personality disorder, conduct disorder, and psychopathy. In J. E. Grant, & M. N. Potenza (Eds.), *Textbook of men's mental health* (pp. 143–170). Washington, DC: American Psychiatric Publishing, Inc.

Blackwell, D. L., & Lichter, D. T. (2004). Homogamy among dating, cohabiting, and married couples. *Sociological Quarterly, 45*(4), 719–737.

Blackwell, T. (2012, March 11). Downside of online dating: More STDs, some experts say. *National Post*. Retrieved from http://news.nationalpost

.com/2012/03/11/downside-of-online-dating-more-stds-some-experts-say/

Blass, E. M., & Camp, C. A. (2003). Changing determinants in 6- to 12-week-old human infants. *Developmental Psychobiology, 42*(3), 312–316.

Blazina, C., Eddins, R., Burridge, A., & Settle, A. G. (2007). The relationship between masculinity ideology, loneliness, and separation- individuation difficulties. *The Journal of Men's Studies, 15*(1), 101–109.

Boccia, M., & Campos, J. J. (1989). Maternal emotional signals, social referencing, and infants' reactions to strangers. In N. Eisenberg (Ed.), *New directions for child development,* No. 44, *Empathy and related emotional responses.* San Francisco: Jossey-Bass.

Bohlmeijer, E., Valenkamp, M., Westerhof, G., Smith, F., & Cuijpers, P. (2005). Creative reminiscence as an early intervention for depression. *Aging & Mental Health, 9*(4), 302–304.

Bohon, C., Garber, J., & Horowitz, J. L. (2007). Predicting school dropout and adolescent sexual behavior in offspring of depressed and nondepressed mothers. *Journal of the American Academy of Child & Adolescent Psychiatry, 46*(1), 15–24.

Boivin, M., Vitaro, F., & Poulin, F. (2005). Peer relationships and the development of aggressive behavior in early childhood. In R. E. Tremblay, W. W. Hartup, & J. Archer (Eds.), *Developmental origins of aggression* (pp. 376–397). New York: Guilford.

Boland, M. (2009). Exclusive breastfeeding should continue to six months. *Paediatrics & Child Health, 10*(3): 148. Retrieved from http://www.cps.ca/english/statements/n/breastfeedingmar05.htm

Bonanno, G. A., & Boerner, K. (2007). The stage theory of grief. *Journal of the American Medical Association, 297,* 2693.

Boom, J., Wouters, H., & Keller, M. (2007). A cross-cultural validation of stage development: A Rasch re-analysis of longitudinal socio-moral reasoning data. *Cognitive Development, 22*(2), 213–229.

Booth-LaForce, C., et al. (2006). Attachment, self-worth, and peer-group functioning in middle childhood. *Attachment & Human Development, 8*(4), 309–325.

Bosi, M. L., & de Oliveira, F. P. (2006). Bulimic behavior in adolescent athletes. In P. I. Swain (Ed.), *New developments in eating disorders research* (pp. 123–133). Hauppauge, NY: Nova Science Publishers.

Boston Children's Hospital. (2011). Newborn senses. Retrieved from http://www.childrenshospital.org/az/Site1356/mainpageS1356P0.html_

Bouchard, T. J., Jr., Lykken, D. T., McGue, M., Segal, N. L., & Tellegen, A. (1990). Sources of human psychological differences: The Minnesota study of twins reared apart. *Science, 250,* 223–228.

Bowlby, J. (1961). Processes of mourning. *International Journal of Psychoanalysis, 42,* 317–339.

Bowlby, J. (1988). *A secure base.* New York: Basic Books.

Bozionelos, N., & Wang, L. (2006). The relationship of mentoring and network resources with career success in the Chinese organizational environment. *International Journal of Human Resource Management, 17*(9), 1531–1546.

Braam, A. W., et al. (2008). God image and mood in old age. *Mental Health, Religion, & Culture, 11*(2), 221–237.

Bracht, M. (2007). Toilet training 101. *ParentsCanada.com.* Retrieved from http://www.parentscanada.com/developing/pre-school/articles.aspx? listingid=181

Bradley, R. H. (2006). The home environment. In N. F. Watt et al. (Eds.), *The crisis in youth mental health: Critical issues and effective programs,* Vol. 4, *Early intervention programs and policies, Child psychology and mental health* (pp. 89–120). Westport, CT: Praeger/Greenwood.

Brady, E. M. (2007). Review of adulthood: New terrain. *Educational Gerontology, 33*(1), 85–86.

Branco, J. C., & Lourenço, O. (2004). Cognitive and linguistic aspects in 5- to 6-year-olds' class-inclusion reasoning. *Psicologia Educação Cultura, 8*(2), 427–445.

Brandstätter, H., & Farthofer, A. (2003). Influence of part-time work on university students' academic performance. *Zeitschrift für Arbeits- und Organisationspsychologie, 47*(3), 134–145.

Brase, G. L. (2006). Cues of parental investment as a factor in attractiveness. *Evolution and Human Behavior, 27*(2), 145–157.

Brazier, A., & Rowlands, C. (2006). PKU in the family: Working together. *Clinical Child Psychology and Psychiatry, 11*(3), 483–488.

Bremner, A., & Bryant, P. (2001). The effect of spatial cues on infants' responses in the AB task, with and without a hidden object. *Developmental Science, 4*(4), 408–415.

Brennan, S., & Taylor-Butts, A. (2008). *Sexual assault in Canada: 2004 and* 2007. (Statistics Canada Catalogue no. 85F0033M). Canadian Centre for Justice Statistics Profile Series, no. 19. Retrieved from http://www.statcan.gc.ca/pub/85f0033m/85f0033m2008019-eng.pdf

Bridges, A. J. (2007). Successful living as a (single) woman. *Psychology of Women Quarterly, 31*(3), 327–328.

Bridges, L. J., Roe, A. E. C., Dunn, J., & O'Connor, T. G. (2007). Children's perspectives on their relationships with grandparents following parental separation: A longitudinal study. *Social Development, 16*(3), 539–554.

Briones, T. L., Klintsova, A. Y., & Greenough, W. T. (2004). Stability of synaptic plasticity in the adult rat visual cortex induced by complex environment exposure. *Brain Research, 1018*(1), 130–135.

British Columbia Ministry of Education. (2010). *Full Day Kindergarten Program Guide*. Retrieved from http://www.bced.gov.bc.ca/early_learning/fdk/pdfs/fdk_program_guide.pdf

Brockman, D. D. (2003). *From late adolescence to young adulthood.* Madison, CT: International Universities Press, Inc.

Bronfenbrenner, U., & Morris, P. A. (2006). The bioecological model of human development. In R. M. Lerner & W. Damon (Eds.), *Handbook of child psychology* (6th ed.), Vol. 1, *Theoretical models of human development* (pp. 793–828). Hoboken, NJ: Wiley.

Bronson, G. W. (1990). Changes in infants' visual scanning across the 2- to 14-week age period. *Journal of Experimental Child Psychology, 49,* 101–125.

Bronson, G. W. (1991). Infant differences in rate of visual encoding. *Child Development, 62,* 44–54.

Bronson, G. W. (1997). The growth of visual capacity: Evidence from infant scanning patterns. *Advances in Infancy Research, 11,* 109–141.

Broomhall, H. S., & Winefield, A. H. (1990). A comparison of the affective well-being of young and middle-aged unemployed men matched for length of unemployment. *British Journal of Medical Psychology, 63*(1), 43–52.

Brown, R. (1973). *A first language: The early stages.* Cambridge, MA: Harvard University Press.

Brown, S. L., Lee, G. R., & Bulanda, J. R. (2006). Cohabitation among older adults. *Journals of Gerontology: Series B: Psychological Sciences and Social Sciences, 61B*(2), S71–S79.

Brownell, C. A., & Carriger, M. S. (1990). Changes in cooperation and self-other differentiation during the second year. *Child Development, 61,* 1164–1174.

Bruck, M., Ceci, S. J., & Principe, G. F. (2006). The child and the law. In K. Renninger, I. E. Sigel, W. Damon, & R. M. Lerner (Eds.), *Handbook of child psychology* (6th ed.), Vol. 4, *Child psychology in practice* (pp. 776–816). Hoboken, NJ: Wiley.

Brunner, L. C., Eshilian-Oates, L., & Kuo, T. Y. (2003). Hip fractures in adults. *American Family Physician, 67*(3), 537–543.

Bryden, P. J., Bruyn, J., & Fletcher, P. (2005). Handedness and health: An examination of the association between different handedness classifications and health disorders. *Laterality: Asymmetries of Body, Brain and Cognition, 10*(5), 429–440.

Budney, A. J., Vandrey, R. G., Hughes, J. R., Moore, B. A., & Bahrenburg, B. (2007). Oral delta-9-tetrahydrocannabinol suppresses cannabis withdrawal symptoms. *Drug and Alcohol Dependence, 86*(1), 22–29.

Bugental, D. B., & Happaney, K. (2004). Predicting infant maltreatment in low-income families: The interactive effects of maternal attributions and child status at birth. *Developmental Psychology, 40*(2), 234–243.

Buhl, H. M., Wittmann, S., & Noack, P. (2003). Child–parent relationship of university students and young employed adults. *Zeitschrift für Entwicklungspsychologie und Pädagogische Psychologie, 35*(3), 144–152.

Buote, V. M., Wood, E., & Pratt, M. (2009). Exploring similarities and differences between online and offline friendships: The role of attachment style. *Human Behavior, 25*, 560–567.

Burke, D. M., & Shafto, M. A. (2008). Language and aging. In F. I. M. Craik, & T. A. Salthouse (Eds.), *The handbook of aging and cognition* (3rd ed.) (pp. 373–443). New York: Psychology Press.

Bushman, B. J. (1998). Priming effects of media violence on the accessibility of aggressive constructs in memory. *Personality and Social Psychology Bulletin, 24*(5), 537–545.

Bushnell, E. W. (1993, June). *A dual-processing approach to cross-modal matching: Implications for development.* Paper presented at the Society for Research in Child Development, New Orleans, LA.

Bushnell, I. W. R. (2001). Mother's face recognition in newborn infants: Learning and memory. *Infant and Child Development, 10*(1–2), 67–74.

Bushnik, T. (2006). *Child care in Canada.* (Statistics Canada, Catalogue no. 89-599-MIE — No. 003). Retrieved from http://www.statcan.gc.ca/pub/89-599-m/89-599-m2006003-eng.pdf

Buss, D. M. (1994). *The evolution of desire: Strategies of human mating.* New York: Basic Books.

Buss, D. M. (Ed.). (2005). *The handbook of evolutionary psychology.* Hoboken, NJ: John Wiley & Sons, Inc.

Buss, D. M., & Duntley, J. D. (2006). The evolution of aggression. In M. Schaller, J. A. Simpson, & D. T. Kenrick (Eds.), *Evolution and social psychology: Frontiers of social psychology* (pp. 263–285). Madison, CT: Psychosocial Press.

Buston, K., Williamson, L., & Hart, G. (2007). Young women under 16 years with experience of sexual intercourse: Who becomes pregnant? *Journal of Epidemiology & Community Health, 61*(3) 221–225.

Butler, M., Tiedemann, M., Nicol, J., & Valiquet, D. (2013). *Euthanasia and assisted suicide in Canada*. Ottawa: Parliamentary Information and Research Service. Retrieved from http://www.parl.gc.ca/Content/LOP/ResearchPublications/2010-68-e.pdf

Butterfield, S. A., & Loovis, E. M. (1993). Influence of age, sex, balance, and sport participation on development of throwing by children in grades K–8. *Perceptual and Motor Skills, 76,* 459–464.

Butler, R. N. (2002). The life review. *Journal of Geriatric Psychology, 35*(1), 7–10.

Buunk, B. P., et al. (2002). Age and gender differences in mate selection criteria for various involvement levels. *Personal Relationships, 9*(3), 271–278.

Bye, D., Pushkar, D., & Conway, M. (2007). Motivation, interest, and positive affect in traditional and nontraditional undergraduate students. *Adult Education Quarterly, 57*(2), 141–158.

Bynum, M. S. (2007). African American mother–daughter communication about sex and daughters' sexual behavior: Does college racial composition make a difference? *Cultural Diversity & Ethnic Minority Psychology, 13*(2), 151–160.

C

Callahan, J. J. (2007). Sandwich anyone? *Gerontologist, 47*(4), 569–571.

Calvert, S. L., & Kotler, J. A. (2003). Lessons from children's television: The impact of the Children's Television Act on children's learning. *Journal of Applied Developmental Psychology, 24*(3), 275–335.

Campanella, J., & Rovee-Collier, C. (2005). Latent learning and deferred imitation at 3 months. *Infancy, 7*(3), 243–262.

Campbell, A., Shirley, L., & Caygill, L. (2002). Sex-typed preferences in three domains: Do two-year-olds need cognitive variables? *British Journal of Psychology, 93*(2), 203–217.

Campbell, A., Shirley, L., Heywood, C., & Crook, C. (2000). Infants' visual preference for sex-congruent babies, children, toys and activities: A longitudinal study. *British Journal of Developmental Psychology, 18*(4), 479–498.

Campbell, D. W., Eaton, W. O., & McKeen, N. A. (2002). Motor activity level and behavioural control in young children. *International Journal of Behavioral Development, 26*(4), 289–296.

Campbell, S. B., et al. (2004). The course of maternal depressive symptoms and maternal sensitivity as predictors of attachment security at 36 months. *Development and Psychopathology, 16*(2), 231–252.

Campos, J. J., Hiatt, S., Ramsey, D., Henderson, C., & Svejda, M. (1978). The emergence of fear on the visual cliff. In M. Lewis & L. Rosenblum (Eds.), *The origins of affect.* New York: Plenum.

Campos, J. J., Langer, A., & Krowitz, A. (1970). Cardiac responses on the visual cliff in prelocomotor human infants. *Science, 170,* 196–197.

Campos, P. (2013). What is the semicolon project? Retrieved from http://kisselpaso.com/what-is-the-semicolon-project/

Camras, L. A., et al. (2007). Do infants show distinct negative facial expressions for fear and anger? Emotional expression in 11-month-old European American, Chinese, and Japanese Infants. *Infancy, 11*(2), 131–155.

Canadian Cancer Society. (2007, January 18). Smoking rates dropping, but lung cancer deaths still leading cause of cancer death. Media release. Retrieved from http://www.cancer.ca/Canada-wide/About%20us/Media%20centre/CW-Media%20releases/CW-2007/Smoking%20rates%20dropping%20%20but%20lung%20cancer%20deaths%20still%20leading%20cause%20of%20cancer%20death.aspx?sc_lang=en

Canadian Cancer Society. (2013). Cancer statistics at a glance. Retrieved from http://www.cancer.ca/en/cancer-information/cancer-101/cancer-statistics-at-a-glance/?region=on

Canadian Cystic Fibrosis Foundation. (2010). About cystic fibrosis. Retrieved from http://www.cysticfibrosis.ca/en/aboutCysticFibrosis/index.php

Canadian Erectile Difficulties Resource Centre. (2013). So how do I know if I have erectile difficulties? Retrieved from http://www.edhelp.ca/en/men/how/

Canadian Federation for Sexual Health. (2007). *Sexual health in Canada: Baseline 2007.* Retrieved from http://www.cfsh.ca/files/publications/sexual_health_in_canada_baseline_2007_final.pdf

Canadian Foundation for the Study of Infant Deaths. (2010). Babies' 'flat heads' can be prevented: Health coalition—Growing public awareness of SIDS prompts concern about positional plagiocephaly. Retrieved from http://www.sidscanada.org/resource-news 4html

Canadian Geographic. (2010). Who we are: Canada by demographics—Top 10 languages. *The Canadian Atlas Online.* Retrieved from http://magazine.canadiangeographic.ca/Atlas/themes.aspx?id=whoweare&sub=whoweare_demographics_work&lang=En

Canadian Hospice Palliative Care Association (2010). *Fact Sheet: Hospice palliative care in Canada.* Retrieved from http://www.chpca.net/resource_doc_library/Fact_Sheet_HPC_in_Canada.pdf

Canadian Institute for Health Information. (2010a). *National Health Expenditure Trends, 1975 to 2010. Table E.1.6–E.1.11 Estimate of Total Provincial/Territorial Government Health Expenditures by Age and Sex, by Province/Territory and Canada (2003–2008).* Ottawa: CIHI.

Canadian Institute for Health Information. (2010b). *National Health Expenditure Trends, 1975 to 2010. Appendix C.9–C.14. Population by Age and Sex, by Province/Territory and Canada (2003–2008).* Ottawa: CIHI.

Canadian Institute for Health Information. (2013). *Canadian Organ Replacement Register Annual Report: Treatment of End-Stage Organ Failure in Canada, 2002 to 2011.* Ottawa: CIHI. Retrieved from https://secure.cihi.ca/free_products/2013_CORR_Annua_Report_EN.pdf

Canadian Institute of Child Health. (2010). The health of Canada's children: A CICH profile—Low birth weight. Retrieved from http://www.cich.ca/PDFFiles/ProfileFactSheets/English/LBWEng.pdf

Canadian Lung Association. (2012). Children and second-hand smoke. Retrieved from http://www.lung.ca/protect-protegez/tobacco-tabagisme/second-secondaire/children-enfants_e.php

Canadian Medical Association. (2007). Euthanasia and assisted suicide (Update 2007). CMA policy. Retrieved from http://policybase.cma.ca/dbtw-wpd/Policypdf/PD07-01.pdf

Canadian Mental Health Association. (2013a). Children and depression. Retrieved from http://www.cmha.ca/mental_health/children-and-depression

Canadian Mental Health Association. (2013b). Eating disorders. Retrieved from http://www.cmha.ca/mental-health/understanding-mental-illness/eating-disorders/

Canadian Mental Health Association. (2013c). Fast facts about mental illness. Retrieved from http://www.cmha.ca/media/fast-facts-about-mental-illness/#.UguRfdKTiSo

Canadian Mental Health Association. (2013d). Youth and suicide. Retrieved from http://www.cmha.ca/mental_health/youth-and-suicide/#.Uicv-tKTiSo

Canadian Paediatric Society. (2007). Bedwetting. Retrieved from http://www.cps.ca/caringforkids/growing&learning/bedwetting.htm

Canadian Paediatric Society. (2010, June 24). When your child is sick. Retrieved from http://www.cps.ca/caringforkids!whensick/colds.htm

Canadian Paediatric Society. (2013a). Growing up: Information for boys about puberty. Retrieved from http://www.caringforkids.cps.ca/handouts/information_for_boys_about_puberty

Canadian Paediatric Society. (2013b). Growing up: Information for girls about puberty. Retrieved from http://www.caringforkids.cps.ca/handouts/information_for_girls_about_puberty

Canadian PKU and Allied Disorders. (2008). About PKU. Retrieved from http://www.canpku.org/

Canadian Psychological Association. (2000). *Canadian code of ethics for psychologists* (3rd ed.). Retrieved (May 12, 2010) from http://www.cpa.ca/cpasite/userfiles/Documents/Canadian%20Code%20of%20Ethics%20for%20Psycho.pdf

Canadian Psychological Association. (2011). Survey findings: Canadians face "significant barriers" to accessing psychological care: National poll. Retrieved from http://www.cpa.ca/polls./

Canadian Women's Health Network. (2006). Hormone therapy (HT). Retrieved from http://www.cwhn.ca/en/print/node/40788

Cancer Care Ontario. (2013). Screen for life. Retrieved from https://www.cancercare.on.ca/pcs/screening/

Candy, T. R., Crowell, J. A., & Banks, M. S. (1998). Optical, receptoral, and retinal constraints on foveal and peripheral vision in the human neonate. *Vision Research, 38*(24), 3857–3870.

Canitano, R. (2007). Epilepsy in autism spectrum disorders. *European Child & Adolescent Psychiatry, 16*(1), 61–66.

Caplan, M., Vespo, J., Pedersen, J., & Hale, D. F. (1991). Conflict and its resolution in small groups of one and two-year-olds. *Child Development, 62,* 1513–1524.

Capron, C., Thérond, C., & Duyme, M. (2007). Brief report: Effect of menarcheal status and family structure on depressive symptoms and emotional/behavioural problems in young adolescent girls. *Journal of Adolescence, 30*(1), 175–179.

Carey, B. (2006). The rules of attraction in the game of love. LiveScience.com. Retrieved from http://www.livescience.com/7023-rules-attraction-game-love.html

Carey, B. (2007a, March 26). Poor behavior is linked to time in day care. *New York Times* online.

Carey, B. (2007b, June 22). Research finds firstborns gain the higher I.Q. *The New York Times* online.

CaringBridge. (2013). About us. Retrieved from http://www.caringbridge.org/about

Carmichael, D. (2008). *Youth sport vs. youth crime.* Retrieved from http://www.isrm.co.uk/news/docs/132 Sport%20and%20Crime.pdf

Carrère, S., Buehlman, K. T., Gottman, J. M., Coan, J. A., & Ruckstuhl, L. (2000). Predicting marital stability and divorce in newlywed couples. *Journal of Family Psychology, 14*(1), 42–58.

Carroll, J. S., et al. (2007). So close, yet so far away: The impact of varying marital horizons on emerging adulthood. *Journal of Adolescent Research, 22*(3), 219–247.

Carver, L. J., & Vaccaro, B. G. (2007). 12-month-old infants allocate increased neural resources to stimuli associated with negative adult emotion. *Developmental Psychology, 43*(1), 54–69.

Casas, J. F., et al. (2006). Early parenting and children's relational and physical aggression in the preschool and home contexts. *Journal of Applied Developmental Psychology, 27*(3), 209–227.

Casini, A., & Sanchez-Mazas, M. (2005). "This job is not for me!": The impact of the gender norm and the organizational culture on professional upward mobility. *Cahiers Internationaux de Psychologie Sociale, Sep-Dec Vol* (67–68), 101–112.

Cassia, V. M., Simion, F., & Umilta, C. (2001). Face preference at birth: The role of an orienting mechanism. *Developmental Science, 4*(1), 101–108.

Caton, D., et al. (2002). Anesthesia for childbirth: Controversy and change. *American Journal of Obstetrics & Gynecology, 186*(5), S25–S30.

Cattell, R. B. (1949). *The culture-fair intelligence test.* Champaign, IL: Institute for Personality and Ability Testing.

Caudle, D. D., et al. (2007). Cognitive errors, symptom severity, and response to cognitive behavior therapy in older adults with generalized anxiety disorder. *American Journal of Geriatric Psychiatry, 15*(8), 680–689.

Caulfield, R. (2000). Beneficial effects of tactile stimulation on early development. *Early Childhood Education Journal, 27*(4), 255–257.

Cavallini, A., et al. (2002). Visual acuity in the first two years of life in healthy term newborns: An experience with the Teller Acuity Cards. *Functional Neurology: New Trends in Adaptive and Behavioral Disorders, 17*(2), 87–92.

Cavell, T. A. (2001). Updating our approach to parent training. I. The case against targeting noncompliance. *Clinical Psychology: Science and Practice, 8*(3), 299–318.

CBC Digital Archives. (2013). Umbilical cord blood: Stem cells for the future? Retrieved from http://www.cbc.ca/archives/categories/science-technology/biotechnology/stem-cells-scientific-promise-ethical-protest-1/umbilical-cord-blood-stem-cells-for-the-future.html

CBC News. (2000, August 20). Mother who killed son dies of injuries. Retrieved from http://www.cbc.ca/news/canada/story/2000/08/20/subway_000820.html

CBC News. (2003, March 17). Father calls sickle cell anemia 'neglected' disease. Retrieved from http://www.cbc.ca/health/story/2003/03/17/sickle_cell030317.html

CBC News. (2007a, September 12). Married people outnumbered for first time: Census. Retrieved from http://www.cbc.ca/canada/story/2007/09/12/censusfamilies.html

CBC News. (2007b, April 20). *Newborn screening.* Retrieved from http://www.cbc.ca/news/background/health/newborn_screen.html

CBC News. (2008, January 14). Life expectancy hits 80.4 years: Statistics Canada. Retrieved from http://www.cbc.ca/canada/story/2008/01/14/death-stats.html

CBC News. (2009a, February 5). Assisted human reproduction: Regulating and treating conception problems. Retrieved from http://www.cbc.ca/health/story/2009/02/05/f-reprotech. html

CBC News. (2009b, February 11). Daycare: The debate over space. Retrieved from http://www.cbc.ca/news/story/2009/02/06/f-daycare.html

CBC News. (2010, July 13). Quebec to pay for IVF treatment. Retrieved from http://www.cbc.ca/canada/montreal/story/2010/07/13/quebec-ivf-treatment.html

CBC News. (2012a, October 12). Inside Gloria Taylor's battle for the right to die. Retrieved from http://www.canada.com/news/Only+cent+doctors+would+perform+euthanasia+legal+poll+finds/7939308/story.html

CBC News. (2012, October 17). Socializing key to "successful aging." Retrieved from http://www.cbc.ca/news/health/socializing-key-to-successful-aging-1.1260922

CBC News. (2013, April 10). Dad shattered over death of Rehtaeh Parsons. Retrieved from http://www.cbc.ca/news/canada/nova-scotia/story/2013/04/10/ns-reteah-parsons-father.html

Cellarius, V. (2008). Terminal sedation and the "imminence condition." *Journal of Medical Ethics, 34*(2), 69–72.

Centers for Disease Control and Prevention. (2005). National Center for Health Statistics. *America's children, 2005. America's children: Key national indicators of well-being 2005*. Childstats.gov. Retrieved from http://www.childstats.gov/amchildren05/hea8.asp.

Centers for Disease Control and Prevention. (2006). HIV/AIDS Surveillance Report, 2005, v. 17. Atlanta: U.S. Department of Health and Human Services, Centers for Disease Control and Prevention. Retrieved from http://www.cdc.gov/hiv/topics/surveillance/ resources/reports/.

Centre for Addiction and Mental Health. (2009). *Responding to older adults with substance use, mental health and gambling challenges.* Retrieved from http://www.camh.net/Publications/Resources_for_Professionals/Older_Adults/index.html

Centre for Research on Youth at Risk. (n.d.). *Restorative justice fact sheet.* Retrieved from http://www.stthomasu.ca/research/youth/restorative.htm

Chalmers, B., Kaczorowski, J., O'Brien, B., & Royle, C. (2012). Rates of interventions in labor and birth across Canada: Findings of the Canadian Maternity Experiences Survey. *Birth: Issues in Perinatal Care, 39*(3), 203–210. doi:10.1111/j.1523-536X.2012.00549.x

Chapman, M., & McBride, M. C. (1992). Beyond competence and performance: Children's class inclusion strategies, superordinate class cues, and verbal justifications. *Developmental Psychology, 28,* 319–327.

Charles, S. T., & Carstensen, L. L. (2007). Emotion regulation and aging. In J. J. Gross (Ed.), *Handbook of emotion regulation* (pp. 307–327). New York: Guilford Press.

Charles, S. T., Reynolds, C. A., & Gatz, M. (2001). Age-related differences and change in positive and negative affect over 23 years. *Journal of Personality and Social Psychology, 80,* 136–151.

Charlton, R. (2004). Ageing male syndrome, andropause, androgen decline or mid-life crisis? *Journal of Men's Health & Gender, 1*(1), 55–59.

Charness, N., & Schaie, K. W. (2003). *Impact of technology on successful aging*. New York: Springer.

Chaudieu, I., et al. (2008). Abnormal reactions to environmental stress in elderly persons with anxiety disorders. *Journal of Affective Disorders, 106*(3), 307–313.

Cheng, H., & Furnham, A. (2002). Personality, peer relations, and self-confidence as predictors of happiness and loneliness. *Journal of Adolescence, 25*(3), 327–339.

Cheng, S-T., & Chan, A. C. M. (2007). Multiple pathways from stress to suicidality and the protective effect of social support in Hong Kong adolescents. *Suicide and Life-Threatening Behavior, 37*(2), 187–196.

Chesley, N., & Moen, P. (2006). When workers care: Dual-earner couples' caregiving strategies, benefit use, and psychological well- being. *American Behavioral Scientist, 49*(9), 1248–1269.

Chess, S., & Thomas, A. (1991). Temperament. In M. Lewis (Ed.), *Child and adolescent psychiatry: A comprehensive textbook.* Baltimore: Williams & Wilkins.

Child Welfare Information Gateway. (2013). *Long-term consequences of child abuse and neglect.* Washington, DC: U.S. Department of Health and Human Services, Children's Bureau.

Choi, J. S., Koren, G., & Nulman, I. Pregnancy and isotretinoin therapy. *CMAJ: Canadian Medical Association Journal, 185*(5), 411–413.

Chong, L., McDonald, H., & Strauss, E. (2004). Deconstructing aging. *Science, 305*(5689), 1419.

Chou, T-L., et al. (2006). Developmental and skill effects on the neural correlates of semantic processing to visually presented words. *Human Brain Mapping, 27*(11), 915–924.

Christian, P., et al. (2003). Effects of alternative maternal micronutrient supplements on low birth weight in rural Nepal: Double blind randomised community trial. *British Medical Journal, 326,* 571–576.

Christophersen, E. R., & Mortweet, S. L. (2003). Establishing bedtime. In E. R. Christophersen & S. L. Mortweet (Eds.), *Parenting that works: Building skills that last a lifetime* (pp. 209–228). Washington, DC: American Psychological Association.

Chronis, A. M., et al. (2007). Maternal depression and early positive parenting predict future conduct problems in young children with attention-deficit/hyperactivity disorder. *Developmental Psychology, 43*(1), 70–82.

Chua, A. (2011). *Battle hymn of the tiger mother*. New York: Penguin Press.

Clancy, B., & Finlay, B. (2001). Neural correlates of early language learning. In M. Tomasello & E. Bates (Eds.), *Language development: The essential readings.* Malden, MA: Blackwell.

Clark, E. V. (1973). What's in a word? On the child's acquisition of semantics in his first language. In E. Moore (Ed.), *Cognitive development and the acquisition of language.* New York: Academic Press.

Clark, E. V. (1975). Knowledge, context, and strategy in the acquisition of meaning. In D. P. Date (Ed.), *Georgetown University roundtable on language and linguistics.* Washington, DC: Georgetown University Press.

Clark, J. (2005). Sibling relationships: Theory and issues for practice. *Child & Family Social Work, 10*(1), 90–91.

Clark, J., & Rugg, S. (2005). The importance of independence in toileting. *British Journal of Occupational Therapy, 68*(4), 165–171.

Clark, R. (1983). *Family life and school achievement: Why poor black children succeed or fail.* Chicago: University of Chicago Press.

Clark, S., & Symons, D. (2000). A longitudinal study of Q-sort attachment security and self-processes at age five. *Infant and Child Development,* 9, 91–104.

Clark, W. (2009). Kids' sports. Retrieved from http://www.statcan.gc.ca/pub/11-008-x/2008001/article/10573-eng.htm

Clayton, R., & Crosby, R. A. (2006) Measurement in health promotion. In R. A. Crosby, R. J. DiClemente, & L. F. Salazar (Eds.), *Research methods in health promotion* (pp. 229–259). San Francisco: Jossey-Bass.

Cleary, D. J., Ray, G. E., LoBello, S. G., & Zachar, P. (2002). Children's perceptions of close peer relationships: Quality, congruence and meta-perceptions. *Child Study Journal, 32*(3), 179–192.

Clode, D. (2006). Review of A left-hand turn around the world: Chasing the mystery and meaning of all things southpaw. *Laterality: Asymmetries of Body, Brain and Cognition, 11*(6) 580–581.

Cnattingius, S. (2004). The epidemiology of smoking during pregnancy: Smoking prevalence, maternal characteristics, and pregnancy outcomes. *Nicotine & Tobacco Research, 6*(Supp. l2), S125–S140.

Coats, A. H., & Blanchard-Fields, F. (2008). Emotion regulation in interpersonal problems: The role of cognitive-emotional complexity, emotion regulation goals, and expressivity. *Psychology and Aging, 23*(1), 39–51.

Cochran, S. V. (2005). Assessing and treating depression in men. In G. E. Good, & G. R. Brooks (Eds.), *The new handbook of psychotherapy and counseling with men* (pp. 121–133). San Francisco: Jossey-Bass.

Cohen, L. S., et al. (2006). Relapse of major depression during pregnancy in women who maintain or discontinue antidepressant treatment. *Journal of the American Medical Association, 295*(5), 499–507.

Cohen, S. (2003). Psychosocial models of the role of social support in the etiology of physical disease. In P. Salovey & A. J. Rothman (Eds.), *Social psychology of health* (pp. 227–244). New York: Psychology Press.

Cohen-Bendahan, C. C. C., Buitelaar, J. K., van Goozen, S. H. M., & Cohen-Kettenis, P. T. (2004). Prenatal exposure to testosterone and functional cerebral lateralization: A study in same-sex and opposite-sex twin girls. *Psychoneuroendocrinology, 29*(7), 911–916.

Cohn, M., Emrich, S. M., & Moscovitch, M. (2008). Age-related deficits in associative memory. *Psychology and Aging, 23*(1), 93–103.

Cole, S., & Lanham, J. (2011). Failure to thrive: An update. *American Family Physician*, *83*(7), 829–834.

Coleman, P. K. (2003). Perceptions of parent–child attachment, social self-efficacy, and peer relationships in middle childhood. *Infant and Child Development, 12*(4), 351–368.

Collaer, M. L., & Hill, E. M. (2006). Large sex difference in adolescents on a timed line judgment task: Attentional contributors and task relationship to mathematics. *Perception, 35*(4), 561–572.

Collins, W. A., & Laursen, B. (2006). Parent–adolescent relationships. In P. Noller & J. A. Feeney (Eds.), *Close relationships: Functions, forms and processes* (pp. 111–125). Hove, England: Psychology Press/Taylor & Francis.

Collins, W. A., Maccoby, E. E., Steinberg, L., Hetherington, E. M., & Bornstein, M. H. (2003). Contemporary research on parenting: The case for nature and nurture. In M. E. Hertzig & E. A. Farber (Eds.), *Annual progress in child psychiatry and child development: 2000–2001* (pp. 125–153). New York: Brunner-Routledge.

Colombo, J. (1993). *Infant cognition.* Newbury Park, CA: Sage.

Commons, M. L. (2004). The state of the art on Perry and epistemological development? *Journal of Adult Development, 11*(2), 59–60.

Commons, M. L., Galaz-Fontes, J. F., & Morse, S. J. (2006). Leadership, cross- cultural contact, socio-economic status, and formal operational reasoning about moral dilemmas among Mexican non- literate adults and high school students. *Journal of Moral Education, 35*(2), 247–267

Conel, J. L. (1959). *The postnatal development of the human cerebral cortex, 5.* Cambridge, MA: Harvard University Press.

Conner, K. R., & Goldston, D. B. (2007). Rates of suicide among males increase steadily from age 11 to 21: Developmental framework and outline for prevention. *Aggression and Violent Behavior, 12*(2), 193–207.

Connolly, J., Furman, W., & Konarski, R. (2000). The role of peers in the emergence of heterosexual romantic relationships in adolescence. *Child Development, 71*(5), 1395–1408.

Connor, P. D., Sampson, P. D., Streissguth, A. P., Bookstein, F. L., & Barr, H. M. (2006). Effects of prenatal alcohol exposure on fine motor coordination and balance: A study of two adult samples. *Neuropsychologia, 44*(5), 744–751.

Conrad, P. (2007). *The medicalization of society: On the transformation of human conditions into treatable disorders.* Baltimore, MD: Johns Hopkins University Press.

Constantino, J. N., et al. (2006). Autistic social impairment in the siblings of children with pervasive developmental disorders. *American Journal of Psychiatry, 163*(2), 294–296.

Cooke, B. M., Breedlove, S. M., & Jordan, C. L. (2003). Both estrogen receptors and androgen receptors contribute to testosterone-induced changes in the morphology of the medial amygdala and sexual arousal in male rats. *Hormones & Behavior, 43*(2), 336–346.

Cooper, J., Appleby, L., & Amos, T. (2002). Life events preceding suicide by young people. *Social Psychiatry and Psychiatric Epidemiology, 37*(6), 271–275.

Coovadia, H. (2004). Antiretroviral agents: How best to protect infants from HIV and save their mothers from AIDS. *New England Journal of Medicine, 351*(3), 289–292.

Coren, S. (1992). *The left-hander syndrome.* New York: Free Press.

Corliss, R. (2003, January 20). Is there a formula for joy? *Time Magazine*, 44–46.

Cornwell, A. A., C., & Feigenbaum, P. (2006). Sleep biological rhythms in normal infants and those at high risk for SIDS. *Chronobiology International, 23*(5), 935–961.

Costello, E. J., Sung, M., Worthman, C., & Angold, A. (2007). Pubertal maturation and the development of alcohol use and abuse. *Drug and Alcohol Dependence, 88*, S50–S59.

Costigan, C. L., Cauce, A. M., & Etchison, K. (2007). Changes in African American mother– daughter relationships during adolescence: Conflict, autonomy, and warmth. In B. J. R. Leadbeater & N. Way (Eds.), *Urban girls revisited: Building strengths* (pp. 177–201). New York: New York University Press.

Courage, M. L., Howe, M. L., & Squires, S. E. (2004). Individual differences in 3.5-month olds' visual attention: What do they predict at 1 year? *Infant Behavior and Development, 27*(1), 19–30.

Cowan, P. A., & Cowan, C. P. (2005). Five- domain models: Putting it all together. In P. A. Cowan, C. P. Cowan, J. C. Ablow, V. K. Johnson, & J. R. Measelle (Eds.), *The family context of parenting in children's adaptation to elementary school, Monographs in parenting series* (pp. 315–333). Mahwah, NJ: Erlbaum.

Cramer, D. (2003). Facilitativeness, conflict, demand for approval, self-esteem, and satisfaction with romantic relationships. *Journal of Psychology, 137*(1), 85–98.

Crenshaw, D. A. (2007). Life span issues and assessment and intervention. In D. Balk, et al. (Eds.), *Handbook of thanatology* (pp. 227–234). New York: Routledge/Taylor & Francis Group.

Crombie, G., & Desjardins, M. J. (1993, March). *Predictors of gender: The relative importance of children's play, games, and personality characteristics.* Paper presented at the meeting of the Society for Research in Child Development, New Orleans, LA.

Crowther, C., et al. (2006). Neonatal respiratory distress syndrome after repeat exposure to antenatal corticosteroids: A randomised control trial. *Lancet, 367*(9526), 1913–1919.

Cruz, N. V., & Bahna, S. L. (2006). Do foods or additives cause behavior disorders? *Psychiatric Annals, 36*(10), 724–732.

CTV News. (2012, November 2). "Ageism" widespread, survey finds. Retrieved from http://www.ctvnews.ca/canada/ageism-widespread-in-canada-survey-finds-1.1021641

Cuellar, J., & Curry, T. R. (2007). The prevalence and comorbidity between delinquency, drug abuse, suicide attempts, physical and sexual abuse, and self-mutilation among delinquent Hispanic females. *Hispanic Journal of Behavioral Sciences, 29*(1), 68–82.

Cumming, S. P., Eisenmann, J. C., Smoll, F. L., Smith, R. E., & Malina, R. M. (2005). Body size and perceptions of coaching behaviors by adolescent female athletes. *Psychology of Sport and Exercise, 6*(6), 693–705.

Cunningham, R. L., & McGinnis, M. Y. (2007). Factors influencing aggression toward females by male rats exposed to anabolic androgenic steroids during puberty. *Hormones and Behavior, 51*(1), 135–141.

Curtis, S. (2012). Early puberty is on the rise. Retrieved from http://www.parentscanada.com/school/early-puberty-is-on-the-rise

D

D'Augelli, A. R., Grossman, A. H., Hershberger, S. L., & O' Connell, T. S. (2001). Aspects of mental health among older lesbian, gay, and bisexual adults. *Aging & Mental Health, 5*(2), 149–158.

Daman-Wasserman, M., Brennan, B., Radcliffe, F., Prigot, J., & Fagen, J. (2006). Auditory-visual context and memory retrieval in 3-month-old infants. *Infancy, 10*(3) 201–220.

Damon, W. (1991). Adolescent self-concept. In R. M. Lerner, A. C. Petersen, & J. Brooks-Gunn (Eds.), *Encyclopedia of adolescence.* New York: Garland.

Dandy, J., & Nettelbeck, T. (2002). The relationship between IQ, homework, aspirations and academic achievement for Chinese, Vietnamese and Anglo-Celtic Australian school children. *Educational Psychology, 22*(3), 267–276.

Dane, S., & Erzurumluoglu, A. (2003). Sex and handedness differences in eye–hand visual reaction times in handball players. *International Journal of Neuroscience, 113*(7), 923–929.

Dang-Vu, T. T., Desseilles, M., Peigneux, P., & Maquet, P. (2006). A role for sleep in brain plasticity. *Pediatric Rehabilitation, 19*(2) 98–118.

Daniels, S. R. (2006). The consequences of childhood overweight and obesity. *The Future of Children, 16*(1), 47–67.

Davis, L., Edwards, H., Mohay, H., & Wollin, J. (2003). The impact of very premature birth on the psychological health of mothers. *Early Human Development, 73*(1–2), 61–70.

De Beni, R., Borella, E., & Carretti, B. (2007). Reading comprehension in aging: The role of working memory and metacomprehension. *Aging, Neuropsychology, and Cognition, 14*(2), 189–212.

De Haan, M., & Groen, M. (2006). Neural bases of infants' processing of social information in faces. In P. J. Marshall & N. A. Fox (Eds.), *The development of social engagement: Neurobiological perspectives. Series in affective science* (pp. 46–80). New York: Oxford University Press.

de Villiers, J. G., & de Villiers, P. A. (1999). Language development. In M. H. Bornstein & M. E. Lamb (Eds.), *Developmental psychology: An advanced textbook* (4th ed.) (pp. 313–373). Mahwah, NJ: Erlbaum.

Deary, I. J., Whiteman, M. C., Starr, J. M., Whalley, L. J., & Fox, H. C. (2004). The impact of childhood intelligence on later life: Following up the Scottish mental surveys of 1932 and 1947. *Journal of Personality and Social Psychology, 86*(1), 130–147.

DeCasper, A. J., & Fifer, W. P. (1980). Of human bonding: Newborns prefer their mothers' voices. *Science, 208,* 1174–1176.

DeCasper, A. J., & Spence, M. J. (1991). Auditorially mediated behavior during the perinatal period: A cognitive view. In M. J. Weiss & P. R. Zelazo (Eds.), *Infant attention* (pp. 142–176). Norwood, NJ: Ablex.

de Guzman, M. R. T. (2007). Friendship, peer influence, and peer pressure during the teenage years. *NebGuide.* Retrieved from http://www.ianrpubs.unl.edu/live/g1751/build/g1751.pdf

Delgado, A. R., & Prieto, G. (2004). Cognitive mediators and sex-related differences in mathematics. *Intelligence, 32*(1), 25–32.

Demont, J. (2012, September 5). It cost a lot to die in Nova Scotia, survey says. *Chronicle Herald.* Retrieved from http://thechronicleherald.ca/business/133001-it-costs-a-lot-to-die-in-nova-scotia-survey-says

Dennerstein, L., & Goldstein, I. (2005). Postmenopausal female sexual dysfunction: At a crossroads. *Journal of Sexual Medicine,* 2(Suppl3), 116–117.

Department of Justice Canada. (2009). *If your child is in trouble with the law.* Retrieved from http://www.justice.gc.ca/eng/pi/yj-jj/information/information.html

Department of Justice Canada. (2013). Age of consent to sexual activity: Frequently asked questions. Retrieved from http://www.justice.gc.ca/eng/rp-pr/other-autre/clp/faq.html

Depp, C. A., & Jeste, D. V. (2006). Definitions and predictors of successful aging: A comprehensive review of larger quantitative studies. *American Journal of Geriatric Psychiatry, 14,* 6–20.

Depression and Bipolar Support Alliance. (n.d.) Postpartum depression. Retrieved from http://www.dbsalliance.org/site/PageServer?pagename=education_depression_postpartum&gclid=CPWSrr3KgrkCFYtDMgodKjoAM

Derby, C. A. (2000, October 2). Cited in Study finds exercise reduces the risk of impotence. *The Associated Press.*

Dezoete, J. A., MacArthur, B. A., & Tuck, B. (2003). Prediction of Bayley and Stanford– Binet scores with a group of very low birth-weight children. *Child: Care, Health and Development, 29*(5), 367–372.

DiLalla, D. L., Gottesman, I. I., Carey, G., & Bouchard, T. J., Jr. (1999). Heritability of MMPI Harris–Lingoes and Subtle–Obvious subscales in twins reared apart. *Assessment, 6*(4), 353–366.

Disabled World. (2008). Height chart of men and women in difference countries. Retrieved from http://www.disabled-world.com/artman/publish/height-chart.shtml#ixzz12uF838KX

Dishion, T. J., & Stormshak, E. A. (2007). Family and peer social interaction. In T. J. Dishion & E. A. Stormshak. (Eds.), *Intervening in children's lives: An ecological, family-centered approach to mental health care* (pp. 31–48). Washington, DC: American Psychological Association.

Doherty, W. J., Carroll, J. S.,& Waite, L. J. (2007). In A. S. Loveless & T. B. Holman (Eds.), Supporting the institution of marriage: Ideological, research, and ecological perspectives. *The family in the new millennium: World voices supporting the "natural" clan Vol 2: Marriage and human dignity* (pp. 21–51). Praeger perspectives. Westport, CT: Praeger Publishers/Greenwood Publishing Group.

Dollfus, S., et al. (2005). Atypical hemispheric specialization for language in right-handed schizophrenia patients. *Biological Psychiatry, 57*(9), 1020–1028.

Dombrowski, M. A. S., et al. (2000). Kangaroo skin-to-skin care for premature twins and their adolescent parents. *American Journal of Maternal/Child Nursing, 25*(2), 92–94.

Donald, M., et al. (2006). Risk and protective factors for medically serious suicide attempts. *Australian and New Zealand Journal of Psychiatry, 40*(1), 87–96.

Donohue, K. F., Curtin, J. J., Patrick, C. J., & Lang, A. R. (2007). Intoxication level and emotional response. *Emotion, 7*(1), 103–112.

Donovan, D. M., & Wells, E. A. (2007). "Tweaking 12-Step": The potential role of 12-Step self-help group involvement in methamphetamine recovery. *Addiction, 102*(Suppl. 1), 121–129 .

Dorling, J., et al. (2006). Data collection from very low birthweight infants in a geographical region: Methods, costs, and trends in mortality, admission rates, and resource utilisation over a five–year period. *Early Human Development, 82*(2), 117–124.

Doron, H., & Markovitzky, G. (2007). Family structure and patterns and psychological adjustment to immigration in Israel. *Journal of Ethnic & Cultural Diversity in Social Work, 15*(1–2), 215–235.

Drasgow, E., Halle, J. W., & Phillips, B. (2001). Effects of different social partners on the discriminated requesting of a young child with autism and severe language delays. *Research in Developmental Disabilities, 22*(2), 125–139.

Drewett, R., Blair, P., Emmett, P., Emond, A., & The ALSPAC Study Team. (2004). Failure to thrive in the term and preterm infants of mothers depressed in the postnatal period: A population-based birth cohort study. *Journal of Child Psychology and Psychiatry and Allied Disciplines, 45*(2), 359–366.

Drigotas, S. M., Rusbult, C. E., & Verette, J. (1999). Level of commitment, mutuality of commitment, and couple well-being. *Personal Relationships, 6*(3) 389–409.

Duberstein, P. R., Pálsson, S. P., Waern, M., & Skoog, I. (2008). Personality and risk for depression in a birth cohort of 70-year-olds followed for 15 years. *Psychological Medicine, 38*(5), 663–671.

Duffy, R. D., & Sedlacek, W. E. (2007). What is most important to students' long-term career choices. *Journal of Career Development, 34*(2), 149–163.

Duggan, A., et al. (2004). Evaluating a statewide home visiting program to prevent child abuse in at-risk families of newborns: Fathers' participation and outcomes. *Child Maltreatment: Journal of the American Professional Society on the Abuse of Children, 9*(1), 3–17.

Dumas, J. A., & Hartman, M. (2003). Adult age differences in temporal and item memory. *Psychology and Aging, 18*(3), 573–586.

Dunn, J., Davies, L. C., O'Connor, T. G., & Sturgess, W. (2001). Family lives and friendships: The perspectives of children in step-, single-parent, and nonstep families. *Journal of Family Psychology, 15*(2), 272–287.

Duplassie, D., & Daniluk, J. C. (2007). Sexuality: Young and middle adulthood. In M S. Tepper & A. F. Owens (Eds.), *Sexual health Vol. 1: Psychological foundations* (pp. 263–289). *Praeger perspectives: Sex, love, and psychology.* Westport, CT: Praeger Publishers/Greenwood Publishing Group.

Dupuis-Blanchard, S. M. (2008). Social engagement in relocated older adults. *Dissertation Abstracts International: Section B: The Sciences and Engineering. 68*(7-B), 4387.

Durkin, S. J., Paxton, S. J., & Sorbello, M. (2007). An integrative model of the impact of exposure to idealized female images on adolescent girls' body satisfaction. *Journal of Applied Social Psychology, 37*(5), 1092–1117.

Dyer, S. J. (2007). The value of children in African countries—Insights from studies on infertility. *Journal of Psychosomatic Obstetrics & Gynecology, 28*(2), 69–77.

E

Eccles, J. S., et al. (2000). Gender-role socialization in the family: A longitudinal approach. In T. Eckes & H. M. Trautner (Eds.), *The developmental social psychology of gender* (pp. 333–360). Mahwah, NJ: Erlbaum.

Eckerman, C. O., Hsu, H.-C., Molitor, A., Leung, E. H. L., & Goldstein, R. F. (1999). Infant arousal in an en-face exchange with a new partner: Effects of prematurity and perinatal biological risk. *Developmental Psychology, 35*(1), 282–293.

Eddleston, M., Dissanayake, M., Sheriff, M. H. R., Warrell, D. A., & Gunnell, D. (2006). Physical vulnerability and fatal self-harm in the elderly. *British Journal of Psychiatry, 189*(3),

Edler, C., Lipson, S. F., & Keel, P. K. (2007). Ovarian hormones and binge eating in bulimia nervosa. *Psychological Medicine, 37*(1), 131–141.

Egerton, A., Allison, C., Brett, R. R., & Pratt, J. A. (2006). Cannabinoids and prefrontal cortical function: Insights from preclinical studies. *Neuroscience & Biobehavioral Reviews, 30*(5), 680–695.

Eimas, P. D., Sigueland, E. R., Juscyk, P., & Vigorito, J. (1971). Speech perception in infants. *Science, 171,* 303–306.

Eisenberg, M. E., Neumark-Sztainer, D., & Paxton, S. J. (2006). Five-year change in body satisfaction among adolescents. *Journal of Psychosomatic Research, 61*(4), 521–527.

Eisner, E. W. (1990). The role of art and play in children's cognitive development. In E. Klugman & S. Smilansky (Eds.), *Children's play and learning: Perspectives and policy implications.* New York: Teachers College Press.

El-Sheikh, M. (2007). Children's skin conductance level and reactivity: Are these measures stable over time and across tasks? *Developmental Psychobiology, 49*(2), 180–186.

Elkind, D. (1967). Egocentrism in adolescence. *Child Development, 38,* 1025–1034.

Elkind, D. (1985). Egocentrism redux. *Developmental Review, 5,* 218–226.

Elkind, D. (2007). *The power of play: How spontaneous imaginative activities lead to happier, healthier children.* Cambridge, MA: Da Capo Press.

Ellis, A., & Dryden, W. (1996). *The practice of rational emotive behavior therapy.* New York: Springer.

Else-Quest, N. M., Hyde, J. S., Goldsmith, H. H., & Van Hulle, C. A. (2006). Gender differences in temperament: A meta-analysis. *Psychological Bulletin, 132*(1), 33–72.

Eltzschig, H., Lieberman, E., & Camann, W. (2003). Regional anesthesia and analgesia for labor and delivery. *New England Journal of Medicine, 348*(4), 319–332.

Emler, N., Tarry, H., & St. James, A. (2007). Post-conventional moral reasoning and reputation. *Journal of Research in Personality, 41*(1), 76–89.

Epel, E. S., et al. (2006). Cell aging in relation to stress arousal and cardiovascular disease risk factors. *Psychoneuroendocrinology, 31*(3), 277–287.

Erikson, E. H. (1963). *Childhood and society.* New York: Norton.

Erikson, E. H. (1968). *Identity: Youth and crisis.* New York: Norton.

Ersner-Hershfield, H., Mikels, J. A., Sullivan, S. J., & Carstensen, L. L. (2008). Poignancy: Mixed emotional experience in the face of meaningful endings. *Journal of Personality and Social Psychology, 94*(1) 158–167.

Escorial, S., et al. (2003). Abilities that explain the intelligence decline: Evidence from the WAIS-III. *Psicothema, 15*(1), 19–22.

Etaugh, C. A., & Bridges, J. S. (2006). Midlife transitions. In J. Worell & C. D. Goodheart (Eds.), *Handbook of girls' and women's psychological health: Gender and well-being across the lifespan* (pp. 359–367). *Oxford series in clinical psychology.* New York: Oxford University Press.

F

Facts About Falling (2008, January 28). *The Washington Post.*

Fagot, B. I. (1990). A longitudinal study of gender segregation: Infancy to preschool. In F. F. Strayer (Ed.), *Social interaction and behavioral development during early childhood.* Montreal: La Maison D'Ethologie de Montreal.

Fagot, B. I., Rodgers, C. S., & Leinbach, M. D. (2000). Theories of gender socialization. In T. Eckes & H. M. Trautner (Eds.), *The developmental social psychology of gender* (pp. 65–89). Mahwah, NJ: Erlbaum.

Fair, R. C. (2007). Estimated age effects in athletic events and chess. *Experimental Aging Research, 33*(1), 37–57.

Fang L., Oliver, A., Jayaraman, G., Wong, T., et al. (2010). Trends in age disparities between younger and middle-age adults among reported rates of chlamydia, gonorrhea, and infectious syphilis infections in Canada: Findings from 1997 to 2007. *Sexually Transmitted Diseases. 37*(1), 18–25.

Fantz, R. L. (1961). The origin of form perception. *Scientific American, 204,* 66–72.

Fantz, R. L., Fagan, J. F., III, & Miranda, S. B. (1975). Early visual selectivity. In L. B. Cohen & P. Salapatek (Eds.), *Infant perception: From sensation to cognition,* Vol. 1. New York: Academic Press.

Faris, M., & McCarroll, E. (2010). Crying babies: Answering the call of infant cries. *Texas Child Care, 34*(2), 14–21.

Farmer, A., Elkin, A., & McGuffin, P. (2007). The genetics of bipolar affective disorder. *Current Opinion in Psychiatry, 20*(1), 8–12.

Feijó, L., et al. (2006). Mothers' depressed mood and anxiety levels are reduced after massaging their preterm infants. *Infant Behavior & Development, 29*(3), 476–480.

Feiring, C. (1993, March). *Developing concepts of romance from 15 to 18 years.* Paper presented at the meeting of the Society for Research in Child Development, New Orleans, LA.

Feldman, R., & Masalha, S. (2007). The role of culture in moderating the links between early ecological risk and young children's adaptation. *Development and Psychopathology, 19*(1), 1–21.

Fergusson, A. (2007). What successful teachers do in inclusive classrooms: Research-based teaching strategies that help special learners succeed. *European Journal of Special Needs Education, 22*(1), 108–110.

Fernandes, L. (2011). Turn off the TV! Why you need to worry about family screen time. Retrieved from http://tvoparents.tvo.org/article/turn-tv-why-you-need-worry-about-family-screen-time

Fernandez-Twinn, D. S., & Ozanne, S. E. (2006). Mechanisms by which poor early growth programs type-2 diabetes, obesity and the metabolic syndrome. *Physiology & Behavior, 88*(3), 234–243.

Féron, J., Gentaz, E., & Streri, A. (2006). Evidence of amodal representation of small numbers across visuo-tactile modalities in 5-month-old infants. *Cognitive Development, 21*(2), 81–92.

Field, A. P. (2006). The behavioral inhibition system and the verbal information pathway to children's fears. *Journal of Abnormal Psychology, 115*(4), 742–752.

Field, T. (1999). Sucking and massage therapy reduce stress during infancy. In M. Lewis & D. Ramsay (Eds.), *Soothing and stress* (pp. 157–169). Hillsdale, NJ: Erlbaum.

Field, T., Hernandez-Reif, M., Feijo, L., & Freedman, J. (2006). Prenatal, perinatal and neonatal stimulation: A survey of neonatal nurseries. *Infant Behavior & Development, 29*(1), 24–31.

Filus, A. (2006). Being a grandparent in China, Greece and Poland. *Studia Psychologiczne, 44*(1), 35–46.

Finkel, E. J., Eastwick, P. W., Karney, B. R., Reis, H. T., & Sprecher, S. (2012). Online dating: A critical analysis from the perspective of psychological science. *Psychological Science in the Public Interest, 13*(1), 3–66.

Finkelman, J. M. (2005). Sexual harassment. In A. Barnes (Ed.). *The handbook of women, psychology, and the law.* (pp. 64–78). Hoboken, NJ: Wiley.

First Nations Pedagogy Online. (2009). Elders. Retrieved from http://firstnationspedagogy.ca/elders.html

Fisch, S. M. (2004). *Children's learning from educational television: Sesame Street and beyond*. Mahwah, NJ: Erlbaum.

Fiske, A. (2006). The nature of depression in later life. In S. H. Qualls, & B. G. Knight (Eds.), *Psychotherapy for depression in older adults* (pp. 29–44). Hoboken, NJ: John Wiley & Sons Inc.

Fitzgerald, H. E., et al. (1991). The organization of lateralized behavior during infancy. In H. E. Fitzgerald, B. M. Lester, &

M. W. Yogman (Eds.), *Theory and research in behavioral pediatrics.* New York: Plenum.

Fivush, R. (2002). Scripts, schemas, and memory of trauma. In N. L. Stein et al. (Eds.), *Representation, memory, and development: Essays in honor of Jean Mandler* (pp. 53–74). Mahwah, NJ: Erlbaum.

Fivush, R., & Hammond, N. R. (1990). Autobiographical memory across the preschool years: Toward reconceptualizing childhood amnesia. In R. Fivush & J. A. Hudson (Eds.), *Knowing and remembering in young children.* Cambridge: Cambridge University Press.

Fivush, R., Sales, J, M., Goldberg, A., Bahrick, L., & Parker, J. (2004). Weathering the storm: Children's long-term recall of Hurricane Andrew. *Memory, 12*(1), 104–118.

Flavell, J. H. (1993). Young children's understanding of thinking and consciousness. *Current Directions in Psychological Science, 2,* 40–43.

Flavell, J. H., Miller, P. H., & Miller, S. A. (2002). *Cognitive development* (4th ed.). Upper Saddle River, NJ: Prentice Hall.

Florsheim, P. (Ed.). (2003). *Adolescent romantic relations and sexual behavior: Theory, research, and practical implications.* Mahwah, NJ: Erlbaum.

Flouri, E., & Buchanan, A. (2003). The role of father involvement and mother involvement in adolescents' psychological well- being. *British Journal of Social Work, 33*(3), 399–406.

Flynn, J. R. (2003). Movies about intelligence: The limitations of g. *Current Directions in Psychological Science, 12*(3), 95–99.

Foley, G. M. (2006). Self and social– emotional development in infancy: A descriptive synthesis. In G. M. Foley & J. D. Hochman (Eds.), *Mental health in early intervention: Achieving unity in principles and practice* (pp. 139–173). Baltimore: Paul H. Brookes.

Fontaine, A-M. (2005). Écologie développementale des premières interactions entre enfants: Effet des matériels de jeu. *Enfance, 57*(2), 137–154.

Food and Drug Administration. (2004, July 20). *Decreasing the chance of birth defects.* Retrieved from http://www.fda.gov/ fdac/ features/996_bd.html.

Forman-Hoffman, V. L., Ruffin, T., & Schultz, S. K. (2006). Basal metabolic rate in anorexia nervosa patients: Using appropriate predictive equations during the refeeding process. *Annals of Clinical Psychiatry, 18*(2), 123–127.

Fortier, J. (2010, April 10). Canada a nation of "satisfied" workers: Survey. *Financial Post.* Retrieved from http://www.working.com/national/sectors/Canada+nation+satisfied+workers+Survey/2901739/story.html

Fouad, N. A., & Arredondo, P. (2007). Implications for Psychologists as Researchers. In N. A. Fouad & P. Arredondo (Eds.), *Becoming culturally oriented: Practical advice for psychologists and educators* (pp. 81–93). Washington, DC: American Psychological Association.

Fozard, J. L., & Gordon- Salant, S. (2001). Changes in vision and hearing with aging. In J. E. Birren, & K. W. Schaie (Eds.), *Handbook of psychology of aging* (5th ed.) (pp. 241–266). San Diego: Academic Press.

Franklin, A., Pilling, M., & Davies, I. (2005). The nature of infant color categorization: Evidence from eye movements on a target detection task. *Journal of Experimental Child Psychology, 91*(3), 227–248.

Frazier, L. D., Newman, F. L., & Jaccard, J. (2007). Psychosocial outcomes in later life. *Psychology and Aging, 22*(4), 676–689.

Frerichs, L., Andsager, J. L., Campo, S., Aquilino, M., & Dyer, C. S. (2006). Framing breastfeeding and formula- feeding messages in popular U.S. magazines. *Women & Health, 44*(1), 95–118.

Freund, A. M., & Baltes, P. B. (2002). The adaptiveness of selection, optimization, and compensation as strategies of life management. *Journals of Gerontology: Series B: Psychological Sciences & Social Sciences, 57B*(5), P426–P434.

Fried, P. A., & Smith, A. M. (2001). A litera-ture review of the consequences of prenatal marijuana exposure: An emerging theme of a deficiency in aspects of executive function. *Neurotoxicology and Teratology, 23*(1), 1–11.

Friedman, R. A. (2008, January 15). Crisis? Maybe he's a narcissistic jerk. *The New York Times online.*

Frisch, R. (1997). Speech reported in N. Angier (1997), Chemical tied to fat control could help trigger puberty, *New York Times,* pp. C1, C3.

Frisch, R. E. (1994). The right weight: Body fat, menarche and fertility. *Proceedings of the Nutrition Society, 53,* 113–129.

Fromkin, V., et al. (2004).*The development of language in Genie: A case of language acquisition beyond the "critical period."* New York: Psychology Press.

Fry, D. P. (2005). Rough-and-tumble social play in humans. In A. D. Pellegrini & P. K. Smith (Eds.), *The nature of play: Great apes and humans* (pp. 54–85). New York: Guilford Press.

Furman, W., Rahe, D., & Hartup, W. W. (1979). Social rehabilitation of low-interactive preschool children by peer intervention. *Child Development, 50,* 915–922.

Furnham, A., Petrides, K. V., & Constantinides, A. (2005). The effects of body mass index and waist-to-hip ratio on ratings of female attractiveness, fecundity, and health. *Personality and Individual Differences, 38*(8), 1823–1834.

G

Gallagher, F., Bell, L., Waddell, G., Benoît, A., & Côté, N. (2012). Requesting cesareans without medical indications: An option being considered by young Canadian women. *Birth: Issues in Perinatal Care, 39*(1), 39–47. doi:10.1111/j.1523-536X.2011.00511.x

Gans, D., & Silverstein, M. (2006). Norms of filial responsibility for aging parents across time and generations. *Journal of Marriage and Family, 68*(4), 961–976.

Gardner, H. (1983). *Frames of mind: The theory of multiple intelligences.* New York: Basic Books.

Gardner, H. (2006). *The development and education of the mind: The selected works of Howard Gardner.* Philadelphia: Routledge/Taylor & Francis.

Garmon, L. (Writer & Director). (1997). Secret of the wild child [Television series episode]. *Nova.* Arlington, VA: PBS.

Gartstein, M. A., Slobodskaya, H. R., & Kinsht, I. A. (2003). Cross-cultural differences in temperament in the first year of life: United States of America (U.S.) and Russia. *International Journal of Behavioral Development, 27*(4), 316–328.

Gathercole, S. E., Pickering, S. J., Ambridge, B., & Wearing, H. (2004a). The structure of working memory from 4 to 15 years of age. *Developmental Psychology, 40*(2), 177–190.

Gathercole, S. E., Pickering, S. J., Knight, C., & Stegmann, Z. (2004b). Working memory skills and educational attainment: Evidence from national curriculum assessments at 7 and 14 years of age. *Applied Cognitive Psychology, 18*(1), 1–16.

Gavin, N. I., et al. (2005). Perinatal depression: A systematic review of prevalence and incidence. *Obstetrics & Gynecology, 106,* 1071–1083.

Ge, X., et al. (2003). It's about timing and change: Pubertal transition effects on symptoms of major depression among African American youths. *Developmental Psychology, 39*(3), 430–439.

Geary, D. C. (2006). Sex differences in social behavior and cognition: Utility of sexual selection for hypothesis generation. *Hormones and Behavior, 49*(3), 273–275.

Georgiades, S., et al. (2007). Structure of the autism symptom phenotype: A proposed multidimensional model. *Journal of the American Academy of Child & Adolescent Psychiatry, 46*(2), 188–196.

Gerard, J. M., Landry-Meyer, L., & Roe, J. G. (2006). Grandparents raising grandchildren: The role of social support in coping with caregiving challenges. *International Journal of Ageing & Human Development, 62*(4), 359–383.

Geschwind, D. H. (2000). Interview cited in D. E. Rosenbaum (2000, May 16), On left- handedness, its causes and costs, *New York Times,* pp. F1, F6.

Gesell, A. (1928). *Infancy and human growth.* New York: Macmillan.

Gesell, A. (1929). Maturation and infant behavior patterns. *Psychological Review, 36,* 307–319.

Ghetti, S., & Alexander, K. W. (2004). "If it happened, I would remember it": Strategic use of event memorability in the rejection of false autobiographical events. *Child Development, 75*(2), 542–561.

Gibson, E. J. (1969). *Principles of perceptual learning and development.* New York: Appleton-Century-Crofts.

Gibson, E. J. (1991). *An odyssey in learning and perception.* Cambridge, MA: MIT Press.

Gibson, E. J., & Walk, R. D. (1960). The visual cliff. *Scientific American, 202,* 64–71.

Gilhooly, M. L., et al. (2007). Real-world problem solving and quality of life in older people. *British Journal of Health Psychology, 12*(4), 587–600.

Gilligan, C. (1982). *In a different voice.* Cambridge, MA: Harvard University Press.

Gilligan, C. (1990). Remapping the moral domain: New images of the self in relationship. In C. Zanardi (Ed.), *Essential papers on the psychology of women. Essential papers in psychoanalysis* (pp. 480–495). New York: New York University Press.

Gilmore, J. (2010). Trends in dropout rates and the labour market outcomes of young dropouts. Ottawa: Statistics Canada. Retrieved from http://www.statcan.gc.ca/pub/81-004-x/2010004/article/11339-eng.htm#b

Giussani, D. A. (2006). Prenatal hypoxia: Relevance to developmental origins of health and disease. In P. Gluckman & M. Hanson (Eds.), *Developmental origins of health and disease* (pp. 178–190). New York: Cambridge University Press.

Gleason, T. R. (2002). Social provisions of real and imaginary relationships in early childhood. *Developmental Psychology, 38*(6), 979–992.

Gleason, T. R. (2004). Imaginary companions and peer acceptance. *International Journal of Behavioral Development, 28*(3), 204–209.

Gleason, T. R., Gower, A. L., Hohmann, L. M., & Gleason, T. C. (2005). Temperament and friendship in preschool-aged children. *International Journal of Behavioral Development, 29*(4), 336–344.

Gleason, T. R., & Hohmann, L. M. (2006). Concepts of real and imaginary friendships in early childhood. *Social Development, 15*(1), 128–144.

Gleason, T. R., Sebanc, A. M., & Hartup, W. W. (2003). Imaginary companions of preschool children. In M. E. Hertzig & E. A. Farber (Eds.), *Annual progress in child psychiatry and child development: 2000–2001* (pp. 101–121). New York: Brunner-Routledge.

Glück, J., & Bluck, S. (2007). Looking back across the life span: A life story account of the reminiscence bump. *Memory & Cognition, 35*(8), 1928–1939.

Gobet, F., & Simon, H. A. (2000). Five seconds or sixty? Presentation time in expert memory. *Cognitive Science, 24*(4), 651–682.

Goel, P., Radotra, A., Singh, I., Aggarwal, A., & Dua, D. (2004). Effects of passive smoking on outcome in pregnancy. *Journal of Postgraduate Medicine, 50*(1), 12–16.

Golan, H., & Huleihel, M. (2006). The effect of prenatal hypoxia on brain development: Short- and long-term consequences demonstrated in rodent models. *Developmental Science, 9*(4), 338–349.

Goldberg A., & Allen, K. (2013). *LGBT-parent families: Innovations in research and implication for practice.* New York: Springer.

Goldman, J. S., Adamson, J., Karydas, A., Miller, B. L., & Hutton, M. (2008). New genes, new dilemmas: FTLD genetics and its implications for families. *American Journal of Alzheimer's Disease and Other Dementias, 22*(6), 507–515.

Goldschmidt, L., Day, N. L., & Richardson, G. A. (2000). Effects of prenatal marijuana exposure on child behavior problems at age 10. *Neurotoxicology and Teratology, 22*(3), 325–336.

Goldsmith, H. H., et al. (2003). Part III: Genetics and development. In R. J. Davidson et al. (Eds.), *Handbook of affective sciences.* London: Oxford University Press.

Goldstein, H. (2004). International comparisons of student attainment. *Assessment in Education: Principles, Policy & Practice, 11*(3), 319–330.

Goldstein, I. (1998). Cited in Kolata, G. (1998, April 4). Impotence pill: Would it also help women? *The New York Times,* pp. A1, A6.

Goldstein, I. (2000). Cited in Norton, A. (2000, September 1). Exercise helps men avoid impotence. *Reuters News Agency online*.

Goldstein, I., & Alexander, J. L. (2005). Practical aspects in the management of vaginal atrophy and sexual dysfunction in perimenopausal and postmenopausal women. *Journal of Sexual Medicine, 2*(Suppl3), 154–165.

Goldstein, I., Meston, C., Davis, S., & Traish, A. (Eds.). (2006). *Female sexual dysfunction.* New York: Parthenon.

Goldstein, S., & Brooks, R. B. (2005). *Handbook of resilience in children*. New York: Kluwer Academic/Plenum.

Gonzalez, V. (2005). Cultural, linguistic, and socioeconomic factors influencing monolingual and bilingual children's cognitive development. In V. Gonzalez & J. Tinajero (Eds.), *Review of research and practice,* Vol. 3 (pp. 67–104). Mahwah, NJ: Erlbaum.

González, Y. S., Moreno, D. S., & Schneider, B. H. (2004). Friendship expectations of early adolescents in Cuba and Canada. *Journal of Cross-Cultural Psychology, 35*(4), 436–445.

Goodman, C. G. (2007a). Intergenerational triads in skipped-generation grandfamilies. *International Journal of Ageing & Human Development, 65*(3), 231–258.

Goodman, C. G. (2007b). Family dynamics in three-generation grandfamilies. *Journal of Family Issues, 28*(3), 355–379.

GoodTherapy.org. (2013). Albert Bandura. Retrieved from http://www.goodtherapy.org/famous-psychologists/albert-bandura.html

Gopnik, A., & Meltzoff, A. N. (1992). Categorization and naming: Basic-level sorting in eighteen-month-olds and its relation to language. *Child Development, 63,* 1091–1103.

Gopnik, A., & Slaughter, V. (1991). Young children's understanding of changes in their mental states. *Child Development, 62,* 98–110.

Gordon-Salant, S., Fitzgibbons, P. J., & Friedman, S. A. (2007). Recognition of time-compressed and natural speech with selective temporal enhancements by young and elderly listeners. *Journal of Speech, Language, and Hearing Research, 50*(5), 1181–1193.

Gormally, S., et al. (2001). Contact and nutrient caregiving effects on newborn infant pain responses. *Developmental Medicine and Child Neurology, 43*(1), 28–38.Gottesman, N. (2012). Generation XL. *Parenting School Years, 26*(7), 72–76.

Gottlieb, B. H., Still, E., & Newby-Clark, I. R. (2007). Types and precipitants of growth and decline in emerging adulthood. *Journal of Adolescent Research, 22*(2), 132–155.

Gottman, J. M., Coan, J., Carrère, S. & Swanson, C. (1998). Predicting marital happiness and stability from newlywed interactions. *Journal of Marriage and the Family, 60,* 5–22.

Graber, J. A., Seeley, J. R., Brooks-Gunn, J., & Lewinsohn, P. M. (2004). Is pubertal timing associated with psychopathology in young adulthood? *Journal of the American Academy of Child and Adolescent Psychiatry, 43*(6), 718–726.

Grandparenting in the twenty-first century: The times they are a changin'. (2005). *Ontario Health Promotion E-Bulletin, 2005*(434). Retrieved from http://www.ohpe.ca/node/6892

Grandi, G., Ferrari, S., Xholli, A., Cannoletta, M., Palma, F., Romani, C., Vope, A., & Cagnacci, A. (2012). Prevalence of menstrual pain in young women: What is dysmenorrhea? *Journal of Pain Research, 5*, 169–174.

Gray, C., Koopman, E., & Hunt, J. (1991). The emotional phases of marital separation: an empirical investigation. *American Journal of Orthopsychiatry, 1991*(61), 138–143.

Gray, S. L., et al. (2008). Antioxidant vitamin supplement use and risk of dementia or Alzheimer's disease in older adults. *Journal of the American Geriatrics Society, 56*(2), 291–295.

Green, R. (1978). Sexual identity of 37 children raised by homosexual or transsexual parents. *American Journal of Psychiatry, 135,* 692–697.

Greene, S. M., Anderson, E. R., Doyle, E. A., Riedelbach, H., & Bear, G. G. (2006). Divorce. In K. M. Minke (Ed.), *Children's needs III: Development, prevention, and intervention* (pp. 745–757). Bethesda, MD: National Association of School Psychologists.

Greenough, W. T., Black, J. E., & Wallace, C. S. (2002). Experience and brain development. In M. H. Johnson, Y. Munakata, & R. O. Gilmore (Eds.), *Brain development and cognition: A reader* (2nd ed.) (pp. 186–216). Malden, MA: Blackwell.

Greidanus, J. A. (2007). A narrative inquiry into the experiences of bereaved children. *Dissertation Abstracts International Section A: Humanities and Social Sciences, 67*(9-A), 3447.

Grigorenko, E. L. (2007). Triangulating developmental dyslexia: Behavior, brain, and genes. In D. Coch, G. Dawson, & K. W. Fischer. (Eds.). *Human behavior, learning, and the developing brain: Atypical development.* (pp. 117–144). New York: Guilford.

Grindrod, C. M., & Baum, S. R. (2005). Hemispheric contributions to lexical ambiguity resolution in a discourse context: Evidence from individuals with unilateral left and right hemisphere lesions. *Brain and Cognition, 57*(1), 70–83.

Grolnick, W. S., McMenamy, J. M., & Kurowski, C. O. (2006). Emotional self-regulation in infancy and toddlerhood. In L. Balter & C. S. Tamis-LeMonda (Eds.), *Child psychology: A handbook of contemporary issues* (2nd ed.) (pp. 3–25). New York: Psychology Press.

Grossman, A. H., D'Augelli, A. R., & O'Connell, T. S. (2003). Being lesbian, gay, bisexual, and sixty or older in North America. In L. D. Garnets, & D. C. Kimmel (Eds.), *Psychological perspectives on lesbian, gay, and bisexual experiences* (2nd ed.) (pp. 629–645). New York: Columbia University Press.

Grossmann, K., et al. (2002). The uniqueness of the child–father attachment relationship: Fathers' sensitive and challenging play as a pivotal variable in a 16-year longitudinal study. *Social Development, 11*(3), 307–331.

Grundy, E., & Henretta, J. C. (2006). Between elderly parents and adult children: A new look at the intergenerational care provided by the "sandwich generation." *Ageing & Society, 26*(5), 707–722.

Grusec, J. E. (2002). Parenting socialization and children's acquisition of values. In M. H. Bornstein (Ed.), *Handbook of parenting* (2nd ed.), Vol. 5, *Practical issues in parenting* (pp. 143–167). Mahwah, NJ: Erlbaum.

Grusec, J. E. (2006). The development of moral behavior and conscience from a socialization perspective. In M. Killen & J. G. Smetana (Eds.), *Handbook of moral development* (pp. 243–265). Mahwah, NJ: Erlbaum.

Guerin, D. W., Gottfried, A. W., & Thomas, C. W. (1997). Difficult temperament and behaviour problems: A longitudinal study from 1.5 to 12 years. *International Journal of Behavioral Development, 21*(1), 71–90.

Guerrini, I., Thomson, A. D., & Gurling, H. D. (2007). The importance of alcohol misuse, malnutrition and genetic susceptibility on brain growth and plasticity. *Neuroscience & Biobehavioral Reviews, 31*(2), 212–220.

Guiaux, M., van Tilburg, T., & van Groenou, M. B. (2007). Changes in contact and support exchange in personal networks after widowhood. *Personal Relationships, 14*(3), 457–473.

Gulli, C. (2009, April 10). Youth survey: Teen girls in charge. *Macleans*. Retrieved from http://www2.macleans.ca/2009/04/10/teen-girls-in-charge/

Güntürkün, O. (2006). Letters on nature and nurture. In P. B. Baltes et al. (Eds.), *Life span development and the brain: The perspective of biocultural co- constructivism* (pp. 379–397). New York: Cambridge University Press.

Gurba, E. (2005). On the specific character of adult thought: Controversies over post- formal operations. *Polish Psychological Bulletin, 36*(3), 175–185.

Gutknecht, L. (2001). Full-genome scans with autistic disorder: A review. *Behavior Genetics, 31*(1), 113–123.

H

Haith, M. M. (1979). Visual cognition in early infancy. In R. B. Kearsly & I. E. Sigel (Eds.), *Infants at risk: Assessment of cognitive functioning.* Hillsdale, NJ: Erlbaum.

Haith, M. M. (1990). Progress in the understanding of sensory and perceptual processes in early infancy. *Merrill–Palmer Quarterly, 36,* 1–26.

Halgin, R. P., & Whitbourne, S. K. (1993). *Abnormal psychology.* Fort Worth, TX: Harcourt Brace Jovanovich.

Hall, D. T. (2004). The protean career: A quarter- century journey. *Journal of Vocational Behavior, 65*(1), 1–13.

Hall, G. S. (1904). *Adolescence: Its psychology and its relations to physiology, anthropology, sociology sex, crime, religion and education, Vol. II.* New York: D Appleton & Company.

Halliday, L. F., & Bishop, D. V. M. (2006). Auditory frequency discrimination in children with dyslexia. *Journal of Research in Reading, 29*(2), 213–228.

Halpern, D. F. (2003). Sex differences in cognitive abilities. *Applied Cognitive Psychology, 17*(3), 375–376.

Halpern, D. F. (2004). A cognitive-process taxonomy for sex differences in cognitive abilities. *Current Directions in Psychological Science, 13*(4), 135–139.

Hamm, J. V. (2000). Do birds of a feather flock together? The variable bases for African American, Asian American, and European American adolescents' selection of similar friends. *Developmental Psychology, 36*(2), 209–219.

Hammer, K. (2012a). Full-day kindergarten in Ontario gets failing grade. Retrieved from http://www.theglobeandmail.com/news/toronto/kindergarten/full-day-kindergarten-in-ontario-gets-failing-grade/article1379499/

Hammer, K. (2012b). The challenge of teaching empathy to stop bullying. Retrieved from http://www.theglobeandmail.com/news/national/education/the-challenge-of-teaching-empathy-to-stop-bullying/article5328473/

Hangal, S., & Aminabhavi, V. A. (2007). Self-concept, emotional maturity, and achievement motivation of the adolescent children of employed mothers and homemakers. *Journal of the Indian Academy of Applied Psychology, 33*(1), 103–110.

Hanlon, T. E., Bateman, R. W., Simon, B. D., O'Grady, K. E., & Carswell, S. B. (2004). Antecedents and correlates of deviant activity in urban youth manifesting behavioral problems. *Journal of Primary Prevention, 24*(3), 285–309.

Hannon, P., Bowen, D. J., Moinpour, C. M., & McLerran, D. F. (2003). Correlations in perceived food use between the family food preparer and their spouses and children. *Appetite, 40*(1), 77–83.

Hansen, J. C., Dik, B. J., & Zhou, S. (2008). An examination of the structure of leisure interests of college students, working-age adults, and retirees. *Journal of Counseling Psychology, 55*(2), 133–145.

Harel, J., & Scher, A. (2003). Insufficient responsiveness in ambivalent mother– infant relationships: Contextual and affective aspects. *Infant Behavior and Development, 26*(3), 371–383.

Harlow, H. F., & Harlow, M. K. (1966). Learning to love. *American Scientist, 54,* 244–272.

Harlow, H. F., Harlow, M. K., & Suomi, S. J. (1971). From thought to therapy: Lessons from a primate laboratory. *American Scientist, 59,* 538–549.

Harris, G. (2004, September 14). *FDA links drugs to being suicidal.* Retrieved from http:// www.nytimes.com.

Harris, S. R., Megens, A. M., Backman, C. L., & Hayes, V. E. (2005). Stability of the Bayley II Scales of Infant Development in a sample of low-risk and high-risk infants. *Developmental Medicine & Child Neurology, 47*(12), 820–823.

Harter, S. (2006). The Self. In K. A. Renninger, I. E. Sigel, W. Damon, & R. M. Lerner (Eds.), *Handbook of child psychology* (6th ed.), Vol. 4, *Child psychology in practice* (pp. 505–570). Hoboken, NJ: Wiley.

Harter, S., & Pike, R. (1984). The pictorial scale of perceived competence and social acceptance for young children. *Child Development, 55,* 1969–1982.

Harter, S., & Whitesell, N. R. (2003). Beyond the debate: Why some adolescents report stable self-worth over time and situation, whereas others report changes in self-worth. *Journal of Personality, 71*(6), 1027–1058.

Hartley, A. (2006). Changing role of the speed of processing construct in the cognitive psychology of human aging. In J. E. Birren & K. W. Schaie (Eds.), *Handbook of the psychology of aging* (6th ed.) (pp. 183–207). Amsterdam, Netherlands: Elsevier.

Hartman, M., & Warren, L. H. (2005). Explaining age differences in temporal working memory. *Psychology and Aging, 20*(4), 645–656.

Hartup, W. W. (1983). The peer system. In P. H. Mussen (Ed.), *Handbook of child psychology,* Vol. 4, *Socialization, personality, and social development.* New York: Wiley.

Hasher, L. (2008, May 20). Cited in Reistad-Long, S. Older brain, wiser brain. *The New York Times online.* Accessed October 5, 2008.

Hassett, J. M., Siebert, E. R., & Wallen, K. (2008). Sex differences in rhesus monkey toy preferences parallel those of children. *Hormone and Behavior, 54*(3), 359–364.

Hassing, L. B., & Johanssom, B. (2005). Aging and cognition. *Nordisk Psykologi, 57*(1), 4–20.

Hastings, P. D., Zahn-Waxler, C., Robinson, J., Usher, B., & Bridges, D. (2000). The development of concern for others in children with behavior problems. *Developmental Psychology, 36*(5), 531–546.

Hatch, L. R., & Bulcroft, K. (2004). Does long-term marriage bring less frequent disagreements? *Journal of Family Issues, 25,* 465–495.

Hatcher, R. A., et al. (Eds.). (2007). *Contraceptive technologies* (18th rev. ed.). New York: Ardent Media.

Hatfield, E., & Rapson, R. L. (2002). Passionate love and sexual desire: Cultural and historical perspectives. In A. L. Vangelisti, H. T. Reis, et al. (Eds.), *Stability and change in relationships. Advances in personal relationships* (pp. 306–324). New York: Cambridge University Press.

Havighurst, R. (1972). In Robert Havighurst: Developmental theorist. Retrieved from http://faculty.mdc.edu/jmcnair/EDF3214.Topic.Outline/Robert.Havighurst.htm. Accessed October 2, 2008.

Hawkley, L. C., Burleson, M. H., Berntson, G. G., & Cacioppo, J. T. (2003). Loneliness in everyday life: Cardiovascular activity, psychosocial context, and health behaviors. *Journal of Personality & Social Psychology, 85*(1), 105–120.

Hay, D. F., Payne, A., & Chadwick, A. (2004). Peer relations in childhood. *Journal of Child Psychology and Psychiatry. 45*(1), 84–108.

Hayes, R., & Dennerstein, L. (2005). The impact of aging on sexual function and sexual dysfunction in women: A review of population-based studies. *Journal of Sexual Medicine, 2*(3), 317–330.

Hayflick, L. (1996) *How and why we age.* New York: Ballantine Books, 1994.

Hayne, H., & Fagen, J. W. (Eds.). (2003). *Progress in infancy research,* Vol. 3. Mahwah, NJ: Erlbaum.

Hayslip, B., Jr., & Kaminski, P. L. (2006). Custodial grandchildren. In G. G. Bear & K. M. Minke (Eds.), *Children's needs III: Development, prevention, and intervention* (pp. 771–782). Washington, DC: National Association of School Psychologists.

Hayslip, B., Jr., Neumann, C. S., Louden, L., & Chapman, B. (2006). Developmental stage theories. In J. C. Thomas, D. L. Segal, & M. Hersen. (Eds.), *Comprehensive handbook of personality and psychopathology, Vol. 1: Personality and everyday functioning* (pp. 115–141). Hoboken, NJ: John Wiley & Sons, Inc.

Health Canada. (2000). *Because life goes on... Helping children and youth live with separation and divorce.* Retrieved from http://www.phac-aspc.gc.ca/publicat/mh-sm/pdf/booklet_e.pdf

Health Canada. (2007a). Breastfeeding. Retrieved from http://www.hc-sc.gc.ca/fn-an/pubs/infant-nourrisson/nut_infant_nourrisson_term_3-eng.php

Health Canada. (2007b). Eating well with Canada's food guide. Retrieved from http://www.hc-sc.gc.ca/fn-an/pubs/res-educat/res-educat_3-eng.php

Health Canada. (2007c). How much food you need every day. Retrieved from http://www.hc-sc.gc.ca/fn-an/food-guide-aliment/basics-base/quantit-eng.php

Health Canada. (2009). Aboriginal Head Start on Reserve. Retrieved from http://www.hc-sc.gc.ca/fniah-spnia/famil/develop/ahsor-papa_intro-eng.php

Health Canada. (2012). Breastfeeding initiation in Canada: Key statistics and graphics. Retrieved from http://www.hc-sc.gc.ca/fn-an/surveill/nutrition/commun/prenatal/initiation-eng.php#a2

Health Disparities, Minority Cancer Awareness. (2004). Cancer Prevention and Control, National Center for Chronic Disease Prevention and Health Promotion, Centers for Disease Control.

The Health Journal. (2010). Canadian women over 30 at risk as infertility rates predicted to double. Retrieved from http://www.thehealthjournal.ca/site/content/view/136/1/

Healy, M. D., & Ellis, B. J. (2007). Birth order, conscientiousness, and openness to experience. Tests of the family-niche model of personality using a within-family methodology. *Evolution and Human Behavior, 28*(1), 55–59.

Heart and Stroke Foundation. (2008). Healthy weight in children and youth. Retrieved from http://www.heartandstroke.com/site/c.iklQLcMWJtE/b.3484293/k.D60A/Healthy_living__Healthy_weight_in_children_and_youth.htm

Heart and Stroke Foundation of Canada. (1993). *Position statement on physical activity.* Unpublished report. Ottawa: Author. Retrieved from http://www.pembinatrails.ca/program/physicaleducation/Documents/MPESA/Articles/Health%20Related/children%20stats.doc

Heart and Stroke Foundation of Canada. (2013). Statistics: Cardiovascular disease deaths. Retrieved from http://www.heartandstroke.com/site/c.iklQLcMWJtE/b.3483991/k.34A8/Statistics.htm

Hebert, T. P. (2000). Gifted males pursuing careers in elementary education: Factors that influence a belief in self. *Journal for the Education of the Gifted, 24*(1), 7–45.

Heilman, K. M., Nadeau, S. E., & Beversdorf, D. O. (2003). Creative innovation: Possible brain mechanisms. *Neurocase, 9*(5), 369–379.

Heindel, J. J., & Lawler, C. (2006) Role of exposure to environmental chemicals in developmental origins of health and disease. In P. Gluckman & M. Hanson (Eds.), *Developmental origins of health and disease* (pp. 82–97). New York: Cambridge University Press.

Held, L. (2010). Profile of Mary Ainsworth. In A. Rutherford (Ed.), *Psychology's feminist voices multimedia Internet archive.* Retrieved from http://www.feministvoices.com/mary-ainsworth/

Henry, D., et al. (2000). Normative influences on aggression in urban elementary school classrooms. *American Journal of Community Psychology, 28*(1) 59–81.

Henzi, S. P., et al. (2007). Look who's talking: developmental trends in the size of conversational cliques. *Evolution and Human Behavior, 28*(1), 66–74.

Heron, M. P. (2007). National Vital Statistics Reports, 56(5). Centers for Disease Control and Prevention. Retrieved from http://www.cdc.gov/nchs/data/nvsr/nvsr56/nvsr56_05.pdf

Hertenstein, M. J., & Campos, J. J. (2004). The retention effects of an adult's emotional displays on infant behavior. *Child Development, 75*(2), 595–613.

Hetherington, E. M. (1989). Coping with family transition: Winners, losers, and survivors. *Child Development, 60,* 1–14.

Hetherington, E. M. (2006). The influence of conflict, marital problem solving and parenting on children's adjustment in nondivorced, divorced and remarried families. In A. Clarke-Stewart & J. Dunn (Eds.), *Families count: Effects on child and adolescent development, The Jacobs Foundation series on adolescence* (pp. 203–237). Cambridge, UK: Cambridge University Press.

Hicks, B. M., et al. (2007). Genes mediate the association between P3 amplitude and externalizing disorders. *Psychophysiology, 44*(1), 98–105.

Hill, R. A., Donovan, S., & Koyama, N. F. (2005). Female sexual advertisement reflects resource availability in twentieth-century UK society. *Human Nature, 16*(3), 266–277.

Hill, S. E., & Flom, R. (2007). 18- and 24-month-olds' discrimination of gender- consistent and inconsistent activities. *Infant Behavior & Development, 30*(1) 168–173.

Hill, S. Y., et al., (2007). Cerebellar volume in offspring from multiplex alcohol dependence families. *Biological Psychiatry, 61*(1), 41–47.

Hinojosa, T., Sheu, C., & Michel, G. F. (2003). Infant hand-use preferences for grasping objects contributes to the development of a hand-use preference for manipulating objects. *Developmental Psychobiology, 43*(4), 328–334.

HIV Edmonton. (2010). *HIV/AIDS.* Retrieved from http://www.hivedmnton.com/hivinfo.htm

Hochwarter, W. A., Ferris, G. R., Perrewé, P. L., Witt, L. A., & Kiewitz, C. (2001). A note on the nonlinearity of the age-job- satisfaction relationship. *Journal of Applied Social Psychology, 31*(6), 1223–1237.

Hoecker, J. L. (2011). Infant and toddler health: Is it okay to play Baby Einstein DVDs for my 6-month-old? I've heard that such programming can promote a child's development. Retrieved from http://www.mayoclinic.com/health/baby-einstein/AN01990

Hoegh, D. G., & Bourgeois, M. J. (2002). Prelude and postlude to the self: Correlates of achieved identity. *Youth and Society, 33*(4), 573–594.

Hoff, E. (2006). Language experience and language milestones during early childhood. In K. McCartney & D. Phillips (Eds.), *Blackwell handbook of early childhood development, Blackwell handbooks of developmental psychology* (pp. 233–251). Malden, MA: Blackwell.

Hoff, E. V. (2005). A friend living inside me—The forms and functions of imaginary companions. *Imagination, Cognition and Personality, 24*(2), 151–189.

Hogan, A. M., de Haan, M., Datta, A., & Kirkham, F. J. (2006). Hypoxia: An acute, intermittent and chronic challenge to cognitive development. *Developmental Science, 9*(4), 335–337.

Hogan, A. M., Kirkham, F. J., Isaacs, E. B., Wade, A. M., & Vargha-Khadem, F. (2005). Intellectual decline in children with moyamoya and sickle cell anaemia. *Developmental Medicine & Child Neurology, 47*(12), 824–829.

Holland, J. J. (2000, July 25). *Groups link media to child violence.* Retrieved from http://www.ap.org/

Holland, J. L. (1997). *Making vocational choices: A theory of vocational personalities and work environments* (3rd ed.). Odessa, FL: Psychological Assessment Resources.

Holland, J. M., Futterman, A., Thompson, L. W., Moran, C., Gallagher-Thompson, D. (2013). Difficulties accepting the loss of a spouse: A precursor for intensified grieving among widowed older adults. *Death Studies, 37*(2), 126–144.

Homer, B. D., & Nelson, K. (2005). Seeing objects as symbols and symbols as objects: Language and the development of dual representation. In B. D. Homer & C. S. Tamis-LeMonda (Eds.), *The development of social cognition and communication* (pp. 29–52). Mahwah, NJ: Erlbaum.

Homish, G. G., & Leonard, K. E. (2007). The drinking partnership and marital satisfaction: The longitudinal influence of discrepant drinking. *Journal of Consulting and Clinical Psychology, 75*(1) 43–51.

Honzik, M. P., Macfarlane, J. W., & Allen, L. (1948). The stability of mental test performance between two and eighteen years. *Journal of Experimental Education, 17,* 309–324.

Höpflinger, F., & Hummel, C. (2006). Heran wachsende Enkelkinder und ihre Großeltern: Im Geschlechtervergleich. *Zeitschrift für Gerontologie und Geriatrie, 39*(1), 33–40.

Hoppmann, C., & Smith, J. (2007). Life- history related differences in possible selves in very old age. *International Journal of Aging & Human Development, 64*(2), 109–127.

Horizons Women's Health Care. (2013). What are STIs? Retrieved from http://www.horizonswomens.com/what-are-stis

Horn, I. B., Brenner, R., Rao, M., Cheng, T. L. (2006). Beliefs about the appropriate age for initiating toilet training: Are there racial and socioeconolmic differences? *The Journal of Pediatrics, 149*(2), 165–168.

Horn, J. L., & Noll, J. (1997). Human cognitive capabilities: Gf-Gc theory. In D. P. Flanagan, J. L. Genshaft, & P. L. Harrison (Eds.), *Contemporary intellectual assessment: Theories, tests, and issues* (pp. 53–91). New York: Guilford Press.

Horton, S. M. (2008). Aging stereotypes: Effects on the performance and health of seniors. *Dissertation Abstracts International Section A: Humanities and Social Sciences. 68*(8-A), 3540.

Hossain, M., Chetana, M., & Devi, P. U. (2005). Late effect of prenatal irradiation on the hippocampal histology and brain weight in adult mice. *International Journal of Developmental Neuroscience, 23*(4), 307–313.

Hostetler, A. J., Sweet, S., & Moen, P. (2007). Gendered career paths: A life course perspective on returning to school. *Sex Roles, 56*(1–2), 85–103.

Hough, M. S. (2007). Adult age differences in word fluency for common and goal-directed categories. *Advances in Speech Language Pathology, 9*(2), 154–161.

Huang, J. (2007). Hormones and female sexuality. In A. F. Owens & M. S. Tepper (Eds.), *Sexual health (Vol 2): Physical foundations* (pp. 43–78). *Praeger perspectives: Sex, love, and psychology.* Westport, CT: Praeger Publishers/Greenwood Publishing Group.

Huestis, M. A., et al. (2002). Drug abuse's smallest victims: in utero drug exposure. *Forensic Science International, 128*(2), 20.

Huizink, A. C., & Mulder, E. J. H. (2006). Maternal smoking, drinking or cannabis use during pregnancy and neurobehavioral and cognitive functioning in human offspring. *Neuroscience & Biobehavioral Reviews, 30*(1), 24–41.

Hultsch, D. F., Hertzog, C., Dixon, R.A., & Small, B. J. (1998). *Memory change in the aged.* New York: Cambridge University Press.

Human Resources and Skills Development Canada. (2010a). *Family life—Age of mother at childbirth.* Retrieved from http://www4.hrsdc.gc.ca/.3ndic.1t.4r@-eng.jsp?iid=75

Human Resources and Skills Development Canada. (2010b). Indicators of Well Being in Canada: Social participation—Volunteering. Retrieved from http://www4.hrsdc.gc.ca/.3ndic.1t.4r@-eng.jsp?iid=74

Human Resources and Skills Development Canada. (2013a). Family life: Age of mother at childbirth. Retrieved from http://www4.hrsdc.gc.ca/.3ndic.1t.4r@-eng.jsp?iid=75

Human Resources and Skills Development Canada. (2013b). Family life: Marriage. Retrieved from http://www4.hrsdc.gc.ca/.3ndic.1t.4r@-eng.jsp?iid=78

Human Resources and Skills Development Canada. (2013c). Health—Low birth rate. Retrieved from http://www4.hrsdc.gc.ca/.3ndic.1t.4r@-eng.jsp?iid=4

Human Resources and Skills Development Canada. (2013d). Health—Self-rated health. Retrieved from http://www4.hrsdc.gc.ca/.3ndic.1t.4r@-eng.jsp?iid=10

Human Rights Campaign Foundation. (2013). *A resource guide to coming out*. Retrieved from http://www.hrc.org/resources/entry/resource-guide-to-coming-out

Hunt, C. E., & Hauck, F. R. (2006). Sudden infant death syndrome. *Canadian Medical Association Journal, 174*(13), 1861–1869.

Huntington Society of Canada. (n.d.). What is Huntington disease? Retrieved from http://www.huntingtonsociety.ca/english/index.asp

Hurd, Y. L., et al. (2005). Marijuana impairs growth in mid–gestation fetuses. *Neurotoxicology and Teratology, 27*(2), 221–229.

Hursting, S. D., Lavigne, J. A., Berrigan, D., Perkins, S. N., & Barrett, J. C. (2003). Calorie restriction, aging, and cancer prevention: Mechanisms of action and applicability to humans. *Annual Review of Medicine, 54*(131–152).

Hussain, A. (2002, June 26) It's official. Men really are afraid of commitment. Reuters.

Hyde, J. S., Fennema, E., & Lamon, S. J. (1990). Gender differences in mathematics performance: A meta-analysis. *Psychological Bulletin, 107,* 139–155.

Hyde, J. S., Lindberg, S. M., Linn, M. C., Ellis, A. B., & Williams, C. C. (2008). Gender similarities characterize math performance. *Science, 321,* 494–495.

Hynes, M., Sheik, M., Wilson, H. G., & Spiegel, P. (2002). Reproductive health indicators and outcomes among refugee and internally displaced persons in postemergency phase camps. *Journal of the American Medical Association, 288,* 595–603.

I

Infant and Toddler Nutrition. (2007, April 10). National Institutes of Health, Department of Health and Human Services. Retrieved from http://www.nlm.nih.gov/medlineplus/infantandtoddlernutrition.html.

International Human Genome Sequencing Consortium (2006). A global map of p53 transcription-factor binding sites in the human genome. *Cell, 124*(1), 207–219.

Ipsos Reid. (2006). 1/2 of Canadians say they have no control over stress levels. Retrieved from http://www.marketwire.com/press-release/-of Canadians-Say-They-Have-No-Control-Over-Stress-Levels-598798.htm

J

Jacobs, D. M., Levy, G., & Marder, K. (2006). Dementia in Parkinson's disease, Huntington's disease, and related disorders. In M. J. Farah & T. E. Feinberg (Eds.), *Patient-based approaches to cognitive neuroscience* (2nd ed.) (pp. 381–395). Cambridge, MA: MIT Press.

Jacobs, J. E., Davis-Kean, P., Bleeker, M., Eccles, J. S., & Malanchuk, O. (2005). "I can, but I don't want to": The impact of parents, interests, and activities on gender differences in math. In A. M. Gallagher & J. C. Kaufman (Eds.), *Gender differences in mathematics: An integrative psychological approach* (pp. 246–263). New York: Cambridge University Press.

Jacobs, S. (1993). *Pathologic grief: Maladaptation to loss.* Washington, DC: American Psychiatric Press.

Jacobsen, J. S., et al. (2006). Early-onset behavioral and synaptic deficits in a mouse model of Alzheimer's disease. *Proceedings of the National Academy of Sciences, 103,* 5161–5166.

Jacobson, P. F., & Schwartz, R. G. (2005). English past tense use in bilingual children with language impairment. *American Journal of Speech-Language Pathology, 14*(4), 313–323.

Jang, Y., Kim, G., Chiriboga, D. A., & Cho, S. (2008). Willingness to use a nursing home. *Journal of Applied Gerontology, 27*(1), 110–117.

Janssen, E. (Ed). (2006). *The psychophysiology of sex.* Bloomington, IN: Indiana University Press.

Janssen, I. (2012). Healthy weights. In Public Health Agency of Canada, *The health of Canada's young people: A mental health focus.* Retrieved from http://www.phac-aspc.gc.ca/hp-ps/dca-dea/publications/hbsc-mental-mentale/weight-poids-eng.php

Janz, T. (2012). Health at a glance: Current smoking trends. Ottawa: Statistics Canada. Retrieved from http://www.statcan.gc.ca/pub/82-624-x/2012001/article/11676-eng.htm

Jayson, S. (2008, June 8). More view cohabitation as acceptable choice. *USA Today.* Retrieved from http://www.usatoday.com/news/nation/2008-06-08-cohabitation-study_N.htm. Accessed October 2, 2008.

Jepsen, D. A., & Choudhuri, E. (2001). Stability and change in 25-year occupational career patterns. *Career Development Quarterly, 50*(1), 3–19.

Johannes, C. B., et al. (2000). Incidence of erectile dysfunction in men 40 to 69 years old: Longitudinal results from the Massachusetts male aging study. *The Journal of Urology, 163,* 460.

Johnson, A. (2011, March 7). Latimer: No regrets about killing disabled daughter. Retrieved from http://www.ctvnews.ca/latimer-no-regrets-about-killing-disabled-daughter-1.615463

Johnson, J. G., Zhang, B., & Prigerson, H. G. (2008). Investigation of a developmental model of risk for depression and suicidality following spousal bereavement. *Suicide and Life-Threatening Behavior, 38*(1), 1–12.

Johnson, K. (2008). Fostering attachment in the child care setting for infants and toddlers. Retrieved from http://www.earlychildhoodnews.com/earlychildhood/article_view.aspx?ArticleID=715

Johnson, W., & Bouchard, T. J., Jr., (2007). Sex differences in mental abilities: g masks the dimensions on which they lie. *Intelligence, 35*(1), 23–39.

Johnson, W., & Krueger, R. F. (2006). How money buys happiness: Genetic and environmental processes linking finances and life satisfaction. *Journal of Personality and Social Psychology, 90*(4), 680–691.

Jones, A., Gulbis, A., & Baker, E. H. (2010). Differences in tobacco use between Canada and the United States. *International Journal of Public Health, 55*(3), 167–175.

Jones B. C., et al. (2008). Effects of menstrual cycle phase on face preferences. *Archives of Sexual Behaviour, 37*(1), 78–84.

Jones, D. C., & Crawford, J. K. (2006). The peer appearance culture during adolescence: Gender and body mass variations. *Journal of Youth and Adolescence, 35*(2), 257–269.

Jones, S. S., & Hong, H-W. (2005). How some infant smiles get made. *Infant Behavior & Development, 28*(2), 194–205.

Jonkman, S. (2006). Sensitization facilitates habit formation: Implications for addiction. *Journal of Neuroscience, 26*(28), 7319–7320.

Jordan, J. V., Kaplan, A. G., Miller, J. B., Stiver, I. P., & Surrey, J. L. (1991). *Women's growth in connection.* New York: Guilford Press.

Jorgensen, G. (2006). Kohlberg and Gilligan: Duet or duel? *Journal of Moral Education, 35*(2), 179–196.

Joshi, R. M. (2003). Misconceptions about the assessment and diagnosis of reading disability. *Reading Psychology, 24*(3–4), 247–266.

Joung, H-M., & Miller, N. J. (2007). Examining the effects of fashion activities on life satisfaction of older females: Activity theory revisited. *Family & Consumer Sciences Research Journal, 35*(4), 338–356.

Judge, T. A., & Klinger, R. (2008). Job satisfaction: Subjective well-being at work. In M. Eid, & R. J. Larsen (Eds.), *The science of subjective well-being* (pp. 393–413). New York: Guilford Press.

K

Kagan, L. J., MacLeod, A. K., & Pote, H. L. (2004). Accessibility of causal explanations for future positive and negative events in adolescents with anxiety and depression. *Clinical Psychology and Psychotherapy, 11*(3), 177–186.

Kaiser Family Foundation, Holt, T., Greene, L., & Davis, J. (2003). *National Survey of Adolescents and Young Adults: Sexual health knowledge, attitudes, and experiences.* Menlo Park, CA: Henry J. Kaiser Family Foundation.

Kaminski, P. L., & Hayslip, B., Jr. (2006). Gender differences in body esteem among older adults. *Journal of Women & Aging, 18*(3), 19–35.

Kaminski, R. A., & Stormshak, E. A. (2007). Project STAR: Early intervention with preschool children and families for the prevention of substance abuse. In P. Tolan, J. Szapocznik, & S. Sambrano (Eds.), *Preventing youth substance abuse: Science-based programs for children and adolescents* (pp. 89–109). Washington, DC: American Psychological Association.

Kanevsky, L., & Geake, J. (2004). Inside the zone of proximal development: Validating a multifactor model of learning potential with gifted students and their peers. *Journal for the Education of the Gifted, 28*(2), 182–217.

Kang, S. (2004). Substance use disorders in pregnancy and postpartum. Retrieved from http://heretohelp.bc.ca/visions/women-vol2/substance-use-disorders-in-pregnancy-and-postpartum

Karatekin, C., Marcus, D. J., & White, T. (2007). Oculomotor and manual indexes of incidental and intentional spatial sequence learning during middle childhood and adolescence. *Journal of Experimental Child Psychology, 96*(2), 107–130.

Karavasilis, L., Doyle, A. B., & Markiewicz, D. (2003). Associations between parenting style and attachment to mother in middle childhood and adolescence. *International Journal of Behavioral Development, 27*(2), 153–164.

Katz, R., Lowenstein, A., Phillips, J., & Daatland, S. O. (2005). Theorizing inter-generational family relations: Solidarity, conflict, and ambivalence in cross-national contexts. In V. L. Bengtson et al. (Eds.), *Sourcebook of family theory & research* (pp. 393–420). Thousand Oaks, CA: Sage.

Katzman, D. K. (2005). Medical complications in adolescents with anorexia nervosa: A review of the literature. *International Journal of Eating Disorders, 37*(Suppl), S52–S59.

Kauff, N. D., & Offit, K. (2007). Modeling genetic risk of breast cancer. *Journal of the American Medical Association, 297,* 2637–2639.

Kavanagh, K., et al. (2007). Characterization and heritability of obesity and associated risk factors in vervet monkeys. *Obesity, 15*(7), 1666–1674.

Kavanaugh, R. D. (2006). Pretend play. In B. Spodek & O. N. Saracho (Eds.), *Handbook of research on the education of young children* (2nd ed.) (pp. 269–278). Mahwah, NJ: Erlbaum.

Kavcic, T., & Zupancic, M. (2005). Sibling relationship in early/middle childhood: Trait- and dyad-centered approach. *Studia Psychologica, 47*(3), 179–197.

Kavšek, M. (2012). The comparator model of infant visual habituation and dishabituation: Recent insights. *Developmental Psychobiology*, doi: 10.1002/dev.21081

Kawas, C. H., & Brookmeyer, R. (2001). Aging and the public health effects of dementia. *The New England Journal of Medicine, 344,* 1160–1161.

Kaye, W. H., et al. (2004). Genetic analysis of bulimia nervosa: Methods and sample description. *International Journal of Eating Disorders, 35*(4), 556–570.

Kazdin, A. E. (2000). Treatments for aggressive and antisocial children. *Child and Adolescent Psychiatric Clinics of North America, 9*(4), 841–858.

Kazui, H., et al. (2008). Association between quality of life of demented patients and professional knowledge of care workers. *Journal of Geriatric Psychiatry and Neurology, 21*(1), 72–78.

Kearney, C. A., & Bensaheb, A. (2007). Assessing anxiety disorders in children and adolescents. In S. R. Smith & L. Handler (Eds.), *The clinical assessment of children and adolescents: A practitioner's handbook* (pp. 467–483). Mahwah, NJ: Erlbaum.

Keen, D., Rodger, S., Doussin, K., & Braithwaite, M. (2007). A pilot study of the effects of a social-pragmatic intervention on the communication and symbolic play of children with autism. *Autism, 11*(1), 63–71.

Keller, H., Kärtner, J., Borke, J., Yovsi, R., & Kleis, A. (2005). Parenting styles and the development of the categorical self: A longitudinal study on mirror self-recognition in Cameroonian Nso and German families. *International Journal of Behavioral Development, 29*(6), 496–504.

Kellman, P. J., & Arterberry, M. E. (2006). Infant visual perception. In D. Kuhn et al. (Eds.), *Handbook of child psychology: Vol. 2, Cognition, perception, and language* (6th ed.) (pp. 109–160). Hoboken, NJ: Wiley.

Kellogg, R. (1959). *What children scribble and why.* Oxford: National Press.

Kellogg, R. (1970). Understanding children's art. In P. Cramer (Ed.), *Readings in developmental psychology today.* Del Mar, CA: CRM.

Kemp, C. L. (2005). Dimensions of grandparent– adult grandchild relationships: From family ties to intergenerational friendships. *Canadian Journal on Aging, 24*(2), 161–178.

Kempes, M., Matthys, W., de Vries, H., & van Engeland, H. (2005). Reactive and proactive aggression in children: A review of theory, findings and the relevance for child and adolescent psychiatry. *European Child & Adolescent Psychiatry, 14*(1), 11–19.

Kendler, K. S., Gardner, C. O., Gatz, M., & Pedersen, N. L. (2007). The sources of co-morbidity between major depression and generalized anxiety disorder in a Swedish national twin sample. *Psychological Medicine, 37*(3), 453–462.

Kennard, J. (2012). Health sperm: Maximize your fertility. Retrieved from http://menshealth.about.com/cs/stds/a/healthy_sperm.htm

Kennedy, B. (2013). Ontario youth soccer to stop keeping score, standings. Retrieved from http://www.thestar.com/sports/soccer/2013/02/16/ontario_youth_soccer_to_stop_keeping_score_standings.html

Keogh, A. F., & Whyte, J. (2006). Exploring children's concepts of intelligence through ethnographic methods. *Irish Journal of Psychology, 27*(1–2), 69–78.

Kerns, K. A., Abraham, M. M., Schlegelmilch, A., & Morgan, T. A. (2007). Mother–child attachment in later middle childhood: Assessment approaches and associations with mood and emotion regulation. *Attachment & Human Development, 9*(1), 33–53.

Khamsi, R. (2007). Active parents make for active kids. Retrieved from http://www.newscientist.com/article/dn12950-active-parents-make-for-active-kids.html#.UheyxNKTiSp

Kidd, E., & Bavin, E. L. (2007). Lexical and referential influences on on-line spoken language comprehension: A comparison of adults and primary-school-age children. *First Language, 27*(1), 29–52.

Kidshealth. (2010). Infections: Toxoplasmosis. Retrieved from http://kidshealth.org/parent/infections/parasitic/toxoplasmosis.html

Killen, M., & Smetana, J. G. (Eds.). (2006). *Handbook of moral development*. Mahwah, NJ: Erlbaum.

Kim, J-Y., McHale, S. M., Osgood, D. W., & Crouter, A. C. (2006). Longitudinal course and family correlates of sibling relationships from childhood through adolescence. *Child Development, 77*(6), 1746–1761.

King, J., MacKay, M., Sirnick, A., & The Canadian Shaken Baby Group. (2003). Shaken baby syndrome in Canada: Clinical characteristics and outcomes of hospital cases. *Canadian Medical Association Journal, 168*(2), 155–159. Retrieved from http://www.cmaj.ca/cgi/content/full/168/2/155

King, P. M., & Kitchener, K. S. (2004). Reflective judgment. *Educational Psychologist, 39*(1), 5–18.

King, V., & Scott, M. E. (2005). A comparison of cohabiting relationships among older and younger adults. *Journal of Marriage and Family, 67*(2), 271–285.

Kingston, A., (2007, January 29). The 27-year itch. *Maclean's*. Retrieved from http://www.macleans.ca/article.jsp?content=20070129_140063_140063

Kinsbourne, M. (2003). The corpus callosum equilibrates the cerebral hemispheres. In E. Zaidel & M. Iacoboni (Eds.), *The parallel brain: The cognitive neuroscience of the corpus callosum* (pp. 271–281). Cambridge, MA: MIT Press.

Kirby, P. G., Biever, J. L., Martinez, I. G., & Gómez, J. P. (2004). Adults returning to school: The impact on family and work. *Journal of Psychology: Interdisciplinary and Applied, 138*(1), 65–76.

Kirkcaldy, B. D., Shephard, R. J., & Siefen, R. G. (2002). The relationship between physical activity and self-image and problem behaviour among adolescents. *Social Psychiatry and Psychiatric Epidemiology, 37*(11), 544–550.

Kirkey, S. (2013). Only 20 per cent doctors would perform euthanasia if legal, poll of MDs finds. Retrieved from CBC News. (2012a, October 12). Inside Gloria Taylor's battle for the right to die. Retrieved from http://www.canada.com/news/Only+cent+doctors+would+perform+euthanasia+legal+poll+finds/7939308/story.html

Kistner, J. (2006). Children's peer acceptance, perceived acceptance, and risk for depression. In T. E. Joiner, J. S. Brown, & J. Kistner (Eds.), *The interpersonal, cognitive, and social nature of depression* (pp. 1–21). Mahwah, NJ: Erlbaum.

Kjelsås, E., Bjornstrom, C., & Götestam, K. G. (2004). Prevalence of eating disorders in female and male adolescents (14–15 years). *Eating Behaviors, 5*(1), 13–25.

Kleiber, D. A., & Kelly, J. R. (1980). Leisure, socialization, and the life cycle. In S. E. Iso-Ahola (Ed.), *Social psychological perspectives on leisure and recreation* (pp. 91–137). Springfield, IL: Charles C. Thomas.

Kliegel, M., Jäger, T., & Phillips, L. H. (2008). Adult age differences in event-based prospective memory: A meta-analysis on the role of focal versus nonfocal cues. *Psychology and Aging, 23*(1), 203–208.

Klein, P. J., & Meltzoff, A. N. (1999). Long-term memory, forgetting and deferred imitation in 12-month-old infants. *Developmental Science, 2*(1), 102–113.

Klier, C. M. (2006). Mother–infant bonding disorders in patients with postnatal depression: The Postpartum Bonding Questionnaire in clinical practice. *Archives of Women's Mental Health, 9*(5), 289–291.

Klintsova, A. Y., & Greenough, W. T. (1999). Synaptic plasticity in cortical systems. *Current Opinion in Neurobiology, 9*(2), 203–208.

Kloep, M., & Hendry, L. B. (2007). Retirement: A new beginning? *The Psychologist, 20*(12), 742–745.

Klohnen, E. C., & Luo, S. (2003). Interpersonal attraction and personality: What is attractive–self similarity, ideal similarity, complementarity or attachment security? *Journal of Personality and Social Psychology, 85*(4), 709–722.

Knaak, S. (2005). Breast-feeding, bottle- feeding and Dr. Spock: The shifting context of choice. *Canadian Review of Sociology and Anthropology, 42*(2), 197–216.

Knafo, A., & Plomin, R. (2006a). Parental discipline and affection and children's prosocial behavior: Genetic and environmental links. *Journal of Personality and Social Psychology, 90*(1), 147–164.

Knafo, A., & Plomin, R. (2006b). Prosocial behavior from early to middle childhood: Genetic and environmental influences on stability and change. *Developmental Psychology, 42*(5), 771–786.

Kniffin, K. M., & Wilson, D. S. (2004). The effect of nonphysical traits on the perception of physical attractiveness: Three naturalistic studies. *Evolution and Human Behavior, 25*(2), 88–101.

Kochanska, G., Coy, K. C., Murray, K. T. (2001). The development of self-regulation in the ?rst four years of life. *Child Development, 72*(4), 1091–1111.

Kohl, C. (2004). Postpartum psychoses: Closer to schizophrenia or the affective spectrum? *Current Opinion in Psychiatry, 17*(2), 87–90.

Kohl, J. V. (2007). The mind's eyes: Human pheromones, neuroscience, and male sexual preferences. *Journal of Psychology & Human Sexuality, 18*(4), 313–369.

Kohlberg, L. (1963). Moral development and identification. In H. W. Stevenson (Ed.), *Child psychology: 62nd yearbook of the National Society for the Study of Education.* Chicago: University of Chicago Press.

Kohlberg, L. (1966). Cognitive stages and preschool education. *Human Development, 9,* 5–17.

Kohlberg, L. (1969). Stage and sequence: The cognitive-developmental approach to socialization. In D. A. Goslin (Ed.), *Handbook of socialization theory and research.* Chicago: Rand McNally.

Kohlberg, L. (1981). *The meaning and measurement of moral development.* Worcester, MA: Clark University Press.

Kohlberg, L. (1985). *The psychology of moral development.* San Francisco: Harper & Row.

Kohlberg, L., & Kramer, R. (1969). Continuities and discontinuities in childhood and adult moral development. *Human Development, 12,* 93–120.

Kolata, G. (2007, May 8). Genes take charge, and diets fall by the wayside. *New York Times online.*

Kolb, B., & Gibb, R. (2007). Brain plasticity and recovery from early cortical injury. *Developmental Psychobiology, 49*(2), 107–118.

Konijn, E. A., Bijvank, M. N., & Bushman, B. J. (2007). I wish I were a warrior: The role of wishful identification in the effects of violent video games on aggression in adolescent boys. *Developmental Psychology, 43*(4), 1038–1044.

Kopp, C. B. (1989). Regulation of distress and negative emotions: A developmental view. *Developmental Psychology, 25,* 343–354.

Korff, S. C. (2006). Religious orientation as a predictor of life satisfaction within the elderly population. *Dissertation Abstracts International: Section B: The Sciences and Engineering. 67*(1-B), 2006, 550.

Krackow, E., & Lynn, S. J. (2003). Is there touch in the game of Twister®? The effects of innocuous touch and suggestive questions on children's eyewitness memory. *Law and Human Behavior, 27*, 589–604.

Krebs, D. L., & Denton, K. (2005). Toward a more pragmatic approach to morality: A critical evaluation of Kohlberg's model. *Psychological Review, 112*(3), 629–649.

Kristensen, P., & Bjerkedal, T. (2007). Explaining the relation between birth order and intelligence. *Science, 313*(5832), 1717.

Kroeger, K. A., & Nelson, W. M., III. (2006). A language programme to increase the verbal production of a child dually diagnosed with Down syndrome and autism. *Journal of Intellectual Disability Research, 50*(2), 101–108.

Krojgaard, P. (2005). Continuity and discontinuity in developmental psychology. *Psyke & Logos, 26*(2), 377–394.

Krueger, C., Holditch-Davis, D., Quint, S., & DeCasper, A. (2004). Recurring auditory experience in the 28- to 34-week-old fetus. *Infant Behavior & Development, 27*(4), 537–543.

Kübler-Ross, E. (1969). *On death and dying.* New York: Macmillan.

Kübler-Ross, E., & Kessler, D. (2005). *On grief and grieving.* New York: Scribner.

Kuczaj, S. A., II (1982). On the nature of syntactic development. In S. A. Kuczaj II (Ed.), *Language development,* Vol. 1, *Syntax and semantics.* Hillsdale, NJ: Erlbaum.

Kuczmarski, R.J., Ogden, C.L., Guo, S.S,, Grummer-Strawn, L.M., Flegal, K.M., Mei, Z., Wei, R., Curtin, L.R., Roche, A.F., & Johnson, C.L. (2002). 2000 Center for Disease Control growth charts for the United States: Methods and development. Center for Disease Control and Prevention, Vital and Health Statistics, Series 11, (no. 246), 1–190.

Kuhl, P. K., et al. (1997). Cross-language analysis of phonetic units in language addressed to infants. *Science, 277*(5326), 684–686.

Kuhl, P. K., et al. (2006). Infants show a facilitation effect for native language phonetic perception between 6 and 12 months. *Developmental Science, 9*(2) F13–F21.

Kuhn, D. (2007). Editorial. *Cognitive Development, 22*(1), 1–2.

Kulick, D. (2006). Regulating sex: The politics of intimacy and identity. *Sexualities, 9*(1), 122–124.

Kulik, L. (2000). Women face unemployment: A comparative analysis of age groups. *Journal of Career Development, 27*(1), 15–33.

Kulik, L. (2004). Perceived equality in spousal relations, marital quality, and life satisfaction. *Families in Society, 85*(2), 243–250.

Kumar, K. (2010). A journey towards creating an inclusive classroom: How Universal Design for Learning has transformed my teaching. *Transformative Dialogues: Teaching & Learning Journal, 4*(2). Retrieved from http://kwantlen.ca/TD/TD.4.2/TD.4.2.5_Kumar_Inclusive_Classroom.pdf

Kunz, J. A. (2007). The life story matrix. In J. A. Kunz, & F. G. Soltys (Eds.), *Transformational reminiscence: Life story work* (pp. 1–16). New York: Springer Publishing Co.

Kunzmann, U., & Baltes, P. B. (2005). The psychology of wisdom: Theoretical and empirical challenges. In R. J. Sternberg, & J. Jordan (Eds.), *A handbook of wisdom: Psychological perspectives* (pp. 110–135). New York: Cambridge University Press.

Kurdek, L. A. (2005). What do we know about gay and lesbian couples? *Current Directions in Psychological Science, 14*(5), 251.

Kurdek, L. A. (2006). Differences between partners from hetersosexual, gay, and lesbian cohabiting couples. *Journal of Marriage and the Family, 68*(2), 509–528.

Kvaal, K., et al. (2008). Co-occurrence of anxiety and depressive disorders in a community sample of older people. *International Journal of Geriatric Psychiatry, 23*(3) 229–237.

Kwok, H-K. (2006). A study of the sandwich generation in Hong Kong. *Current Sociology, 54*(2), 257–272.

Kwok, H. W. M. (2003). Psychopharmacology in autism spectrum disorders. *Current Opinion in Psychiatry, 16*(5), 529–534.

L

Labouvie-Vief, G. (2006). Emerging structures of adult thought. In J. J. Arnett & J. L. Tanner (Eds.). *Emerging adults in America.* (pp. 59–84). Washington, DC: American Psychological Association.

Labouvie-Vief, G., & González, M. M. (2004). Dynamic integration: Affect optimization and differentiation in development. In D. Y. Dai & R. J. Sternberg (Eds.), *Motivation, emotion, and cognition* (pp. 237–272). Mahwah, NJ: Erlbaum.

Labrell, F., & Ubersfeld, G. (2004). Parental verbal strategies and children's capacities at 3 and 5 years during a memory task. *European Journal of Psychology of Education, 19*(2), 189–202.

Lachman, M. E. (2004). Development in midlife. *Annual Review of Psychology, 55,* 305–331.

Laflamme, D., Pomerleau, A., & Malcuit, G. (2002). A comparison of fathers' and mothers' involvement in childcare and stimulation behaviors during free-play with their infants at 9 and 15 months. *Sex Roles, 47*(11–12), 507–518.

Lai, H-L., et al. (2006). Randomized controlled trial of music during kangaroo care on maternal state anxiety and preterm infants' responses. *International Journal of Nursing Studies, 43*(2), 139–146.

Lam, K. S. L., Aman, M. G., & Arnold, L. E. (2006). Neurochemical correlates of autistic disorder: A review of the literature. *Research in Developmental Disabilities, 27*(3), 254–289.

Lam, T. H., Shi, H. J., Ho, L. M., Stewart, S. M., & Fan, S. (2002). Timing of pubertal maturation and heterosexual behavior among Hong Kong Chinese adolescents. *Archives of Sexual Behavior, 31*(4), 359–366.

Lamb, M. E., & Ahnert, L. (2006). Nonparental child care: Context, concepts, correlates, and consequences. In K. A. Renninger, I. E. Sigel, W. Damon, & R. M. Lerner (Eds.), *Handbook of child psychology* (6th ed.), Vol. 4, *Child psychology in practice* (pp. 950–1016). Hoboken, NJ: Wiley.

Lamers, C. T. J., Bechara, A., Rizzo, M., & Ramaekers, J. G. (2006). Cognitive function and mood in MDMA/THC users, THC users and non-drug using controls. *Journal of Psychopharmacology, 20*(2), 302–311.

Langlois, C. (2013). Stages of puberty: Help your children feel positive about the changes in their body. Retrieved from http://www.canadianliving.com/moms/teens/stages_of_puberty.php

Langlois, J. H., et al. (2000). Maxims or myths of beauty? A meta-analytic and theoretical review. *Psychological Bulletin, 126*(3), 390–423.

Lansford, J. E., Malone, P. S., Castellino, D. R., Dodge, K. A., Pettit, G. S., & Bates, J. E. (2006). Trajectories of internalizing, externalizing, and grades for children who have and have not experienced their parents' divorce or separation. *Journal of Family Psychology. 20*(2), 292–301.

Lantolf, J. P., & Thorne, S. L. (2007). Sociocultural theory and second language learning. In B. VanPatten & J. Williams (Eds.), *Theories in second language acquisition: An introduction* (pp. 201–224). Mahwah, NJ: Erlbaum.

LaPointe, L. L. (Ed.). (2005). Feral children. *Journal of Medical Speech-Language Pathology, 13*(1), vii–ix.

Lapsley, D. K. (2006). Moral stage theory. In K. Killen & J. G. Smetana (Eds.), *Handbook of moral development* (pp. 37–66). Mahwah, NJ: Erlbaum.

Larroque, B., et al. (2005). Temperament at 9 months of very preterm infants born at less than 29 weeks' gestation: The Epipage study. *Journal of Developmental & Behavioral Pediatrics, 26*(1), 48–55.

Latham, G. P., & Budworth, M.-H. (2007). The study of work motivation in the 20th century. In L. L. Koppes, (Ed.), *Historical perspectives in industrial and organizational psychology* (pp. 353–381). Mahwah, NJ: Erlbaum.

Lattanzi-Licht, Marcia. (2007). Religion, spirituality, and dying. In D. Balk, et al. (Eds.), *Handbook of thanatology* (pp. 11–17). New York: Routledge/Taylor & Francis Group.

Lau, A. S., Litrownik, A. J., Newton, R. R., Black, M. M., & Everson, M. D. (2006). Factors affecting the link between physical discipline and child externalizing problems in Black and White families. *Journal of Community Psychology, 34*(1), 89–103.

Laumann, E. O., et al. (2006). Sexual activity, sexual disorders and associated help-seeking behavior among mature

Meltzoff, A. N. (1988). Imitation, objects, tools, and the rudiments of language in human ontogeny. *Human Evolution, 3*(1–2), 45–64.

Meltzoff, A. N., & Moore, M, K. (1977). Imitation of facial and manual gestures by human neonates. *Science, 198*, 75–78.

Meltzoff, A. N., & Prinz, W. (Eds.). (2002). *The imitative mind: Development, evolution, and brain bases.* New York: Cambridge University Press.

Mendle, J., et al. (2006). Family structure and age at menarche: A children-of-twins approach. *Developmental Psychology, 42*(3), 533–542.

Mendleson, R. (2009, April). Youth survey: The surprising optimism of Aboriginal teams. *Macleans*. Retrieved from http://www2.macleans.ca/2009/04/02/the-surprising-optimism-of-aboriginal-youth/

Mental Health Canada. (2013). Children and adolescents with conduct disorder. Retrieved from http://www.mentalhealthcanada.com/ConditionsandDisordersDetail.asp?lang=e&category=69#204

Metcalfe, J. S., et al. (2005). Development of somatosensory-motor integration: An event-related analysis of infant posture in the first year of independent walking. *Developmental Psychobiology, 46*(1), 19–35.

Metzger, K. L., et al. (2007). Effects of nicotine vary across two auditory evoked potentials in the mouse. *Biological Psychiatry, 61*(1), 23–30.

Meyerhoff, M. (2005). *A Parent's Guide to Avoiding the Super Baby Syndrome*. Tallahassee, FL: William Gladden Foundation.

Michael, R., Gagnon, J., Laumann, E., & Kolata, G. (1994). *Sex in America: A definitive survey.* Boston: Little Brown.

Milgram, R. M., & Livne, N. L. (2006). Research on creativity in Israel: A chronicle of theoretical and empirical development. In J. C. Kaufman & R. J. Sternberg (Eds.), *The international handbook of creativity* (pp. 307–336). New York: Cambridge University Press.

Millar, W. J., & Maclean, H. (2005). Breastfeeding practices. *Health Reports* (Statistics Canada, Catalogue 82-003-XIE) *16*(12): 23–31. Retrieved from http://www.statcan.gc.ca/pub/82-003-x/82-003-x2004002-eng.pdf

Miller, C. F., Trautner, H. M., & Ruble, D. N. (2006). The role of gender stereotypes in children's preferences and behavior. In L. Balter & C. S. Tamis-LeMonda (Eds.), *Child psychology: A handbook of contemporary issues* (2nd ed.) (pp. 293–323). New York: Psychology Press.

Miller, S. M., Boyer, B. A., & Rodoletz, M. (1990). Anxiety in children: Nature and development. In M. Lewis & S. M. Miller (Eds.), *Handbook of developmental psychopathology.* New York: Plenum.

Mills, B., Reyna, V. F., & Estrada, S. (2008). Explaining contradictory relations between risk perception and risk taking. *Psychological Science, 19*(5), 429–433.

Miner, R. (2010). *People without Jobs, Jobs without People: Ontario's Labour Market Future*. Retrieved from http://www.collegesontario.org/policy-positions/MinerReport.pdf

Minino, A. M., Heron, M. P., Murphy, S. L., & Kochanek, K. D. (2007, October 10). Deaths: Final data for 2004. *National vital statistics reports, 55*(19). Retrieved from http://www.cdc.gov/nchs/data/nvsr/nvsr55/nvsr55_19.pdf

Minkler, M., & Fuller-Thomson, E. (2005). African American grandparents raising grandchildren: A national study using the Census 2000 *American Community Survey. Journals of Gerontology: Series B: Psychological Sciences and Social Sciences, 60B*(2), S82–S92.

Miscarriage. (2007, January 11). Retrieved from http://www.nlm.nih.gov/medlineplus/ency/article/001488.htm. Accessed February 23, 2007.

Mischo, C. (2004). Fördert Gruppendiskussion die Perspektiven-Koordination? *Zeitschrift für Entwicklungspsychologie und Pädagogische Psychologie, 36*(1), 30–37.

Mitchell, A. L. (2006). Medical consequences of cocaine. *Journal of Addictions Nursing, 17*(4), 249.

Mitchell, D. D., & Bruss, P. J. (2003) Age differences in implicit memory: Conceptual, perceptual, or methodological? *Psychology and Aging, 18*(4), 807–822.

Mock, S. E., & Cornelius, S. W. (2007). Profiles of interdependence: The retirement planning of married, cohabiting, and lesbian couples. *Sex Roles, 56*(11–12), 793–800.

Mock, S. E., Taylor, C. J., & Savin- Williams, R. C. (2006). Aging together: The retirement plans of same-sex couples. In D. Kimmel, T. Rose, & S. David (Eds.), *Lesbian, gay, bisexual, and transgender aging: Research and clinical perspectives* (pp. 152–174). New York: Columbia University Press.

Moen, P., Huang, Q., Plassmann, V., & Dentinger, E. (2006). Deciding the future. *American Behavioral Scientist, 49*(10), 1422–1443.

Moen, P., Kim, J. E., & Hofmeister, H. (2001). Couples' work/retirement transitions, gender, and marital equality. *Social Psychology Quarterly, 64,* 55–71.

Moens, E., Braet, C., & Soetens, B. (2007). Observation of family functioning at mealtime: A comparison between families of children with and without overweight. *Journal of Pediatric Psychology, 32*(1), 52–63.

Mohan, R., & Bhugra, D. (2005). Literature update. *Sexual and Relationship Therapy, 20*(1), 115–122.

Molinari, L., & Corsaro, W. A. (2000). Le relazioni amicali nella scuola dell'infanzia e nella scuola elementare: Uno studio longitudinale. *Eta Evolutiva, 67,* 40–51.

Monat, A., Lazarus, R. S , & Reevy, G. (Eds.). (2007). *The Praeger handbook on stress and coping* (Vol. 2). Westport, CT: Praeger Publishers/Greenwood Publishing Group.

Monette, M. (2012, October 15). Senior suicide: An overlooked problem. *Canadian Medical Association Journal*. Retrieved from http://www.cmaj.ca/site/earlyreleases/15oct12_senior_suicide.xhtml

Monte, L. (2013). Portion size, then and now. Retrieved from http://www.divinecaroline.com/self/wellness/portion-size-then-vs-now

Moore, D. R. & Heiman, J. R. (2006). Women's sexuality in context: Relationship factors and female sexual functioning. In I. Goldstein, C. Meston, S. Davis, & A. Traish (Eds.), *Female sexual dysfunction.* New York: Parthenon.

Moretti. M. M., & Peled, M. (2004). Adolescent-parent attachment: Bonds that support healthy development. *Pediatrics and Child Health, 9*(8): 551–555.

Morrell, J., & Steele, H. (2003). The role of attachment security, temperament, maternal perception, and care-giving behavior in persistent infant sleeping problems. *Infant Mental Health Journal, 24*(5), 447–468.

Morrow, A. (2010, Sept. 7). Canadians are among the best educated in the world. *Globe and Mail*. Retrieved from http://www.theglobeandmail.com/news/national/canadians-among-best-educated-in-the-world-report/article4326151/

Morry, M. M., & Gaines, S. O. (2005). Relationship satisfaction as a predictor of similarity ratings: A test of the attraction-similarity hypothesis. *Journal of Social and Personal Relationships, 22*(4), 561–584.

Morton, S. M. B. (2006). Maternal nutrition and fetal growth and development. In P. Gluckman & M. Hanson (Eds.), *Developmental origins of health and disease* (pp. 98–129). New York: Cambridge University Press.

Moses, L. J., & Flavell, J. H. (1990). Inferring false beliefs from actions and reactions. *Child Development, 61,* 929–945.

Moshman, D. (2005). *Adolescent psychological development (2nd ed.).* Mahwah, NJ: Erlbaum.

Mueller, R., Pierce, K., Ambrose, J. B., Allen, G., & Courchesne, E. (2001). Atypical patterns of cerebral motor activation in autism: A functional magnetic resonance study. *Biological Psychiatry, 49*(8) 665–676.

Muhlbauer, V., & Chrisler, J. C. (Eds.). (2007). *Women over 50: Psychological perspectives.* New York: Springer Science + Business Media.

Muraco, A. (2006). Intentional families: Fictive kin ties between cross-gender, different sexual orientation friends. *Journal of Marriage and Family, 68*(5), 1313–1325.

Muris, P., Bodden, D., Merckelbach, H., Ollendick, T. H., & King, N. (2003). Fear of the beast: A prospective study on the effects of negative information on childhood fear. *Behaviour Research and Therapy, 41*(2), 195–208.

Murray, D. (2013). Breastfeeding and infant growth. Retrieved from http://breastfeeding.about.com/od/breastfeedingbystage/a/Breastfeeding-And-Infant-Growth.htm

Myers, J. E., Madathil, J., & Tingle, L. R. (2005). Marriage satisfaction and wellness in India and the United States: A preliminary comparison of arranged marriages and marriages of choice. *Journal of Counseling & Development, 83*(2), 183–190.

Myers, S. M. (2006). Religious homogamy and marital quality: Historical and generational patterns, 1980–1997. *Journal of Marriage and Family, 68*(2): 292–304.

N

Nadeau, L., et al. (2003). Extremely premature and very low birthweight infants: A double hazard population? *Social Development, 12*(2), 235–248.

Nagin, D. S., & Tremblay, R. E. (2001). Parental and early childhood predictors of persistent physical aggression in boys from kinder-garten to high school. *Archives of General Psychiatry, 58*(4), 389–394.

National Center for Children in Poverty. (2004). Low-income children in the United States (2004). Retrieved from http://cpmcnet.columbia.edu/dept/nccp/.

National Center for Education Statistics. (2007, June). Dropout rates in the United States: 2005. Retrieved from http://nces.ed.gov/pubs2007/dropout05/. Accessed July 20, 2007.

National Center for Injury Prevention and Control, Office of Statistics and Programming, Centers for Disease Control and Prevention. (2007a, March 29). National Center for Health Statistics (NCHS), National Vital Statistics System. Accessed May 7, 2007. Available at http://webappa.cdc.gov/cgi-bin/broker.exe.

National Center for Injury Prevention and Control. (2007b, July 11). Suicide: Fact sheet. Available at http://www.cdc.gov/ncipc/ factsheets/suifacts.htm.

National Eating Disorder Information Centre. (2012). Statistics: Eating disorders and disordered eating. Retrieved from http://www.nedic.ca/knowthefacts/statisticsArchive.shtml

National Guideline Clearinghouse. (2007). Use of clomiphene citrate in women. Available at http://www.guideline.gov/summary/summary.aspx?ss=15&doc_id=4843&nbr=3484. Last updated January 29, 2007. Accessed February 6, 2007.

National Institutes of Health. (2002). Available at http://cerhr.niehs.nih.gov/genpub/topics/ vitamin_a-ccae.html.

National Sleep Foundation. (2011). Children and sleep. Retrieved from http://www.sleepfoundation.org/article/sleep-topics/children-and-sleep

Natsopoulos, D., Kiosseoglou, G., & Xeromeritou, A. (1992). Handedness and spatial ability in children: Further support for Geschwind's hypothesis of "pathology of superiority" and for Annett's theory of intelligence. *Genetic, Social, and General Psychology Monographs, 118*(1) 103–126.

Nauert, R. (2013). National survey finds big jump in teen abuse of prescription drugs. Retrieved from http://www.habitude.ca/national-survey-finds-big-jump-in-teen-abuse-of-prescription-drugs/

Nauta, M. M. (2007). Career interests, self- efficacy, and personality as antecedents of career exploration. *Journal of Career Assessment, 15*(2), 162–180.

Naveh-Benjamin, M., Brav, T. K., & Levy, O. (2007). The associative memory deficit of older adults: The role of strategy utilization. *Psychology and Aging, 22,* 202–208.

Neisser, U., et al. (1996). Intelligence: Knowns and unknowns. *American Psychologist, 51,* 77–101.

Nelson, C. A., de Haan, M., & Thomas, K. M. (2006). Neuroscience of cognitive development: The role of experience and the developing brain. Hoboken, NJ: Wiley.

Nelson, C. A., & Luciana, M. (Eds.). (2001). *Handbook of developmental cognitive neuroscience.* Cambridge, MA: MIT Press.

Nelson, C. A., & Ludemann, P. M. (1989). Past, current, and future trends in infant face perception research. *Canadian Journal of Psychology, 43,* 183–198.

Nelson, K. (1973). *Structure and strategy in learning to talk.* Monographs for the Society for Research in Child Development, 38(1–2, ser. 149).

Nelson, K. (1981). Individual differences in language development: Implications for development of language. *Developmental Psychology, 17,* 170–187.

Nelson, K. (2005). Cognitive functions of language in early childhood. In B. D. Homer & C. S. Tamis-LeMonda (Eds.), *The development of social cognition and communication* (pp. 7–28). Mahwah, NJ: Erlbaum.

Nelson, K. (2006). Advances in pragmatic developmental theory: The case of language acquisition. *Human Development, 49*(3), 184–188.

Nelson, K., & Fivush, R. (2004). The emergence of autobiographical memory: A social cultural developmental theory. *Psychological Review, 111*(2), 486–511.

Nelson, M. (2013). Neonatal abstinence syndrome: The nurse's role. *International Journal of Childbirth Education, 28*(1), 38–42.

Nelson, T. D. (2005). Ageism: Prejudice against our feared future self. *Journal of Social Issues, 61*(2), 207–221.

Nesdale, D., & Lambert, A. (2007). Effects of experimentally manipulated peer rejection on children's negative affect, self-esteem, and maladaptive social behavior. *International Journal of Behavioral Development, 31*(2), 115–122.

Newburn-Cook, C. V., et al. (2002). Where and to what extent is prevention of low birth weight possible? *Western Journal of Nursing Research, 24*(8), 887–904.

Newman, R., Ratner, N. B., Jusczyk, A. M., Jusczyk, P. W., & Dow, K. A. (2006). Infants' early ability to segment the conversational speech signal predicts later language development: A retrospective analysis. *Developmental Psychology, 42*(4), 643–655.

News-Medical.Net. (2013). Culture plays role in deciding what makes a mate attractive, says researcher. Retrieved from http://www.news-medical.net/news/20130531/Culture-plays-role-in-deciding-what-makes-a-mate-attractive-says-researcher.aspx?page=2

Neyer, F. J. (2002). Twin relationships in old age. *Journal of Social and Personal Relationships, 19*(2), 155–177.

NIAAA (National Institute on Alcohol Abuse and Alcoholism). (2005). Cage questionnaire. Available at http://pubs.niaaa.nih.gov/publications/Assesing%20Alcohol/InstrumentPDFs/16_CAGE.pdf

Nielsen, S., & Palmer, B. (2003). Diagnosing eating disorders: AN, BN, and the others. *Acta Psychiatrica Scandinavica, 108*(3), 161–162.

Nielsen, S. J., & Popkin, B. M. (2003). Patterns and trends in food portion sizes, 1977–1998. *Journal of the American Medical Association, 289*(4), 450–453.

Niemeier, H. M., Raynor, H. A., Lloyd- Richardson, E. E., Rogers, M. L., & Wing, R. R. (2006). Fast food consumption and breakfast skipping: Predictors of weight gain from adolescence to adulthood in a nationally representative sample. *Journal of Adolescent Health, 39*(6), 842–849.

Nigg, J. T., Goldsmith, H. H., & Sachek, J. (2004). Temperament and attention deficit hyperactivity disorder: The development of a multiple pathway model. *Journal of Clinical Child and Adolescent Psychology, 33*(1), 42–53.

Nigg, J. T., Hinshaw, S. P., & Huang-Pollock, C. (2006). Disorders of attention and impulse regulation. In D. Cicchetti & D. J. Cohen (Eds.), *Developmental psychopathology,* Vol. 3, *Risk, disorder, and adaptation* (2nd ed.) (pp. 358–403). Hoboken, NJ: Wiley.

Nimrod, G. (2007). Retirees' leisure. *Leisure Studies, 26*(1), 65–80.

Nisbett, R. E. (2007, December 9). All brains are the same color. *The New York Times online.*

Nixon, R. (2011). Midlife crisis is a myth. LiveScience.com. Retrieved from http://www.livescience.com/12930-midlife-crisis-total-myth.html

Nock, M. K., Kazdin, A. E., Hiripi, E., & Kessler, R. C. (2006). Prevalence, subtypes, and correlates of DSM-IV conduct disorder in the National Comorbidity Survey Replication. *Psychological Medicine, 36,* 699–710.

Nolen-Hoeksema, S., Stice, E., Wade, E., & Bohon, C. (2007). Reciprocal relations between rumination and bulimic, substance abuse, and depressive symptoms in female adolescents. *Journal of Abnormal Psychology, 116*(1), 198–207.

Nomaguchi, K. M. (2006). Maternal employment, nonparental care, mother–child interactions, and child outcomes during preschool years. *Journal of Marriage and Family, 68*(5), 1341–1369.

Nonaka, A. M. (2004). The forgotten endangered languages: Lessons on the importance of remembering from Thailand's Ban Khor Sign Language. *Language in Society, 33*(5), 737–767.

Nonnemaker, J. M., & Homsi, G. (2007). Measurement properties of the Fagerström Test for nicotine dependence adapted for use in an adolescent sample. *Addictive Behaviors, 32*(1), 181–186.

Noppe, I. C., & Noppe, L. D. (2004). Adolescent experiences with death: Letting go of immortality. *Journal of Mental Health Counseling, 26*(2), 146–167.

Norlander, T., Erixon, A., & Archer, T. (2000). Psychological androgyny and creativity: Dynamics of gender-role and personality trait. *Social Behavior and Personality, 28*(5), 423–435.

Norton, A., et al. (2005). Are there pre- existing neural, cognitive, or motoric markers for musical ability? *Brain and Cognition, 59*(2), 124–134.

Nurnberg, H. G., et al. (2008). Sildenafil treatment of women with antidepressant-associated sexual dysfunction. *Journal of the American Medical Association, 300*(4), 395–404.

Nuttman-Shwartz, O. (2007). Is there life without work? *International Journal of Aging & Human Development, 64*(2) 129–147.

O

O'Boyle, M. W., & Benbow, C. P. (1990). Handedness and its relationship to ability and talent. In S. Coren (Ed.), *Left-handedness: Behavior implications and anomalies.* Amsterdam: North-Holland.

O'Brien, B., Chalmers, B., Fell, D., Heaman, M., Darling, E. K., & Herbert, P. (2011). The experience of pregnancy and birth with midwives: Results from the Canadian Maternity Experiences Survey. *Birth: Issues in Perinatal Care, 38*(3), 207–215. doi:10.1111/j.1523-536X.2011.00482.x

O'Dea, J. A. (2006). Self-concept, self-esteem and body weight in adolescent females: A three-year longitudinal study. *Journal of Health Psychology, 11*(4), 599–611.

O'Doherty, J., et al. (2003). Beauty in a smile: The role of medial orbitofrontal cortex in facial attractiveness. *Neuropsychologia, 41*(2), 147–155.

O'Donnell, L., et al. (2003). Long-term influence of sexual norms and attitudes on timing of sexual initiation among urban minority youth. *Journal of School Health, 23*(2), 68–75.

O'Keeffe, M. J., O'Callaghan, M., Williams, G. M., Najman, J. M., & Bor, W. (2003). Learning, cognitive, and attentional problems in adolescents born small for gestational age. *Pediatrics, 112*(2), 301–307.

O'Neill, D. K., & Chong, S. C. F. (2001). Preschool children's difficulty understanding the types of information obtained through the five senses. *Child Development, 72*(3), 803–815.

O'Neill, D. K., & Gopnik, A. (1991). Young children's ability to identify the sources of their beliefs. *Developmental Psychology, 27,* 390–397.

O'Shea, R. P., & Corballis, P. M. (2005). Binocular rivalry in the divided brain. In D. Alais & R. Blake (Eds.), *Binocular rivalry*. (pp. 301–315). Cambridge, MA: MIT Press.

Oates, J., & Messer, D. (2007). Growing up with TV. *The Psychologist, 20*(1), 30–32.

Office of National Statistics. (2006). Available at http://www.multiplebirths.org.uk/media.asp. Accessed February 6, 2007.

Office of the Commissioner of Official Languages. (2005). Bilingualism in Canada. Retrieved from http://www.ocol-clo.gc.ca/html/biling_e.php

Ogunfowora, O. B., Olanrewaju, D. M., & Akenzua, G. I. (2005). A comparative study of academic achievement of children with sickle cell anemia and their healthy siblings. *Journal of the National Medical Association, 97*(3), 405–408.

Oliveira, M. (2010, March 25). Canada a hotbed of online dating. *Globe and Mail*. Retrieved from http://www.theglobeandmail.com/technology/canada-a-hotbed-of-online-dating/article4312016/

Olivo, L., Cotter, R., & Bromwich, R. (2007).*Youth and the law: New approaches to criminal justice and child protection.* Toronto: Emond Montgomery Publications Ltd.

Olson, S. L., Bates, J. E., Sandy, J. M., & Lanthier, R. (2000). Early developmental precursors of externalizing behavior in middle childhood and adolescence. *Journal of Abnormal Child Psychology, 28*(2), 119–133.

Oltjenbruns, K. A., & Balk, D. E. (2007). Life span issues and loss, grief, and mourning: Part 1: The importance of a developmental context: childhood and adolescence as an example. In D. Balk, et al. (Eds.), *Handbook of thanatology* (pp. 143–163). New York: Routledge/Taylor & Francis Group.

Olweus Bullying Prevention Program. (2010). What is bullying? Retrieved from http://www.olweus.org/public/bullying.page

Omori, M., & Ingersoll, G. M. (2005). Health-endangering behaviours among Japanese college students: A test of psychosocial model of risk-taking behaviours. *Journal of Adolescence, 28*(1), 17–33.

Ontario Association of Children's Aid Societies. (2010). Your duty to report. Retrieved from http://www.oacas.org/childwelfare/duty.htm

Ontario Ministry of Education. (2004). *The individual education plan (IEP): A resource guide.* Retrieved from http://www.edu.gov.on.ca/eng/general/elemsec/speced/guide/resource/iepresguid.pdf

Orel, N. (2006). Lesbian and bisexual women as grandparents: The centrality of sexual orientation in the grandparent – grandchild relationship. In D. Kimmel, T. Rose, & S. David (Eds.), *Lesbian, gay, bisexual, and transgender ageing: Research and clinical perspectives* (pp. 175–194). New York: Columbia University Press.

Organisation for Economic Co-operation and Development. (2005). *OECD urges Canadian governments to increase funding for childcare.* Retrieved from http://www.oecd.org/canada/rgescanadiangovernmentstoincreasefundingforchildcare.htm

Örnkloo, H., & von Hofsten, C. (2007). Fitting objects into holes: On the development of spatial cognition skills. *Developmental Psychology, 43*(2), 404–416.

Orstavik, R. E., Kendler, K. S., Czajkowski, N., Tambs, K., & Reichborn-Kjennerud, T. (2007). Genetic and environmental contributions to depressive personality disorder in a population-based sample of Norwegian twins. *Journal of Affective Disorders, 99*(1–3), 181–189.

Ortega, V., Ojeda, P., Sutil, F., & Sierra, J. C. (2005). Culpabilidad sexual en adolescentes: Estudio de algunos factores relacionados. *Anales de Psicología, 21*(2), 268–275.

language abilities, working memory, and executive functioning. *Cognitive Development, 20*, 427–447.

Roeser, R. W., Peck, S. C., & Nasir, N. S. (2006). Self and identity processes in school motivation, learning, and achievement. In P. A. Alexander & P. H. Winne (Eds.), *Handbook of educational psychology* (pp. 391–424). Mahwah, NJ: Erlbaum.

Roffwarg, H. P., Muzio, J. N., & Dement, W. C. (1966). Ontogenetic development of the human sleep–dream cycle. *Science, 152,* 604–619.

Rogue Community College. (2012). Holland code quiz. Retrieved from http://www.roguecc.edu/counseling/hollandcodes/test.asp

Rondal, J. A., & Ling, L. (2006). Neurobehavioral specificity in Down's Syndrome. *Revista de Logopedia, Foniatría y Audiología, 26*(1), 12–19.

Roopnarine, J. L., Krishnakumar, A., Metindogan, A., & Evans, M. (2006). Links between parenting styles, parent–child academic interaction, parent–school interaction, and early academic skills and social behaviors in young children of English-speaking Caribbean immigrants. *Early Childhood Research Quarterly, 21*(2), 238–252.

Roots of Empathy. (2013). What we do: Research and effectiveness of the program. Retrieved from http://www.rootsofempathy.org/en/what-we-do/research.html

Rose, A. J., Swenson, L. P., & Carlson, W. (2004). Friendships of aggressive youth: Considering the influences of being disliked and of being perceived as popular. *Journal of Experimental Child Psychology, 88*(1), 25–45.

Rose, S. A., Feldman, J. F., & Jankowski, J. J. (2001). Visual short-term memory in the first year of life: Capacity and recency effects. *Developmental Psychology, 37*(4), 539–549.

Rose, S. A., Feldman, J. F., & Jankowski, J. J. (2005). The structure of infant cognition at 1 year. *Intelligence, 33*(3), 231–250.

Rose, S. A., Feldman, J. F., & Wallace, I. F. (1992). Infant information processing in relation to six-year cognitive outcomes. *Child Development, 63,* 1126–1141.

Rosen, T., Pillemer, K., & Lachs, M. (2008). Resident-to-resident aggression in long-term care facilities. *Aggression and Violent Behavior, 13*(2), 77–87.

Rosenstein, D., & Oster, H. (1988). Differential facial responses to four basic tastes. *Child Development, 59,* 1555–1568.

Rosenthal, R., & Jacobson, L. (1968). *Pygmalion in the classroom.* New York: Holt, Rinehart & Winston.

Rospenda, K. M., et al. (2005). Is workplace harassment hazardous to your health? *Journal of Business and Psychology, 20*(1), 95–110.

Ross, H., Ross, M., Stein, N., & Trabasso, T. (2006). How siblings resolve their conflicts: The importance of first offers, planning, and limited opposition. *Child Development. 77*(6) 1730–1745.

Ross, J. L., Roeltgen, D., Feuillan, P., Kushner, H., & Cutler, W. B. (2000). Use of estrogen in young girls with Turner syndrome: Effects on memory. *Neurology, 54*(1), 164–170.

Rotenberg, K. J., et al. (2004). Cross-sectional and longitudinal relations among peer-reported trustworthiness, social relationships, and psychological adjustment in children and early adolescents from the United Kingdom and Canada. *Journal of Experimental Child Psychology, 88*(1), 46–67.

Roterman, M. (2012). Sexual behaviour and condom use of 15 - to 24-year-olds in 2003 and 2009/10. *Statistics Canada*. Retrieved from http://www.statcan.gc.ca/pub/82-003-x/2012001/article/11632-eng.htm

Roth, G. S., et al. (2004). Aging in rhesus monkeys: Relevance to human health interventions. *Science, 305*(5689), 1423–1426.

Rothbart, M. K., Ellis, L. K., & Posner, M. I. (2004). Temperament and self-regulation. In R. F. Baumeister & K. D. Vohs (Eds.), *Handbook of self-regulation: Research, theory, and applications.* New York: Guilford.

Rothbart, M. K., & Sheese, B. E. (2007). Temperament and emotion regulation. In J. J. Gross (Ed.), *Handbook of emotion regulation* (pp. 331–350). New York: Guilford.

Rottinghaus, P. J., Betz, N. E., & Borgen, F. H. (2003). Validity of parallel measures of vocational interests and confidence. *Journal of Career Assessment, 11*(4), 355–378.

Rottinghaus, P. J., Coon, K. L.,Gaffey, A. R., & Zytowski, D. G. (2007). Thirty-year stability and predictive validity of vocational interests. *Journal of Career Assessment, 15*(1), 5–22.

Roulet-Perez, E., & Deonna, T. (2006). Autism, epilepsy, and EEG epileptiform activity. In R. Tuchman & I. Rapin (Eds.), *Autism: A neurological disorder of early brain development* (pp. 174–188). *International review of child neurology*. London: Mac Keith Press.

Rowland, D. T. (2009). Global population aging: History and prospects. In P. Uhlenberg (Ed.), *International handbook of population aging* (pp. 37–65). New York: Springer Science + Business Media.

Rubia, K., et al. (2006). Progressive increase of frontostriatal brain activation from childhood to adulthood during event-related tasks of cognitive control. *Human Brain Mapping, 27*(12), 973–993.

Rubin, K. H., Bukowski, W. M., & Parker, J. G. (2006). Peer interactions, relationships, and groups. In N. Eisenberg, W. Damon, & R. M. Lerner (Eds.), *Handbook of child psychology* (6th ed.), Vol. 3, *Social, emotional, and personality development (*pp. 571–645). Hoboken, NJ: Wiley.

Ruble, D. N., Martin, C. L., & Berenbaum, S. A. (2006). Gender development. In N. Eisenberg, W. Damon, & R. M. Lerner (Eds.), *Handbook of child psychology* (6th ed.), Vol. 3, *Social, emotional, and personality development.* (pp. 858–932). Hoboken, NJ: Wiley.

Rudolph, K. D., & Flynn, M. (2007). Childhood adversity and youth depression: Influence of gender and pubertal status. *Development and Psychopathology, 19*(2), 497–521.

Rudy, D., & Grusec, J. E. (2006). Authoritarian parenting in individualist and collectivist groups: Associations with maternal emotion and cognition and children's self-esteem. *Journal of Family Psychology, 20*(1), 68–78.

Rumbold, A. R., et al. (2006). Vitamins C and E and the risks of preeclampsia and perinatal complications. *New England Journal of Medicine, 354*, 1796–1806.

Runyon, M. K., & Kenny, M. C. (2002). Relationship of attributional style, depression, and posttrauma distress among children who suffered physical or sexual abuse. *Child Maltreatment: Journal of the American Professional Society on the Abuse of Children, 7*(3), 254–264.

Rusconi, A. (2004). Different pathways out of the parental Home: A comparison of West Germany and Italy. *Journal of Comparative Family Studies, 35*(4), 627–649.

Rushton, J. P., & Bons, T. A. (2005). Mate choice and friendship in twins: Evidence for genetic similarity. *Psychological Science, 16*(7), 555–559.

Rushton, J. P., & Jensen, A. R. (2005). Thirty years of research on race differences in cognitive ability. *Psychology, Public Policy and Law, 11*(2), Retrieved from http://psychology.uwo.ca/faculty/rushtonpdfs/PPPL1.pdf

Rushton, J. P., Skuy, M., & Fridjhon, P. (2003). Performance on Raven's Advanced Progressive Matrices by African, East Indian, and White engineering students in South Africa. *Intelligence, 31*(2), 123–137.

Russ, S. W. (2006). Pretend play, affect, and creativity. In P. Locher, C. Martindale, & L. Dorfman (Eds.), *New directions in aesthetics, creativity and the arts, Foundations and frontiers in aesthetics* (pp. 239–250). Amityville, NY: Baywood.

Rybash, J. M., & Hrubi-Bopp, K. L. (2000). Source monitoring and false recollection: A life span developmental perspective. *Experimental Aging Research, 26*(1), 75–87.

Ryff, C. D., Singer, B. H., & Seltzer, M. M. (2002). Pathways through challenge: Implications for well-being and health. In L. Pulkkinen, & A. Caspi (Eds.), *Paths to successful development: Personality in the life course* (pp. 302–328). New York: Cambridge University Press.

S

Sabattini, L., & Leaper, C. (2004). The relation between mothers' and fathers' parenting styles and their division of labor in the home: Young adults' retrospective reports. *Sex Roles, 50*(3–4), 217–225.

Sabia, J. J. (2008). There's no place like home: A hazard model analysis of aging in place among older homeowners in the PSID. *Research on Aging, 30*(1), 3–35.

Sadker, D. M., & Silber, E. S. (Eds.) (2007). *Gender in the classroom: Foundations, skills, methods, and strategies across the curriculum.* Mahwah, NJ: Erlbaum.

Saffran, J. R., Werker, J. F., & Werner, L. A. (2006). The infant's auditory world: Hearing, speech, and the beginnings of language. In D. Kuhn, R. S. Siegler, W. Damon, & R. M. Lerner (Eds.), *Handbook of child psychology,* Vol. 2, *Cognition, perception, and language* (6th ed.) (pp. 58–108). Hoboken, NJ: Wiley.

Saggino, A., Perfetti, B., Spitoni, G., & Galati, G. (2006). Fluid intelligence and executive functions: New Perspectives. In L. V. Wesley (Ed.), *Intelligence: New research* (pp. 1–22). Hauppauge, NY: Nova Science Publishers.

Saigal, S., et al. (2006). Transition of extremely low-birth-weight infants from adolescence to young adulthood: Comparison with normal birth-weight controls. *Journal of the American Medical Association, 295*(6), 667–675.

Saiki, J., & Miyatsuji, H. (2007). Feature binding in visual working memory evaluated by type identification paradigm. *Cognition, 102*(1), 49–83.

Saito, S., & Miyake, A. (2004). On the nature of forgetting and the processing–storage relationship in reading span performance. *Journal of Memory and Language, 50*(4), 425–443.

Salapatek, P. (1975). Pattern perception in early infancy. In L. B. Cohen & P. Salapatek (Eds.), *Infant perception: From sensation to cognition.* New York: Academic Press.

Sales, J. M., Fivush, R., & Peterson, C. (2003). Parental reminiscing about positive and negative events. *Journal of Cognition and Development, 4*(2), 185–209.

Salmivalli, C., Ojanen, T., Haanpää, J., & Peets, K. (2005). "I'm OK but you're not" and other peer-relational schemas: Explaining individual differences in children's social goals. *Developmental Psychology, 41*(2), 363–375.

Salthouse, T. A. (2001). Structural models of the relations between age and measures of cognitive functioning. *Intelligence, 29*(2), 93–115.

Salthouse, T. A., & Babcock, R. L. (1991). Decomposing adult age differences in working memory. *Developmental Psychology, 27*(5), 763–776.

Salthouse, T. A., & Berish, D. E. (2005). Correlates of within-person (across-occasion) variability in reaction time. *Neuropsychology, 19*(1), 77–87.

Salthouse, T. A., & Davis, H. P. (2006). Organization of cognitive abilities and neuropsychological variables across the lifespan. *Developmental Review, 26*(1), 31–54.

Salthouse, T. A., & Siedlecki, K. L. (2007). Efficiency of route selection as a function of adult age. *Brain and Cognition, 63*(3), 279–286.

Salthouse, T. A., Siedlecki, K. L., & Krueger, L. E. (2006). An individual differences analysis of memory control. *Journal of Memory and Language, 55*(1), 102–125.

Salzarulo, P., & Ficca, G. (Eds.). (2002). *Awakening and sleep–wake cycle across development.* Amsterdam: John Benjamins.

Sandman, C., & Crinella, F. (1995). Cited in Margoshes, P. (1995). For many, old age is the prime of life. *APA Monitor, 26*(5), 36–37.

Santelli, J. S., Lindberg, J. D., Abma, J., McNeely, C. S., & Resnick, M. (2000). Adolescent sexual behavior: Estimates and trends from four nationally representative surveys. *Family Planning Perspectives, 32*(4), 156–165, 194.

Santos, D. C. C., Gabbard, C., & Goncalves, V. M. G. (2000). Motor development during the first 6 months: The case of Brazilian infants. *Infant and Child Development, 9*(3), 161–166.

Saroglou, V., & Galand, P. (2004). Identities, values, and religion: A study among Muslim, other immigrant, and native Belgian young adults after the 9/11 attacks. *Identity, 4*(2), 97–132.

Sarrazin, P., Trouilloud, D., & Bois, J. (2005a). Attentes du superviseur et performance sportive du pratiquant. Amplitude et fonctionnement de l'effet Pygmalion en contexte sportif. *Bulletin de Psychologie, 58*(1), 63–68.

Sarrazin, P., Trouilloud, D., Tessier, D., Chanal, J., & Bois, J. (2005b). Attentes de motivation et comportements différenciés de l'enseignant d'éducation physique et sportive à l'égard de ses élèves: une étude en contexte naturel d'enseignement. *Revue Européenne de Psychologie Appliquée, 55*(2), 111–120.

Sasaki, C. (2007). Grounded-theory study of therapists' perceptions of grieving process in bereaved children. *Dissertation Abstracts International: Section B: The Sciences and Engineering, 68*(1-B), 635.

Save the Children. (2004). *State of the world's mothers 2004.* Available at http://www.savethechildren.org/mothers/report_2004/index.asp. Accessed June 2004.

Savickas, M. L. (2005). The theory and practice of career construction. In S. D. Brown & R. W. Lent (Eds.). *Career development and counseling.* (pp. 42–70). Hoboken, NJ: Wiley.

Savin-Williams, R. C. (2007). Girl-on-girl sexuality. In B. J. R. Leadbeater & N. Way (Eds.), *Urban girls revisited: Building strengths* (pp. 301–318). New York: New York University Press.

Savin-Williams, R. C., & Diamond, L. M. (2004). Sex. In R. M. Lerner & L. Steinberg (Eds.), *Handbook of adolescent psychology* (2nd ed.) (pp. 189–231). Hoboken, NJ: Wiley.

Schaie, K. W. (1994). The course of adult intellectual development. *American Psychologist, 49,* 304–313. Copyright © American Psychological Association.

Schaie, K. W. (2005). What can we learn from longitudinal studies of adult development? *Research in Human Development, 2*(3), 133–158.

Schaie, K. W., Willis, S. L., & Caskie, G. I. L. (2004). The Seattle longitudinal study: Relationship between personality and cognition. *Aging, Neuropsychology, and Cognition, 11*(2–3), 304–324.

Scharf, M., Shulman, S., & Avigad-Spitz, L. (2005). Sibling relationships in emerging adulthood and in adolescence. *Journal of Adolescent Research, 20*(1), 64–90.

Schmidtke, A., Sell, R., & Lohr, C. (2008). Epidemiology of suicide in older persons. *Zeitschrift für Gerontologie und Geriatrie, 41*(1), 3–13.

Schneewind, K. A., & Kupsch, M. (2007). Patterns of neuroticism, work-family stress, and resources as determinants of personal distress: A cluster analysis of young, dual-earner families at the individual and couple level. *Journal of Individual Differences, 28*(3), 150–160.

Schonfeld, A. M., Mattson, S. N., & Riley, E. P. (2005). Moral maturity and delinquency after prenatal alcohol exposure. *Journal of Studies on Alcohol, 66*(4), 545–554.

Schoppe-Sullivan, S. J., Mangelsdorf, S. C., Brown, G. L., & Sokolowski, M. S. (2007). Goodness-of-fit in family context: Infant temperament, marital quality, and early coparenting behavior. *Infant Behavior & Development, 30*(1), 82–96.

Schraf, M., & Hertz-Lazarowitz, R. (2003). Social networks in the school context: Effects of culture and gender. *Journal of Social and Personal Relationships, 20*(6), 843–858.

Schuetze, P., Lawton, D., & Eiden, R. D. (2006). Prenatal cocaine exposure and infant sleep at 7 months of age: The influence of the caregiving environment. *Infant Mental Health Journal, 27*(4), 383–404.

Schultz, D. P., & Schultz, S. E. (2008). A history of modern psychology (9th Ed.). Belmont, CA: Thomson/Wadsworth.

Schultz, W. W., et al. (2005). Women's sexual pain and its management. *Journal of Sexual Medicine, 2*(3), 301–316.

Schumacher, D., & Queen, J. A. (2007). *Overcoming obesity in childhood and adolescence: A guide for school leaders.* Thousand Oaks, CA: Corwin Press.

Schuurmans, J., et al. (2006). A randomized, controlled trial of the effectiveness of cognitive-behavioral therapy and sertraline versus a waitlist control group for anxiety disorders in older adults. *American Journal of Geriatric Psychiatry, 14*(3), 255–263.

Schwartz, S. J. (2001). The evolution of Erik sonian and neo-Eriksonian identity theory and research: A review and integration. *Identity, 1*(1), 7–58.

Science Daily. (2001). A second language gives toddlers an edge. Retrieved from http://www.sciencedaily.com/releases/2011/01/110119120409.htm

Science Daily. (2013). Children with autism show increased positive social behaviors when animals are present. Retrieved from http://www.sciencedaily.com/releases/2013/02/130227183504.htm

Scoffield, H. (2012). Canada family census 2011: New structure means new rules. Retrieved from http://www.huffingtonpost.ca/2012/09/19/canada-family-census-2011_n_1896307.html

Scott, J. R. (2006). Preventing eclampsia. *Obstetrics & Gynecology, 108,* 824–825.

Scourfield, J., Van den Bree, M., Martin, N., & McGuffin, P. (2004). Conduct problems in children and adolescents: A twin study. *Archives of General Psychiatry, 61,* 489–496.

Sears, W., & Sears, M. (2001). *The attachment parenting book: A commonsense guide to understanding and nurturing your baby.* Boston: Little, Brown & Co.

Secker-Walker, R. H., & Vacek, P. M. (2003). Relationships between cigarette smoking during pregnancy, gestational age, maternal weight gain, and infant birthweight. *Addictive Behaviors, 28*(1), 55–66.

Sefcek, J. A., Brumbach, B. H., Vasquez, G., & Miller, G. F. (2007). The evolutionary psychology of human mate choice: How ecology, genes, fertility, and fashion influence mating strategies. *Journal of Psychology & Human Sexuality, 18*(2–3) 125–182.

Segrin, C., Powell, H. L., Givertz, M., & Brackin, A. (2003). Symptoms of depression, relational quality, and loneliness in dating relationships. *Personal Relationships, 10*(1), 25–36.

Seidah, A., & Bouffard, T. (2007). Being proud of oneself as a person or being proud of one's physical appearance: What matters for feeling well in adolescence? *Social Behavior and Personality, 35*(2), 255–268.

Selman, R. L. (1976). Social-cognitive understanding. In T. Lickona (Ed.), *Moral development and behavior: Theory, research, and social issues.* New York: Holt, Rinehart & Winston.

Selman, R. L. (1980). *The growth of interpersonal understanding: Developmental and clinical analysis.* New York: Academic Press.

Selman, R. L., & Dray, A. J. (2006). Risk and prevention. In K. A. Renninger, I. E. Sigel, W. Damon, & R. M. Lerner (Eds.), *Handbook of child psychology* (6th ed.), Vol. 4, *Child psychology in practice* (pp. 378–419). Hoboken, NJ: Wiley.

Serbin, L. A., Poulin-Dubois, D., Colburne, K. A., Sen, M. G., & Eichstedt, J. A. (2001). Gender stereotyping in infancy: Visual preferences for and knowledge of gender-stereotyped toys in the second year. *International Journal of Behavioral Development, 25*(1), 7–15.

Service Canada. (2013). Employment insurance maternity and parental benefits. Retrieved from http://www.servicecanada.gc.ca/eng/ei/types/maternity_parental.shtml

Sessoms, G. (2010). Activities for obese children to lose weight. Retrieved from http://www.livestrong.com/article/320821-activities-for-obese-children-to-lose-weight/

Seward, R. R. (2005). Family and community in Ireland. *Journal of Comparative Family Studies, 36*(2), 343–344.

Sexual Information and Education Council of Canada (SIECCAN). (2004). Sexual health education in the schools: Questions and answers. *Canadian Journal of Human Sexuality,* 13(3–4): 129–144. Retrieved from http://www.sieccan.org/pdf/sexual_health_qs.pdf

Sexton, S. A. (2008). The influence of social support systems on the degree of PTSD symptoms in the elderly. *Dissertation Abstracts International: Section B: The Sciences and Engineering, 68*(7-B), 2008, 4846.

Shafto, M. A., Burke, D. M., Stamatakis, E. A., Tam, P. P., & Tyler, L. K. (2007). On the tip-of-the-tongue: Neural correlates of increased word-finding failures in normal aging. *Journal of Cognitive Neuroscience, 19*(12), 2060–2070.

Shatz, K. H. (2006). The widow who wasn't a bride. *Dissertation Abstracts International Section A: Humanities and Social Sciences, 67*(2-A), 739.

Shaw, G. (2013, March 13). Amanda Todd's mother speaks out about her daughter, bullying (with video). *Vancouver Sun*. Retrieved from http://www.vancouversun.com/news/Amanda+Todd+speaks+about+daughter+death/7384521/story.html

Shaywitz, B. A., Lyon, G. R., & Shaywitz, S. E. (2006a). The role of functional magnetic resonance imaging in understanding reading and dyslexia. *Developmental Neuropsychology, 30*(1), 613–632.

Shaywitz, S. E., Mody, M., & Shaywitz, B. A. (2006b). Neural mechanisms in dyslexia. *Current Directions in Psychological Science, 15*(6), 278–281.

Sheeber, L. B., Davis, B., Leve, C., Hops, H., & Tildesley, E. (2007). Adolescents' relationships with their mothers and fathers: Associations with depressive disorder and subdiagnostic symptomatology. *Journal of Abnormal Psychology, 116*(1), 144–154.

Sherwin-White, S. (2006). The social toddler: Promoting positive behaviour. *Infant Observation, 9*(1), 95–97.

Shinohara, H., & Kodama, H. (2012). Relationship between duration of crying/fussy behavior and actigraphic sleep measures in early infancy. *Early Human Development, 88*(11): 847–852.

Shiota, M. N., & Levenson, R. W. (2007). Birds of a feather don't always fly farthest. *Psychology and Aging, 22*(4), 666–675.

Shirk, S., Burwell, R., & Harter, S. (2003). Strategies to modify low self-esteem in adolescents. In M. A. Reinecke et al. (Eds.), *Cognitive therapy with children and adolescents: A casebook for clinical practice* (2nd ed.) (pp. 189–213). New York: Guilford.

Shneidman, E. S. (1977). Aspects of the dying process. *Psychiatric Annals, 17*(8), 391–397.

Shroff, H., et al. (2006) Features associated with excessive exercise in women with eating disorders. *International Journal of Eating Disorders, 39*(6), 454–461.

Shultz, K. S., & Adams, G. A. (Eds.). (2007). *Aging and work in the 21st century.* New York: Lawrence Erlbaum Associates, Inc.

Siegel, L. S. (1992). Infant motor, cognitive, and language behaviors as predictors of achievement at school age. In C. Rovee-Collier & L. P. Lipsitt (Eds.), *Advances in infancy research,* Vol. 7. Norwood, NJ: Ablex.

Siegler, R. S., & Alibali, M. W. (2005). *Children's thinking* (4th ed.). Upper Saddle River, NJ: Prentice Hall.

Siegrist, J., Von Dem Knesebeck, O., & Pollack, C. E. (2004). Social productivity and well- being of older people. *Social Theory & Health, 2*(1), 1–17.

Sierra, F. (2006). Is (your cellular response to) stress killing you? *Journals of Gerontology: Series A: Biological Sciences and Medical Sciences, 61A*(6), 557–561.

Signal Hill. (2009). *Healthy sexuality.* Retrieved from http://www.prolifebc.ca/hs-std.html

Signorello, L. B., & McLaughlin, J. K. (2004). Maternal caffeine consumption and spontaneous abortion: A review of the epidemiologic evidence. *Epidemiology, 15*(2), 229–239.

Silbereisen, R. K. (2006). Development and ecological context: History of the psychological science in a personal view and experience—An interview with Urie Bronfenbrenner. *Psychologie in Erziehung und Unterricht, 53*(1), 241–249.

Silventoinen, K., et al. (2007). Genetic and environmental factors in relative weight from birth to age 18: The Swedish young male twins study. *International Journal of Obesity, 31*(4), 615–621.

Silver, R. C., & Wortman, C. B. (2007). The stage theory of grief. *Journal of the American Medical Association,* 297, 2692.

Simion, F., Cassia, V. M., Turati, C., & Valenza, E. (2001). The origins of face perception: Specific versus nonspecific mechanisms. *Infant and Child Development, 10*(1–2), 59–65.

Simonelli, A., Monti, F., & Magalotti, D. (2005). The complex phenomenon of failure to thrive: Medical, psychological and relational-affective aspects. *Psicologia Clinica dello Sviluppo, 9*(2), 183–212.

Simonelli, A., Vizziello, G. F., Bighin, M., De Palo, F., & Petech, E. (2007). Transition to triadic relationships between parenthood and dyadic adjustment. *Età Evolutiva, 86,* 92–99.

Simon Fraser University. (2011). The Silver Surfer Project. Retrieved from http://www.sfu.ca/silversurfers/?page_id=26

Simonton, D. K. (2006a). Creative genius, knowledge, and reason: The lives and works of eminent creators. In J. C. Kaufman & J. Baer (Eds.). *Creativity and reason in cognitive development.* (pp. 43–59). New York: Cambridge University Press.

Simonton, D. K. (2006b). Creativity around the world in 80 ways … but with one destination. In J. C. Kaufman & R. Sternberg (Eds.), *The international handbook of creativity* (pp. 490–496). New York: Cambridge University Press.

Simonton, D. K. (2007). Creative life cycles in literature: Poets versus novelists or conceptualists versus experimentalists? *Psychology of Aesthetics, Creativity, and the Arts, 1*(3), 133–139.

Sims, C. S., Drasgow, F., & Fitzgerald, L. F. (2005). The effects of sexual harassment on turnover in the military. *Journal of Applied Psychology, 90*(6), 1141–1152.

Singer, L. T., et al. (2005). Prenatal cocaine exposure and infant cognition. *Infant Behavior & Development, 28*(4), 431–444.

Sinnema, J. (2009, March 12). Bad habits priming kids for chronic diseases: Study. *Edmonton Journal.* Retrieved from http://www.canada.com/health/healthy-living/habits+pri-ming+kids+chronic+diseases+Study/1385622/story.html

Sirrs, S. M., et al. (2007). Normal-appearing white matter in patients with phenylketonuria: Water content, myelin water fraction, and metabolite concentrations. *Radiology, 242,* 236–243.

Skinner, B. F. (1957). *Verbal behavior.* New York: Appleton.

Skinner, R., & McFaull, S. (2012). Suicide among children and adolescents in Canada: Trends and sex differences, 1980–2008. *CMAJ, 184*(9), 1029–1034.

Skoczenski, A. M. (2002). Limitations on visual sensitivity during infancy: Contrast sensitivity, vernier acuity, and orientation processing. In J. W. Fagen & H. Hayne (Eds.), *Progress in infancy research,* Vol. 2. Mahwah, NJ: Erlbaum.

Slaughter, V., & Griffiths, M. (2007). Death understanding and fear of death in young children. *Clinical Child Psychology and Psychiatry, 12*(4), 525–535.

Slavin, R. E. (2006). *Educational psychology: Theory and practice* (8th ed.). Boston: Allyn & Bacon.

Sloan, S., Sneddon, H., Stewart, M., & Iwaniec, D. (2006). Breast is best? Reasons why mothers decide to breastfeed or bottlefeed their babies and factors influencing the duration of breastfeeding. *Child Care in Practice, 12*(3), 283–297.

Slobin, D. I. (2001). Form/function relations: How do children find out what they are? In M. Tomasello & E. Bates (Eds.), *Language development: The essential readings.* Malden, MA: Blackwell.

Smetana, J. G. (1990). Morality and conduct disorders. In M. Lewis & S. M. Miller (Eds.), *Handbook of developmental psychopathology.* New York: Plenum.

Smetana, J. G. (2005). Adolescent–parent conflict: Resistance and subversion as developmental process. In L. Nucci (Ed), *Conflict, contradiction, and contrarian elements in moral development and education* (pp. 69–91). Mahwah, NJ: Erlbaum.

Smetana, J. G., Campione-Barr, N., & Metzger, A. (2006). Adolescent development in interpersonal and societal contexts. *Annual Review of Psychology, 57,* 255–284.

Smiley, P. A., & Johnson, R. S. (2006). Self- referring terms, event transitivity and development of self. *Cognitive Development, 21*(3), 266–284.

Smith, C. L., Calkins, S. D., Keane, S. P., Anastopoulos, A. D., & Shelton, T. L. (2004). Predicting stability and change in toddler behavior problems: Contributions of maternal behavior and child gender. *Developmental Psychology, 40*(1), 29–42.

Smith, P. K. (2005). Play: Types and functions in human development. In B. J. Ellis & D. F. Bjorklund (Eds.), *Origins of the social mind: Evolutionary psychology and child development* (pp. 271–291). New York: Guilford Press.

Smolka, E., & Eviatar, Z. (2006). Phonological and orthographic visual word recognition in the two cerebral hemispheres: Evidence from Hebrew. *Cognitive Neuropsychology, 23*(6), 972–989.

Snarey, J. R., & Bell, D. (2003). Distinguishing structural and functional models of human development. *Identity, 3*(3), 221–230.

Snedeker, J., Geren, J., & Shafto, C. L. (2007). Starting over: International adoption as a natural experiment in language development. *Psychological Science, 18*(1), 79–87.

Snegovskikh, V., Park, J. S., & Norwitz, E. R. (2006). Endocrinology of parturition. *Endocrinology and Metabolism Clinics of North America, 35*(1), 173–191.

Snow, C. (2006). Cross-cutting themes and future research directions. In D. August & T. Shanahan (Eds.), *Developing literacy in second-language learners: Report of the National Literacy Panel on Language-Minority Children and Youth* (pp. 631–651). Mahwah, NJ: Erlbaum.

Snyderman, M., & Rothman, S. (1990). *The IQ controversy.* New Brunswick, NJ: Transaction.

Society of Obstetricians and Gynaecologists of Canada. (2009a). Facts and statistics: Sexual health and Canadian youth–Teen pregnancy rates. Retrieved from http://www.sexualityandu.ca/teachers/data-6.aspx

Society of Obstetricians and Gynaecologists of Canada. (2009b). Fact sheets: Sex facts in Canada 2006. Retrieved from http://www.sexualityandu.ca/media-room/fact-sheets-1.aspx

Society of Obstetricians and Gynaecologists of Canada. (2012a). Sexual health: Masturbation. Retrieved from http://www.sexualityandu.ca/sexual-health/what_is_masturbation

Society of Obstetricians and Gynaecologists of Canada. (2012b). Sexual health: Sexual orientation and coming out. Retrieved from http://www.sexualityandu.ca/sexual-health/sexual-orientation-and-coming-out

Society of Obstetricians and Gynaecologists of Canada. (2012c). Statistics on Canadian teen pregnancies. Retrieved from Society of Obstetricians and Gynaecologists of Canada. (2012c). Statistics on sexual intercourse experience among Canadian teenagers. Retrieved from http://www.sexualityandu.ca/sexual-health/statistics1/statistics-on-canadian-teen-pregnancies

Society of Obstetricians and Gynaecologists of Canada. (2012d). Statistics on sexual intercourse experience among Canadian teenagers. Retrieved from http://www.sexualityandu.ca/sexual-health/statistics1/statistics-on-sexual-intercourse-experience-among-canadian-teenagers

Society of Obstetricians and Gynaecologists of Canada. (2012e). Types of STIs–STDs. Retrieved from http://www.sexualityandu.ca/stis-stds/types-of-stis-stds

Solano, C. H., Batten, P. G., & Parish, E. A. (1982). Loneliness and patterns of self- disclosure. *Journal of Personality and Social Psychology, 43,* 524–531.

Soliz, J. (2007). Communicative predictors of a shared family identity: Comparison of grandchildren's perceptions of family-of-origin grandparents and stepgrandparents. *Journal of Family Communication, 7*(3), 177–194.

Sommerfeld, J. (2000, April 18). Lifting the curse: Should monthly periods be optional? MSNBC online.

Sommers, M. S. (2008). Age-related changes in spoken word recognition. In D. B. Pisoni, & R. E. Remez (Eds.), *The handbook of speech perception. Blackwell handbooks in linguistics* (pp. 469–493). Malden, MA: Blackwell Publishing.

Sonnentag, S. (2003). Recovery, work engagement, and proactive behavior. *Journal of Applied Psychology, 88,* 518–528.

Sontag, L. W., & Richards, T. W. (1938). *Studies in fetal behavior: Fetal heart rate as a behavioral indicator.* Child Development Monographs, *3*(4).

Sorce, J., Emde, R. N., Campos, J. J., Klinnert, M. D. (2000). Maternal emotional signaling: Its effect on the visual cliff behavior of 1-year-olds. In D. Muir & A. Slater, (Eds.), *Infant development: The essential readings. Essential readings in developmental psychology* (pp. 282–292). Malden, MA: Blackwell.

Sousa, L., & Figueiredo, D. (2002). Dependence and independence among old persons. *Reviews in Clinical Gerontology, 12*(3), 269–273.

Soussignan, R., & Schaal, B. (2005). Emotional processes in human newborns: a functionalist perspective. In J. Nadel, & D. Muir (Eds.), *Emotional development: Recent research advances* (pp. 127–159). New York: Oxford University Press.

South, S. J., Haynie, D. L., & Bose, S. (2007). Student mobility and school dropout. *Social Science Research, 36*(1), 68–94.

Spelke, E. S., & Owsley, C. (1979). Inter-modal exploration and knowledge in infancy. *Infant Behavior and Development, 2,* 13–27.

Spieker, S. J., et al. (2003). Joint influence of child care and infant attachment security for cognitive and language outcomes of low-income toddlers. *Infant Behavior and Development, 26*(3), 326–344.

Sprecher, S. (1998). Insiders' perspectives on reasons for attraction to a close other. *Social Psychology Quarterly, 61*(4), 287–300.

Sroufe, L. A. (1998). Cited in S. Blakeslee (1998, August 4), Re-evaluating significance of baby's bond with mother, *New York Times,* pp. F1, F2.

Sroufe, L. A., Waters, E., & Matas, L. (1974). Contextual determinants of infant affectional response. In M. Lewis & L. Rosenblum (Eds.), *The origins of fear.* New York: Wiley.

Staff, J., Mortimer, J. T., & Uggen, C. (2004). Work and leisure in adolescence. In R. Lerner & L. Steinberg, (Eds.), *Handbook of adolescent psychology* (2nd ed.) (pp. 429–450). Hoboken, NJ: Wiley.

Stagnitti, K., Unsworth, C., & Rodger, S. (2000). Development of an assessment to identify play behaviours that discriminate between the play of typical preschoolers and preschoolers with pre-academic problems. *Canadian Journal of Occupational Therapy, 67*(5), 291–303.

Stahmer, A. C., Ingersoll, B., & Koegel, R. L. (2004). Inclusive programming for toddlers autism spectrum disorders: Outcomes from the Children's Toddler School. *Journal of Positive Behavior Interventions, 6*(2), 67–82.

Stams, G. J. M., Juffer, F., & IJzendoorn, M. H. van (2002). Maternal sensitivity, infant attachment, and temperament in early childhood predict adjustment in middle childhood: The case of adopted children and their biologically unrelated parents. *Developmental Psychology, 38*(5), 806–821.

Stanford, J. N., & McCabe, M. P. (2005). Sociocultural influences on adolescent boys' body image and body change strategies. *Body Image, 2*(2), 105–113.

Stankoff, B., et al. (2006). Imaging of CNS myelin by positron-emission tomography. *Proceedings of the National Academy of Sciences of the United States of America, 103*(24), 9304–9309.

Stanley, M. A., & Beck, J. G. (2000). Anxiety disorders. *Clinical Psychology Review, 20*(6), 731–754.

Statistics Canada. (2005). Divorces. *The Daily.* Retrieved from http://www.statcan.gc.ca/daily-quotidien/050309/dq050309b-eng.htm

Statistics Canada. (2008a). Back-to-school factbook: Working while in school. Retrieved from http://www.statcan.gc.ca/pub/81-004-x/2006003/9341-eng.htm#e

Statistics Canada. (2008b). *Leading causes of death in Canada.* (Statistics Canada, Catalogue no. 84-215-X.) Retrieved from www.statcan.gc.ca/pub/84-215-x/2008000/hl-fs-eng.htm#3

Statistics Canada. (2008c). *National longitudinal study of children and youth (NLSCY).* Record no. 4450. Retrieved from http://www.statcan.gc.ca/cgi-bin/imdb/p2SV.pl?Function=getSurvey&SDDS=4450&lang=en&db=imdb&adm=8&dis=2

Statistics Canada. (2009a). Gay pride...by the numbers. Retrieved from http://www42.statcan.ca/smr08/smr08_118-eng.htm

Statistics Canada. (2009b). Ten leading causes of death by selected age groups, by sex, Canada—65 to 74 years. Retrieved from http://www.statcan.gc.ca/pub/84-215-x/2008000/tbl/t008-eng.htm

Statistics Canada. (2009c). *2006 Census: The evolving linguistic portrait, 2006 Census: Sharp increase in population with a mother tongue other than English or French*. Retrieved from http://www12.statcan.ca/census-recensement/2006/as-sa/97-555/p2-eng.cfm

Statistics Canada. (2010a). Aboriginal seniors in Canada. In *A portrait of seniors in Canada*. Retrieved from http://www.statcan.gc.ca/pub/89-519-x/2006001/4122091-eng.htm

Statistics Canada. (2010b). Infant mortality rates, by province and territory (Table 102-0504). Retrieved from http://www40.statcan.gc.ca/101/cst01/health21a-eng.htm

Statistics Canada. (2010c). Internet use by individuals, by selected frequency of use and age. Retrieved from http://www.statcan.gc.ca/tables-tableaux/sum-som/l01/cst01/comm32a-eng.htm

Statistics Canada. (2012a). Body mass index of Canadian children and youth, 2009 to 2011. Retrieved from http://www.statcan.gc.ca/pub/82-625-x/2012001/article/11712-eng.htm

Statistics Canada. (2012b). 2011 Census: Age and sex. *The Daily*, May 29. Retrieved from http://www.statcan.gc.ca/daily-quotidien/120529/dq120529a-eng.pdf

Statistics Canada. (2012c). 2011 Census of Population: Linguistic Characteristics of Canadians. Retrieved from http://www.statcan.gc.ca/daily-quotidien/121024/dq121024a-eng.htm

Statistics Canada. (2013a). Canadian Households in 2011: Type and growth. Retrieved from http://www12.statcan.gc.ca/census-recensement/2011/as-sa/98-312-x/98-312-x2011003_2-eng.cfm

Statistics Canada. (2013b). Distribution (number and percentage) and percentage change of census families by family structure, Canada, provinces and territories, 2011. Retrieved from http://www12.statcan.ca/census-recensement/2011/as-sa/98-312-x/2011001/tbl/tbl2-eng.cfm

Statistics Canada. (2013b). Fifty years of families in Canada: 1961 to 2011. Retrieved from http://www12.statcan.gc.ca/census-recensement/2011/as-sa/98-312-x/98-312-x2011003_1-eng.cfm

Statistics Canada. (2013c). Generations in Canada. Retrieved from http://www12.statcan.gc.ca/census-recensement/2011/as-sa/98-311-x/98-311-x2011003_2-eng.cfm

Statistics Canada. (2013d). Linguistic characteristics of Canadians. Retrieved from http://www12.statcan.gc.ca/census-recensement/2011/as-sa/98-314-x/98-314-x2011001-eng.cfm

Statistics Canada. (2013e). Police-reported crime statistics, 2012. *The Daily*, July 25. Retrieved from http://www.statcan.gc.ca/daily-quotidien/130725/dq130725b-eng.htm

Statistics Canada. (2013e). The Canadian incidence study of reported child abuse and neglect. Retrieved from http://www5.statcan.gc.ca/bsolc/olc-cel/olc-cel?catno=85-224-X20010006459&lang=eng

Stauffacher, K., & DeHart, G. B. (2006). Crossing social contexts: Relational aggression between siblings and friends during early and middle childhood. *Journal of Applied Developmental Psychology, 27*(3), 228–240.

Steele, H. (2005a). Editorial. *Attachment & Human Development, 7*(4), 345.

Steele, H. (2005b). Editorial: Romance, marriage, adolescent motherhood, leaving for college, plus shyness and attachment in the preschool years. *Attachment & Human Development, 7*(2), 103–104.

Stein, D. J., Collins, M., Daniels, W., Noakes, T., & Zigmond, M. (2007). Mind and muscle: The cognitive–affective neuroscience of exercise. *CNS Spectrums, 12*(1), 19–22.

Stemberger, J. P. (2004). Phonological priming and irregular past. *Journal of Memory and Language, 50*(1), 82–95.

Sternberg, R. J. (2000). In search of the zipperump-a-zoo. *Psychologist, 13*(5), 250–255.

Sternberg, R. J. (2006a). A duplex theory of love. In R. J. Sternberg, & K. Weis (Eds.), *The new psychology of love* (pp. 184–199). New Haven, CT: Yale University Press.

Sternberg, R. J. (2006b). The nature of creativity. *Creativity Research Journal, 18*(1), 87–98.

Sternberg, R. J. (2007). A systems model of leadership: WICS. *American Psychologist, 62*(1), 34–42.

Sternberg, R. J., & Williams, W. M. (1997). Does the Graduate Record Examination predict meaningful success in the graduate training of psychologists? *American Psychologist, 52,* 630–641.

Stevenson, H. W., Chen, C., & Lee, S. (1993). Mathematics achievement of Chinese, Japanese, and American children: Ten years later. *Science, 259,* 53–58.

Stifter, C. A., & Wiggins, C. N. (2004). Assessment of disturbances in emotion regulation and temperament. In R. DelCarmen-Wiggins & A. Carter (Eds.), *Handbook of infant, toddler, and preschool mental health assessment* (pp. 79–103). New York: Oxford University Press.

Stipek, D., & Hakuta, K. (2007). Strategies to ensure that no child starts from behind. In J. L. Aber et al. (Eds.), *Child development and social policy: Knowledge for action, APA Decade of Behavior volumes* (pp. 129–145). Washington, DC: American Psychological Association.

Stipek, D., Recchia, S., & McClintic, S. (1992). *Self-evaluation in young children.* Monographs of the Society for Research in Child Development, 57(1, ser. 226).

Stoel-Gammon, C. (2002). Intervocalic consonants in the speech of typically developing children: Emergence and early use. *Clinical Linguistics and Phonetics, 16*(3), 155–168.

Storch, E. A., et al. (2007). Peer victimization, psychosocial adjustment, and physical activity in overweight and at-risk-for-overweight youth. *Journal of Pediatric Psychology, 32*(1), 80–89.

Stores, G., & Wiggs, L. (Eds.). (2001). *Sleep disturbance in children and adolescents with disorders of development: Its significance and management.* New York: Cambridge University Press.

Strassberg, D. S., & Holty, S. (2003). An experimental study of women's Internet personal ads. *Archives of Sexual Behavior, 32*(3), 253–260.

Stratton, T. D., et al. (2005). Does students' exposure to gender discrimination and sexual harassment in medical school affect specialty choice and residency program selection? *Academic Medicine, 80*(4), 400–408.

Strayer, J., & Roberts, W. (2004). Children's anger, emotional expressiveness, and empathy: Relations with parents' empathy, emotional expressiveness, and parenting practices. *Social Development, 13*(2), 229–254.

Streri, A. (2002). Hand preference in 4-month-old infants: Global or local processing of objects in the haptic mode. *Current Psychology Letters: Behaviour, Brain and Cognition, 7,* 39–50.

Stright, A. D., Neitzel, C., Sears, K. G., & Hoke-Sinex, L. (2001). Instruction begins in the home: Relations between parental instruction and children's self-regulation in the classroom. *Journal of Educational Psychology, 93*(3), 456–466.

Strock, M. (2004). *Autism spectrum disorders (pervasive developmental disorders).* NIH Publication NIH-04–5511. Bethesda, MD: National Institute of Mental Health, National Institutes of Health, U.S. Department of Health and Human Services. Available at http://www.nimh.nih.gov/publicat/autism.cfm.

Sukhodolsky, D. G., Golub, A., Stone, E. C., & Orban, L. (2005). Dismantling anger control training for children: A randomized pilot study of social problem-solving versus social skills training components. *Behavior Therapy, 36*, 15–23.

Sullivan, S. E., Martin, D. F., Carden, W. A., & Mainiero, L. A. (2003). The road less traveled. *Journal of Leadership & Organizational Studies, 10*(2), 34–42.

Sulloway, F. J. (2007). Birth order and intelligence. *Science, 316*(5832), 1711–1712.

Sun, S. S., et al. (2005). Is sexual maturity occurring earlier among U.S. children? *Journal of Adolescent Health, 37*(5), 345–355.

Suomi, S. J., Harlow, H. F., & McKinney, W. T. (1972). Monkey psychiatrists. *American Journal of Psychiatry, 128,* 927–932.

Supple, A. J., & Small, S. A. (2006). The influence of parental support, knowledge, and authoritative parenting on Hmong and European American adolescent development. *Journal of Family Issues, 27*(9), 1214–1232.

Sylva, K., et al. (2007). Curricular quality and day-to-day learning activities in pre-school. *International Journal of Early Years Education, 15*(1), 49–65.

Szaflarski, J. P., et al. (2006). A longitudinal functional magnetic resonance imaging study of language development in children 5 to 11 years old. *Annals of Neurology, 59*(5), 796–807.

T

Takahashi, M., & Sugiyama, M. (2003). Improvement and prevention of misbehavior in a junior high school student: An analysis of behavioral contingency and change of stimulus function in a social setting. *Japanese Journal of Counseling Science, 36*(2), 165–174.

Talbot, L. A., Morrell, C. H., Fleg, J., L., & Metter, E. J. (2007). Changes in leisure time physical activity and risk of all-cause mortality in men and women. *Preventive Medicine: An International Journal Devoted to Practice and Theory, 45*(2–3), 169–176.

Tamis-LeMonda, C. S., Bornstein, M. H., & Baumwell, L. (2001). Maternal responsiveness and children's achievement of language milestones. *Child Development, 72*(3), 748–767.

Tamis-LeMonda, C. S., Cristofaro, T. N., Rodriguez, E. T., & Bornstein, M. H. (2006). Early language development:

Social influences in the first years of life. In L. Balter & C. S. Tamis-LeMonda (Eds.), *Child psychology: A handbook of contemporary issues* (2nd ed.) (pp. 79–108). New York: Psychology Press.

Tan, R. S. (2002). Managing the andropause in aging men. *Clinical Geriatrics.* Available at http://www.mmhc.com/cg/articles/CG9907/Tan.html.

Tan, R. S., & Culberson, J. W. (2003). An integrative review on current evidence of testosterone replacement therapy for the andropause. *Maturitas, 45*(1), 15–27.

Tanner, J. L. (2006). Recentering during emerging adulthood: A critical turning point in life span human development. In J. J. Arnett & J. L. Tanner (Eds.), *Emerging adults in America: Coming of age in the 21st century* (pp. 21–55). Washington, DC: American Psychological Association.

Tanner, J. M. (1989). *Fetus into man: Physical growth from conception to maturity.* Cambridge, MA: Harvard University Press.

Tapper, K., & Boulton, M. J. (2004). Sex differences in levels of physical, verbal, and indirect aggression amongst primary school children and their associations with beliefs about aggression. *Aggressive Behavior, 30*(2), 123–145.

Tashiro, T., Frazier, P., & Berman, M. (2006). Stress-related growth following divorce and relationship dissolution. In M. A. Fine & J. H. Harvey (Eds.), *Handbook of divorce and relationship dissolution* (pp. 361–384). Mahwah, NJ: Erlbaum.

Tassi, F., Schneider, B. H., & Richard, J. F. (2001). Competitive behavior at school in relation to social competence and incompetence in middle childhood. *Revue Internationale de Psychologie Sociale, 14*(2), 165–184.

Taylor, C., & Peter, T. (2011). *Every class in every school: The first national climate survey on homophobia, biphobia, and transphobia in Canadian schools. Final report.* Toronto: Egale Canada Human Rights Trust.

Taylor, M. (1999). *Imaginary companions and the children who create them.* London: Oxford University Press.

Taylor, M., & Hort, B. (1990). Can children be trained in making the distinction between appearance and reality? *Cognitive Development, 5*(1), 89–99

Taylor, M. F., Clark, N., & Newton, E. (2008). Counselling Australian baby boomers. *British Journal of Guidance & Counselling, 36*(2), 189–204.

Teen Challenge Canada. (2013). Alcohol abuse facts. Retrieved from http://www.teenchallenge.ca/get-help/educational-resources/alcohol-abuse-facts

Terracciano, A., Costa Jr., P. T., & McCrae, R. R. (2006). Personality plasticity after age 30. *Personality and Social Psychology Bulletin, 32*(8), 999–1009.

Thapar, A., Langley, K., Asherson, P., & Gill, M. (2007). Gene-Environment interplay in attention-deficit hyperactivity disorder and the importance of a developmental perspective. *British Journal of Psychiatry, 190*(1), 1–3.

The Infinity Project. (2013). Retrieved from https://www.facebook.com/TogetherWeCanbeInfinite?filter=3

Thomas, A., & Chess, S. (1989). Temperament and personality. In G. A. Kohnstamm, J. E. Bates, & M. K. Rothbart (Eds.), *Temperament in childhood.* Chichester, England: Wiley.

Thompson, A. M., Baxter-Jones, A. D. G., Mirwald, R. L., & Bailey, D. A. (2003). Comparison of physical activity in male and female children: Does maturation matter? *Medicine and Science in Sports and Exercise. 35*(10), 1684–1690.

Thompson, I. M., et al. (2005). Erectile dysfunction and subsequent cardiovascular disease. *Journal of the American Medical Association, 294*(23). 2996–3002.

Thompson, R. A. (2006). The development of the person: Social understanding, relationships, conscience, self. In N. Eisenberg, W. Damon, & R. M. Lerner (Eds.), *Hand-book of child psychology* (6th ed.), Vol. 3, *Social, emotional, and personality development* (pp. 24–98). Hoboken, NJ: Wiley.

Thompson, R. A., Easterbrooks, M. A., & Padilla-Walker, L. M. (2003). Social and emotional development in infancy. In R. M. Lerner et al. (Eds.), *Handbook of psychology: Developmental psychology.* New York: Wiley.

Thompson, R. A., & Limber, S. P. (1990). "Social anxiety" in infancy: Stranger and separation reactions. In H. Leitenberg (Ed.), *Handbook of social and evaluation anxiety.* New York: Plenum.

Thompson, R. A., & Meyer, S. (2007). Socialization of emotion regulation in the family. In J. J. Gross (Ed.), *Handbook of emotion regulation* (pp. 249–268). New York: Guilford.

Thomson, J., Ahluwalia, M., & Huang, S. (2013, April 15). Gay seniors struggling to find "safe" retirement housing. Retrieved from http://www.cbc.ca/news/canada/gay-seniors-struggling-to-find-safe-retirement-housing-1.1405867

Thornton, L. M., Andersen, B. L., Crespin, T. R., & Carson, W. E. (2007). Individual trajectories in stress covary with immunity during recovery from cancer diagnosis and treatments. *Brain, Behavior, and Immunity, 21*(2), 185–194.

Timmerman, L. M. (2006). Family care versus day care: Effects on children. In B. M. Gayle et al. (Eds.), *Classroom communication and instructional processes: Advances through meta-analysis* (pp. 245–260). Mahwah, NJ: Erlbaum.

Tjepkema, M. (2005). *Adult obesity in Canada: Measured height and weight* (Statistics Canada, Catalogue no. 82-620-MWE). Retrieved from http://www.statcan.gc.ca/pub/82-620-m/2005001/article/adults-adultes/8060-eng.htm

Tobbell, J. (2003). Students' experiences of the transition from primary to secondary school. *Educational and Child Psychology, 20*(4), 4–14.

Togsverd, M., et al. (2008). Association of a dopamine beta-hydroxylase gene variant with depression in elderly women possibly reflecting noradrenergic dysfunction. *Journal of Affective Disorders, 106*(1-2), 169–172.

Tomaka, J., Thompson, S., & Palacios, R. (2006). The relation of social isolation, loneliness, and social support to disease outcomes among the elderly. *Journal of Aging and Health, 18*(3), 359–384.

Tomiyama, T., et al. (2008). A new amyloid ß variant favoring oligomerization in Alzheimer's-type dementia. *Annals of Neurology, 63*(3), 377–387.

Ton, M., & Hansen, J. C. (2001). Using a person-environment fit framework to predict satisfaction and motivation in work and marital roles. *Journal of Career Assessment, 9,* 315–331.

Toneguzzi, M. (2011, August 17). Nearly half of Canada's baby boomers still paying. *Calgary Herald*. Retrieved from http://blogs.calgaryherald.com/2011/08/17/nearly-half-of-canadas-baby-boomers-still-paying-down-mortgage/

Toronto District School Board. (2013). International Day of Silence. Retrieved from http://www2.tdsb.on.ca/_site/ViewItem.asp?siteid=15&menuid=35317&pageid=29911

Towse, J. (2003). Lifespan development of human memory. *Quarterly Journal of Experimental Psychology: Human Experimental Psychology, 56A*(7), 1244–1246.

Towse, J., & Cowan, N. (2005). Working memory and its relevance for cognitive development. In W. Schneider, R. Schumann- Hengsteler, & B. Sodian (Eds.), *Young children's cognitive development: Interrelationships among executive functioning, working memory, verbal ability, and theory of mind* (pp. 9–37). Mahwah, NJ: Erlbaum.

Trainor, L. J., & Desjardins, R. N. (2002). Pitch characteristics of infant-directed speech affect infants' ability to discriminate vowels. *Psychonomic Bulletin & Review, 9*(2), 335–340.

Trehub, S. E., & Hannon, E. E. (2006). Infant music perception: Domain-general or domain-specific mechanisms? *Cognition, 100*(1), 73–99.

Trevarthen, C. (2003). Conversations with a two-month-old. In J. Raphael-Leff (Ed.), *Parent–infant psychodynamics: Wild things, mirrors, and ghosts.* London: Whurr.

Troxel, W. M., & Matthews, K. A. (2004). What are the costs of marital conflict and dissolution to children's physical health? *Clinical Child and Family Psychology Review, 7*(1), 29–57.

Trudel, G. A., Goldfarb, M. R., Preville, M., & Boyer, R. (2007). Relationship between psychological distress and marital functioning in the elderly. American Psychological Association, Conference abstract.

Tsuneishi, S., & Casaer, P. (2000). Effects of preterm extrauterine visual experience on the development of the human visual system: A flash VEP study. *Developmental Medicine and Child Neurology, 42*(10), 663–668.

Turkheimer, E., Haley, A., Waldron, M., D'Onofrio, B., Gottesman, I. I. (2003). Socioeconomic status modifies heritability of IQ in young mothers. *Psychological Science, 14*(6), 623–628.

Twist, M. (2005). Review of relationship therapy with same-sex couples. *Journal of Marital & Family Therapy, 31*(4), 413–417.

U

U.S. Bureau of the Census. (2008). *Statistical abstract of the United States* (128th ed.). Washington, DC: U.S. Government Printing Office.

U.S. Department of Education, (2006). *Teaching children with attention deficit hyperactivity disorder: Instructional strategies and practices*. Washington, DC.

Umek, L. M., Podlesek, A., & Fekonja, U. (2005). Assessing the home literacy environment: Relationships to child language comprehension and expression. *European Journal of Psychological Assessment, 21*(4), 271–281.

UNAIDS. (2006). *Report on the global AIDS epidemic: Executive summary.* Joint United Nations Programme on HIV/AIDS (UNAIDS). UNAIDS. 20 Avenue Appia. CH-1211. Geneva 27 Switzerland.

UNICEF. (2006). *The state of the world's children: 2007*. New York: United Nations.

UNICEF. (2010). The Breastfeeding Initiative Exchange: Facts and figures. Retrieved from http://www.unicef.org/programme/breastfeeding/facts.htm

UNICEF Canada. (2009). *Canadian supplement to The State of the World's Children 2009: Aboriginal children's health: Leaving no child behind.* Toronto: Author. Retrieved from http://www.unicef.ca/portal/Secure/Community/502/WCM/HELP/take_action/Advocacy/Leaving%20no%20child%20behind%2009.pdf

University of Ottawa. (2013). Suicide in Canada: Facts and figures. Retrieved from http://www.med.uottawa.ca/sim/data/Suicide_e.htm

USDHHS. (2005, January 10). *Bone health and osteoporosis: A report of the Surgeon General*. http://www.surgeongeneral.gov/library/bonehealth. Accessed October 5, 2008.

Uylings, H. B. M. (2006). Development of the human cortex and the concept of "critical" or "sensitive" periods. *Language Learning, 56*(Suppl. 1), 59–90.

V

van IJzendoorn, M. H., & Juffer, F. (2006). The Emanuel Miller Memorial Lecture 2006: Adoption as intervention. Meta-analytic evidence for massive catch-up and plasticity in physical, socio-emotional, and cognitive development. *Journal of Child Psychology and Psychiatry, 47*(12), 1228–1245.

van Solinge, H., & Henkens, K. (2005). Couples' adjustment to retirement: A Multi-Actor Panel Study. *Journals of Gerontology: Series B: Psychological Sciences and Social Sciences, 60B*(1), S11–S20.

Vandello, J. A., & Cohen, D. (2003). Male honor and female fidelity: Implicit cultural scripts that perpetuate domestic violence. *Journal of Personality & Social Psychology, 84*(5), 997–1010.

Vander Ven, T., & Cullen, F. T. (2004). The impact of maternal employment on serious youth crime: Does the quality of working conditions matter? *Crime & Delinquency, 50*(2), 272–291.

Vares, T., Potts, A., Gavey, N., & Grace, V. M. (2007). Reconceptualizing cultural narratives of mature women's sexuality in the Viagra era. *Journal of Aging Studies, 21*(2), 153–164.

Vartanian, O., Martindale, C., & Kwiatkowski, J. (2003). Creativity and inductive reasoning: The relationship between divergent thinking and performance on Wason's 2-4-6 task. *Quarterly Journal of Experimental Psychology: Human Experimental Psychology. 56A*(4), 641–655.

Vastag, B. (2003). Many questions, few answers for testosterone replacement therapy. *Journal of the American Medical Association, 289,* 971–972.Vellas, B., Gillette-Guyonnet, S., & Andrieu, S. (2008). Memory health clinics—A first step to prevention. *Alzheimer's & Dementia, 4*(1, Suppl 1), S144–S149.

Vellutino, F. R., Fletcher, J. M., Snowling, M. J., & Scanlon, D. M. (2004). Specific reading disability (dyslexia): What have we learned in the past four decades? *Journal of Child Psychology and Psychiatry, 45*(1), 2–40.

Verissimo, M., & Salvaterra, F. (2006). Maternal secure-base scripts and children's attachment security in an adopted sample. *Attachment & Human Development, 8*(3), 261–273.

Virji-Babul, N., Kerns, K., Zhou, E., Kapur, A., & Shiffrar, M. (2006). Perceptual-motor deficits in children with Down syndrome: Implications for intervention. *Down Syndrome: Research & Practice, 10*(2), 74–82.

Visscher, W. A., Feder, M., Burns, A. M., Brady, T. M., & Bray, R. M. (2003). The impact of smoking and other substance use by urban women on the birthweight of their infants. *Substance Use and Misuse, 38*(8), 1063–1093.

Vitiello, B. (Ed.). (2006). Guest editorial: Selective serotonin reuptake inhibitors (SSRIs) in children and adolescents. *Journal of Child and Adolescent Psychopharmacology, 16*(1–2), 7–9.

Volkova, A., Trehub, S. E., & Schellenberg, E. G. (2006). Infants' memory for musical performances. *Developmental Science, 9*(6), 583–589.

Volling, B. L. (2003). Sibling relationships. In M. H. Bornstein et al. (Eds.), *Well-being: Positive development across the life course* (pp. 205–220). Mahwah, NJ: Erlbaum.

Volterra, M. C., Caselli, O., Capirci, E., & Pizzuto, E. (2004). Gesture and the emergence and development of language. In M. Tomasello & D. I. Slobin (Eds.), *Beyond nature–nurture.* Mahwah, NJ. Erlbaum.

von Gontard, A. (2007). Encopresis. *Praxis der Kinderpsychologie und Kinderpsychiatrie, 56*(6),492–510.

VonDras, D. D., Powless, D. R., Olson, A. K., Wheeler, D., & Snudden, A. L. (2005). Differential effects of everyday stress on the episodic memory test performances of young, mid-life, and older adults. *Aging & Mental Health, 9*(1), 60–70.

Vorauer, J. D., Cameron, J. J., Holmes, J. G., & Pearce, D. G. (2003). Invisible overtures: Fears of rejection and the signal amplification bias. *Journal of Personality & Social Psychology, 84*(4), 793–812.

Vukman, K. B. (2005). Developmental differences in metacognition and their connections with cognitive development in adulthood. *Journal of Adult Development, 12*(4), 211–221.

Vygotsky, L. S. (1962). *Thought and language.* Cambridge, MA: MIT Press.

Vygotsky, L. S. (1978). *Mind in society: The development of higher psychological processes.* Cambridge, MA: Harvard University Press.

W

Wachs, T. D. (2006). The nature, etiology, and consequences of individual differences in temperament. In L. Balter & C. S. Tamis- LeMonda (Eds.), *Child psychology: A handbook of contemporary issues* (2nd ed.) (pp. 27–52). New York: Psychology Press.

Wahler, R. G., Herring, M., & Edwards, M. (2001). Coregulation of balance between children's prosocial approaches and acts of compliance: A pathway to mother–child cooperation? *Journal of Clinical Child Psychology, 30*(4), 473–478.

Wainright, J. L., Russell, S. T., & Patterson, C. J. (2004). Psychosocial adjustment, school outcomes, and romantic relationships of adolescents with same-sex parents. *Child Development, 75*(6), 1886–1898.

Wald, J., & Losen, D. J. (2007). Out of sight: The journey through the school-to-prison pipeline. In S. Books (Ed.), *Invisible children in the society and its schools* (3rd ed.) (pp. 23–37). Mahwah, NJ: Erlbaum.

Walitza, S., et al. 2006). Genetic and neuroimaging studies in attention deficit hyperactivity disorder. *Nervenheilkunde: Zeitschrift für interdisziplinaere Fortbildung, 25*(6), 421–429.

Wall, A. (2007). Review of Integrating gender and culture in parenting. *The Family Journal, 15*(2), 196–197.

Wall, G., & Arnold, S. (2007). How involved is involved fathering? *Gender & Society, 21*(4), 508–527.

Wallerstein, J., Lewis, J., Blakeslee, S., Hetherington, E. M., & Kelly, J. (2005). Issue 17: Is divorce always detrimental to children? In R. P. Halgin (Ed.), *Taking sides: Clashing views on controversial issues in abnormal psychology* (3rd ed.) (pp. 298–321). New York: McGraw-Hill.

Walter, J. L., & LaFreniere, P. J. (2000). A naturalistic study of affective expression, social competence, and sociometric status in preschoolers. *Early Education and Development, 11*(1), 109–122.

Wang, L. (2005). Correlations between self- esteem and life satisfaction in elementary school students. *Chinese Mental Health Journal, 19*(11), 745–749.

Wang, S.-H., Baillargeon, R., & Paterson, S. (2005). Detecting continuity violations in infancy: A new account and new evidence from covering and tube events. *Cognition, 95*(2), 129–173.

Washburn, D. A. (Ed,). (2007). *Primate perspectives on behavior and cognition.* Washington, DC: American Psychological Association.

Watson, J. B. (1924). *Behaviorism.* New York: Norton.

Waxman, S. R., & Lidz, J. L. (2006). Early word learning. In D. Kuhn, R. S. Siegler, W. Damon, & R. M. Lerner (Eds.), *Handbook of child psychology* (6th ed.), Vol. 2, *Cognition, perception, and language* (pp. 299–335). Hoboken, NJ: Wiley.

WebMD. (2010). Tay-Sachs test. Retrieved from http://www.webmd.com/parenting/baby/tay-sachs-test

WebMD. (2012). 10 surprising health benefits of sex. Retrieved from http://www.webmd.com/sex-relationships/guide/10-surprising-health-benefits-of-sex?page=1

WebMD. (2013). What's it like in the womb? Retrieved from http://www.webmd.com/baby/features/in-the-womb

Wechsler, D. (1975). Intelligence defined and undefined: A relativistic appraisal. *American Psychologist, 30,* 135–139.

Weckerly, J., Wulfeck, B., & Reilly, J. (2004). The development of morphosyntactic ability in atypical populations: The acquisition of tag questions in children with early focal lesions and children with specific- language impairment. *Brain and Language, 88*(2), 190–201.

Weeks, C. (2009, March 30). Interracial relationships rise 30 per cent in five years. *Globe and Mail.* Retrieved from http://www.theglobeandmail.com/life/article 677491.ece

Weinberg, R. A. (2004). The infant and the family in the twenty-first century. *Journal of the American Academy of Child and Adolescent Psychiatry, 43*(1), 115–116.

Weinshenker, M. N. (2006). Adolescents' expectations about mothers' employment: Life course patterns and parental influence. *Sex Roles, 54*(11–12), 845–857.

Weisler, R. H., & Sussman, N. (2007). Treatment of attention-deficit/hyperactivity disorder. *Primary Psychiatry, 14*(1), 39–42.

Wellman, H. M., Cross, D., & Bartsch, K. (1986). *Infant search and object permanence: A meta-analysis of the A-not-B error.* Monographs of the Society for Research in Child Development, 5(3, ser. 214).

Wellman, H. M., Fang, F., Liu, D., Zhu, L., & Liu, G. (2006). Scaling of theory-of-mind understandings in Chinese children. *Psychological Science, 17*(12), 1075–1081.

Weng, X., Odouli, R., & Li, D-K. (2008, January 25). Maternal caffeine consumption during pregnancy and the risk of miscarriage: a prospective cohort study. *American Journal of Obstetrics and Gynecology, available online.*

Wenger, G. C., Dykstra, P. A., Melkas, T., & Knipscheer, K. C. P. M. (2007). Social embeddedness and late-life parenthood: Community activity, close ties, and support. *Journal of Family Issues, 28*(11), 1419–1456.

Wenger, G. C., & Jerrome, D. (1999). Change and stability in confidant relationships. *Journal of Aging Studies, 13*(3), 269–294.

Wennergren, A.-C., & Rönnerman, K. (2006). The relation between tools used in action research and the zone of proximal development. *Educational Action Research, 14*(4), 547–568.

Wentworth, N., Benson, J. B., & Haith, M. M. (2000). The development of infants' reaches for stationary and moving targets. *Child Development, 71*(3), 576–601.

Wentzel, K. R., Barry, C. M., & Caldwell, K. A. (2004). Friendships in middle school: Influences on motivation and school adjustment. *Journal of Educational Psychology, 96*(2), 195–203.

Werker, J. F. (1989). Becoming a native listener. *American Scientist, 77,* 54–59.

Werker, J. F., et al. (2007). Infant-directed speech supports phonetic category learning in English and Japanese. *Cognition, 103*(1), 147–162.

Werker, J. F., & Tees, R. C. (2005). Speech perception as a window for understanding plasticity and commitment in language systems of the brain. *Developmental Psychobiology, 46*(3), 233–234.

Werner, E. E. (1988). A cross-cultural perspective on infancy. *Journal of Cross-Cultural Psychology, 19,* 96–113.

Werner, L. A., & Bernstein, I. L. (2001). Development of the auditory, gustatory, olfactory, and somatosensory systems. In E. B. Goldstein (Ed.), *Blackwell handbook of perception., Handbook of experimental psychology series* (pp. 669–708). Boston: Blackwell.

Wethington, E., Kessler, R. C., & Pixley, J. E. (2004). Turning points in adulthood. In O. G. Brim, C. D. Ryff, & R. C. Kessler (Eds.), *How healthy are we?: A national study of well-being at midlife* (pp. 586–613). *The John D. and Catherine T. MacArthur foundation series on mental health and development. Studies on successful midlife development.* Chicago: University of Chicago Press.

Whitehouse, E. M. (2006). Poverty. In G. G. Bear & K. M. Minke (Eds.), *Children's needs III: Development, prevention, and intervention* (pp. 835–845). Washington, DC: National Association of School Psychologists.

Wickwire Jr., E. M., Roland, M. M. S., Elkin, T. D., & Schumacher, J. A. (2008). Sleep disorders. In M. Hersen & D. Michel (Eds.), *Handbook of psychological assessment, case conceptualization, and treatment. Vol 2: Children and adolescents* (pp. 622–651). Hoboken, NJ: Wiley.

Wierzalis, E. A., Barret, B., Pope, M., & Rankins, M. (2006). Gay men and aging: Sex and intimacy. In D. Kimmel, T. Rose, & S. David (Eds.), *Lesbian, gay, bisexual, and transgender aging: Research and clinical perspectives* (pp. 91–109). New York: Columbia University Press.

Willett, W. C. (2005). Diet and cancer. *JAMA: Journal of the American Medical Association, 293,* 233–234.

Willetts, M. C. (2006). Union quality comparisons between long-term heterosexual cohabitation and legal marriage. *Journal of Family Issues, 27*(1), 110–127.

Williams, M. S. (2004). The psychology of eating. *Psychology and Health, 19*(4), 541–542.

Willis, S. L., & Schaie, K. W. (2006). Cognitive functioning in the baby boomers: Longitudinal and cohort effects. In

S. K. Whitbourne, & S. L. Willis (Eds.), *The baby boomers grow up: Contemporary perspectives on midlife* (pp. 205–234). Mahwah, NJ: Lawrence Erlbaum Associates Publishers.

Wilson, D. R., Langlois, S., & Johnson, J. (2007). Mid-trimester amniocentesis fetal loss rate: Committee opinion. *Journal of Obstetrics and Gynaecology Canada, 29*(7):586–590). Retrieved from http://www.sogc.org/guidelines/documents/gui194CPG0707.pdf

Wilson, E. O. (2004). *On Human Nature*. Cambridge, MA: Harvard University Press.

Wilson, J. M. B., Tripp, D. A., & Boland, F. J. (2005). The relative contributions of waist-to-hip ratio and body mass to judgments of attractiveness. *Sexualities, Evolution & Gender, 7*(3), 245–267.

Wilson, P. (2004). A preliminary investigation of an early intervention program: Examining the intervention effectiveness of the Bracken Concept Development Program and the Bracken Basic Concept Scale–Revised with Head Start students. *Psychology in the Schools, 41*(3), 301–311.

Windsor, T. D., Anstey, K. J., Butterworth, P., & Rodgers, B. (2008). Behavioral approach and behavioral inhibition as moderators of the association between negative life events and perceived control in midlife. *Personality and Individual Differences, 44*(5), 1080–1092.

Winner, E. (2000). The origins and ends of giftedness. *American Psychologist, 55,* 159–169.

Witherington, D. C., Campos, J. J., Anderson, D. I., Lejeune, L., & Seah, E. (2005). Avoidance of heights on the visual cliff in newly walking infants. *Infancy, 7*(3), 285–298.

Witkowska, E., & Gådin, K. G. (2005). What female high school students regard as harassment. International Journal of *Adolescent Medicine and Health, 17*(4), 391–406.

Wocadlo, C., & Rieger, I. (2006). Educational and therapeutic resource dependency at early school-age in children who were born very preterm. *Early Human Development, 82*(1), 29–37.

Wodrich, D. L. (2006). Sex chromosome anomalies. In L. Phelps (Ed.), *Chronic health-related disorders in children: Collaborative medical and psychoeducational interventions* (pp. 253–270). Washington, DC: American Psychological Association.

Wojslawowicz Bowker, J. C., Rubin, K. H., Burgess, K. B., Booth-Laforce, C., & Rose- Krasnor, L. (2006). Behavioral characteristics associated with stable and fluid best friendship patterns in middle childhood. *Merrill-Palmer Quarterly, 52*(4), 671–693.

Wolfenden, L. E., & Holt, N. L. (2005). Talent development in elite junior tennis: Perceptions of players, parents, and coaches. *Journal of Applied Sport Psychology, 17*(2), 108–126.

Woolfolk, A. (2008). *Educational psychology, Active learning edition* (10th ed.). Boston: Allyn & Bacon.

World Health Organization. (2004). *HIV transmission through breastfeeding: A review of available evidence*. Retrieved from http://www.unfpa.org/webdav/site/global/shared/documents/publications/2004/hiv_transmission.pdf

Worell, J., & Goodheart, C. D. (Eds.), (2006). *Handbook of girls' and women's psychological health: Gender and well-being across the lifespan*. New York: Oxford University Press.

Wozniak, J. R., & Lim, K. O. (2006). Advances in white matter imaging: A review of in vivo magnetic resonance methodologies and their applicability to the study of development and aging. *Neuroscience & Biobehavioral Reviews, 30*(6), 762–774.

Wright, C., & Birks, E. (2000). Risk factors for failure to thrive: A population-based survey. *Child: Care, Health, and Development, 26*(1), 5–16.

Wright, D. W., & Young, R. (1998). The effects of family structure and maternal employment on the development of gender-related attitudes among men and women. *Journal of Family Issues, 19*(3), 300–314.

Wulff, K., & Siegmund, R. (2001). Circadian and ultradian time patterns in human behaviour. Part 1: Activity monitoring of families from prepartum to postpartum. *Biological Rhythm Research, 31*(5), 581–602.

X

Xie, H. L., Yan, B., Signe M., Hutchins, B. C., & Cairns, B. D. (2006). What makes a girl (or a boy) popular (or unpopular)? African American Children's perceptions and developmental differences. *Developmental Psychology, 42*(4), 599–612.

Y

Yaffe, K., Haan, M., Byers, A., Tangen, C., & Kuller, L. (2000). Estrogen use, APOE, and cognitive decline: Evidence of gene- environment interaction. *Neurology, 54*(10), 1949–1953.

Yamada, H., et al. (2000). A milestone for normal development of the infantile brain detected by functional MRI. *Neurology, 55*(2), 218–223.

Yang, H.-C., & Noel, A. M. (2006). The developmental characteristics of four- and five-year-old pre-schoolers' drawing: An analysis of scribbles, placement patterns, emergent writing, and name writing in archived spontaneous drawing samples. *Journal of Early Childhood Literacy,6*(2), 145–162.

Yeo, J. (2010). Childbirth experience of participants in Lamaze childbirth education [Korean]. *Korean Journal of Women Health Nursing, 16*(3), 215–223

Yost, M. R., & Zurbriggen, E. L. (2006). Gender differences in the enactment of sociosexuality. *Journal of Sex Research, 43*(2), 163–173.

Z

Zacks, R. T., Hasher, L., & Li, K. Z. H. (2000). Human memory. In F. I. M. Craik & T. A. Salthouse (Eds.), *Age-related changes in memory: A cognitive neuroscience perspective. The handbook of aging and cognition* (2nd ed.) (pp. 293–357). Mahwah, NJ: Lawrence Erlbaum Associates Publishers.

Zaidi, A. U., & Shyraydi, M. (2002). Perceptions of arranged marriages by young Pakistani Muslim women living in a Western society. *Journal of Comparative Family Studies, 33*(4), 495–514.

Zajonc, R. B. (2001). The family dynamics of intellectual development. *American Psychologist, 56*(6/7), 490–496.

Zan, B., & Hildebrandt, C. (2003). First graders' interpersonal understanding during cooperative and competitive games. *Early Education and Development, 14*(4), 397–410.

Zarbatany, L., McDougall, P., & Hymel, S. (2000). Gender-differentiated experience in the peer culture: Links to intimacy in preadolescence. *Social Development, 9*(1), 62–79.

Zeifman, D. M. (2004). Acoustic features of infant crying related to intended caregiving intervention. *Infant and Child Development, 13*(2), 111–122.

Zeintl, M., Kliegel, M., & Hofer, S. M. (2007). The role of processing resources in age- related prospective and retrospective memory within old age. *Psychology and Aging, 22*(4), 826–834.

Zelazo, P. R. (1998). McGraw and the development of unaided walking. *Developmental Review, 18*(4), 449–471.

Zimmerman, B. J. (2000). Self-efficacy: An essential motive to learn. *Contemporary Educational Psychology, 25*(1), 82–91.

Zimmermann, P., Maier, M. A., Winter, M., & Grossmann, K. E. (2001). Attachment and adolescents' emotion regulation during a joint problem-solving task with a friend. *International Journal of Behavioral Development, 25*(4), 331–343.

Zweigenhaft, R. L., & Von Ammon, J. (2000). Birth order and civil disobedience: A test of Sulloway's "born to rebel" hypothesis. *Journal of Social Psychology, 140*(5), 624–627.

Name Index

Aalsma, M. C., 202
Aartsen, M. J., 314
Abdelaziz, Y. E., 155
Aber, J. L., 183
Abraham, L., 143
Abravanel, E., 86
Acevedo, A., 298
Adams, G. A., 281
Adams, G. R., 210
Adams, R. G., 285
Adler, J. M., 279
Adolph, K. E., 38, 73, 74
Aguiar, A., 84
Ahnert, L., 109
Ainsworth, M. D. S., 99, 100, 101, 103
Ajdacic-Gross, V., 314, 332
Akman, Y., 210
Alexander, J. L., 267
Alexander, K. W., 131
Alfirevic, Z., 30
Alibali, M. W., 11, 81, 85
Alipuria, L. L., 211
Allain, P., 301
Allen, L., 169
Alloway, T. P., 162
Almeida, D. M., 278
Alphonso, C., 122
Amato, P. R., 181, 313
Ambert, A.-M., 251, 256
Aminabhavi, V. A., 182
Ammaniti, M., 101
Amodio, D. M., 246
Andersen, M. L., 287
Anderson, C. A., 177
Anderson, J., 199
Andreou, G., 121
Angier, N., 32
Annett, M., 121
Antonucci, T. C., 285
Appel, J. M., 321, 322
Appleyard, K., 104, 140
Aquilino, W. S., 282
Arai, A., 316
Archer, J., 144
Archibald, L. M. D., 162
Ardelt, M., 302, 306, 330
Arija, V., 67
Arnett, J. J., 225, 255
Arnold, S., 255
Arnon, S., 52
Aronson, E., 215
Arranz, L., 264
Arredondo, P., 15
Arterberry, M. E., 57, 58
Aschermann, E., 172
Ash, D., 14
Asherson, P., 156
Aslin, R. N., 69
Aspy, C. B., 218
Atkinson, G., 155
Auger, R. W., 238, 239
August, D., 93
Avioli, P. S., 285
Axford, J., 295, 296

B., N., 323
Bäckström, T., 234
Bahna, S. L., 156
Bahrick, H. P., 298, 299
Bahrick, L., 131
Bailey, J. M., 232
Baillargeon, R., 84, 85
Bajor, J. K., 318
Bakker, D. J., 157
Balk, D., 327, 329
Balk, D. E., 329
Ball, J., 174
Ball, V., 316
Ballmaier, M., 310
Baltes, M. M., 317
Baltes, P. B., 302, 317, 318
Bancroft, J., 266
Bandura, A., 9, 145, 146, 177, 180
Barnard, C. J., 264
Barnett, J. E., 291
Barr, M., 62
Barr, R. G., 61, 86
Barry, C. M., 182
Bartsch, K., 85
Barua, B., 293
Batsche, G. M., 184
Bauer, K. W., 153
Baum, S. R., 118
Bauman, M. L., 108
Baumrind, D., 137, 139, 140, 179
Baumwell, L., 95
Bavin, E. L., 95
Bayley, N., 87
Beaulieu, M-D., 311
Beck, E., 141, 142
Beck, J. G., 310
Becker, D., 277
Bedford, V. H., 285
Beidel, D. C., 188
Beilei, L., 155
Bell, D., 210, 211
Bell, J. H., 202
Belsky, J., 100, 101, 109
Beltrame, J., 276
Bem, S. L., 150
Benbow, C. P., 121, 172
Bender, H. L., 137
Bengtson, V. L., 313
Bensaheb, A., 188
Berg, C. J., 44
Berger, S. E., 38, 73, 74
Berish, D. E., 270
Berndt, T. J., 183
Bernstein, I. L., 58
Bernstein, I. M., 43
Berscheid, E., 246
Bertoni, A., 253
Bertrand, L. D., 220
Berzonsky, M. D., 210, 211
Bhugra, D., 309
Bialystok, E. K., 131, 173
Bibby, R., 252, 256
Bielski, Z., 236
Bigler, R. S., 147
Binet, A., 4, 165, 166
Bird, A., 113
Birks, E., 67
Bishop, D. V. M., 157
Bishop-Josef, S. J., 183
Bissell, M., 33
Bjerkedal, T., 141
Bjornstrom, C., 200
Black, D. W., 186
Blackwell, D. L., 253
Blackwell, T., 291
Blanchard-Fields, F., 302
Blass, E. M., 59
Blazina, C., 243
Block, S. D., 332
Bluck, S., 300
Boccia, M., 111
Boerner, K., 332
Bohlmeijer, E., 306
Bohon, C., 200, 205
Boivin, M., 182
Boland, M., 67
Bonanno, G. A., 332
Bons, T. A., 246
Boom, J., 204
Booth-LaForce, C., 147, 183
Bornstein, M. H., 89, 90, 91, 92, 93, 94, 95, 132, 133, 180
Bose, S., 205
Bosi, M. L., 197
Bouchard, T. J., Jr., 31, 171, 202, 203
Bouffard, T., 212
Boulton, M. J., 144
Bourgeois, M. J., 8
Bowlby, J., 99, 103, 332
Bozionelos, N., 239
Braam, A. W., 312
Bracht, M., 125
Bradbury, T. N., 254
Bradley, R. H., 172
Brady, E. M., 272
Branco, J. C., 129
Brandstätter, H., 207
Brase, G. L., 148
Brazier, A., 27
Breitner, J. C. S., 298
Bremner, A., 85
Brennan, S., 235
Bridges, A. J., 265
Bridges, J. S., 278, 279
Bridges, L. J., 284
Briones, T. L., 71
Brockman, D. D., 243
Bronfenbrenner, U., 12, 13
Bronson, G. W., 76
Brookmeyer, R., 287
Broomhall, H. S., 282
Brown, R., 91, 93
Brown, S. L., 313
Brownell, C. A., 112
Bruck, M., 164
Brunner, L. C., 290
Bruss, P. J., 299
Bryant, P., 85, 130
Bryden, P. J., 121
Buchanan, A., 213
Buckley, K. E., 177
Budney, A. J., 230
Budworth, M.-H., 141
Bugental, D. B., 52
Buhl, H. M., 243
Bukowski, W. M., 142
Buote, V. M., 215
Burke, D. M., 301
Bushman, B. J., 146, 212
Bushnell, E. W., 78
Bushnell, I. W. R., 76
Bushnik, T., 108
Buss, D. M., 148, 245, 253
Buston, K., 218
Butler, R. N., 306
Butterfield, S. A., 155
Buunk, B. P., 245
Bye, D., 272
Bynum, M. S., 217

Callahan, J. J., 285
Calvert, S. L., 130
Camp, C. A., 59
Campanella, J., 86
Campbell, A., 111, 114, 143
Campbell, D. W., 119, 143
Campbell, S. B., 148, 149

Campos, J. J., 76, 77, 110, 111
Campos, P., 222
Camras, L. A., 110
Candy, T. R., 57
Canitano, R., 107
Caplan, M., 144
Capron, C., 196
Carey, B., 108, 142, 245
Carmichael, D., 221
Carrère, S., 256, 257
Carriger, M. S., 112
Carroll, J. S., 225, 255
Carstensen, L. L., 307, 308, 317, 318
Carver, L. J., 110
Casaer, P., 71
Casas, J. F., 140
Caserta, M. S., 314
Casini, A., 281
Cassia, V. M., 76
Caton, D., 50
Cattell, R. B., 168
Caudle, D. D., 311
Caulfield, R., 52
Cavallini, A., 75
Cavell, T. A., 187
Cellarius, V., 325
Chalmers, B., 49, 50
Chapman, B., 243, 244
Chapman, M., 159
Charles, S. T., 306, 307
Charlton, R., 266
Charness, N., 268
Chaudieu, I., 311
Cheng, H., 249
Cheng, S-T., 221
Chesley, N., 256
Chess, S., 112
Choi, J. S., 41
Chong, L., 295
Chong, S. C. F., 130
Chou, T-L., 118
Choudhuri, E., 281
Chrisler, J. C., 285
Christian, P., 39
Christophersen, E. R., 124
Chronis, A. M., 186
Clancy, B., 96
Clark, B. F. C., 293
Clark, E. V., 91
Clark, J., 141, 309
Clark, N., 314
Clark, R., 134
Clark, S., 147
Clark, W., 155
Clarke-Stewart, K. A., 100
Clayton, R., 56
Cleary, D. J., 183
Clode, D., 121
Cnattingius, S., 43
Coan, J. A., 256, 257
Coats, A. H., 302
Cochran, S. V., 310
Cohen, D., 248
Cohen, L. S., 54
Cohen, S., 264
Cohen-Bendahan, C. C. C., 149
Cohn, M., 299
Cole, S., 67
Coleman, P. K., 100
Collaer, M. L., 203
Collins, M., 229
Collins, W. A., 180, 213, 214
Colombo, J., 88
Commons, M. L., 204, 237
Conner, K. R., 222
Connolly, J., 215
Connor, P. D., 42
Conrad, P., 266
Constantino, J. N., 107
Cooke, B. M., 122
Cooper, J., 222
Coovadia, H., 39
Corballis, P. M., 118
Coren, S., 121
Corliss, R., 238
Cornelius, S. W., 315
Cornwell, A. A. C., 60
Corsaro, W. A., 182
Costa, P. T., Jr., 279, 280
Costello, E. J., 197
Costigan, C. L., 213, 214
Courage, M. L., 88
Cowan, C. P., 180
Cowan, N., 162, 163, 164
Cowan, P. A., 180
Craik, F. I. M., 173
Cramer, D., 249
Crawford, J. K., 198
Crenshaw, D. A., 329
Crinella, F., 318
Cristofaro, T. N., 89, 90, 91, 92, 93, 94, 132, 133
Crockenberg, S. C., 55
Crombie, G., 143
Crook, C., 111, 114
Crosby, R. A., 56
Crowther, C., 52
Cruz, N. V., 156
Csikszentmihalyi, M., 318
Cuellar, J., 222
Cullen, F. T., 182
Cumming, S. P., 155
Cunningham, R. L., 144
Curry, T. R., 222
Curtis, S., 198

Da Costa, L.A., 299
Daman-Wasserman, M., 85
Damon, W., 212
Dandy, J., 171
Dane, S., 121
Dang-Vu, T. T., 61
Daniels, S. R., 154
Daniels, W., 229
Daniluk, J. C., 264
Darwin, C., 12
D'Augelli, A. R., 313, 314
Davenne, D., 155
Davis, H. P., 269, 270
Davis, L., 52
Davis, S., 265, 266
De Beni, R., 301
de Groh, M., 121
de Guzman, M. R. T., 214
de Haan, M., 51, 75, 118
de Oliveira, F. P., 197
De Thomas, C., 156
de Villiers, J. G., 90
de Villiers, P. A., 90
Deary, I. J., 169
DeCasper, A. J., 38, 60, 85
DeHart, G. B., 144
Delgado, A. R., 203
DelVecchio, W. F., 280
Demont, J., 331
Dennerstein, L., 266, 267
Denton, K., 160
Deonna, T., 107
Depp, C. A., 317
Derby, C. A., 267
Desjardins, M. J., 143
Desjardins, R. N., 95
DeYong, N. G., 86
Dezoete, J. A., 88
Diamond, L. M., 216
Dik, B. J., 316, 317
DiLalla, D. L., 31
Dishion, T. J., 142, 218
Doherty, W. J., 255
Dollfus, S., 121
Dombrowski, M. A. S., 52
Donald, M., 257
Donohue, K. F., 230
Donovan, D. M., 205
Dorling, J., 51
Doron, H., 284
Doucet, E., 228
Drasgow, E., 108
Dray, A. J., 178, 180
Drewett, R., 52
Drigotas, S. M., 247
Dryden, W., 188
Dube, W. V., 9
Duberstein, P. R., 310
Duffy, R. D., 238
Duggan, A., 106
Dumas, J. A., 299
Dunn, J., 182, 284
Dunning, C., 291
Duntley, J. D., 148
Duplassie, D., 264
Dupuis-Blanchard, S. M., 311
Durkin, S. J., 199, 212
Duyme, M., 196
Dyer, C. S., 68
Dyer, S. J., 255

Eastwood, C., 282
Eaton, W. O., 119, 143
Eccles, J. S., 114, 179
Eckerman, C. O., 52
Eddleston, M., 310
Edler, C., 200
Egerton, A., 230
Eimas, P. D., 77
Eisenberg, M. E., 198
Eisner, E. W., 120
Elkind, D., 89, 142, 202
Ellis, A., 188
Ellis, B. J., 141
Else-Quest, N. M., 142, 143
El-Sheikh, M., 182
Eltzschig, H., 50
Emler, N., 204
Epel, E. S., 292
Erikson, E. H., 5, 6–8, 99, 102, 104, 137, 177, 209, 241, 243, 275–277, 305, 309
Ersner-Hershfield, H., 308
Escorial, S., 269
Etaugh, C. A., 278, 279
Eviatar, Z., 172

Fagen, J. W., 85, 86
Fagot, B. I., 114, 143
Fair, R. C., 236
Fang L., 265
Fantz, R. L., 75
Faris, M., 104
Farmer, A., 23
Farthofer, A., 207
Feigenbaum, P., 60
Feijó, L., 52
Feiring, C., 183, 215
Feldman, R., 126
Fergusson, A., 157
Fernandes, L., 130
Fernandez-Twinn, D. S., 39
Féron, J., 78
Ficca, G., 60, 61
Fichner-Rathus, L., 39, 150, 218
Field, A. P., 147
Field, T., 52, 62
Fifer, W. P., 38, 60, 85
Figueiredo, D., 309
Filus, A., 283
Finkel, E. J., 250
Finkelman, J. M., 236
Finlay, B., 96
Fisch, S. M., 130
Fiske, A., 310
Fitzgerald, H. E., 120
Fivush, R., 131, 132, 163
Flavell, J. H., 11, 81, 130, 131, 164
Florsheim, P., 215
Flouri, E., 213
Flynn, J. R., 268
Flynn, M., 205
Fogassi, L., 86
Foley, G. M., 112
Fontaine, A-M., 142
Forman-Hoffman, V. L., 200
Fortier, J., 281
Fouad, N. A., 15
Fozard, J. L., 226
Franklin, A., 58
Frazier, L. D., 307
Frazier, P., 181
Freeman, S., 58
Frerichs, L., 68
Freud, S., 5–6, 16, 102
Freund, A. M., 318

Fried, P. A., 42
Friedman, R. A., 278
Friedman, S. A., 301
Frisch, R., 197
Frisch, R. E., 197
Fromkin, V., 96
Fry, D. P., 119
Fucito, L. M., 267
Fuller-Thomson, E., 242
Furman, W., 104, 215
Furnham, A., 244, 249
Fu-xi, F., 327

Gådin, K. G., 236
Gaines, S. O., 246
Galand, P., 210
Gallagher, F., 50
Gans, D., 285
Gardner, H., 165
Garmon, L., 96
Gartstein, M. A., 112
Gathercole, S. E., 162, 163
Gavin, N. I., 54, 55
Ge, X., 197
Geake, J., 14
Geary, D. C., 148
Georgiades, S., 107
Gerard, J. M., 284
Geschwind, D. H., 121
Gesell, A., 5, 74
Ghetti, S., 131
Gibb, R., 118
Gibson, E. J., 76, 78
Gilhooly, M. L., 302
Gilligan, C., 205, 243
Gilmore, J., 205
Giussani, D. A., 39
Glazer, J. P., 327
Gleason, T. R., 126, 142, 183
Glück, J., 300
Gobet, F., 163
Goel, P., 43
Golan, H., 51
Goldberg, A., 131, 284
Goldman, J. S., 297
Goldschmidt, L., 42
Goldsmith, H. H., 112, 142, 143, 156
Goldstein, H., 195
Goldstein, I., 265, 266, 267
Goldstein, S., 180
González, M. M., 237
Gonzalez, V., 173
González, Y. S., 214
Goodheart, C. D., 114
Goodman, C. G., 284
Gopnik, A., 130, 131, 134
Gordon-Salant, S., 226, 301
Gormally, S., 61
Gosling, S. D., 308, 309
Gottlieb, B. H., 225
Gottman, J. M., 256, 257
Graber, J. A., 197
Grandi, G., 234
Gray, C., 332
Gray, S. L., 298
Green, R., 180
Greenberg, J. S., 284
Greene, L., 218
Greene, S. M., 18
Greenough, W. T., 71, 79
Greidanus, J. A., 329
Griffiths, M., 327
Grigorenko, E. L., 157
Grindrod, C. M., 118
Grolnick, W. S., 111
Grossman, A. H., 313, 314
Grossmann, K., 101
Grundy, E., 285
Grusec, J. E., 138, 139, 140, 142
Guerin, D. W., 113
Guerrini, I., 39, 42, 43
Guiaux, M., 314
Gulli, C., 218
Güntürkün, O., 71
Gurba, E., 237
Gutknecht, L., 107

Haith, M. M., 73, 75, 76
Hakuta, K., 129
Halgin, R. P., 186
Hall, D. T., 281
Hall, G. S., 4, 193
Hall, L. K., 299
Halliday, L. F., 157
Halpern, D. F., 203
Hamm, J. V., 183
Hammer, K., 146, 161
Hammond, N. R., 131
Hangal, S., 182
Hanlon, T. E., 182
Hannon, E. E., 58
Hannon, P., 122
Hansen, J. C., 316, 317
Happaney, K., 52
Harel, J., 100
Harlow, H. F., 102, 104
Harlow, M. K., 102, 104
Harris, G., 188
Harris, S. R., 88
Harter, S., 147, 179, 180, 212
Hartley, A., 270
Hartman, M., 299
Hartup, W. W., 104, 126, 144, 183
Hasher, L., 270, 302
Hassett, J. M., 143
Hassing, L. B., 301
Hastings, P. D., 143
Hatch, L. R., 312, 313
Hatcher, R. A., 33
Hatfield, E., 246, 248
Havighurst, R., 241, 275–276
Hawkley, L. C., 249
Hay, D. F., 143
Hayes, R., 266
Hayes, V. E., 88
Hayflick, L., 292
Hayne, H., 85, 86
Haynie, D. L., 205
Hayslip, B., Jr., 243, 244, 284, 309
Healy, M. D., 141
Hebert, T. P., 150
Heilman, K. M., 171
Heiman, J. R., 266
Heindel, J. J., 43
Held, L., 103
Hen, R., 23
Hendry, L. B., 315
Henkens, K., 316
Henretta, J. C., 285
Henry, D., 144
Henzi, S. P., 214
Herbert, P., 50
Heron, M. P., 262, 294
Hershberger, S. L., 314
Hertenstein, M. J., 110, 111
Hertz-Lazarowitz, R., 214
Hess, T. M., 271
Hetherington, E. M., 18, 180, 182
Hicks, B. M., 144
Hildebrandt, C., 177
Hilden, K., 162
Hill, E. M., 203
Hill, R. A., 244
Hill, S. E., 114
Hill, S. Y., 23
Hinojosa, T., 121
Hochwarter, W. A., 281
Hoecker, J. L., 87
Hoegh, D. G., 8
Hoff, E. V., 90, 126
Hogan, A. M., 28, 51
Holland, J. J., 146
Holland, J. L., 206
Holland, J. M., 314, 332, 333
Holt, N. L., 180
Holty, S., 244
Homer, B. D., 132, 134
Homish, G. G., 253
Homsi, G., 230
Hong, H-W., 103
Honzik, M. P., 169
Höpflinger, F., 283
Hoppmann, C., 314
Horn, I. B., 125
Horn, J. L., 268–269
Horn, M. C., 278
Hort, B., 131
Horton, S. M., 288
Hossain, M., 44
Hostetler, A. J., 272
Hough, M. S., 301
Houts, A. C., 125
Howe, M. L., 88
Hrubi-Bopp, K. L., 299
Huang, J., 232
Huestis, M. A., 42
Huizink, A. C., 42
Huleihel, M., 51
Hultsch, D. F., 270
Hummel, C., 283
Hunt, C. E., 62
Hurd, Y. L., 42
Hursting, S. D., 295
Hussain, A., 251
Hyde, J. S., 142, 143, 203

Inder, T., 51
Ingersoll, B., 108
Ingersoll, G. M., 202
Isaacs, E. B., 28
Iwaniec, D., 68

Jackendoff, R., 94
Jacklin, C. N., 114
Jacobs, D. M., 27
Jacobs, J. E., 179
Jacobs, S., 332
Jacobsen, J. S., 297
Jacobson, L., 185
Jacobson, P. F., 133
Jang, Y., 311
Janssen, E., 266
Janssen, I., 198, 200
Janz, T., 230
Jayson, S., 252
Jensen, A. R., 171
Jepsen, D. A., 281
Jerrome, D., 314
Jeste, D. V., 317
Johannes, C. B., 266
Johanssom, B., 301
Johnson, A., 323
Johnson, J. G., 310
Johnson, K., 108
Johnson, R. S., 112
Johnson, W., 23, 202, 203
Jones, A., 230
Jones, B. C., 244
Jones, D. C., 198
Jones, S. S., 103
Jonkman, S., 230
Jordan, J. V., 243
Jorgensen, G., 205
Joshi, R. M., 156
Joung, H-M., 307, 330
Judge, T. A., 281
Juffer, F., 67, 101

Kagan, L. J., 187
Kaminski, P. L., 284, 309
Kaminski, R. A., 13, 14
Kanevsky, L., 14
Kang, S., 43
Karapetsas, A., 121
Karatekin, C., 155
Karavasilis, L., 101
Katz, R., 180
Katzman, D. K., 200
Kauff, N. D., 263
Kauffmann, M., 301
Kavanagh, K., 228
Kavanaugh, R. D., 142
Kavcic, T., 141
Kavšek, M., 86
Kawas, C. H., 287
Kaye, W. H., 200
Kazdin, A. E., 186
Kazui, H., 311
Kearney, C. A., 188
Keen, D., 126
Keller, H., 111
Kellman, P. J., 57, 58
Kellogg, R., 120
Kelly, J., 182

Kelly, J. R., 316
Kemp, C. L., 315
Kempes, M., 144
Kendler, K. S., 188
Kennard, J., 32
Kennedy, B., 179
Kenny, M. C., 187
Keogh, A. F., 169
Kerns, K., 26
Kerns, K. A., 100
Khamsi, R., 119
Kidd, E., 95
Killen, M., 184
Kim, J-Y., 141
King, J., 63
King, N., 147
King, P. M., 237
King, V., 313
Kingston, A., 279
Kinsbourne, M., 118
Kirby, P. G., 272
Kirkcaldy, B. D., 155
Kirkey, S., 326
Kistner, J., 187
Kitchener, K. S., 237
Kjelsås, E., 200
Kleiber, D. A., 316
Klein, P. J., 86
Kliegel, M., 301
Klier, C. M., 55
Klinger, R., 281
Klintsova, A. Y., 71
Kloep, M., 315
Klohnen, E. C., 246
Knaak, S., 68
Knafo, A., 23, 143, 144
Kniffin, K. M., 244
Kochanek, K. D., 262
Kochanska, G., 138
Kohl, C., 54
Kohl, J. V., 232
Kohlberg, L., 149, 159–161, 204, 205
Kolata, G., 154, 253
Kolb, B., 118
Konijn, E. A., 212
Kopp, C. B., 111
Korff, S. C., 312
Kotler, J. A., 130
Krackow, E., 164
Kramer, R., 205
Krebs, D. L., 160
Kristensen, P., 141, 293
Kroeger, K. A., 93
Krojgaard, P., 85
Krueger, C., 38
Krueger, R. F., 23
Kübler-Ross, E., 321, 322, 332
Kuczaj, S. A., II, 93
Kuczmarski, R.J., 117, 153
Kuhl, P. K., 77, 78
Kuhn, D., 85
Kuk, L. S., 211
Kulick, D., 250
Kulik, L., 282, 313
Kumar, K., 158
Kunz, J. A., 306
Kunzmann, U., 302
Kupsch, M., 256
Kurdek, L. A., 254
Kurowski, C. O., 111
Kvaal, K., 309, 310
Kwok, H. W. M., 108
Kwok, H-K., 285

Labouvie-Vief, G., 237
Labrell, F., 132
Lachman, M. E., 236, 259, 278
Laflamme, D., 101
LaFreniere, P. J., 144
Lai, H-L., 52
Lam, K. S. L., 108
Lam, T. H., 197, 198
Lamb, M. E., 109
Lambert, A., 179
Lamers, C. T. J., 230
Langlois, C., 196
Langlois, J. H., 182, 197, 244
Lansford, J. E., 18
Lantolf, J. P., 129
LaPointe, L. L., 96
Lapsley, D. K., 159, 202
Larroque, B., 52
Latham, G. P., 141
Lattanzi-Licht, M., 327, 329
Lau, A. S., 137, 138
Laumann, E. O., 251, 253, 264, 265, 266, 291, 292
Launslager, D., 31, 34
Laurendeau, M., 127
Laursen, B., 213, 214
Lawler, C., 43
Lawrence, E., 255
Lawrence, E. B., 254
Leaper, C., 143, 149
Lecanuet, J. P., 38
Leclerc, C. M., 271
Leder, S., 284
Leerkes, E. M., 55
Lefkowitz, E. S., 150
Legro, R. S., 33
Lei, L., 155
Leinbach, M. D., 114
Lejeune, C., 42
Lemaire, P., 301
Le Mare, L., 74
Lengua, L. J., 129
Lenneberg, E. H., 90
Leonardo, E. D., 23
Leone, J. L., 285
Leung, C., 138
Levenson, R. W., 312, 313
Lever, N., 205
Levine, D., 246
Levinson, D. J., 243, 244, 277, 280, 306
Levinthal, B. R., 172
Levpušcek, M. P., 243
Lewin, A. C., 313
Lewinsohn, P. M., 187, 197
Lewis, B. A., 42
Lewis, H. L., 211
Lewis, M., 183
Li, Q., 184
Lichter, D. T., 253
Lickliter, R., 89
Lidz, J. L., 132, 134
Lim, K. O., 71
Limber, S. P., 110
Lin, Y., 77
Lindau, S. T., 264, 265
Lindberg, L. D., 217
Ling, L., 26
Lipman, E. L., 140
Lippa, R. L., 297
Lipsitt, L. P., 59, 62
Li-qi, Z., 327
Livne, N. L., 171
Lleras, A., 172
Locke, J., 3, 16
Löckenhoff, C. E., 318
Loewenstein, D. A., 298
Lohr, C., 310
Loovis, E. M., 155
Lorant, V., 257
Lorenz, F. O., 278
Lorenz, K., 12, 103
Losen, D. J., 205
Louden, L., 243, 244
Lourenço, O., 129
Lovaas, O. I., 108
Lubinski, D., 165, 172
Lucariello, J. M., 163
Luciana, M., 117, 118
Ludemann, P. M., 76
Ludwick, R., 294
Ludwig, F. M., 284
Lunau, K., 232
Lund, D. A., 314
Luo, S., 246
Lupien, S. J., 300
Lykken, D. T., 31, 144, 171, 318
Lynne, S. D., 197
Lyon, G. R., 156, 157

Maccoby, E. E., 114, 180
MacDonald, N., 198
Macfarlane, A., 58
Maciejewski, P. K., 332
Mackic-Magyar, J., 107
Maclean, A. M., 204
Maclean, H., 68
MacLeod, A. K., 187
MacQueen, K., 212
Madon, S., 185
Magolda, M. B. B., 237
Mahay, J., 251, 253, 291, 292, 313
Mahler, M. S., 112
Maimburg, R. D., 107
Major, G. C., 228
Malone, P. S., 18, 181
Mangina, C. A., 298
Mann, D., 66
Manning, M. A., 212, 213
Maratsos, M. P., 85
Marchione, M., 263
Marcia, J. E., 209
Marcovitch, S., 85
Marean, G. C., 78
Markham, B., 226
Markovitzky, G., 284
Marks, L., 312
Marquis, C., 251
Marron, D. J., 272
Martin, C. L., 114, 132, 143, 149, 150
Marwick, C., 265
Masalha, S., 126
Matlin, M. W., 113, 148
Matthews, A. K., 254, 266
Matthews, K. A., 181
Matthews, R. A., 256
Mauro, E., 215
Maxwell, C. D., 235
McBride, M. C., 159
McCabe, M. P., 198, 267
McCall, R. B., 169
McCarthy, B. W., 267
McCartney, K., 100
McClellan, J. M., 108
McCormick, B., 179
McCracken, J., 107
McCracken, M., 226
McCrae, R. R., 279, 280
McDevitt, T. M., 118
McDonald, H., 295
McDonough, L., 91
McGinnis, M. Y., 144
McGrath, M., 52
McHale, J. P., 255
McHale, S. M., 141
McIlvane, W. J., 9
McKay, A., 33
McKee-Ryan, F., 282
McLaughlin, J. K., 43
McManus, C., 121
McManus, I. C., 121
Meaney, K. S., 155
Meier, B. P., 146
Meijer, A. M., 254
Meinert, C. L., 298
Melamed, S., 316
Mellon, M. W., 125
Meltzoff, A. N., 85, 86, 134
Mendle, J., 196
Mendleson, R., 221
Merrill, M., 166
Metcalfe, J. S., 73
Metzger, A., 213, 214
Metzger, K. L., 23
Meyer, S., 111
Meyerhoff, M., 72
Michael, R., 253
Michael, R. T., 266
Michaels, S., 266
Milgram, R. M., 171
Millar, W. J., 68
Miller, C. F., 148, 149
Miller, N. J., 307, 330
Miller, S. M., 147
Mills, B., 327, 330

Miner, R., 281
Minino, A. M., 262
Minkler, M., 242
Mischo, C., 177
Mitchell, A. L., 230
Mitchell, D. D., 299
Miyake, A., 162
Miyatsuji, H., 84
Mock, S. E., 315
Moen, P., 256, 272, 312, 315
Moens, E., 154
Mohan, R., 309
Mohay, H., 52
Moilanen, I., 126
Molinari, L., 182
Monat, A., 264
Monette, M., 310
Monte, L., 121
Moore, D. R., 266
Moran, P., 121
Moretti, M. M., 213, 214
Morrell, J., 101
Morris, P. A., 12, 13
Morrison, T., 271
Morrow, A., 15
Morry, M. M., 246
Morton, S. M. B., 39
Mortweet, S. L., 124
Moses, L. J., 130
Moshman, D., 237
Mozart, W. A., 271
Mueller, R., 108
Muhlbauer, V., 285
Mulder, E. J. H., 42
Muraco, A., 314
Muris, P., 147
Murphy, S. L., 262
Murray, D., 66
Mutran, E. J., 315, 316
Myers, J. E., 252

Nadeau, L., 51
Nagin, D. S., 144
Natsopoulos, D., 121
Nauert, R., 199
Nauta, M. M., 206, 239
Naveh-Benjamin, M., 299
Neisser, U., 165, 171
Nelson, C. A., 76, 117, 118
Nelson, K., 90, 93, 131, 132, 133, 134, 277
Nelson, M., 42
Nelson, T. D., 134
Nesdale, D., 179
Nettelbeck, T., 171
Newburn-Cook, C. V., 43
Newman, R., 86, 90
Neyer, F. J., 314
Nielsen, S., 200
Nielsen, S. J., 153
Niemeier, H. M., 199
Nigg, J. T., 156
Nimrod, G., 307
Nisbett, R. E., 268
Nixon, R., 277
Nock, M. K., 186
Nolen-Hoeksema, S., 200
Noll, J., 269
Nomaguchi, K. M., 182
Nonaka, A. M., 95
Nonnemaker, J. M., 230
Noppe, I. C., 330
Noppe, L. D., 330
Norlander, T., 150
Norton, A., 271
Nurnberg, H. G., 266
Nuttman-Shwartz, O., 316

Oates, J., 177
O'Boyle, M. W., 121
O'Brien, B., 49, 50
O'Dea, J. A., 212
O'Doherty, J., 244
O'Donnell, L., 218
Offit, K., 263
Ogunfowora, O. B., 28
O'Keeffe, M. J., 51
Oliveira, M., 250
Olivo, L., 220
Ollendick, T. H., 147
Olson, S. L., 143, 144
Oltjenbruns, K. A., 329
Omori, M., 202
O'Muircheartaigh, C. A., 264, 265
O'Neill, D. K., 130
Ong, A. D., 211
Orel, N., 284
Ormrod, J. E., 118
Örnkloo, H., 114
Orstavik, R. E., 188
Ortega, V., 217
Osgood, D. W., 141
O'Shea, R. P., 118
Oster, H., 58, 110
Ouellette, G. P., 89
Outram, S., 278
Owsley, C., 77
Ozanne, S. E., 39
Oztop, E., 86

Paavola, L., 126
Palmer, B., 200
Park, H-O. H., 284
Park, N. S., 312
Parke, R. D., 141
Patenaude, J., 204
Paterson, D. S., 62
Patrick, S., 253
Patterson, C. J., 180
Patterson, G. R., 144
Patterson, M. M., 147
Pauli-Pott, U., 112
Paulussen-Hoogeboom, M. C., 138
Paus, T., 117, 118
Pausch, R., 334
Paxton, S. J., 198, 199, 212
Peck, R. C., 305–306
Pei, M., 149
Pelphrey, K. A., 86
Penn, H. E., 108
Perls, T. T., 292
Perrault, S., 220
Perrig-Chiello, P., 309
Perrone, K. M., 253
Perry, P. J., 291
Perry-Jenkins, M., 255
Persson, G. E. B., 144
Philip, J., 30
Phillips, B., 108
Phinney, J. S., 211
Phipps, M. G., 44
Piaget, J., 10–11, 16, 81, 82, 83, 85, 125–129, 134, 142, 158–159, 164, 177, 201–202
Picard, A., 49
Picasso, P., 271
Pichichero, M. E., 233
Pickert, K., 104
Piek, J. P., 72, 147
Pierce, K., 108
Pierce, K. M., 109
Pike, R., 147
Pillard, R. C., 232
Pinard, A., 127
Pinker, S., 94
Pinquart, M., 316
Pittman, G., 50
Pizzuto, E., 89
Plomin, R., 23, 107, 143, 144, 157
Poisson, J., 151
Pollack, C. E., 316
Poltorak, D. Y., 327
Popenoe, D., 255
Popkin, B. M., 153
Popma, A., 144
Porfeli, E. J., 207
Porter, L. J., 184
Posey, D. J., 156
Posner, M., 112–113
Posner, M. I., 71
Post, L. A., 235
Pote, H. L., 187
Potter, J., 308, 309
Powlishta, K. K., 114, 149
Prato-Previde, E., 95
Pratt, C., 130
Pressley, M., 162
Pressman, S. D., 249
Previti, D., 313
Prieto, G., 203
Prigerson, H. G., 310, 332
Priner, R., 58
Prinz, W., 86
Prull, M. W., 270
Puente, S., 248
Pujol, J., 69
Pulverman, R., 134

Qin, W., 298
Queen, J. A., 154
Quigley, N. R., 239

Radotra, A., 43
Radvansky, G. A., 270
Raikes, H., 173
Ramage-Morin, P. L., 296
Ramchandani, P. G., 115
Ramey, C. T., 39
Randel, B., 171
Rapin, I., 108
Rapson, R. L., 246, 248
Rat-Fisher, L., 121
Rathus, S. A., 39, 150, 218
Rattan, S. I. S., 293
Rayman, J. R., 272
Reddy, L. A., 156
Redshaw, M., 255
Reef, S., 40
Rees, S., 51
Reijneveld, S. A., 61
Reis, O., 215
Reitzes, D. C., 315, 316
Rennie, S., 242
Rest, J. R., 204
Retsinas, J., 322
Reynolds, C. A., 253, 306
Richards, J. C., 264
Richards, T. W., 38
Rizzolatti, G., 86
Roberts, B. W., 280
Roberts, K. C., 121
Roberts, W., 143, 144
Robins, R. W., 308, 309
Robins Wahlin, T., 27
Robinson, M., 253
Rodriguez, E. T., 89, 90, 91, 92, 93, 94, 132, 133
Rodriguez, S., 323, 325
Roebers, C. M., 164
Roeser, R. W., 209
Roffwarg, H. P., 60
Rogers, M. L., 199
Rogers, S. J., 313
Rohde, P., 187
Rondal, J. A., 26
Rönnerman, K., 129
Roopnarine, J. L., 138
Rose, A. J., 182
Rose, S. A., 86, 88
Rosen, T., 311
Rosenstein, D., 58
Rosenthal, R., 185
Rospenda, K. M., 236
Ross, H., 141
Ross, J. L., 265
Rotenberg, K. J., 183, 214
Roterman, M., 219
Roth, G. S., 295
Rothbart, M. K., 71, 111, 112–113
Rothman, S., 168
Rotman, T., 255
Rottinghaus, P. J., 206, 239
Roulet-Perez, E., 107
Rousseau, J.-J., 3
Rovee-Collier, C., 86
Rovere, M., 293
Rowland, D. T., 287
Rowlands, C., 27
Rubia, K., 162
Rubin, K. H., 142, 183
Ruble, D. N., 114, 148, 149, 150
Rudolph, K. D., 205
Rudy, D., 138
Rugg, S., 309

Rumbold, A. R., 40
Runyon, M. K., 187
Rusconi, A., 283
Rushton, J. P., 168, 171, 246
Russ, S. W., 126
Russell, S. T., 180
Rybash, J. M., 299
Ryff, C. D., 278

Sabattini, L., 149
Sabia, J. J., 311
Sadker, D. M., 186
Saffran, J. R., 77
Saggino, A., 298
Saigal, S., 52
Saiki, J., 84
Saito, S., 162
Salapatek, P., 76
Sales, J. M., 131
Salkind, S. J., 134
Salmivalli, C., 147
Salthouse, T. A., 269, 270
Salvaterra, F., 101, 103
Salzarulo, P., 60, 61
Sanchez-Mazas, M., 281
Sandman, C., 318
Santelli, J. S., 217, 233
Santos, D. C. C., 72
Saroglou, V., 210
Sarrazin, P., 185
Sasaki, C., 329
Savickas, M. L., 239
Savin-Williams, R. C., 216, 315
Scanlon, D. M., 157
Schaal, B., 110
Schaie, K. W., 267, 268, 269, 270
Scharf, M., 141
Scher, A., 100
Schindler, I., 316
Schlaggar, B. L., 69
Schmidtke, A., 310
Schneewind, K. A., 256
Schonfeld, A. M., 43
Schoppe-Sullivan, S. J., 113
Schraf, M., 214
Schuetze, P., 42
Schultz, D. P., 6
Schultz, S. K., 200
Schultz, W. W., 267
Schumacher, D., 154
Schuurmans, J., 310
Schwartz, S. J., 210
Scoffield, H., 181
Scott, J. R., 41
Scott, M. E., 313
Scourfield, J., 186
Sears, W., 104
Secker-Walker, R. H., 43
Sedlacek, W. E., 238
Sefcek, J. A., 232
Segrin, C., 249
Seidah, A., 212
Sell, R., 310
Selman, R. L., 178, 180, 183
Senman, L., 131
Serbin, L. A., 114, 149
Sessoms, G., 154
Seward, R. R., 252
Sexton, S. A., 311
Shafto, C. L., 95
Shafto, M. A., 301
Shakespeare, W., 248
Shatz, K. H., 332
Shaw, G., 215
Shaw, G. B., 252
Shaywitz, B. A., 156, 157
Shaywitz, S. E., 156, 157
Sheeber, L. B., 213
Sheese, B. E., 111
Sherwin-White, S., 142
Shinohara, H., 61
Shiota, M. N., 312, 313
Shirk, S., 212
Shneidman, E. S., 322
Showers, C. J., 246
Shroff, H., 200
Shultz, K. S., 281
Shyraydi, M., 252
Siegel, L. S., 88
Siegler, R. S., 11, 81, 85
Siegmund, R., 60
Siegrist, J., 316
Sierra, F., 293
Sierra, J. C., 217
Signorello, L. B., 43
Sigueland, E. R., 77
Silbereisen, R. K., 13
Silva, M. C., 294
Silventoinen, K., 228
Silver, R. C., 332
Silverstein, M., 285
Simion, F., 76
Simon, H. A., 163
Simon, T., 4, 165, 166
Simonelli, A., 67, 255
Simonton, D. K., 171, 271
Sims, C. S., 236
Singer, B. H., 278
Singer, L. T., 42
Sinnema, J., 123
Sirrs, S. M., 69
Skinner, B. F., 8, 93
Skinner, R., 222
Skoczenski, A. M., 75
Slaughter, V., 131, 327
Slavin, R. E., 184, 185
Sloan, S., 68
Slobin, D. I., 92
Small, S. A., 179
Smetana, J. G., 184, 193, 204, 213, 214
Smiley, P. A., 112
Smith, A. M., 42
Smith, C. L., 112
Smith, J., 314
Smith, P. K., 119
Smolka, E., 172
Smoll, F. L., 155
Snarey, J. R., 210, 211
Snedeker, J., 95
Snegovskikh, V., 47
Snow, C., 93, 96
Snyderman, M., 168
Sokolov, E. N., 298
Solano, C. H., 249
Soliz, J., 284
Sommerfeld, J., 233
Sommers, M. S., 289
Sonnentag, S., 316
Sontag, L. W., 38
Sorce, J., 77
Sousa, L., 309
Soussignan, R., 110
South, S. J., 205
Spearman, C., 165
Spelke, E. S., 77
Spence, M. J., 60, 85
Spieker, S. J., 100
Spock, B., 104
Sprecher, S., 246, 250
Sroufe, L. A., 100, 110
Staff, J., 207, 215
Stagnitti, K., 126
Stahmer, A. C., 108
Stams, G. J. J. M., 101, 138
Stanford, J. N., 198
Stankoff, B., 69
Stanley, M. A., 310
Stauffacher, K., 144
Steele, H., 100, 101, 242
Stein, D. J., 229
Steinberg, L., 180
Stemberger, J. P., 133
Sternberg, R. J., 165, 171, 247–248
Stevenson, H. W., 171
Stewart, M., 68
Stewart, S. M., 197, 198
Stifter, C. A., 112
Stipek, D., 112, 129
St. James, A., 204
Stoel-Gammon, C., 89
Storch, E. A., 154
Stores, G., 124
Stormshak, E. A., 13, 14, 142, 218
Strassberg, D. S., 244
Stratton, T. D., 236
Strayer, J., 143, 144
Streri, A., 78, 121
Stright, A. D., 164
Strock, M., 108
Styfco, S. J., 172
Sugiyama, M., 9
Sukhodolsky, D. G., 186
Sullivan, S. E., 281
Sulloway, F. J., 141
Sun, S. S., 195
Suomi, S. J., 104
Super, D., 238
Supple, A. J., 179
Sussman, N., 156
Sylva, K., 129
Szaflarski, J. P., 118

Takahashi, M., 9
Talbot, L. A., 307, 330
Tamis-LeMonda, C. S., 89, 90, 91, 92, 93, 94, 95, 132, 133
Tan, R. S., 266
Tanner, J. L., 243
Tanner, J. M., 117
Tapper, K., 144
Tashiro, T., 181
Tassi, F., 179
Taylor, C., 217
Taylor, H. H., 287
Taylor, M., 126, 131
Taylor, M. F., 314
Taylor-Butts, A., 235
Tees, R. C., 96
Terman, L., 166
Terracciano, A., 279
Thapar, A., 156
Thomas, A., 112
Thompson, A. M., 155
Thompson, I. M., 267
Thompson, R. A., 101, 110, 111, 179
Thomson, J., 314
Thorne, S. L., 129
Thornton, L. M., 264
Tiedemann, M., 323
Timmerman, L. M., 109
Tinbergen, N., 12
Tobbell, J., 205
Togsverd, M., 310
Tomaka, J., 249
Tomiyama, T., 297
Ton, M., 316
Toneguzzi, M., 276
Towse, J., 162, 163, 164
Tracy, J. L., 308, 309
Trainor, L. J., 95
Trehub, S. E., 58
Tremblay, R. E., 144
Trevarthen, C., 95
Troxel, W. M., 181
Trudeau, M., 54
Trudel, G. A., 291
Trzesniewski, K. H., 308, 309
Tsuneishi, S., 71
Turkheimer, E., 170
Turner, S. M., 188
Twist, M., 254
Tworkov, J., 298
Tymon, W. G., Jr., 239

Ubersfeld, G., 132
Ueno, K., 285
Umek, L. M., 14
Uylings, H. B. M., 96

Vaccaro, B. G., 110
Vacek, P. M., 43
Valiquet, D., 323
van den Akker, O., 255
van den Wittenboer, G. L. H., 254
van IJzendoorn, M. H., 67
van Solinge, H., 316
Vandell, D. L., 100, 109
Vandello, J. A., 248
Vander Ven, T., 182
Vares, T., 264, 265
Vartanian, O., 171
Vastag, B., 266

Vellutino, F. R., 157
Verissimo, M., 101, 103
Virji-Babul, N., 26
Visscher, W. A., 42
Vitiello, B., 188
Volkova, A., 58
Volling, B. L., 141
Volterra, M. C., 89
Von Ammon, J., 142
Von Dem Knesebeck, O., 316
VonDras, D. D., 279
von Gontard, A., 125
von Hofsten, C., 114, 155
Vorauer, J. D., 249
Vukman, K. B., 237
Vygotsky, L. S., 10, 14, 135

Wachs, T. D., 112
Wahler, R. G., 180
Wainright, J. L., 180
Wald, J., 205
Walitza, S., 156
Walk, R. D., 76
Wall, A., 256
Wall, G., 255
Wallace, I. F., 88
Wallerstein, J., 182
Walter, J. L., 144
Wang, L., 179, 239
Wang, S.-H., 85
Warren, L. H., 299
Washburn, D. A., 12
Watson, J. B., 4, 8
Waxman, S. R., 132, 134
Wechsler, D., 167
Weckerly, J., 172
Weeks, C., 253
Weinberg, R. A., 71
Weinshenker, M. N., 256
Weisler, R. H., 156
Wellman, H. M., 85, 130
Wells, E. A., 205
Weng, X., 43
Wenger, G. C., 314
Wennergren, A.-C., 129
Wentworth, N., 73
Wentzel, K. R., 182
Werker, J. F., 77, 78, 96
Werner, E. E., 85
Werner, L. A., 58, 77, 78
Werry, J. S., 108
Wethington, E., 277
Whitbourne, S. K., 186
Whitehouse, E. M., 129
Whiteman, M. C., 169
Whyte, J., 169
Wickwire, E. M., Jr., 290
Wierzalis, E. A., 314
Wiggins, C. N., 112
Wiggs, L., 124
Wilde, O., 238
Willett, W. C., 263
Willetts, M. C., 253
Williams, M. S., 200
Williams, W. M., 171
Willis, S. L., 267, 269
Wilson, D. R., 30
Wilson, D. S., 244
Wilson, E. O., 144
Wilson, J. M. B., 244
Wilson, P., 129
Wilson, T. D., 215
Windsor, T. D., 279
Winefield, A. H., 282
Winner, E., 172
Winter, M., 111
Witherington, D. C., 77
Witkowska, E., 236
Wocadlo, C., 51
Wodrich, D. L., 27
Wogrin, C., 327, 329
Wojslawowicz Bowker, J. C., 183
Wolfenden, L. E., 180
Woolfolk, A., 184, 185
Worell, J., 114
Wortman, C. B., 332
Wozniak, J. R., 71
Wright, C., 67
Wright, D. W., 182
Wulff, K., 60

Xie, H. L., 182

Yaffe, K., 265
Yamada, H., 117
Yeo, J., 50
Yost, M. R., 235
Youm, Y., 251, 253, 291, 292
Young, R., 182
Youniss, J., 215

Zacks, R. T., 270
Zaidi, A. U., 252
Zajonc, R. B., 141
Zan, B., 177
Zarbatany, L., 183
Zeifman, D. M., 61
Zeintl, M., 301
Zelazo, P. D., 85
Zelazo, P. R., 74
Zeldow, P. B., 150
Zhang, B., 310, 332
Zhou, S., 316, 317
Zimmerman, B. J., 180
Zimmermann, P., 111
Zupancic, M., 141
Zurbriggen, E. L., 235
Zweigenhaft, R. L., 142

Subject Index

Aboriginal people. *See also* Inuit children
- adolescence, 221
- Head Start program, 129
- infant mortality and, 53, 63
- language and, 96
- late adulthood, 318
- restorative justice, 221

abortion, 218
abstinence syndrome, 229
abuse, 105–106
accidents, 123, 198, 225, 297
accommodation, 11, 81
accutane, 41
achieved ethnic identity, 211
achievement, 164
activity theory, 307
adaptation, 11, 96
adaptive thermogenesis, 228
ADHD (attention-deficit/hyperactivity disorder), 155–156
adolescence
- overview, 193
- career development, 206–207
- cognitive abilities and sex differences, 202–203
- cognitive development, 201–202
- death and view of, 329–330
- health and illness, 198–201
- identity development, 209–213
- parents, relationships with, 213–214
- peer relationships, 214–215
- puberty, 193–198
- school and, 204–206
- sexuality, 216–219
- suicide, 221–222
- youths in conflict with the law, 220–221

adoption, 34
adoption studies, 31
adulthood. *See* early adulthood; late adulthood; middle adulthood
advanced directives, 323
age homogamy, 253
age of parents
- Down syndrome and, 26
- fertility and, 33
- low birth weight and, 51
- multiple births and, 25
- prenatal development and, 44

age-30 transition, 244
ageism, 277, 288
aggression, development of, 144–146
aging theories, 292–293
agoraphobia, 310
AIDS/HIV, 39, 68
alcohol, 42–43, 199, 230, 296–297
alleles, 25
alpha-fetoprotein (AFP) assays, 30
altruism, 143–144
Alzheimer's Disease, 297–298
ambivalent/resistant attachment, 100
amenorrhea, 234
amniocentesis, 29–30
amniotic fluid, 37, 47
amniotic sacs, 37
amphetamines, 230
amplitude, 58
anal stage, 6
analytical intelligence, 165
androgens, 37
androgyny, 150
anesthesia, 50
angular gyrus, 157
animals, for autism treatment, 108
animism, 127
anorexia nervosa, 200
A-not-B errors, 85
anoxia, 51
antibodies, 264
anxiety disorders, 231, 310–311
Apgar scale, 56
appearance–reality distinction, 131
arranged marriages, 252
arteriosclerosis, 264
arthritis, 295–296
artificial insemination, 34
artificialism, 127
ASD (autism spectrum disorders), 106–108
Asperger disorder, 106
assimilation, 11, 81
assisted suicide, 325
associative memory, 299
asynchronous growth, 194–195
atherosclerosis, 264
attachment, 99–104, 140
attachment-in-the-making phase, 101
Attachment Parenting Book (Sears), *The*, 104
attention-deficit/hyperactivity disorder (ADHD), 155–156
attraction, 244–246
attraction–similarity hypothesis, 246
attributional style, 187
auditory acuity, 77
authoritarian style, 139
authoritative style, 138–139, 179, 214
autism spectrum disorders (ASDs), 106–108
autobiographical memory, 131
autosome pairs, 24
avoidant attachment, 100
axons, 69–70

babbling, 89
Babinski reflex, 57
baby blues, 53–54
baby boomers, 259
Baby Storm, 151
basal metabolic rate (BMR), 260
Battle Hymn of the Tiger Mother (Chua), 104
Bayley Scales of Infant Development (BSID-II), 87–88
beauty, 244–245
Because Life Goes On (Health Canada), 140
bed-wetting, 125
behaviour modification for autism, 108
behaviourism, 4
benign tumours, 262
bereavement, 331–333
"big five" personality traits, 280
bilingualism, 173–174
Binet-Simon scale, 165–166
binge eating and purging, 200
birth. *See* childbirth
birth order, 141–142
birth rate, 31, 109
blastocysts, 35
blood sugar tolerance, 261
blood testing, 30
BMR (basal metabolic rate), 260
Bobo doll experiment, 145
body esteem, 309
body image, 198
body mass index (BMI), 154, 227–228, 260
bonding, 55
bone density, 260, 289–290
boomerang kids, 242, 276
bottle feeding, 68
brain death, 321
brain development, 69–70, 117–118. *See also* cognitive development
Braxton-Hicks contractions, 47
Brazelton Neonatal Behavioural Assessment Scale, 56
breast feeding, 67–68
breech (bottom-first) presentation, 51
British Columbia Full Day Kindergarten Program Guide, 146
BSID-II (Bayley Scales of Infant Development), 87–88
bulimia nervosa, 200
bullying, 161, 184
burials, 331

CA (chronological age), 166
caffeine, 43
calorie restriction, 295
Canadian Human Rights Code, 157
Canadian Incidence Study of Reported Child Abuse and Neglect, 105
Canadian Medical Association, 325–326
Canadian Psychological Association, 17
canalization, 67
cancer, 262–263
cannabis, 42
career development, 206–207, 238–239
career typology, 206–207
carriers, 25
case studies, 17
cataracts, 288–289
categorical self, 147
celibacy, 250
cellular clock theory, 292
centration, 128
cephalocaudal development, 36, 65–66
cerebellum, 70
cerebral cortex, 70
cerebrum, 70
cesarean sections, 50
character education, 161
child abuse and neglect, 105–106
childbirth
- overview, 47
- methods of, 49–50
- postpartum period, 53–55
- problems with, 50–53
- stages of, 47–49

childhood. *See* adolescence; early childhood; middle childhood
childhood disintegrative disorder, 107
children with disabilities, 155–158
chlamydia, 33, 234
chorionic villus sampling (CVS), 30
chromosomal abnormalaties, 26–27
chromosomes, 23–25
chronological age (CA), 166
chronosystems, 13–14
churchgoing, 311–312
cigarettes, 43, 123, 230
circular reactions, 82–83
class inclusion, 128–129, 159
classical conditioning, 8, 59–60
classroom inclusion, 157–158
clear-cut-attachment phase, 101

climacteric, 265
cliques, 214
cocaine, 42, 230
Code of Ethics, 20
codominance, 25
cognitive assimilation, 11, 81
cognitive development. *See also* memory
adolescence, 201–202
early adulthood, 236–238
early childhood, 125–131
information processing approach, 85–86
intelligence and, 86–88
language development and, 134–135
late adulthood, 298–302
middle adulthood, 267–271
middle childhood, 158–159
Piaget and, 81–85, 125–129
play and, 142
cognitive development theory, 10–12
cognitive–affective complexity, 237
cohabitation, 251, 313, 332
cohort effects, 20, 268
colour blindness, 28–29
colour perception, 58
coming out, 216–217
commitment, 210, 247
conception, 31–35
concrete-operational stage, 158–159, 177–178
condoms, 34
conduct disorders, 186–187
congenital, 39
conjoined twins, 24
conscientiousness, 312
conservation, 128, 158
constructive play, 142
consummate love, 248
contact comfort, 102–103
continuity versus discontinuity, 16
control groups, 19
conventional stage, 160–161
convergence, 58
convergent thinking, 171
cooing, 89
coordination of secondary schemes, 82–83
co-regulation, 180
corpus callosum, 118
correlation coefficients, 18
correlations, 18
crawling, 73
creative intelligence, 165
creativity, 171, 271
creeping, 73
cremations, 331
crime, 220–221, 235
critical periods of development, 39–40, 103
cross-linking theory, 293
cross-sectional research, 20
crowds, 214
crowning, 48
crying, 61–62, 89
crystallized intelligence, 236, 269, 298
cultural bias, 168–169
cultural–familial developmental challenges, 170
Culture-Fair Intelligence Test, 168–169
culture-free tests, 168–169
CVS (chorionic villus sampling), 30
cystic fibrosis, 28

dating, 215, 217, 235–236
day care, 108–109, 129
death
adolescence, 198
coping with, 330–334
defined, 321–322
euthanasia, 325–327
lifespan perspectives on, 327–330
low birth weight and, 51
maternal and infant rates of, 52–53, 63
middle adulthood, 261–262
overview, 321
places for, 323–325
understanding of, 321–323
decentration, 158–159
deferred imitation, 85
dementia, 297–298
dendrites, 69–70
deoxyribonucleic acid (DNA), 23–24
dependent variables, 19
depressants, 229–230
depression, 54–55, 187–188, 309–310
depth perception, 76–77
DES (diethylstilbestrol), 42
development theories
behavioural theory, 8–9
biopsychosocial framework and, 4
cognitive development theory, 10–12
debates in, 15–17
ecological systems theory, 12–14
ethology, 12
history of, 3–4
overview, 4–5
psychosexual development theory, 5–6
psychosocial development theory, 6–8
research methods for, 17–20
social cognitive theory, 9–10
sociocultural theory, 14–15
developmental psychology, 4
DHEAS (dehydroepiandrosterone sulfate), 295
diethylstilbestrol (DES), 42
dieting, 228
differentiation, 66, 96
difficult temperament, 112–113
dilate, 47
disabilities, children with, 155–158
discontinuity versus continuity, 16
disengagement theory, 307
dishabituation, 85–86
disinhibit, 146
disorganized–disoriented attachment, 100
divergent thinking, 171
diversity, 15, 237–238
divorce, 181–182, 256–257, 279, 313
dizygotic (DZ) twins, 24–25
DNA (deoxyribonucleic acid), 23–24
doctor-assisted suicide, 326
dominant traits, 25–26
dowager's humps, 290
Down syndrome, 26–27
dramatic play, 142
drawings, 120
"dream, the," 243–244
dropouts, 205–206
drugs and drug use, 41–43, 199, 229–231, 296–297
dual-earner families, 256
dualistic thinking, 237
Duchenne muscular dystrophy, 28
Duncker Candle Problem, 301–302
dying. *See also* death
defined, 321
euthanasia, 325–327
places for, 323–325
stages of, 322
support of, 324–325
understanding of, 321–323
dyslexia, 157
dysmenorrhea, 197, 233–234

early adulthood
attraction, 244–246
career development, 238–239
cognitive development, 236–238
cohabitation, 251
death and view of, 330
divorce, 256–257
the dream, 243–244
as emerging adulthood, 225
health and fitness, 226–231
intimacy versus isolation, 241, 243
loneliness, 249
love, 246–248
marriage, 251–254
overview, 225, 241
parenthood, 255–256
physical growth and development, 226
separation and individuation, 242–243
sexuality, 232–236
single life, 249–250
early childhood
cognitive development factors, 129–130
death and view of, 327–329
elimination disorders, 125
emotional development, 146–147
gender roles and sex differences, 148–151
health and illness, 123
language development, 132–135
memory, 131–132
motor development, 118–121
nutrition, 121–122
parenting style and, 137–141
personality development, 146–147
physical growth and development, 117–118
preoperational stage and, 125–129
sleep, 124–125
social behaviour and, 141–146
easy temperament, 112–113
eating disorders, 199–201
echolalia, 89, 107
ecological systems theory, 12–14
ecology, 12
Ecstasy, 230
ectoderm, 36
education, 204–206, 237–238, 271–272
efface, 47
ego, 5
ego integrity or despair, 305–306
egocentrism, 126–127
elaborative rehearsal, 270
elaborative strategies, 162
elder bias, 294–295
elderly people. *See* late adulthood
elimination disorders, 125
embryonic disks, 35
embryonic stage, 36–37
emerging adulthood, 225. *See also* early adulthood
emotional development, 109–111, 146–147, 177–180, 186–190
emotional regulation, 111
empathy, 143, 161
empirical, 17
employment, 207, 280–282
empty nest syndrome, 278
encode, 162
encopresis, 125
endoderm, 36
endometriosis, 33–34
endometrium, 32
enuresis, 125
environment, 30–31, 38–41, 43–44
epiphyseal closure, 195
episiotomies, 48–49
equilibrium, 11
erectile dysfuncion, 266–267
Erikson's theory of psychosocial development
adolescence, 209
early adulthood, 241
early childhood, 137
infancy, 99
late adulthood, 305
middle adulthood, 275–277
middle childhood, 177
overview, 6–8
estrogen, 265–266, 291
ethics
child abuse reporting, 107
code for, 20
monkeys and, 19
reproductive technology and, 44–45
stem cells, 51
ethnic identity, 211
ethnic identity search, 211
ethnicity, 15, 211
ethologists, 103

ethology, 12
euthanasia, 325–327
exercise, 155, 229
exosystems, 13
experimental groups, 19
experiments, 18–19
explicit memories, 298–299
exploration, 210
expressive language style, 90–91
expressive vocabulary, 89
extinction, 9–10, 93
extrajudicial measures, 220

factor theories, 164–165
failure to thrive (FTT), 67
false beliefs, 130
false labour, 47
families, middle childhood and, 180–182
fantasy stage of career development, 238
FAPs (fixed action patterns), 12
FASD (fetal alcohol spectrum disorder), 42–43
fast mapping, 132
fathers, 101, 114–115, 213
fear of strangers, 110
fears, early childhood, 147
feedback loops, 193
fertility, 44
fertility drugs, 33
fertilization, 24
fetal alcohol spectrum disorder (FASD), 42–43
fetal stage, 37–38
Fifty Years of Families in Canada (Statistics Canada), 181
fine motor skills, 120, 155
First Nations, infant deaths, 63
five-factor model of personality, 280
fixation, 5
fixed action patterns (FAPs), 12
fluid intelligence, 236, 269, 298, 301
Flynn Effect, 268
foreclosure, 210–211
formal games, 142
formal operations, 201–202
formula versus breast milk, 68
fraternal twins, 24–25
free-radical theory, 293
Freud's theory of psychosexual development, 5–6
friendships
  adolescence, 214–215
  early childhood, 142
  late adulthood, 315
  love and, 247–248
  middle adulthood, 285
  middle childhood, 183
FTT (failure to thrive), 67
functional play, 142
funerals, 330–331

GAD (generalized anxiety disorder), 188–189, 310–311
Gardner's multiple intelligences, 165–166
gays, 180, 216
gender, 15
gender constancy, 149
gender identity, 149
gender roles, 148–151
gender-schema theory, 149–150
gender stability, 149
gender stereotypes, 203
general anesthesia, 50
general nominals, 90
generalized anxiety disorder (GAD), 188–189, 310–311
generativity, 276–277
genes, 23
genetic abnormalities, 27–28
genetic counselling, 29–30
genetics, 23. *See also* heredity
Genie Project, 96
genital herpes, 234
genital stage, 6
genital warts, 234
genotypes, 30
German measles, 40
germinal (zygotic) stage, 35–36
giftedness, 170
glaucoma, 288–289
global disabilities, 170
glucose, 261
gonorrhea, 234
goodness of fit, 113
grammar, 132–133, 172. *See also* language development
grandparenting, 283–284, 315
grasping reflex, 57
grief, 331–333
gross motor skills, 118–119, 154–155
growth spurts, 153
gynecomastia, 195

habituation, 77, 85–86, 88, 146
handedness, 37, 120–121
Havighurst's developmental tasks, 275–276
HD (Huntington disease), 27
health and illness
  adolescence, 198–201
  early adulthood, 226–231
  early childhood, 123
  late adulthood, 293–298
  longevity and, 287–288
  middle adulthood, 261–264
  minor versus major, 123
  statistics on, 54
  unemployment and, 282
health care directives (living wills), 323, 326–327, 328
hearing, 58, 71, 77–78, 289
heart disease, 263–264
height, 66–67, 117, 194–195
hemophilia, 28
heredity
  environment and, 30–31
  influence on development of, 23–30
  IQ and, 171–172
  weight, 228
heritability, 171
heritage language programs, 174
heroin, 42
heterozygous, 25
HIV/AIDS, 39, 68, 233–234
Holland's Career Inventory, 206–207
Holland's career typology, 206–207
holophrases, 91–92
homogamy, 253
homosexuality
  adolescence, 216–219
  grandparenting and, 284
  late adulthood, 313–314
  same-sex parents and, 180
  sexuality and, 232–233
homozygous, 25
hormonal stress theory, 292–293
hormone replacement therapy (HRT), 266
hormones
  adolescence, 193–194
  DHEAS, 295
  early childhood, 149
  late adulthood, 291
  middle adulthood, 265–266
  ova and, 32
  to prevent miscarriage, 41–42
hospice care, 323–324
hospitals, 323
HRT (hormone replacement therapy), 266
Huntington disease (HD), 27
hyperactivity, 156
hypothesis, 19
hypothetical thinking, 201
hypoxia, 51

id, 5
identical twins, 24–25
identity achievement, 210–211
identity crisis, 8
identity development, 209–213, 215
identity diffusion, 210–211
identity statuses, 209–211
IEPs (Individual Education Plans), 157
illegal activities, adolescence and, 220–221
illnesses, 123. *See also* health and illness
imaginary audiences, 202
imaginary friends, 126
imitation, 85–86, 92–93
imitation reflex, 86
immigrants, 212
immune system, 264
immunological theory, 293
implantation, 35–36
implicit memories, 298–299
imprinting, 103
inclusion in classrooms, 157–158
incubators, 52
independent variables, 19
Individual Education Plans (IEPs), 157
individuation, 242–243
inductive methods, 138
infancy. *See also* newborns
  attachment and, 99–104
  autism spectrum disorders and, 106–108
  brain and nervous system development, 69–72
  child abuse and neglect, 105–106
  day care and, 108–109
  emotional development, 109–111
  mortality rates, 52–53, 63
  motor development, 72–74
  personality development, 111–115
  physical growth and development, 65–68
  sensory development, 74–79
  social deprivation during, 105
  spoiling babies during, 104
infertility, 33–34
Infinity Project, 184
inflammation, 264
information-processing theory, 11–12
initial-preattachment phase, 101
inner speech, 135
insomnia, 290
instruction directives, 323
intelligence, 86–88, 164–172
intelligence quotient (IQ), 165, 170–171
intelligence tests, 18, 165–169
interindividual variability, 259, 268
internalization, 5
International Day of Silence, 217
Internet, 215, 250, 308
intimacy, 247
intimacy versus isolation, 241, 243
intonation, 89
intrinsic rewards, 238
Inuit children, 79
invention of new means through mental combinations, 83
in vitro fertilization, 34
in-voluntary euthanasia, 325
irreversibility, 128
isotretinoin, 41

jealousy, 248
job satisfaction, 281

kangaroo care, 52
kinship studies, 30–31
Kohlberg's theory of moral development, 159–161, 204–205

Labouvie-Vief's theory of pragmatic thought, 237
Lamaze method, 50
language development
  autism and, 107
  bilingualism, 173–174
  cognitive development and, 134–135
  early childhood, 132–135
  heritage language programs, 174
  late adulthood, 301
  middle childhood, 172–174

process of, 89–96
referential and expressive styles in, 90–91
screen time and, 87
speech sound perception and, 77–78
languages, 94–96
lanugo, 51
late adulthood
aging theories, 292–293
cognitive development, 298–302
health concerns, 293–298
physical development, 287–292
psychological development, 308–311
retirement, 239, 315–317
social and emotional development theories, 305–308
social aspects, 311–315
successful aging, 317–318
latency stage, 6
leading questions, 164
learned helplessness, 180
learning disabilities, 156–158
leisure activities, 316–317
lesbians, 180, 216, 284
leukocytes, 263
Levinson's seasons, 277
LGBTQ, 216. *See also* homosexuality
life crisis, 7
life-events approach to middle adulthood, 278–279
life expectancy, 287–288
life reviews, 306
life span, 287–288
literacy, 172–174
living wills, 323, 326–327, 328
local anesthesia, 50
locomotion, 73–74
loneliness, 249
longevity, 287–288
longitudinal research, 19–20
long-term care facilities, 311–312
long-term memory, 162–163, 299–300
love, 246–248
low-birth weight infants, 51–53
LSD, 230

macrosystems, 13
maintenance stage of career development, 239
malignant tumours, 262
marijuana, 42, 230
marriage, 251–254, 283, 312–313
masturbation, 217
mathematical ability in adolescence, 203
maturation, 5
mean length of utterance (MLU), 92
media, 130, 145
medication
abuse of, 296–297
adolescence, 199
for autism, 108
for depression, 188
for school phobia, 189
medulla, 70
meiosis, 23–24
memory
early childhood, 131–132
of infants, 85–86, 88
information-processing theory and, 11–12
late adulthood, 298–301
middle adulthood, 270
middle childhood, 162–164
visual recognition memory, 88
menarche, 196–197
menopause, 265–266
menstruation
amenorrhea, 234
dysmenorrhea, 197, 233–234
menarche, 196–197
menopause, 265–266
PMS, 234–235
mental age (MA), 166
mental combinations, 83
mental illness, 18
mental repetition, 132
mercy killing, 325–327
mesoderm, 36
mesosystems, 13
metabolism, 260
metacognition, 164
metamemory, 164
metastases, 262
methadone, 42
methamphetamines, 230
microsystems, 13
middle adulthood
cognitive development, 267–271
creativity, 271
death and view of, 330
employment and, 280–282
health and illness, 261–264
immune system, 264
learning abilities, 271–272
overview, 259, 275–276
physical development, 259–261
relationships during, 282–285
sexuality, 264–267
stability and change in, 279–280
theories of development in, 276–279
middle childhood
cognitive development, 158–159
death and view of, 329
emotional development theories, 177–180
families and, 180–182
growth and, 153–154
information processing and memory, 162–164
intellectual development, 164–172
language development, 172–174
moral development, 159–161
motor development, 154–155
peer relationships, 182–183
school and, 183–186
social and emotional problems during, 186–190
social development theories, 177–180
midlife crises, 277–278
midlife transitions, 277
midwives, 49–50
Minnesota Study of Twins Reared Apart, 31
mirror neurons, 86
mirror technique, 111–112
miscarriage, 36, 41–42
mitosis, 23–24
MLU (mean length of utterance), 92
models, 10, 92
monogamous marriages, 252–253
monogamy, 251
monozygotic (MZ) twins, 24–25
moral development, 159–161, 204–205
moratorium, 210–211
Moro reflex, 56–57
mortality. *See* death
Motherese, 95
mothers, 101, 182, 213
motility, 33
motor development, 72–74, 118–121, 154–155. *See also* physical growth and development
mourning, 331–333
multidirectionality, 268
multifactorial problems, 25
multiple births, 31
multiple intelligences, 165–166
multiple sclerosis, 69
muscular dystrophy, 28
mutations, 24
mutism, 107
myelin sheath, 69
myelination, 69, 71, 117–118

National Longitudinal Survey of Children and Youth (NLSCY), 20
natural childbirth, 50
naturalistic observations, 17
nature/nurture debate
autism and, 107
brain development and, 71–72
cognitive development and, 85
language development and, 92–96
motor development and, 73–74
overview, 16
perceptual development and, 79
negative correlations, 18
negative reinforcers, 9–10
neglect, 105–106
nerves, 69
neural tubes, 36
neurons, 12, 69–70, 86
neurotransmitters, 69
newborns. *See also* infancy
crying by, 61–62
health assessments of, 56
learning by, 59–60
preterm infants, 51
reflexes, 56–57
sensory capabilities of, 57–59
shaken baby syndrome, 63
sleeping and waking states, 60–62
sudden infant death syndrome, 62–63
nicotine, 43
nightmares, 124
NLSCY (National Longitudinal Survey of Children and Youth), 20
nocturnal emissions, 195
nominals, 90
nonorganic FTT, 67
non-voluntary euthanasia, 325
nursing homes, 311–312
nutrition
adolescence, 198–199
early childhood, 121–122
fetal development and, 39
infancy and, 67–68
middle childhood, 153–154

obesity, 121–122, 153–154, 227–228
object permanence, 84–85, 101–102
observational learning, 10
online dating, 250
online friendships, 215
operant conditioning, 8–9, 60
oral stage, 5
organ donation, 327
organic FTT, 67
origins of knowledge, 130–131
osteoarthritis, 295–296
osteoporosis, 200, 289–290
ova, 24, 32
overextensions, 91
overregularization, 133
ovulation, 25
oxygen deprivation, 51
oxytocin, 47

palliative care, 324
palmar grasp, 72
palmar reflex, 57
panic disorders, 231
parental leave, 55
parenthood, 255–256
parents. *See also* age of parents; fathers; mothers
activity levels of, 119
adolescence and cognitive abilities, 213–214
aggression and, 144
early childhood and, 137–141
middle adulthood and, 282–283
preterm newborns and, 52
same-sex parents, 180
self-esteem and, 212–213
sexuality of adolescents and, 217–218
social development and involvement of, 101
taking care of, 284–285
working mothers, 182
passion, 247
PCBs (polychlorinated biphenyls), 43–44
Peck's developmental tasks, 305–306
peers, 182–183, 214–215, 218. *See also* friendships

pelvic inflammatory disease (PID), 33
perceptual development, 74–79
perimenopause, 265–266
"period of purple crying", 62
periods (menarche). *See* menstruation
peripheral vision, 75
permissive–indulgent style, 139–140
personal fables, 202
personality development,
  111–115, 146–147, 279–280
perspective-taking skills, 143–144, 178
PGD (preimplantation genetic diagnosis),
  35
phallic stage, 6
phenotypes, 30
phenylalanine, 27
phenylketonuria (PKU), 27, 69
pheromones, 245
phobias, 188–190
phobic disorder, 310
phonetic method, 173
phonological processing, 157
physical growth and development
  adolescence, 193
  early adulthood, 226
  early childhood, 117–121
  infancy, 65–72
  late adulthood, 287–292
  middle adulthood, 259–261
  middle childhood, 153–154
Piaget's theory of cognitive
  development
  concrete-operational stage,
    158–159, 177–178
  formal operations, 201–202
  overview, 10–11
  preoperational stage, 125–129
  sensorimotor stage, 81–85
PID (pelvic inflammatory
  disease), 33
pincer grasp, 72–73
Pink Shirt Day, 184
pitch, 58
PKU (phenylketonuria), 27, 69
placentas, 37
plaque, 264
plasticity of the brain, 118, 268
play, 125–126, 142–143
PMDD (premenstrual dysphoric
  disorder), 234
PMS (premenstrual syndrome),
  234–235
polyamory, 253
polychlorinated biphenyls (PCBs),
  43–44
polygenic, 23
portion sizes, 121–122
positive correlations, 18
positive reinforcers, 9
postconventional stage,
  160–161, 204–205
postformal thinking, 237
postpartum depression (PPD), 54–55
postpartum period, 53–55
PP (precocious puberty), 198
PPD (postpartum depression), 54–55
practical intelligence, 165
pragmatic thought theory, 237
pragmatics, 133–134
precausal, 127
precocious puberty (PP), 198
preconventional stage, 160–161
pregnancy, 218. *See also*
  prenatal development
preimplantation genetic diagnosis
  (PGD), 35
prelinguistic vocalizations, 89
premature birth, 40, 51–53
premenstrual dysphoric
  disorder (PMDD), 234
premenstrual syndrome (PMS),
  234–235
prenatal development
  brain development, 70
  embryonic stage, 36–37
  environmental influences on,
    38–41, 43–44
  fetal stage, 37–38
  germinal (zygotic) stage, 35–36
  overview, 35
prenatal testing, 29–30
preoperational stage, 125–129
presbycusis, 289
presbyopia, 260
preschoolers. *See* early childhood
prescription medication. *See*
  medication
pretend play, 126
preterm infants, 51
prewiring, 94
primary circular reactions, 82
primary sex characteristics, 194
procedural memory, 270
programmed theories of aging, 292–293
prosocial behaviour, 143–144
prospective memory, 300–301
prostaglandins, 47, 234
proximodistal development, 36, 66
proxy directives, 323
psychoanalytic perspective, 5–8
psychologically androgynous
  people, 150
psychosocial development theory, 6–8.
  See also Erikson's theory of
  psychosocial development
psychotherapy, 188
puberty, 193–198
pubic lice, 234
punishments, 9–10
PURPLE crying, 62
Pygmalion effect, 185

questions, 133
quieting of egos, 306

radiation, 44
random assignment, 19
rapid-eye movement (REM) sleep,
  60–61
reaction ranges, 30, 74
reaction time, 260, 270
reading skills, 172–173
realistic choice stage of career
  development, 239
recall, 163
receptive vocabulary, 89
recessive traits, 25–26
reciprocity, 246
reduction division, 24
referential language style, 90–91
reflexes, 56–57, 81, 86
regression, 141
rehearsal, 132, 162
reinforcement, 8–10, 93–94
rejecting–neglecting style, 139–140
relativistic thinking, 237
religion, 311–312
reminiscence, 306
research methods, 17–20
Resource Guide to Coming Out, A
  (Human Rights Campaign
  Foundation), 217
respiratory distress syndrome, 52
restorative justice, 221
retirement stage of career development, 239, 315–317
Rett disorder, 106
Rh incompatibility, 41
rheumatoid arthritis, 296
*Rising Tide: The Impact of Dementia
  on Canadian Society* (Alzheimer
  Society), 297–298
romantic love, 246–248
rooting reflex, 56–57
Roots of Empathy, 161
rote rehearsal, 270
rough-and-tumble play, 119
rubella, 40

SAD (separation anxiety
  disorder), 188–189
same-sex marriages, 253
same-sex parents, 180
sandwich generation, 285
SBS (shaken baby syndrome), 63
scaffolding, 14, 129
schemes, 11, 81
school and education
  adolescence, 204–206
  dropping out, 205–206
  early adulthood, 237–238
  middle adulthood, 271–272
  middle childhood, 183–186
school phobia, 189–190
school refusal, 189–190
screen time, 130
scribbles, 120
scripts, 131
Second Careers, 281
secondary circular reactions, 82
secondary sex characteristics, 194
second-hand smoke, 123
"Secret of the Wild Child," 96
secular trend, 195
secure attachment, 100, 140
selective attention, 162
selective optimization with compensation, 317–318
self-concept
  adolescence, 212
  early childhood, 147
  infancy, 111–112
  middle childhood, 178–180
  social media and, 215
self-esteem, 147, 179, 212–213,
  308–309
self-fulfilling prophecies, 185
semen, 195
seniors' residences, 311
senses, 59, 71, 226. *See also* hearing;
  smell; taste; vision
sensitive periods of development,
  39–40, 96
sensorimotor stage, 81–85
sensory development, infancy and,
  74–79
sensory memory, 162
sensory register, 162
sensory stimulation, 52–53, 71–72
sentence development, 91–92
separation anxiety, 99
separation anxiety disorder (SAD),
  188–189
separation–individuation
  process, 112, 242–243
serial monogamy, 250
seriation, 158–159
serotonin, 188
serving sizes, 121–122
Sesame Street, 130
sex chromosomes, 24
sex determinations, 24
sex differentiation, 36–37
sex hormones, 149
sex selection, 35
sexes, differences between
  adolescence and cognitive abilities,
    202–203
  attractiveness and, 245
  body esteem, 309
  conception and, 32
  early childhood, 148–151
  life expectancy, 288
  middle adulthood and, 283–284
  middle childhood and, 153, 155
  moral development and, 205
  play and, 142–143
  separation from parents, 243–244
  sexuality attitudes and, 218
  social behaviour and, 113–115
  weight, 228
sexism, 186
sex-linked chromosomal
  abnormalities, 26–27
sex-linked genetic
  abnormalities, 28
sexual assault, 235
sexual dysfunction, 266–267
sexual harassment, 236
sexuality. *See also* homosexuality
  adolescence, 217–218
  early adulthood, 232–236
  late adulthood, 290–292
  middle adulthood, 264–267

Sexuality & U website, 219
sexually transmitted infections (STIs). *See also* HIV/AIDS
early adulthood, 233–234
fetal development and, 39
late adulthood, 291
middle adulthood, 265
statistics on, 219
shaken baby syndrome (SBS), 63
shaping, 93
siblings, 141, 285, 314–315
sickle-cell anemia, 27–28
SIDS (sudden infant death syndrome), 62–63
sight vocabulary, 173
silver tsunami, 293
simple reflex stage, 81
single people, 249–250
sleep, 60–61, 66, 124–125, 290
sleep apnea, 290
sleep terrors, 124
sleepwalking, 124–125
"slow to warm up" temperament, 112–113
small for dates, 51
smell, 58, 289
smoking, 43, 123, 230
social and emotional problems, 186–190
social clocks, 277
social cognition, 178
social cognitive theory, 9–10, 177
social deprivation, 104
social development
attachment and, 99–104
day care and, 108–109
early childhood, 141–146
failure of attachment, 104–108
middle childhood, 177–180
social media, 215, 250
social referencing, 110–111
social smiles, 103
sociocultural theory, 14–15
socioemotional selectivity theory, 307–308
somnambulism, 124–125
soothing, 62
specific nominals, 90
spectrum, 106
speech. *See* language development
sperm, 24, 32–33
spontaneous abortions, 32
sports, 155, 179
stage theory, 5–6
stagnation, 277
stalking, 235
standardized tests, 17
standing, 73
Stanford–Binet Intelligence Scale (SBIS), 165–167
startle reflex, 56–57
stem cells, 51
stepping reflex, 57
Sternberg's theory of intelligence, 165
Sternberg's triangular theory of love, 247–248
stillbirth, 39
stimulants, 156, 230
STIs. *See* sexually transmitted infections (STIs)
stranger anxiety, 110
strange-situation method, 100
stress
early adulthood, 230–231, 249, 255, 257
middle adulthood, 264, 278–279
substance abuse, 229. *See also* drugs and drug use
substance dependence, 229
successful aging, 317–318
sucking, 62
sucking reflex, 56
sudden infant death syndrome (SIDS), 62–63
suicide, 221–222, 310, 332
Super Baby Syndrome, 72
superego, 5
surveys, 17
swaddling, 59
symbolic play, 126, 142
symbolism, 125
symbols, 201–202
symmetry, 245
syntax, 92
syphilis, 39, 234

tabula rasa, 3
taste, 58–59, 289
Tay-Sachs disease, 28
teachers, 185–186
teenagers. *See* adolescence
telegraphic speech, 91
television, 130
telomeres, 292
temperament, 112–113
tentative choice stage of career development, 238–239
teratogens, 39
terminal sedation, 325
tertiary circular reactions, 83
testosterone, 266
thalidomide, 41
"the dream," 243–244
theory of mind, 130–131
theory of pragmatic thought, 237
3-D ultrasound, 30
three-mountains test, 126–127
toddlers, 73. *See also* early childhood
toilet training, 6, 125
tolerance, 229
tonic-neck reflex, 57
touch, newborns and, 59
toxemia, 40–41
toxoplasmosis, 44
traits. *See* heredity
transductive reasoning, 127
transgendered, 216
transition, 48
transivity, 158–159
transsexuals, 180, 216
triangular theory of love, 247–248
triarchic theory of intelligence, 165–166
twin studies, 31
twins, 24–25

ultrasound, 30
umbilical cords, 37, 49
unemployment, 281–282
unexamined ethnic identity, 211
universal design, 158
uterus, 30

variables, 19
vasomotor instability, 265
verbal ability in adolescence, 202–203
vernix, 51
violence, 144–146, 235–236
vision, 57–58, 71, 75–77, 288–289
visual accommodation, 58
visual acuity, 75
visual cliffs, 76–77
visual habituation–dishabituation model, 85–86
visual preferences, 75–76
visual recognition memory, 88
visual–spatial ability in adolescence, 203
vitamins, 42
vocabulary, 89–91, 132, 172. *See also* language development
vocalizations, 89
voluntary euthanasia, 325
volunteering, 308
Vygotsky's sociocultural theory, 14–15

waist-to-hip ratio, 245
walking, 73
Watson's behavioural theory, 8–9
wear-and-tear theory, 293
Wechsler scales, 167–168
weight
adolescence, 194–195
early adulthood, 227–228
early childhood, 117, 121–122
infancy, 66–67
middle childhood, 153–154
wet dreams, 195
white blood cells, 264
widowhood, 314
wisdom, 302
word-recognition method, 173
work, 207, 280–282
working memory (short-term), 162

X-rays, 44

youths in conflict with the law, 220–221

zone of proximal development (ZPD), 14, 129
zygotes, 23
zygotic stage, 35–36

Chapter in Review

LO1 developmental psychology
the biological, psychological, and sociocultural study of human change across the lifespan. (p. 4)

LO2 behaviourism
Watson's view that science must study observable behaviour only and investigate relationships between stimuli and responses. (p. 4)

maturation
the unfolding of genetically determined traits, structures, and functions. (p. 5)

psychosexual development
the process by which libidinal energy is expressed through different erogenous zones during different stages of development. (p. 5)

stage theory
a theory of development characterized by distinct periods of life. (p. 5)

psychosocial development
Erikson's theory, which emphasizes the importance of social relationships and conscious choice throughout eight stages of development. (p. 6)

life crisis
an internal conflict that attends each stage of psychosocial development. (p. 7)

identity crisis
according to Erikson, a period of inner conflict during which individuals examine their values and make decisions about their life roles. (p. 8)

classical conditioning
a simple form of learning in which one stimulus comes to bring forth the response usually brought forth by a second stimulus as a result of being paired repeatedly with the second stimulus. (p. 8)

operant conditioning
a simple form of learning in which an organism learns to engage in behaviour that is reinforced. (p. 8)

reinforcement
the process of providing stimuli following responses in an effort to increase the frequency of the responses. (p. 8)

positive reinforcer
a reinforcer that, when applied, increases the frequency of a response. (p. 9)

negative reinforcer
a reinforcer that, when removed, increases the frequency of a response. (p. 9)

extinction
the cessation of a response that is performed in the absence of reinforcement. (p. 9)

punishments
aversive events that suppress or decrease the frequency of the behaviour they follow. (p. 9)

LO1 Relate the history of the study of human development.

In centuries past, children often were viewed as innately evil, and discipline was harsh. The philosopher John Locke focused on the role of experience in development. Jean-Jacques Rousseau argued that children are good by nature, and if allowed to express their natural impulses, will develop into moral people. G. Stanley Hall founded child development as an academic discipline. Alfred Binet developed the first standardized intelligence test. All these theories are integrated to form a definition of developmental psychology, which is the biological, psychological, and sociocultural study of development across the lifespan. It is this approach to lifespan development that provides the organization for your textbook.

LO2 Compare and contrast theories of human development.

Psychoanalytic theory focuses on the roles of internal conflict. Sigmund Freud believed that children undergo five stages of psychosexual development. Erik Erikson focused on social relationships and included adulthood by extending Freud's five developmental stages to eight.

Erikson's Stages

0–18 months	Trust vs. Mistrust
19 months–3 years	Autonomy vs. Shame and Doubt
4–5 years	Initiative vs. Guilt
6–11 years	Industry vs. Inferiority
Adolescence (12–18 years)	Identity vs. Role Confusion
Young Adulthood (19–39 years)	Intimacy vs. Isolation
Middle Adulthood (40–64 years)	Generativity vs. Stagnation
Later Life (65 years to death)	Ego Integrity vs. Despair

Learning theorists focus on how learning influences behaviour. John B. Watson and B. F. Skinner stress classical and operant conditioning. Social cognitive theorists, such as Albert Bandura, argue that much learning occurs by observation and that we choose whether we engage in learned behaviour.

Jean Piaget's cognitive developmental theory hypothesizes that children's cognitive processes develop in an invariant series of stages, culminating with *formal operational* reasoning. Information-processing theory deals with how we encode information, manipulate it, place it in memory, and retrieve it.

The biological perspective refers to genetics and developments such as conception, puberty, and peak performance and decline in adulthood. Ethology involves instinctive behaviour patterns.

Urie Bronfenbrenner's ecological theory explains development in terms of the *reciprocal interaction* between children and the settings where development occurs. Lev Semenovich Vygotsky's sociocultural perspective includes the key concepts of the *zone of proximal development (ZPD)* and *scaffolding*. The sociocultural perspective broadly addresses the richness of diversity by noting the influences of ethnicity and gender on development. This perspective is of particular importance to Canadians, given the more than 200 cultures within our borders.

LO3 Enumerate key controversies in human development.

Theories of human growth and development have led to three major debates:

Nature and Nurture	What aspects of behaviour are determined by our genetic programming (nature)? What aspects of behaviour can be traced to nutrition, cultural and family backgrounds, and learning opportunities (nurture)?

social cognitive theory
a cognitively oriented learning theory that emphasizes observational learning. (p. 9)

cognitive-developmental theory
the stage theory that suggests children's abilities to mentally represent the world and solve problems are a result of the interaction of experience and the maturation of neurological structures. (p. 10)

scheme
an action pattern or mental structure involved in the acquisition and organization of knowledge. (p. 11)

adaptation
the interaction between the organism and the environment, consisting of assimilation and accommodation. (p. 11)

assimilation
the incorporation of new events or knowledge into existing schemes. (p. 11)

accommodation
the modification of existing schemes to permit the incorporation of new events or knowledge. (p. 11)

equilibration
the creation of an equilibrium, or balance, between assimilation and accommodation. (p. 11)

ethology
the study of behaviours that are specific to a species. (p. 12)

fixed action pattern (FAP)
a stereotyped pattern of behaviour that is evoked by a "releasing stimulus"; an instinct. (p. 12)

ecology
the branch of biology that studies the relationships between living organisms and their environment. (p. 12)

ecological systems theory
the view that explains child development in terms of the reciprocal influences between children and their environmental settings. (p. 12)

microsystem
the immediate settings with which the child interacts, such as the home, the school, and peers. (p. 13)

mesosystem
the interlocking settings that influence the child, such as the interaction of the school and the larger community. (p. 13)

exosystem
community institutions and settings that indirectly influence the child, such as the school board and the parents' workplaces. (p. 13)

macrosystem
the basic institutions and ideologies that influence the child. (p. 13)

chronosystem
the environmental changes that occur over time and have an effect on the child. (p. 13)

zone of proximal development (ZPD)
Vygotsky's term for the range of tasks a child can carry out with the help of someone who is more skilled. (p. 14)

Continuity and Discontinuity	Maturational, psychoanalytic, and cognitive-developmental theorists see development as discontinuous (occurring in stages), whereas learning theorists see development as a continuous process.
Active and Passive Roles	Some educators, such as John Locke, view children as passive, requiring external motivation to learn. Other educators, many of them more modern, view children as active, having a natural love of learning.

LO4 Describe ways in which researchers study human development.

Development is studied by first gathering sound information and conducting research. Naturalistic observation is conducted in "the field"—the settings in which people develop. The case study is a carefully drawn account or biography of behaviour. Correlational studies reveal relationships between variables but not cause and effect, as demonstrated in Figure 1.5. Experiments seek to determine cause and effect by exposing subjects to treatments and observing the results.

Researchers have devised different strategies for comparing children of one age with children or adults of other ages. Longitudinal research, such as Canada's National Longitudinal Survey of Children and Youth (NLSCY), studies the same people repeatedly over time. Cross-sectional research observes and compares people of different ages. A drawback to cross-sectional research is the cohort effect. Ethical standards outlined by the Canadian Psychiatric Association require that researchers not use treatments that harm participants.

Please visit the CourseMate at www.nelson.com/4ltrpress/icanhdev2ce to view the Emerging Canada boxes that supplement this chapter.

scaffolding
Vygotsky's term for temporary cognitive structures or methods of solving problems that help children as they learn to function independently. (p. 14)

LO3

nature
the processes within an organism that guide it to develop according to its genetic code. (p. 16)

nurture
environmental factors that influence development. (p. 16)

LO4

empirical
based on observation and experimentation. (p. 17)

case study
a carefully written account of the behaviour of an individual. (p. 17)

standardized test
a test that compares an individual's score with the scores of a group of similar individuals. (p. 17)

correlation coefficient
a number ranging from +1.00 to −1.00 that expresses the direction (positive or negative) and strength of the relationship between two variables. (p. 17)

positive correlation
a relationship between two variables in which one variable increases as the other increases. (p. 17)

negative correlation
a relationship between two variables in which one variable increases as the other decreases. (p. 17)

experiment
a method of scientific investigation that seeks to discover cause-and-effect relationships by introducing independent variables and observing their effects on dependent variables. (p. 19)

hypothesis
a proposition to be tested. (p. 19)

independent variable
a condition in a scientific study that is manipulated so that its effects can be observed. (p. 19)

dependent variable
a measure of an assumed effect of an independent variable. (p. 19)

experimental group
a group of subjects who receive a treatment in an experiment. (p. 19)

control group
a group of subjects in an experiment who do not receive the treatment but for whom all other conditions are comparable with those of the experimental group. (p. 19)

longitudinal research
the study of developmental processes by taking repeated measures of the same group of participants at various stages of development. (p. 19)

cross-sectional research
the study of developmental processes by taking measures of participants of different age groups at the same time. (p. 20)

cohort effect
similarities in behaviour among a group of peers as a result of being of approximately the same age. (p. 20)

HEREDITY AND PRENATAL DEVELOPMENT

2 Chapter in Review

LO1 **genetics** the branch of biology that studies heredity. (p. 23)

chromosomes
rod-shaped structures that are composed of genes and are found within the nuclei of cells. (p. 23)

genes
the basic units of heredity. Genes are composed of deoxyribonucleic acid (DNA). (p. 23)

polygenic
resulting from many (poly) genes. (p. 23)

deoxyribonucleic acid (DNA)
genetic material that takes the form of a double helix and is composed of phosphates, sugars, and bases. (p. 23)

mitosis
the form of cell division in which each chromosome splits lengthwise to double in number. Half of each chromosome combines with chemicals to retake its original form and then moves to the new cell. (p. 23)

mutation
a sudden, or accidental, variation in a heritable characteristic that affects the composition of genes. (p. 24)

meiosis
the form of cell division in which each pair of chromosomes splits so that one member of each pair moves to the new cell. As a result, each new cell has 23 chromosomes. (p. 24)

autosome
a pair of chromosomes (with the exception of sex chromosomes). (p. 24)

sex chromosome
a chromosome in the shape of a Y (male) or X (female) that determines the sex of the child. (p. 24)

monozygotic (MZ) twins
twins that derive from a single zygote that has split into two; identical twins. Each MZ twin carries the same genetic code. (p. 24)

dizygotic (DZ) twins
twins that derive from two separate zygotes; fraternal twins with separate genetic codes. (p. 24)

ovulation
the releasing of an ovum from an ovary. (p. 25)

allele
a member of a pair of genes. (p. 25)

homozygous
having two identical alleles. (p. 25)

heterozygous
having two different alleles. (p. 25)

dominant trait
a trait that is expressed. (p. 25)

recessive trait
a trait that is not expressed when the gene or genes involved have been paired with dominant genes. (p. 25)

LO1 Describe the influences of heredity on development.

Heredity is the biological transmission of traits from one generation to another. People normally have 46 strands of deoxyribonucleic acid (DNA) called chromosomes, which are organized into 23 pairs (see Figure 2.2). Genes, which regulate the development of traits, are segments of chromosomes.

FIGURE 2.2

The 23 Pairs of Human Chromosomes

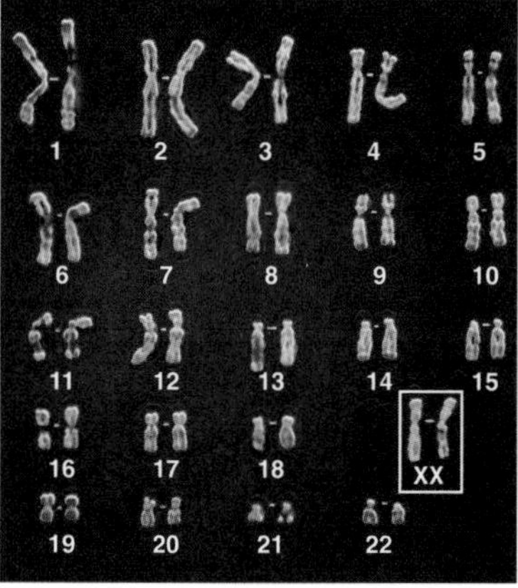

Female

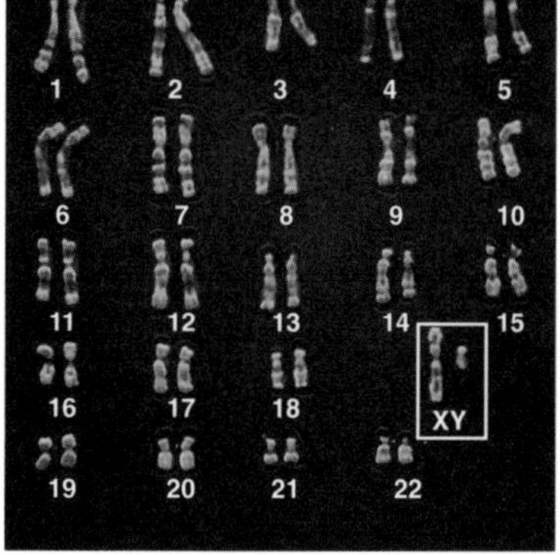

Male

Sperm and ova are produced by meiosis and have 23 rather than 46 chromosomes. Monozygotic (MZ), or identical, twins develop from a single fertilized ovum that splits in two. Dizygotic (DZ), or fraternal, twins develop from two fertilized ova. Traits are determined by pairs of genes, either from "averaging" the genetic instructions, or by dominant genes. Carriers of a trait bear one dominant gene and one recessive gene for it.

Chromosomal abnormalities in offspring are more likely as parents age. Down syndrome is caused by an extra chromosome on the 21st pair. People with sex-linked disorders experience many differences, some of them associated with "maleness" or "femaleness." Genetic disorders include phenylketonuria (PKU), Huntington's disease, sickle-cell anemia, Tay-Sachs disease, cystic fibrosis, and hemophilia. Prenatal blood tests, ultrasound, and amniocentesis can determine the presence of various genetic and chromosomal abnormalities.

LO2 Describe the influences of the environment on development.

Our genotypes are the sets of traits that we inherit. But environmental conditions can vary their expression, resulting in our phenotypes. Researchers can study the heritability of a trait by observing its expression among relatives who differ in genetic closeness. Parents and children have a 50 percent overlap in genes, as do siblings, with the exception of monozygotic (MZ) twins, who have 100 percent overlap. MZ twins resemble each other more closely than dizygotic (DZ) twins on physical and psychological traits, even when reared apart. Traits are likely to have a strong genetic basis if adopted children are closer to their natural parents than to their adoptive parents in their expression.

LO3 Explain what happens in the process of conception.

Conception is the union of an ovum and a sperm cell and usually occurs in a fallopian tube (see Figure 2.7). More boys are conceived than girls, but they have a higher rate of miscarriage. Once a sperm cell has entered an ovum, the chromosomes from the sperm cell line up across from the corresponding chromosomes in the egg cell. They form 23 new pairs with a unique set of genetic instructions.

FIGURE 2.7

Female Reproductive Organs

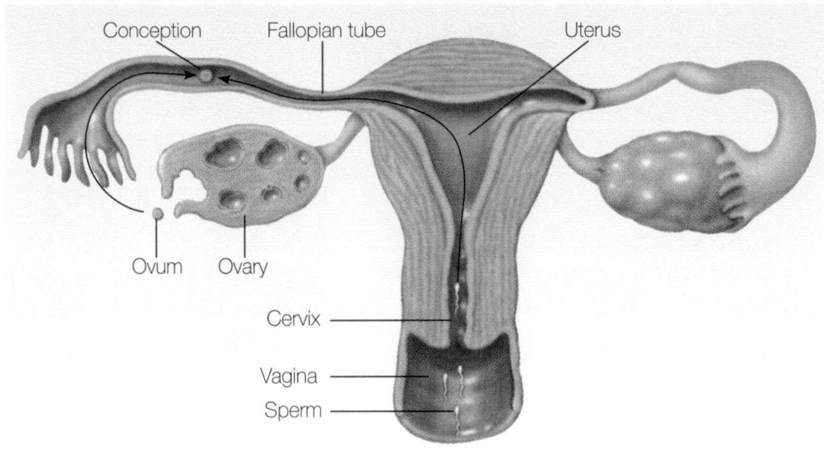

carrier
a person who carries and transmits characteristics but does not exhibit them. (p. 25)

multifactorial problems
problems that stem from the interaction of heredity and environmental factors. (p. 25)

Down syndrome
a chromosomal abnormality characterized by intellectual challenges and caused by an extra chromosome in the 21st pair. (p. 26)

sex-linked chromosomal abnormalities
abnormalities that are transmitted from generation to generation and are carried by a sex chromosome. (p. 26)

phenylketonuria (PKU)
a genetic abnormality in which phenylalanine builds up and causes intellectual challenges. (p. 27)

Huntington disease (HD)
a fatal genetic neurologic disorder whose onset takes place is in middle age. It is a dominant trait, which is rare for a fatal genetic disorder. (p. 27)

sickle-cell anemia
a genetic disorder that decreases the blood's capacity to carry oxygen. (p. 27)

Tay-Sachs disease
a fatal genetic neurological disorder that causes degeneration and premature death. (p. 28)

cystic fibrosis
a fatal genetic disorder in which mucus obstructs the lungs and pancreas. (p. 28)

hemophilia
a genetic disorder in which blood does not clot properly. (p. 28)

sex-linked genetic abnormalities
abnormalities resulting from genes that are found on the X sex chromosome. They are more likely to be shown by male offspring (who do not have an opposing gene from a second X chromosome) than by female offspring. (p. 28)

muscular dystrophy
a chronic disease characterized by a progressive wasting away of the muscles. (p. 28)

prenatal
before birth. (p. 29)

amniocentesis
a procedure for drawing and examining fetal cells sloughed off into amniotic fluid to determine the presence of various disorders. (p. 29)

chorionic villus sampling (CVS)
a method for the prenatal detection of genetic abnormalities that samples the membrane enveloping the amniotic sac and fetus. (p. 30)

uterus
the hollow organ within females in which the embryo and fetus develop. (p. 30)

ultrasound
sound waves too high in pitch to be sensed by the human ear. (p. 30)

alpha-fetoprotein (AFP) assay
a blood test that assesses the mother's blood level of alpha-fetoprotein, a substance that is linked to fetal neural tube defects. (p. 30)

LO2

reaction range
the interaction between nature (genetic potential) and nurture (the set of circumstances that we encounter in life). (p. 30)

genotype
the genetic form or constitution of a person as determined by heredity. (p. 30)

phenotype
the actual form or constitution of a person as determined by heredity and environmental factors. (p. 30)

LO3

conception
the union of a sperm cell and an ovum that occurs when the chromosomes of each of these cells combine to form 23 new pairs. (p. 31)

endometrium
the inner lining of the uterus. (p. 32)

spontaneous abortion
unplanned miscarriage of the developing organism. (p. 32)

motility
self-propulsion. (p. 33)

pelvic inflammatory disease (PID)
an infection of the abdominal region that may have various causes and may impair fertility. (p. 33)

endometriosis
inflammation of endometrial tissue sloughed off into the abdominal cavity rather than out of the body during menstruation; the condition is characterized by abdominal pain and sometimes infertility. (p. 33)

artificial insemination
injection of sperm into the uterus to fertilize an ovum. (p. 34)

in vitro fertilization (IVF)
fertilization of an ovum in a laboratory dish. (p. 34)

donor IVF
the transfer of a donor's ovum, fertilized in a laboratory dish, to the uterus of another woman. (p. 34)

LO4

germinal (zygotic) stage
the period of development between conception and the implantation of the embryo. (p. 35)

blastocyst
a stage within the germinal period of prenatal development in which the zygote has the form of a sphere of cells surrounding a cavity of fluid. (p. 35)

embryonic disk
the platelike inner part of the blastocyst that differentiates into the ectoderm, mesoderm, and endoderm of the embryo. (p. 35)

embryonic stage
the stage of prenatal development that lasts from implantation through the eighth week of pregnancy; it is characterized by the development of the major organ systems. (p. 36)

cephalocaudal
from head to tail. (p. 36)

proximodistal
from the inner part (or axis) of the body outward. (p. 36)

ectoderm
the outermost cell layer of the newly formed embryo from which the skin and nervous system develop. (p. 36)

neural tube
a hollowed-out area in the blastocyst from which the nervous system develops. (p. 36)

endoderm
the inner layer of the embryo from which the lungs and digestive system develop. (p. 36)

mesoderm
the central layer of the embryo from which the bones and muscles develop. (p. 36)

androgens
male sex hormones. (p. 37)

amniotic sac
the sac containing the fetus. (p. 37)

amniotic fluid
fluid within the amniotic sac that suspends and protects the fetus. (p. 37)

fetal stage
the stage of development that lasts from the beginning of the ninth week of pregnancy through birth; it is characterized by gains in size and weight and by maturation of the organ systems. (p. 37)

stillbirth
the birth of a dead fetus. (p. 39)

teratogens
environmental influences or agents that can damage the embryo or fetus. (p. 39)

critical periods
in this usage, periods during which an embryo is particularly vulnerable to a certain teratogen. (p. 39)

syphilis
a sexually transmitted infection that, in advanced stages, can attack major organ systems. (p. 39)

congenital
present at birth; resulting from the prenatal environment. (p. 39)

HIV/AIDS
HIV stands for human immunodeficiency virus, which cripples the body's immune system. AIDS stands for acquired immunodeficiency syndrome, a condition in which the immune system is weakened such that it is vulnerable to diseases it would otherwise be able to fight off. (p. 39)

rubella
a viral infection that can cause retardation and heart disease in the embryo. Also called German measles. (p. 40)

toxemia
a life-threatening disease that can afflict pregnant women; characterized by high blood pressure. (p. 40)

premature
born before the full term of gestation. Also referred to as preterm. (p. 40)

FIGURE 2.10

A Human Embryo at 7 Weeks

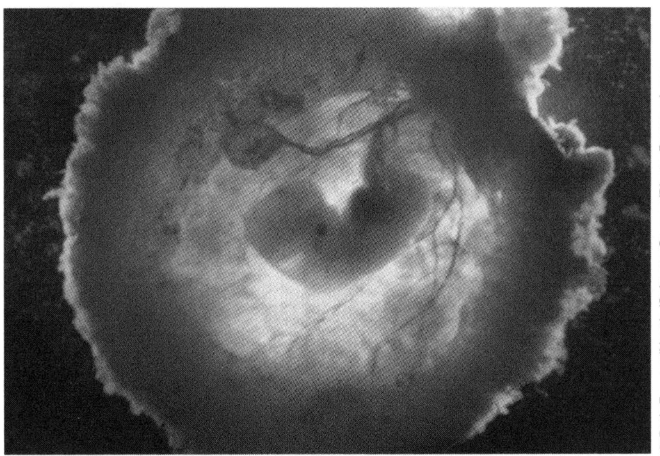

© Petit Format/Nestle/Science Source/Photo Researchers

A low sperm count—or lack of sperm—is the most common infertility problem in men. The most common infertility problem in women is irregular ovulation or lack of ovulation; other reasons for infertility include infections such as pelvic inflammatory disease (PID), endometriosis, and obstructions. Fertility drugs regulate ovulation. Other ways of conceiving include artificial insemination and in vitro fertilization (IVF).

LO4 Recount the major events of prenatal development. During the germinal stage, the zygote divides repeatedly and travels through a fallopian tube to the uterus, where it implants. Before implantation, it is nourished by the yolk of the original egg cell. Once implanted in the uterine wall, it is nourished by the mother. The embryonic stage lasts from implantation until the eighth week of development, during which the major organ systems differentiate. Development follows cephalocaudal and proximodistal trends. The heart begins to beat during the fourth week. By the end of the second month, facial features are becoming distinct, teeth buds have formed, the kidneys are working, and the liver is producing red blood cells. Male sex hormones spur development of the male reproductive system. The embryo and fetus exchange nutrients and wastes with the mother through the placenta. Some disease organisms, such as those that cause syphilis and rubella, can pass through the placenta. Some drugs also pass through, including aspirin, narcotics, and alcohol.

Rh incompatibility
a condition in which antibodies produced by the mother are transmitted to the child, possibly causing brain damage or death. (p. 41)

accutane (isotretinoin)
a frequently prescribed acne medication that can cause significant physical and neurological birth defects. (p. 41)

thalidomide
a sedative used in the 1960s that has been linked to birth defects, especially deformed or absent limbs. (p. 41)

progestin
a hormone used to maintain pregnancy that can cause masculinization of the fetus. (p. 41)

DES
diethylstilbestrol, an estrogen that has been linked to cancer in the reproductive organs of children of women who used the hormone when pregnant. (p. 42)

fetal alcohol spectrum disorder (FASD)
a cluster of symptoms shown by children of women who drank heavily during pregnancy, including characteristic facial features and intellectual challenges. (p. 42)

The fetal stage is characterized by maturation of organs and gains in size. It lasts from the end of the embryonic stage until birth. The fetus begins to turn at the ninth or tenth week. It responds to sound waves by the 13th week of pregnancy. By the end of the second trimester, the fetus opens and shuts its eyes, sucks its thumb, and alternates between wakefulness and sleep. During the third trimester, it becomes increasingly capable of sustaining independent life.

Maternal malnutrition is linked to low birth weight, prematurity, and cognitive and behavioural problems. Teratogens are most harmful during critical periods, when certain organs are developing. Women who contract rubella may bear children who suffer from deafness, intellectual challenges, heart disease, or cataracts. Syphilis can cause miscarriage or stillbirth. Toxemia is characterized by high blood pressure and is often seen in preterm or small babies. In Rh incompatibility, the mother's antibodies cause brain damage or death. Environmental agents that can harm the embryo and fetus include accutane, thalidomide, tetracycline, DES (diethylstilbestrol), toxoplasmosis, high doses of vitamins A and D, narcotics, marijuana, cocaine, alcohol, cigarette smoke, heavy metals, PCBs (polychlorinated biphenyls), and radiation.

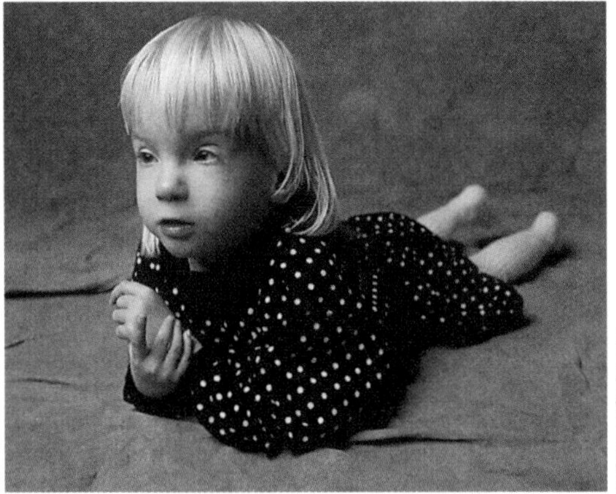

Teenage mothers have a higher incidence of infant mortality and children with low birth weight. Older parents run an increasing risk of chromosomal abnormalities and stillborn or preterm babies.

The rapid pace of scientific technology has caused Canadians to closely examine medical ethics and to enact legislation to ensure that research in reproductive technology remains ethically sound.

Please visit the CourseMate at www.nelson.com/4ltrpress/icanhdev2ce to view the Emerging Canada boxes that supplement this chapter.

Chapter in Review

Braxton-Hicks contractions
the first, usually painless, contractions of childbirth. (p. 47)

prostaglandins
hormones that stimulate uterine contractions. (p. 47)

oxytocin
a hormone that stimulates labour contractions. (p. 47)

LO1 efface
to become thin. (p. 47)

dilate
to widen. (p. 47)

transition
movement of the head of the fetus into the birth canal. (p. 48)

LO2 midwife
an individual who helps women in childbirth. (p. 49)

anesthetics
agents that lessen pain. (p. 50)

general anesthesia
an agent that eliminates pain by putting a person to sleep. (p. 50)

local anesthetic
an agent that reduces pain in an area of the body. (p. 50)

natural childbirth
childbirth without anesthesia. (p. 50)

Lamaze method
a childbirth method in which women are educated about childbirth, breathe in patterns that reduce pain during birth, and have a coach present. (p. 50)

cesarean section
delivery of a baby by abdominal surgery. (p. 50)

LO3 anoxia
absence of oxygen. (p. 51)

hypoxia
less oxygen than required. (p. 51)

breech (bottom-first) presentation
buttocks-first childbirth. (p. 51)

preterm
born prior to 37 weeks of gestation. (p. 51)

small for dates
description of newborns who are small for their age. (p. 51)

lanugo
fine, downy hair on premature babies. (p. 51)

vernix
oily white substance on the skin of premature babies. (p. 51)

respiratory distress syndrome
weak and irregular breathing, typical of preterm babies. (p. 52)

LO1 **Identify the stages of childbirth.** An expectant woman's first uterine contractions are Braxton-Hicks contractions, or false labour contractions. A day or so before labour begins, women may spot blood. About 1 woman in 10 has a rush of amniotic fluid. Maternal hormones stimulate contractions strong enough to expel the baby.

Childbirth begins with the onset of regular contractions of the uterus, which efface and dilate the cervix. The first stage may last from hours to more than a day. During transition, the head of the fetus moves into the birth canal. The second stage begins when the baby appears at the opening of the birth canal and ends with birth of the baby. Mucus is suctioned from the baby's mouth so that breathing is not obstructed. The umbilical cord is severed. During the third stage, the placenta is expelled.

LO2 **Describe the different methods of childbirth.** General anesthesia and analgesics put the woman to sleep, but they decrease the strength of uterine contractions and lower the responsiveness of the newborn. Local anesthetics deaden pain in parts of the body. Prepared childbirth teaches women relaxation exercises to help deal with the discomfort of contractions. A coach aids the mother. A cesarean section (C-section) delivers a baby surgically through the abdomen. C-sections are most likely when the baby is large or in distress. Herpes and HIV infections can be bypassed by using C-section.

LO3 **Discuss potential problems with childbirth.** Prenatal oxygen deprivation can impair development of the nervous system and can be fatal. A baby is preterm when birth occurs at or before 37 weeks of gestation. A baby has a low birth weight when it weighs less than 2.5 kg (5.5 lb.). Risks of prematurity include infant mortality and delayed neurological and motor development. Preterm babies are relatively thin. Their sucking may be weak, and they may show respiratory distress. Preterm babies usually remain in the hospital in incubators, but they profit from early stimulation. Canadians want to ensure that all children have an equal opportunity to access health care services. The UNICEF Report, *Leaving No Child Behind,* looks at disparities between health statistics of Aboriginal and non-Aboriginal children in Canada.

LO4 **Describe the key events of the postpartum period.** Women may encounter the baby blues, or postpartum depression. These problems probably reflect hormonal changes following birth, although stress can play a role.

Postpartum depression symptoms include the following:

- feelings of hopelessness, helplessness, and worthlessness
- mood swings
- abnormal sleep patterns (frequently insomnia)

Early infant bonding has not been shown to be critical but does have advantages for both the baby and the mother.

LO5 **Describe the characteristics of the newborn.** The newborn's health is usually evaluated by the Apgar scale, displayed below. The Brazelton Neonatal Behavioural Assessment Scale screens for behavioural and neurological problems. The newborn's rooting and sucking reflexes are basic to survival. Other key reflexes include the startle reflex, the grasping reflex, the stepping reflex, the Babinski reflex, and the tonic-neck reflex. Most reflexes disappear or are replaced by voluntary behaviour within months. Newborns are nearsighted. Newborns are particularly responsive to the sounds and rhythms of speech. The taste preferences of neonates are similar to those of older children and adults. The sensations of skin against skin may contribute to attachment.

incubators
heated, protective containers for premature infants. (p. 52)

LO4 postpartum period

the period immediately following childbirth. (p. 53)

postpartum depression (PPD)
serious maternal depression following delivery; characterized by sadness, apathy, and feelings of worthlessness. (p. 54)

bonding
formation of parent–infant attachment. (p. 55)

LO5 Apgar scale

a measure of a newborn's health that assesses appearance, pulse, grimace, activity level, and respiratory effort. (p. 56)

Brazelton Neonatal Behavioural Assessment Scale
a measure of a newborn's motor behaviour, response to stress, adaptive behaviour, and control over physiological state. (p. 56)

reflexes
unlearned responses to a stimulus. (p. 56)

rooting reflex
the response of turning the mouth and head toward the stroking of the cheek or the corner of the mouth. (p. 56)

Moro reflex
the response of arching the back, flinging out the arms and legs, and drawing them back to the chest in response to a sudden change in position. (p. 56)

grasping reflex
the response of grasping objects that touch the palms. (p. 57)

stepping reflex
the response of taking steps when held under the arms and leaned forward so the feet press the ground. (p. 57)

Babinski reflex
the response of fanning the toes when the soles of the feet are stroked. (p. 57)

tonic-neck reflex
the response of turning the head to one side, extending the arm and leg on that side, and flexing the limbs on the opposite side. (p. 57)

visual accommodation
automatic adjustments of the lenses to focus on objects. (p. 58)

convergence
inward movement of the eyes to focus on an object that is drawing nearer. (p. 58)

amplitude
loudness (of sound waves). (p. 58)

pitch
highness or lowness (of a sound), as determined by the frequency of sound waves. (p. 58)

rapid-eye-movement (REM) sleep
a sleep period when dreams are likely, as suggested by rapid eye movements. (p. 60)

Newborns are capable of classical and operant conditioning. Neonates spend two-thirds of their time in sleep, distributing their sleep throughout the day and night in a series of naps. Neonates spend about half their time sleeping in rapid-eye-movement (REM) sleep, but as time goes on, REM sleep accounts for less of their sleep. REM sleep may be related to brain development. Babies cry mainly because of pain and discomfort. Crying communicates hunger, anger, pain, and the presence of health problems. "Purple Crying" can be frightening for parents but is developmentally normal.

Sudden infant death syndrome (SIDS) is the most common cause of death in infants between the ages of 1 month and 1 year. SIDS is more common among babies who are put to sleep on their stomachs, preterm and low-birth-weight infants, male infants, and infants whose mothers smoked during or after pregnancy. Shaken Baby Syndrome (SBS) is the impulsive act of an exhausted or frustrated caregiver. Harm to a child is preventable when caregivers seek help and the proper support systems are in place.

TABLE 3.1

The APGAR Scale

POINTS	0	1	2
Appearance: Colour	Blue, pale	Body pink, extremities blue	Entirely pink
Pulse: Heart Rate	Absent (not detectable)	Slow—below 100 beats/minute	Rapid—100–140 beats/minute
Grimace: Reflex Irritability	No response	Grimace	Crying, coughing, sneezing
Activity level: Muscle tone	Completely flaccid, limp	Weak, inactive	Flexed arms and legs; resists extension
Respiratory effort: Breathing	Absent (infant is apneic)	Shallow, irregular, slow	Regular breathing; lusty crying

Please visit the CourseMate at www.nelson.com/4ltrpress/icanhdev2ce to view the Emerging Canada boxes that supplement this chapter.

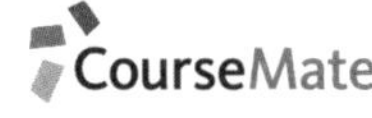

non-rapid-eye-movement (non-REM) sleep
a sleep period when dreams are unlikely. (p. 60)

pacifier
a device such as an artificial nipple or teething ring that soothes babies when sucked. (p. 62)

sudden infant death syndrome (SIDS)
the death, while sleeping, of apparently healthy babies who stop breathing. (p. 62)

4 Chapter in Review

LO1

differentiation
the processes by which behaviours and physical structures become specialized. (p. 66)

failure to thrive (FTT)
a disorder of infancy and early childhood characterized by variable eating and inadequate gains in weight. (p. 67)

canalization
the tendency of growth rates to return to normal after undergoing environmentally induced change. (p. 67)

LO2

nerves
bundles of axons from many neurons. (p. 69)

neurons
cells in the nervous system that transmit messages. (p. 69)

dendrites
rootlike parts of neurons that receive impulses from other neurons. (p. 69)

axon
a long, thin part of a neuron that transmits impulses to other neurons through branching structures called axon terminals. (p. 69)

neurotransmitters
chemicals that transmit neural impulses across a synapse from one neuron to another. (p. 69)

myelin sheath
a fatty, whitish substance that encases and insulates axons. (p. 69)

myelination
the coating of axons with myelin. (p. 69)

multiple sclerosis
a disorder in which hard fibrous tissue replaces myelin, impeding neural transmission. (p. 69)

medulla
an area of the hindbrain involved in heartbeat and respiration. (p. 70)

cerebellum
the part of the hindbrain involved in coordination and balance. (p. 70)

cerebrum
the part of the brain responsible for learning, thought, memory, and language. (p. 70)

LO1 Describe trends in the physical development of the infant. Three key sequences of physical development are cephalocaudal development, proximodistal development, and differentiation. Infants usually double their birth weight in 5 months and triple it by their first birthday. Height increases by about half in the first year and usually occurs in spurts after extended periods of sleep. Infants grow another 10 to 15 cm (4 to 6 in.) and gain another 1.8 to 3.2 kg (4 to 7 lb.) in their second year. The head diminishes in proportion to the rest of the body. Failure to thrive (FTT) impairs growth in infancy and early childhood. FTT can have organic causes or nonorganic causes, possibly including deficiencies in caregiver-child interaction.

Infants require breast milk or an iron-fortified formula. Introduction of solid foods is recommended at 4–6 months. Breast feeding is related to the mother's availability, knowledge of the advantages of breast feeding, support in caregiving, and availability of alternatives. Breast milk is tailored to human digestion, contains essential nutrients, contains the mothers' antibodies, helps protect against infant diarrhea, and is less likely than formula to lead to allergies.

LO2 Describe the physical development of the brain and the nervous system. Neurons receive and transmit messages in the form of neurotransmitters. As the child matures, axons grow in length, dendrites and axon terminals proliferate, and many neurons become wrapped in myelin, making them more efficient. The brain triples in weight by the first birthday, reaching nearly 70 percent of its adult weight. The brain has two major prenatal growth spurts: neurons proliferate during the first, and the second spurt is due mainly to the proliferation of dendrites and axon terminals. Sensory and motor areas of the brain begin to develop because of maturation, but sensory stimulation and motor activity spur development. Malnutrition is connected with a small brain, fewer neurons, and less myelination.

FIGURE 4.2

Structures of the Brain

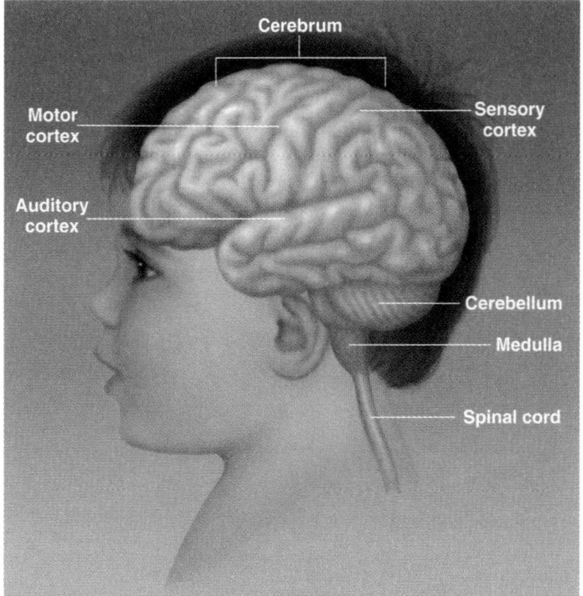

LO3 palmar grasp
grasping objects between the fingers and the palm. (p. 72)

pincer grasp
grasping objects between the fingers and the thumb. (p. 72)

locomotion
movement from one place to another. (p. 73)

toddler
a child who walks with short, uncertain steps. (p. 73)

LO4 habituation
becoming used to a stimulus and therefore paying less attention to it. (p. 77)

FIGURE 4.5

Eye Movements of 1- and 2-Month-Olds

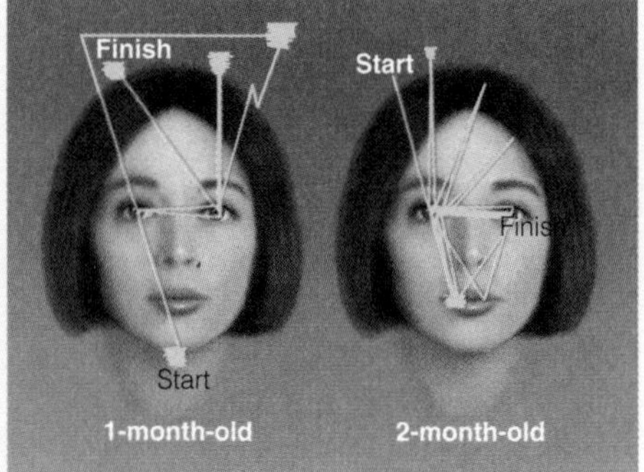

Source: Salapatek (1975).

Go to www.nelson.com/4ltrpress/icanhdev2ce to access an interactive version of this figure.

LO3 Describe the key events in the motor development of the infant.

Motor development is related to changes in posture, movement, and coordination. Children gain the ability to move their bodies through a sequence of activities that includes rolling over, sitting up, crawling, creeping, walking, and running. Although the sequence remains stable, some children skip a step. Both maturation (nature) and experience (nurture) play roles in motor development. Development of motor skills can be accelerated by training, but the effect is generally slight. Extreme deprivation can be overcome as seen in the example of Romanian orphans adopted by Canadians.

LO4 Describe patterns of sensory and perceptual development in infancy.

Newborns are nearsighted and have poor peripheral vision. Their acuity and peripheral vision approximate adult levels by the age of 6 months. Newborns look longer at stripes than at blobs, and by 8 to 12 weeks of age, they prefer curved lines to straight ones. Two-month-olds fixate longer on the human face than on other stimuli. Infants can discriminate their mother's face from a stranger's after about 8 hours of contact. Newborns direct their attention to the edges of objects, but 2-month-olds scan objects from the edges inward.

Researchers use the visual cliff apparatus to study depth perception. Most infants refuse to venture out over the cliff by the time they can crawl. Perhaps infants need some experience crawling before they develop a fear of heights. Newborns reflexively orient their heads toward a sound. Infants discriminate caregivers' voices by 31/2 months of age. Early infants can perceive most of the speech sounds throughout the languages of the world, but by 10 to 12 months of age, this ability diminishes.

Newborns seem to be at the mercy of external stimuli, but later intentional action replaces "capture." Systematic search replaces unsystematic search, attention becomes selective, and irrelevant information gets ignored. Sensory changes are linked to maturation of the nervous system (nature), but experience (nurture) also plays a crucial role. Children have critical periods in their perceptual development when their sensory experience is required to optimize—or maintain—sensory capacities.

Please visit the CourseMate at www.nelson.com/4ltrpress/icanhdev2ce to view the Emerging Canada boxes that supplement this chapter.

FIGURE 4.7

Declining Ability to Discriminate the Sounds of Foreign Languages

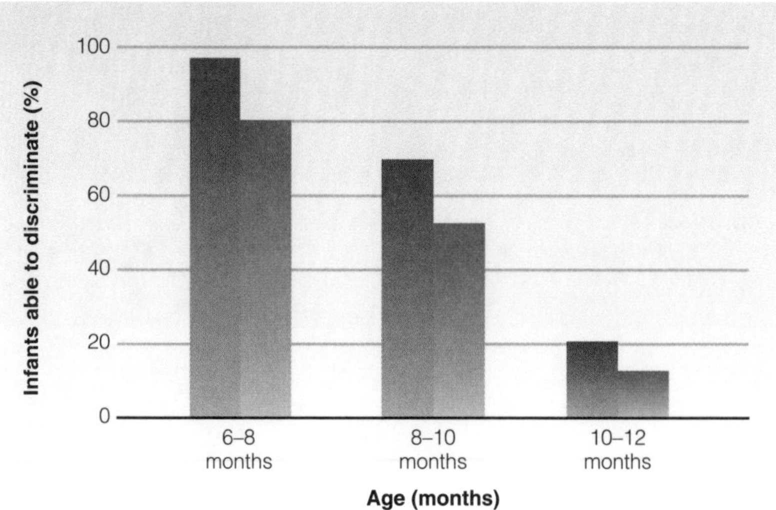

Source: Werker (1989).

INFANCY: COGNITIVE DEVELOPMENT

5 Chapter in Review

LO1 primary circular reactions the repetition of actions that first occurred by chance and that focus on the infant's own body. (p. 82)

secondary circular reactions the repetition of actions that produce an effect on the environment. (p. 82)

tertiary circular reactions the purposeful adaptation of established schemes to new situations. (p. 83)

object permanence recognition that objects continue to exist when they are not in view. (p. 84)

deferred imitation the imitation of previously encountered people and events. (p. 85)

LO3 visual recognition memory the kind of memory shown in an infant's ability to discriminate previously seen objects from novel objects. (p. 88)

LO4 prelinguistic vocalizations made by the infant before the use of language. (p. 89)

cooing prelinguistic vowel-like sounds that reflect feelings of positive excitement. (p. 89)

babbling the child's first vocalizations that have the sounds of speech. (p. 89)

echolalia the automatic repetition of sounds or words. (p. 89)

intonation the use of pitches of varying levels to help communicate meaning. (p. 89)

receptive vocabulary the number of words one understands. (p. 89)

expressive vocabulary the number of words one can use in the production of language. (p. 89)

referential language style use of language primarily as a means for labelling objects. (p. 91)

expressive language style use of language primarily as a means for engaging in social interaction. (p. 91)

overextension use of words in situations in which their meanings become extended. (p. 91)

telegraphic speech type of speech in which only the essential words are used. (p. 91)

holophrase a single word that is used to express complex meanings. (p. 91)

LO1 Examine Jean Piaget's studies of cognitive development. Piaget hypothesized that cognitive processes develop in an orderly sequence of four stages: sensorimotor, preoperational, concrete operational, and formal operational. The sensorimotor stage refers to the first 2 years of cognitive development and involves the progression from responding to events with reflexes to displaying goal-oriented behaviour (see table below). A critical milestone in the sensorimotor stage is the appearance of early signs of object permanence, or the ability of an infant to appreciate that an object continues to exist physically even when out of view.

Researchers who question the validity of Piaget's claims argue the following:

- development is not tied to discrete stages
- adult and peer influences play a role in cognitive development
- infants are more competent than Piaget estimated.

Piaget's Stages of Cognitive Development

STAGE	AGE	HALLMARKS
1. Simple reflexes	0–1 month	Assimilation of new objects into reflexive responses. Infants "look and see." Inborn reflexes can be modified by experience.
2. Primary circular reactions	1–4 months	Repetition of actions that may have initially occurred by chance but that have satisfying or interesting results. Infants "look in order to see." The focus is on the infant's body. Infants do not yet distinguish between themselves and the external world.
3. Secondary circular reactions	4–8 months	Repetition of schemes that have interesting effects on the environment. The focus shifts to external objects and events. Infants gain initial cognitive awareness that schemes influence the external world.
4. Coordination of secondary schemes	8–12 months	Coordination of secondary schemes, such as looking and grasping to attain specific goals. Infants' activities show signs of the beginning of intentionality and means–end differentiation. Infants demonstrate an imitation of actions not already in their repertoires.
5. Tertiary circular reactions	12–18 months	Purposeful adaptation of established schemes to specific situations. Infants' behaviour takes on an experimental quality. Infants exhibit overt trial and error in problem solving.
6. Invention of new means through mental combinations	18–24 months	Mental trial and error in problem solving. Infants take "mental detours" based on cognitive maps. Infants engage in deferred imitation and symbolic play. Infants' cognitive advances are made possible by mental representations of objects and events and by the beginnings of symbolic thought.

syntax
the language rules for placing words in an order to form sentences. (p. 92)

models
in learning theory, those whose behaviours are imitated by others. (p. 92)

extinction
decrease in the frequency of a response due to the absence of reinforcement. (p. 93)

shaping
gradual building of complex behaviour by reinforcing successive approximations to the target behaviour. (p. 93)

sensitive period
the period from about 18 months to puberty when the brain is especially capable of learning language. (p. 96)

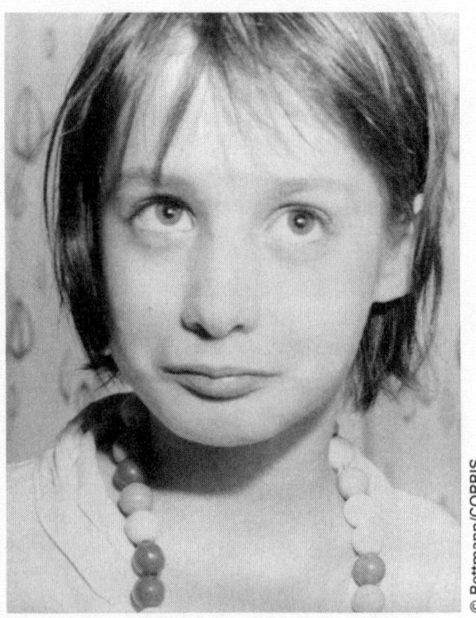

Genie's tragically unique experience provides support for the *sensitive period hypothesis* of language development.

LO2 **Discuss the information-processing approach.** The information-processing approach focuses on how children manipulate or process information from the environment or already stored in the mind. Two primary tools used in this processing are memory and imitation. Even newborns demonstrate memory to stimuli, and between 2 and 6 months of age, infants' memory develops dramatically. Infant memory can be improved if infants receive a reminder before given a memory test. Deferred imitation occurs as early as 6 months of age.

LO3 **Identify individual differences in intelligence among infants.** The Bayley Scales of Infant Development are one of the most important tests of intellectual development among infants. A total of 287 scale items test for mental skills (verbal communication, perceptual skills, learning and memory, and problem-solving skills) and motor skills (gross and fine). Infant intelligence is tested to determine the presence of handicaps, and although the Bayley scales can identify gross lags in development and relative strengths and weaknesses, infant intelligence scores are generally poor predictors of intelligence scores taken more than a year later.

Assessing visual recognition memory is another way of studying infant intelligence. Longitudinal studies by Susan Rose and her colleagues showed that the capacity for visual recognition memory is stable and the trait shows predictive validity for broad cognitive abilities throughout childhood, including intelligence and language ability.

LO4 **Examine language development in children.** Children develop language according to an invariant sequence of steps or stages. The first stage involves prelinguistic vocalizations, such as cooing, babbling, and echolalia. Once children can express themselves with words, they try to talk about more objects than they have words for. Just as their first words are simple syllabic combinations, first sentences are often single words that express simple but complete ideas. In early language acquisition, children use telegraphic speech to communicate full ideas.

Theories on language development are divided into those emphasizing nurture and those emphasizing nature. Proponents of nurture theories build on the work of B. F. Skinner and cite the roles of imitation and reinforcement in language development. Proponents of the nativist view, like Noam Chomsky, argue that the ability to acquire language is innate and therefore biological. The work of Steven Pinker, among others, shows, however, that language acquisition results from an interaction of biological and environmental factors (in other words, it results from a combination of nature and nurture). This notion is reinforced through the tragic story studied in *The Genie Project*, which allows us to see the impact of severe environmental conditions on language acquisition.

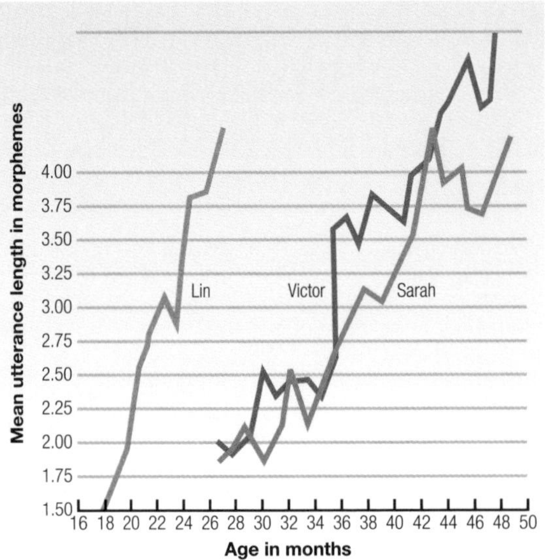

FIGURE 5.3

Mean Length of Utterance for Three Children

Please visit the CourseMate at www.nelson.com/4ltrpress/icanhdev2ce to view the Emerging Canada boxes that supplement this chapter.

Chapter in Review

LO1

attachment an affectional bond characterized by seeking closeness with another and distress upon separation. (p. 99)

separation anxiety fear of separation from a target of attachment. (p. 99)

secure attachment a type of attachment characterized by mild distress at leave-takings and being readily soothed by reunion. (p. 100)

avoidant attachment a type of insecure attachment characterized by apparent indifference to leave-takings by and reunions with an attachment figure. (p. 100)

ambivalent/resistant attachment a type of insecure attachment characterized by severe distress at leave-takings by and ambivalent behaviour at reunions. (p. 100)

disorganized–disoriented attachment a type of insecure attachment characterized by dazed and contradictory behaviours toward an attachment figure. (p. 100)

initial-preattachment phase the first phase in development of attachment, characterized by indiscriminate attachment. (p. 101)

attachment-in-the-making phase the second phase in development of attachment, characterized by preference for familiar figures. (p. 101)

clear-cut-attachment phase the third phase in development of attachment, characterized by intensified dependence on the primary caregiver. (p. 101)

contact comfort the pleasure derived from physical contact with another. (p. 103)

ethologists scientists who study the behaviour patterns characteristic of various species. (p. 103)

social smile a smile that occurs in response to a human voice or face. (p. 103)

critical period a period during which imprinting can occur. (p. 103)

imprinting the process by which waterfowl become attached to the first moving object they follow. (p. 103)

LO2

autism spectrum disorders (ASDs) developmental disorders characterized by impairment in communication and social skills, and by repetitive, stereotyped behaviour. (p. 106)

PSYCHOSOCIAL STAGE	PERSONALITY CRISIS (CHALLENGE)	IMPORTANT LIFE EVENT	OUTCOME
Infancy (birth to 18 months)	Trust vs. Mistrust	Feeding	Trust is developed when caregivers are reliable and affectionate. Mistrust is developed when care is unpredictable and/or lacking in affection.

LO1 Describe the development of attachment in infancy and theoretical views of how it occurs. Most infants in Canada and the United States are securely attached. In the Strange Situation, secure infants mildly protest the mother's departure and, on her return, are readily comforted by her. The two major types of insecure attachment are avoidant attachment and ambivalent/resistant attachment. Compared with insecure infants, secure infants are happier, more sociable, and more competent. They use their mother as a secure base from which to explore their environment. Parents of securely attached infants are more likely to be affectionate and sensitive to their needs.

According to Ainsworth's studies of the development of attachment, the initial-preattachment phase lasts from birth to about 3 months and is characterized by indiscriminate attachment. The attachment-in-the-making phase occurs at about 3 or 4 months and is characterized by a preference for familiar figures. The clear-cut-attachment phase occurs at 6 or 7 months and involves dependence on the primary caregiver.

Cognitive theorists suggest that an infant must develop object permanence before specific attachment is possible. Behaviourists suggest that infants become attached to caregivers because caregivers meet their physical needs. Psychoanalysts suggest that the primary caregiver becomes a love object. The Harlows' experiments with monkeys suggest that contact comfort is a key to attachment. Ethologists view attachment as an instinct (i.e., a fixed-action pattern) that occurs during a critical period.

LO2 Discuss the effects of social deprivation, abuse and neglect, and autism spectrum disorders on attachment. The Harlows found that rhesus infants reared in isolation later avoided contact with other monkeys. Isolated females who later had offspring tended to neglect or abuse them. Many institutionalized children who receive little social stimulation temporarily develop withdrawal and depression. Mistreated children are less intimate with peers and are more aggressive, angry, and noncompliant than other children. Child abuse tends to run in families, perhaps because abusive parents serve as role models. The 2008 Canadian Incidence Study of Reported Child Abuse and Neglect (Public Health Agency of Canada, 2010) concluded that incidents of child abuse are under-reported and remain a significant Canadian social issue.

Autism spectrum disorders (ASDs) are characterized by impairment in communication skills and social interactions, and repetitive, stereotyped behaviour. The most striking feature of autism is the child's aloneness. Other features include communication problems, intolerance of change, and self-harm. Studies of twins suggest that autism may involve heredity, and neurological impairment is also suspected. Behaviour modification has been used to increase social play and the child's attention to others. The Autism Society of Canada reminds us that individuals with autism should be valued for their differences and not viewed as persons that should be changed. Avoid referring to "an autistic child," but instead refer to "a child with autism" to avoid having the disorder define the individual.

autism
a disorder characterized by extreme aloneness, communication problems, preservation of sameness, and ritualistic behaviour. (p. 107)

mutism
refusal to speak. (p. 107)

echolalia
automatic repetition of sounds or words. (p. 107)

LO4 **social referencing**
using another person's reaction to a situation to form one's own response. (p. 110)

emotional regulation
techniques for controlling one's emotional states. (p. 111)

LO5 **separation–individuation**
the process of becoming separate from and independent of the mother. (p. 112)

temperament
individual difference in style of reaction that is present early in life. (p. 112)

goodness of fit
agreement between the parents' expectations of a child and the child's temperament. (p. 113)

LO3 **Discuss the effects of day care.** Day care was once seen as a second alternative to home care but research now shows that day care has many advantages. Infants with day-care experience are more independent, self-confident, outgoing, affectionate, and more cooperative with peers and adults than infants who are not in day care. In terms of cognitive development, children in high-quality day care outperform children who remain in the home. Children in day care are more aggressive than other children, but some aggression may indicate independence, not maladjustment. A population increase will require a closer examination of Canadian day cares.

LO4 **Describe the emotional development of the infant.** Researchers debate whether the emotional expression of newborns begins in an undifferentiated state of diffuse excitement or whether several emotions are present. Infants' initial emotional expressions appear to comprise either a positive attraction to pleasant stimulation or withdrawal from aversive stimulation. By the age of 2 to 3 months, social smiling has replaced reflexive smiling. Most infants develop a fear of strangers at about 6 to 9 months.

Infants display social referencing as early as 6 months of age, when they use caregivers' facial expressions or tones of voice for information on how to respond in novel situations. Emotional regulation is emotional self-control. Securely attached children are more likely to regulate their emotions well.

LO5 **Describe the personality development of the infant, focusing on the self-concept, temperament, and sex differences.** Research using the mirror technique finds that the self-concept develops by about 18 months of age. Self-awareness enables the child to develop concepts of sharing and cooperation and emotions such as embarrassment, envy, empathy, pride, guilt, and shame.

Infants' temperament (see Table 6.2) involves their activity level, regularity, approach or withdrawal, adaptability, response threshold, response intensity, quality of mood, distractibility, attention span, and persistence. Thomas and Chess found that most infants can be classified as having one of three temperaments: easy, difficult, or slow-to-warm-up. Temperament remains moderately consistent from infancy through young adulthood.

Female infants sit, crawl, and walk earlier than boys do. By 12 to 18 months of age, girls prefer to play with dolls and similar toys, whereas boys prefer sports equipment and transportation toys.

Please visit the CourseMate at www.nelson.com/4ltrpress/icanhdev2ce to view the Emerging Canada boxes that supplement this chapter.

CourseMate

FIGURE 6.3

Contact Comfort

© Martin Rogers/Stock, Boston

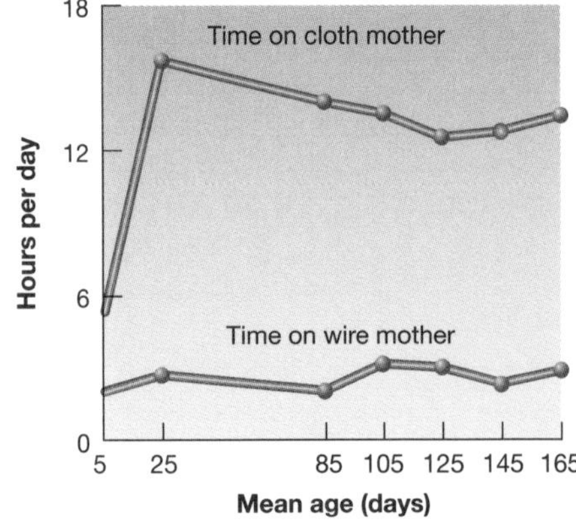

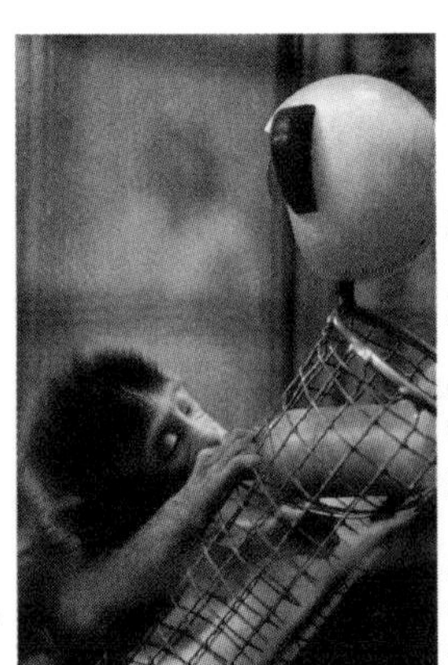
© Martin Rogers/Woodfin Camp & Associates

EARLY CHILDHOOD: PHYSICAL AND COGNITIVE DEVELOPMENT

7 Chapter in Review

LO1 **corpus callosum** the thick bundle of nerve fibres that connects the left and right hemispheres of the brain. (p. 118)

plasticity the tendency of new parts of the brain to take up the functions of injured parts. (p. 118)

LO2 **gross motor skills** skills employing the large muscles used in locomotion. (p. 118)

fine motor skills skills employing the small muscles used in manipulation, such as those in the fingers. (p. 120)

LO5 **sleep terrors** frightening dreamlike experiences that occur during the deepest stage of non-REM sleep, shortly after the child has gone to sleep. (p. 124)

somnambulism sleepwalking. (p. 124)

LO6 **enuresis** failure to control the bladder (urination) once the normal age for control has been reached. (p. 125)

bed-wetting failure to control the bladder during the night. (p. 125)

encopresis failure to control the bowels once the normal age for bowel control has been reached. Also called soiling. (p. 125)

LO7 **preoperational stage** the second stage in Piaget's scheme, characterized by inflexible and irreversible mental manipulation of symbols. (p. 125)

symbolic play play in which children make-believe that objects and toys are other than what they are. Also called pretend play. (p. 126)

egocentrism putting oneself at the centre of things such that one is unable to perceive the world from another person's point of view. (p. 126)

precausal a type of thought in which natural cause-and-effect relationships are attributed to will and other preoperational concepts. (p. 127)

transductive reasoning faulty reasoning that links one specific isolated event to another specific isolated event. (p. 127)

animism the attribution of life and intentionality to inanimate objects. (p. 127)

LO1 **Describe trends in physical development in early childhood.** Children gain about 5 to 8 cm (2 to 3 in.) in height and 2 to 3 kg (4 to 6 lb.) in weight per year in early childhood. Boys are slightly larger than girls. The brain develops more quickly than any other organ in early childhood, in part because of myelination. The left hemisphere is relatively more involved in logical analysis, language, and computation. The right hemisphere is usually superior in visual–spatial functions, emotional responses, and creative mathematical reasoning. But the hemispheres work together. The brain shows plasticity in early childhood. Two factors involved in the brain's plasticity are the growth of new dendrites and the redundancy of neural connections.

LO2 **Describe motor development in early childhood.** Preschoolers make great strides in the development of gross motor skills. Girls tend to be better in balance and precision; boys have some advantage in throwing and kicking. Physically active parents are likely to have physically active children. Fine motor skills develop gradually. Kellogg identified 20 scribbles that she considers the building blocks of art. Free drawing should be encouraged. Handedness emerges by 6 months. Left-handedness may be related to some language and health problems, yet a disproportionately large number of artists, musicians, and mathematicians are left-handed.

LO3 **Describe nutritional needs in early childhood.** Health Canada recommends that young children's diet should focus on food servings rather than caloric intake. During the second and third years, children's appetites typically wane and grow erratic. Many children eat too much sugar and salt. Experts are concerned about the rising trend in childhood obesity. They recommend the main prevention

LO4 **Describe trends in health and illness in early childhood.** The incidence is high for minor illnesses, such as colds, nausea and vomiting, and diarrhea. In developing countries, diarrheal diseases are a leading cause of death and are almost always related to unsafe drinking water and lack of adequate sanitation. Immunization and antibiotics reduce the incidence of disease.

LO5 **Describe sleep patterns in early childhood.** Most 2- and 3-year-olds sleep about 10 hours at night and nap during the day. Sleep terrors are more severe than nightmares. Sleep terrors and sleepwalking usually occur during deep sleep. Sleepwalkers' eyes are usually open; if awakened, they may show confusion but are unlikely to be violent. Adequate sleep is necessary, as a lack of sleep is associated with behavioural difficulties.

LO6 **Discuss elimination disorders.** Most Canadian children are toilet trained by age 2 or 3 but may continue to have "accidents." Enuresis is apparently related to slowed physical development and stress. Encopresis can stem from constipation and stress. Most of these concerns are outgrown.

LO7 **Describe Piaget's preoperational stage.** Piaget's preoperational stage lasts from about age 2 to 7 and is characterized by the use of symbols. Preoperational thinking is characterized by pretend play, egocentrism, precausal thinking, confusion between mental and physical events, and ability to focus on only one dimension at a time. Conservation is lacking because it requires focusing on two aspects of a situation at once.

artificialism
the belief that environmental features were made by people. (p. 127)

conservation
in cognitive psychology, the principle that properties of substances such as weight and mass remain the same (are conserved) when superficial characteristics such as their shapes or arrangement are changed. (p. 128)

LO8

scaffolding
Vygotsky's term for temporary cognitive structures or methods of solving problems that help the child as he or she learns to function independently. (p. 129)

zone of proximal development (ZPD)
Vygotsky's term for the situation in which a child carries out tasks with the help of someone who is more skilled, frequently an adult who represents the culture in which the child develops. (p. 129)

LO9

theory of mind
a commonsense understanding of how the mind works. (p. 130)

appearance–reality distinction
the difference between real events on the one hand and mental events, fantasies, and misleading appearances on the other hand. (p. 131)

LO10

scripts
abstract, generalized accounts of familiar repeated events. (p. 131)

autobiographical memory
the memory of specific episodes or events. (p. 131)

rehearsal
a strategy that uses repetition to remember information. (p. 132)

LO11

fast mapping
a process of quickly determining a word's meaning, which facilitates children's vocabulary development. (p. 132)

overregularization
the application of regular grammatical rules for forming inflections to irregular verbs and nouns. (p. 133)

pragmatics
the practical aspects of communication, such as adaptation of language to fit the social situation. (p. 133)

inner speech
Vygotsky's concept of the ultimate binding of language and thought. Inner speech originates in vocalizations that may regulate the child's behaviour and become internalized by age 6 or 7. (p. 135)

LO8 Discuss influences on cognitive development in early childhood. Vygotsky envisions scaffolding and the zone of proximal development as two factors in cognitive development. When caregivers provide appropriate play materials and stimulating experiences, children show gains in social and language development. For example, First Nation Head Start programs enhance children's academic readiness and skills while instilling a sense of pride and an eagerness to learn. Canadians are increasingly concerned about the quality control in day cares and an increasing baby population. Television and screen time continue to be primary focuses in children's learning. Fortunately, some viewing (e.g., *Sesame Street*) shows mild to productive influences on cognitive development.

LO9 Explain how "theory of mind" affects cognitive development. Children come to understand the distinctions between external and mental events and between appearances and realities. By age 3, most children begin to realize that people gain knowledge through the senses, and by age 4, they understand which senses provide certain kinds of information.

LO10 Describe memory development in early childhood. Preschoolers recognize more items than they can recall. Autobiographical memory is linked to language skills. Factors affecting memory include what the child is asked to remember, interest level and motivation, the availability of retrieval cues, and the memory measure being used. When preschoolers are trying to remember, they engage in behaviour such as looking, pointing, and touching.

LO11 Describe language development in early childhood. Preschoolers acquire about nine new words per day, some of which occur due to fast mapping. During the third year, children usually add articles, conjunctions, possessive adjectives, pronouns, and prepositions. Between the ages of 3 and 4, children combine phrases and clauses into complex sentences. Preschoolers overregularize irregular verbs and nouns as they learn grammar. To Vygotsky, inner speech is the ultimate binding of language and thought.

Please visit the CourseMate at www.nelson.com/4ltrpress/icanhdev2ce to view the Emerging Canada boxes that supplement this chapter.

Chapter in Review

8

LO1

inductive
based on an attempt to foster understanding of the principles behind parental demands; characteristic of disciplinary methods, such as reasoning. (p. 138)

authoritative
a child-rearing style in which parents are restrictive and demanding yet communicative and warm. (p. 139)

authoritarian
a child-rearing style in which parents demand submission and obedience. (p. 139)

permissive–indulgent
a child-rearing style in which parents are warm and not restrictive. (p. 139)

rejecting–neglecting
a child-rearing style in which parents are neither restrictive and controlling nor supportive and responsive. (p. 139)

secure attachment
a type of attachment characterized by mild distress when caregivers physically leave a space, and being readily soothed upon their return. (p. 140)

LO2

regression
a return to behaviour characteristic of earlier stages of development. (p. 141)

dramatic play
play in which children enact social roles. (p. 142)

disinhibit
stimulate a response that has been suppressed by showing a model engaging in that response. (p. 146)

PSYCHOSOCIAL STAGE	PERSONALITY CRISIS (CHALLENGE)	IMPORTANT LIFE EVENT	OUTCOME
Early Childhood (19 months to 3 years)	Autonomy vs. Shame and Doubt	Toilet Training	Children develop a sense of personal control, skill, and independence. Success leads to feelings of self-rule and independence, whereas failure results in feelings of shame and self-doubt.
Preschool (4 to 5 years)	Initiative vs. Guilt	Exploration	Children need to take control over their own environment, which leads to a sense of purpose. If children exert too much power, they will encounter disapproval and resulting guilt. Failure to control their environment will lead to a sense of inadequacy.

LO1 Describe the dimensions of child rearing and styles of parenting.

Approaches to child rearing can be classified according to the dimensions of warmth–coldness and restrictiveness–permissiveness. Consistent control and firm enforcement of rules can lead to positive consequences for the child. To enforce rules, parents tend to use inductive methods, power assertion, and withdrawal of love. Inductive methods use "reasoning," or explaining why one sort of behaviour is good and another is not. Authoritative parents are restrictive but warm and tend to have the most competent and achievement-oriented children. Authoritarian parents are restrictive and cold. The sons of authoritarian parents tend to be hostile and defiant; the daughters tend to be low in independence. Children of neglectful parents show the least competence and maturity. Young children experience divorce much differently from adults. They are helped through this family transition when parents talk to them about the separation. Securely attached children use their parents as a home base for exploration, which builds a foundation for their independence.

LO2 Explain how siblings, birth order, peers, and other factors affect social development during early childhood.

Siblings provide caregiving, emotional support, advice, role models, social interaction, restrictions, and cognitive stimulation. However, they are also sources of conflict, control, and competition. First-born and only children are generally more highly motivated to achieve, more cooperative, more helpful, more adult-oriented, and less aggressive, but later-born children tend to have greater social skills with peers. From their peers, children learn social skills, such as sharing, taking turns, and coping with conflict. Peers also provide emotional support. Preschoolers' friendships are characterized by shared activities and feelings of attachment.

Play develops motor, social, and cognitive skills. Children show preferences for gender-stereotyped toys by 15 to 30 months of age. Boys also prefer vigorous outdoor activities and rough-and-tumble play. Girls are more likely to prefer arts and crafts. These preferences were thought to be primarily due to socialization but monkeys also show the same sex-based biases in toy preference. Preschool children generally prefer playmates of their own sex, partly

LO3 **categorical self** the definitions of the self that refer to external traits. (p. 147)

LO4 **gender roles** clusters of traits and behaviours that are considered stereotypical of females and males. (p. 148)

gender identity knowledge that one is female or male. (p. 149)

gender stability the concept that one's sex is unchanging. (p. 149)

gender constancy the concept that one's sex remains the same despite changes in appearance or behaviour. (p. 149)

gender-schema theory the view that society's gender-based concepts shape our assumptions of gender-typed preferences and behaviour patterns. (p. 149)

psychologically androgynous having both stereotypical feminine and masculine traits. (p. 150)

because of shared interest in activities. Boys' play is more oriented toward dominance, aggression, and rough play. Prosocial behaviour begins to develop in the first year, when children begin to share. The development of prosocial behaviour is linked to the development of empathy and perspective taking. Girls show more empathy than boys do. Preschool aggression is often instrumental. By age 6 or 7, aggression can become hostile. Aggressive behaviour appears to be stable and can predict problems in adulthood. Genetic factors may be involved in aggressive behaviour. Social cognitive theory suggests that children become aggressive as a result of frustration and observational learning. Aggressive children are often rejected by their less aggressive peers. Children who are physically punished are more likely to behave aggressively. Observing aggressive behaviour teaches aggressive skills, disinhibits children, and habituates them to violence. Those who view aggression as socially acceptable behaviour are more likely to be aggressive themselves. All-day kindergarten in Canada has been found to lead to higher achievement and greater independence, but critics wonder whether children are being rushed through their early childhood.

LO3 **Discuss personality and emotional development during early childhood, focusing on the self, Erikson's views, and fears.** Children as young as age 3 can describe themselves in terms of their behaviour and their internal states. Secure attachment and competence contribute to self-esteem. Preschoolers are most likely to fear animals, imaginary creatures, and the dark.

LO4 **Discuss the development of gender roles and sex differences.** Females are stereotyped as dependent, gentle, and home-oriented. Males are stereotyped as aggressive, self-confident, and independent. Cultural expectations of females and males are called gender roles. Stereotypical gender preferences for toys and play activities are in evidence at an early age. Males are more aggressive than females. Social cognitive theorists explain the development of gender-typed behaviour in terms of observational learning and socialization. According to Kohlberg's cognitive-developmental theory, gender-typing involves the emergence of gender identity, gender stability, and gender constancy. According to gender-schema theory, preschoolers attempt to conform to the cultural gender schema. Psychological androgyny, according to Bem, indicates future adult success.

TABLE 8.1

Baumrind's Patterns of Parenting

	Parental Behaviour Patterns	
Parental Style	***Restrictiveness and Control***	***Warmth and Responsiveness***
Authoritative	↑	↓
Authoritarian	↑	↓
Permissive–Indulgent	↓	↓
Rejecting–Neglecting	↓	↓

Please visit the CourseMate at www.nelson.com/4ltrpress/icanhdev2ce to view the Emerging Canada boxes that supplement this chapter.

9 Chapter in Review

LO1 **growth spurt** a period during which growth advances at a dramatically rapid rate compared with other periods. (p. 153)

LO2 **reaction time** the amount of time required to respond to a stimulus. (p. 155)

LO3 **attention-deficit/hyperactivity disorder (ADHD)** a disorder characterized by excessive inattention, impulsiveness, and hyperactivity. (p. 156)

hyperactivity excessive restlessness and overactivity; a characteristic of ADHD. (p. 156)

stimulants drugs that increase the activity of the nervous system. (p. 156)

learning disabilities disorders characterized by inadequate development of specific academic, language, and speech skills. (p. 156)

dyslexia a reading disorder characterized by letter reversals, mirror reading, slow reading, and reduced comprehension. (p. 157)

classroom inclusion placing children with disabilities in classrooms with children without disabilities. (p. 157)

LO4 **concrete operations** the third stage in Piaget's scheme, characterized by flexible, reversible thought concerning tangible objects and events. (p. 158)

decentration simultaneous focusing on more than one aspect or dimension of a problem or situation. (p. 158)

transitivity the principle that if A > B and B > C, then A > C. (p. 158)

seriation placing objects in an order or series according to a property or trait. (p. 158)

LO5 **preconventional level** according to Kohlberg, a period during which moral judgments are based largely on expectations of rewards or punishments. (p. 161)

conventional level according to Kohlberg, a period during which moral judgments largely reflect social rules and conventions. (p. 161)

LO1 **Describe trends in physical development in middle childhood.** Children tend to gain a little over 5 cm (2 in.) in height and 2 to 3 kg (5 to 7 lb.) in weight per year during middle childhood. Boys are slightly heavier and taller than girls through ages 9 or 10, until girls begin the adolescent growth spurt. Overweight children usually do not outgrow their baby fat. Parents can promote children's healthy living by eliminating unhealthy snack foods from the home, controlling portion sizes, and acting as a positive role model. Heredity plays a role in weight. Sedentary habits also foster weight gain. Healthy food choices from the Canada's Food Guide should be coupled with regular physical activity.

Monkey Business Images/Shutterstock.com

LO2 **Describe changes in motor development in middle childhood.** Middle childhood is marked by increases in speed, strength, agility, and balance. Children improve in gross and fine motor skills as the pathways that connect the cerebellum to the cortex become more myelinated. Reaction time decreases. Boys have slightly greater overall strength, whereas girls have better coordination and flexibility. Many Canadian children are not physically fit, in part because of the amount of time spent watching TV. Cuts to Canadian physical education programming have also hurt the health of our children.

LO3 **Discuss ADHD and learning disabilities.** Attention-deficit/hyperactivity disorder (ADHD) runs in families and may involve differences in the brain. Children with ADHD are sometimes treated with stimulants, which trigger the cerebral cortex to inhibit more primitive areas of the brain. When working with children with ADHD, give one direction at a time, make directions short and clear, and take frequent breaks. Dyslexia also runs in families. Some children with learning disabilities benefit from being in mainstream classrooms. Universal classroom design and individual education plans are two strategies implemented to meet the needs of Canada's diverse classrooms.

LO4 **Describe Piaget's concrete-operational stage.** By the age of 11, children's thought processes become more logical and complex. Piaget characterized children during this period as entering the concrete-operational stage, in which children begin to think in logical terms but focus on tangible objects rather than abstract ideas. Concrete-operational children are less egocentric, engage in decentration, and understand concepts such as conservation, transitivity, seriation, and class inclusion.

postconventional level
according to Kohlberg, a period during which moral judgments are derived from moral principles, and people look to themselves to set moral standards. (p. 161)

LO6 **sensory memory**
the structure of memory first encountered by sensory input. Information is maintained in sensory memory for only a fraction of a second. (p. 162)

sensory register
another term for sensory memory. (p. 162)

working memory
the structure of memory that can hold a sensory stimulus for up to 30 seconds after the trace decays. (p. 162)

encode
to transform sensory input into a form that is more readily processed. (p. 162)

rehearsing
repeating that aids in recall. (p. 162)

long-term memory
the memory structure capable of relatively permanent storage of information. (p. 162)

elaborative strategy
a method for increasing retention of new information by relating it to well-known information. (p. 162)

metacognition
awareness of and control of one's cognitive abilities. (p. 164)

metamemory
knowledge of the functions and processes involved in one's storage and retrieval of information. (p. 164)

LO7 **intelligence**
defined by Wechsler as the "capacity ... to understand the world [and the] resourcefulness to cope with its challenges." (p. 164)

achievement
acquired competencies that are attained by one's efforts and are presumed to be made possible by one's abilities. (p. 164)

intelligence quotient (IQ)
(1) a ratio obtained by dividing a child's mental age on an intelligence test by his or her chronological age; (2) a score on an intelligence test. (p. 165)

mental age (MA)
the score that a person earns on the Stanford–Binet Intelligence Scale. (p. 166)

chronological age (CA)
a person's actual age. (p. 166)

cultural bias
a factor in intelligence tests that provides an advantage for test takers from certain cultural backgrounds. (p. 168)

culture-free
descriptive of a test in which cultural biases have been removed. (p. 168)

cultural–familial developmental challenges
substandard intellectual performance stemming from lack of opportunity to acquire knowledge and skills. (p. 170)

creativity
a trait characterized by flexibility, ingenuity, and originality. (p. 171)

convergent thinking
a thought process that attempts to focus on the single best solution to a problem. (p. 171)

divergent thinking
free and fluent association to the elements of a problem. (p. 171)

heritability
the degree to which the variations in a trait from one person to another can be attributed to genetic factors. (p. 171)

LO8 **word-recognition method**
a method for learning to read in which children come to recognize words through repeated exposure to them. (p. 173)

phonetic method
a method for learning to read in which children decode the sounds of words based on their knowledge of the sounds of letters and letter combinations. (p. 173)

sight vocabulary
words that are not decoded but are immediately recognized because of familiarity with their overall shapes. (p. 173)

bilingual
using or capable of using two languages with equal or nearly equal facility. (p. 173)

LO5 **Discuss Kohlberg's theories of moral development.** Kohlberg concluded that moral reasoning in children was related to overall cognitive development. Kohlberg's theory emphasized the importance of being able to view a situation from multiple perspectives. The reasoning on which people base their judgments reflects their level of moral development. At a preconventional level, moral judgments are based on the positive or negative consequences of one's actions. At the conventional level, moral judgments are based on conformity to conventional standards. At a postconventional level, moral judgments are based on personal moral standards. Roots of Empathy is a character-based curriculum being taught in Canadian classrooms. It aims to reduce the incidence of aggression and bullying and to promote behaviour based on empathy.

LO6 **Describe developments in information processing in middle childhood.** Key elements in children's information-processing capabilities include development in selective attention; development in the storage and retrieval of sensory, short-term, and long-term memory; development of recall memory; and development of metacognition and metamemory.

LO7 **Describe intellectual development in middle childhood, focusing on theories of intelligence.** Intelligence is usually perceived as a child's underlying competence or *learning ability,* whereas achievement involves a child's acquired competencies or *performance*. Factor theorists view intelligence as consisting of one or more major mental abilities. Sternberg proposed a three-part theory of intelligence (see Figure 9.5). Gardner theorized that intelligence reflected more than academic achievement, with nine different categories of intelligence, or "talents" (see Figure 9.6).

The Wechsler and SBIS scales have been developed to measure intelligence. Many psychologists and educational specialists have developed culture-free tests to avoid cultural biases they feel are present in the Wechsler scale and the Stanford–Binet Intelligence Scale (SBIS). About half of children score between 90 and 110 on IQ (intelligence quotient) tests. Those who score below 70 are labelled "intellectually challenged" and those scoring above 130 are labelled "gifted." Most tests indicate only a moderate relationship between IQ scores and creativity. Intelligence tests usually rely on convergent thinking, whereas creativity is generally based on divergent thinking.

LO8 **Describe language development in middle childhood, including reading and bilingualism.** Children's language ability grows more sophisticated in middle childhood. During this stage, most children learn to read. Exposure to a variety of languages affects children's cognitive development. Bilingualism is of special interest in Canada, where more than 100 languages are spoken.

Please visit the CourseMate at www.nelson.com/4ltrpress/icanhdev2ce to view the Emerging Canada boxes that supplement this chapter.

MIDDLE CHILDHOOD: SOCIAL AND EMOTIONAL DEVELOPMENT

Chapter in Review

LO1 **social cognition** our understanding of the relationship between ourself and others. (p. 178)

learned helplessness an acquired (hence, learned) belief that one is unable to control one's environment. (p. 180)

LO2 **co-regulation** a gradual transferring of control from parent to child, beginning in middle childhood. (p. 180)

transsexuals persons who prefer to be of the other sex and who may undergo hormone treatments, cosmetic surgery, or both to achieve the appearance of the other sex. (p. 180)

LO4 **Pygmalion effect** a self-fulfilling prophecy; an expectation that is confirmed because of the behaviour of those who hold the expectation. (p. 185)

self-fulfilling prophecy an event that occurs because of the behaviour of those who expect it to occur. (p. 185)

sexism discrimination or bias on the basis of a person's sex. (p. 186)

LO5 **conduct disorders** disorders marked by persistent breaking of the rules and violations of the rights of others. (p. 186)

attributional style one's disposition toward interpreting outcomes (successes or failures), as in tending to place blame or responsibility on oneself or on external factors. (p. 187)

serotonin a neurotransmitter that is involved in mood disorders such as depression. (p. 188)

generalized anxiety disorder (GAD) an anxiety disorder in which anxiety appears to be present continuously and is unrelated to the situation. (p. 188)

phobias irrational, excessive fears that interfere with one's functioning. (p. 188)

separation anxiety disorder (SAD) an extreme form of separation anxiety characterized by anxiety about separating from parents; SAD often takes the form of refusal to go to school. (p. 188)

school phobia fear of attending school, marked by extreme anxiety at leaving parents. (p. 189)

PSYCHOSOCIAL STAGE	PERSONALITY CRISIS (CHALLENGE)	IMPORTANT LIFE EVENT	OUTCOME
School Age (6 to 11 years)	Industry vs. Inferiority	School	Children learn to cope with new social and academic demands. Success leads to a sense of ability and accomplishment. Failure leads to a sense of inferiority.

LO1 **Explain theories of social and emotional development in middle childhood.** Erikson saw middle childhood as the stage of industry versus inferiority. Social cognitive theorists note that children in middle childhood depend less on external rewards and punishments and increasingly regulate their own behaviour. Cognitive-developmental theory notes that concrete operations enhance social development. In middle childhood, children become more capable of taking the role or perspective of another person. Selman theorizes that children move from egocentricity to seeing the world through the eyes of others in five stages.

In early childhood, children's self-concepts focus on external traits. In middle childhood, children begin to include abstract internal traits. Social relationships and group membership assume importance. In middle childhood, competence and social acceptance contribute to self-esteem, but self-esteem tends to decline because the self-concept becomes more realistic. Authoritative parenting fosters self-esteem. Children with "learned helplessness" tend not to persist in the face of failure. Erikson's developmental focus on industry versus inferiority provides perspective on the issue of whether scoring in organized sport can lead to loss of self-esteem.

LO2 **Discuss the influences of the family on social development in middle childhood.** In middle childhood, the family continues to play a key role in socialization. Parent–child interactions focus on school-related issues, chores, and peers. Parents do less monitoring of children, as children's "co-regulation" develops. The Canadian family has evolved to the point that there is no longer a "typical" family. Research does not indicate a difference in development when a child is raised by same-sex parents. The sexual orientation of these children is generally heterosexual. Divorce disrupts children's lives and usually lowers the family's financial status. Children are likely to greet divorce with sadness, shock, and disbelief. Children of divorce fare better when parents cooperate in child rearing. Children appear to suffer as much from marital conflict as they do from divorce. Having both parents in the workforce may lead to lack of supervision, but there is little evidence that maternal employment harms children. Research shows that having a mother who works fosters children's greater independence and flexibility in their gender-role stereotypes.

LO3 **Discuss the influences of peers on social development in middle childhood.** Peers take on increasing importance in middle childhood and exert pressure to conform. Peers provide practice in social skills, sharing, relating to leaders, and coping with aggressive impulses. Early in middle childhood, friendships are based on proximity. Between the ages of 8 and 11, children become more aware of the value of friends as meeting each other's needs and having traits such as loyalty.

LO4 **Discuss the influence of the school on development in middle childhood.** Schools make demands for mature behaviour and nurture positive physical, social, and cognitive development. Readiness for school is related to children's early life experiences, individual differences in development and learning, and the school's expectations. An effective school has an orderly atmosphere, empowers teachers and students, holds high expectations of children, and has solid academics. Teachers' expectations can become self-fulfilling prophecies.

LO5 **Discuss social and emotional problems that tend to develop in middle childhood.** Conduct disorders may have a genetic component, but other contributing factors are sociopathic models in the family, deviant peers, and inconsistent discipline. Depressed children tend to complain of poor appetite, insomnia, lack of energy, and feelings of worthlessness. They blame themselves excessively for any shortcomings. Psychotherapy focuses on cognitive errors; antidepressants are sometimes helpful but controversial. Separation anxiety disorder (SAD) is diagnosed when separation anxiety is persistent and excessive and interferes with daily life. Children may refuse school due to school phobia or because they find it to be unpleasant or hostile. The central aspect of treatment of school refusal is to insist that the child attend school.

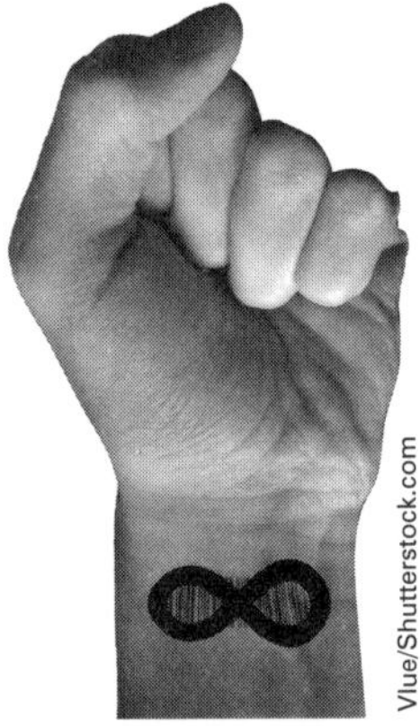
Vlue/Shutterstock.com

The Infinity Project is a youth initiative encouraging each other to speak out if they are struggling with depression, self-harm, anxiety or any issue that overwhelms them.

Please visit the CourseMate at www.nelson.com/4ltrpress/icanhdev2ce to view the Emerging Canada boxes that supplement this chapter.

11 Chapter in Review

LO1

puberty
the biological stage of development characterized by changes that lead to reproductive capacity. (p. 193)

feedback loop
a system in which glands regulate each other's functioning through a series of hormonal messages. (p. 193)

primary sex characteristics
the structures that make reproduction possible. (p. 194)

secondary sex characteristics
physical indicators of sexual maturation—such as changes to the voice and growth of bodily hair—that do not directly involve reproductive structures. (p. 194)

asynchronous growth
imbalanced growth, such as the growth that occurs during the early part of adolescence and causes many adolescents to appear gawky. (p. 194)

secular trend
a historical trend toward increasing adult height and earlier puberty. (p. 195)

semen
the fluid that contains sperm and substances that nourish and help transport sperm. (p. 195)

nocturnal emission
emission of seminal fluid while asleep. (p. 195)

gynecomastia
enlargement of breast tissue in males. (p. 195)

epiphyseal closure
the process by which the cartilage that separates the long end of a bone from the main part of the bone turns to bone. (p. 195)

menarche
the onset of menstruation. (p. 196)

LO2

anorexia nervosa
an eating disorder characterized by irrational fear of weight gain, distorted body image, and severe weight loss. (p. 200)

osteoporosis
a condition involving progressive loss of bone tissue. (p. 200)

bulimia nervosa
an eating disorder characterized by cycles of binge eating and vomiting as a means of controlling weight gain. (p. 200)

LO3

formal operations
the fourth stage in Piaget's cognitive-developmental theory, characterized by the capacity for flexible, reversible operations concerning abstract ideas and concepts, such as symbols, statements, and theories. (p. 201)

LO1 Describe the key events of puberty and their relationship to social development. G. Stanley Hall believed that adolescence is marked by "storm and stress." Current views challenge the idea that storm and stress are normal or beneficial. Puberty is a stage of physical development that is characterized by reaching sexual maturity. Sex hormones trigger the development of primary and secondary sex characteristics. Adolescents grow about 20 cm (8 inches) but puberty is a process that takes a long time. Precocious puberty (or early onset puberty) is becoming a common trend in Canada. Adolescents may look gawky because of asynchronous growth. Having a resource that is knowledgeable and non-judgmental is important for teens who experiencing so many physical changes. The effects of early maturation are generally positive for boys and often negative for girls.

LO2 Discuss health in adolescence, focusing on causes of death and eating disorders. Unintentional injuries are the number one cause of death for Canadian adolescents. Car accidents are the most common cause of death. To fuel the adolescent growth spurt, adolescents need to increase their food intake by making more healthy choices from Canada's Food Guide. The use of recreational drugs (both illegal and prescription) is a social reality for the Canadian teenager. Other issues that workers with teens should be aware of include eating disorders such as anorexia nervosa and bulimia nervosa, which may develop because of fear of gaining weight resulting from cultural idealization of the slim female. Genetic factors may connect eating disorders with perfectionistic personality styles.

LO3 Discuss adolescent cognitive development and the key events of Piaget's stage of formal operations. In Western societies, formal operational thought begins at about the time of puberty. The major achievements of the stage involve classification, logical thought (deductive reasoning), and the ability to hypothesize. Adolescent egocentrism is shown in the concepts of the imaginary audience and the personal fable.

LO4 Discuss sex differences in cognitive abilities. The stage of formal operations is Piaget's final stage of development. Many children, but not all, reach this stage during adolescence. The formal operational stage is characterized by the individual's increased ability to classify objects and ideas, engage in logical thought, hypothesize, and demonstrate a sophisticated use of symbols.

Adolescents show a new egocentrism in which they comprehend the ideas of other people, but have difficulty sorting out those things that concern other people from the things that concern themselves.

LO5 Discuss Kohlberg's theory of moral development in adolescence. Females tend to excel in verbal ability. Males tend to excel in visual–spatial ability. Females and males show equal ability in math. Boys are more likely than girls to have reading problems. Sex differences in cognitive abilities have been linked to biological factors and to gender stereotypes and social influences. In the postconventional level, according to Kohlberg, moral reasoning is based on the person's own moral standards. In Kohlberg's scheme, males reason at higher levels of moral development than females do, but Gilligan argues that this sex difference reflects patterns of socialization, with girls being encouraged to take a more "caring" orientation.

imaginary audience
the belief that others around us are as concerned with our thoughts and behaviours as we are; one aspect of adolescent egocentrism. (p. 202)

personal fable
the belief that our feelings and ideas are special and unique and that we are invulnerable; one aspect of adolescent egocentrism. (p. 202)

LO5 **postconventional level**
according to Kohlberg, a period during which moral judgments are derived from moral principles and people look to themselves to set moral standards. (p. 204)

LO6 **Discuss the roles of the school in adolescence, focusing on dropping out.** The school has a significant role in the adolescent's life. The transition to middle school, junior high, or high school generally involves a shift to a larger, more impersonal setting. This transition is often accompanied by a decline in grades and a drop in self-esteem. More Canadian teenagers are graduating than in previous generations, but we must continue to address the issue of dropping out. High-school dropouts are more likely to be unemployed and to earn lower salaries in their adult lives.

Pink Candy/Shutterstock.com

LO7 **Discuss career development and work experience during adolescence.** Student employment can be a positive influence if working is kept to a reasonable amount (10 hours per week). If employment hours are greater than 10, or if the employment takes place late at night, working can be another barrier to completing high school. The Holland Inventory is a tool that students can use to match their personal interests and strengths with possible future careers.

Please visit the CourseMate at www.nelson.com/4ltrpress/icanhdev2ce to view the Emerging Canada boxes that supplement this chapter.

Chapter in Review

LO1 **ego identity** according to Erikson, one's sense of who one is and what one stands for. (p. 209)

psychological moratorium a time-out period when adolescents experiment with different roles, values, beliefs, and relationships. (p. 209)

identity crisis a turning point in development during which one examines one's values and makes decisions about life roles. (p. 209)

identity diffusion an identity status that characterizes those who have no commitments and who are not in the process of exploring alternatives. (p. 210)

foreclosure an identity status that characterizes those who have made commitments without considering alternatives. (p. 210)

moratorium an identity status that characterizes those who are actively exploring alternatives in an attempt to form an identity. (p. 210)

identity achievement an identity status that characterizes those who have explored alternatives and have developed commitments. (p. 210)

ethnic identity a sense of belonging to an ethnic group. (p. 211)

unexamined ethnic identity the first stage of ethnic identity development; similar to the diffusion or foreclosure identity statuses. (p. 211)

ethnic identity search the second stage of ethnic identity development; similar to the moratorium identity status. (p. 211)

achieved ethnic identity the final stage of ethnic identity development; similar to the identity achievement status. (p. 211)

LO2 **clique** a group of five to ten individuals who hang around together and who share activities and confidences. (p. 214)

crowd a large, loosely organized group of people who may or may not spend much time together and who are identified by the activities of the group. (p. 214)

LO3 **homosexual** an erotic orientation toward members of one's own sex. (p. 216)

masturbation sexual self-stimulation. (p. 217)

PSYCHOSOCIAL STAGE	PERSONALITY CRISIS (CHALLENGE)	IMPORTANT LIFE EVENT	OUTCOME
Adolescence (12 to 18 years)	Identity vs. Role Confusion	Social Relationships	Teens develop a sense of their personal identity. Success leads to their ability to clearly define themselves and to stay true to who they believe they are. Failure leads to unclear standards and a weak sense of self.

LO1 Discuss the formation of identity in adolescence. Erikson's adolescent stage of psychosocial development is identity versus identity diffusion. The primary task of this stage is for adolescents to develop a sense of who they are and what they stand for. Marcia's identity statuses represent the four combinations of the dimensions of exploration and commitment: identity diffusion, foreclosure, moratorium, and identity achievement. Development of identity is more complicated for adolescents who belong to ethnic minority groups; they are faced with two sets of cultural values that may conflict.

Self-esteem tends to decline as the child progresses from middle childhood into early adolescence, perhaps because of increasing recognition of the disparity between the ideal self and the real self. Self-esteem then gradually improves.

LO2 Discuss relationships with parents and peers during adolescence. During adolescence, children spend much less time with parents than during childhood. Although adolescents become more independent of their parents, they generally continue to love and respect them. The role of peers increases markedly during the teen years. Adolescents are more likely than younger children to stress intimate self-disclosure and mutual understanding in friendships. The two major types of peer groups are cliques and crowds. Romantic relationships begin to appear during early and middle adolescence. Dating is a source of fun, prestige, and experience in relationships. Dating is also a preparation for adult intimacy. Online friendships are important to teens, although insecure attachment has been linked to unsafe disclosures in online relationship. Cyber bullying is a concern, although social media can also support positive social messages.

LO3 Discuss sexuality during adolescence, focusing on sexual identity and teenage pregnancy. Issues regarding lesbian, gay, bisexual, trans (gendered, sexual, twin-spirited), and questioning (LGBTQ) youth are becoming part of our mainstream Canadian culture. The process of "coming out" may be a painful struggle but as society becomes more inclusive, these adjustments will likely become a more positive experience. Early onset of puberty can lead to earlier sexual activity, though teen sexual activity is not increasing. Adolescents who have close relationships with their parents are less likely to initiate sexual activity early. Peer pressure is a powerful contributor to adolescent sexual activity.

LO4 youth in conflict with the law
a child or adolescent whose behaviour is characterized by illegal activities. (p. 220)

Many girls who become pregnant have received little advice about how to resist sexual advances. Many do not have access to contraception. Others misunderstand reproduction or miscalculate the odds of conception. Graduating from high school becomes more difficult for these young mothers, which lowers their potential for future income earning. Young Canadian women are becoming much more comfortable with their sexuality.

Albert Ziganshin/Shutterstock

Sexual experience

© cisale/iStockphoto

Sexually transmitted infections (STIs)

LO4 **Discuss the statistics specific to youth in conflict with the law and measures that can reduce youth crime in Canada.** Although Canada is experiencing a decrease in national crime rates, youth crimes (assaults, drug-related crimes, and school-related offences) are on the rise. The important link between youth and crime seems to be socioeconomic deprivation, not race or ethnicity; however, more Canadian studies are needed.

Empowerment and community involvement are primary philosophies of the Youth Criminal Justice Act (2003), which favours community programs (such as those involving sports) over incarceration as a way to reduce these crime trends. Restorative justice focuses on community ownership and involvement, giving a voice to the victims, the offenders, the family and friends of both, and society as a whole. Aboriginal youth report feeling optimistic about their futures, despite their over representation in the youth justice system.

LO5 **Discuss risk factors in adolescent suicide.** Suicide is the second leading cause of death among Canadian adolescents. Most suicides among adolescents and adults are linked to stress, feelings of depression, identity problems, impulsivity, and social problems. Warning signs of suicide include sudden changes in behaviour, isolation, withdrawal, and feelings of hopelessness. Suicide rates are increasing among female children and adolescents and decreasing among male children and adolescents..

Please visit the CourseMate at www.nelson.com/4ltrpress/icanhdev2ce to view the Emerging Canada boxes that supplement this chapter.

Chapter in Review

LO1

emerging adulthood
a theoretical period of development, spanning the ages of 18 to 25, when young people in developed nations engage in extended role exploration. (p. 225)

LO3

adaptive thermogenesis
the process by which the body converts food energy (calories) to heat at a lower rate when a person eats less, because of, for example, famine or dieting. (p. 228)

substance abuse
a persistent pattern of use of a substance characterized by frequent intoxication and impairment of physical, social, or emotional well-being. (p. 229)

substance dependence
a persistent pattern of use of a substance that is accompanied by physiological addiction. (p. 229)

tolerance
habituation to a drug such that increasingly higher doses are needed to achieve similar effects. (p. 229)

abstinence syndrome
a characteristic cluster of symptoms that results from a sudden decrease in the level of usage of a substance. (p. 229)

hallucinogenics
drugs that give rise to hallucinations. (p. 230)

LO4

dysmenorrhea
painful menstruation. (p. 233)

prostaglandins
hormones that cause muscles in the uterine wall to contract, as during labour. (p. 234)

amenorrhea
the absence of menstruation. (p. 234)

premenstrual syndrome (PMS)
the discomforting symptoms that affect many women during the 4–6 day interval preceding their periods. (p. 234)

premenstrual dysphoric disorder (PMDD)
a condition similar to but more severe than PMS. (p. 234)

dating violence
assaults such as verbal threats, pushing, and slapping committed by an individual in an intimate relationship and often leading to injuries that require first aid. (p. 235)

sexual harassment
deliberate or repeated unwanted comments, gestures, or physical contact. (p. 236)

LO5

crystallized intelligence
one's intellectual attainments, as shown, for example, by vocabulary and accumulated knowledge. (p. 236)

LO1 Discuss the (theoretical) stage of emerging adulthood. Emerging adulthood is a period of development, spanning the ages of 18 to 25, in which young people engage in extended role exploration. Many developmental theorists consider emerging adulthood to be a new stage of development that bridges adolescence and early adulthood.

LO2 Describe trends in physical development in early adulthood. Physical development peaks in early adulthood. During this stage, most people are at their height of sensory sharpness, strength, reaction time, and cardiovascular fitness. Peak fitness is followed by gradual declines in the cardiovascular, respiratory, and immune systems but regular exercise can reduce these effects. Fertility in both sexes declines as early adulthood progresses.

LO3 Discuss health in early adulthood, focusing on causes of death, diet, exercise, and substance abuse. Accidents are the leading cause of death in early adulthood. Most young adults do not eat the recommended five fruits and vegetables each day. About four in ten report insufficient exercise and being overweight, which has become a Canadian health concern. Substance abuse is use of a substance despite its social, occupational, psychological, or physical effects. Depressants such as alcohol, narcotics, and barbiturates are addictive substances that slow the activity of the nervous system. Alcohol also lowers inhibitions, relaxes, and intoxicates. Stimulants such as nicotine, cocaine, and amphetamines accelerate the heartbeat and other bodily functions but depress the appetite. Hallucinogenics such as marijuana and LSD give rise to perceptual distortions called hallucinations. Stress is a concern in a busy Canadian lifestyle.

LO4 Discuss sexuality in early adulthood, focusing on homosexuality, STIs, menstrual problems, and sexual coercion. Sexual activity with a partner tends to peak in the 20s. An international report found that Canadians are quite comfortable with their sexuality, reporting more partners and more time spent on sex than people in most other countries. Researchers have found evidence for genetic and hormonal factors in sexual orientation. Sexually transmitted infections (STIs) include bacterial infections such as chlamydia, gonorrhea, and syphilis; viral infections such as HIV/AIDS (human immunodeficiency virus/acquired immune deficiency syndrome), HPV (human papillomavirus), and genital herpes; and some others. Risk factors for contracting STIs include sexual activity with multiple partners and without condoms, and substance abuse. Most women experience at least some discomfort prior to or during menstruation. Sexual assault is significantly underreported in Canada, perhaps partly because victims usually know their attackers. Dating violence is also increasing at an alarming rate. At the root of this issue are social attitudes that minimize aggressive sexual behaviour.

LO5 Discuss cognitive development in early adulthood, focusing on "post-formal" developments and effects life after high school. Young adults are more cognitively complex than adolescents. They are able to weigh several factors at one time, and they encounter diverse ideas and people when attending postsecondary education, as a majority of Canadian youth do. Their previous dualistic thinking may be replaced by relativistic thinking. Labouvie-Vief's theory of pragmatic thought notes that "cognitively healthy" adults are more willing than egocentric adolescents to compromise and deal within the world as it is, not as they would like it to be; they develop cognitive–affective complexity that enables them to harbour both positive and negative feelings about their choices.

fluid intelligence
mental flexibility; the ability to process information rapidly. (p. 236)

dualistic thinking
dividing the cognitive world into opposites, such as good and bad, or us versus them. (p. 237)

relativistic thinking
recognition that judgments are often not absolute but made from a certain belief system or cultural background. (p. 237)

pragmatic thought
decision making characterized by willingness to accept reality and compromise. (p. 237)

cognitive–affective complexity
a mature form of thinking that permits people to harbour positive and negative feelings about their career choices and other matters. (p. 237)

LO6 Describe career choice and development during early adulthood. Careers are central to the lives of Canadian adults. People work for extrinsic rewards, such as money and benefits, and for intrinsic rewards, such as self-identity and self-fulfillment. Stages of career development include a fantasy stage, a realistic-choice stage, a maintenance stage, perhaps job-changing or retraining stages, and a retirement stage. Developmental tasks when beginning a job include accepting subordinate status, learning to get along with co-workers and supervisors, finding a mentor, and showing progress.

Boule/Shutterstock.com

DO YOU HAVE A PROBLEM WITH ALCOHOL?

How can you tell whether you may have a drinking problem? Answering the following questions can help you find out (NIAAA, 2005):

Yes	No	Have you ever felt you should cut down on your drinking?
Yes	No	Have people annoyed you by criticizing your drinking?
Yes	No	Have you ever felt bad or guilty about your drinking?
Yes	No	Have you ever had a drink first thing in the morning (as an "eye opener") to steady your nerves or get rid of a hangover?
Yes	No	Has drinking ever caused a social difficulty for you?
Yes	No	Have you ever missed school or work because of drinking?

Just one "yes" answer suggests a possible alcohol problem. Two or more "yeses" make it highly likely that a problem exists. In either case, it is advisable to discuss your answers with your doctor or another health care provider.

Please visit the CourseMate at www.nelson.com/4ltrpress/icanhdev2ce to view the Emerging Canada boxes that supplement this chapter.

14 Chapter in Review

LO1 individuation the young adult's process of becoming an individual by means of integrating his or her own values and beliefs with those of his or her parents and society at large. (p. 242)

LO2 intimacy versus isolation according to Erik Erikson, the central conflict or life crisis of early adulthood, in which a person develops an intimate relationship with a significant other or risks heading down a path toward social isolation. (p. 243)

LO3 the dream according to Daniel Levinson and his colleagues, the drive to become someone, to leave one's mark on history, which serves as a tentative blueprint for the young adult. (p. 243)

LO4 attraction–similarity hypothesis the view that we tend to develop romantic relationships with people who are similar to ourselves in physical attractiveness and other traits. (p. 246)

reciprocity the tendency to respond in kind when we feel admired and complimented. (p. 246)

romantic love a form of love fuelled by passion and feelings of intimacy. (p. 246)

intimacy the experience of warmth toward another person that arises from feelings of closeness and connectedness. (p. 247)

passion intense sexual desire for another person. (p. 247)

commitment the decision to devote oneself to a cause or another person. (p. 247)

PSYCHOSOCIAL STAGE	PERSONALITY CRISIS (CHALLENGE)	IMPORTANT LIFE EVENT	OUTCOME
Young Adulthood (19 to 39 years)	Intimacy vs. Isolation	Relationships	Young adults need to form intimate and loving relationships. Success leads to patterns of strong relationship building. Failure to enter into loving relationships results in loneliness and isolation.

LO1 Examine the issues involved in early adulthood separation. Havighurst's "tasks" for early adulthood include getting started in an occupation and finding a life partner, though his view might now be seen as a dated notion of early adulthood. Traditional or insecure parents may find a child's—especially a daughter's—leaving for college or university to be stressful. Young adults are returning home (the boomerang generation) in very high numbers, making the "empty nest" not so empty anymore. Adult children most often return because of financial troubles or relationship issues. Young adults need to become individuals by integrating their own values with those of their parents and society.

LO2 Describe the conflict between intimacy and isolation. Erikson's core conflict for early adulthood is intimacy versus isolation. Young adults who develop ego identity during adolescence are more ready to marry and develop friendships. A variety of different types of relationships are available to young Canadians starting out in life.

LO3 Discuss the stage of life for entry into adulthood. Levinson labels the ages of 17 to 33 the entry phase of adulthood for young men—when they leave home and strive for independence. Many young adults adopt "the dream," which serves as a tentative blueprint for life. Young adults undergo an age-30 transition, when they commonly reassess their lives. Young adults often settle down during their later 30s.

LO4 Examine the emotional forces of attraction and love. Physical appearance is a key in selection of romantic partners. People tend to prefer slenderness in both sexes. Women are more likely to prefer socially dominant men, but many men are put off by assertive women. Women find physical attractiveness less important than men do, but they prefer steady workers. Some psychologists believe that sex differences in preferences for mates provide reproductive advantages. People prefer partners who are similar to them in attractiveness and attitudes. People tend to reciprocate feelings of attraction. Berscheid and Hatfield define romantic love in terms of arousal and cognitive appraisal of that arousal as love. Sternberg's "triangular theory" of love includes the building blocks of intimacy, passion, and commitment. Jealousy can lead to insecurity and loss of feelings of affection.

LO5 Explain why people get lonely and what they do in response. Loneliness is related to low self-confidence, depression, and physical health problems. Lonely people tend to lack social skills, interest in other people, and empathy. Many people remain lonely because of fear of rejection. There is an important difference between being lonely and being alone.

Vadym Zaitsev/Shutterstock.com

The Internet has become both a potential source of comfort and difficulty for socially isolated people.

LO6 **serial monogamy** a series of exclusive sexual relationships. (p. 250)

celibacy abstention from sexual activity, whether from choice or lack of opportunity. (p. 250)

LO7 **cohabitation** living together with a romantic partner without being married. (p. 251)

LO8 **monogamy** the practice of having a sexual relationship with only one person at a time. (p. 252)

polyamory the practice of consenting partners who maintain an "open" sexual relationship. (p. 253)

same-sex marriage marriage between two gay males or between two lesbians. (p. 253)

homogamy marriage between two similar individuals. (p. 253)

LO6 **Discuss the lifestyle of being single.** Being single is the most common Canadian lifestyle of people in their early 20s. Many people postpone marriage to pursue educational and career goals. Many choose to live together without being married. Some have not found the right partner. Some single people are lonely, but most are well adjusted. Online dating is becoming a common way to meet potential partners in Canada. Many singles engage in serial monogamy.

LO7 **Describe the practice of living together.** The number of people living together in Canada has surged in the last two decades. In 2006, Statistics Canada recorded same-sex unions for the first time, as a result of Canada's legalization of same-sex marriages. Relationships are much more likely to dissolve when cohabitation precedes marriage. Cohabitants tend to have less traditional views of marriage and gender roles.

LO8 **Describe the practice of marriage.** Families, for all of their different descriptions and labels, remain our most common form of Canadian lifestyle. Marriage legitimizes sexual relations, provides an institution for rearing children, and permits the orderly transmission of wealth from one generation to another. Types of marriage include monogamy, arranged marriage and same-sex marriages. Similarity in physical attractiveness, attitudes, background, and interests plays a role in marital choices. Most marriages where partners are very similar in physical attractiveness, values, and family backgrounds enjoy a higher rate of stability than other unions. Intimacy and support of one's spouse are related to marital satisfaction. Couple satisfaction does not seem to be measurably different between same-sex couples and opposite-sex couples, but household chores are more evenly distributed in same-sex unions, leading to less bickering.

FIGURE 14.2

Types of Households, Canada, 2011 (percent)

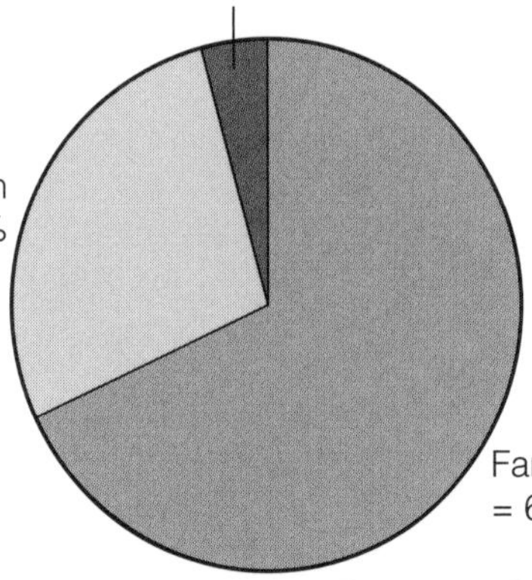

Unrelated-persons households = 4.1%

One-person households = 27.6%

Family households = 68.3%

Source: Statistics Canada. (2013a). Canadian Households in 2011: Type and growth. Description for Figure 1. 2011 Census. Ottawa, 2013. found at http://www12.statcan.gc.ca/census-recensement/2011/as-sa/98-312-x/98-312-x2011003_2-eng.cfm

LO9 **Discuss the state of parenthood.** Young Canadians are delaying parenthood into their later 20s. Most Canadians choose to have children for personal happiness but having a child is unlikely to save a troubled marriage. The mother is usually the primary caregiver and encounters more stress and role overload than fathers do when the mother is also in the workforce. Workplace tension affects home life, and vice versa.

LO10 **Discuss divorce and its repercussions.** In a survey of Canadian teenagers, 90 percent stated that when they marry it will be forever; yet the Canadian divorce rate is currently 38 percent. Changes in divorce laws and increased economic independence of women contribute to the divorce rate. Divorce hits women in the pocketbook harder than men, especially when women do not have careers. Divorced and separated people have the highest rates of physical and mental illness.

Please visit the CourseMate at www.nelson.com/4ltrpress/icanhdev2ce to view the Emerging Canada boxes that supplement this chapter.

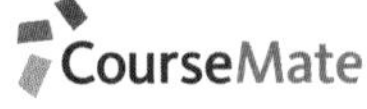

Chapter in Review

15

LO1 **baby boomers** postwar babies whose births between 1946 and 1965 spiked the Canadian population 11%. (p. 259)

interindividual variability the notion that people do not age in the same way or at the same rate. (p. 259)

presbyopia loss of elasticity in the lens that makes it harder to focus on nearby objects. (p. 260)

LO2 **metastases** the transference of malignant or cancerous cells to other parts of the body. (p. 262)

arteriosclerosis hardening of the arteries. (p. 264)

atherosclerosis the buildup of fatty deposits (plaque) on the lining of arteries. (p. 264)

LO3 **leukocytes** white blood cells. (p. 264)

LO4 **menopause** the cessation of menstruation. (p. 265)

perimenopause the beginning of menopause, usually characterized by 3 to 11 months of amenorrhea or irregular periods. (p. 265)

climacteric the gradual decline in reproductive capacity of the ovaries, generally lasting about 15 years. (p. 265)

sexual dysfunctions persistent or recurrent problems in becoming sexually aroused or reaching orgasm. (p. 266)

LO1 **Describe trends in physical development in middle adulthood.** The baby boomers have grown up and are now Canada's middle-aged generation. In middle adulthood, hair begins to grey, and hair loss accelerates. The skin loses elasticity. It becomes harder for eyes to focus on nearby objects or fine print. Reaction time takes longer. Breathing capacity declines. Fat replaces lean tissue and the basal metabolic rate declines. Strength decreases. Bone begins to lose density and strength. The cardiovascular system becomes less efficient. There is an increased risk of adult onset diabetes.

LO2 **Discuss the major health concerns of middle adulthood, including cancer and heart disease.** In middle adulthood, cancer and heart disease are the two leading causes of death in Canada. Risk factors for cancer include heredity, problems in the immune system, hormonal factors, and carcinogens. Positive lifestyle habits can reduce the risks associated with cancer. The risk factors for heart disease include family history, high blood pressure, high serum cholesterol, smoking, sedentary lifestyle, and arteriosclerosis.

TABLE 15.1

Leading Causes of Death in Middle Adulthood*

Age group	45–54	55–64
Cancer	119.0	333.4
Heart diseases	90.2	218.8
Accidents	40.7	33.2
Chronic liver diseases	18.0	22.6
Suicide	16.6	13.8
Strokes & other cerebrovascular diseases	14.9	34.3
Diabetes	13.4	37.1
Chronic respiratory diseases	8.4	40.4
Blood poisoning	5.4	12.9
Kidney diseases	5.0	13.6
Homicide	4.8	3.0
Influenza & pneumonia	4.6	10.8

*Annual deaths per 100,000 people.

Source: Arialdi M. Minino, Melanie P. Heron, Sherry L. Murphy, & Kenneth D. Kochanek. (2007, October 10). Deaths: Final data for 2004. *National vital statistics reports, 55*(19). Adapted from Table 9, pp. 27–29. http://www.cdc.gov/nchs/data/nvsr/nvsr55/nvsr55_19.pdf

LO3 **Discuss the functioning of the immune system.** The immune system combats disease by producing white blood cells (leukocytes), which engulf and kill pathogens. Leukocytes recognize foreign substances (antigens), deactivate them, and mark them for destruction. Stress suppresses the immune system. Stress hormones connected with anger can constrict the blood vessels to the heart, leading to a heart attack.

LO4 **Discuss sexuality in middle adulthood, focusing on menopause and sexual difficulties.** Most people in middle adulthood lead rich sex lives, but the frequency of sex tends to decline. The climacteric generally lasts about 15 years and is caused by decline in estrogen production. Menopause is part of the climacteric and is a normal process lasting about two years, which results in the female no longer ovulating. Estrogen deficiency can cause night sweats, hot flashes, hot flushes—even dizziness, headaches, joint pain, tingling in the hands

LO5 multidirectionality in the context of cognitive development, the notion that some aspects of intellectual functioning may improve while others remain stable or decline. (p. 268)

plasticity the capability of intellectual abilities to be modified, as opposed to being absolutely fixed. (p. 268)

crystallized intelligence a cluster of knowledge and skills that depend on accumulated information and experience, awareness of social conventions, and good judgment. (p. 269)

fluid intelligence a person's skills at processing information. (p. 269)

© Shauna Longmuir

Mature learners in higher education are likely to be highly motivated and to find the subject matter interesting for its own sake. Ironically, women with the greatest family and work demands are most likely to return to school. Canada has the second highest rate of postsecondary attainment in the world.

or feet, burning or itchy skin, heart palpitations, and brittleness and porosity of the bones (osteoporosis). Hormone replacement therapy (HRT) can help women deal with these symptoms but using HRT comes with considerable health risks. Men show a more gradual decline in sex hormones and fertility. Sexual difficulties often begin in middle adulthood. Sexual activity can, however, yield surprising health benefits. There is an increase in sexually transmitted infections (STIs) in middle age, possibly because condom use tends to be associated with preventing pregnancy, which is no longer an issue for middle-aged women; a shift toward more single, sexually active people; greater use of male impotence medication; and middle-aged adults' mistaken belief that they are not at risk for STIs. Condoms must continue to be used to protect against STIs.

LO5 Describe cognitive development in middle adulthood, distinguishing between crystallized and fluid intelligence. Intellectual development in adulthood shows multidirectionality, interindividual variability, and plasticity. Schaie's Seattle Longitudinal Study found that adults born more recently were superior to those born at earlier times in inductive reasoning, verbal meaning, spatial orientation, and word fluency. The earlier cohorts performed better in numeric ability. Neurological factors apparently play a powerful role in fluid intelligence. Crystallized intelligence tends to increase with age through middle adulthood, but a decline occurs in fluid intelligence, which relates to perceptual speed, spatial orientation, and numeric ability. Verbal ability and reasoning mainly reflect crystallized intelligence; they increase through middle adulthood and hold up in late adulthood. Good health and staying intellectually active help stem cognitive decline in late adulthood.

LO6 Discuss opportunities for exercising creativity and continuing education in middle adulthood. The middle-aged decline in processing speed apparently reflects changes in the nervous system. Most researchers find that people in middle and late adulthood perform less well than young adults at memorizing lists. In later middle adulthood, we are less able both to learn by rote repetition and to screen out distractions. Elaborative rehearsal may suffer since we are less capable of rapid classification. Yet, we tend to retain or expand our general knowledge. Procedural memories can be retained for a lifetime. Middle-aged people have the verbal abilities of young adults, have lost little fluid intelligence, and have a greater store of expertise.

TABLE 15.2

Deaths Due to Cancer and Heart Disease in Middle Adulthood and Late Adulthood*

AGE GROUP	45–54	55–64	65–74	75–84	85 AND OVER
Cancer	119.0	333.4	755.1	1,280.4	1,653.3
Heart diseases	90.2	218.8	541.6	1,506.3	4,895.9

*Annual deaths per 100,000 people.

Source: Arialdi M. Minino, Melanie P. Heron, Sherry L. Murphy, & Kenneth D. Kochanek. (2007, October 10). Deaths: Final data for 2004. *National vital statistics reports, 55*(19). Adapted from Table 9, pp. 27–29. Retrieved from http://www.cdc.gov/nchs/data/nvsr/nvsr55/nvsr55_19.pdf.

Please visit the CourseMate at www.nelson.com/4ltrpress/icanhdev2ce to view the Emerging Canada boxes that supplement this chapter.

MIDDLE ADULTHOOD: SOCIAL AND EMOTIONAL DEVELOPMENT

16 Chapter in Review

LO1 generativity
The ability to generate or produce, as in bearing children or contributing to society. (p. 276)

stagnation
the state of no longer developing, growing, or advancing. (p. 277)

social clock
the social norms that guide our judgment regarding the age-related "appropriateness" of certain behaviours. (p. 277)

midlife transition
a psychological shift into middle adulthood that is theorized to occur between the ages of 40 and 45, as people begin to believe they have more to look back on than to look forward to. (p. 277)

midlife crisis
a time of dramatic self-doubt and anxiety, during which people sense the passing of their youth and become concerned with their own aging and mortality. (p. 277)

empty nest syndrome
a feeling of loneliness or loss of purpose that parents, and especially mothers, are theorized to experience when the youngest child leaves home. (p. 278)

LO2 "big five" personality traits
basic personality traits derived from contemporary statistical methods: extraversion, agreeableness, conscientiousness, neuroticism (emotional instability), and openness to experience. (p. 280)

PSYCHOSOCIAL STAGE	PERSONALITY CRISIS (CHALLENGE)	IMPORTANT LIFE EVENT	OUTCOME
Middle Adulthood (40 to 64 years)	Generativity vs. Stagnation	Work and Parenthood	Adults thrive when they create and nurture things that will outlast them. Raising children, or creating a positive change, leads to feelings of usefulness and accomplishment. Failure results in shallow involvement, and a realization that they will leave nothing lasting behind.

LO1 Discuss theories of development in middle adulthood. Havighurst's tasks for middle adulthood include helping our children establish themselves, adjusting to physical changes, and adjusting to caring for aging parents. Erikson believed that the major psychological challenge of the middle years is generativity versus stagnation. Canadian Elliott Jaques developed the concept of a midlife crisis. Levinson characterizes the years of 40 to 45 as a midlife transition that is often accompanied by a midlife crisis, but many people at this age are at the height of their productivity and resilience. Although it was once assumed that women without children in the home would undergo an "empty nest syndrome," this time can be a positive event. The social clock has begun and ageism colours much of middle life.

David Svetlik/Shutterstock.com

LO2 Discuss stability and change in social and emotional development in middle adulthood. Longitudinal research finds that the "big five" personality traits show a good deal of stability after age 30, but the traits of agreeableness and conscientiousness tend to increase and neuroticism declines.

LO3 Discuss career developments typical of middle adulthood. A study of university employees found that job satisfaction increased through middle adulthood. Most career changes in midlife involve shifts into related fields. Unemployed middle-aged people show lower well-being than unemployed young adults. Second Careers is a provincial government initiative designed to send middle-aged workers back to school, creating a more vital economy.

LO4 **sandwich generation** the term for middle-aged people who need to meet the demands of both their own children and their aging parents. (p. 285)

© Warner Bros. Pictures/Sunset Boulevard/Corbis

After working for more than 15 years as a television and film actor, Clint Eastwood took his place behind the camera to guide the next generation of actors.

LO4 **Discuss trends in relationships in middle adulthood, focusing on grandparenting and being in the "sandwich generation."** When their children take partners or get married, middle-aged people need to adjust to having in-laws. Research generally finds that grandchildren are beneficial to grandparents socially and psychologically. Parents spend a higher proportion of their time with their children in child-care activities, whereas grandparents spend relatively more time in recreational and educational activities. Grandchildren spend more time in activities with their grandmothers than with their grandfathers, and are relatively more involved with their mother's parents. In some cases, grandparents bear the primary responsibility for rearing grandchildren, and sometimes they are the sole caregivers. Such arrangements typically begin when the grandchild has a single parent. Acting as the parent again can be highly stressful for grandparents. The timing of grandparents "coming out" to their grandchildren seems to met with greater acceptance when the grandchildren are in early childhood rather than in the teen years, when the aging adult is viewed as being asexual.

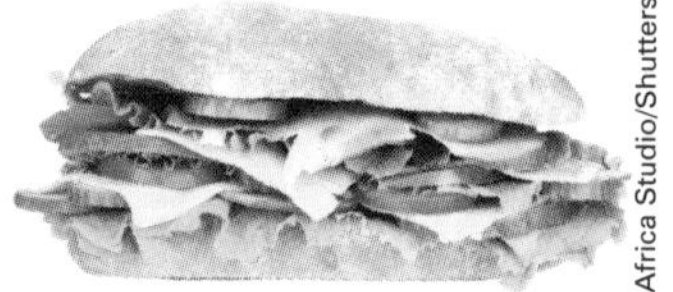

Africa Studio/Shutterstock.com

When aging parents need help, the task usually falls to a middle-aged daughter, who then becomes "sandwiched" between caring for her parents while also caring for or helping her children (and sometimes her grandchildren). Sibling relationships that were antagonistic in childhood can grow closer in middle adulthood if the siblings cooperate in caring for parents. In middle adulthood, the number of friends tends to decline, and people tend to place more value on the friends they retain.

Please visit the CourseMate at www.nelson.com/4ltrpress/icanhdev2ce to view the Emerging Canada boxes that supplement this chapter.

LATE ADULTHOOD: PHYSICAL AND COGNITIVE DEVELOPMENT

Chapter in Review

LO1 **life span (longevity)**
the maximum amount of time a person can live under optimal conditions. (p. 287)

life expectancy
the amount of time a person can actually be expected to live in a given setting. (p. 287)

ageism
prejudice against people because of their age. (p. 288)

cataract
a condition characterized by clouding of the lens of the eye. (p. 288)

glaucoma
a condition involving abnormally high fluid pressure in the eye. (p. 288)

presbycusis
loss of acuteness of hearing due to age-related degenerative changes in the ear. (p. 289)

osteoporosis
a disorder in which bones become more porous, brittle, and subject to fracture, due to loss of calcium and other minerals. (p. 289)

sleep apnea
temporary suspension of breathing while asleep. (p. 290)

LO2 **cellular clock theory**
a theory of aging focusing on the limits of cell division. (p. 292)

telomeres
protective segments of DNA located at the tips of chromosomes. (p. 292)

hormonal stress theory
a theory of aging that suggests stress hormones, left at elevated levels, make the body more vulnerable to chronic conditions. (p. 292)

immunological theory
a theory of aging that holds that the immune system is preset to decline by an internal biological clock. (p. 293)

wear-and-tear theory
a theory of aging that suggests that over time our bodies become less capable of repairing themselves. (p. 293)

free-radical theory
a theory of aging that attributes aging to damage caused by the accumulation of unstable molecules called free radicals. (p. 293)

cross-linking theory
a theory of aging that holds that the stiffening of body proteins eventually breaks down bodily processes, leading to aging. (p. 293)

LO3 **arthritis**
inflammation of the joints. (p. 295)

LO1 **Describe trends in physical development in late adulthood, focusing on life expectancy.** Old age is divided into the young-old, the old-old, and the oldest-old. One in eight North Americans is over the age of 65. The life span of a species depends on its genetic programming. Our life expectancy is the number of years we can actually expect to live. Disease prevention and treatment contribute to longevity. The average Canadian baby can expect to live about 80 years, but there are differences due to sex, race, geographic location, and behaviour. Men's life expectancy trails women's by about 4 years. Leading causes of death include cancer, heart disease, respiratory disease, brain disease, diabetes, and accidents. After we reach our physical peak in our 20s, our biological functions gradually decline. Chemical changes of aging can lead to vision disorders such as cataracts and glaucoma. Presbycusis affects one senior citizen in three. Taste and smell become less acute. Osteoporotic hip fractures consume more hospital bed days in Canada than strokes or heart attacks. Insomnia and sleep apnea become more common in later adulthood.

Sexual daydreaming, sex drive, and sexual activity decline with age, but sexual satisfaction may remain high. Many of the physical changes in older women stem from a decline in estrogen production. Sexual frequency declines with age.

LO2 **Compare programmed and cellular theories of aging.** Theories of aging have two main categories: (1) programmed theories such as cellular clock theory, hormonal stress theory, and immunological theory, and (2) cellular damage theories such as wear-and-tear theory, free-radical theory, and cross-linking theory.

LO3 **Identify common health concerns associated with late adulthood.** The three major causes of death of Canadians age 65 and older are cancer, heart disease, and respiratory disease (see Table 17.1). Hypertension is a major risk factor for heart attacks and strokes. Arthritis becomes more common with advancing age and is more common in women. Many older adults are addicted to prescription drugs; many have adverse drug reactions. Older adults have a greater risk of accidents, especially falls. Dementia is not a normal result of aging, however, Alzheimer's disease (AD) is the leading cause of dementia.

TABLE 17.1

Ten Leading Causes of Death in Canada by Gender, 65 Years and Over

MEN	WOMEN
1. Cancer	1. Cancer
2. Heart disease	2. Heart disease
3. Respiratory disease	3. Respiratory disease
4. Brain disease	4. Brain disease
5. Diabetes	5. Diabetes
6. Accidents	6. Accidents
7. Liver disease	7. Pneumonia
8. Aneurysm	8. Alzheimer's disease
9. Pneumonia	9. Liver disease
10. Nephritis	10. Nephritis

Source: Statistics Canada. (2009b). Ten leading causes of death by selected age groups, by sex, Canada — 65 to 74 years. Retrieved from http://www.statcan.gc.ca/pub/84-215-x/2008000/tbl/t008-eng.htm

osteoarthritis
a painful, degenerative disease characterized by wear and tear on joints. (p. 295)

rheumatoid arthritis
a painful, degenerative disease characterized by chronic inflammation of the membranes that line the joints. (p. 296)

dementia
a condition characterized by deterioration of cognitive functioning. (p. 297)

Alzheimer's disease (AD)
a severe form of dementia characterized by memory lapses, confusion, emotional instability, and progressive loss of cognitive functioning. (p. 297)

LO5

implicit memory
automatic memories based on repetition and apparently not requiring any conscious effort to retrieve. (p. 299)

prospective memory
memory of things one has planned for the future. (p. 300)

As AD progresses, people find it harder to manage daily tasks and may eventually no longer recognize family members. Memory loss may be caused by accumulation of plaque. The potential cost of our aging population is staggering and is referred to as the "silver tsunami."

LO4 Discuss cognitive development in late adulthood. Fluid intelligence is most vulnerable to decline in late adulthood. Crystallized intelligence can improve throughout much of late adulthood. Older adults have relatively more difficulty naming public figures than uncommon objects. The working memories of older adults hold less information than the working memories of young adults. The temporal memory of older adults may become confused. They may have trouble telling apart memories of actual events from illusory events. Older adults usually do as well as younger adults in tasks that measure implicit memory, such as memory of multiplication tables or the alphabet. Aging has a more detrimental effect on associative memory than on memory for single items, perhaps because of impairment in binding and in use of strategies for retrieval. Long-term memories are subject to distortion, bias, and even decay. Older people recall events from their teens and 20s in greatest detail and emotional intensity, perhaps because of the effects of sex hormones. Age-related declines in processing speed and working memory (fluid intelligence) impair retrospective memory. Distractibility also plays a role.

Knowledge of meanings of words can improve well into late adulthood, but a decline in reading comprehension is related to a decrease in working memory. Because of the decline in working memory and also because of impairments in hearing, many older adults find it more difficult both to understand the spoken language and to produce language. Older people are more likely to experience the "tip-of-the-tongue" phenomenon.

Problem solving requires executive functioning to select strategies, working memory to hold the elements of the problem in mind, and processing speed to accomplish the task while the elements remain in mind. All of these have fluid components that decline with age. Older adults tend to regulate their emotional responses when they experience conflict.

The greater distractibility of older adults may encourage them to take a broader view of situations, contributing to wisdom. People with wisdom tend to tolerate other people's views and to admit that life has its uncertainties and that we seek workable solutions in an imperfect world.

Please visit the CourseMate at www.nelson.com/4ltrpress/icanhdev2ce to view the Emerging Canada boxes that supplement this chapter.

Chapter in Review

18

LO1 **ego integrity or despair**
Erikson's eighth life crisis, defined by maintenance of the belief that life is meaningful and worthwhile despite physical decline and the inevitability of death versus depression and hopelessness. (p. 305)

disengagement theory
the view that older adults and society withdraw from one another as older adults approach death. (p. 307)

activity theory
the view that older adults fare better when they engage in physical and social activities. (p. 307)

LO2 **socioemotional selectivity theory**
the view that we place increasing emphasis on emotional experience as we age but limit our social contacts to regulate our emotions. (p. 307)

generalized anxiety disorder
general feelings of dread and foreboding. (p. 310)

phobic disorder
irrational, exaggerated fear of an object or situation. (p. 310)

agoraphobia
fear of open, crowded places. (p. 310)

PSYCHOSOCIAL STAGE	PERSONALITY CRISIS (CHALLENGE)	IMPORTANT LIFE EVENT	OUTCOME
Later Life (65 years to death)	Ego Integrity vs. Despair	Reflection on Life (Life Review)	Older adults need to actively look back on life and feel a sense that their life mattered. Success at this stage leads to feelings of wisdom and contribution. Death is the logical next step and is received with grace. Failure to navigate this stage results in regret, bitterness, and despair. Death is feared.

LO1 **Evaluate various theories of social and emotional development in late adulthood.** Erikson's final stage is ego integrity versus despair; the challenge is to continue to see life as meaningful and worthwhile in the face of physical decline and the approach of death. Peck's three developmental tasks of late adulthood are ego differentiation versus work-role preoccupation, body transcendence versus body preoccupation, and ego transcendence versus ego preoccupation. Butler proposes that reminiscence, or life reviews, attempt to make life meaningful and accept the end of life. Well-being among older adults is generally predicted by pursuing goals rather than withdrawal. Activity theory argues that older adults are better adjusted when they are more active and involved. According to socioemotional selectivity theory, older people limit their social contacts to regulate their emotional lives.

LO2 **Discuss psychological development in late adulthood, focusing on self-esteem and maintaining independence.** Self-esteem is highest in childhood, dips sharply in middle childhood and into adolescence, rises gradually throughout middle adulthood, and declines again in late adulthood, as shown in Figure 18.2.

Age differences in self-esteem may result from life changes such as retirement, loss of a spouse or partner, and declining health. Older adults who are independent see themselves as normal, whereas adults who are dependent on others tend to worry more about physical disabilities and stress. Volunteerism in Canada increases with age: those aged 65 and older contribute more volunteer hours to their communities than any other age group. Approximately 10 percent of older adults are affected by depression, which may be related to neuroticism, imbalances in norepinephrine, illness, loss of loved ones, and cognitive impairment. Depression can lead to suicide which is sometimes underestimated, likely due to ageism. The most common anxiety disorders among older adults are generalized anxiety disorder and phobic disorders.

© Shauna Longmuir

LO3 **Discuss the social contexts in which people age, focusing on housing, religion, and family.** Older Canadians prefer to remain in their homes as long as their physical and mental conditions permit. Older Canadians worry about crime, although they are less likely than younger people to be victimized. Older people who cannot live alone may hire in-house care, move in with adult children, or enter assisted-living residences or nursing homes (also called long-term facilities). Relocation disrupts social networks. Religious involvement often provides social, educational, and charitable activities as well as the promise of an afterlife. Religious involvement in late adulthood is usually associated with less depression and more life satisfaction. A majority of Canadians will fulfill their marital commitment "until death do us part." A study of the Big Five personality factors and

LO5 selective optimization with compensation reshaping of one's life to concentrate on what one finds to be important and meaningful in the face of physical decline and possible cognitive impairment. (p. 317)

© Thinkstock

marital satisfaction found that similarity in conscientiousness and extraversion predicts marital satisfaction for couples in their 60s. By that age, many midlife responsibilities such as child rearing and work have declined, and intimacy re-emerges as a central issue. As compared with couples in midlife, older couples are more affectionate when they discuss conflicts, and they disagree less. Sharing power in the relationship and dividing household tasks contributes to satisfaction. Older adults are less likely than younger adults to seek divorce. As with heterosexuals, gay men and lesbians in long-term partnerships tend to enjoy higher self-esteem and less depression. Losing one's spouse in late adulthood is a traumatic experience and can lead to a decline in health. Widowed men are more likely to remarry than widowed women. Older sibling pairs support each other emotionally. Older people often narrow their friendships to people who are most like them. Grandparents and their adult grandchildren often have very close relationships.

LO4 Discuss factors that contribute to adjustment to retirement. Retirement planning is a key to successful retirement—e.g., putting money aside and investigating areas where one might relocate. The best adjusted and most satisfied retirees are involved in a variety of activities.

LO5 Discuss factors in "successful aging." Definitions of successful aging often focus on physical activity, social contacts, the absence of cognitive impairment and depression, and health. Baltes and Carstensen focus on person–environment fit and see successful aging in terms of selective optimization with compensation, which is related to socioemotional selectivity theory. Successful agers also tend to be optimistic and to challenge themselves.

Please visit the CourseMate at www.nelson.com/4ltrpress/icanhdev2ce to view the Emerging Canada boxes that supplement this chapter.

FIGURE 18.2

Mean Level of Self-Esteem as a Function of Age, for Total Sample, Males, and Females

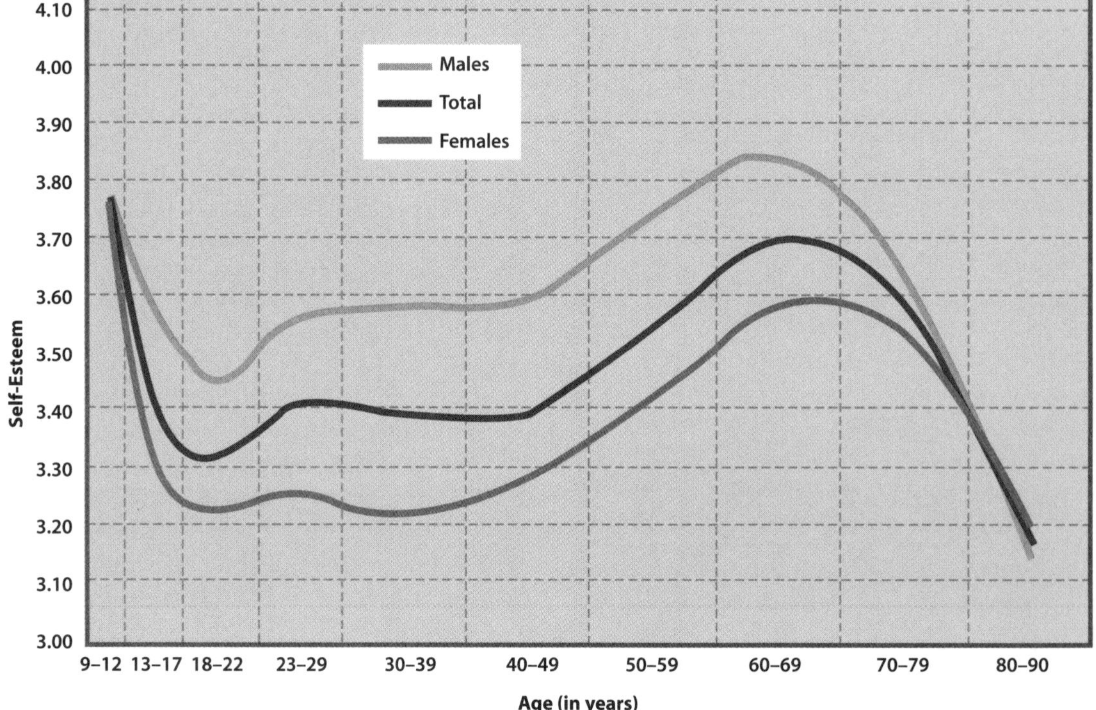

Source: Richard W. Robins, Kali H. Trzesniewski, Jessica L. Tracy, Samuel D. Gosling, & Jeff Potter. (2002). Global self-esteem across the lifespan. *Psychology and Aging, 17*(3), 423–434.

LIFE'S FINAL CHAPTER

19 Chapter in Review

LO1 **death**
the irreversible cessation of vital life functions. (p. 321)

dying
the end-stage of life in which bodily processes decline, leading to death. (p. 321)

brain death
cessation of activity of the cerebral cortex. (p. 321)

whole brain death
cessation of activity of the cerebral cortex and brain stem. (p. 322)

LO2 **hospice**
an organization that treats dying patients by focusing on palliative care rather than curative treatment. (p. 323)

palliative care
treatment focused on the relief of pain and suffering, not on a cure. (p. 324)

LO3 **euthanasia**
the purposeful taking of life to relieve suffering. (p. 325)

voluntary euthanasia
the intentional ending of life as a result of a competent, informed person having made a personal decision to have an assisted death. (p. 325)

non-voluntary euthanasia
the intentional ending of the life of a person who has not expressed his or her preference in terms of an assisted death. (p. 325)

in-voluntary euthanasia
the intentional ending of the life of a person who made an informed choice and expressed his or her refusal to have an assisted death. (p. 325)

assisted suicide
a self-inflicted death as a result of someone intentionally providing the knowledge or means to die by suicide. (p. 325)

terminal sedation
the practice of relieving distress in the last hours or days of life with the use of sedatives. (p. 325)

living will
a document prepared when a person is well, directing medical care providers to terminate life-sustaining treatment in the event of incapacitation or inability to speak; also known as a health care directive. (p. 326)

LO1 **Define death and dying, and evaluate views on stages of dying.** Death is the end of life, but *dying* is a part of life. Medical authorities usually use brain death—absence of activity in the cerebral cortex—as the standard for determining whether a person has died. Whole brain death includes death of the brain stem. Kübler-Ross hypothesized five stages of dying: denial, anger, bargaining, depression, and final acceptance. But Kübler-Ross's view applies only to people who have been diagnosed with terminal illness, and other investigators find that dying does not necessarily follow a progression of stages.

FIGURE 19.1

How Do Doctors Feel about Euthanasia?

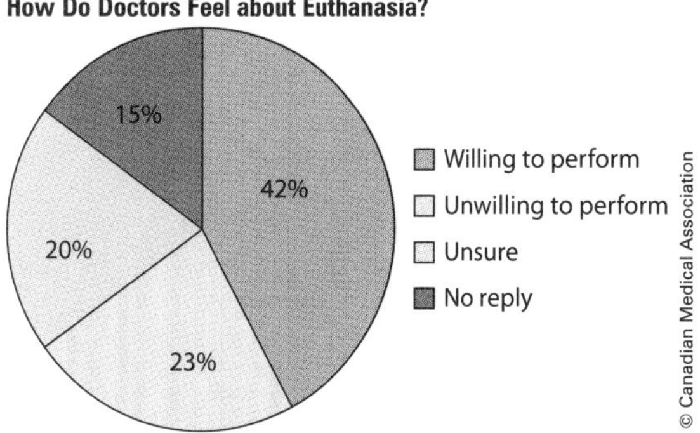

LO2 **Identify settings in which people die, distinguishing between hospitals and hospices.** About 70 percent of all Canadians die in hospitals. Only a few die at home —usually those who are very old or terminally ill. Between 16 and 30 percent of Canadians who die have access to hospice services or receive hospice services. Hospices provide palliative care, not curative care, and they help the whole family, not just the patient. People who are dying often want to focus on topics other than their situation and may enjoy hearing about humorous events or a companion's life experiences. Social-media websites such as CaringBridge can assist in creating a support group for those who are ill, while minimizing the energy needed to stay in touch with loved ones.

LO3 **Discuss the various types of euthanasia and their controversies.** The Canadian Medical Association has taken a leadership role in end-of-life medical issues. This organization has defined voluntary euthanasia (requested by a competent patient), non-voluntary euthanasia (the patient's consent has not been received and his or her preference is unknown), and involuntary euthanasia (the patient does not want intervention). Terminal sedation, or continuous sedation, can be administered to the dying person to prevent discomfort but some argue that it might hasten death.

Physicians are not unified on end-of-life issues. Many doctors say that, although they have been asked to assist in a death, they are unsure they would do so even if it were legal. Gloria Taylor had her right to obtain physician-assisted suicide upheld in British Columbia—if she could find a doctor who would help. She passed away before she could exercise her right. Canadian opinion polls indicate that 67 percent of Canadians support legalizing medically assisted euthanasia. The declaration of the wish to forego aggressive treatment can be in the form of a living will. Every competent Canadian has the right to refuse medical treatment.

LO4 **Discuss people's perspectives on death at various stages of development.** Preschoolers may think that death is reversible or temporary, but their view of death becomes progressively more realistic at the ages of 4, 5, and 6. Death of a parent is usually most difficult for a child to bear. It is normal for children to fear death. Adolescents know that when someone dies, life cannot be restored, but they may construct

LO5 bereavement the state of deprivation brought about by the death of a family member or close friend. (p. 331)

grief emotional suffering resulting from a death. (p. 331)

mourning customary methods of expressing grief. (p. 331)

magical, spiritual, or pseudoscientific theories to try to explain how some form of life or thought might survive. Most young adults in developed nations need not think too much about death. In middle adulthood, death comes more to the fore, often when screening for various deadly diseases is prescribed. Older people may come to fear disability almost as much as death. Some theorists suggest that ego transcendence enables some people to begin to face death with calmness.

Scape/Shutterstock

LO5 **Discuss coping with death, focusing on the funeral, and possible stages of grieving.** If you are present at someone's death, call the family doctor, the police, or 911. Funerals provide an organized response to death that is tied to religious and cultural traditions. Ritual allows people to grieve publicly and bid farewell to the deceased person. In multicultural Canada, this ritual can be expressed in many forms. The family of a deceased person may find it difficult to focus on financial and legal matters such as organ donation or the costs of funerals. A death can lead to bereavement and mourning. Grief can involve a variety of feelings—depression, loneliness, emptiness, numbness, fear, guilt, even anger. A person's early responses to grief can be predictors of their later experiences of grief. Bowlby proposed a stage theory of grief, and Maciejewski and his colleagues found some research evidence for five stages: disbelief, yearning, anger, depression, and acceptance. Death is universal—a developmental event that we all encounter. Fittingly, those who have taken us by the hand in life—in death—often serve as our most insightful teachers. Death holds the gift of wisdom and teaches us that, through memories, loved ones live on forever.

Please visit the CourseMate at www.nelson.com/4ltrpress/icanhdev2ce to view the Emerging Canada boxes that supplement this chapter.